The Golden Homes
Encyclopedia of Garden Plants

A
Golden Hands book

Marshall Cavendish, London

Pamela Booth
J. K. Burras
N. Chaffer
P. R. Chapman
Bruce Coleman Ltd.
K. Collier
R. J. Corbin
J. K. B. Cowley
G. Douglas
J. E. Downward
Alan Duns
V. Finnis
B. Furner
S. Grubb
A. P. Hamilton
R. M. Hatfield
J. C. W. Howden (Royal National Rose Society)
P. Hunt
A. J. Huxley
G. E. Hyde
Lesley Jackson
Leslie Johns
Reginald Kaye
D. J. Kesby
John Markham
Elsa M. Megson
H. A. Morrison
Opera Mundi
Orchid Society of Great Britain
Sheila J. Orme
Ronald Parrett
Picturepoint
Ray Procter
M. C. F. Procter (NHPA)
Gerald Rodway
E. R. Rotherham
E. S. Satchell
Miki Slingsby
D. Smith
Harry Smith
Violet Stevenson
Tourist Photo Library
Colin Watmough
D. Wildridge
Henry J. Wood
Dennis Woodland

Edited by Peter Shanks

*Published by Marshall Cavendish Publications
Limited,
58 Old Compton Street, London W1V 5PA*
© *Marshall Cavendish Limited, 1968, 1970 and
1973*

*This material was first published by
Marshall Cavendish Limited in the partwork*
Encyclopedia of Gardening

*This volume was first published 1973
Printed by Henri Proost, Turnhout, Belgium*

ISBN 0 85685 026 8

*This volume is not to be sold in the USA,
Canada and the Philippines*

INTRODUCTION

This compact and authoritative reference book of popular flowers and vegetables for the garden is designed to fill a gap on the bookshelf of all keen gardeners. It is a lavishly illustrated guide to most of the common plants that can be grown today. It identifies them with hundreds of beautiful colour illustrations, tells you how to cultivate them and where they will flourish best.

Because the *Golden Homes Encyclopedia of Garden Plants* is in alphabetical order, you will be able to refer quickly to whichever plant interests you. The entries are listed under the botanical names, but there is a comprehensive Index to the book, which includes all the common names of the hundreds of plants as well, and will tell you where to look if you do not know the Latin name.

You will find all of your favourites here – Carnations, Dahlias, Irises – even the common vegetables such as Beans, Peas and Onions. There is a special thirty-page section on Roses to satisfy even the keenest grower of this most popular of species. With the *Encyclopedia of Garden Plants* in your collection you will never again be at a loss for information on the plants and vegetables you can enjoy growing in your own garden.

Acanthus (ak-an-thus)

From the Greek *akanthos*, a spine (*Acanthaceae*). Bear's breech. Handsome hardy perennials known to the Greeks and Romans, who used the leaf form of *Acanthus mollis* for the decoration of the Corinthian column.

Species cultivated *A. caroli-alexandri,* 1–1½ feet, white or rose flowers in July. *A. longifolius,* up to 3–4 feet, purple flowers in June. *A. mollis,* the best-known species, 3–4 feet, with white, pink or mauve flowers and great bold leaves 2 feet long; vars. *latifolius* with wider leaves and white flowers, *nigrum,* with glossy, spineless leaves and lilac-white flowers. *A. spinosus,* 4 feet, very prickly deeply divided leaves, a handsome plant with purple, green and white flowers in July and August.

Cultivation Excellent as specimen plants where their form and character can be appreciated, acanthus stand erect without support. Tenacious because of their stout roots, they can withstand both drought and wind. The foliage of the young plants is less pointed and not as deeply cut as that of mature plants, and root cuttings taken from young plants will produce plants of less jagged leaf shape. Grow them in well-drained loam, preferably, but not necessarily, in a sunny position. Propagate by seed sown in gentle heat in spring, or root cuttings in winter or spring, or division in autumn or spring.

Achillea (ak-ill-e-a)

Named after Achilles, who is said to have used it as a treatment for his wounds (*Compositae*). Yarrow, Milfoil. Hardy perennials, for the border or border rock garden.

Species cultivated: Border *A. filipendulina,* large, plate-like heads of yellow flowers in summer; Cultivars include 'Gold Plate', 4–5 feet, 'Flowers of Sulphur', 2½ feet, soft sulphur yellow flowers and powdered leaves, and 'Canary Bird', 1½–2 feet. *A. millefolium,* form of the native 'Old Man's Pepper'; cultivars are 'Cerise Queen', 2 feet, with rose-cerise flowers in July in a loose head, 'Crimson Beauty', 2½ feet, and 'Fire King', 2–2½ feet (probably the best). *A. ptarmica* (sneezewort), 2 feet, a white-flowered native, has several good cultivars of which 'The Pearl' 2½ feet, with small tightly double flowers is the best. *A. sibirica,* 1½ feet, white flowers; 'Perry's White', 2–3 feet, is a fine variety. **Rock Garden** *A. ageratifolia,* 4 inches, grey-white leaves and white flowers. *A. chrysocoma,* mats of grey leaves, flowers yellow on 4–6 inch stems. *A. huteri,* silvery tufts, short-stemmed white flowers. *A.* 'King Edward' (syn. *A. x lewisii*) 4 inches, grey-green mats, buff-yellow flowers all summer. *A. portae,* 4 inches, grey leaves, white flowers. *A. prichardii* 4 inches, grey mats, white flowers. *A. rupestris,* 4–6 inches, foliage creeping, sprays of white flowers, May. *A. tomen-*

Achillea filipendulina 'Gold Plate'

tosa, 9 inches, leaves grey, flowers golden-yellow; needs protection from winter dampness; var. *aurea* flowers deeper yellow.

Herb Garden *A. decolorans.* Mace (but not the mace of commerce), 1 foot, dark green aromatic leaves, yellowish-white flowers. Leaves used occasionally for flavouring soups, curries, etc.

Cultivation Achilleas flourish in almost any soil, provided it is not sour or waterlogged, and revel in sunshine. They prefer lime but are quite tolerant of acid conditions. They have tiny or double daisy-like flowers collected in loose clusters or flat heads and bloom in summer. Foliage is fern-like, stems stiff and unbreakable and the fragrance somewhat pungent. Some varieties are recommended for winter arrangements of dried flowers, the best being *A. filipendula,* 'Gold Plate', and if the heads are stored in powdered alum until quite dry they last well and retain all their colour. Plant in autumn or spring or divide the plants at this time. Sow seed ¼ inch deep in early summer. Border kinds ought to be lifted and divided every three or four years and the shoots cut down in winter.

Aconitum (ak-on-i-tum)

An ancient Greek name for a poisonous plant (*Ranunculaceae*). Monkshood. Attractive herbaceous perennials, flowering in the late summer in various shades of blue and, rarely, yellow. Poisonous, especially when in contact with open scratches or if eaten by children or animals. The English name well describes the helmet-shaped flowers.

Species cultivated *A. anglicum,* 2–3 feet, a native plant, bluish-lilac, mid-summer. *A. anthora,* 3 feet, yellow, July. *A. carmichaelii,* 4 feet, purple-blue flowers late summer to autumn. *A. napellus,* 3–4 feet, the best-known species, used in medicine. Very handsome, deeply cut leaves and rich blue or purplish flowers in July and August; vars. *album,* white, *bicolor,* blue and white and *roseum,* pink, are all well worth growing. There are also cultivars 'Spark's Variety' and 'Newry Blue', both with rich blue flowers and 'Bressingham Spire', 3 feet, violet-blue with useful secondary spikes. *A. uncinatum* (syn. *A. volubile*), up to 8 feet, dark blue flowers in autumn and slender twining stems. Useful for planting by porches. *A. variegatum* (syn. *A. cammarum*) 2–5 feet, blue to white, summer; var. *bicolor,* blue and white flowers. *A. wilsonii,* 5–6

feet, blue, September and October; 'Bakers Variety', similar but better.

Cultivation Aconitums are tolerant of shade which makes them useful garden plants, though they prefer sunshine provided that the soil is not too heavy. They can be left undisturbed for many years, when they will form attractive clumps. No staking is required except in very exposed gardens.

Autumn or spring planting is best, when the roots can be split up to increase stock. Seed is slow to germinate and may be more successful if sown as soon as it is ripe rather than in the early summer.

Agapanthus (ag-a-pan-thus)

From the Greek *agape*, love, *anthos*, flower (*Liliaceae*). African lily. Half-hardy or, in some places, hardy evergreen herbaceous perennials from South Africa.

Species cultivated *A. africanus*, 1½–3 feet, summer, deep violet-blue flowers; vars. *albus*, white, *nanus*, a dwarf kind. *A. campanulatus* (syn. *A. umbellatus mooreanus*), 1½ feet, sky blue flowers, July to September; var. *albus* has white flowers. *A. inapertus*, 3 feet, blue, drooping, bell-shaped flowers, summer. *A. orientalis*, erroneously known as *Agapanthus umbellatus*, presumably because the flowers grow in a great umbel, sometimes as many as 30–60 flowers in a head in a season. 1½–2 feet, rather variable but most commonly grown; var. *albus*, 1½–2 feet, white flowers.

The 'Headbourne Hybrids', of complex parentage developed in recent years, are hardier than the species. Colours range from pale blue to deep violet blue.

Cultivation Plants are conveniently grown in tubs because the vigorous roots tend to break pots. A suitable compost consists of 3 parts of loam, 1 part of decayed manure, 1 part of leafmould, and ½ part of sand. Firm planting is essential and ample water is needed from spring to autumn, with weak liquid feeds before and during the flowering period. The tubs may be used for sun lounge decoration or put in strategic positions out of doors all summer.

Propagation is by division of the plants in early spring, although plants should not be disturbed more often than is necessary. There is increasing proof that some species are hardy, especially in southern England, and plants require only slight protection out of doors in winter. In the open ground or in the border, plants do best in rich soil and require plenty of water in summer.

Ageratum (aj-er-a-tum)

From the Greek *a*, not, *geras*, old, a reference to the non-fading flowers (*Compositae*). Floss flower. Half-hardy compact annuals from Mexico. Useful for summer bedding schemes, carpeting, edging and window boxes. The English name floss flower well describes the blue-mauve tassel-like flowers borne in fluffy heads, which last well.

Species cultivated *A. houstonianum* (syn. *A. mexicanum*) 1½ feet when grown naturally. Heart-shaped leaves in rosette formation. Cultivars include 'Florist Blue', 'Little Dorrit' azure blue, 'Mexican White', 'Fairy Pink', 'Blue Ball'.
Cultivation Ageratums like a sunny spot and need to be planted not less than 6 inches apart to be effective. Propagation is by seed sown in pans in March in a temperature of 55°F (13°C). Prick off, and about ten days later pinch out the tips of the shoots to ensure branched and compact specimens. Harden off and plant out in late May or early June. The flowering season will be prolonged if the dead flower-heads are removed from time to time. When a really good colour is obtained cuttings may be taken in spring from a plant that has been potted up in the late summer and flower-buds removed. Pot up and harden off once the cuttings have rooted and plant out in May.

Ajuga (a-ju-ga)

From an old Latin name *abiga* (*Labiatae*). Bugle. Hardy perennial, herbaceous plants of creeping habit, producing upstanding flowering spikes.
Species cultivated *A. genevensis*, 6–12 inches, Geneva bugle, flowers blue, rose or white, June, coarsely toothed leaves; var. *brockbankii*, 6 inches, has deep blue flowers. Both need sunshine to flower well. *A. reptans*, 6–12 inches, spreads quickly, needs curbing, blue, white or rose flowers in June; vars. *atropurpurea*,

Alchemilla mollis, the Lady's Mantle, bears delicate flowers and is a ground cover plant for shady situations

6 inches, bronze purple flowers and purple leaves, *multicolor*, sometimes known as 'Rainbow', leaves metallic bronze with buff and purple markings, blue flowers in spring, *variegata*, 6 inches, blue flowers in May and variegated leaves.

Cultivation Bugles are particularly useful as ground cover, flourishing in almost any position, but those with variegated foliage benefit from full sun. Propagation is by division in autumn or spring, or seed sown outdoors in April.

Alchemilla (al-kem-il-a)

From *alkemelych*, an Arabic word, indicating the plant's use in alchemy (*Rosaceae*). Lady's mantle. Hardy herbaceous low-growing plants suitable for use on rock gardens, or at the fronts of borders. The flowers are in clusters, in shades of green or yellow, in July.

Species cultivated *A. alpina*, 6 inches, handsome foliage, grey green above, silvery below, flowers pale greenish-yellow. When grown on the rock garden, it is best planted in crevices between rocks. *A. mollis*, 12 inches, attractive, with kidney-shaped, wavy-edged, softly hairy leaves and greenish-yellow flowers, good for cutting. Contrasts well when grown in association with *Campanula poscharskyana*. Inclined to be invasive when established, but well worth growing, especially as ground cover in shady or semi-shady places, such as under trees.

Cultivation Drainage must not be impaired for alchemillas to thrive well, otherwise any ordinary garden soil suits them. They are best transplanted in autumn or spring. As they are spreading plants, division is a simple means of propagation and they set seed freely. This may be collected with the aid of polythene bags, placed over the faded flower heads, and sown in spring.

Allium (Al-le-um)

Taken from *all*, the Celtic word for pungent, or from the Latin name for garlic, *Allium sativum* (*Liliaceae*). A large genus of bulbous plants mainly with spherical flower heads, mostly with a strong onion-like odour. As perennials they are grown in cultivation under glass, in ornamental borders and as food crops. *A. neapolitanum* is especially suitable as a pot plant or for cutting when forced in a greenhouse.

Greenhouse species cultivated *A. acu-*

7

minatum, 10 inches, rose-purple flowers, May–June. *A. amabile*, 4–8 inches, bell-shaped flowers, deep rose spotted with purple, August–September. *A. cyaneum*, 10 inches, dull blue flowers with protruding stamens, August. *A. farreri*, 6–12 inches, reddish purple flowers, June. *A. neapolitanum*, 9–12 inches, white flowers, March–May (will also grow outdoors). *A. oreophilum*, 6 inches, deep rose flowers, May (will also grow outdoors). *A. subhirsutum*, 8 inches, white flowers, lavender midrib, May.

Hardy species cultivated *A. aflatunense*, 2½–3 feet, purple-lilac flowers, late May. *A. albopilosum*, 18 inches, large purple flowers with metallic sheen, June. *A. azureum*, 2 feet, sky-blue flowers, July. *A. beesianum*, 12 inches, blue flowers, July. *A. breweri*, 3 inches, violet-purple flowers, June. *A. caeruleum*, 1–3 feet, attractive light blue flowers, June–July. *A. elatum*, 3 feet, rosy-lilac flowers, late May. *A. flavum*, 12 inches, glistening sulphur-yellow flowers, July. *A. giganteum*, 3–4 feet, lilac flowers, July. *A. karataviense*, 9 inches, pink flowers, broad leaves, May. *A. moly*, golden garlic, 12 inches, bright yellow flowers, June. *A. narcissiflorum*, 10 inches, red-purple flowers, June. *A. ostrowskianum*, 10 inches, light rose flowers, May. *A. paradoxicum*, 12 inches, white flowers, April. *A. pulchellum*, 18 inches, reddish violet flowers, July–August. *A. ramosum*, 2 feet, white and rose flowers, June–July. *A. rosenbachianum*, 4 feet, purple-rose flowers, May; var. *album*, white flowers. *A. roseum*, 18 inches, light rose flowers, June; var. *grandiflorum*, larger flowers. *A. schubertii*, 12 inches, pink flowers, April–May. *A. sphaerocephalum*, 2 feet, purple-lilac, June–July. *A. triquetrum*, 6–12 inches, white, summer, suitable for naturalising in partial shade. *A. uniflorum*, 15 inches, pink flowers, May. *A. ursinum*, 10 inches, white flowers, May. *A. victorialis*, 1–2 feet, white or yellowish flower, May. *A. zebadense*, 1–2 feet, white flowers.

Cultivation Dormant bulbs are planted closely in well-drained compost in pans in the cool greenhouse or alpine house. The containers are plunged in an ash-bed until growth begins, then removed to a cold-frame until well developed, to flower in the greenhouse. *A. neapolitanum* may be forced in a temperature of 60°F (16°C). Dry off the bulbs after flowering. Propagation is by seed or by separating young bulbs, in spring.

Outdoor cultivation is very easy. Alliums require only ordinary, well-drained garden soil; most thrive in full sun. They may be used in flower borders, shrubberies or rock gardens. Plant in October or November, at a depth equal to twice the diameter of the bulbs. Increase in spring by small bulbs or seed planted in gritty soil and well fed.

Alstroemeria (al-stro-meer-e-a)
In honour of Baron Clas Alstroemer, a

Swedish botanist (*Amaryllidaceae*). Peruvian lily. Attractive South American plants liable to injury by severe cold if not protected in bad winters. The popular species and hybrids provide large heads of brightly coloured summer flowers, long lasting and good for cutting. They are sometimes grown as pot plants.

Species cultivated *A. aurantiaca*, 2–3 feet, flowers in shades of red and carmine; var. *lutea*, yellow. There are some good named varieties. *A. brasiliensis*, 3–4 feet, red flowers tinged yellow and spotted brown. *A. campaniflora*, erect stems to 4 feet, heads of 10–23 flowers, green with dark spots. *A. chilensis*, 2–3 feet, blood red or pink flowers. *A. haemantha*, to 3 feet, red flowers, green spotted purple. *A. ligtu*, to 2 feet, flowers

These decorative relatives of the onion, Allium pulchellum 1 Allium albopilosum 2 and Allium moly 3 are hardy bulbs

in shades of lilac or pink, and white, striped purple. *A. pelegrina*, to 2 feet, individual flowers, 2 inches in shades of lilac, yellow based and spotted red-purple, has white form, *alba* (lily of the Incas), fairly tender, *A. pulchella* (syn. *A. psittacina*), 3 feet, or more, flowers dark red tipped green, spotted brown. *A. versicolor*, 1 foot, rather tender with mainly yellow flowers spotted and flecked purple. *A. violacea*, 1–2 feet, bright lilac flowers, spotted, up to 2 inches long.

Cultivars 'Dover Orange', 'Dr Slater's Hybrids', shades of pink and salmon; 'Ligtu Hybrids', 'Moerheim Orange', 'Walter Fleming', yellow, rose and maroon.

Cultivation Alstroemerias are best obtained as pot-grown plants because they resent root disturbance. Plant 6 inches deep for permanency. They require a sun-baked position in well-drained soil.

Propagate by seeds with minimum disturbance to young plants, if necessary breaking the pots to avoid damage to the brittle, glass-like roots, and planting the contents without separating the plants.

Althaea (al-the-a)

Referring to its medicinal use, from the Greek *althaea*, to cure (*Malvaceae*). A genus of easily grown plants comprising annuals, biennials and perennials.
Biennial species cultivated *A. ficifolia* (fig-leaved or Antwerp hollyhock), to 6 feet, single or double flowers in spikes of mostly yellow, June. *A. rosea*, hollyhock, erect-growing, to 9 feet or sometimes a good deal more. Tall spikes of single or double flowers, sometimes 3 inches or more across, in shades of red, pink, yellow and white, July (see below). This is strictly a perennial but is often treated as a biennial.
Perennial species cultivated *A. cannabina*, 5–6 feet, rose flowers, June; var. *narbonensis*, red flowers. *A. officinalis* (marsh mallow), 4 feet, blush-coloured flowers, July, native to British marshes.
Cultivars of hollyhock 'Chater's Improved', fully double flowers, mixed colours. 'Apple Blossom', apple-blossom pink. 'Carmine Rose', double cherry-red flowers; and other separate colours. 'Allegheny Mammoth', mixed colours, single and semi-double. 'Begonia Flowered', fringed petals with central rosette, mixed. Annual hollyhock: 'Triumph Supreme', to 4 feet, compact growing.
Cultivation Hollyhocks will succeed in most soils, but prefer the heavier kinds, especially if they are enriched. They need plenty of water in dry periods and should be firmly staked with stout stakes 7 feet or more long, driven well into the ground, to prevent wind damage, particularly in exposed gardens. Stems should be cut down to within about 6 inches of the ground after flowering is over.

Propagation is by seed sown in a sunny seed-bed in June. Seedlings should be transplanted to their flowering quarters in September or October, except in cold districts or where the soil is very heavy and liable to become very wet in winter, when they should be lifted, potted up and overwintered in a cold frame until they can be planted out in April.

In spring older plants will start to produce new growths and these may be cut off and rooted in a propagating case with a little bottom heat. When well rooted and hardened off they may be planted out of doors. Late summer cuttings will root in a closed frame. The other species described are propagated

Althaea rosea, the well-known Hollyhock, one of the tallest of hardy perennial plants, available in various colours

by seed sown out of doors in a sunny position in April.

Alyssum

From the Greek *a*, not, and *lyssa*, madness: once thought to cure madness or rage (*Cruciferae*). Madwort. The dwarf perennial species in cultivation, mostly with grey foliage and yellow flowers, are chiefly confined to the rock garden; the taller-growing kinds are best in borders. The popular sweet alyssum or sweet Alison, is now correctly called *Lobularia maritima*.

Species cultivated *A. alpestre*, 3 inches, of tufted habit, flowering in June. *A. argenteum*, to 18 inches, becomes woody at the base. Deep yellow flowers in clustered heads, May–July. *A. flexi-caule*, 3 inches, tufts of fragrant yellow flowers, spring. *A. idaeum*, of trailing habit, soft yellow flowers, May–June. *A. moellendorfianum*, 6 inches, silvery plant, flowers in long racemes. *A. montanum*, to 10 inches, usually much lower, fragrant flowers, bright yellow, in loose racemes. *A. pyrenaicum*, 8–10 inches, dwarf shrubby growth, white velvety leaves, white flowers, summer. *A. saxatile*, gold dust, to 12 inches, spreading habit, numerous heads of golden-yellow flowers, April–June, vars. *citrinum*, lemon-yellow, *compactum*, 4–6 inches, 'Dudley Neville', 6–9 inches, biscuit yellow, *plenum*, double flowers, dwarf, 'Tom Thumb', *variegatum*, variegated foliage, yellow and green. *A. spinosum*, (see Ptilotrichum spinosum). *A. wulfenianum*, 3 inches, round, thick, silver

leaves, pale yellow flowers in large, loose heads borne in summer.

Cultivation Alyssums require only ordinary, well-drained soils in the open. *A. saxatile* is often grown vertically in walls or on banks. It should be trimmed back after flowering to prevent it from straggling unduly. Young plants are occasionally used in spring bedding schemes. Propagation is by seed, division or by 2–3 inch long cuttings taken in early summer and rooted in shade.

Amaranthus (am-a-ran-thus)

So named (from the Greek *a*, not, and *maraino*, to fade) because of the lasting qualities of the flowers (*Amaranthaceae*). Half hardy annuals grown in sub-tropical bedding schemes, some for their coloured foliage, in shades of red, crimson and green. They are good for pot culture under glass. *A. caudatus*, love-lies-bleeding, and *A. hypochondriacus*, prince's feather, are two of the hardiest and can be treated as hardy annuals in warmer areas.

Species cultivated *A. caudatus*, 2–3 feet, long, red, drooping tail-like flowers, August; vars. *albiflorus*, greenish white, *atropurpureus*, blood red. *A. gibbosus*, dwarf, slender flowers in red clusters. *A. hypochondriacus*, 4–5 feet, flowers in dense spikes, deep crimson, July, purplish green foliage; vars. *atropurpureus*, dark, *sanguineus*, blood red throughout, *sanguineus nanus*, dwarf form, *splendens*, good crimson foliage. *A. melancholicus*, 1–3 feet, grown chiefly for its variable coloured foliage; vars. *ruber*, leaves crimson, *bicolor*, leaves green streaked yellow, *tricolor*, Joseph's coat, 18 inches, purple and green leaves, yellow stalks, *salicifolius*, 3 feet, narrow, brightly coloured leaves, bronze-green with orange and crimson markings. Cultivars: 'Fire King', 'Molten Torch', Pygmy Torch'.

Cultivation Plant out in June in sunny beds. Propagate by seed sown in a temperature of 55–60°F (13–16°C) in March. Harden off young plants carefully before planting out.

Anagallis (an-a-gal-is)

From the Greek *anagelao*, meaning delightful (*Primulaceae*). Pimpernel. Though some species are naturally perennials, it is usual to treat all as annuals in cultivation. As such they are a delight at the front of the annual border, as they are usually low or even trailing in habit. *A. tenella* may be used to great advantage in a moist or boggy spot.

Species cultivated *A. arvensis* (poor man's weather glass), of prostrate growth, flowers $\frac{1}{4}$ inch wide, variable shades between scarlet and white, late

Amaranthus 'Molten Torch' 1 and Amaranthus caudatus, Love-lies-Bleeding 2 are two half-hardy annuals used to provide foliage and flower colour in sub-tropical bedding schemes

summer; vars. *caerulea*, blue; *phoenicea*, red; *latifolia*, blue. *A. linifolia*, 12 inches, flowers blue, red undersides, ½ inch wide, July; vars. *breweri*, red; *collina*, flowers rosy purple; *lilacina*, lilac; *monellii*, flowers larger than the species; *phillipsii*, deep gentian-blue. *A. tenella* (bog pimpernel), 2–4 inches, bell-shaped flowers, ½ inch across, pink with darker veins, summer.

Cultivation A sunny spot suits these charming plants, in ordinary garden soil; a moist place for *A. tenella*. Seed may either be sown in heat in March and planted out in June, or sown direct into flowering positions in April. *A. linifolia* may be propagated by division in March if kept as a perennial.

Anaphalis (an-af-a-lis)
Said to be an old Greek name for a similar plant (*Compositae*). Hardy perennials with white woolly foliage and flowers which can be cut before maturity and dried for use as 'everlastings', sometimes being dyed.

Species cultivated *A. margaritacea* (pearly everlasting), 1 foot, white throughout, flowering June–August. *A. nubigena*, 6–9 inches, silvery white foliage, flowers white, summer. *A. triplinervis*, 12–18 inches, soft woolly silver foliage, pearly-white flowers, June–August. *A. yedoensis*, 2 feet, leaves grey above, white below, flowers white, summer.

Cultivation Anaphalis are suitable for the rock garden or for borders, according to size. An ordinary garden soil and a sunny position suits them. They do well on chalky soils. Plant out in autumn or spring. Established plants may be increased by division at the same seasons. New plants may also be raised from seed sown outside in April

Anchusa (an-chu-sa)
The name originates from the Greek *anchousa*, a cosmetic paint (*Boraginaceae*). Alkanet, bugloss. Cultivated species are usually perennials or biennials, noteworthy for their blue flowers. The plant long known as *Anchusa myosotidiflora* is now correctly known as *Brunnera macrophylla*.

Biennial species cultivated *A. capensis*, 18 inches, flowers in panicles at tips of stems, July. *A. officinalis*, 1–2 feet, flowers sometimes purple in double spikes, May; var. *incarnata*, flowers pale pink.

Perennial species cultivated *A. azurea* (syn. *A. italica*), 3–5 feet, bright blue flowers summer. *A. barrelieri*, 2 feet, flowers, blue and white, yellow throats, May. *A. caespitosa* (syn. *A. angustissima*), 12–15 inches, tufted plant with gentian-blue flowers from May to July, rock garden or alpine house. *A. sempervirens*, 1½–2 feet, rich blue flowers, May; var. *variegata*, foliage cream and green.

Cultivars *A. azurea*—'Dropmore', 'Loddon Royalist', 'Morning Glory', 'Opal',

Anchusa azurea, a good border plant

'Pride of Dover', 'Suttons Bright Blue' 'Suttons Royal Blue' *A. capensis*–'Blue Bird'.

Cultivation Sunny borders in ordinary soil. Plant out in autumn or spring. Perennials may be raised from seed, from root cuttings taken in February, or by dividing established plants in October. Biennials are raised from seed sown under glass in heat in March, or outside in April.

Androsace (an-dros-a-se)
From the Greek *aner*, a man, *sakos*, buckler, referring to the resemblance of the anther to an old type of buckler (*Primulaceae*). Rock jasmine. A genus of alpine plants of which the perennial species are chiefly grown, though there are also annuals. The flowers more or less resemble miniature primulas.

Species cultivated *A. alpina*, 1 inch, flowers pink, summer. *A. carnea*, 3 inches, pink, June–July; var. *laggeri*, pink, March–April. *A. chamaejasme*, 3 inches, white flowers, May–June; var. *ciliata*, rose-pink. *A. helvetica*, 1 inch, flowers pink at first then white, June–July. *A. hirtella*, 1 inch, white, May–June. *A. imbricata*, 1 inch, white, June. *A. lactea*, 6 inches, white flowers with yellow eyes, June–August. *A. lanuginosa*, 6 inches, rose flowers, July; var. *leichtlinii*, white flowers with crimson eye. *A. sarmentosa*, 3–4 inches, rose flowers, May; vars. *chumbyi*, more brightly coloured, *watkinsii*, 6 inches, rose-red, *yunnanensis*, pink. 'Galmont', with larger pink flowers and 'Salmon', a larger and more vigorous plant, are two cultivars of this species. *A. semper-*

vivoides, 3 inches, rose-pink, May–June.
Cultivation Not all are easy: those listed above are generally not difficult in cultivation. They require an open compost of leafmould and sandy loam with plenty of sharp grit added. Plant in March or April. Propagate by seed in well-drained shallow pans. Cuttings may be taken or roots divided in spring. New plants form on stolons.

Anemone (an-em-o-ne)

Derived from the Greek words *anemos,* wind, and *mone,* habitation, because some species are found in windy places (*Ranunculaceae*). Windflower. A fairly large genus of hardy, attractively flowered herbaceous plants, some tuberous rooted. Some previously known as anemones are now included under *Hepatica* or *Pulsatilla.*

Species cultivated *A. apennina,* 6 inches, flowers pink, blue and white, March. Many varieties, including some with double flowers. *A. baldensis,* 6 inches, mainly white flowers, part pink, May–June. *A. blanda,* 6 inches, blue flowers, January–March. Vars. *atrocaerulea,* deeper blue, *rosea,* rosy-pink. *A. canadensis,* 2½ feet, white flowers, June. *A. coronaria,* poppy anemone, 9–12 inches, variously coloured flowers, spring, tuberous rooted. *A. fanninii,* 3–4 feet, flowers white, June, greenhouse. *A. × fulgens,* scarlet windflower, 1 foot, flowers scarlet, May. *A. glauciifolia,* 1–3 feet, flowers lilac, summer. *A. hortensis,* 1 foot, various colours, spring, tuberous rooted. *A. hupehensis,* Japanese anemone, 2–3 feet, rose flowers, August–October; var. *alba,* white; *elegans,* pale rose; *japonica,* carmine, semi-double. *A. × hybrida,* Japanese anemone, 4–5 feet, pink, August–October. *A. magellanica,* 6 inches, creamy-white flowers, June; var. *major* flowers larger. *A. multifida,* 6–12 inches, flowers red through white to yellow, June. *A. narcissiflora,* 12 inches, creamy-white or pink flowers, May–June. *A. nemorosa,* wood anemone, 6 inches, flowers white, spring, native plant; var. *alba major* (*grandiflora*), large white; *alba plena,* double white; *alleni,* soft blue; *robinsoniana,* lavender blue; *rosea, rubra, rubra plena,* change from white to red; *A. palmata,* 6 inches, white or golden yellow flowers, May, tuberous rooted. *A. pavonina* 1 foot, flowers variable in shades of red to nearly white, March–April, tuberous rooted; vars.: *typica,* scarlet; *ocellata,* scarlet, yellow eye; *purpureo-violacea,* violet or rose-red. *A. ranunculoides,* 9–12 inches, flowers golden-yellow, March; var. *pleniflora,* double form. *A. rivularis,* 2 feet, white flowers, May. *A. rupicola,* 12 inches, flowers white, May–June. *A. sylvestris,* snowdrop windflower, 1 foot, white flowers, April. *A. tetrasepala,* 3 feet, white flowers, May–June. *A. vitifolia,* 2 feet, white flowers, summer, fairly tender.
Cultivars *A. blanda:* 'Blue Pearl', large,

Four Anemones: **1** Anemone narcissiflora has white or pink flowers **2** Anemone fulgens, the Scarlet Windflower **3** The De Caen Anemones make splendid cut flowers **4** Anemone blanda in its various colour forms, may be grown in pots

mid-blue with yellow centres; 'Bridesmaid', pure white; 'Charmer', rosy-red; 'Pink Star', cyclamen-pink with yellow centres. *A. coronaria:* de Caen, a strain with large single flowers in mainly red and blue shades; 'His Excellency', scarlet; 'Mr. Fokker', blue; 'St. Brigid', a semi-double strain, mixed colours; 'Sylphide', violet; 'The Bride', white. *A. hupehensis:* 'September Charm', clear pink; 'Bressingham Glow', ruby rose, semi-double; 'Lorelei', soft rose-pink; 'Louise Uhink', white; 'Krimhilde', rose-pink, semi-double; 'Margarita', deep pink, semi-double; 'Mont Rose', clear pink, large, semi-double. *A. × hybrida:* 'Honorine Jobert', white.

Cultivation Anemones, generally, prefer a well enriched soil. Most of them like lime, but will also grow in acid soils. Most will tolerate partial shade, making them a good choice for open woodland planting. They may be planted in autumn or spring. The dwarf species are excellent rock garden plants.

The tubers of the popular florists' anemones, varieties of *A. coronaria*, which are excellent cut flowers, together with other tuberous species, may be planted in October and November, or February and March, 3 inches deep, 6 inches apart. Tubers of these may be lifted and stored after their foliage has died down, and kept in a cool place until replanted. Choose a well-drained sheltered spot, previously well manured. Herbaceous species may be raised from seed sown in cold frame in spring, by division in October or March, or by root cuttings made in spring. Tuberous species are best increased by seed in July or early spring.

Antirrhinum (an-tir-i-num)

From the Greek, *anti*, like, *rhinos*, snout, a reference to the curiously shaped flowers (*Scrophulariaceae*). The most important of these nearly hardy perennials is the snapdragon, *Antirrhinum majus*, which is grown extensively as a half-hardy annual for bedding purposes.

Antirrhinum majus 'Fiery Red'

In some districts it will prove hardy and remain perennial but as the plants are inclined to become straggly after the first year they are nearly always treated as annuals, although plants are sometimes naturalised in the crannies of old walls. *A. majus* originally came from the Mediterranean region where it grows to 3 feet, in height. It has been considerably developed for bedding purposes by plant breeders. Species suitable for the rock garden are *A. asarina* and *A. glutinosum*, but like *A. majus* they are not reliably hardy.

Species cultivated *A. asarina*, a trailing plant with yellow flowers, from June to September. *A. glutinosum*, low growing with yellow and cream flowers in summer. *A. majus*, 3 feet, the well-known snapdragon. Flowers pink in the species. Many garden forms have developed from this species by natural variation. It has also been hybridised to produce plants in a wide range of colours and of various heights including dwarf spreading plants. Plants remain in flower over a long period, through summer and autumn.

Some good cultivars *Tall* (3–4 feet): 'Cloth of Gold', golden yellow. 'Giant Ruffled Tetra' strain mixed colours, large. 'Rocket Hybrids', mixed large flowers, vigorous plants. *Intermediate* (1½ feet): 'Dazzler' brilliant scarlet. 'Eldorado', deep, rich golden yellow. 'Fire King', orange and white. 'Malmaison', silver pink, dark foliage, 'Orange Glow', deep orange, cerise throat, 'Purity' white. 'Regal Rose', an F.1 rust-resistant hybrid; rich rose red. *Dwarf* (9 inches): 'Floral Carpet' Mixed F.1 Hybrids, extremely colourful. 'Magic Carpet Strain' mixed colours. 'Tom Thumb', 9 inches, available in various colours or mixed. *Rust resistant:* 'Amber Monarch', golden amber. 'Orange Glow', deep orange, cerise throat. 'Rust Resistant Roselight', rich glowing salmon. 'Toreador', deep crimson. 'Victory', buff pink, suffused orange. 'Wisley Golden Fleece', yellow. Seedsmen list many more and new ones appear regularly.

Cultivation The low growing species, *A. asarina* and *A. glutinosum*, need plenty of sun and good drainage and may be planted in April in any ordinary soil. It is wise to take cuttings in August, inserting them in sandy soil in a pot in case the parent plants are killed by frost in the winter. The garden forms of *A. majus* grown as half-hardy annuals, are sown in March in a temperature of 70° F (21°C); the seedlings are pricked out into boxes and then hardened off and planted out in May or the beginning of June. They may be used to fill gaps in borders but look best when planted in drifts in the garden or in bedding displays in public parks. Seed may also be sown outdoors in April. Plants may also be grown in pots in the cool greenhouse for spring display, for which purpose seed is sown in August.

13

Plenty of ventilation should be given at all times. The height of these snapdragons varies a great deal, from the 9 inches of the dwarf kinds to the 4 feet of the tall varieties. Under glass, in pots, the latter may, by careful feeding and attention to watering, be induced to grow even taller.

Antirrhinum rust is a troublesome disease but there are rust resistant cultivars now (see above and seedsmen's lists). A great deal of hybridising has been carried out with these popular bedding plants and there are now tetraploid cultivars which have larger flowers on robust plants.

Aquilegia (ak-wil-e-je-a)

The flower form resembles an eagle's claw, hence the probable origin of this name from *aquila* the Latin for eagle (*Ranunculaceae*). Columbine. Hardy, herbaceous perennials for the herbaceous border and rock garden. The flowers and leaves are very dainty. Unfortunately they are inclined to be short lived in heavy, wet soils, but they are easily increased by seed. The flowers appear in May and June in a wide range of colours from yellows and creams to blues and reds and purples. The garden hybrids have been raised from various species, e.g. the long-spurred hybrids from *A. longissima*. Mrs Scott Elliott's is a well-known strain, and more recently there are the McKana Giant hybrids, with larger flowers and long spurs.

Species cultivated *A. alpina*, 1 foot, flowers blue, white centre. *A. atrata*, 9 inches, purple-red flowers. *A. bertolonii*, 6 inches, flowers deep violet-blue. *A. caerulea*, 1½–2½ feet, flowers pale blue and white; various named forms, such as 'Blue King', 'Crimson Star, *candidissima* ('Snow Queen'), pure white, *cuprea* ('Copper Queen') coppery, 'Dragon Fly',

a dwarf strain in various colours. *A. canadensis*, 1½ feet, pale yellow. *A. chrysantha*, 2–4 feet, golden-yellow. *A. clematiflora hybrida*, 1½ feet, spurless flowers in pink and blue shades. *A. discolor*, 3 inches, blue and white flowers. *A. flabellata*, 9 inches, white, tinged pink; var. *nana alba*, 6 inches, flowers white. *A. formosa*, 1½ feet, yellow or yellow and red flowers; var. *truncata*, smaller flowers. *A. fragrans*, 1½–2 feet, white or purple fragrant; needs a sunny, sheltered position. *A. glandulosa*, 1 foot, lilac and white flowers. *A. helenae*, 1½ feet, blue and white. *A. longissima*, 2 feet, long-spurred yellow flowers. *A. skinneri*, 2 feet, crimson flowers. *A. viridiflora*, 9 inches, green and brown, fragrant. *A. vulgaris*, the common columbine, 1½–2½ feet, various colours and forms including the very double *flore pleno*, sometimes known as Granny Bonnets.

Cultivation The requirements are sun or partial shade and a loamy soil enriched with leafmould and not too heavy or dry. Dwarf species, grown on the rock garden, need well-drained soil and full sun. Plants do well on chalky soils. Seed is sown in May or June in the open, in August in a frame or the plants may be divided in spring or autumn.

Arabis (ar-ab-is)

Rock plants from Arabia, hence the name from the Greek *arabis*, Arabia (*Cruciferae*). Wall cress, rock cress. Well-known plants for the rock garden and dry wall, these hardy perennials flower in the spring and early summer when the plants are covered with the small blooms.

Species cultivated *A. albida*, the widely grown, grey-leaved trailing plant, smothered with white flowers in spring; vars. *coccinea*, crimson flowers; *flore pleno*, the double form and a better plant; 'Snowflake', larger, pure white flowers;

variegata, pretty white-edged leaves *A. alpina*, 6 inches, small white flowers; vars. *grandiflora*, larger flowers; *rosea*, rosy-pink flowers. *A. aubrietioides*, 6 inches, a summer-flowering purple-lilac species. *A. blepharophylla*, 3–4 inches, flowers pink or intense carmine, early spring. *A. bryoides olympica*, 1 inch, rosettes of silvery leaves, white flowers. Needs a sunny scree. *A.* × *kellereri*, 2–3 inches, rosettes of grey leaves, white flowers. *A. petraea*, 3 inches, white, early summer.

Cultivation Plant in the autumn in a sunny place on the rock garden or dry wall. All species do well on lime. If it is not grown in a scree, *A. bryoides olympica* makes a good plant for the alpine house in a pot of very well-drained gritty soil. *A. albida* may be used as an edging plant in the herbaceous border or as a carpeting plant in spring bedding schemes. Propagate the single varieties by seed sown in a frame in March or outdoors in late spring or by cuttings or division of plants. The double varieties may be propagated either by cuttings or by division.

Arctotis (ark-to-tis)

From *arktos*, a bear in Greek and *ous*, an ear, probably referring to the shaggy fruits of this annual (*Compositae*). Decorative half-hardy annuals and perennials, mostly from South Africa, that flower from July to September and like being baked in the sun on a warm sunny bank.

Perennial species cultivated *A. acaulis*, 6 inches, orange-carmine.

Annual species cultivated *A. breviscapa*, 6 inches, orange. *A. grandis*, 1½ feet, silvery flowers with blue reverse. *A. laevis*, 8 inches, flowers brownish, suffused red. *A. stoechadifolia*, 2 feet, flowers white, blue reverse.

Hybrids There are large-flowered hybrids, half-hardy annuals listed as *A.* × *hybrida*, in a wide colour range, including yellows, oranges, reds, crimsons, purples and whites. All are about 1–1½ feet tall. 'Crane Hill', which can grow up to 2 feet, has white flowers with a blue centre and a yellow zone.

Cultivation Sow seeds in heat in March, prick out the seedlings and harden them off before planting them out 1 foot apart when frosts are over. They make excellent plants for the unheated greenhouse in pots containing loam and leafmould in equal parts, plus a little sharp sand. These should start in a sunny place and should be watered moderately from October to March, freely at other times. Cuttings may be taken in early summer and rooted and overwintered in a frame or greenhouse, but propagation by seed is the usual method. *A. acaulis* needs cloche or frame protection in winter.

Armeria (ar-meer-e-a)

This genus has retained the old Latin name for pink although it is not related to the true pink, a species of dianthus (*Plumbaginaceae*). Perennials mainly for the rock garden though the taller kinds are sometimes used at the front of the herbaceous border. They all need well-drained, sunny positions and grow well in seaside gardens; the common thrift does, in fact, grow wild in extensive colonies on cliffs by the sea.

Species cultivated *A. caespitosa*, 2 inches, a true alpine so it must have good drainage, flowers pale lilac in early summer, a good plant for the alpine house; vars. *alba*, flowers white; *rubra*, ruby-red. *A. corsica*, 6 inches, brick-red. *A. maritima*, the common thrift or sea pink, 6 inches, flowers pink in early summer. There are good varieties of this species such as *laucheana*, 9 inches, bright red flowers; *nana alba*, with large, white flowers in May and June; 'Merlin', rich pink, and 'Vindictive', masses of reddish-pink flowers. *A. pseudoarmeria*, sea pink, thrift, 1 foot, a handsome plant for the herbaceous border; the bright rose-coloured flowers appear in June. The cultivar 'Bees Ruby' was developed from this species and is taller, at 2 feet, and bears rounded heads of deep rose flowers in early summer. *A. splendens*, 3–4 inches, pale pink, summer.

Cultivation Any good, sandy loam suits these plants which must have well-drained positions either in the herbaceous border or on the rock garden. Propagate by division of roots in autumn or spring when they should also be planted. Seeds can be sown in spring in sandy soil.

Artemisia (ar-tem-ees-e-a)

Named after Artemis the Greek goddess (*Compositae*). A large genus, widely distributed over the world, of shrubs, sub-shrubs, herbaceous perennials and annuals, grown mainly for their dainty, aromatic foliage which is very finely cut in some species. The genus shows a great diversity of habit and leaf shape: the flowers are very small and are seldom of much account, though they are often borne in large panicles or plumes. The herb used for flavourings and tarragon vinegar is a member of this family. Most of the artemisias are sun lovers, but *A. lactiflora*, with its sprays of creamy white flowers, will grow in semi-shade and is a useful plant for the herbaceous border.

Annual species cultivated *A. sacrorum viridis*, summer fire, 4 feet, strictly a sub-shrub but grown as an annual.

Herbaceous and sub-shrubs *A. absinthium*, wormwood, 1½ feet, flowers yellow, summer. There is a good form, 'Lam-

Artemisia gnaphalodes, a hardy perennial with whitish leaves, makes a good foil for warmer colours in the border

brook Silver' useful for the grey border. *A. baumgartenii*, 9 inches, silvery leaves, yellow flowers, late summer. *A. canescens*, 1 foot, makes a dome of silvery leaves and is suitable for the rock garden. *A. dracunculus*, tarragon, 2 feet, whitish-green. *A. filifolia*, dwarf carpeting plant with bright silvery foliage. *A. glacialis*, 3–6 inches, silvery leaves, yellow flowerheads. A plant for a scree in the rock garden or for the alpine house. **Rock Garden** *A. ludoviciana*, 3 feet, silvery leaves, yellow flowers, summer. *A. maritima*, sea wormwood, 1–1½ feet, silvery-white leaves, yellowish to reddish flowers, summer. *A. nutans*, 1½–2 feet, finely cut silver-grey leaves. *A. pedemontana*, 6 inches, silvery leaves, rock garden. *A. pontica*, 1–2 feet, grey foliage, whitish-yellow flowers, late summer. *A. stelleriana*, 2–3 feet, silvery leaves, yellow flowers. *A. purshiana*, 2½ feet, white leaves, used as a foliage plant. *A. vulgaris*, mugwort, 2–4 feet, purplish or yellow flowers, autumn, a native plant.

Shrubs *A. abrotanum*, 3–4 feet, the well-known old man, southernwood, or lad's love, fragrant, grey, filigree foliage. *A. arborescens*, 3 feet, silvery foliage retained throughout the year. The flowers of both these shrubs, when produced, are insignificant. They are grown for their foliage.

Cultivation Plant in autumn or spring in sunny borders in ordinary soil. Propagate shrubby species by summer cuttings and herbaceous by cuttings or division. Seeds may be sown in spring of annual and herbaceous species.

Artichokes

The flavours of these vegetables are acquired tastes and are not every gardener's choice. Jerusalem and Chinese artichokes are easy enough to grow and yield a good crop, taking up little space, but the globe artichoke is rather wasteful of space and it does require a little extra skill to grow it well.

Chinese artichokes (*Stachys affinis*) The tuberous roots, which are knobbly, are eaten as a root vegetable during the winter. The tubers should be planted 4 inches deep in any ordinary soil, that has been well prepared, in spring, spacing them 9 inches apart in rows 18 inches apart. No further cultivation is required except occasional hoeing. The tubers are lifted as they are required but in severe weather cover the ground to prevent it from freezing too hard. Plants grow 1–1½ feet tall. See also *Stachys affinis*.

Globe artichokes (*Cynara scolymus*) These plants are very ornamental; they grow to about 5 feet and produce large flower-heads which are gathered just as the scales are beginning to open. The flower-heads are boiled and the fleshy portion at the base of each scale is eaten, together with the base of the flower.

To grow these plants well the ground must be deeply dug and manured. Plant

the off-sets in the spring at least 3 feet apart each way and choose a sunny position. Keep the plants well watered during dry weather and mulch the beds in the spring. The beds should be renewed about every three years, so it is a good plan to detach off-sets from the parent plants every spring and make a new plantation, discarding any beds that are over three years old. It is important to protect the plants in the winter by placing some bracken or other protective material over them in October. If the soil is too heavy or wet they are liable to rot in the winter; the ideal is a sandy loam.

Seed is another method of propagation but a slower one. Seed should be sown in an unheated greenhouse or frame in March or outdoors in April. As soon as the seedlings can be handled, transplant them but wait until the following spring before you transfer them to their final quarters.

Jerusalem artichokes (*Helianthus tuberosus*). The tubers of Jerusalem artichokes are very similar to Chinese artichokes but they are larger and more irregular in shape (those of the French variety 'Fusean' are larger and less irregular as well as being more palatable). The tubers are planted in February, or earlier if the ground is workable. Space the tubers about 18 inches apart in rows 3 feet apart, in ground that has been well dug and manured. They will grow in any odd, rough corner of the garden, but they appreciate a well-cultivated site. See also *Helianthus tuberosus*.

These artichokes grow to about 5 feet in height and look very like the sunflowers to which they are related; they make an excellent screen for an old shed, manure heap, compost heap or other unsightly part of the garden. The top growth should be cut down in the autumn, leaving the tubers in the ground. These are then lifted as they are required or they may be lifted and stored in some dry soil or peat in a shed. If they are left out of the ground for long they will shrivel.

During the summer the ground between them should be hoed occasionally but they do not need any further attention.

Tubers for planting the following year can be selected from those lifted in the late winter and replanted almost immediately.

Asparagus (as-par-ag-us)

The prickles on some species are said to give this genus its name, from the Greek *a*, intensive, and *sparasso*, to tear (*Liliaceae*). A genus which includes perennial climbers and shrubs for the greenhouse as well as a vegetable for the epicure. The greenhouse species with their diversity of fine foliage are invaluable to the florist. They also make excellent pot plants and are specially useful for hanging baskets. The hardy herbaceous asparagus has feathery foliage which

grows to about 4 feet, but this species is grown for the plump young shoots which are cut for eating when they are about 4 inches long.

Greenhouse species cultivated *A. asparagoides*, climber to 10 feet, known as smilax by the florist. *A. plumosus*, climber to 10 feet, very fine foliage and known as asparagus fern, used extensively in bouquets. There is also a dwarf variety, *nanus*. *A. sprengeri*, climber to 6 feet, a good species for hanging baskets.

Hardy *A. officinalis*, the edible asparagus.

Cultivation of greenhouse species Greenhouse species are largely grown for the florist trade, but *A. plumosus* and *A. sprengeri* are also grown as house plants and used to plant up hanging baskets. The compost should be made up of 2 parts of loam to 1 part of a mixture made up of sand, peat and leafmould in equal quantities. They should be potted in March. They need a greenhouse temperature of about 55 F (13 C) in winter and rather more in summer. Keep them syringed during the summer and feed with liquid manure or a balanced fertiliser regularly to encourage growth. It is important to keep a humid atmosphere in the greenhouse during the summer. When cutting the foliage do not cut too drastically. Propagation is by division of the roots in spring or by seeds sown in a temperature of 70 F (21 C) in spring.

Cultivation of Edible Asparagus This delicious vegetable is rather expensive to buy but easy to grow. The shoots are cut below the soil level when they are about 4 inches long, but all cutting must cease soon after the middle of June to allow the plants to develop over the summer and build up the crowns for the following spring. Asparagus plants must not be cropped until they are at least three years old and then only moderately until they are well established.

An asparagus bed will last for a good many years, so it should be dug to a depth of 2 feet, incorporating manure in the second spit, and if the soil is heavy add some cinders or other material that will break up the soil and improve the drainage as the crowns are liable to rot in heavy, wet soils. It is advisable on heavy, ill-drained soils, to raise the level of the beds about 6 inches to improve the drainage. The beds are usually made about 4 feet wide with an alley of 2 feet or so between them.

Crowns are planted in spring or seed may be sown. If planting crowns make sure the roots are spread out well and then cover them with 3 inches of soil. They should be spaced about 1 foot apart, in rows 15 inches apart.

Seeds may be sown either directly into the permanent beds or in a seed bed or frame and then thinned out eventually leaving the plants 9 inches apart. They will be ready for planting into their permanent bed the following spring. Female plants, which are berry-bearing, do not produce such good crops as the male plants and should be discarded, replacing them with male plants. It is not possible to distinguish between them until the plants are two years old so the rogueing must be done when the plants are in their permanent beds, or the seedlings can be kept in the seed bed and planted out as soon as they can be sorted out.

Topdress the beds in the spring with a thick layer of well-rotted manure and keep them weeded but do not use a hoe as the roots are so near the surface. The top growth must be cut down in the autumn when it turns yellow.

Plants may be forced in a warm greenhouse by packing some crowns into boxes containing soil or by planting them in a hotbed outdoors. They are kept close and moist until the shoots appear when they should be ventilated. After forcing the crowns are discarded.

There are several varieties on the market, one of the best being 'Connover's Colossal', an old American variety. 'Purple Argentinil' is a French variety said to be one of the best for flavour; 'Webb's New Market Favourite' is a newer, early variety.

Aster (as-ter)
From the Greek *aster*, star, describing the flower shape (*Compositae*). Michaelmas daisy. Among the most useful herbaceous perennials, most of the asters flower in late summer right into the aut-

1 'Beechwood', a useful form of Aster alpinus. 2 Aster pappei flowers throughout summer. 3 'Aubrey', a good dwarf for the front of the border

umn and are extremely hardy and easy to grow. They increase so rapidly, in fact, that many of them have to be lifted and divided about every second year. There are a great many cultivars suitable for the back of the herbaceous border, growing to about 6 feet in height, derived from *A. novi-belgii* and *A. novae-angliae* but there are also shorter, bushier cultivars, up to 3 feet in height that have been raised from *A. amellus* and *A. frikartii*. These dwarfer varieties are also earlier flowering than the taller kinds. The really dwarf cultivars, from 9–15 inches tall, are excellent plants for the front of a border, as they are compact and very free flowering.

There are asters, too, for the rock garden, such as *A. subcaeruleus*, which flowers in June; the bright violet-blue flowers are produced on 9 inch stems and stand up above the foliage which makes small clumps as it spreads.

The two groups, *A. novi-belgii* and *A. novae-angliae* are very similar, but the foliage in the *novi-belgii* group is smooth, whereas that of *novae-angliae* is downy.

A great deal of hybridising has been carried out with Michaelmas daisies, the largest variations are to be seen in the *novi-belgii* group where the colours range from white, pinks, mauves, to deep rose-pink and purple. There are double and single flowers, and some of the varieties are short and bushy, more like the *amellus* group. In the *nova-angliae* group the colours are confined to deep pinks and purples and the flowers have an unfortunate habit of closing at sundown.

Species cultivated *A. acris*, 3 feet, masses of lavender-blue flowers in mid-summer. *A. alpinus*, 6 inches, purple flowers in mid-summer; 'Beechwood' is a fine cultivar. *A. amellus*, 2 feet, purple flowers in mid-summer. *A. cordifolius*, 2 feet, mauve flowers on arching stems in summer. *A. ericoides*, 2–3 feet, abundant white flowers in autumn, angular branching habit; 'Perfection', 4 feet, white and 'Ringdove' 4 feet, rosy mauve, are two cultivars. *A. farreri*, 1½ feet, flowers long rayed, violet-blue in summer. *A. × frikartii*, 3 feet, flowers lavender-blue in mid-summer; 'Wonder of Staff', lavender-blue, is a popular cultivar. *A. linosyris*, goldilocks, 1½ feet, a native with showy golden-yellow flowers in late summer. *A. novae-angliae*, 5–6 feet, autumn-flowering, purple flowers. *A. novi-belgii*, 4 feet, blue flowers in autumn. *A. pappei*, 1 foot, bright blue flowers throughout summer and early autumn. Not reliably hardy except in milder places. *A. subcaeruleus*, 9 inches, violet-blue flowers on 9 inch stems above the foliage; 'Wendy', 1½ feet, pale blue with orange centre, a fine cultivar. *A. thomsonii*, 15 inches, pale blue, a parent, with *A. amellus*, of the hybrid *A. × frikartii*. *A. tradescantii*, 4 feet, white flowers in autumn. *A. yunnanensis*, 1 foot, lilac-blue flowers in summer; 'Napsbury' has larger flowers of heliotrope-blue.

Cultivars Named varieties of the major groups are numerous and new ones seem to appear each year and it is worth visiting a nursery or consulting an up-to-date catalogue before ordering plants. Among the best are the following:

Amellus 'Blue King', 2½ feet, bright blue. 'King George', 2½ feet, bright blue; an old favourite. 'Sonia', 2 feet, clear pink.

Novae-angliae 'Barr's Pink', 4 feet, 'Harrington's Pink', 4½ feet, clear pink, both old varieties. 'Lye End Beauty', 4 feet, pale plum and 'September Glow', 5 feet, ruby, are both newer varieties.

Novi-belgii 'Apple Blossom', 3 feet, cream, overlaid pink. 'Blue Radiance', 3 feet, large flowers, soft blue. 'Crimson Brocade', 3 feet, bright red, double. 'Little Pink Boy', 2 feet, deep pink. 'Marie Ballard', 3 feet, mid-blue, large fully double. 'My Smokey', 6 feet, deep mulberry, vigorous. 'Orlando', 3½ feet, clear pink, single. 'Peerless', 4 feet, soft heliotrope, semi-double. 'Sailing Light', 3 feet, deep rose. 'Sweet Seventeen', 4 feet, lavender-pink, fully double. 'The Cardinal', 5 feet, rose-red. 'The Rector', 3½ feet, claret. 'White Lady', 5–6 feet, pure white. 'Winston Churchill', 2½ feet, ruby-crimson.

Dwarf 'Audrey', 15 inches, large, pale blue. 'Lilac Time', 1 foot, soft lilac. 'Pink Lace', 15 inches, double pink. 'Professor A. Kippenburg', 15 inches, light blue, semi-double. 'Snow Cushion', 10 inches, white. 'Victor', 9 inches, light blue.

Cultivation Their cultivation is simple: plant in the autumn or spring except the *amellus* group which dislike autumn planting and so must be planted and divided in the spring. They like a sunny position but will tolerate a little shade,

and though they will repay good cultivation they are not fussy about soil. They are readily increased by division. Attacks by powdery mildew often whiten the leaves and make them unsightly. Spraying in summer with dilute lime-sulphur (1 part in 80 parts of water) will check this trouble.

Astilbe (as-til-be)

Many of the older species had colourless flowers which may be the origin of the name, from the Greek *a*, no, *stilbe*, brightness (*Saxifragaceae*). A small genus of herbaceous perennials with feathery plumes composed of myriads of minute flowers in white, many in shades of pink and deep crimson. They are delightful waterside plants but they will grow in the herbaceous border if given a good, rich, moist soil. They will grow well in partial shade and there are dwarf species suitable for the rock garden.

Species cultivated *A. chinensis pumila*, 1 foot, rose-lilac flowers in late summer. *A. crispa*, 6 inches, salmon-pink flowers, summer. *A. davidii*, 4–5 feet, rose pink flowers in late summer. *A. japonica*, 2 feet, white flowers in spring. *A. simplicifolia erecta*, 9 inches, pink flowers in arching sprays in summer. *A. thunbergii*, 1–2 feet, white flowers in May.

Cultivars 'Amethyst', 3 feet, lilac-purple. 'Cattleya', 3 feet, orchid-pink. 'Fanal', 2 feet, garnet red. 'Feuer', crimson with deep crimson foliage. 'Granat', 3 feet, rose-crimson. 'Professor Van der Weilan', 3 feet, white. 'Red Sentinel', 2 feet, brick red. 'Rhineland', 2½ feet, rich rose pink. 'Venus', 3 feet, deep pink. 'White Queen', 2½ feet. All these are known as *A. × arendsii* hybrids and are of complex parentage. Others will be found in nurserymen's lists.

Cultivation Plant in autumn or spring and water well in dry weather. Propagate by division or seeds. Astilbes may also be grown as early-flowering greenhouse plants. They should be potted up in the early autumn in a compost of loam, leafmould and sand. Pots should be kept plunged outdoors until December when they may be brought into the greenhouse and forced into early flower in a temperature of 55–60° F (13–16° C). After flowering is over the plants should be hardened off, after which they may be planted outdoors again in May.

Astrantia (as-tran-te-a)

Starlike flowers, hence the name from the Greek *aster*, a star (*Umbelliferae*). Masterwort. Summer-flowering perennials with fascinating papery-looking flowers in shades of green, white and pink. The actual flowers are insignificant but they are surrounded by parchment-like bracts that give them colour. They make excellent and unusual cut flowers. **Species cultivated** *A. biebersteinii*, 2 feet, flowers light lilac. *A. carinthiaca*, 1–2 feet, very similar to *A. major* with which it is often confused, flowers fragrant of marzipan. *A. carniolica*, 2 feet, white or bluish-pink flowers; var. *rubra*, reddish. **Cultivation** Plant astrantias in the autumn or spring in ordinary soil in a shady position in the border or woodland garden. They will grow in more open positions provided they are not hot and dry. Propagate by division at planting time or grow from seeds sown in sandy loam in April in a cold frame.

Aubrieta (aw-bre-she-a)

Commemorating M. Claude Aubriet, a French botanical artist (*Cruciferae*). Purple rock-cress. The most widely grown of all rock garden plants the aubrieta (usually misspelt aubretia) is a hardy perennial. Apart from its use in the rock garden it may also be grown as a border edging, in spring bedding schemes, or on dry banks or walls.

Species cultivated *A. deltoidea*, 2 inches, purple flowers in spring, is probably the only species seen in cultivation and even this is uncommon since it has been superseded by its numerous cultivars in a wide range of colours. Interesting varieties of *A. deltoidea* are *argenteo-variegata*, light purple flowers, white variegated foliage, and *aureo-variegata*, bright yellow variegated foliage. **Cultivars** 'Barker's Double', red, semi-double; 'Bonfire', bright crimson; 'Bressingham Pink', deep pink, semi-double; 'Cambria', bright red, early; 'Dream', light blue; 'Dr Mules', an old, rich purple

3

4

1 'White Queen' and 2 'Fanal' are two of the astilbe hybrids. 3 Aubrietas are shown to their best advantage when grown in this way. 4 'Riverslea' is a late-flowering aubrieta hybrid

variety; 'Gurgedyke', rich violet; 'Hartswood', rich purple; 'Lissadell Pink', pink with white eye; 'Magnificent', red with darker eye; 'Mrs Rodewald', dark red, late flowering, a very fine aubrieta; 'Riverslea', mauve-pink, late; 'Stock-flowered Pink', clear pink, semi-double; 'Studland', lavender.

Cultivation Plant in the autumn or spring in any open sunny position in the rock garden or in crevices in a dry wall. After flowering plants benefit from a hard clipping. Cuttings may be taken in June and rooted in a sandy soil in a cold frame which should be kept closed until they have rooted. They can also be raised from seed but they do not always come true to type, so divide the roots in spring or take cuttings for true-to-type plants.

Auriculas

These hardy plants of the primula family (*Primulaceae*) have the most quaint and diverse colourings in their flowers. The alpine kinds (probably bred from *Primula pubescens*) have flowers of one colour with a white or yellow eye and they are quite free from the powdery covering ('meal') found on the flowers and stems of the florists' auriculas. The florists' auriculas (almost certainly bred from *Primula auricula*) are usually grown in a frame or cool greenhouse and this protects the mealy powder from damage by the weather.

In both kinds the leaves are evergreen and leathery, clustered at the base of the flower stems which are anything from 3–9 inches in height. The flowers are in heads of seven or so very similar in habit to the polyanthus. The most unusual colourings are to be found in the florists' auriculas with distinct colour bands on their petals in all shades of greens, greys, russets, reds, blues, yellows and other colours not generally associated with flowers. They have been grown for well over 350 years and in that time certain standards of excellence, defining the formation of the perfect flower, have been laid down, and five different types are recognised.

Cultivars: Alpine 'Blue Velvet', deep blue, white eye. 'Celtic King', yellow, white eye. 'Jean Walker', mauve, cream eye. 'Old Yellow Dusty Miller', yellow, powdery flowers. 'W. A. Cook', deep red.

Florists' There is a very wide range of these listed by specialist growers, one of the most famous growers is Douglas of Bookham, Surrey.

Cultivation The hardy, border kinds do not need pampering but they appreciate rich soil. Plant in early spring and divide the clumps when they become too overgrown. Propagate by seed or division.

The florists' auriculas need greenhouse or frame protection, but should be given ample ventilation at all times. Only in very severe weather should the ventilators be entirely closed. Frames will need added protective covering in such weather. The compost should consist of turfy loam, rotted manure, leaf-mould and sand. Pot the plants into 3 inch pots in February or March and keep them well watered in the summer. When in flower give them a feed with liquid manure and provide some shade. They propagate easily by seeds sown in spring or by division after flowering.

Beans

All beans provide in their low-grade protein a very rich source of food. They are of very ancient cultivation. Below they are listed in their various categories.

Broad beans (*Vicia faba*) These were certainly known to the Ancient Egyptians and are probably natives of northern and western Asia. These are grown solely for their seeds, unlike the french bean and scarlet runner. They are among the hardiest of our bean crop.

Cultivation A good rich loam suits these beans, though they are not difficult to grow on any soil. This crop may well follow cabbages and potatoes, or manure may be dug in sparingly. A certain amount of chemical fertiliser may be added as follows: 3 oz per square yard of superphosphate and 1 oz per square yard of sulphate of potash. These beans prefer a neutral or alkaline soil to one which is acid. On acid soil lime or chalk should be applied.

In January or February seed may be sown in boxes or individual pots and started under glass. In April the young plants are set out and the crop becomes mature in June. Another method is to plant outdoors in April for the main summer crop or a May sowing becomes ready in September. At one time autumn sowing was popular, but a number of bad winters in succession has made this method unpopular.

In sowing, the seeds are spaced at 6 inch intervals in rows 2 feet apart. The beans may be put 1½ inches deep or, on clay soil, be placed on the surface and soil ridged up to cover them. When the first bean pods are showing the tip of the main shoot should be broken off and removed.

Haricot beans and french beans (*Phaseolus vulgaris*) The difference between the french bean and the haricot bean is merely that in the former the pod containing immature seeds is eaten, while the haricots are the ripe seeds without the pods. The details of cultivation are the same for both french and haricot forms of the bean.

Though in Britain the runner bean is more often grown than the french, on the continent the reverse is true. It is not always known that a climbing form of the french bean is available though the dwarf kind is certainly more popular and has some advantages.

Cultivation Soil should be rich and light and well dug, with a dusting of superphosphate of lime at 3 oz per square yard and manure at the rate of 1 cwt to each 8 square yards. For early crops seeds may be sown in boxes during April and started under glass to be hardened off and planted out in May. Outdoors it is unwise to sow before the end of April.

The secret of a good crop of succulent beans is speedy raising without check. Water freely and mulch if dry weather occurs. It is essential with this bean to begin picking while the beans are still tender and not more than 4 inches long. It seems a British trait to produce the heaviest crop of the largest vegetables, and this is why the best qualities of flavour and texture are sometimes lacking from our vegetables.

The outdoor beans should be spaced 6

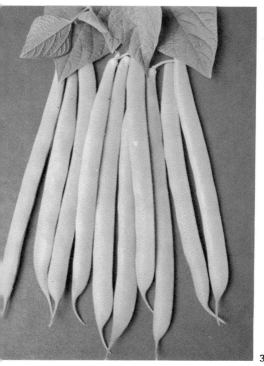

1 'Prizewinner Enorma', a popular runner bean. 2 Dwarf bean 'The Prince'. 3 Dwarf french bean 'Cherokee'.

inches apart in drills 1 inch deep, 18 inches apart.

At the end of the season the plants may well be allowed to ripen their remaining seeds as these when shelled and dried are really the haricots of commerce. They may be used as seed for next year's crop, but as long as they are kept dry they may be kept for over a year for use in cookery.

French beans may be forced under glass to have them at a time when they are unobtainable in the shops. From a January sowing under glass with a maintained temperature of 60°F (16°C) beans may be had by May. Early March sowings give beans in June. Soil should be as for tomato culture and an even temperature and state of moisture must be maintained throughout (see Tomato culture).

Named kinds include: 'Brown Dutch', 'Canadian Wonder', 'Cherokee', 'Fin de Bagnols', 'Masterpiece' and 'Black Prince'.

Runner beans (*Phaseolus coccineus*) This plant is a native of tropical America, and when first introduced into Britain it was grown for the beauty of its bright scarlet blossoms. It is actually a tender perennial, but is commonly grown as an annual; though it is possible to take a plant and overwinter it, nothing is gained.

Those who use the railways running into London will, in late summer, have noted in almost all the suburban backyards abutting upon the line thriving plants of the beloved scarlet runner, and it is notable that this is often the only vegetable grown. All of which speaks eloquently of the merits of this most pop-

ular amateur's plant.

Cultivation It would be most unwise to plant runner beans before May as they will not take the least frost. Should an early crop be required the same method may be used as advised for the french bean and sow the seed in boxes under glass. It is not necessary to sow these seeds before April since they may not be put out before late May or the beginning of June.

The method of planting for those plants which will be staked is that of two double rows 10 inches apart separated by a space of at least 5 feet. It is in this central area that the strong supports must be placed. The individual seeds must be placed at 8 inch intervals.

The poles or stakes should be quite 8 feet long and should be connected by a strong horizontal structure firmly lashed to the uprights. The rest of the framework is merely a net or an arrangement of strings. The weight of a row of runner beans in full growth is considerable and they present a large surface to be shaken by the wind. To avoid all this scaffolding it is quite possible to convert the plants into shrubby masses by a routine of pinching out the growing shoots. However, when this plan is adopted the individual seeds must be spaced at 2 foot intervals, with a distance of 3 feet between the rows. Naturally a given number of plants will occupy considerably more ground space under these conditions.

When runner beans are in full production pick them frequently. As with french beans, they should be picked when they are young and tender.

Named kinds include: 'Best of All', 'Giraffe', 'Kentucky Wonder', 'Painted Lady', 'Prizewinner', 'Streamline'.

Beetroot

This sweet salad-vegetable has a high food value. It needs good deep soil, and is best suited to occupy a place where a previous non-root crop has been grown. Do not add fresh manure as this is inclined to cause forking of the root. If, instead of growing vegetables in the kitchen garden, they are grown in the old-fashioned cottager's way interspersed with flowering plants, the beetroot is a most suitable plant, since the round or turnip-shaped beet has generally fine decorative crimson leaves. In addition to the round beet there are two other forms obtainable, a long-rooted, and an intermediate type, called tankard or canister-shaped. Good named kinds are: 'Crimson Globe', 'Veitch's Intermediate', 'Cheltenham Green Top' and 'Nutting's Red Globe'. All are forms of *Beta vulgaris* (see also Beta).

Cultivation The soil must be of an open well-worked, but not recently manured type. Ammonium sulphate should be given at the rate of 1 oz. per square yard, potassium sulphate at the same rate, and 4 oz of calcium superphosphate also to each square yard.

Sow the globe-rooted beet in April; the others may follow in May. Make drills, 12 inches apart, space seeds 5 inches apart. A point to note is that each so-called 'seed' is, in fact, a 'seed-ball' containing several seeds and more than one may germinate. It is necessary to single the seedlings to one at each point when they are 1 inch high.

Another most important point to remember with this crop is the extreme care required when the roots are harvested. On no account should root or top growth be damaged, or the result is quite likely to be a most unpalatable ,anaemic-

looking thing instead of the rich wine-red and appetising vegetable it should be. The roots should be only shaken free of soil as they are dug in August or September, and then stored in a shed, giving some cover in the form of dry soil, peat or leaves. Top growth may be carefully twisted off to avoid damage. Do not leave the roots to get hard and woody before digging them. After the beets have been cooked they may be cut without damaging the appearance of them, but if they are cut before cooking their appearance will certainly be spoiled.

Beet, Seakale
This is cultivated in the same way as spinach beet (see Beet, Spinach), but in use only the broad white midrib is cooked and served as if it were seakale or asparagus, with a melted butter sauce.
Cultivation Both crops should be thinned to 1 foot in the rows to get big succulent leaves, and generous watering greatly improves the crop.

The seakale beet should be treated rather in the manner of celery, by earthing-up the plants and securing thus some well-blanched leaves with broad tender midribs. Do not allow the plant to produce flowering shoots. If this happens scrap the crop and prepare the bed for a new planting, as an elderly flowering plant will not give the sweet succulent growth required.

Both seakale beet and spinach beet are known botanically as *Beta vulgaris cicla*

Beet, Spinach
This is one of the easiest of all vegetable crops to grow, and the longest available, as it may be picked at any time in the year (see Beet, Seakale; Beta).

The large succulent leaves are treated as if they were spinach, which they somewhat resemble in flavour.
Cultivation Similar to that of beetroot, but instead of harvesting the roots, the outer leaves are picked while they are still in a young state and are then cooked without added water, and served with melted butter. The cooked leaves may also be reduced to a puree.

Begonia (be-go-ne-a)
Commemorating Michel Bégon, 1638–1710, Governor of Canada, patron of botany (*Begoniaceae*). These half-hardy herbaceous and sub-shrubby plants are natives of moist tropical countries, apart from Australia. They need greenhouse treatment, though a large number are now used in summer bedding schemes.

The genus begonia is usually divided into two groups; those species with fibrous roots and those with tubers. Other classifications give special treatment to the winter-flowering forms, and to those grown exclusively for the interest of their leaves. A notable feature of begonias is their oblique, lop-sided or uneven sided leaves.

There has been so much hybridising in this genus that the naming has become quite complicated, and the custom of giving Latin specific names has not made matters easier.

The begonia, unlike the majority of plants, has, instead of hermaphrodite blooms, separate male and female blossoms on the same plant; the female flowers are generally removed as not being of much interest, though if seed is required, they must, of course, be retained. The seed is dust-fine and needs no covering of soil, in fact the raising of begonias from seed has something in common with the art of raising ferns from spores.

Species cultivated The best-known begonias are the hybrids of the tuberous species: *B. boliviensis, B. clarkei, B. cinnabarina, B. davisii, B. pearcei, B. rosaeflora, B. veitchii.*

Another important group consists of the hybrids and varieties of *B. rex*, a plant from Assam with most interesting, colourful foliage. The winter-flowering and fibrous-rooted varieties derived from *B.* 'Gloire de Lorraine', a variety originally raised in France in 1891 by the plant breeder Victor Lemoine, who crossed *B. socotrana* and *B. dregei*, form a most valuable group as they furnish the greenhouse at a difficult time of the year.

Fibrous-rooted species include: *B. acutifolia*, white, spring. *B. angularis*, white-veined leaves. *B. coccinea*, scarlet, winter. *B. evansiana*, pink, almost hardy (possibly hardy in the south-west). *B. fuchsioides*, scarlet, winter. *B. froebelli*, scarlet, winter. *B. foliosa*, white and rose, summer. *B. glaucophylla*, pink and pendulous, winter. *B. haageana*, pink, autumn. *B. hydrocotylifolia*, pink, summer. *B. incarnata*, rose, winter. *B. manicata*, pink, winter. *B. scharffiana*, white, winter. *B. semperflorens*, rose (has important large-flowered vars.). *B. socotrana*, pink, winter.

Nurserymen's catalogues contain long lists of hybrids of the above, too numerous to mention here, but in various shades of pink, red, cream and white with enormous double flowers in a number of different forms.

Species with ornamental leaves include: *B. albo-picta, B. argenteo-guttata*, white and pink speckled leaves. *B. heracleifolia*, leaves deeply lobed. *B. imperialis*, velvety-green leaves. *B. boeringiana*, foliage purplish and green. *B. maculata*, foliage spotted white. *B. masoniana*, ('Iron Cross'), leaves green with a prominent dark 'iron cross' marking, popular as a houseplant. *B. metallica*, foliage has metallic lustre. *B. olbia*, bronze leaves spotted white. *B. rex*, foliage metallic silver and purple. *B. ricinifolia*, bronze leaves. *B. sanguinea*, leaves blood-red beneath. There are, in addition to the species given, many hybrids with beautiful leaves, especially named garden hybrids derived from *B.*

rex and its varieties and other species, all known as Rex begonias.

Cultivation The fibrous-rooted begonias are usually obtained from seed, which should be sown in January in a temperature of 60°F (16°C). It is also possible to root growths from the base of the plant. The sub-shrubby perennial forms will come easily from normal cuttings, or all begonias may be raised by leaf cuttings. Leaf cuttings are single leaves which are pegged down in sandy compost, the undersides of all the main veins having been nicked with a razor blade. The temperature should be around 60–70°F (16–21°C). Little plants should form where veins were cut, and these may later be detached and potted-on separately. Most begonias need a winter temperature of about 60°F (16°C). The ornamental Rex type must not be exposed to full sunlight, and many of the other classes will be happy with much less light than suits other greenhouse plants.

The tuberous begonias may, of course, be grown from tubers. These are usually started into growth by placing them in shallow boxes of peat or leafmould in February or March, hollow side uppermost, in a temperature of 60–70°F (16–21°C). After roots have formed the tubers are potted up in small pots and later moved into larger ones. A compost of equal parts of loam, leafmould, well-rotted manure and silver sand is suitable. Do not start to feed these tuberous plants till they have formed roots, or they will decay, but after they are rooted a bi-weekly dose of liquid manure is helpful. The tuberous begonias may also be raised from seed, and if this is sown in February plants may flower from July to October. These seed-raised plants are popular for summer bedding.

Tuberous begonias when their season is over must be gradually dried out. They may be left in their pots in a frost-proof shed, or knocked-out and stored in clean dry sand.

Bergenia (ber-gen-i-a)

Named for Karl August von Bergen, 1704–60, German botanist (*Saxifragaceae*). These hardy perennial herbaceous plants with large evergreen leaves were at one time called megasea, and were at another time included with the saxifrages. The flowers which come in early spring are showy in white, pink or red-purple, borne in large heads on long stems. The large leathery, glossy leaves are also decorative, especially as in some kinds the foliage is suffused with reddish colour, in winter.

Species cultivated *B. cordifolia*, 1 foot, pink, spring; var. *purpurea*, flowers purplish-pink. *B. crassifolia*, 1 foot, pink, spring. *B. delavayi*, 9 inches, leaves turn crimson in winter, flowers purplish-rose, March. *B. ligulata*, 1 foot, white or pink, January or February onwards. *B.* ×

schmidtii, 1 foot, flowers pink spring. *B. stracheyi*, 1 foot, pink, April.

Cultivars 'Ballawley Hybrid', 1½ feet, crimson flowers, dark purplish leaves in winter. 'Delbees', 1 foot, leaves turn red in winter, flowers rosy, March–April. 'Evening Glow', 15–18 inches, dark purple flowers, reddish-bronze foliage. 'Silberlicht', ('Silver Light'), 1 foot, flowers white flushed pink, spring. Others are available and more are likely to be seen in cultivation as time goes on.

Cultivation These members of the saxifrage family are in no way difficult, thriving in any soil, in sun or shade. However, to get full colour in the winter leaves (and this can be very fine), it will be necessary to give the bergenias full sun exposure; and under those conditions they will also produce their flowers somewhat earlier.

Beta (be-ta)

From the Latin *beta*, beetroot, or *bett*, the Celtic word for red (*Chenopodiaceae*). A small genus known principally for the species *Beta vulgaris*, a biennial or perennial, of which beetroot, seakale beet, spinach beet, sugar beet, and mangold are distinct forms. In addition, there are certain forms with highly coloured foliage which are used for ornamental purposes, sometimes in sub-tropical bedding schemes (see Beetroot, Seakale; Beet, Spinach).

Species cultivated *B. vulgaris*, beetroot, etc., 1 foot; vars. *cicla*, seakale beet, spinach beet; *dracaenaefolia*, narrow, dark-red leaves. Other ornamental forms may be found in seedsmen's lists from time to time.

Cultivation For cultivation of vegetable kinds see Beetroot.

Seeds of ornamental beet are sown

1 Bergenia cordifolia. 2 Brachycome 'Purple King', a striking annual.

¼ inch deep in boxes of John Innes seed compost under glass in March, in a temperature of 60–70°F (16–21°C). The seedlings are pricked off into pots and moved to the cold frame in April to be hardened off and planted out in May.

Brachycome (brak-e-ko-me)

From the Greek *brachys*, short, *comus*, hair (*Compositae*). A genus of half-hardy Australian annual or perennial herbs. The species usually cultivated is *B. iberidifolia*, the Swan River daisy, which grows 9–12 inches tall and has 1 inch wide daisy flowers in shades of blue, pink and white in summer. Named hybrids in separate colours are available, including: 'Little Blue Star', 'Purple King' and 'Red Star'.

Cultivation These plants are easily grown in a dry, sunny bed. Sow seed under glass in March in boxes of light soil and plant out in May, or sow in the open in early May where the plants are to flower. When sown under glass in August or September they will make good pot plants for early spring display under glass.

Brassica (bras-sik-a)

The Latin name for the cabbage plant (*Cruciferae*). A genus, mainly from the Mediterranean area, of annual, biennial or perennial herbs of economic importance; the cabbages and allied plants.

Species cultivated *B. campestris* var. *rapa*, the turnip. *B. cernua*, the Chinese cabbage or Petsai. *B. napus*, the swede. *B. nigra*, mustard. *B. oleracea* var. *acephala*, kale; var. *bullata*, savoy cabbage; var. *capitata*, cabbage, colewort; var. *costata*,

24

couve tronchuda; var. *gemmifera*, brussels sprouts; red cabbage; var. *gongyloides*, kohlrabi; var. *botrytis cauliflora*, broccoli, cauliflower; *botrytis cymosa*, sprouting broccoli.

Cultivation The cultivation of all these is described under the common names (see Cabbage, etc.).

Broccoli

Broccoli, known botanically as *Brassica oleracea* var. *botrytis (Cruciferae)*, are frequently mistaken for cauliflowers, and although there is now little difference between them owing to hydridisation, they both have their own seasons of use. Broccoli usually have a stronger flavour, are coarser leaved and hardy, maturing between October and June, while the season for cauliflowers is roughly between June and October, although there are exceptions. The best crops are obtained on rather heavy soils. With careful timing of sowing, combined with choice of varieties to mature in succession, cutting may continue from October to May or June.

Cultivation Some of the finest compact heads are produced on loam or clay soils which have been well manured and deeply cultivated for the previous crop. The addition of fresh manure to the ground and the resulting spongy nature of the soil could cause open, poorly shaped heads and lush growth, more liable to damage from severe weather. On light, hungry soil incorporate well-decayed manure when winter digging, and apply a good compound fertiliser ten days prior to planting. Firm the ground well by treading. A constant supply of heads can be maintained by sowing varieties from the different groups in succession during March and April, in

a sheltered seed bed. Sow thinly in rows 10–12 inches apart, thin the seedlings when necessary to produce sturdy plants. Plant out in May and June 2 feet apart each way. There are many excellent varieties but the 'Roscoff' varieties 1, 2, 3, 4, 5, and 6 produce a continuous supply until the cauliflower heads are ready for cutting in early summer. Alternative varieties are 'Veitch's Self Protecting', November to December; 'Snow's Winter White', January to February; 'Knight's Protecting', April; 'Late Queen', May.

Broccoli, Sprouting

This is another variety, *italica*, of *Brassica oleracea*. Both purple and white sprouting produce a profusion of young shoots invaluable for prolonging the supplies of winter greens. Purple sprouting is the most hardy and will safely overwinter in most open situations. Young shoots may be produced for Christmas, but it is in March and April that the vegetable is most useful. White sprouting is perhaps a little less strong in flavour, not so hardy and can only be grown in sheltered gardens. The small curds which sprout forth in profusion are white instead of purple. Seed should be sown thinly in the open from the middle of April, in drills ¼ inch deep and 9 inches apart. Thin seedlings when they are large enough to handle. Plant out in June or July 2 feet 6 inches apart, in rows allowing 3 feet between the rows. This is a useful crop to plant in July after an early crop of potatoes. The ground must be in good heart, preferably well manured for the previous crop. Otherwise, dig in decayed manure or compost with the addition of extra phosphates and potash, for example 3 oz

of superphosphate and 1 oz of sulphate of potash. Really firm ground will help to keep the plants upright through spells of severe weather, but it may be found necessary to draw soil towards the stems to give extra protection or even to stake the largest of the plants. Varieties are named by type, such as Early or Late Purple or White Sprouting.

Brodiaea (bro-de-e-a)
Named in honour of James Brodie, of Morayshire, Scotland (*Liliaceae*). Hardy bulbs or corms from North and South America, with large clusters of flowers.

Species cultivated *B. californica*, 9–12 inches, blue-purple, June, California. *B. coronaria* (syn. *Hookera coronaria*), 6–18 inches, lilac or violet, June, western North America. *B. ida-maia*, 1½ feet, bright red, yellow and white, June, California. *B. pulchella* (syn. *Hookera pulchella*), 1 foot, blue, summer, California. *B. uniflora* (see Ipheion uniflorum).

Cultivation Plant in September or October in a well-drained sunny bed of rich sandy loam. Depth and distance apart, 4 inches. Propagation is by offsets in the autumn, or by seed sown in a cold frame in March in sandy soil, covering the seed very lightly.

Brussels Sprouts

This important member of the cabbage family, known botanically as *Brassica oleracea* var. *gemmifera (Cruciferae)*, originated in Belgium. The popularity of the vegetable is due not only to the fact that picking can be extended over a long period, but it can stand up to severe winter weather. It is indeed one of the most valued of brassica crops. Brussels sprouts need a deeply-worked, rich, firm soil, plenty of room for development and a long season of growth.

Cultivation To produce compact, firm sprouts, it is essential to have firm ground and an attempt should be made to follow a crop for which the ground has already been well manured. Alternatively, dig in well-decayed manure in the autumn. Late preparation, loose soil or fresh manure results only in lush growth and loose sprouts. If manure is not available apply 3 oz of superphosphate and 1 oz of sulphate of potash per square yard prior to planting. Even when manuring has been carried out the addition of half the recommended quantities of fertiliser will be found beneficial. For early or late varieties, sow in a prepared seed bed in a sheltered position in the middle of March. Transplant to permanent positions in late May and firm well. Under normal growing conditions allow 2½ feet between the plants and in the rows, but with vigorous growing varieties on good growing soil allow 3 feet between the rows and 2½ feet between the plants. As a precaution against cabbage root maggot and club root disease, dip the washed roots of the young plants into a thin paste using 4

25

per cent calomel dust and water. Water the young plants if the weather is hot and dry. Hoe the soil frequently to keep down weeds. Apply 1 oz of Nitro-chalk in September or October. In open windy areas it is as well to stake plants in the autumn if growth is at all vigorous. Remove yellow leaves as they appear. Pick the sprouts as they are ready. Do not remove the tops until the end of the winter as this helps in the formation of sprouts and gives protection during severe weather.

Varieties 'Cambridge No. 1' (early); 'Cambridge No. 2' (mid-season); 'Cambridge No. 5' (late); 'Harrison's XXX', a good heavy cropping early; 'Jade Cross', a newer F.1. hybrid, very early, producing a heavy crop of dark green sprouts; 'The Aristocrat', an excellent mid-late variety producing medium-sized sprouts with perfect flavour, over a long period.

Cabbage

The origin of the cultivated cabbage is unknown, but it has been grown for many hundred of years and was highly regarded by the herbalists of old. The cabbage is known botanically as *Brassica oleracea capitata,* and is a member of the *Cruciferae* family. There are three main types, and with careful choice of varieties within these, cabbages may be produced all the year round. Spring sowing can be divided into two groups, producing heads from June to February. Autumn sowing will produce plants to overwinter and develop compact heads or greens in the spring.

Cultivation Cabbages are gross feeders and require adequate quantities of manure dug in well before planting. Firm ground is essential. Apply 3 oz of superphosphate and 1 oz of sulphate of potash prior to planting. A slightly alkaline soil with a *p*H 7 0 or over is best. On an acid soil apply lime, but never at the same time as manure. Apply a good basic dressing for autumn planting, such as 4 oz of basic slag and 1 oz of sulphate of potash. A dressing of 1 oz of nitrate of soda per square yard in early spring will provide the necessary tonic to start the plants into active growth. The earliest sowing may be under glass in January or early February, and the seedlings pricked off into a protected cold frame 2–3 inches apart. Plant out when hardened off in early May and apply 1 oz of nitrate of soda six weeks later. Cutting should begin in late June. When the ground is in a suitable state in March or early April make a main sowing, using two varieties, one for autumn use and the other for winter cutting. Sow thinly in drills ½ inch deep. Plant these out when ready in early June to 18 inches apart in the rows and 2 feet between the rows. Plants for autumn planting to produce spring cabbages should be sown from the middle of July to the middle of August

Calendulas, sometimes called marigolds, are hardy annuals growing 12 to 15 inches in height. The many cultivars available include **1** 'Geisha Girl' with incurved blooms. **2** One of the strain known as 'Art Shades'. These are a vast improvement over those with single blooms

depending on weather, soil, and locality. Two separate sowings a fortnight apart can prove helpful if the precise sowing time is doubtful. Plant out in September and firm well. Plants must be hard and sturdy. Distance of planting for spring cabbage should be 18 inches apart each way, or 18 inches between the rows, cutting alternate plants first as spring greens. A useful spring crop may be obtained by planting 12 inches between the rows and 9 inches in the rows using the crop as spring greens.

Varieties Early frame sowing, 'Primo' and 'Greyhound'. April sowing for summer and autumn cutting, 'Winningstadt' and 'Wheeler's Imperial', or for winter cabbage 'Christmas Drumhead' and 'January King'. Sowing July–August for summer cutting, 'Harbinger', 'Early Offenham' and 'Flower of the Spring'.

Red cabbage, also known as pickling cabbage, is usually sown in July or August, and thereafter treated in the same way as spring cabbage, although it is better to plant out at 3 feet apart to get better heads. Alternatively it may be sown in March. There are few varieties: those that are available have 'Red' as part of their name e.g. 'Red Drumhead', 'Large Bloodred', although 'Stockley's Giant' is an exception.

Ornamental cabbage The appreciation of

the value of ornamental cabbage and kale leaves for decorative purposes owes much to the activities of floral arrangement societies. The crinkled leaves are most effective when used with arrangements in a vase and the plants are also colourful and long lasting in the garden. The plants are easily raised from seeds which are obtainable as variegated silver, variegated purple and variegated mixed. Sow the seeds in April or May and transplant the seedlings about 18 inches apart. Cultivation, for which firm ground is essential, is the same as for ordinary cabbage.

Calendula (kal-en-du-la)

From the Latin *calendae,* the first day of the month, probably referring to the fact that some species flower almost perpetually *(Compositae).* Natives of Europe. One species only is widely grown, *C. officinalis,* the English, or pot marigold; the latter name is derived from its use in the past as a herb for flavouring soups etc., the specific name *officinalis* also means it was once considered to have medicinal properties. A hardy annual, the species grows 12–15 inches tall and bears single, orange daisy-like flowers on branching stems. Through hybridisation there are now many attractive cultivars from cream to deep orange, double, semi-double and quilled, mainly taller than the type, reaching about 2 feet, and blooming continuously throughout the summer and early autumn.

Cultivars 'Art Shades', a strain in apricot, orange, cream, etc.; 'Campfire', deep orange, long stems; 'Crested mixed', various colours; 'Flame Beauty'; 'Geisha Girl', like an incurved chrysanthemum; 'Indian Maid', pale orange, maroon centre; 'Pacific Beauty mixed', large flowers, various shades; 'Radio', quilled; 'Rays of Sunshine', various colours; 'Twilight', cream.

Cultivation Any ordinary soil which is not too rich is suitable and though plants will bloom in the shade, they tend to become leggy, and a sunny site is best. Seed is sown thinly out of doors in March or April where plants are to flower and the seedlings thinned to 9 inches apart. Seed may also be sown in September, slightly more thickly. The seedlings are then left to stand the winter and thinned in the spring. Losses occur more through wet and cold winds than hard frosts, choose a sheltered site and well-drained soil. Grown this way plants are useful for cloching if wished.

Callistephus (kal-is-tef-us)

From the Greek *kallistos,* most beautiful, *stephos,* a crown, a reference to the flower *(Compositae).* A genus of a single species, introduced from China by a Jesuit Missionary in 1731. This is *C. chinensis,* commonly known as the China or annual aster, a half-hardy annual. The original plants had single purple

Various colour forms of the China aster, Callistephus chinensis. These half-hardy annuals will flourish in most soils, in open, sunny positions

flowers on 2 foot stems but *C. chinensis* has been greatly hybridised to give a wide variety of flower form, in which the petals may be quilled, shaggy, plumed or neat. Colours range from white through pinks and reds to purples and blues and recently yellow has been introduced; heights vary from 6 inches to 2½ feet. Among the most important are the wilt–resistant strains bred in this country and the USA. These flowers may be used for exhibition, bedding, cut-flowers and some strains make useful pot plants.

Cultivation China asters grow on a wide range of soils provided they have been well cultivated and manured and the lime content maintained. Open sunny sites give best results. Seed is sown in March in a temperature of 55 F (13°C), and the seedlings subsequently pricked out and hardened off, for planting out in May. Seed may also be sown later (April) in the cold frame. Plant out 6–12 inches apart according to the height of the variety. When flower buds show give a feed of weak liquid manure. Never allow the plants to receive a check in

any way. When raising plants keep them growing the whole time.

Many new cultivars may be bought in separate colours, and several are wilt-resistant. A good seedsman's catalogue should be consulted.

Named strains, in mixed colours include:

Single flowered, all 2–2½ feet: 'Southcote Beauty', long petals; 'Super Chinensis', good for cutting; 'Upright Rainbow', attractive mixture of colours.

Semi-double and double, dwarf: 'Bedder' series, 6 inches; 'Feather Cushion', 6 inches; 'Thousand Wonders', 6 inches; 'Dwarf Cartmel', wilt-resistant, 10 inches; 'Dwarf Chrysanthemum-Flowered', 12 inches; 'Dwarf Queen', 12 inches; 'Dwarf Waldersee', carpet effect, semi-double, wilt-resistant; 'Lilliput', 15 inches, cut-flower.

From 2–3 feet: 'Bouquet Powderpuff', densely petalled, centre quilled; 'Californian Giants', good for exhibition; 'Comet', mid season, curling petals; 'Crego', branching, long-stemmed, fluffy appearance; 'Duchesse', American introduction, vigorous, inward curving like a chrysanthemum, includes yellow; 'Mammoth Victoria', bedding and cutting; 'Ostrich Plume', old favourite, now with wilt-resistant varieties; 'Paeony-flowered', incurved, pale colours; 'Rayonantha', new, quilled, wilt-resistant; 'Super Princess', similar to 'Bouquet Powderpuff'.

Camassia (kam-as-e-a)

From the North American word *Quamash*, used for the edible species *(Liliaceae)*. A genus of a few species of hardy bulbs with handsome flowers in early summer, natives of North America. They may be grown in the border or naturalised in woodland or watermeadows. All bear loose racemes of small flowers and are good for cutting.

Species cultivated *C. cusickii*, 2 feet, numerous pale lavender, star-like flowers, an easy grower, bulb very large. *C. leichtlinii*, 2–3 feet, deep mauve-blue flowers or purple; var. *alba* has the contrast of creamy or white flowers with glaucous foliage. *C. quamash* (syn. *C. esculenta)*, camass, 1½ feet, flowers a good blue, but variable in colour, naturalises well, bulb large.

Cultivation These bulbs prefer a moist soil in sun or light shade. They should be planted 3 inches deep in the autumn, fairly close together for good display. If conditions are right, they will seed themselves in time. In the flower border lift and divide every third year. Propagation is by offsets detached at planting time or by seed sown out of doors in March, in a warm site.

Campanula (kam-pan-u-la)

From the Latin *campanula*, a little bell, hence the common name bellflower *(Campanulaceae)*. A large genus of annuals, biennials and perennials for growing in the border, wild garden, rock garden and greenhouse; widely distributed over the Northern Hemisphere, some native to the British Isles.

Border species cultivated *C. × burghaltii*, 2½ feet, large lavender bells, June and July, sandy soil. *C. carpatica*, 9 inches, edging plant, also rock garden, flowers blue, July and August, plant in the autumn before leaves die down, avoiding dormant season; vars. 'Ditton Blue', 6 inches, indigo; 'Harvest Moon', violet-blue; 'Queen of Somerville', 15 inches, pale blue; *turbinata*, 6 inches, purple-blue; *turbinata pallida*, 6 inches, china-blue; 'White Star', 1 foot. *C. grandis* (syn. *C. latiloba)*, 3 feet, sturdy, rather stiff growth, flowers close-set in spikes, open flat, blue, June and July, creeping root-stock, lift every third year, grows in shade. *C. lactiflora*, the finest of the bellflowers, 4–5 feet, establishes well in good moist soil, stem erect, covered with foliage, branching to trusses of lavender flowers, July and August; vars. 'Loddon Anna', pale pink; 'Pritchard's Variety', deep blue; 'Pouffe', 1 foot, dwarf variety, light blue. *C. latifolia*, 2½ feet, blue, June to August, easy to grow, tolerates shade; vars. *alba*, white flowers; 'Brantwood', 4 feet, violet-purple; *macrantha*, deep violet flowers, this species some-

times attracts blackfly. *C. persicifolia*, the peach-leaved bellflower, 2½–3 feet, best species to grow in the shade, sends out stolons and forms rosettes of leaves from which the wiry flowering stem grows, producing lavender flowers in June and July; vars. 'Fleur de Neige', 2 feet, semi-double white; 'Snowdrift', single white; 'Telham Beauty', large, single, lavender-blue; 'Wedgwood Blue'; 'Wirral Belle', good double deep blue; also mixed 'Giant Hybrids'. *C. rotundifolia*, 3–4 inches, the English harebell and Scottish bluebell, well-known on chalk and light soils, bears single nodding delicate flowers, July and August; var. *olympica*, 9 inches, lavender-blue, June to September. *C. sarmatica*, 1½ feet, spikes of pale blue flowers, July, greyish leaves.

Rock garden These are mainly dwarf species which require a gritty, well-drained soil and an open, sunny position, except where noted. All are summer-flowering unless otherwise stated. *C. abietina*, 6 inches, violet. *C. alliariaefolia*, 2 feet, white. *C. arvatica*, 3 inches, deep violet, needs scree conditions; var. *alba*,

1 Campanula trachelium, an autumn flowering perennial for the wild garden.
2 C. medium, Canterbury bells. The flowers vary in colour from violet-blue to white and appear in July.

white. *C. aucheri*, 4–6 inches, tufted habit, deep purple, early. *C. bellidifolia*, 4 inches, purplish blue. *C. calaminthifolia*, prostrate, grey leaves, soft blue flowers, alpine house. *C. carpatica* (as border species). *C. cochlearifolia* (syn. *C. pusilla*), 3 inches, bright blue; vars. *alba*, white; 'Jewel' 4 inches, large, blue; *pallida*, pale blue. *C. elatines*, 6 inches, purple blue. *C. formaneckiana*, 15 inches, silver-grey leaves, pale blue or white flowers, monocarpic, best in the alpine house. *C. garganica*, 4 inches, blue, good wall plant; vars. *hirsuta*, light blue, hairy leaves, May onwards; 'W. H. Paine', dark blue, white centres. *C. hallii*, 4 inches, white. *C. herzegovinensis nana*, 1 inch, deep blue. *C. jenkinsae*, 6 inches, white. *C. kemmulariae*, 9–12 inches, mauve-blue. *C. linifolia*, 9 inches, purple. *C. nitida* (syn. *C. planiflora*), 9 inches, blue; var. *alba*, 6 inches, white. *C. portenschlagiana* (syn. *C. muralis*) 6 inches, trailing, purple, good wall plant. *C. poscharskyana*, 6 inches, powder blue, walls or banks; var. *lilacina*, lilac. *C. pulla*, 4 inches, violet, likes limy soil. *C. raddeana*, 1 foot, deep violet. *C. raineri*, 1 inch, china-blue, scree plant. *C. sarmatica*, 9 inches, grey-blue leaves and flowers. *C. saxifraga*, 4 inches, deep purple. *C. speciosa*, 9 inches, purple blue. *C. stansfieldii*, 4 inches, violet. *C. tridentata*, 4–6 inches, deep blue. *C. valdensis*, 9 inches, grey leaves, violet flowers. *C. warleyensis*, 3 inches, blue, double.

Rock garden: cultivars 'Birch Hybrid' (*C. portenschlagiana* × *C. poscharskyana*), 9 inches, purple blue; 'G. F. Wilson', 4 inches, violet-blue; 'Patience Bell', 3–4 inches, rich blue; 'Profusion', 4–5 inches, blue; 'R. B. Loder', semi-double, mid-blue.

Wild garden The growth of these is too rampant for the border. *C. barbata*, 1 foot, clear pale blue flowers. *C. glomerata*, native plant, 1½ feet, head of closely-packed deep purple flowers, June to August; vars. *acaulis*, 6 inches, violet-blue flowers; *dahurica*, 1 foot, violet; *superba*, 1 foot, purple. *C. rapunculoides*, 5 feet, drooping flowers, deep blue, spreads rapidly. *C. thyrsoides*, 1 foot, yellow bells in closely-packed spike, summer, monocarpic. *C. trachelium*, 2 feet, purple-blue flowers on erect stems, June and July.

Greenhouse *C. pyramidalis*, the chimney bellflower, a biennial, 4–5 feet, spectacular, covered with white or lavender flowers. *C. isophylla*, a trailing plant for hanging baskets or edge of greenhouse staging, lilac-blue flowers, summer; vars. *alba*, white flowers, *mayi*, woolly variegated leaves.

Biennial *C. medium*, Canterbury bell, 2½

1 Campanula latifolia alba, the white form that flowers in July. 2 Campanula raineri, a tufted perennial for the rock garden which produces its tiny, china-blue flowers in June.

feet, in shades of pink and blue, and also white forms; vars. *calycanthema,* the cup-and-saucer type; *flore pleno,* double, 3 feet, with white, blue or pink flowers. Cultivars include 'Dean's Hybrids' with single or double flowers.

Annual *C. ramosissima,* 6–12 inches, pale blue to violet, this is not often grown but may be used to fill gaps in borders. Sow seed in early April and thin seedlings to 4–6 inches apart.

Cultivation: Border Many of the border campanulas may be grown in partial shade; most like a well-cultivated soil. Plant in spring or autumn. Stake tall species. They are propagated by seed sown in pans in very fine compost, with no covering of soil, put in a shaded frame. Prick out seedlings and harden them off before planting out. Propagate plants with creeping roots by division in autumn.

Rock garden Propagate these kinds by seed sown in March in frames, by division in spring, or by cuttings after flowering.

Wild garden Plant out kinds suitable for the wild garden in spring or autumn, in sun or partial shade. Propagate them by seed or division as for border kinds.

Biennial Seed of *C. pyramidalis,* is sown in pans in a cold frame in May and the seedlings potted up singly. Pot on until they are finally in 8 inch pots. Grow them in cool conditions, giving them ample ventilation. Plants may also be used out of doors in the border. Canterbury bells (*C. medium*) are raised in a shady site from seed sown in May or June. The bed should have a very fine tilth, and seed drills should be shallow; or sow in boxes in finely sieved soil and put the boxes in a frame, transplant seedlings to a nursery bed, 6 inches apart. Set out in autumn where the plants are to flower, having added lime to the soil. *C. isophylla* and its varieties are propagated by cuttings taken in early summer and rooted in a greenhouse propagating frame. John Innes potting compost is a suitable growing medium; the plant does best in a cold greenhouse or conservatory as it is nearly hardy and, indeed, may survive out of doors in sheltered gardens. It may be used for planting up hanging baskets intended for outdoor decoration.

Carnations

The large and diverse genus *Dianthus* (*Caryophyllaceae*) has been cultivated for generations. It takes its name from the Greek *dios,* a god or divine, and *anthos,* a flower. The original species, *D. caryophyllus,* was described by Theophrastus as early as 300 B.C. In the

1 The Show Pink 'Timothy'. **2** A group of Show Pinks, which indicate the range of colour that is available. These carnations are grown out of doors and bloom once, in the summer.

sixteenth century the border carnation was already a popular flower in English gardens, but the perpetual-flowering, or greenhouse carnation, is of much more recent origin. Its development started in the early 1800s in the USA and the popular present-day blooms owe their origin mainly to *D. caryophyllus* and *D. sinensis*. It is probable that other species have also been made use of by breeders over the years. During the present century a great deal of work has been done by breeders in this country, as well as by continental nurserymen and by several large growers in the USA. As a result the perpetual-flowering carnation is a most important market flower, in great demand for decorative purposes on formal occasions, such as weddings, banquets and other festivities. The modern border carnation is a connoisseur's flower, tended and grown to perfection by amateurs, rather than in quantity by commercial growers. The range of colour of border carnations is now remarkably varied and beautiful, many having the additional charm of a spicy clove fragrance.

Perpetual-flowering carnations These are grown in greenhouses in this country, usually in pots by amateur growers, or in raised beds by commercial growers. While the plants will withstand quite low temperatures artificial heat is required to keep carnations flowering during the winter months. In mild areas of southern France and Italy they are grown commercially in the open, with the emphasis on quantity. This is evidence that the plants require plenty of air and when grown under glass a free circulation of air is most important whenever the weather permits. Excessive humidity must be avoided, although during hot summer days the staging and greenhouse floor should be 'damped down' once, or perhaps twice, a day, but the atmosphere should not be damp at night. If the pots are stood on a layer of small shingle damping can easily be done with a watering can or a syringe. Spraying the plants used to be the practice as a check to red spider mite, but water spots the blooms and the pest is better controlled by the use of a greenhouse aerosol.

It is of the utmost importance to start with cuttings or plants obtained from disease-free stock. In recent years 'cultured' cuttings have been available commercially and these form an excellent nucleus on which to start a collection. Cuttings may be taken over many months from October to February, and the strongest shoots from about half-way up a stem which has produced blooms should be chosen. As the propagating period is long this makes it possible to take time in selecting the best cuttings. Cuttings taken in January and February have the advantage of lengthening days. The cutting should bear about four or five pairs of fully developed leaves and

The predominant parent of the hybrid Pinks is Dianthus plumarius, which has been crossed with perpetual-flowering carnations to produce modern Pinks. This is the Pink 'Show Beauty'.

should be severed from the parent plant with a sharp knife and not pulled, as this may damage the stem on which it was growing. Insert the cuttings in pots, or in a propagating frame, containing clean sharp silver sand. Make the base of the cutting firm with the dibber, placing the cuttings about 1½ inches apart. Water the cuttings and stand them in a frame with gentle bottom heat 55–60 F (13–16°C). Keep the frame shaded and closed for about two weeks, after which a chink of air can be admitted. During the third week the cuttings should start rooting and in the fourth week the glass should be removed if growth is by then obvious. Cuttings may be rooted without bottom heat, but this takes longer and more care must be taken to see that they do not damp off.

A horticultural grade of vermiculite, or perlite, may also be used as rooting media, but care must be taken not to get such material too wet. The first potting is into clay or peat/fibre pots (size about 2½ inch) using John Innes potting compost No. 1. When the plants are well rooted they are moved into 3½ inch pots using a similar compost. Later when the plants have produced about eight pairs

of fully developed leaves they should receive their first 'stopping'. This means that the leading growth is pinched out to encourage new growths to break at the lower joints. These sidegrowths are later stopped when they are about 6–7 inches long. This stopping should not be done all at once, but when the growths are at the right stage. With experience the time of the flowering can be regulated by this means. From the 3½ inch pot stage the plants can be moved on to 4 inch size or straight into 6 inch pots, using John Innes potting compost No. 2. If it is intended to flower the plants for three years grow them in 8 inch pots.

Varieties are numerous and as new ones appear regularly it is advisable to consult the descriptive lists issued by specialist growers.

Border carnations These are in the main hardy but some exhibition varieties will not tolerate winter wet when planted in the open. Such varieties make admirable pot-grown plants for a cold greenhouse where they can be carefully watered. An experienced carnation nurseryman will always recommend plants suitable for either purpose. Good drainage is essential for border carnations and for this reason they are often planted in beds raised a few inches above the surrounding level. They are sun-loving plants and should be planted about 15 inches apart, either in the autumn or in

April. Planted firmly but not too deep, a mistake often made by the novice, which may lead to stem rot. The ideal soil for border carnations growing in the open is a sandy loam, rather on the heavier side than light. Where the soil is heavy and inclined to be wet it should be deeply dug before planting and a dressing of pulverized limestone will help break down the soil and improve the drainage. On such a soil spring planting is recommended. For pot-grown border carnations use a compost consisting of 3 parts of good maiden loam, and 1 part of sharp silver sand. To each bushel of this compost add a 5 inch pot of small limestone chippings, or old mortar rubble. When potting the plants on into 3 or 3½ inch pots use 4 parts of good maiden loam, 1 part of old manure, and a quarter part of wood or bonfire ash. A similar quantity of limestone chippings or mortar rubble should also be incorporated as with the first potting compost. Propagation of border carnations is usually done by means of layers during the summer as soon as the plants have finished flowering. The side stems are pegged down with a layering pin, after the stems have been partially severed in an upward direction. Moist sandy soil is first placed around the mother plant. The lower leaves of the layer should be stripped off before pegging down. In dry weather the layers should be watered and after about five or six weeks they will have made sufficient roots for the layers to be severed from parent plant and potted singly. It is a good idea to leave them in the ground for about a week after cutting the stem, rather than to lift and pot immediately. One important difference between the cultivation of borders and perpetuals is that border carnations are never stopped. They may be disbudded, but this should not be overdone or the blooms may become over large and out of character, making the calyx more liable to split.

There are many named varieties in cultivation. The following is a mere selection: 'Border Fancy', white ground, rose markings; 'Bridesmaid', pink, scarlet centre; 'Desert Song', apricot pink, with lavender-grey overlay; 'Ettrickdale', clear yellow; 'Fair Maiden', white, scarlet edge; 'Lavender Clove', lavender-grey; 'Montrose', scarlet; 'Oakfield Clove', crimson; 'White Ensign', pure white (see Dianthus and Pinks).

Carrots

The carrot, a hardy annual or biennial, known botanically as *Daucus carota sativa* (*Umbelliferae*), was introduced to England from Europe in the reign of Queen Elizabeth, by the Flemings. There are four distinct types varying in shape, suitability to different seasons, conditions, and time of maturity.

Types 1 Short-horn: short conical or globe-shaped for early forcing in hot bed for sowing November–February, or summer catch crops.

2 Stump-rooted: cylindrical blunt-rooted for frames, cloches and first early sowings out of doors.

3 Intermediate: slender in shape but shorter than the long rooted. Used as a main crop for storing where soil is shallow or heavy clay.

4 Long-rooted: tapering roots for storing and exhibition.

Cultivation Carrots do best in deep, well-cultivated sandy loam, preferably well manured for the previous crop. Fresh manure causes forking and excessive top growth. Apply a good compound fertiliser 7–10 days prior to sowing. This may be fish meal or 3 parts of superphosphate, 2 parts of sulphate of potash and 1 part of sulphate of ammonia, applied at 3 oz. per square yard. Sow early crops thinly in drills ¼ inch deep and 9 inches apart from November onwards in heat or under cloches in January or February as soon as the soil is workable. Thin the seedlings as required, using the young roots as they become fit for use. Outdoor sowing may begin in early March or when the ground is suitably dry. Successive sowings of short-horn and stump-rooted types made at 3 week intervals until the middle of June provide a continuous supply of young carrots throughout the summer. Make drills for the main crop ½ inch deep and 12–15 inches apart. Postpone sowings of main crop for storing until late May or June where carrot fly is troublesome. Thin main crop to 2 inches when the seedlings are large enough to handle, finally thinning to 6 inches. As a precaution against carrot fly, draw soil towards the rows after thinning, and dust with an approved insecticide. For winter storing, lift the roots in October with a fork and cut their tops to ½ inch above the root. Store in layers of dry sand or ash in a cool shed or where the quantity is large, use the clamp method as for potatoes. The store must not be damp or soft rot will result. Where cloches or frames are available, make a sowing of a stump-rooted variety in August out of doors and place the cloches in position in October for pulling November and December. Hoe throughout the season to keep down weeds and to keep the soil surface crumbly. Careful watering throughout the season obviates root cracking which occurs when a period of drought is followed by heavy rain. As a result slugs and millipedes find their way into the root, and are blamed for the severe damage. With good crop rotation and cultivation there should be little difficulty with pests or diseases. Carrot fly, however, can cause serious damage.

Catananche (kat-an-an-kee)

From the Greek *katananke*, a strong incentive, referring to its use in love potions (*Compositae*). A small genus of annuals or perennials of which C. caerulea is the only species likely to be found in cultivation. This is commonly known as Cupid's dart or blue cupidone and was introduced in 1596. It is a hardy perennial, 2½ feet tall, somewhat similar to a cornflower in habit of growth with grey-green leaves and light blue flowers surrounded by papery, silver-coloured bracts. It is a good border plant and is also an excellent cut-flower, fresh, or dried for winter decoration. It flowers from July to September. Improved forms are *major* and 'Wisley Variety'; var. *bicolor* has blue and white flowers; var. *alba*, a plant of very vigorous growth has large white flowers; 'Perry's White' is the best white variety, 'Snow White' is another excellent white kind.

Cultivation This perennial likes well-drained soil and is not averse to lime. It should be given an open sunny position. Plant in October or March and provide adequate staking when plants are in full growth. It survives the winter best if a proportion of the flower stems are removed at the end of August. Propagation is by division in March, or by seed sown during April in a cold frame.

Cattleya (kat-le-a)

Commemorating William Cattley of Barnet, who died in 1832, an enthusiastic orchid collector (*Orchidaceae*). A genus of about 40–50 species of epiphytic orchids, natives of tropical America. The fine large flowers of both species and the many thousands of hybrids, make this a very important genus. Hybridists have made many crosses within the group and with the closely related genera such as *Laelia*, *Brassavola*, *Sophronitis* and *Epidendrum*. Two broad sections are recognised, those having often long, thin pseudobulbs carrying two leaves and those with stout pseudobulbs and a single leaf. The former usually have clusters of more or less waxy, long-lasting flowers while the latter have often large, 6–8 inch wide flowers. All are very colourful.

Species cultivated C. aclandiae, purple, spotted olive-green, with rich purple lip, very fragrant, summer, Brazil. C. amethystoglossa, rose, spotted purple, spring, Brazil. C. aurantiaca, many small orange red flowers, summer, Mexico. C. bicolor, bronze-green and purplish, variable, Brazil. C. bowringiana, rose-purple, autumn, Honduras. C. dormanniana, olive-brown and rose-purple, autumn, Brazil. C. elongata, dark rose, spring, Brazil. C. forbesii, yellowish-green or whitish, summer, Brazil. C. granulosa, olive-green spotted purple, lip crimson, summer, Brazil. C. guttata, yellowish, rose-purple and white, autumn, Brazil. C. harrisoniana, light rose mauve, summer, Brazil. C. loddigesii, as in the last but paler, summer, Brazil. C. schilleriana, olive-green marked red, lip red-purple, summer, Brazil. C. skinneri, rose-purple, summer, Brazil. C. velutina, orange-yellow, spotted purple, summer, Brazil.

C. violacea, violet-purple, summer, British Guiana. *C. walkeriana*, soft rose and purple, winter, Brazil. The above have slender bulbs while the following have stout bulbs: *C. dowiana*, yellow marked red, summer, Brazil. *C. gaskelliana*, rose to purple, summer, Brazil. *C. labiata*, very variable, light to dark rose, autumn, Brazil. *C. lueddemanniana*, light rose and amethyst, summer, Brazil. *C. luteola*, small, yellowish, dwarf growing, autumn, Brazil. *C. maxima*, pale rose, autumn, Peru. *C. medelii*, pinkish and crimson-purple, summer, Brazil. *C. mossiae*, rose, yellow and crimson, summer, Venezuela. *C. percivaliana*, rose, magenta and yellow, winter, Venezuela. *C. trianae*, blush white and purplish, often deep purplish, winter Brazil. *C. warneri*, rose to purple red, summer, Brazil. *C. warscewiczii*, large, rose and purple, summer, Brazil.

Cultivars (a small selection) Unless otherwise stated the colour is typical of the cattleyas, i.e. pink to purplish-mauve. 'Admiration'; 'Amabilis.; 'Ann Sander'; 'Bob Betts', a fine white; 'Bow Bells', another white; 'Dupreana', a large summer flowering form; 'Estelle', white; 'Fabia', a strong coloured, old hybrid; 'Lord Rothschild', white with mauve lip; 'Nigritian'; 'New Era', bifoliate type; 'Norman's Bay', a modern hybrid of very fine shape; 'Portia' bifoliate type, very attractive; 'Edgar van Belle', yellow.

Cultivation Provide compost of 3 parts of osmunda fibre and 1 part of sphagnum moss in well-crocked pans; firm potting is essential. In summer cattleyas need a temperature of 65–80 F (18–27 C), frequent watering, a moist atmosphere and shading to prevent scorching. The winter temperature should be 55–60 F (13–16 C). When the plants are resting, give little water, only sufficient to prevent shrivelling of pseudobulbs and leaves. Shading can be removed in September and the plants exposed to maximum light to ripen the pseudobulbs. Propagation is by division at potting time in the spring. Dormant buds on the rhizome can be brought into growth by severing the rhizome behind the fourth pseudobulb. Small pieces of one or two bulbs can also be encouraged into growth by placing them in moss.

Cauliflower

The origin of the cauliflower known botanically as *Brassica oleracea botrytis cauliflora* (Cruciferae) is unknown, but even 300 years ago strains of an inferior quality were cultivated in England.

1 Cattleya 'Clifton Down'. 2 Cattleya loddigesii introduced from Brazil in 1815 flowers in August and September. Cattelyas were named in honour of William Cattley who died in 1832. The genus comprises at least 40 species, all epiphytes and is allied to laelia, epidendrum, brassavola and sophronitis with which crosses can be made to produce improved hybrids

Grown as an annual, the plant has a relatively short season of growth, and is essentially a summer vegetable, although cutting may extend until severe frost in the autumn. In appearance the heads are similar to those of broccoli but are more tender and delicate in flavour. It is not a vegetable to attempt to grow on hot, dry soils. A rich, deeply-dug soil with organic content to help retain moisture is essential; it does best on neutral or alkaline soils.

Cultivation A deeply-dug well-manured soil in an open sunny position is best, but the ideal condition is when the crop follows a heavily manured one such as early potatoes. Apply a dressing of superphosphate at 2 oz per square yard prior to planting. As for other brassicas the soil must be well firmed. The earliest cauliflowers for June cutting are raised from seed sown in boxes in a heated greenhouse in January or February. Prick off the seedlings into boxes, or pot up individually and gradually harden off until plants are ready for setting out in rows 18 inches apart with 18 inches between the plants in April or May as weather and locality permit. If heat is not available sow seed in a cold frame in September, prick out seedlings at 3 inch intervals and plant out in the spring. Caterpillars rarely attack this early crop. Sow seed for the main crop in March in drills ¼ inch deep and 9 inches apart in a sheltered seed bed and plant out in May, 2 feet apart and 2½ feet between the rows. An adequate supply of water, and continuous hoeing to keep a surface dust mulch, will go a long way to ensure a good crop. As soon as a head or curd appears a leaf may be broken over it to provide shade from the sun, because otherwise the curd is likely to become discoloured.

As with broccoli there is a wide choice of varieties with varying periods of maturity, but careful planning is required to ensure a succession of heads throughout the season. Among the best-known varieties are 'Early Snowball' and 'Delfter Market', for cutting during June or July; 'Early London' and 'Dwarf Mammoth', which mature in August; 'Majestic', which is ready in September; 'Walcheren', an old variety, ready October to December; 'Veitch's Self Protecting', for late October cutting; 'Canberra' a newer Australian variety, maturing in November and December (see also *Brassica*).

Celery

Celery was originally a British wild plant with poisonous properties growing in marshland close to the sea. Extensive plant breeding has removed much of the bitterness and celery is now a popular vegetable. It is known botanically as *Apium graveolens dulce* (*Umbelliferae*). Celery grows best in a slightly acid soil which is deep,

easily worked and has a high organic content. Adequate soil moisture must be available throughout the season, but the ground must not be waterlogged. The main winter crops are grown in trenches. The self-blanching type is grown on the flat in blocks to exclude the brightest light but must be used before the onset of frost. It lacks the flavour and tenderness of the blanched celery but is nevertheless welcome and is useful for cooking.

Cultivation Sow celery thinly in pots or boxes in heat in March for early varieties, or in a cold house in mid-April for the main crop. Prick off into deep seed boxes as soon as the seedlings are large enough to handle, at 2 inch intervals. After hardening off, plant out from mid May to the end of June, in prepared trenches. This is not only helpful in earthing but enables watering to be carried out by flooding the trench.

Prepare the trench some time before planting by removing soil 8–12 inches deep, depending on the situation, placing the soil in equal amounts on either side of the trench. Keep the sides of the bank as upright as possible patting them with the back of the spade. This forms neat ridges which can be used for growing other vegetables—lettuce, spinach, radish. Place a good depth of manure in the trench and dig this into the bottom soil. Firm well by treading and leave the trench as long as possible to settle before planting. For single rows plant 10–12 inches apart, 12 inches each way for double rows staggering the plants. Immediately after planting, flood the trench and repeat this operation in dry weather. Feed occasionally with weak manure water or dried blood, and also apply two dressings of superphosphate at 1 oz per 6 foot run, by mid August.

Start to earth up when the plants are fully grown in August or September, after removing any sideshoots and low-growing leaves which would otherwise be completely covered. Tie the stems with raffia and place soil from the side bank around the plants up to the base of the leaves. Slugs can cause much damage and it is wise to scatter slug bait round the plants before earthing up, especially if paper collars, black plastic or drainpipes are used, as they sometimes are, to ensure long, well-blanched stems. Pat the sides of the ridge to encourage rain to run down, rather than penetrate into the celery hearts. Celery fly can cause serious damage from May to September if precautionary measures are not taken.

Digging may begin six to eight weeks after earthing.

'Clayworth Prize Pink' produces a good crisp head. Good white varieties include 'Sandringham White' and 'Wright's Giant White'. White varieties which need no earthing up include

'Golden Self Blanching' and 'Tall Utah'.

Celosia (se-lo-se-a)

From the Greek *kelos*, burnt, referring to the burnt appearance of the flowers of some species (*Amaranthaceae*). A genus of half-hardy annuals with brilliant flowers of golden-yellow, and glowing shades of red, which look more like bright grasses.

Species cultivated *C. argentea*, 2 feet, tapering spikes of creamy-white flowers all summer; var. *linearis*, leaves narrower, bronze-red in autumn. *C. cristata*, the cockscomb, has tightly packed flowers in rather congested form. There are many cultivars of this, including *nana* 'Empress', 1 foot, dark foliage, crimson 'comb'; 'Golden Beauty', 1 foot, flowers dark golden yellow; *nana* 'Jewel Box', very dwarf and compact, wide colour range, orange, cream, pink, red, and bronze, new; 'Kurume Scarlet', 3 feet, foliage bright red; 'Toreador', 1½ feet, bright red, good form, can be dried and retains colour if kept away from light. *C. plumosa*, 2½ feet, Prince of Wales's Feather, the feathery species with graceful spikes of flowers; vars. 'Golden Plume'; 'Scarlet Plume'; 'Lilliput Firebrand', 1 foot. Both *C. cristata* and *C. plumosa* are sometimes looked upon as varieties of *C. argentea* and may sometimes be so listed in catalogues.

Cultivation Celosias are very good greenhouse plants. Sow seed in John Innes seed compost in a temperature of 65 F (18 C) in February. Pot up the seedlings singly, never allowing them to become potbound. Keep the atmosphere moist and plants gently growing without any check. Pot finally into 6-inch pots. Plants should be shaded throughout the summer. Bedding plants should be hardened off and planted out in the second week in June.

Centaurea (sen-taw-re-a)

From the classical myths of Greece; the plant is said to have healed a wound in the foot of Chiron, one of the Centaurs (*Compositae*). A genus of annual and perennial plants with flowers not unlike those of a thistle in structure. The annuals (cornflowers and sweet sultan) are good for cutting; some species of perennials are used as foliage plants for the silvery-white leaves.

Species cultivated: Perennial *C. argentea*, semi-erect, fernlike silvery leaves, pale yellow flowers, half-hardy. *C. dealbata*, 3 feet, lobed leaves, silvery white beneath, pinkish-purple flowers, summer; var. *steenbergii*, flowers rosy-crimson. *C. glastifolia*, 5 feet, upright branching stems, pale yellow flowers, June and July. *C. gymnocarpa*, 1½ feet, sub shrub, much lobed white leaves, half-hardy. *C. jacea*, 3–3½ feet, narrow leaves, rosy-purple flowers, summer. *C. macrocephala*, 2–3 feet, large yellow

flowers, June to August, a good border plant. *C. maculosa,* 2½ feet, mauve flowers, summer. *C. montana,* 2 feet, deep blue flowers, April to June, easy to grow, one of the most popular; vars. *alba,* white; *rosea,* pink; *rubra,* rosy-red. *C. pulcherrima,* 2½ feet, narrow leaves, grey beneath, flowers bright rose pink, May to July. *C. ruthenica,* 4 feet, finely cut leaves, graceful plant, yellow flowers on long stems, summer. *C. rutifolia,* 3 feet, silver foliage, yellow flowers, summer. *C. simplicicaulis,* 1 foot.

Annual *C. cyanus,* the cornflower, 2½ feet, a native plant, blue flowers, summer. There are garden varieties in many colours, including *caerulea fl. pl.,* double blue; 'Julep', good reds, pinks and a white; 'Mauve Queen'; *nana* 'Polka Dot', 1 foot, mixed colours, good for bedding or edging, excellent range of colours including maroon; *nana* 'Rose Gem'; *rosea fl. pl.,* double pink; 'White Lady'. *C. moschata,* sweet sultan, 1½ feet, pale lilac purple, fringed petals, sweetly scented. The strain *imperialis*

Cheiranthus allionii, the Siberian wall-flower, is a hardy perennial

(Imperial Sweet Sultan), 3 feet, branching stems, mixed colours, is one of the best. Other cultivars are *alba,* white; *flava,* yellow; *rosea,* pink; 'The Bride', pure white.

Cultivation: Perennial Plant in November or March in fairly light soil including chalky soils. Propagation is by division in spring.

Annual These need a light friable soil with good lime content. Seed is sown in March or April where the plants are to flower and the seedlings thinned 9–12 inches apart. Tall kinds need staking. For early cut flowers, sow in August or September, keep the soil cultivated between the rows, but leave thinning until the spring.

Cheiranthus (ki-ran-thus)
Origin of name doubtful, possibly from the Arabic *kheyri,* a name for a fragrant red flower, combined with the Greek *anthos,* flower *(Cruciferae).* These are the

wallflowers; there are minor botanic differences only between this genus and the genus *Erysimum.*

Species cultivated *C. allionii,* Siberian wallflower, 1 foot, bright orange, spring, hybrid, thought by some botanists to be an erysimum. *C. alpinus,* 6 inches, yellow flowers, May, Scandinavia. *C. cheiri,* the wallflower or gillyflower (note: in the eighteenth century the gillyflower was the carnation), 1–2 feet, various colours, spring, Europe, including Britain. *C. × kewensis,* 1 foot, sulphur yellow, orange and purple flowers, November to May, a hybrid. *C. semperflorens* (syn. *C. mutabilis),* 1 foot, purple flowers, spring, Morocco (see also Erysimum).

Cultivars Dwarf: 'Golden Bedder'; 'Blood Red'; 'Orange Bedder'; 'Golden Monarch'; 'Ruby Gem'; 'Vulcan', crimson; all about 1 foot. 'Tom Thumb', mixed colours, blood red and golden-yellow; 'Harpur Crewe', golden yellow, all about 9 inches.

Early flowering: 'Yellow Phoenix'; 'Early flowering Fire King'; 'Early

35

Flowering Vulcan'; 'Feltham Early',
red and brown.

Tall and sweet-scented: 'Blood Red';
'Scarlet Emperor'; 'Cranford Beauty',
yellow; 'Eastern Queen', salmon and
apricot; 'Fire King', intense flame
colour; 'Primrose'; 'Cloth of Gold';
'Ellen Willmott', ruby; 'Rose Queen';
'Carter's White'; 'Bacchus', wine red;
'Carmine King', all 1½–2 feet.

Cultivation Wallflowers grow well in
an ordinary, not too heavy, well-drained
soil. The plants like chalk, so lime or
old mortar may be added with advantage.
Put them in sunny borders or beds
and into old walls, where plants may
remain perennial. Sow seed broadcast
or in drills, ½ inch deep, 6 inches apart,
in May. When the third leaf has formed
transplant the seedlings 6 inches apart
both ways in a previously limed bed of
firm soil. Seedlings may be attacked
by insects, such as the turnip flea
beetle, and it is wise to take some
precautionary measures by dusting the
soil and the seedlings with derris or a
proprietary flea beetle dust, repeating
the operation at weekly intervals for
several weeks. Transplant them to their
final quarters in September or October
at least 1 foot apart either way and make
the soil firm around the roots. It is
usual, though not essential, to discard
plants after flowering. To grow them
in walls add a little soil and well-rotted
manure to holes and sow a pinch of
seeds in each hole in May, or transplant
young seedlings to the sites.

Wallflowers make useful early-flowering pot plants for the greenhouse.
Sow seed in ordinary good soil in 6 inch
pots in September, put them in a cold
frame until the flower buds form and
then transfer them to a greenhouse;
water them moderately only and supply
weak liquid manure when in flower.
Discard the plants after flowering.

Wallflowers may also be propagated
by cuttings made from side shoots
rooted in sandy soil. *C. alpinus, C.*
× *kewensis* and *C. semperflorens* are
best grown in sunny rock gardens in a
mixture of loam soil and old mortar.
They may be topdressed every year with
well-rotted manure.

Chionodoxa (chi-on-o-dok-sa)

From the Greek *chion*, snow, *doxa*,
glory, the plants flower early in the year
as the snow melts *(Liliaceae)*. Glory
of the snow. A small genus of bulbous
plants, flowering in early spring, related
to the scillas. They are very suitable as
edging plants for the rock garden and
form a carpeting for taller spring
flowers such as daffodils. They may
also be planted in the wild garden or in
copses.

Species cultivated *C. cretica*, 6 inches,
blue and white. *C. luciliae*, 6 inches,
blue and white. *C. sardensis*, 6 inches,
intense blue almost throughout, with

white stamens.

Cultivation These small bulbs are not
fussy about soil, although they do best
on lighter, sandy soils. Plant them in
informal drifts, 3 inches deep and
about 1 inch apart, in September.
Ideally they should be lifted and replanted every third year as they form
extensive colonies, seeding themselves
freely. After chionodoxas have become
established borders may be dug without
doing much harm as some bulbs always
survive and bloom. Propagate from
seeds or bulbs. Sow seeds ¼ inch deep
in boxes in August and raise in a cold
frame. Treat the offset bulbs as mature
bulbs and plant in the ordinary way.
For pot culture use a compost of equal
parts of peat, loam, leafmould, and sand.
In a well-crocked 3 inch pot plant
12 bulbs 1 inch deep in September.
Set the pot out of doors in the open or
in a cold frame and cover with ashes
until January and then bring into the
greenhouse or a window indoors. Water
moderately from January to April afterwards freely till June when watering
should cease.

Chlorophytum (klor-o-fi-tum)

From the Greek *chloros*, green, *phyton*, a
plant *(Liliaceae)*. Greenhouse plants with
long narrow leaves, some with variegated leaves. They are interesting in that
they produce long drooping flower
stems ending in a tuft of leaves, forming
an offset. These offsets may be detached
and rooted for propagation purposes.

Species cultivated *C. comosum (syn. C.
sternbergianum)*, 1–2 feet, white flowers
in summer. *C. elatum* (syns. *C. antheri-
cum, C. capense* and *Phalangium elatum)*,

Above **Chionodoxa luciliae, small bulbs
from Asia Minor and Crete, which flower
in early spring.** *Opposite* **Chrysanthemum
'Cloth of Gold'.**

1–1½ feet, white flowers in summer;
var. *variegatum* has creamy white
longitudinal variegations on the leaves.

Cultivation Grow the variegated and tall
kinds in pots in a compost composed of
equal parts of loam, leafmould, peat and
sand. The drooping kinds should be
grown in baskets or pots suspended in a
greenhouse or window. Plants can be
used for bedding out of doors from June
to September. Pot up the young plants
in March, and from March to October
keep them at temperatures of 55–65 F
(13–18 C), for the remainder of the year
at 45–50 F (7–10 C). Water freely during
the summer but only moderately during
winter. Propagate by seeds sown ⅛
inch deep in pots containing well-drained
light soil at a temperature of 65 F (18 C)
in March, by offshoots taken in April
and placed singly in pots under a bell jar
put in a window or greenhouse, or by
division of roots when repotting.

Chrysanthemum (kris-an-the-mum)

From the Greek *chrysos*, gold, *anthemon*,
flower *(Compositae)*. A genus of over 100
species of annuals, herbaceous perennials and sub-shrubs, distributed over
Africa, America, Asia and Europe, including Britain. The well-known greenhouse and early-flowering (outdoor)
chrysanthemums are descended from *C.
indicum*, found in China and Japan, and
C. morifolium (syn. *C. sinense)*, from
China, two closely related, variable
plants. For full details of the cultivation

36

of these chrysanthemums see Chrysanthemum cultivation.

Annual species cultivated *C. carinatum*, 2 feet, white and yellow flowers, summer, Morocco; cultivars include *burridgeanum*, white with a crimson ring; *flore pleno hybridum*, fringed double flowers, mixed colours; 'John Bright', pure yellow; 'Lord Beaconsfield', bronze-red and bronze rings on various ground colours; 'Northern Star', white, sulphur yellow ring; 'The Sultan', coppery-scarlet; 'W. E. Gladstone', coppery-scarlet; 'White Queen'. *C. coronarium*, 1–4 feet, yellow and white, double, southern Europe; vars. 'Golden Crown', 3–4 feet, butter-yellow; 'Cream Gen', 'Golden Gem', 1 foot; 'Golden Glory', 2 feet, single. *C. frutescens*, Paris daisy, marguerite, shrubby half-hardy plant, strictly a perennial but usually treated as an annual, 2½–3 feet, white, blooming continuously, valuable greenhouse pot plant for winter, or out of doors in summer, Canary Islands; var. 'Etoile d'Or', lemon-yellow. *C. inodorum*, 9 inches, white, summer, good for cutting. *C. multicaule*, 9 inches, single golden yellow flowers, summer, Algeria. *C. nivellii*, 1 foot, white, summer, Morocco. *C. segetum*, corn marigold, yellow boy, 1½ feet, golden-yellow, summer Europe (including Britain), Africa, Asia; vars. 'Eastern Star', yellow; 'Evening Star', golden-yellow; 'Golden Glow', double;

1 Chrysanthemum segetum, the hardy annual that grows 12 to 15 inches in height. 2 Chrysanthemum rubellum, a hardy perennial of which 'Clara Curtis', deep pink, 'Duchess of Edinburgh', fiery red, 'Mary Stoker', soft yellow and 'Paul Boissier', orange bronze are good forms

'Morning Star', pale yellow.

Hardy perennials *C. alpinum* (syn. *Leucanthemum alpinum*) 3–6 inches, white flowers, summer, Pyrenees, Carpathians, scree in rock garden. *C. argenteum* (syns. *Matricaria argentea*, *Pyrethrum argenteum*, *Tanacetum argenteum*), 6 inches, sub-shrubby, grey-white stems and leaves, solitary white flowers, summer. *C. cinerariifolium*, 1–2 feet, white flowers, July and August. This is the species which produces pyrethrum insecticidal powder and is widely cultivated for this purpose in Japan and Kenya. *C. coccineum* (syn. *Pyrethrum roseum*), 2–3 feet, the pyrethrum of gardens, variable in colour; the origin of the garden pyrethrum (see *Pyrethrum*). *C. haradjanii*, 6 inches, silvery leaves, rock garden foliage plant. *C. leucanthemum*, oxeye daisy, 2–3 feet, white flowers, summer, Europe (including Britain), North America, a good cut flower. *C. maximum*, Shasta daisy, 1½–3 feet, white flowers, summer, Pyrenees; vars. 'Beauté Nivelloise', fringed petals; 'Esther Read' double, the most popular; 'Horace Read', creamy-white, double; 'Ian

Murray', anemone-centred; 'Jennifer Read', later flowering; 'Mount Everest', large flowered; 'Thomas Killin', large, anemone-centred; 'Wirral Pride', double, lemon-centred when first open; 'Wirral Supreme', large, double. Many others are to be found in catalogues and new varieties appear from time to time. *C. nipponicum*, 12–15 inches, white flowers, summer, Japan. *C. parthenium*, feverfew, 2 feet, pungent stems and leaves, white flowers, summer, Europe (including Britain), best in its double form; var. *aureum*, golden feather, dwarf, yellow leaves, used in bedding. Flower-heads should be removed when they appear. *C. praeteritum*, 9 inches, sub-shrubby, grey, finely divided aromatic foliage; foliage plant. *C. ptarmicaefolium*, 1 foot, silvery-white, much divided foliage, white flowers, summer, Canary Islands. *C. rubellum*, 2–3 feet, single flowers, in shades of lilac and pink, September and October, of unknown origin; var. 'Clara Curtis', clear pink. *C. sibiricum* (syns. *C. coreanum* and *Leucanthemum sibiricum*), Korean chrysanthemum, 2–3 feet, variously coloured flowers, single and double, September and October, Korea. *C. uliginosum*, giant daisy, moon daisy, 5 feet, single white flowers, autumn, good for cutting, eastern Europe.

Cultivation The annuals, with the exception of *C. frutescens*, are hardy and seed is sown out of doors in April or May where the plants are to flower, in open, sunny positions and ordinary soil. An earlier start may be made by sowing under glass in spring, hardening off the seedlings and planting out in May, 6 inches apart. They may also be grown as pot plants, planting four seedlings to a 5 inch pot, seven to a 6 inch pot, growing them on in a cold frame for indoor decoration, or in the greenhouse for display purposes.

C. frutescens is propagated from cuttings taken in summer and rooted in heat in the greenhouse. The rooted cuttings are potted on, kept in a sunny place out of doors until September then moved into a cold frame until November when they are brought into the greenhouse to flower in a temperature of 50–55°F (10–13°C). Moderate watering only is required, but plants should be fed with weak liquid manure when their pots are full of roots. For outdoor cultivation in the summer cuttings are taken early in the year, grown on, hardened off and planted out in May.

The taller hardy perennials are useful border plants which will grow in any ordinary soil and sunny position. They may be planted in spring or autumn and clumps should be lifted, divided and replanted every third year. The dwarf kinds are suitable for sunny rock gardens. All are propagated either by division in March or by seeds sown in the greenhouse at the same time.

Chrysanthemum cultivation

There are very many different kinds of chrysanthemum (see Chrysanthemum); however, this article is concerned only with those garden and greenhouse plants which are descended from two original species, *Chrysanthemum indicum* and *Chrysanthemum morifolium* (syn. *C. sinense*).

These hybrids may be divided into three classes according to their season of blooming. The Early-flowering type blooms in the open garden before October 1st. Mid-season varieties flower in October and November under glass and are followed in December and January by the true Late-flowering section. The glasshouse types are normally grown in pots but may be planted in the open garden for the summer and lifted into the greenhouse for blooming. Flowers may, therefore, be had from August to January and there is a great variety of form and colour.

Propagation of all types is by division or cuttings, the latter giving the best results particularly for exhibition. The stools are taken up a few weeks after flowering and when the old soil has been removed by washing they are boxed up in fresh compost, John Innes potting compost No. 1 being very suitable. Since a period of dormancy is essential the boxes are kept in a cool airy place such as a cold frame and the stools kept only

just moist for about a month. Slight frost will do no harm but some protection should be given when conditions· are severe. Cold wet soil will cause more loss than frost.

The stronger light and higher temperatures of the spring season will cause the stools to start into growth but when cuttings have to be rooted early in the year, this process must be accelerated. Once the new growth appears, watering can be increased, and the amount should be regulated according to the speed of growth. Cuttings are taken in the usual way when they are about 3 inches long (see Propagation). They root easily on an open bench if some muslin is stretched a few inches above them. The temperature range is as mentioned above. The time for inserting the cuttings will vary according to the facilities available and the varieties involved. Generally speaking, the early flowering-types are struck in February and March, together with those flowering in December. The mid-season varieties can be rooted from January to March.

The treatment of the young plants will vary according to the method by which they are to be grown. Plants intended for the open garden are best planted up in boxes 4 inches deep filled with John Innes potting compost No. 1 or the equivalent soilless compost. Another plan is to make up a bed of compost on the floor of the cold frame. In either case, space out well at not less than 4 inches to avoid thin spindly growth. If the plants are to be flowered in large pots they should be transplanted from the cutting bed into 3 inch pots using the same compost as for boxes.

At this stage it is important to keep the plants cool and a cold frame is quite suitable in most areas from the middle of March. Plenty of light and air will keep the growth sturdy. Water the plants moderately and allow the pots and boxes to dry out between waterings. Soil kept wet all the time will encourage soft growth but overdryness produces a hard plant which can never give satisfaction. The hardening off process will aim at fully exposing the plants to unsheltered conditions by the end of April or early May.

Plants in pots will require repotting before this time and as soon as the small pot is full of roots the plant should be moved to a 5 inch or 6 inch size, using a richer compost such as John Innes potting compost No. 2 or the equivalent soilless compost. Again the emphasis should be on good spacing for maximum light while the plants should only be watered sparingly, particularly for the first few weeks. A short stake is usually needed at this time, with the stem lightly looped to it.

Plants in boxes will normally grow well until planting out time, but if there are any signs· of starvation, give a few

dilute liquid feeds at weekly intervals.

From early May the treatment of plants varies according to type and it is necessary to follow each method separately.

Early-flowering chrysanthemums These are flowered in the open garden and the ground must be well prepared during the winter. The main aims are to provide plenty of humus for moisture retention and sufficient nourishment to sustain the plants in full growth for a period of several months. The basic method is to dig the land one spit deep incorporating farmyard manure or compost at the rate of one bucket per square yard. At the same time, dust the trenches with bonemeal, using $\frac{1}{2}-\frac{3}{4}$ lb per square yard. The ground is left rough for weathering until the middle of April when a light forking over is given. This should never go deeper than 3–4 inches but this surface layer must be enriched by working in a base fertiliser such as Growmore or a similar general fertiliser at $\frac{1}{4}$ lb. per square yard. This programme provides nourishment immediately available at the surface for the young roots and slow acting organic material at lower levels to serve the mature plant. Lime is required only if the soil is rather acid (*p*H less than 6·5). Where plants are to be grown in rows on a separate plot, this cultivation should be given to the whole area but if plants are to form groups in a border the same kind of preparation may be given to the actual planting sites.

A careful raking will level the soil and prepare a good planting tilth in early May and the actual moving of the plants may be done from about May 10th in the south if the weather is suitable. The first step is to place the canes either in rows or groups according to the site. Plants should never be closer than 18 inches and rows can be double, leaving paths $2\frac{1}{2}$ feet wide between each pair. Planting may be done when the soil is nicely moist without being sticky. A hole is taken out close to the cane and large enough to contain the root ball without cramping. If soil preparation was not well done or the soil tends to be poor it is a good thing to incorporate a handful of peat and a sprinkling of base fertiliser in the bottom of the hole. Water the boxes some hours beforehand so that the plants may be removed from them with little damage to the roots. Plant firmly at the same level and immediately give one loose tie around the cane to avoid breakages. It is better not to water in but if the weather is dry try to keep the plants going with overhead sprays of water until a shower comes. When watering is essential give a substantial amount so as to wet the soil quite deeply.

Slugs may still be troublesome and appropriate action must be taken. In built-up areas birds may become a problem, as they peck at leaves and

weeding after mid-June to avoid damaging the surface roots. Pests will cause trouble, and particular attention should be given in July and August when **capsid bugs are active. Regular use of approved pesticides will minimize damage. Tying-in of the stems is also** very important. They may either be looped to a strong central cane or enclosed in a framework of three canes. In either case allow some movement of the stems for in this way they will bend before the wind. Too rigid a support often results in breakage.

The pinching and disbudding process for large blooms follows the same pattern for early-flowering and late-flowering and will be described fully in a later paragraph.

Late-flowering chrysanthemums These plants are grown on in the 5–6 inch pots for several weeks but before they become pot bound they must be potted on to their final sizes. The 9 inch size is the most useful pot but both 8 inch and 10 inch may be used. For the very best results the following crop may be taken:

Large exhibition blooms Two blooms in a 10 inch pot or one only to an 8 inch.

Incurveds and decoratives Three blooms in an 8 inch pot or four to a 9 inch. The 10 inch size is only used for the very vigorous plants when up to six blooms may be taken.

Singles Best quality is obtained when four blooms are taken from an 8 inch and two more for every inch increase in the size of pot.

These figures are for blooms of exhibition quality but for good cut-flowers one may safely increase the crop by 50 per cent in each instance.

The final potting which is usually necessary in early June, must be done carefully. John Innes potting compost No. 4 is advised, or the equivalent soil-less compost. The first step is to provide adequate drainage in the bottom of the pot, covering the bottom layer of large crocks with smaller ones and placing on top of this a thin layer of peat or the coarser material of the compost. Place the root ball on the coarse material and add compost until the final level is some 3 inches below the rim. New compost is added and if it is of the John Innes type, some gentle firming must be done as each handfull is placed. Modern practice does not favour the heavy ramming which was once the custom. When peat/sand composts are used, no firming of any kind is necessary.

If the plants were watered several hours before potting there will be no need to water them in, indeed it is best to place the newly potted stock in a cool, shady place and provide them with overhead sprays of water as long as

growing points with unfortunate results. Black cotton stretched in criss-cross fashion a few inches above the tips still seems to be the best answer. The birds stop attacking the plants after a few weeks and the cotton can be removed to make hoeing easier.

It is important to keep the plants growing steadily without any check and in dry weather a thorough watering may be necessary every week though a mulch of compost, peat or lawn mowings may help on light soils. Feeding will also help, but it should not be overdone. One application of fertiliser at the end of May and another at the end of June should be quite enough if the winter cultivation was well done. Each time use a fertiliser containing about twice the amount of nitrogen as potash. Throughout the growing season keep the ground free of weeds but resort to hand possible. Under good conditions it may not be necessary to water for between four to seven days. When water is obviously needed give sufficient to fill the whole 3 inches of free space which has been left at the top of the pot. Thereafter, each plant should be watered according to its needs, allowing the soil to dry out almost to the point of causing the plant to flag a little before watering again. It is difficult to describe the precise state the soil should have reached, but the grower will soon become expert at judging the correct time to water.

Once the plants are established in their new pots they may be stood out in rows for the summer. The standing ground should be in full sun and the rows of plants set out with wide paths for easy access. The maximum room available should be given to each plant and it is best to stand the pots on slates, planks or gravel to discourage the entry of worms and to ensure free drainage of surplus water. The canes, inserted at final potting must be securely tied to a straining wire stretched about 3½ feet above the pots. If these wires are supported by firm end posts there will be no fear of damage by the gales which always come in September when the plants are large.

Pest control, tying and watering will all need attention through the growing season but a major concern will be feeding since the roots, being confined to a limited volume of soil, will need extra help to produce fine plants. Much could be written on this subject but a basic programme involves the application of dry fertiliser once weekly at the rate of one teaspoonful per pot or at such rates as the manufacturer may specify. This begins about the first week in July and the fertiliser should be of a fairly high nitrogen content to encourage the growth of leaf and stem. Later on when the bud arrives, the fertiliser is changed to one which has about equal quantities of nitrogen and potash. Liquid fertilisers are probably better and here one may give a feed every two days using a quarter strength dilution. All feeding should stop when the plants are taken inside to flower.

This process of housing takes place about the end of September and is preceded by a thorough cleaning of the **house, which should be followed with a thorough fumigation to keep it rid of all pests. The plants themselves** require preparation and this involves the removal of the old leaves at the base and a spraying of all foliage with a combination of insecticide and fungicide. A good combination would be dinocap and BHC. It is important to wet the undersides of the foliage where many mildew troubles begin.

Once the plants are dry they may be taken inside and arranged in convenient rows, giving them as much space as

Chrysanthemums with quilled petals

possible to allow light and air to flow around the lower leaves. For the first fortnight, every ventilator and door can be left open by day and night but as the buds begin to open it will be necessary to regulate ventilation in conjunction with gentle heat to keep the air dry and moving and at a temperature of 50–55°F (10–13°C). Shading on the roof is an added refinement to prevent scorching from very bright morning sunshine. Indoors the plants may not require so much watering but it should be done carefully and early in the day, so that the air is dry before closing some of the ventilators at night. There must always be some ventilators left open except in very foggy conditions and even then it is better to have a little ventilation with enough heat to exclude the moisture. Pests may be controlled by the use of an aerosol or by routine fumigations.

Stopping If left to grow naturally the chrysanthemum plant will extend its single stem until a bud forms at the tip. This is the break bud which causes the plant to break into branching growth. Usually the grower will pinch out the tip of his plant before this bud forms and this process is sometimes called 'stopping'. It has the same result in the formation of lateral branches and is a useful device to help in timing flowers for a particular date. Each of the side branches ultimately forms a bud at its tip and this is the first crown bud and this is usually the one which is 'taken' or allowed to flower (see Crown bud). In the few instances—such as the singles—where the second crown is the desired bud, the plant may be pinched or stopped a second time, thus producing further laterals and increasing the potential flower crop. Most chrysanthemum catalogues give the best dates on which to pinch each variety to obtain blooms at the normal show season, but the gardener

who is growing for cut-flowers may ignore these dates and follow the following alternative plan.

Early flowering: Pinch the plants when they are about 6–9 inches high and take on four to six stems. For decorative plants in the border, double this number of stems may be kept. For exhibition quality three only are retained.

Mid season: Pinch when plants are about 9 inches high and allow the required number of stems to grow on. If the number produced is not sufficient, pinch again and allow the requisite number to extend to bud.

Late flowering: Pinch for the first time at 9 inches high and give a further pinch at the end of July.

Disbudding If left to develop naturally, the chrysanthemum will flower in sprays but if it is desired to produce large specimen blooms the buds must be restricted to one per stem. Unless it has been damaged, the central or crown bud is retained and all the buds or sideshoots clustered around it removed. The removal should begin when the sideshoots are about ½ inch long and it is advisable to take out one each day over a period. The sideshoots which are produced lower down the plant, together with the suckers appearing from the soil, may be removed as soon as they are seen so that all the energies of the plant are directed to the flowering stems.

Timing Production of blooms for a specific date is not the easiest task, since it is controlled by many factors. The dates on which the plants are rooted and pinched will have some bearing and the optimum dates for each variety can usually be ascertained from catalogues and other publications.

The buds of Early-flowering types to give bloom in the first half of September should arrive from mid-July to the first week of August. The mid-seasons normally bloom in the first two weeks of November and buds should appear at the following times according to type:

Large Exhibition	**August 10-20th**
Incurveds and Decoratives	
	end of August
Singles	**around September 7-14th**

There is little one can do to hurry a bud which is late but early buds can be dealt with in one of three ways. If the bud is more than three weeks earlier than desired it is best to pinch each stem and allow the next crown bud to form. Buds only two to three weeks early may be 'run on.' This means that the bud is removed together with all the side shoots around it except for the topmost one. This is allowed to grow on as an extension of the main stem to form another bud in a few weeks. Buds which are only a few days early may be delayed somewhat by leaving the sideshoots around the bud to grow to an inch or so before disbudding begins.

Protecting blooms In exposed gardens or in areas of polluted air it may be necessary to protect the choicer outdoor blooms from damage. Light wooden frames covered with polythene may be firmly fixed over the beds. Another method widely used by exhibitors consists of enclosing individual blooms within paper bags specially made with waterproof glue. Two bags, one within the other are used, and after being inflated with the breath they are placed over the opening bud which has previously been sprayed and allowed to dry. The mouth of the bag is gathered up to the stem and secured firmly with two green twist ties about 2 inches apart. No protection of any kind should be placed on the buds until the stem immediately below is firm and strong and the first colour is seen in the florets. White and yellow blooms bag well but other colours tend to fade badly.

Soilless composts It is not always possible to rely on the quality of John Innes Composts bought from the shops and the supply of good quality loam for home mixing is very limited. For these reasons it may be profitable to use the new Soilless Composts for all pot work. Experience suggests that either Alexpeat or Levington Compost will satisfy most requirements but the grower must be ready to follow the instructions quite closely. These composts are not recommended for boxing up the Early-flowering plants for the root action is so vigorous that it is almost impossible to separate the plants at planting-out time without causing very serious damage to the roots.

Recommended cultivars Because of the large number of cultivars available and the steady stream of novelties each year, the following list can only indicate some of the best varieties at the present time.

They are set out according to the National Chrysanthemum Society's Classification.

Indoor varieties: Section 1 Large Exhibition 'Duke of Kent' white, 3½ feet, reflexed, stop May 15th for first crown; 'Yellow Duke' is also very fine and treatment is the same. 'Gigantic', salmon, 4½ feet, reflexed, stop May 7th for first crown. 'Majestic', light bronze, 3 feet, reflexed, stop May 7th for first crown; 'Yellow Majestic' and 'Red Majestic' are equally as good and should be treated in the same way, 'Shirley Primrose', yellow, 5–6 feet, interlacing florets. Root in January and allow the plants to break twice to give second crown buds.

Section 2 Medium Exhibition 'Cosack', red, 4 feet, very reliable. Root in January and February and stop at mid-June for first crown. 'Connie Mayhew', yellow, 5 feet, deep primrose incurved bloom. Let plants form their break naturally and take the first crown.

Section 3 Exhibition Incurveds: *Large-flowered* 'Audrey Shoesmith', pink, 5 feet, strong healthy grower, blooms are very tight. Stop on June 1st for first crown. There is a 'White Audrey Shoesmith' which responds to the same treatment. 'Lilian Shoesmith' is a bronze. The plants are dwarfer at 4 feet and should be pinched at mid-June. 'Shirley Model' is of recent introduction. The rich pink blooms are borne on upright plants of about 4 feet. Stop third week of May.

Medium-flowered 'Maylen', white, 4 feet, is the parent of a large family including yellow, golden and buff coloured sports. All give good blooms if stopped twice, June 1st and July 7th for second crowns. 'Vera Woolman', yellow, is similar in height and stopping requirements. 'Minstrel Boy', light bronze, is possibly the best in this section. Reaching 4½ feet, this one also needs two stops, June 1st and June 30th.

Section 4 Reflexed Decoratives: *Large-flowered* There is a shortage of good cultivars in this section. 'Stuart Shoesmith' light bronze, 4½ feet, is a very easy grower. Stop June 15th for first crown. 'Elizabeth Woolman' pink, and the salmon sport reach only 3 feet, and should be allowed to make a natural break or be stopped in late June.

Medium-flowered 'Joy Hughes', pink, 4½ feet, deeply reflexing spiky florets. Root in February and allow to make a natural break for first crown. Often needs frequent watering. 'Princess Anne', pink, 3½ feet. Its only fault is a spreading habit which calls for careful tying-in. There are several sports including 'Yellow Princess Anne' which is probably the best of the family. The whole family produces its best flowers on second crown buds after the plants have been stopped on June 1st and July 7th. 'Woking Scarlet', red, 3½ feet, an excellent cut flower when stopped about mid-June allowing the first crown

bud to form and then rubbing it out to run-on for second crown.

Section 5 Intermediate Decoratives These are neither incurved nor fully reflexing. *Large-flowered* 'Balcombe Perfection', bronze, 3½ feet, parent of a family including red, and golden sports. For November flowering stop once only on June 1st. For December a second stop may be given at the end of July. 'Fair Lady', pink, 3½ feet, a most beautiful incurving form in carnation pink, with very neat habit. Stop June 15th for first crown. The bronze and orange sports are also highly desirable. 'Goldfoil', yellow, 3½ feet, clear yellow and very resistant to damping. Stop end of June. 'Daily Mirror', purple, 4½ feet, a recent introduction of great worth though not everyone's choice of colour. Stop twice, June 1st and 30th.

Medium-flowered 'Leslie Tandy', purple, 4 feet, very full blooms with a touch of silver. There is also a red sport. Stop June 7th for first crown. 'Woking Perfection', red, 4½ feet, hard, long-lasting blooms. Best rooted in February and stopped once only in mid-June.

Section 7 Singles: *Large-flowered* 'Albert Cooper', yellow, 4½ feet; 'Broadacre', white, 3½ feet; 'Preference', pink, 4½ feet; 'Woolman's Glory', bronze, 4½ feet; 'Red Woolman's Glory', red, 4½ feet. All should be stopped twice, mid-May and late-June.

Medium-flowered 'Golden Seal', yellow, 3 feet; 'Mason's Bronze', bronze, 5 feet, and several colour sports including 'Chesswood Beauty', red 'Jinx', white, 4 feet. Stopping times are as for the Large-flowered.

Decoratives for December and Christmas 'Christmas Wine', pink; 'Bellona', pink; the Favourite family including white, golden, pink and red; 'Fred Shoesmith', and its sports; 'Loula', red. These should all be stopped twice, the first time when they are about 9 inches high and again at the end of July. 'Mayford Perfection', and its many sports are also very good but these must be grown on natural first crowns.

The so-called American Sprays are useful for the November–December period and there is a variety of form ranging from singles to pompons. It is best to obtain young plants in June, for early rooting leads to excessive height. Stop once only when they are about 9 inches high and then leave them to branch naturally. No disbudding is practised and the flowers come in dainty sprays. 'American Snow', white; 'Christmas Greeting', red; 'Corsair', yellow; 'Galaxy', bronze; 'Minstrel', pink, can all be recommended.

Section 23 Incurved Decoratives: *Large-flowered* 'Ermine', white, 4½ feet, stands alone in this section. Thin stems but strong and healthy. There is a yellow sport of less quality. Stop June 7th. Bags well.

1 Chrysanthemum 'Pretty Polly' a medium-flowered reflexed decorative. 2 Cascade chrysanthemums popular for conservatory decoration in Victorian times are once again returning to popularity. Flowering is over a six month period

Medium-flowered 'Martin Riley', yellow, 4 feet, long-lasting blooms tending to come in August. Stop at mid-June. 'Yellow Nugget', yellow, 3½ feet, excellent flowers on a sturdy plant, bags well.

Section 24 Reflexed Decoratives: *Large-flowered* 'Ken Cooper', yellow, 3½ feet, of immaculate form and clear colour. Stop June 15th. 'Polaris', white, 3 feet, a quality flower with long, plunging florets, stop June 1st. 'Standard', bronze, 4 feet. Bright orange-bronze and top of its class, stop May 20th. 'Tracy Waller', pink with salmon, bronze and cherry sports, all at 5 feet. The height makes these a little difficult but the flowers are superb. Stop on June 1st.

Medium-flowered 'Early Red Cloak', red, 3½ feet, strong prolific grower. Flowers of fine form and the colour fades but little. Stop June 7th. 'Morley Jones', 3 feet, colour is rich amber with peach suffusion. Perfectly weather-proof and suitable for exhibition or bedding. Stop June 15th. 'Pretty Polly', purple, 2½ feet. Good for all purposes, the flowers being weatherproof. Stop June 1st. 'Sonny Riley', yellow, 4 feet, possibly the best in this section with high quality flowers. Bags well and always blooms well. Stop June 1st.

Section 25 Intermediate Decoratives: *Large-flowered* 'Evelyn Bush', white, 4½ feet, mainly an exhibitor's flower as it comes best out of bags. Stop June 1st. 'Gladys Sharpe', yellow, 3 feet, very strong grower with large foliage and full blooms. Stop mid-May. 'Harry James', bronze, 4 feet, reddish bronze florets which are broad and closely incurving. Blooms late in September, so stop mid-May. 'Keystone', purple, and its sport Red Keystone' reach about 4 feet. 'Highly resistant to weather damage Stop in early June.

Medium-flowered 'Cricket', white, with yellow and primrose sports, 4 feet, blooms last well after cutting. Stop June 7th. 'Jane Rowe', pale pink, 3½ feet, new but very promising though the delicate colour fades in bright sunshine. Stop June 15th. 'People', purple, 4½ feet, of exquisite form showing the reverse of the florets. Tends to bloom in the second half of September so stop mid-May. 'Topper', light bronze, 3½ feet, a lovely flower which bags well with little loss of colour. Stop June 1st.

Outdoor Singles are not very distinguished but 'Kitty' may be tried, while 'Premiere', an anemone-centred type is also worth a place.

Any of the Pompons are good and they are available in varying heights and colour. Give one pinch when the plants are established outside, and then leave them to develop naturally.

A selection for bedding In addition to the shorter cultivars among those already listed, the following are recommended: August-flowering. 'Sweetheart', pink, and its many sports, 3 feet; 'Capstan', bronze, 2½ feet; 'Sunavon', yellow, 3 feet; 'Red flare', red, 3 feet.

September-flowering. 'Whiteball', white, 2½ feet; 'Catherine Porter', pink, 3 feet; 'Packwell', bronze, 3½ feet: 'J. R. Johnson', yellow, 3½ feet.

All these should be stopped about June 7th. They may be allowed to flower in sprays or be disbudded for larger blooms.

Cimicifuga (sim-is-e-fu-ga)
From the Latin *cimex*, a bug, *fugio*, to run away; one species has insecticidal properties and was used in Russia to drive away bed bugs (*Ranunculaceae*). Bugbane. A genus of hardy herbaceous perennials with small flowers, borne very freely, in long spikes.
Species cultivated *C. americana* (syn. *C. cordifolia),* 3 feet, creamy-white flowers,

July and August, North America. *C. dahurica*, 4 feet, white flowers, July, China. *C. elata*, 4–5 feet, white flowers, July, China. *C. foetida*, 4–5 feet, greenish-white flowers, July, Russia, Japan; vars. *intermedia* (syn. *C. simplex*), white flowers, July and August; 'White Pearl', pearly-white. *C. racemosa*, 5 feet, broad spikes of white flowers, July and August, eastern North America.

Cultivation The bugbanes grow well in ordinary soil in moist, shady borders. Plant them in October, November or March. They are propagated by sowing seed $\frac{1}{16}$th inch deep in boxes placed in a cold frame in September, or by division of the roots in March.

Cineraria (sin-er-air-e-a)

From the Latin *cinereus*, ash-coloured, referring to the colour of the undersides of the leaves. All but a very few species (none of which are likely to be found in cultivation) have been transferred to the genus *Senecio* and for information on cinerarias other than the florist's cinerarias (see Senecio).

Florist's cinerarias The florist's cinerarias, obtainable in a very wide range of beautiful colours, have been derived from *Senecio cruentus* (once known as *Cineraria cruenta*), a herbaceous peren-

Cinerarias are colourful and deservedly popular as house plants but must be given cool, airy conditions with full light during the winter months

nial from the Canary Islands. Although the plants are strictly perennials they are almost invariably grown as half-hardy annuals or biennials, for greenhouse display or for spring window boxes. Seed is obtainable of various strains in mixed colours, under such names as *hybrida grandiflora*, producing plants about 18–24 inches tall; 'Berlin Market', not quite so tall, in various rich shades; 'Hansa Strain', 18 inches, bright colours, compact plants; 'Rainbow', 18 inches, pinks and pale blues; 'Cremer's Prize', 18 inches, medium-sized flowers, freely produced; *stellata*, $2\frac{1}{2}$ feet, large heads of small, star-shaped flowers in very varied colours; *multiflora nana*, 1 foot, dwarf plants, self-coloured flowers. In addition there are certain named colour cultivars growing to about 21 inches tall, including *atroviolacea*, large dark violet flowers; 'Matador', coppery scarlet; *sanguinea*, blood-red.

Cultivation To produce winter-flowering plants seed should be sown in April or early May in the heated greenhouse, in a temperature of 55–60°F (13–16°C). Seed

for spring-flowering plants should be sown in an unheated frame in June or early July. Sow thinly in John Innes seed compost, covering the seed only lightly. When the seedlings have developed three leaves pot them up into deep seed boxes. Give them plenty of light and air; pot them on again singly into 3 inch pots before they become crowded, then into 6 inch pots when the 3 inch pots are filled with roots. Large, vigorous plants may need a further potting into 7 or 8 inch pots; this should be done by the end of October. John Innes potting composts are perfectly suitable. Once they have been potted singly the plants should be moved out into the cold frame and kept shaded. They may remain there until about mid-October, given plenty of ventilation, both by day and by night. They will still need ample ventilation after they have been brought into the greenhouse where they should be placed on the staging as near to the glass as possible. Feed the plants with weak liquid manure or fertiliser, twice weekly from September onwards and spray them against attacks by aphids and leaf miners. From late October until the plants have finished flowering and are either discarded or used to provide cuttings, the temperature in the green-

house should be 45–50°F (7–10°C). However, cuttings are hardly ever used to
propagate these plants, unless it is to
increase a specially desirable variety.

Clarkia (klar-ke-a)

Commemorating Captain William
Clark, who with Captain Meriwether
Lewis made a famous journey through
America and across the Rocky Mountains
early in the nineteenth century
(*Onagraceae*). A small genus of hardy
annuals from North America, of which
one species only, the popular *C. elegans*, is
likely to be encountered in general
cultivation. Of this, however, there are
many fine cultivars in a good colour range.
They include 'Brilliant', double carmine;
'Enchantress', double salmon-pink; 'Firebrand', scarlet; 'Glorious', bright
crimson, dark leaves; 'Illumination',
orange and rose-pink; 'Lady Satin
Rose', double; 'May Blossom', double
pink; 'Orange King'; 'Purple King',
double; 'Salmon Bouquet'. All these
grow to about 2 feet tall. There are also
mixed strains available as well as the
'Royal Bouquet' mixed strain, slightly
dwarfer.

Cultivation Clarkias do best in a light
rich soil in a sunny border or bed.
Space the plants well apart to obtain
the best results. Propagate from seed
sown ⅛ inch deep in April, May or June
in rows or clumps where the plants
are required to flower, as they do
not transplant well. Thin the seedlings
to 8 inches apart when they are 3 inches
high. Clarkias may also be grown as
greenhouse plants. Sow seeds in small
pots of loamy soil in September and grow
the plants on in cool, airy conditions
until spring, when they should be repotted into loamy soil for flowering.
The stems, whether grown in pots or
out of doors, may need a few twigs
among them for support.

Cobaea (ko-be-a)

Commemorating Father Barnadez Cobo,
a Spanish Jesuit and naturalist, who
lived in Mexico, the home of these
plants (*Polemoniaceae*). A small genus
of tender perennial plants, climbing by
means of tendrils, usually grown as
annuals. One species only is likely to
be found in cultivation. This is *C.
scandens*, the cup and saucer vine, so
named because of the shape of the
beautiful long-stemmed flowers, which
resemble those of a Canterbury bell.
They open cream and gradually turn
deep purple. They appear continuously
from May to October, or even throughout the winter. A quick-growing evergreen climber to 20 feet, this is particularly useful for large conservatories
where two or three plants can soon
cover a wall. There is a white-flowered
form, *flore albo*, and a variegated form,
variegata.

Cultivation Seed should be sown
(edgeways in the pots) in a temperature

of 50–55°F (10–13°C) in late February,
or in a frame in April and young plants
potted up singly when they have made
two or three leaves. They can then
either be planted out of doors in June
in sheltered gardens or planted in a cold
greenhouse or conservatory border.
Alternatively, they can be potted in
large pots or tubs in a compost of equal
parts of leafmould and loam with a
scattering of sand, and the laterals
pinched back to two or three buds to
prevent straggly growth. Water regularly and feed weekly with a liquid
feed during the early summer.

Plants occasionally survive the winter
out of doors in the south but are usually
so slow to make new growth that much
quicker results are obtained by raising
new plants from seed. They may be
grown in a light warm living room, but
need ample space and adequate support
for their tendrils. A sticky nectar is

*Cineraria hybrida grandiflora is
typical of modern strains.*

liable to drop from the open flowers, so
the position indoors should be chosen
with some care.

Colchicum (kol-chee-kum)

From a province in Asia Minor called
Colchis, whence many colchicums sprang
(*Liliaceae*). Autumn crocus. Hardy bulbous plants with crocus-like flowers,
though with no botanical connection
with the crocus family. Flowers, several
inches high, appear throughout autumn
and on towards the end of the year,
without foliage. This appears the following spring, dies down by the summer
and is generally rather large.

Species cultivated *C. atropurpureum*,
purplish red. *C. autumnale*, purple; vars.
album, white; *minor*, rosy-purple; *roseum
plenum*, rosy lilac, double. *C. byzan-*

tinum, pink and purple. *C. giganteum*, pink and white. *C. speciosum*, purplish lilac; vars. *album*, white; *bornmueueri*, rosy lilac and white. *C. variegatum*, pink and purple.

Cultivation Reasonably good soil suits colchicums. They do well in sunny places, though they will thrive in thin shade. They may be planted among and beneath ground cover plants such as ajugas or naturalised in lawns or in rough grass, although the grass should not be cut until the leaves have died down in summer. Bulbs should be planted 3 inches deep in groups a few inches apart during July and August, choosing a similar time to split clumps when overcrowded. Propagation is by seed sown ⅛ inch deep in fine soil out of doors or in a cold frame during August or September. Plant out when two years old. Four or five years will pass before newly-raised bulbs flower.

Coleus (ko-le-us)

From the Greek, *koleos*, a sheath, referring to the combined stamens (*Labiateae*). Warm greenhouse plants from the tropics, of which one, *C. blumei*, is grown mainly for its highly ornamental nettle-like foliage; variegated, self-coloured and often brilliantly edged. Colours include green, purple, bronze, white, scarlet, pink and yellow.

Species cultivated *C. blumei*, 1–1½ feet perennial, giving rise to the many brilliant colour variations. *C. frederici*, to 4 feet, annual or biennial, deep blue flowers, December. *C. thyrsoideus*, 3 feet, perennial, bright blue flowers, winter.

Cultivation Use John Innes potting compost in 5–6 inch pots. Keep adequately warm and moist. Summer temperatures, 60–65°F (16–18°C), winter, 55°F (13°C), minimum, 45°F (7°C). Water well during the warm season, less so during the cooler months. Ventilate when temperatures exceed the summer optimum. Weak liquid feeding is beneficial throughout summer. Shade only when essential. Higher temperatures are required for the winter flowerers, especially during winter, 50–60°F (10–16°C). Propagation is by seed sown February, March and April, barely covered in a temperature of 70°F (21°C), or by cuttings of young shoots taken at almost any time and rooted in a propagating frame with bottom heat. Stop young plants by pinching out the growing point to induce bushiness. Strike cuttings of winter flowerers from April to June. Named coleus with decorative foliage, which can be raised from seed include: 'Autumn Splendour', buff-brown with green edge; 'Candidus', green and ivory; 'Red Velvet'; 'Rembrandt', wine, scarlet and bronze.

Convallaria (kon-va-lair-e-a)

Derived from *convallis*, the Latin for a valley (*Liliaceae*). Lily-of-the-valley. Hardy herbaceous, tuberous-rooted

Colchicum autumnale, the leafless Autumn Crocus, or Meadow Saffron, will tolerate light shade and competition of thin grass

perennial. The only species in the genus is *C. majalis*, which grows to 6 inches and bears deliciously fragrant white flowers in spring. There are varieties *fortunei*, with large flowers, and *rosea*, striped rose. 'Fortin's Giant' is a large-flowered, very fragrant cultivar.

Cultivation The lily-of-the-valley thrives in any good garden soil; it grows to perfection with adequate moisture and some shade. Plant October and November, 6 inches by 9 inches and 1 inch deep. Plants are best allowed to spread in a bed of their own. Lift and replant only when congestion reduces flower quality. A mulch of well-rotted manure or compost in spring is beneficial. Cover crowns with frame lights early in the year for early flowers. Obtain winter blossom by boxing strong crowns in peat. Keep very moist in darkness, at a temperature of 80°F (27°C). Introduce light when flower stems appear. Sub-

sequently discard the forced plants. Crowns can also be potted in September, kept in a frame till December, then brought into a cool greenhouse at 55–60°F (13–16°C) rising to 70°F (21°C) when the flower spikes appear. Such plants may subsequently be replanted. Retarded crowns can be purchased and forced quickly for Christmas. General temperature when successful flowering occurs in the greenhouse after forcing should be about 55°F (13°C) to keep flowers in condition. Propagation is by seed sown ¼ inch deep outside in light soil during March, or preferably by lifting and splitting clumps during autumn or spring.

Convolvulus (kon-vol-vu-lus)

From the Latin *convolvo*, to entwine, as some of the species do (*Convolvulaceae*). A valuable race of plants both annual and perennial, herbaceous or sub-shrubby. Flowers are bell-shaped throughout and highly attractive.

Hardy perennial species cultivated *C. althaeoides*, 1–2 feet, pink flowers, summer.

C. cantabrica, 1 foot, pink flowers, mid to late summer. *C. cneorum*, 1–2 feet, silvery leaves, pinkish-white flowers, summer, sub-shrubby, a little tender. *C. incanus*, 6 inches, trailing, silvery leaves, bluish-white flowers, summer. *C. mauritanicus*, trailing, with blue flowers, summer, hardy in warm places, otherwise a fine plant for a greenhouse hanging basket. *C. tenuissimus*, 6 inches, silvery-grey leaves, bright pink flowers, late summer.

Hardy annual *C. tricolor* (syn. *C. minor*), 1 foot, blue, pink and white flowers, late summer; cultivars include 'Cambridge Blue'; 'Crimson Monarch', cherry red with white and gold centre; 'Lavender Rosette'; 'Royal Ensign', Wedgwood blue with gold centre; 'Royal Marine', rich blue. For *C. major* see *Ipomoea purpurea*.

Cultivation These convolvulus can be grown in beds and borders and appreciate good soil and sun. Trailing species may be provided with support if preferred. A sunny, sheltered rock garden is especially suitable for *C. cneorum*, *C. mauritanicus* and other dwarf and trailing species. Propagation of hardier kinds is by seed sown out of doors in spring. Strike cuttings of *C. cneorum* and *C. mauritanicus* in sandy soil in a frame in July and August. Bottom heat is an advantage.

Coreopsis (kor-e-op-sis)

From the Greek *koris*, a bug or tick, *opsis*, like, a reference to the appearance of the seeds *(Compositae)*. Tickseed. The annual species are often catalogued under *Calliopsis*. Hardy perennials and annuals with showy flowers, excellent for borders.

Perennial species cultivated *C. grandiflora*, 2–3 feet, yellow flowers, summer; var. *flore pleno*, double. Cultivars include 'Baden Gold', large golden yellow flowers; 'Mayfield Giant', orange-yellow; 'Sunburst', double yellow; 'Perry's Variety' semi-double, clear yellow; 'Baby Sun', 1½ feet, golden-yellow. *C. lanceolata*, 2–3 feet, yellow flowers, summer; var. *grandiflora*, large-flowered form. *C. major*, 2–3 feet, yellow flowers, mid to late summer. *C. palmata*, 1½–3 feet, orange-yellow flowers, mid to late summer. *C. pubescens* (syn. *C. auriculata superba*), 2 feet, yellow and crimson flowers, summer. *C. rosea*, 9 inches–2 feet, pink flowers, summer. *C. verticillata*, 1½ feet, yellow flowers, summer; var. *grandiflora*, 2 feet, larger flowers.

Annual *C. atkinsoniana*, 2–4 feet, yellow and purple flowers, summer. *C. basalis* (syn. *C. cardaminifolia*), 6 inches–2 feet, yellow and purplish flowers, summer. *C. coronata*, 2 feet, orange and crimson flowers, summer. *C. drummondii*, 2 feet,

1 The many forms of Coleus blumei are all grown for their brilliant leaves. 2 Coreopsis verticillata, hardy perennial

47

yellow and crimson flowers, summer; a cultivar is 'Golden Crown'. *C. tinctoria* (syn. *C. bicolor*), 2 feet, yellow and crimson flowers, summer; cultivars include 'Crimson King', 9 inches; 'Fire King' 9 inches, scarlet; 'Golden Sovereign', 9 inches; 'Dazzler', 9 inches, crimson and yellow; 'Star of Fire', 9–12 inches, red; 'Evening Star', 9 inches, yellow and scarlet; 'The Garnet', 1½ feet, crimson-scarlet; 'Tiger Star', 12 inches, bronze and yellow; 'Golden Blaze', 2–3 feet, gold and maroon, yellow and maroon; 'Sovereign', 9 inches, golden-yellow.

Cultivation Coreopsis do well in ordinary well drained garden soil and in sunny positions. Plant perennials during autumn and spring. Propagate single perennial species from cuttings in April, or seed sown a month later; double forms by cuttings in April. Split large clumps in autumn. The annuals are raised from seed sown out of doors during spring and early summer, where they are intended to flower, thinning the seedlings to 9 inches. Alternatively, seed may be sown under glass in a temperature of 65°F (18°C) in March.

Cosmos (koz-mos)

From the Greek *kosmos*, beautiful *(Compositae)*. Half-hardy annuals and perennials, mainly from tropical America, with ferny foliage and broad-petelled, daisy flowers, single and sometimes double. They are sometimes found in catalogues under the name *Cosmea*.

Species cultivated *C. atrosanguineus*, 1–3 feet, dark brownish-red flowers, late

---

Cosmos bipinnatus, an annual introduced from Mexico in 1799, which reaches 3 feet and flowers in late summer

summer to early autumn, perennial, treated as an annual. *C. bipinnatus*, 3 feet, rose or purple, late summer. *C. diversifolius* (syn. *Bidens dahlioides*), 3 feet, lilac flowers, late summer to early autumn. *C. sulphureus*, 3–4 feet, pale yellow flowers, mid to late summer. Cultivars and strains in many hues are numerous. Those of *C. bipinnatus* include 'Early Flowering Crimson-Scarlet'; 'Fairy Queen', bright rose; 'Sensation', pink and white; 'Sensation Purity', white; 'Sensation Radiance', rose and crimson bicolor; 'Crested Mixed', double, in varied colours. Cultivars of *C. sulphureus* are 'Klondyke Orange Flare' and 'Klondyke Yellow Flare'.

Cultivation Cosmos will grow in almost any good garden soil, especially the lighter kinds and should be given a sunny position. Propagation is by seed sown in a temperature of 55–60°F (13–16°C) from February to March. Prick out the seedlings into boxes in which they are grown on and finally hardened off. Plant out at the end of May, at 1 foot apart. Plants will become large and, in high summer, are loaded with flowers, which are ideal for cutting.

Crocosmia (kro-koz-me-a)

From the Greek *krokos*, saffron, and *osme*, small, a reference to the smell of the dried flowers when immersed in water *(Iridaceae)*. There are five species and one well-known hybrid in this

---

genus which is closely allied to *Tritonia*, and sometimes included in it. Natives of South Africa, these plants are nearly hardy, but may be killed in cold districts or in severe winters out of doors. The hybrid is the familiar montbretia, hardy in most parts of the country. All flower in late summer.

Species cultivated *C. aurea*, 2–3 feet, yellow turning reddish. *C. × crocosmiiflora (C. aurea × C. pottsii)*, montbretia, 2–3 feet, various shades of yellow, orange or red. *C. masonorum*, 3 feet, large bright orange-red flowers. *C. pottsii*, 3 feet, orange-yellow. Cultivars of *C. × crocosmiiflora* include: 'Emily McKenzie', large flowers, orange with brownish-red markings; 'James Coey', deep orange-red; 'Lady Oxford', bright orange, one of the tallest; 'Rheingold', pure yellow.

Cultivation The best soil is sandy loam, but the plants are fairly adaptable, especially montbretias. Good drainage is essential and full sunshine desirable. The corms should be planted in March or April, 3 inches deep and 3 inches apart. They can be lifted in autumn in the same way as gladioli and stored for the winter, but they usually survive out of doors. They should be lifted and replanted every three years. Propagation is by the natural increase of the corms, or seed may be sown in pans of light soil as soon as ripe in a cold greenhouse or frame. The species come true from seed, but montbretias do not, and seed of them is mainly used for producing new varieties.

Crocus (kro-kus)

From the Greek *krokos*, probably derived from an Arabic word connected with saffron, a product of *C. sativus (Iridaceae)*. The familiar and easy grown garden crocuses are hybrids of Dutch origin, largely derived from *C. aureus*. There are also many species from Europe, North Africa and western Asia, which flower in autumn, winter and spring. Those that flower in autumn are confused by many people with colchicums, which are usually known as autumn crocuses. However, colchicums belong to the lily family, and there are many differences, the most obvious being that the flowers have 6 stamens, whereas true crocuses have 3. Most of the crocus species are not so easy to grow as the Dutch hybrids, but few are really difficult. Moreover they are cheap and last for many years.

Species cultivated: Autumn-flowering *C. asturicus*, 4–5 inches, violet-purple, variable, September to November. *C. karduchorum* (probably a form of *C. zonatus*) 4–5 inches, lavender-blue, September and October. *C. medius*, 4 inches, bright purple, scarlet stigmas, October and November. *C. nudiflorus*, 6 inches, purple-violet, autumn. *C. ochroleucus*, 4 inches, pale cream, orange throat, late autumn. *C. pulchellus*, 4 inches,

1 Crocus vernus, flowers from February to April and forms vary from white to purple. The orange stigmas are attractively fringed. 2 Crocus tomasinianus at close quarters. 3 Crocus sativus elwesii, a form of the Saffron Crocus that flowers in September and October. This is the source of the saffron of commerce. 4 Crocus vernus comes from Europe and there are many named forms

lavender, yellow throat, September and November, foliage appears in spring. *C. salzmanni*, 3–4 inches, silvery-lilac, October and November. *C. sativus*, saffron crocus, 6 inches, bright lilac, purple at base, stigmas long, bright scarlet, September and October. The dried powdered stigmas are saffron. *C. speciosus*, 6 inches, bright lilac, feathered purple, September and October; vars. *albus*, white, scarlet stigmas; 'Artabir', light blue, darker veins; 'Cassiope', blue, yellow bases to the petals; 'Conqueror', sky blue; *globosus*, bright blue, later to flower; 'Oxonian', deep violet blue. *C. zonatus* (syn. *C. kotschyanus*), 4 inches, rosy lilac,

September and October, foliage appears in spring.

Winter-flowering *C. ancyrensis*, Golden Bunch, 3 inches, orange-yellow, many flowers from each corm, January and February. *C. aureus*, Dutch yellow crocus, 5 inches, bright orange, February and March. *C. balansae*, 2–3 inches, orange, flushed bronze or brown, March; 'Zwanenburg' is a bronze cultivar. *C. biflorus*, Scotch crocus, 5 inches, white to lilac, February and March; vars. include *argenteus*, lilac with purplish featherings; *parkinsonii*, creamy-white, purplish striped; *weldenii albus*, pure white outside; *weldenii* 'Fairy', silvery-white faintly flushed lilac; 'White Lady', pure white. *C. candidus*, 2½ inches, white to orange, purple outside, March; var. *subflavus*, yellow, spotted bronze—purple outside. *C. chrysanthus*, 3 inches, bright orange, bronze featherings, February. Cultivars are numerous: they include 'Blue Pearl', pale blue, milky white inside; 'Cream Beauty', ivory white; 'E. P. Bowles', buttercup yellow; 'Snow

Crocus chrysanthus flowers in February and occurs naturally in Greece. There are many fine cultivars such as **1** 'Blue Pearl' and **2** 'E. A. Bowles'. **3** Crocus biflorus wildenii 'Fairy' is one of the number of forms of the Scotch Crocus, sometimes called the Cloth of Silver. It flowers in the spring and the type is found in the wild in the lowlands of Italy east to Persia. **4** Crocus medius flowers in October and November and came from the Riviera in 1843. Crocuses are hardy cormous plants. The autumn-flowering species deserve to be better known as they flower as freely as the many spring-flowering cultivars. The corms of both should be planted as early in the autumn as possible, 3 inches deep and 3 inches apart. Crocuses grow well in grass, the rock garden, and pots. They can also be planted under Mossy Saxifrages to good effect

Bunting', white; 'Zwanenburg Bronze', deep yellow, bronze outside. *C. dalmaticus*, 2 inches, lilac, yellow throat, February and March. *C. etruscus*, 2–3 inches, lilac-purple, striped lilac, throat yellow, March; var. 'Zwanenburg' bluish-violet. *C. fleischeri*, pale yellow or purple flowers, February. *C. imperati*, 4 inches, purple, outside buff, feathered purple, January. *C. korolkowii*, 3 inches, yellow inside, striped bronze-purple outside, February to March. *C. laevigatus*, 2 inches, white to lilac, flowering period variable. *C. minimus*, 1½–2 inches, purple, February and March. *C. olivieri*, 1½–2 inches, rich orange-yellow, March. *C. sieberi*, 4 inches, bright lilac, golden base, stigmas orange-scarlet, February and March. Cultivars include: 'Firefly',

lilac-pink; 'Hubert Edelsten', purple, lilac featherings; 'Violet Queen' lavender-blue. *C. stellaris*, 2–2½ inches, bright orange with bronze lines, March. *C. susianus*, cloth of gold crocus, 4 inches, deep orange, brown outside, February and March. *C. tomasinianus*, 3–4 inches, sapphire-lavender, March. Cultivars include: 'Barr's Purple'; 'Lilac Beauty'; 'Ruby Giant'; 'Taplow Ruby'; 'Whitewell Purple'.

Spring-flowering *C. corsicus*, 2–2½ inches, pale purple, April. *C. vernus*, 4 inches, varying from white to purple, sometimes feathered, March and April; 'Vanguard', blue inside, grey outside, is a cultivar. *C. versicolor picturatus*, 6 inches, white with purple feathering, March and April.

Cultivars of the large Dutch crocuses flowering in March and April, and all about 6 inches tall, include: 'Cinderella', lilac mauve and dark mauve; 'Early Perfection', deep mauve-purple; 'Flower Record', bluish-violet; 'Jeanne d'Arc', white; 'Kathleen Parlow', pure white; 'Little Dorrit', silvery blue; 'Negro Boy', blackish-purple; 'Pickwick', silvery blue, deep lilac stripes; 'Paulus Potter', ruby-purple, 'Queen of the Blues', lavender, purple at the base; 'Remembrance', soft purple-blue; 'Yellow Mammoth', yellow.

Cultivation Crocuses will grow in any soil and in partial shade, but do best in full sun in a light, rich soil with good drainage. Plant the corms 3 inches deep and 3 inches apart in August and September for autumn-flowering species, but spring-flowering crocuses can be planted up to December. Leave them undisturbed until they become overcrowded, then lift and separate the corms when the foliage has died down, about June or July, replanting them at once. Seed may be sown in sandy soil in a cold frame in autumn, spacing the seeds 1 inch apart and leaving them undisturbed until August of the second year, when the young corms are planted out. Crocuses can be grown in pots in a cold greenhouse, but they must not be forced artificially in heat.

Cucumbers

In the greenhouse The English type, long cucumber, *Cucumis sativus anglicus*, needs glass protection. Sow the seeds singly in small clay pots between January and mid-March at a temperature of 65–70 F (18–21 C). In the meantime, construct a special bed in the greenhouse. The drainage must be very good indeed but the texture of the compost must be spongy so that it holds moisture. A suitable compost consists of turfy loam and partially decayed stable manure containing a high percentage of rotted straw. Mix the manure and the loam in the proportion of 2 barrowloads of loam to 1 of manure. Add 1 lb of fine bonemeal and 1 lb of hydrated lime to each barrowload of loam when mixing. Build the compost into an 18 inch deep, flat-topped bed. Provided the staging is quite rigid, it may be covered with galvanized iron sheets on which the bed may be constructed. Alternatively, make the bed in the greenhouse border.

At planting out time, the bed should have a temperature of at least 65°F (18°C). Set the plants 3 feet apart and leave ½ inch of the soil ball above the level of the bed. Water freely, using water from a tank in the greenhouse. During the growing period, the temperature must not be allowed to fall below 60°F (16°C). It may, of course, rise to 80°F (27°C) or more with sun heat. Tie the growing plants to bamboo canes or to wires. The sideshoots are tied to horizontal wires. Stop the plants when they are 7 or 8 feet high and pinch out all sideshoots at the second leaf beyond the small cucumbers forming on them. Stop all secondary shoots on the first sidegrowths at two leaves beyond the fruits. Remove any flowers on the main stem and all male flowers on any part of the plant. Unless the males are removed, the cucumbers are liable to develop seeds and be less palatable.

To prevent red spider mites from breeding, keep the atmosphere very moist by syringeing with tepid water. During the season, topdress the plants by spreading a 1 inch layer of well-rotted stable manure mixed with good loam over the bed. Although the plants benefit from all possible sunshine in winter and spring, some shade should be given them in summer. To encourage the plants to continue cropping, cut cucumbers as soon as they are of edible size. 'Improved Telegraph' and 'Butcher's Disease Resisting' are recommended varieties. The hardier variety, 'Conqueror', is generally chosen for growing in the unheated greenhouse. Cultivation is as for a heated greenhouse but the plants should not be set out until late May.

In the frame 'Conqueror' is also suitable for cold frame growing in warmer parts of the country. A rich bed should be prepared and the plants set out in early June. A frame, measuring 6 × 4 feet, will take one plant which should be set in the centre. Pinch out the plants when six leaves have been made and guide the four sideshoots to the corners of the frame. Stop all other sidegrowths when they reach the sides of the frames.

A hardy outdoor variety such as 'Burpee F.1 Hybrid' should be chosen for the cold frame in northern areas. Plants are raised in a similar way as described for the longer, frame varieties. Do not sow before late April because the plants should not be set out in the frame until late May or early June. In other districts, set the plants out of doors in early to mid-June. The site must be open and sunny and the bed reasonably rich and well drained. Space the plants 15 inches apart and stop them by pinching out the growing point when six leaves have been made. No other pruning is necessary and no flowers should be removed.

Plants of 'Kaga', 'Kariha' and other recent introductions from Japan are grown alongside and trained to a 6 foot high trellis. The plants must be tied-in regularly and stopped when they reach the top of the supports.

Out of doors There are two types of hardy ridge cucumbers, those grown on the flat and those needing tall supports. Both kinds may be grown out of doors in the southern part of the country. In other areas, plants in the first group need frame or cloche protection. The climbing kinds may also be grown in the cold greenhouse.

In late April or early May sow two or three seeds in 3½ inch pots filled with John Innes seed compost. Stand the pots in the greenhouse, the cold frame or beneath a cloche. Water now and then with a fine rose to prevent drying out and pinch out the weaker seedlings to leave a strong plant in each pot.

The bed should be well drained and reasonably fertile. The application of a 1 inch thick mulch of garden compost just prior to planting out in June is helpful. The plants need to be spaced 18 inches apart in rows 2 feet apart.

Plants growing on the flat are pinched out when seven true leaves have been made. This encourages the production of sub-lateral shoots. Tie the new growth of climbing plants to the supports and pinch out at 6 feet. Keep down weeds by hoeing or mulching, water in dry weather and feed with liquid manure when the first fruits set. Fertilization of the female flowers is necessary so do not remove the male blooms. Harvest the cucumbers regularly to encourage more flowers to set.

Vars. for growing on the flat: 'King of the Ridge', 'Burpee F.1 Hybrid', 'Bedfordshire Prize'. Climbing kinds: 'Kaga', 'Kariha', 'Ochiai Long Day'.

Cucumis (ku-ku-mis)
The Latin for cucumber (*Cucurbitaceae*). A genus of about 30 plants, annuals or herbaceous perennials, which climb by tendrils. The most important species are *C. melo*, a very variable species which includes the cultivated melons, and *C. sativus*, which includes cucumbers. All require greenhouse treatment in the early stages, but some can be planted out of doors in summer. The male and female flowers occur on different parts of the plant, and to get fruit the female flower must be pollinated, usually by picking off a male flower and putting it into a female one. Mostly they are natives of tropical Africa and Asia, but a few are found in America and Australia (see Cucumbers and Melons).

Cyclamen (sik-la-men)
From the Greek *kyklos*, a circle, referring to the coiling of the flower stems of some species after flowering (*Primulaceae*). Sowbread. A valuable genus of dwarf tuberous plants, natives of the

Mediterranean area, some flowering in autumn and early spring out of doors, others in the greenhouse or conservatory for winter decoration. Showy, neat and easy to cultivate, they belong to the same family as the primrose. Most species are on the borderline of hardiness in the British Isles, and whereas some flourish happily in sheltered gardens, the beauty of others may be best appreciated in an alpine house or cold greenhouse, or a sheltered sink garden or scree frame. In many species the flower stalk twists like a spring after the flowers have faded, to draw the seed capsules down to ground level.

Species cultivated *C. africanum*, 6 inches, white or whitish tinged pale rose-purple, or rose-purple flowers, September and October. *C. balearicum*, 4 inches, white, tinged with rose at the mouth, slightly fragrant flowers, February and March, silver markings and mottlings on the leaves. *C. cilicium*, 3–5 inches, pale rose, with a red spot on each petal, October and November. Hardier than is generally realised. *C. creticum*, 6 inches, flowers white, petals slightly waved, spicy fragrance, February and March, somewhat ivy-shaped leaves, crimson on the undersurface and slightly toothed. *C. cyprium*, 4 inches, white or pinkish white flowers, October, leaves very dark green, crimson below with yellowish markings on upper surface. *C. europaeum*, 3 inches, deep carmine fragrant flowers, July to September, leaves kidney shaped with distinct silver markings on the upper surface; var. *album*, white flowers, quite hardy in all but the coldest areas. *C. graecum*, 4 inches, flowers pale pink or whitish with deeper pink base, September. *C. libanoticum*, 5 inches, salmon pink flowers, fading to a pinkish blue, February and March. Leaves appear before the flowers, marked with broad creamy blotches. *C. neapolitanum* (syn. *C. hederaefolium*), 4–6 inches, flowers range from pure white through pale pink to deep mauvish-pink, sometimes appearing as early as July, in warm damp weather, before the leaves; the flowering season proper is from September onward and the leaves are delightful and vary in shape and form, marbled with silver, splashed with pale cream or a lovely deep self green. They last throughout the winter forming good ground cover in extensive plantings. *C. orbiculatum* (syn. *C. atkinsii, C. coum, C. hiemale, C. vernum, C. ibericum*), 3–5 inches, rosy pink flowers starting in December and going on until March, before the leaves appear (some authorities consider *C. coum*, 3 inches, with shorter flowering stems and magenta flowers early in the new year as a separate form). *C. persicum*, 6–15 inches, varying shades of pink and white, winter to spring; the flower stalk does not curl up like a spring in this species. This is the parent of the

greenhouse cyclamen of which many strains have been produced with large, showy flowers appearing between November and March. *C. repandum,* 4 inches, flowers scented, pink with darker mouth and carried well above the leaves, March to early May. Hardy in all districts.

Cultivation For the hardy species grown out of doors choose a loam rich in leafmould in partially shaded nooks of the rock garden or turf bordering shrub borders or under trees, including conifers. Plant the tubers 1–2 inches deep and 4–5 inches apart in June or July, for the autumn-flowering kinds, and in September for the spring-flowering ones. *C. neapolitanum* needs to be planted a little deeper, say 3 inches. Protect with leaves or bracken in winter if necessary.

For alpine house or cold greenhouse cultivation plant the tubers of hardy species in summer for the autumn-flowering kinds and in late September or October for the winter and spring-flowering species, in a compost of 2 parts of loam to 1 part of leafmould and sand, and let the snout of the tuber show above the soil level. Cover the compost with limestone chippings to ensure surface drainage. Water as required up to and during flowering time, gradually reducing watering after flowering. Plunge the pots in peat or ashes out of doors during the summer months to make room in the greenhouse and to rest the tubers. Repot, start to water and return to the greenhouse in September. Propagation is from seed sown in pans in the autumn in a temperature of 45–55°F (7–13°C), but germination is often slow. The small plants are pricked off and potted up singly once the tubers swell.

Cultivation of Cyclamen persicum A cold greenhouse or living room windowsill is suitable for *C. persicum,* when cultivation is as described for cold greenhouse sorts. These plants are extensively forced for winter decoration and have come to be known as florists' cyclamen. In August soak the pot and tuber that have previously been dried off all summer and once the tiny leaves begin to sprout, repot in a fresh compost of 2 parts of loam to 1 part of leafmould and sand. The tuber should be potted so that the level of the soil surrounds its circumference, no deeper. Keep close for a few days until growth starts again.

1 Cyclamen are deservedly popular as pot plants for winter and spring decoration. Easily raised from seed sown under glass, high temperatures are not required. 2 This group shows the sturdy growth and the wide variety in colour. 3 The modern strains produce large, elegant blooms on strong stems. 4 The 'Salmon Pink' strain

Syringe daily, keep the plants shaded and maintain a moist atmosphere and temperature of 55–60°F (13–16°C). Water moderately and feed weekly with a liquid feed throughout the flowering period which, with a selection of plants, can be from November to March. Remove old blossoms and leaves by tugging them out from the base of the stem. After flowering, gradually dry off, resting the tubers out of doors in a dry frame or plunge bed during the summer months. Propagation is from seed sown in very fine compost between mid-August and mid-November in a temperature of 50–60°F (10–16°C). Prick off the seedlings and then pot them into thumb pots. Subsequently pot them on, with the necks of the tubers well above soil level. In August gentle forcing can begin. One-year old plants give the finest flowers, though tubers can be grown on from year to year, but it is advisable to raise a fresh supply of plants each autumn for good results the following winter.

Numerous strains have been produced, many of which come true from seed. Seed of mixed colours is usually sown and the resultant range of colour is very wide. Strains of self colour can be purchased under such names as 'Bonfire', scarlet; 'Mauve Queen', purple-mauve; 'Pink Pearl', deep salmon pink; 'Salmon King', pale salmon pink.

Cymbidium (sim-bid-e-um)

From the Greek *kymbe*, a boat, referring to the boat-shaped hollow of the lip (*Orchidaceae*). A large and important genus of terrestrial, semi-epiphytic and epiphytic orchids. Many thousands of hybrids have been raised in this very popular cool house group. The long stems which are upright or gracefully pendent, carry up to 30 large, long-lasting flowers in many attractive shades of colour and are much appreciated by the amateur grower as well as the cut-flower producer, mainly because they are of easy cultivation and require minimum heating.

Species cultivated (A selection only) *C. devonianum,* pendent spikes, greenish and purple, spring, Assam. *C. eburneum,* large, white, fragrant, winter, northern India. *C. erythrostylum,* white, red column, autumn, Annam. *C. findlay-sonianum,* a warm house species, small flowers on a pendent spike, reddish, Malaya. *C. insigne,* whitish, flushed rose, crimson spotted, spring, Annam. *C. lowianum,* yellowish-green, lip with a dark red bar, spring, Burma. *C. tracyanum,* large fragrant, yellowish with reddish-brown lines, autumn, Burma.

Named cultivars Great variation of spike

1 A typical Cymbidium, a genus of orchids which came originally from north India, Burma and China. 2 Cymbidium 'Cambria', one of the thousands of hybrids

habit and flower colour exists in the many hybrids because of their complex breeding. New crosses are continually being made, these are offered by trade growers usually with a stated expectancy of colour, etc. Seedlings near to flowering are usually the cheapest to buy, and with flowered plants, especially if of good quality the price can be considerably more. A number of cultivars have become famous as stud plants and seedlings derived from them are often of very fine quality; a few of these are 'Pauwelsii', 'Compte de Hemptine', 'Babylon', 'Castle Hill', 'Alexandri', Westonbirt', 'Rosanna', 'Pinkie'.

Cultivation A basic compost consists of 3 parts of osmunda fibre and 1 part of sphagnum moss, but various mixtures using loam fibre, old cow manure, dry bracken stems, fibrous peat, with the addition of sand and sphagnum, can be found to suit the individual requirements. Moisture retention plus free drainage is the essential compost condition. In winter an ideal minimum night temperature is 50°F (10°C) but this can fall to 45°F (7°C) or lower for a short time if conditions are dry; 50–55°F (10–13°C) should be the daytime temperature. Growths and spikes are present in winter so it is advisable to water the plants carefully and not to dry them off completely. Ventilation should be given when outside conditions permit. In summer the heating can be dispensed with, night temperatures can be retained at 55°F (13°C) and by day can rise by sun heat to 70–80°F (21–27°C). Lightly shade to prevent scorching only; abundant light is vital for regular flowering. Moist, airy conditions should be aimed at; water freely and syringe. Repot after flowering in the spring if necessary. Plants can remain in large pots for several years. Propagation is by division of large plants; 4–5 pseudobulbs the growth from which will make a new plant. Single pseudobulbs can be started off in moist sphagnum moss.

Dahlia (day-le-a or dah-le-a)

Commemorating Andreas Dahl, a Swedish botanist who was a pupil of Linnaeus *(Compositae)*. Half-hardy, tuberous-rooted perennials from Mexico, first introduced into Britain in 1789 by Lord Bute.

Species cultivated (Few of the following original species are available although they may occasionally be seen in botanic gardens and the like) *D. coccinea,* 4 feet, scarlet, September, the parent of the single dahlia. *D. coronata,* 4 feet, fragrant scarlet flowers on long stems, autumn. *D. excelsa,* 15–20 feet, purplish-pink flowers, summer. *D. gracilis,* 5 feet, scarlet-orange flowers, September. *D.*

juarezii, 3 feet, parent of the cactus dahlias, flowers scarlet, late August and September. *D. merckii,* 3 feet, lilac and yellow flowers, October (together with *D. variabilis* the parent of most modern double dahlias). *D. variabilis,* 4 feet, (syns. *D. pinnata, D. rosea, D. superflua),* variable flower colours, even a green form was suspected at the end of the nineteenth century. The parent of show, fancy and pompon dahlias.

Cultivation Nowadays dahlias are comparatively easy to grow. They tolerate all soils between the moderately acid and alkaline and for ordinary garden purposes need little or no specialised attention, yet will flower profusely. In their evolution they have produced multiple types and hundreds of thousands of varieties simply because they are a cross-pollinated plant. This means that it is possible to produce unusual and original cultivars by raising plants from seed, which is an additional asset. Furthermore, with correct culture, plants will flower continuously from July until the first autumn frosts, providing a colourful display over a range of several months.

Soil Preparation This begins by winter or early spring digging of the site, at the same time incorporating plenty of bulky organic materials such as peat, leaf-mould, spent hops, vegetable compost, or well-rotted horse, pig or cow manure, but not poultry manure which encourages too much growth at the expense of

flowers. Put any of these into the top foot of soil, because dahlias make a mass of fibrous roots in this region. The organic materials can be mixed into the planting holes if a few tubers or plants only are grown, or if dahlias follow spring bedding plants, but generally it is better to dig them in the ground overall.

A fortnight before planting, topdress the ground with a general granular fertiliser containing a higher amount of potash in comparison with the nitrogen and phosphate content. Root crop fertilisers have this analysis, and potato fertilisers are very good for the purpose. This application will provide the extra plant food needed during growth, the organic materials previously supplied mainly providing humus for improving the soil conditions and water retention.

Type of Stock The choice of stock will depend on the purpose which the plants are to fulfil. Dormant tubers are best for a general garden display, for they flower earlier than dahlia plants and produce more flowers over the season as a whole. If you want extremely early flowers, for instance blooming in May, you can plant tubers in pots, or even in the greenhouse border, in February. If you have cloches you can plant tubers out of doors in April and they will start to flower during early July. Remove the cloches in mid-June. In both these instances the best flowers will be over before the growing season has finished. For the best results over the whole

Dahlia 'Beauty of Baarn' a medium semi-Cactus, reaches 3½ feet. It holds its blooms high above the foliage.

season, plant dormant tubers during the first half of May out of doors. They will not usually need protection, because by the time the shoots emerge above ground level it is likely that the threat of any late spring frosts will be past. Nevertheless keep sacks, pots, polythene bags or other materials handy in case of occasional night frost at this time. Flowering will start in late July and early August.

There are two types of tuber, one being the ground root, a large bulky root resulting from growing a dahlia out of doors without restricting the roots. If replanted from year to year, the number of tubers tends to increase to excess, too many poor quality flowers result, and vigour and tuber formation decrease. Division every second year into several portions is advisable; each portion containing several growth buds, or eyes, and having at least one complete healthy tuber to start them into growth. (At this point, it may be noted that, unlike the potato, dahlia eyes are not on each individual tuber, but are congregated at the base of the old stems). An easy way to judge how many portions a root can be divided into is to put it in the greenhouse for a fortnight or three weeks. Spray overhead with water every second day until the shoots are about $\frac{1}{2}$ inch long. Do not bury the tuber in any material as this will encourage unwanted root growth. With a small hacksaw cut the root into portions according to where the emerging shoots are grouped, or lever it apart with an old screwdriver.

The other type of dahlia tuber, the pot-grown or pot tuber, is often sold in general garden shops and multiple stores in the spring. It is produced from cuttings struck in early spring and grown in pots all through the season so that the roots are restricted and the tuber forms into a neat rounded mass. Although pot tubers are easy to store and transport, forming very good stock for the garden, they are not so good as ground roots for producing cuttings, generally having insufficient bulk to be divided. Pot tubers become ground roots after a season of growth out of doors and their planting times are the same as for ground roots. Before actual planting, chip away some of the wax coating if present to allow moisture to swell the tuber. All tubers can be planted until mid-June.

The dahlia plant itself, which provides a type of stock commonly sold by dahlia nurseries, is formed by rooting dahlia cuttings. Plants grown from cuttings flower later than those grown from tubers, though if you need early flowers before mid-August, it is a good idea to specify on the order sheet 'April Delivery'. If you have a greenhouse or frame, you can then pot the plants into 5 inch pots and they will grow into fine

Dahlia 'Comet', an Anemone-flowered type which is becoming popular.

bushy specimens by planting out time. This is standard technique for large and giant-flowered varieties.

You cannot plant unprotected dahlia plants out of doors until late May, or even safer, the first ten days in June. With cloches or in sheltered situations, free from late spring frosts, you can plant out in late April or early May. In the north and in Scotland, mid-June.

Planting Out This stage is best tackled by taking out a hole in the ground with a small spade. Stakes should be inserted at this time to avoid damage to the tubers which would occur if they were put in later. The hole should be wide enough to prevent cramping and deep enough to allow the upper surfaces of the tubers to be about 2 inches below ground level. Replace the earth on top, shaking the tuber to settle it round the root as you proceed, firming it in by gentle treading. This applies to both ground and pot tubers. Planting distances are 2 feet apart for pompons, $2\frac{1}{2}$ feet for ball dahlias and all others, except the large and giant decoratives, such as cactus and semi-cactus, which should be 3 feet apart.

Keep the soil watered periodically to swell the tubers and to start the shoots into growth. Shoots should emerge above the soil within five weeks; if not, dig up the tuber and inspect it for decay and slug damage. Slug pellets applied above soil level round the root when planting both tubers and plants are an advisable precaution. Dahlia plants are placed in a hole taken out with a trowel and their roots set so that the potting soil is just below ground level. Bituminised paper, or fibre pots, should be carefully removed from the plants before planting out. (With peat pots especially, make sure to keep the soil moist enough to encourage the roots to penetrate into the open ground, since failure to do this is a frequent cause of stunted, poorly growing plants). Again, it is important to plant to a stake, previously driven in, thus avoiding damage to the roots. Moreover, arranging the stakes in a desired pattern can be a useful guide to design.

Summer Care The main requirement is copious watering, not a lot of feeding. Provided that you have prepared the soil as suggested, all that will be needed during the growing period will be two topdressings of sulphate of potash, each at the rate of $\frac{1}{4}$ oz per square yard. One should be given at the first sign of the petal colour opening from the bud, to improve stem strength and flower colour; the other during early September to improve tuber formation. Monthly feeds of liquid manures made from seaweed extracts are also very good and give excellent results even if used for foliar feeding. The dahlia makes a lot of leaves in August and even in very wet weather the soil may remain dry round the roots. The need to water very frequently can

be largely avoided even in the hottest weather if a thick mulch of straw is provided at the roots in mid-July. This keeps down weeds as well as encouraging better root growth.

Tubers will need at least one strong stake, but dahlia plants are better if they are supported by a triangle of three canes or stakes. Such plants have to carry all the weight of stems, leaves and flowers on one main stem or 'leg', so are very prone to wind damage. Tubers on the other hand, push out rigid shoots from below soil level and are much less likely to be broken by the wind in the early stages of growth. These shoots should be tied to the stake every 18 inches, whereas the dahlia plant needs tying every 6 inches for additional protection. A good average length for dahlia supports is 5 feet; these are knocked in to the ground to a depth of 1 foot. Avoid having the stakes higher than the blooms because the wind will knock the flowers against them.

Ground tubers can be left to produce flowers on the tips of their main stems. Allow about eight main stems per division to emerge, and cut off any others below soil level carefully with a knife. Large and giant-flowered varieties should be allowed to produce about five stems only.

Pot tubers, unless they produce sufficient main shoots from below soil level, will have to be treated like green plants. The leading growth tip of the plant is pinched out, or 'stopped', about a month after planting out, usually when about six pairs of leaves have developed. This encourages sideshoots to be produced so plenty of flowers come into bloom as a start; otherwise, if not stopped in advance, dahlia plants produce one central flower only at first. Take notice which are the strongest emerging sideshoots after stopping, and when they are 3 inches long, remove the excess ones by snapping them out from their joints with the main stem. Retain five shoots only, however, with large and giant-flowered varieties. The technique with the pot tuber is to select initially the strongest main shoot, similar to that of the dahlia plant as the central growing stem, removing the others. This main shoot will be stopped and the sideshoots selected in exactly the same way. A ground tuber is not usually stopped, the flowers being borne on the terminal, or crown buds of each stem. It can, however, be treated like a pot tuber or green plant as far as shoot growth is concerned, but by stopping and selecting one main stem, the flowers, through having to be produced on sideshoots, will be about three weeks later than on the tips of the main stems. Pompon varieties need no de-shooting or disbudding.

Disbudding should be done to all other types when the flower buds are about the size of a pea. Allow the main, centrally placed, largest bud to remain and flower

on each shoot, removing the others, together with the fresh secondary shoots which will emerge from each leaf joint on the stem as the flowers mature. Leave just one, fairly low down, on each stem to produce the successive flower, again disbudding and de-shooting. This technique is adopted throughout the flowering period and is the only way to achieve a long flowering season combined with good quality flowers with long stems for cutting.

Left to their own devices, dahlias produce a mass of buds and flowers and soon become uncontrollable, their very tiny, poor blossoms often becoming single by the end of the season. If you need small-flowered dahlias, grow special small-flowered varieties.

Lifting and Storing Ideally this is done once frost has blackened the foliage. If, however, the autumn continues without frost, it does no harm to lift dahlias in late October and early November. Only in the mildest of places, in very sheltered situations or during unusually gentle winters can dahlias be left out of doors in the ground all winter. They can be put into a clamp in the same way as potatoes, but the disadvantage here is that they may be killed if the weather becomes very severe. Furthermore, you cannot examine them for signs of rotting or put them in the greenhouse to take cuttings.

To lift dahlia roots, first cut off the stems just above soil level. Then lift by prising in a circle with a broad-tined fork, working well away from the stems. After lifting the roots clear of the soil, pick off as much adhering earth as possible. Then place the roots upside down in a well-ventilated greenhouse, frame or shed for at least a fortnight. During this period they will lose excess moisture and by the time the remaining soil becomes dust dry, they will be ready to be put into winter storage. There they should be covered with sacks or straw at night if frost threatens. Only in very wet autumns should artificial heat be used, never exceeding 70°F (21°C).

Before placing them in store, retrim the stems as low as possible, without actually cutting into the tubers. Retie the labels on one of the tubers, because in store the stems will become paper dry and will actually drop off. Most dahlia roots need no covering in store, and in fact, a frequent cause of loss during the winter is covering them up, putting them away in a cupboard and forgetting about them until the spring. Lay them on racks in a frost-proof shed, cellar, or in a greenhouse which can be kept frost free. Straw bales provide good frost protection.

Very tiny tubers, however, should be covered in boxes or pots with material such as garden soil or sand. During the winter, sprinkle the surface with water very occasionally if it gets dust dry, but avoid giving sufficient water to start the tubers into growth. A good temperature

to aim at in store is 40–50°F (4–10°C); failing that, it should never fall below 34°F (1°C) nor exceed 50°F (10°C). If you have to store them in a warm place, shrivelling is likely, so all tubers must then be covered with sand or soil in boxes, but keep the boxes separated and put only one layer of tubers in each box. Avoid any store that is subject to drips or draughts, or is so airtight that it encourages fungus rot.

Every month inspect the tubers and if any parts are rotting, cut them out with a sharp knife. Dry the surfaces left with a rag and smear on captan or zineb to prevent further rot. Occasionally fumigate with smoke pellets to deal with aphids which may have hatched out in store or bulb flies which sometimes attack the roots.

Pests and diseases As a general precaution, always spray dahlias with insecticides every three weeks during the season of growth, including those growing in the greenhouse and frame.

Sometimes the soil becomes infected with verticillium wilt, when the stock must be burnt and a fresh growing site found. Cauliflower-like outgrowths, due to crown gall, also mean that affected stock must be destroyed, but it is slow to spread and healthy stock can still be grown in the same ground.

A common leaf disease, especially in humid summers, is dahlia leaf spot, causing light green ringed spots which later turn brown. In this event, treat the leaves with zineb.

Plants are sometimes attacked by virus diseases, of which light green patches or yellowing bands up the veins and perhaps dark green blisters on the leaves are symptoms. A more certain sign is dwarfing of the plant, which becomes very close-jointed and bushy, producing small flowers. Burn stock affected in this way, for there is no cure at present.

Propagation The preparation for growing from seed is a simple matter. Remove the petals as they fade and take the seed pods indoors before the frost, later extracting the seed and placing it in envelopes. The seed is sown in boxes in mid-March, and the seedlings are potted off in May and planted out in June. The best breeding, however, is done by crossing selected varieties by hand, and covering the blooms with old nylon stockings to prevent chance pollination by bees and other insects. It should be remembered that dahlias do not come true to type or variety from seed, though dwarf bedding types, such as 'Coltness Gem' or 'Unwins Hybrids' are commonly grown in this way as they come reasonably true.

Years ago dahlia shoots were grafted on to tubers to produce plants, but only research into virus control now employs this technique. Nowadays dahlias are commonly propagated from cuttings. Tubers are packed close together in

1 Dahlia 'Lady Tweedsmuir', a Small-flowered Decorative with blooms over 4 inches in diameter, but not exceeding 6 inches. 2 Dahlia 'Coltness Gem'.

boxes of soil in February, put on the greenhouse bench with bottom heat of about 60°F (16°C) and watered. When the shoots, produced after some three weeks, are about 2½ inches long, they are cut off close to the tuber just below a leaf joint, and after removing the lower leaves, they are inserted into holes round the edge of 3 inch pots. The holes are made by inserting a pencil-sized dibber 1½ inches deep into the rooting medium in the pots, commonly sand or a mixture of equal parts of peat and sand. Five cuttings are placed in each pot. The pots are then placed over bottom heat from soil-warming wires, boiler pipes, or paraffin or electrical heating. The temperature should be about 60°F (16°C) round the pots. Cover the pots by suspending polythene sheeting above them in the daytime, plus brown paper if the sun shines, and spray them gently with water morning and night, removing the covers over night. Do not make the mistake of overwatering the pots during the rooting period, or rotting may take place. Add water to the pot only when the sand surface dries out and then dip it in a bucket of water with a finger over the drainage hole until bubbles cease to rise. Otherwise, rely on overhead spraying on the cuttings themselves.

After two or three weeks, when new tip growth is evident, the cuttings will have rooted and can be potted off individually in ordinary potting compost. For the first ten days afterwards, keep them in a warm part of the greenhouse, but for the rest of the time until planting out they grow much better if kept cool. Certainly they should be ready to be put into a cold frame three weeks after potting off.

The division of tubers described earlier is the other method of propagation.

Types of dahlias On January 1st 1966, a new system of dahlia classification came into being. As far as Britain is concerned the National Dahlia Society is the authority for domestic classification. Periodically the society issues a classified list of varieties showing the type or size to which any named variety belongs.

There are now ten main groups, some being subdivided into sizes according to flower diameter. These include single-flowered, anemone-flowered, collerette, paeony-flowered and miscellaneous (containing such types as orchid-flowered). As far as the gardener is concerned the most popular groups are the decorative dahlia, with flat broad petals; the cactus dahlia with petals that roll backwards to form a quill; semi-cactus dahlias,

1 'Rotterdam', a medium-flowered Semi-Cactus dahlia. Other dahlias in this category are 2 'Homespun' and 3 'Hamari Bride'. 4 'Grand Prix', a Giant Decorative dahlia. 5 'Worton Pride' 6 'Devil du Roi Albert'.

which have part only of their petal length rolled; pompon dahlias, like drumsticks, their flowers having blunt, tubular petals, under 2 inches in diameter; and the new group of ball dahlias which comprise all the previously known groups of medium and large pompons and the similar, but larger, double show varieties, plus any globular shaped varieties which were previously small or miniature decoratives.

Size groups are: pompons one size only; ball dahlias are divided into miniature balls, 2–4 inches, and balls over 4 inches, decorative, cactus and semi-cactus dahlias are each divided into five groups; miniature, under 4 inches, small, 4–6 inches, medium 6–8 inches, large-flowered 8–10 inches, giant-flowered over 10 inches. Bedding dahlias are put where their flower shape designates them.

Exhibiting Cultural technique varies little from that described. Cuttings are mostly used for propagation purposes; they flower during late August and the first half of September when most dahlia shows are held. Tubers of the large-flowered and giant varieties are started into growth in the greenhouse in mid-January, cuttings being taken for rooting during early March; plants, when put in the frame, later on, should be put into 5 inch pots by early May. All other varieties are started off in mid-February, the best plants being obtained from cuttings rooted during the end of March and the first three weeks in April. Those taken before this period will usually flower much too early for the shows. For show work, it is much better to grow at least six plants of each good variety, so restricting the number of varieties to the capacity of the outdoor space available to grow them in. When garden plants are grown for display, distances should be 2 feet apart for pompons, 2½ feet apart for ball dahlias and all others, except the large and giant decoratives cactus and semi-cactus which should be placed 3 feet apart. Many exhibitors mulch the giant varieties with manure in July; for the others, a straw mulch is used. During flowering it is common practice to protect the flowers of the large and giant varieties either with cones of builder's bituminised brown paper, or even by erecting metal uprights to support a roof made of corrugated vinyl clear plastic sheeting, giving the effect of an open-sided greenhouse.

Always cut the flowers the evening before and stand them in a cool, dark place in water over night. Large and giant blooms must have a 2 foot cane tied along the stem when it is cut to prevent the bloom toppling over in transit. Common methods of transport include oil or distemper drums with holes drilled round the edge to which the individual blooms can be tied; milk crates with one bloom in each corner resting in a water-filled bottle, or old butcher's liver tins especially for pompons. It is always advisable to carry flowers to a show in water.

The best way to pick up showing technique is to join a dahlia society if there is one in the locality, or if not, to contact the National Dahlia Society.

Recommended varieties It is always unwise to be dogmatic about recommending varieties as they quickly pass out of favour, but those mentioned here are likely to remain attractive in the garden, as well as being suitable for exhibition, for years to come. The small flowered decoratives, medium and small cactus and semi-cactus, the ball dahlias and poms are the best to choose for cutting and flower arrangement. .

Giant decoratives These do not necessarily grow tall and in fact many are dwarf growers. If you allow up to eight flowers per tuber or plant you will get quite small blooms which are preferred by those who object to a very large size: 'Black Monarch', deep maroon; 'Bona-fide', yellow; 'Evelyn Rumbold', light purple; 'Go American', orange bronze; 'Grand Prix', very bright yellow tipped, white; 'Hamari Girl', a dwarf, pale rose pink; 'Holland Festival', popular orange and white; 'Jacondo', wine purple; 'Kelvin Floodlight', yellow; 'Kidd's Climax', pale lavender and cream; 'Lavengro', outstanding lavender; 'Liberator', deep crimson; 'Margaret Bowyer', white.

Large decoratives These are not so widely grown but very good varieties include: 'Enfield Salmon', orange-pink; 'Hamari Boldness', a tall variety, glowing crimson; 'Moon Probe', very attractive golden variety with long stems; 'Ovation', a golden-bronze with pointed petals; and 'Polyand', lilac.

Medium decoratives 'Betty Russell', bright yellow; 'Breckland Joy', orange-pink; 'Crossfield Standard', bright orange, an improvement on 'House of Orange'; and 'Pattern', bright lilac, tipped white.

Small decoratives 'Amethyst', pale bluish-lavender; 'Angora', white with split petal tips; 'Chinese Lantern', orange and gold; 'Dedham', deep lilac and white; 'Hamari Fiesta', very bright yellow and red; 'Marie Rust', bright orange; 'Mrs Silverstone', pale silvery-pink; 'Procyon', orange and red; 'Rosy Cloud', glowing cerise-pink; 'Snow Queen', white; 'Twiggy', a bright pink water-lily type; 'Worton Gold', golden-yellow; and 'Vicky Crutchfield', a very pretty pale pink water lily variety.

Miniature decoratives 'David Howard', golden-orange with purple foliage; 'Horn of Plenty', scarlet; 'Jo's Choice', deep crimson; and 'Schweitzer's Kokarde', bright orange.

Giant or large cactus or semi-cactus 'Frontispiece', white with frilly petal tips; 'Hamari Dream', pale primrose; 'Nantenan', deep yellow; 'Miss Universe', bright burnt-orange; 'Paul Critchley', lavender, and 'Respectable', an early-flowering, compact, gold.

Medium cactus or semi-cactus 'Autumn Fire', orange-red; 'Exotica', deep pink and cream; 'Frigid Friend', white fimbriated; 'Hamari Bride', white; 'Hill's Delight', red tipped yellow; 'Homespun', buff-primrose and red; 'Lucky Fellow', deep pink; 'Piquant', red and white; 'Rotterdam', crimson; 'Sure Thing', scarlet with needle-like petals; 'Westminster', bright golden-bronze.

Small cactus or semi-cactus 'Combo', pink and primrose; 'Doris Knight', deep purple sport of 'Doris Day', which is deep crimson; 'Goya's Venus', light orange-pink; 'Orange Nymph', golden-orange with finely-cut foliage; 'Paul Chester', yellow and orange; 'Temptress', cream and lilac; 'White Swallow', white; and 'Worton Sally Ann', lavender-pink.

Ball dahlias 'Blossom', pale pink; 'Dr. John Grainger', burnt-orange; 'Florence Vernon', lavender, tipped white; 'Ian Patterson', lilac; 'Rothesay Superb', scarlet; 'Rev. Colwyn Vale', purple; and 'Worton Pride', yellow.

Pompons 'Andrew Lockwood', lavender; 'Czar Willo', purple; 'Kym Willo', orange and yellow; 'Little Sally', scarlet; 'Whale's Rhonda', purple, tipped silver; 'Winnie', pink, tipped silver; 'Py', yellow.

Delphinium (del-fin-e-um)

From the Greek *delphin,* a dolphin, the flowerbuds having some resemblance to that sea creature *(Ranunculaceae).* Larkspur. The genus consists of annual, biennial and herbaceous perennial plants, mostly hardy and showy plants for border cultivation, with some dwarf species suitable for the rock garden.

Species cultivated: Annual D. ajacis, 1–2 feet, blue, violet, rose-pink or white, summer, Europe. D. consolida, branching larkspur, 2 feet, purple or deep violet, summer, Europe. D. paniculatum, Siberian larkspur, up to 3 feet, single, violet, July to September, also grown as a biennial. Seedsmen list many beautiful varieties of these annual larkspurs, mainly 2½–3 feet tall, derived mainly from D. ajacis and D. consolida. They include such strains as 'Giant Hyacinth-flowered'; 'Giant Imperial'; 'Regal', 4 feet; 'Supreme', 4 feet, and named cultivars such as 'Blue Spire', dark blue; 'Carmine King'; 'Dazzler', bright scarlet; 'Exquisite Pink'; 'Lilac Spire'; 'Los Angeles', rose and salmon; 'Miss California', salmon rose; 'Rosamond', bright rose and 'White Spire'.

Perennial D. brunonianum, 1–1½ feet, light purple, June and July, western China. D. cardinale, 2–3 feet, bright red, July and August, California, somewhat tender. D. denudatum, 2½ feet, yellow and blue, summer, Himalaya. D. elatum, 2–3 feet, blue, June, Alps, Pyrenees eastwards, the plant from which most garden delphiniums have been derived.

D. formosum, 3 feet, purple-blue, August, Caucasus, Asia Minor. *D. grandiflorum* (syn. *D. chinense*), 1–3 feet, violet-blue or white, long spurred, summer, Siberia. *D. nudicaule*, 1–1½ feet, red and yellow, April to June, California. *D. speciosum* (syn. *D. caucasicum*), 6 inches–2 feet, blue and purple, summer, Himalaya. *D. tatsienense*, 1½ feet, violet-blue, July, Szechwan. *D. vestitum*, 2 feet, pale and deep blue, summer, northern India. *D. zalil* (syn. *D. sulphureum*), 1–2½ feet, lemon-yellow, summer, Persia, requires a well-drained soil.

Cultivation Sow annual varieties in a sunny, open border in April where they are to flower, or in boxes of light soil under glass in March in a temperature of 55°F (13°C). Prick out seedlings when large enough to handle and transplant in the open in May. Perennials should be planted out in the spring or autumn in beds of rich, deeply cultivated soil; dwarf varieties are suitable for rock gardens. Feed with liquid manure in the early summer. Lift and replant every

third year. Propagation of perennial varieties is by means of cuttings of young shoots in early spring, inserted in sandy soil in pots in a shaded propagating frame, or by seeds sown in the open ground in late spring or under glass in spring.

Cultivation of modern hybrid delphiniums
Fast-growing plants, delphiniums require a deeply-dug, rich soil with adequate drainage. A medium loam is preferable to a light sandy soil. Where the soil is light dig in deeply plenty of compost or old farmyard manure before planting and during the summer a mulch of garden compost is excellent. Nitrogenous fertilisers should be used with care as they may only result in producing weak stems. If the stems are cut back immediately after flowering a second crop of spikes may be produced, but these should only be encouraged with strong-growing varieties. Adequate

moisture will be required to produce this second crop during what may be hot, summer weather. Slugs can be a menace with the tender young delphinium shoots, especially in the early spring, so precautions should be taken with slug pellets or other repellents. Varieties that grow to about 4–5 feet in height are more suitable for small gardens than those that tower to 7 feet or more, and they are less liable to damage by summer gales. Pea sticks, brushwood or twigs can be used to support the young growths but these should be put in position around the plants in good time so that the stems grow up through them. This is often left too late with the result that the tender stems get broken when the sticks are being pushed into the soil. Staking for exhibition spikes must be carefully done, using one stout cane to each spike. When growing the large flowering varieties it is usual to restrict one-year-old plants to one spike and two-year-old plants to two or three spikes. Pea sticks, however, provide adequate support for the lighter, less tall graceful belladonna types of delphinium, with their branching stems, which are also so attractive for floral arrangement. Exhibition spikes should be straight, tapering and well filled with large circular florets but not overcrowded, and bearing few laterals. The foliage should be clean, healthy and undamaged. Immediately spikes are cut they should be placed in deep containers filled with water and stood in a cool, but not draughty place. There they should remain for some hours or overnight. Each stem should be wrapped in a large sheet of tissue paper (30×40 inches) before being taken to the show. A further step to ensure that the spike does not

flag is to turn it upside down, immediately before final staging, fill the hollow stem with cold water and plug with cotton wool.

As they are easily raised from seed the delphinium has been of much interest to the plant breeder who has produced many stately varieties. The era of immense spikes has passed its zenith and the trend is to develop a range of hybrids not exceeding about 4½ feet in height. These are of much more general use in gardens which are ever becoming smaller, but more numerous.

1 Delphinium 'Daily Express', a fine garden plant. 2 Delphinium 'Silver Moon', one of the finest cultivars ever raised.

From the glorious shades of blue the colour range has been extended from white and cream through pink, carmine, mauve, lavender, purple and violet. Now, thanks to the work done by Dr Legro, the celebrated Dutch hybridist, the range includes shades of cerise, orange, peach and tomato-red. Our garden hybrids have been mainly derived from *Delphinium elatum,* a natural tetraploid species, but Dr Legro succeeded in overcoming the sterility barrier when he made a number of species crosses at diploid level, tetraploided the resulting plants and then successfully married them to hybrid elatums. A recent development, the rediscovery of the white African species, *D. leroyi*, which has a

1

2

freesia-like fragrance, also opens up pleasing possiblities. First crosses at diploid level have shown that this quality is not recessive, so hopes are high, but all this work takes time. In this country Dr B. J. Langdon has also been working on these problems and during the next few years we should see a truly remarkable range of hybrid delphiniums.

Recommended tall varieties 'Alice Artindale', light blue, 6 feet; 'Ann Page', deep cornflower blue, 5½ feet; 'Bridesmaid', silvery-mauve, white eye, 7 feet; 'Charles F. Langdon', mid-blue, black eye, 6½ feet; 'Daily Express', bright sky-blue, black eye, 6 feet; 'Janet Wort', pure white, 6½ feet; 'Jennifer Langdon', pale blue and mauve, 5½ feet; 'Mogul', rosy-purple, 6½ feet; 'Purple Ruffles', deep purple, overlaid royal blue, 5 feet; 'Royalist', deep blue, 6 feet; 'Silver Moon', silvery-mauve, white eye, 5½ feet; 'Swanlake', pure white, black eye, 5 feet.

Shorter-growing varieties 'Blue Bees', pale blue, 4 feet; 'Blue Tit', indigo blue, black eye, 3½ feet; 'Blue Jade', pastel blue, dark brown eye, 4 feet; 'Cliveden Beauty', pale blue, 4 feet; 'Naples', bright blue, 4 feet; 'Peter Pan', deep blue, 3½ feet; 'Wendy', gentian-blue, 4–5 feet, the most popular of the belladonna type.

The Pacific Hybrids raised in America, growing 4–6 feet tall, include 'Astolat', lilac and pink; 'Black Knight' series, shades of violet; 'Blue Jay', mid-blue; 'Cameliard' series, lavender shades; 'Elaine', rose-pink; 'Galahad' series, whites; 'Guinevere' series, shades of lavender-pink; 'King Arthur' series, shades of violet-purple; 'Lancelot' series, shades of lilac; 'Percival', white with a black eye; 'Round Table', including various colours as above; 'Summer Skies', good true blues.

Dendrobium (den-dro-be-um)

From the Greek *dendron*, a tree, *bios*, life, the plants growing on trees in their native habitats *(Orchidaceae)*. A very large genus of approximately 1100 species of epiphytic orchids, which are widely distributed throughout eastern regions and the Southern Hemisphere. Considerable variation is found in flower and plant habit, from small tufted plants to stout pseudobulbed plants, several feet tall. Many hybrids have been produced particularly in the *D. nobile* and *D. phalaenopsis* sections.

Species cultivated (A selection only) *D. aggregatum*, yellow, spring, requires a decided rest, Burma. *D. atroviolaceum*, creamy white, purple spotted, spring, New Guinea. *D. aureum*, amber-yellow and brown, very fragrant, autumn, India, etc. *D. bigibbum*, magenta-purple, winter, Australia. *D. brymerianum*, bright yellow with densely fringed lip, spring, Burma. *D. chrysanthum*, orange-yellow, maroon blotched, autumn, India. *D. chrysotoxum*, orange-yellow, spring, requires a decided rest, Burma. *D. dearei*,

white, summer, Philippines. *D. densiflorum*, clusters of orange-yellow flowers, spring, Burma. *D. fimbriatum*, orange-yellow, various, Burma. *D. findlayanum*, white, yellow and magenta, winter, Burma. *D. formosum*, large, white and yellow, fragrant, autumn, Burma, etc. *D. jamesianum*, large, white, spring, Burma. *D. kingianum*, small purplish flowers, spring, Australia. *D. moschatum*, yellow, flushed rose, black blotches, spring, Burma. *D. parishii*, purplish-rose, spring, Burma. *D. phalaenopsis*, rose-red to magenta-purple, autumn and various, Australia and New Guinea. *D. regium*, large, rose, spring, India. *D. superbum*, large, rose-purple, spring, Philippines. *D. thyrsiflorum*, white and yellow, spring, Burma. *D. victoria-reginae*, whitish approaching blue, one of the very few orchids having a near blue colour. *D. wardianum*, white, purplish-yellow and rose-red, winter, Burma.

Named cultivars run into many thousands. A few are given here from the *nobile* section, all having fine large, strongly coloured flowers derived mainly from *D. nobile*, *D. findlayanum* and their early hybrids. 'Fort Noble', 'Fort Alan', 'Winifred Fortescue', 'Montrose', 'Margaret Illingworth', 'Sunburst', 'Ann-Marie', 'Gatton Monarch'.

Cultivation General directions only can be given for this large and varied genus. The plants require a general compost of 3 parts of osmunda fibre and 1 part of sphagnum moss, in well-drained pots or pans. An important factor with most types is maximum light in autumn to

Dendrobium 'Lady Coleman'.

ripen the growths. Water freely in summer and rest carefully in winter. The *nobile* types, especially, require cooler conditions in winter to initiate flower buds; temperatures should be about 50–55°F (10–13°C). For other types they should be 55–60°F (13–16°C). Summer temperatures can for most species rise to 80–85°F (27–29°C) and moist conditions should prevail. Propagation is by division at potting time; *nobile* types and some others produce adventitious growths from the stems; these can be potted up in small pots. The stems of some species can be cut up into small pieces of about one node (joint) and placed in warm conditions; these will produce small plants.

Dianthus (di-an-thus)

From the Greek *dios*, a god or divine, *anthos*, a flower, divine flower, flower of Jupiter or Zeus *(Caryophyllaceae)*. A large genus of hardy annual, biennial and perennial plants, which falls into three main groups: pinks, carnations and dianthus proper (see Carnation cultivation and Pinks). The greatest number of species come from the Balkans and Asia Minor, some from the Iberian Peninsula and North Africa, a few from China and Japan and two are natives of the British Isles. Many plants in the genus are very fragrant, with a unique perfume, predominantly clove, strongest among the pinks and carnations. Many of the dwarf kinds are excellent rock garden plants; the taller kinds are suitable for the front

of sunny borders, banks or other places.
Species cultivated (All are perennials unless otherwise stated) *D.* × *allwoodii*, 6 inches– 2½ feet, very variable in colour, single and double, summer, hybrid. *D. alpinus*, 3 inches, rose-red, May and June. *D. arvernensis*, 4–6 inches, clear pink, May and June. *D. barbatus*, Sweet William, 6 inches – 1½ feet, perennial usually grown as a biennial, variable in colour, summer. *D.* × *boydii*, 3–6 inches, rose-pink, May and July. *D. carthusianorum*, 1–1½ feet, rose-purple, June to August. *D. caryophyllus*, carnation, clove pink, picotee, 9 inches–3 feet, red, but very variable in cultivation, parent, with *D. chinensis,* of annual carnations and Chinese and Indian pinks (see Carnation cultivation and Pinks). *D. chinensis* (syn. *D. sinensis*), Chinese or Indian pink, 9 inches, annual, variable in colour, summer. *D. deltoides,* maiden pink, 6 inches, purple to crimson, spotted and striped, summer, native; vars. *albus,* white; *erectus,* rich red. *D. fragrans,* 1–1½ feet, white, summer. *D. gratianopolitanus* (syn. *D. caesius*), Cheddar pink, 1 foot, pink, May and June; vars. *albus,* white; *flore-pleno,* double or semi-double. *D. haematocalyx,* 4–6 inches, bright pink, July. *D. knappii,* 1 foot, pure yellow, July and August. *D. microlepis,* 2–3 inches, pink, flowers small, spring, scree plant. *D. monspessulanus,* 6–12 inches, pink, summer. *D. musalae,* 2 inches, bright pink, spring, scree. *D. myrtinervis,* 2–3 inches, pink, small, spring. *D. neglectus,* 3 inches, rose-red, June, dislikes lime. *D. nitidus,* 6 inches– 2 feet, rose-pink, July and August. *D. noeanus,* 6–8 inches, white, July and August. *D. petraeus* (syn. *D. kitaibelii*), 8–12 inches, pink, June; var. *albus,* 6 inches, double white. *D. pindicola,* 2 inches, deep pink, summer, scree. *D. plumarius,* pink, Scotch pink, 1 foot, variable in colour, May to July. Parent of the garden pinks (see Pinks). *D. squarrosus,* 1 foot, white, summer. *D. sternbergii,* 6 inches, rose-red, June. *D. strictus,* 6 inches, white, June and July. *D. subacaulis,* 3 inches, rose-pink, June to August.

Cultivars are numerous (for those of carnations and pinks see Carnations and Pinks). Those of species described above include 'Ariel' ('Crossways'), 4–6 inches, cherry-red, July and August; 'Baker's Variety', 6 inches, large, deep pink, June and July; *D. deltoides* 'Brilliant', 6 inches, crimson, summer, and 'Huntsman', 6 inches, bright red, June and July; 'Charles Musgrave', 9 inches, white with green eye, summer; 'Cherry Ripe', 6–9 inches, rose-red, summer; *D. gratianopolitanus* 'Prichard's Variety', 4–6 inches, rose pink; 'La Bourboulle', 3 inches, deep pink, summer, and 'Double Ruby', 9 inches, summer; 'F. C. Stern', 6 inches,

Dianthus barbatus, Sweet William, is naturally a perennial but usually grown as a biennial. The colour varies.

1 Dianthus neglectus forms a dense mat and flowers in July and August. Unlike most varieties of dianthus it dislikes lime in the soil. 2 Dianthus 'Charles Musgrave'.

rosy-red, June to September; 'Fusilier', 3 inches, shining crimson, summer; 'F. W. Millward', 9 inches, double pink, summer; 'Highland Queen', 1 foot, deep rose, summer; 'Holmsted', 6 inches, soft pink, summer; 'Inchmery', 1 foot, soft pink, double, summer; 'Isolde', 9 inches, pink and white, double, summer; 'Len Hutton', 1 foot, claret-red, edge laced white, summer; 'Little Jock', 4 inches, rose-pink with darker eye, semi-double, summer; 'Little Jock Hybrids', various colours; 'Margaret Curtis', 1 foot, white, crimson zone, summer; 'Mars', 4 inches, rich red, double; 'Spencer Bickham', 4 inches, deep pink, summer; 'Sweet Wivelsfield' (*D.* × *allwoodii* × *D. barbatus*), 18 inches, half-hardy annuals in many bright colours, summer; 'Windward Rose', 6 inches, light rose, summer.
Cultivation Sharp drainage and preferably a limy soil in a sunny position is needed for most dianthus, except perhaps

D. alpinus which likes less sun and tolerates an acid soil fairly well, and *D. neglectus* which dislikes lime. All do well in sandy loam. When the alpine species are grown in pots in the alpine house a compost ensuring brisk drainage but at the same time sufficiently retentive of moisture is needed. Make it up of 2 parts of coarse sand or crushed gravel, 2 parts of leafmould or spent hops, 1 part of loam and a scattering of bonemeal. Cover the surface of the pots with limestone chippings for attractiveness, to present the plant as a perfect cushion and to guarantee surface drainage. Propagation is from seed for annual and biennial kinds and those species that set seed, or by pipings and cuttings taken immediately flowering ends, and inserted in pure sand round the edges of a pot and protected until rooting has taken place.

Dicentra (di-sen-tra)

From the Greek *di,* two, *kentron,* a spur, referring to the two spurs on the petals (*Fumariaceae*). Hardy herbaceous perennials formerly known as *Dielytra.* Fibrous and tuberous rooted, they generally transplant badly because the roots are as brittle as glass. The flowers are pendent from arching stems, like lanterns hung along a cord.
Species cultivated *D. cucullaria,* Dutchman's breeches, 6 inches, very divided pale green foliage, flowers pearl white, tipped yellow, May and June. *D. eximia,* 1–1½ feet, reddish-purple flowers, May and September and intermittently between; var. *alba,* white flowers. *D. formosa,* 1–1½ feet, pink or light red, long flowering period; 'Bountiful' is a larger-flowered cultivar, with deep pink flowers. *D. oregana,* 6 inches, flowers creamy-pink, tipped purple, May and June. *D. peregrina* (syn. *D. pusilla*), 3 inches, rose-pink flowers in June and July, a good plant for a scree in the rock garden. *D. spectabilis,* Chinaman's breeches, bleeding heart, lyre flower, 1½–2 feet, flowers rose-red, May and June; var. *alba,* white, a garden hybrid (*D. eximia* × *D. formosa*), 9–12 inches, has deep red flowers.
Cultivation Dicentras will grow in light shade or full sun provided the soil does not dry out at the roots. A rich loam is best with shelter from cold winds. Some protection may be needed in winter. Propagation is by root cuttings in March or April raised in a temperature of about 55°F (13°C). Division of plants is possible in spring, but difficult because the roots are very brittle. *D. spectabilis* is sometimes grown in pots and forced in a compost of equal parts of loam, peat and sand. The plants are kept frost free all winter and taken into a temperature of 55–65°F (13–18°C) during February and started into growth. Water, and feed moderately with a liquid feed once the buds begin to show. Forced plants should be planted out in the open ground after they have flowered.

Digitalis (dij-it-ay-lis)

From the Latin *digitus*, a finger, referring to the resemblance of the flower to
the finger of a glove *(Scrophulariaceae)*.
Foxglove. A genus of hardy biennial and
perennial plants, the common foxglove
growing wild extensively in Britain.
They are excellent woodland plants,
useful both for borders and wild gardens
where they will seed themselves
profusely.

Species cultivated *D. davisiana,* 2 feet,
bronze flowers, summer, perennial. *D.
ferruginea,* 4–6 feet, rust-red flowers,
July, biennial. *D. grandiflora* (syn. *D.
ambigua),* 2–3 feet, pale yellow blotched
brown, July and August, a poor perennial, best grown as a biennial. *D.
laevigata,* 3 feet, bronze-yellow, white-
lipped flowers, July, perennial. *D. lanata,*

Foxgloves are known botanically as Digi-
talis. They are excellent woodland plants,
useful for borders and wild gardens.

2–3 feet, cream-yellow with deeper
markings, July and August, a good
biennial. *D. lutea,* 3 feet, yellow, July,
perennial. *D. × mertonensis,* 3 feet,
large attractive crushed strawberry-
coloured flowers, summer, perennial,
hybrid which comes true from seed. *D.
orientalis,* 1 foot, pale cream, July and
August. *D. purpurea,* common foxglove,
3–5 feet, flowers purple with deeper
spots, July to September; var. *gloxinae-
flora* (gloxinia-flowered or *gloxinoides*
of the nurserymen's catalogues), flowers
more open than the type. Many good
strains and varieties are available now,
including the 'Shirley Strains' and 'Ex-

celsior Hybrids', in which the flowers are
borne all round the stem and do not
droop. Beautiful 'art shades' are available ranging through cream and yellow
to pink and purple.

Cultivation Rich moist soil is ideal for
foxgloves and they are most effective
when planted in drifts. The perennials
are planted in spring or autumn and
none are long lived so replacements may
be necessary to maintain an effect. The
biennials, and those perennials treated
as biennials are raised from seed sown in
April or May, the seedlings being transplanted to a shady reserve bed in July
and to their final positions in October.
Propagation of the perennial kinds is
from seed treated as for biennials or by
division of the crowns into separate
rosettes in autumn after flowering.

Dimorphotheca (di-mor-foth-e-ka)
From the Greek *di*, two, *morphe*, shape, *theca*, seed, because the flower produces two different shapes of seed, one from the disk florets and another from the ray florets (*Compositae*). Cape marigold, star of the veldt, Namaqualand daisy. A genus of half-hardy annual, herbaceous perennial and sub-shrubby plants from South Africa, grown for their long-lasting daisy-like flowers in bright colours. Considerable confusion in naming exists in many books and catalogues and according to some authorities those plants known as dimorphothecas should be split up between the genera *Castalis*, *Chrysanthemoides*, *Dimorphotheca* and *Osteospermum*. Here, for the sake of convenience, they are all treated as belonging to the genus *Dimorphotheca*.
Species cultivated *D. aurantiaca* (syn. *Castalis tragus*, *D. flaccida* and apparently the true name for many of the plants grown in gardens under the names of *D. calendulacea* and *D. sinuata*), 1–1½ feet, bright orange flowers with a dark brown disk, edged with metallic blue, June to September, a perennial usually treated as a half-hardy annual. This species has given rise to several garden hybrids (listed in catalogues) such as 'Buff Beauty'; 'Goliath', extra large, mainly orange flowers; 'Lemon Queen'; 'Orange Glory'; 'Glistening White' and 'White Beauty'. *D. barberiae* (syn. *Osteospermum barberiae*), 1½ feet, aromatic foliage, long stemmed rosy-lilac flowers, summer to autumn, with occasional flowers appearing at almost any time, sub-shrubby. This plant is hardier than is generally supposed and will usually survive out of doors in the south of England, making large spreading clumps. There is a dwarf form, *compacta*, which is said to be hardier still. *D. calendulacea* see *D. aurantiaca*. *D. ecklonis*, 2–3 feet, flowers white with reverse of petals purple and a deep purple zone on the petals, perennial treated as annual. *D. pluvialis* (syn. *D. annua*), 1 foot, almost hardy, white above, purple below; var. *ringens*, violet ring round disk, June onwards. *D. sinuata* see *D. aurantiaca*.
Cultivation Sun is essential for all species and in a poor, cloudy summer nothing can be done to improve the results since the flowers of most kinds open only in sunny weather, closing or failing to open when the sky is overcast, or in late afternoon. Out of doors they do best in the lighter soils, although *D. barberiae* will thrive on any kind of soil, even heavy clay. In the sunny greenhouse dimorphothecas are grown in pots containing a compost of 3 parts of sandy loam, 1 part of leafmould, plus silver sand. The minimum temperature in winter, when they need moderate watering only, should be 40°F (4°C). Propagation is by seed sown in March in pans or boxes in heat and, after hardening off, the seedlings may be put out in the

Dimorphotheca barbariae will do well out of doors in sheltered gardens

border in late May or early June. The plants grow quickly and will start flowering in June. Perennial species may be propagated by cuttings taken in late summer and rooted in a greenhouse or frame. *D. pluvialis* is probably the hardiest of those grown as annuals and seed of this species may be sown out of doors in early April in fine soil, the seedlings later thinned, to start flowering at the end of June.

Doronicum (dor-on-ik-um)
From the Arabic name *doronigi* (*Compositae*). Leopard's bane. Hardy herbaceous perennials, natives of Europe and Asia, early-flowering, with long-stemmed, daisy-like yellow flowers. The sap from the root of *D. pardalianches* is said to be poisonous. Doronicums last well as cut-flowers.
Species cultivated *D. austriacum*, 18 inches, golden-yellow, spring. *D. carpetanum*, 2 feet, yellow, May and June. *D. caucasicum*, 1 foot, yellow, April and May; var. *magnificum*, flowers larger.

D. clusii, 1 foot, yellow, May and June. *D. cordatum*, 6–9 inches, deep yellow, April and May. *D. orientale*, 1 foot, yellow, April, *D. plantagineum*, 2–3 feet, yellow, spring; var. *excelsum* (syn, 'Harpur Crewe') larger, bright yellow flowers, April to June. Other good named varieties will be found in nurserymen's catalogues. The new German hybrid 'Fruhlingspracht', or 'Spring Splendour', 1 foot, is an interesting introduction with double yellow flowers during April and May.
Cultivation Plant in the autumn or spring in ordinary garden soil in sun or partial shade. Propagation is by division of the roots in October or March. Doronicums are adaptable plants which may be moved or divided without damage even when they are in bud, provided this is done in moist weather.

Draba (dra-ba)
From the Greek *drabe*, acrid, a reference to the taste of the leaves (*Cruciferae*). A genus of over 250 annual, biennial and perennial plants from the colder areas of the world. Those cultivated are perennials for the rock garden or alpine house.

Species cultivated *D. aiziodes,* 3 inches, yellow, March, the earliest to flower, Europe. *D. aizoon,* 3 inches, yellow, April, Europe. *D. alpina,* 3 inches, yellow, April, Europe and Asia. *D. brunifolia,* 3 inches, yellow, June, Caucasus. *D. bryoides,* 2 inches, hard green cushions, tiny golden flowers, April, Caucasus; var. *imbricata,* 1 inch, both scree plants or for alpine house. *D. carinthiaca* (syn. *D. johannis*), 3 inches, white, May, Carpathians and Pyrenees. *D. dedeana,* 3 inches, little cushions of grey-green with white flowers, May, Spain. *D. mollissima,* 2 inches, grey-green cushion with clusters of yellow, fragrant flowers on tiny stems, April, sensitive to damp, suitable for the alpine house, Caucasus. *D. olympica,* 3 inches, golden flowers, April, Asia Minor. *D. polytricha,* 2 inches, pale yellow, April, for the alpine house, Turkish Armenia. *D. rigida,* 2 inches, yellow flowers in clusters, Armenia.

Cultivation Plant in March or April between rocks in sandy soil and in a sunny position. Good drainage is essential for these cushion-forming plants. Any dead rosettes should be removed or the rot may spread. Propagation is by seed sown in pans of sandy soil in March; by careful division of the roots in March, or by rosettes taken in June and rooted in a propagating frame in sandy soil.

Dryas (dri-as)

From the Greek *dryas,* a dryad or wood nymph or goddess, or from the Greek *drus,* an oak, since the leaves are somewhat reminiscent of oak leaves (*Rosaceae*). Three species of hardy, evergreen creeping plants from the mountainous regions of the Northern Hemisphere. They are admirable plants for a sunny rock garden or a gravelly bank, forming a mat of attractive foliage throughout the year, with pleasing flowers, like small single roses, in May and June.

Species cultivated *D. drummondii,* 3 inches, yellow, bell-shaped flowers, June, North America. *D. octopetala,* mountain avens, 3 inches, white, May and June, northern Europe, Britain, North America. *D.* × *suendermannii* (*D. drummondii* × *D. octopetala*) 3–4 inches, white, flowers, yellow in the bud stage, June, hybrid.

Cultivation These little plants thrive in a sunny position in a peaty compost. *D. octopetala* is found mainly in limestone mountainous areas. Nurserymen supply pot-grown plants which may be planted at any time during favourable weather. Propagation is by seed sown in pans of sandy peat and placed in a cold frame in April or May. Cover the seed very lightly. Transplant the seedlings carefully as the roots are easily damaged. Seedlings may flower in the second year. Cuttings about 2 inches long may also be rooted in sandy soil in a cold frame in August or plants may be increased by division of self-rooted branchlets

Eccremocarpus (ek-re-mo-kar-pus)

From the Greek *ekkremes,* pendant, and *karpos,* fruit, describing the pendulous seed vessels (*Bignoniaceae*). An attractive evergreen half-hardy annual climbing plant. There are very few species and of these one only is in cultivation. This is *E. scaber,* the Chilean glory flower. It grows up to 15–20 feet, clinging to suitable supports by means of tendrils at the ends of the leaves. The flowers, borne in clusters from late spring to autumn, are tubular in shape, scarlet or orange-red and yellow in colour. There is a golden-flowered variety, *aureus,* and an orange-red variety, *ruber.*

Cultivation *E. scaber* is very easily raised from seed sown in pots of sandy soil in March or April and germinated in a temperature of about 60°F (16°C). Seed will even germinate out of doors in milder gardens if sown in April or May. Plant out in June in a light, rich soil against south or southwest facing walls, with trellis, wires, etc., for support. The growths are weak, so that they will do no harm if the plant is allowed to scramble over shrubs. In mild winters the roots are hardy, but in exposed gardens should be covered with old ashes or matting in severe weather. In favoured gardens, even in the south Midlands, and extreme southeast, the plant appears to be quite hardy except, perhaps, in very severe winters, when it may be cut to the ground only to spring again from the base. Seed is set very freely in long capsules which turn dark brown as they ripen. Self-sown seedlings occasionally appear in the spring, particularly where they have germinated between paving stones and thus the seed has had some protection during the winter.

Echinops (ek-in-ops)

From the Greek *echinos,* a hedgehog, *opsis,* like, referring to the spiky appearance of the flower heads which resemble a rolled-up hedgehog (*Compositae*). Globe thistle. Hardy herbaceous perennial and biennial plants for the border.

Species cultivated (All perennial) *E. bannaticus,* 2–3 feet, violet-blue globular heads of flowers, summer, Hungary. *E. humilis,* 3–5 feet, large blue heads, September, Asia; var. *nivalis,* white. The cultivar 'Taplow Blue' has bright blue heads in summer. *E. ritro,* 3–4 feet, steel-blue, summer, southern Europe. *E. sphaerocephalus,* 6 feet, flowers silvery-grey, summer, Europe and western Asia.

Cultivation Plant in autumn or spring in ordinary soil, in sun or partial shade. Echinops are trouble-free plants for a large border or for a wild garden. The metallic lustre of the flower heads keeps them decorative for a long time when dried. The species *E. ritro* is probably the best for this purpose. Propagation is by root cuttings or division in October or March, or by seed sown in the open in a sunny position in April.

Echium (ek-e-um)

From the Greek *echis,* a viper, referring either to the supposed resemblance of the seed to a viper's head or the belief that the plant was efficacious against the adder's bite (*Boraginaceae*). Viper's bugloss. Hardy and half-hardy annual, biennial and perennial plants mainly from the Mediterranean region and the Canary Islands.

Species cultivated: Annual and biennial *E. creticum,* 1–1½ feet, violet, July, annual. *E. plantagineum,* 2–3 feet, rich bluish-purple, summer, annual or biennial. *E. vulgare,* 3–4 feet, purple or blue, summer, biennial, native. *E. wildpretii,* 2–3 feet, rose-pink, summer, biennial.

Perennial *E. albicans,* 6–18 inches, rose, becoming violet, summer. *E. fastuosum,* 2–4 feet, deep blue, April to August, greenhouse, but hardy in the Isles of Scilly. *E.* × *scilloniensis,* 4–6 feet, blue, May onwards, hybrid originating in the gardens of Tresco Abbey, Isles of Scilly, where other half-hardy species are also grown out of doors.

Cultivation Plant out the perennial kinds in ordinary well-drained soil and in a sunny position in May. Seed of the annual kinds is sown in a sunny position in the open in April or August. The perennials are propagated by seed sown out of doors in spring.

Endymion (en-dim-e-on)

Named for *Endymion,* a beautiful youth in Greek mythology, who slept perpetually on Mount Latimus, kissed by *Silene,* the moon (*Liliaceae*). Bulbous plants usually included in *Scilla,* sometimes described as *Hyacinthus,* commonly known as bluebells, but botanically now a small separate genus.

Species cultivated *E. hispanicus,* Spanish bluebell, 12–18 inches, variable, deep blue, pale blue, pinkish and white, scentless. Individual bells are larger than those of our native bluebell and the stems are stouter, May, Spain and Portugal. There are various named hybrids, including the pure white *alba maxima,* the porcelain blue 'Blue Queen', the deep blue 'Excelsior' and the rosy-lilac 'Rose Queen'. *E. non-scriptus,* bluebell (but not the bluebell of Scotland, which is *Campanula rotundifolia,* the English harebell), 12–18 inches, misty blue, occasionally pink or white, nodding, slightly fragrant, bell-shaped flowers, May, Britain and western Europe.

Cultivation These plants are ideal for naturalising in dappled woodland or partially shaded areas where the large bulbs should be planted about 3–4 inches deep in the autumn. Once planted they should be left undisturbed until they have formed thick clumps, when they may be divided. Lifting is quite a task. They thrive best in a heavyish loamy soil, and are not averse to clay, provided it is not waterlogged.

Epilobium (ep-e-lo-be-um)
From the Greek *epi*, upon, *lobos*, a pod; the flowers appear to grow on the seed pod *(Onagraceae)*. Willow herb. Hardy perennial plants for the wild garden. The willow herbs comprise some pretty plants, but the majority are far too rampant and some seed themselves with abandon. The rosebay willow herb or fireweed, *Epilobium angustifolium (Chamaenerion angustifolium)*, can become a menace and is the plant which became a dominant feature on bombed sites during and after the war years. The seeds are readily carried by the wind and once the plant is established it quickly spreads by means of its long, underground stolons.

Species cultivated *E. dodonaei* (syns. *E. rosmarinifolium, Chamaenerion palustre)*, 1 foot, rose-purple, June to August, Europe. *E. hirsutum*, great willow herb, or codlins and cream, 3–5 feet, rose-purple, July and August, clammy to touch. Britain, central and southern Europe. *E. obcordatum*, 3–6 inches, creeping, large rosy-purple flowers, summer, California.

Cultivation Plant from October to March in ordinary soil, in sun or shade, or by the waterside, dwarf species on a sunny rock garden. Propagation is by seed sown out of doors in a shady position in the spring or in August or by division of the roots in October or March.

Epimedium (ep-im-ee-de-um)
From *epimedion* the ancient Greek name used by Pliny *(Berberidaceae)*. Decorative hardy perennials for the rock garden or wild garden. In the spring the small shield-shaped leaves are pale green with pink, rose and pale lemon tints. They become deeper green in the summer and are attractively veined; by the autumn they take on rich tints of deeper colouring. The light, arching sprays of flowers are borne in spring and early summer.

Species cultivated *E. alpinum*, bishop's hat, 9 inches, rose-purple and yellow on branching stems, June, southern Europe. *E. diphyllum* (syn. *Aceranthus diphyllus)*, 6 inches, white, drooping, April and May, Japan. *E. grandiflorum*, 9–15 inches, a most attractive species with variable flowers, white, pale yellow, deep rose to violet, June, Japan. The hybrid 'Rose Queen' has crimson-carmine flowers. *E. perralderianum*, 1 foot, bright yellow, June, young leaves rich bronze, Algeria. *E. pinnatum*, barrenwort, 1 foot, arching stems of bright yellow flowers, May to July; var. *colchicum (elegans)*, larger flowers more numerous, Persia. *E. pubigerum*, 1½ feet, pale yellow or white, May, Balkans, Asia Minor. *E. × rubrum* (syn. *E. alpinum rubrum)*, 9 inches, crimson and yellow, April, a hybrid. *E. × versicolor*, 1 foot, red when young, becoming pale yellow, a hybrid; var. *sulphureum*,

flowers pale yellow. *E. × youngianum*, 6–12 inches, white, tinged with green, April, a hybrid; vars. *niveum*, white flowers; *rubrum*, rose-red. *E. × warleyense*, 9 inches, coppery-red, April and May, a hybrid.

Cultivation Plant in the autumn or spring in sandy loam enriched with leafmould or peat. Choose a cool shady border or rock garden. They do well under trees, provided the situation is not too dry, where they retain their leaves throughout the winter. They are useful for suppressing weeds. Propagation is by division of the roots in the autumn.

Eranthis (er-an-this)
From the Greek *er*, Spring, *anthos*, flower *(Ranunculaceae)*. Winter aconite. Hardy tuberous-rooted dwarf perennials. The cup-shaped yellow flowers with their conspicuous ruffs of green leaves are among the earliest to appear in the garden, where once planted, they should be left undisturbed.

Species cultivated *E. cilicica*, 4–5 inches, bright yellow, February and March, Greece and Asia Minor. *E. hyemalis*, 3–4 inches, lemon-yellow, February and March, western Europe. *E. × tubergenii*, 3–5 inches, golden-yellow, a hybrid raised in Holland, with larger, long-

Eranthis x tubergenii produces larger flowers than the common winter Aconite

lasting flowers. 'Guinea Gold' is another hybrid with 2 inch wide, fragrant flowers, deep yellow, flushed with bronze.

Cultivation Plant from October to December about 2 inches deep and 2 inches apart in ordinary soil, in partially shaded borders or under trees. They may also be grown in pans containing a compost of loam, leafmould and sharp sand in equal parts, and flowered in a cool greenhouse or not too sunny window. For this purpose plant the tubers close together and cover them with ½ inch of compost in October or November. After flowering plant the tubers in the garden. Propagation is by division of the tubers in October or November, or by seed which will germinate freely when sown in the open, where the plants are to grow, as soon as the seed is ripe.

Eremurus (er-e-mur-us)
From the Greek *eremos*, solitary, *oura*, a tail, a reference to the single flower spike *(Liliaceae)*. Imposing hardy herbaceous perennials with a curious, thick brittle rootstock, like a giant starfish. These natives of western Asia and the

Himalaya region are best planted when quite young, although this may mean waiting three years or so before they flower, and once planted they should remain undisturbed for several years. They vary in height from 3–10 feet. There is a delightful range of colour.

Species cultivated *E. bungei* (syn. *E. stenophyllus bungei*), 3–4 feet, yellow, early July, Persia. *E. elwesii*, 6–9 feet, pink, May; var. *albus*, white. *E. himalaicus*, 6–8 feet, white, May and June, Himalaya. *E.* × *himrob* (*E. himalaicus* × *E. robustus*), 6–8 feet, pale pink, May and June, hybrid. *E. kaufmanniana*, 3–4 feet, yellow, June, Turkestan. *E. olgae*, 2–4 feet, white flushed with lilac, fragrant, July, Turkestan. *E. robustus*, fox-tail lily, 8–10 feet, peach-pink, June, Turkestan. *E. spectabilis*, 2–4 feet, pale yellow tinted orange, June, Siberia. *E.* × *tubergenii*, 5–7 feet, light yellow, May and June, hybrid. Named cultivars include 'Dawn', 6–8 feet, rose pink, June and July; 'Flair', 8 feet, golden yellow, flushed pink, June and July; 'Highdown Hybrids', 6–7 feet, various shades, summer; 'Shelford Hybrids', 6–7 feet, pink, coppery-yellow, etc., June and July; 'Sir Arthur Hazlerigg', 5 feet, coppery-orange, June and July.

Cultivation Plant in August, September or October in well-drained, rich, sandy loam in a warm, sunny bed, sheltered as much as possible from wind; a background of evergreens is admirable. Mulch each autumn with well-decayed manure. The lush green leaves appear in early spring and may be liable to damage by frost unless protected with cut heather, bracken or sand. If sand is placed over the crown in January or February the leaves will grow through it; the sand can easily be brushed away, and slug damage is not so likely as when other material is used. Propagation is by seed sown thinly in a cold frame in the early autumn. The seedlings should remain undisturbed for two years before transplanting. Germination of old seed is unpredictable. Division of the roots may be done carefully in October or March. The roots are easily broken when lifting and any damaged roots should be cut clean and dusted with lime.

Erigeron (er-ij-er-on)

From the Greek *eri*, early or *ear*, spring, *geron*, old, possibly referring to the hoary leaves of some species (*Compositae*). Fleabane. Hardy herbaceous, daisy-flowered perennials some of which continue to flower intermittently throughout the summer.

Species cultivated *E. alpinus*, 9 inches, purple and yellow, August, northern Alps. *E. aurantiacus*, orange daisy, 12–18 inches, orange, summer, Turkestan. *E. aureus*, 4 inches, bright gold, spring onwards, North America. *E. compositus*, 3 inches, purple, summer, North America. *E. glaucus*, 6–12 inches, purple to pink, summer, North America. *E. coulteri*, 15

The Shelford Hybrid Eremurus are imposing hardy, herbaceous perennials, growing to 7 feet and flowering in June.

inches, white or pale mauve, summer, North America. *E. leiomerus*, 4 inches, small, lavender-blue, North America. *E. macranthus* (syn. *E. mesa-grande*), 2 feet, violet, yellow centres, summer, North Africa. *E. mucronatus*, 9 inches, white, deep and pale pink, summer and autumn, Mexico, a useful wall plant. *E. philadelphus*, 2 feet, lilac-pink, summer, North America. *E. speciosus*, 18 inches, violet-blue, summer, North America. *E. trifidus*, 2 inches, pale lavender, summer, North America. *E. uniflorus*, 4 inches, white or purplish, summer, North America.

Cultivars include: 'B. Ladhams', 1½ feet, bright rose; 'Bressingham Strain', (*E. aurantiacus*), 1–1½ feet, orange to yellow shades, May to July; 'Charity', 2 feet, pale pink; 'Darkest of All', 2 feet, deep violet; 'Dignity', 2 feet, mauve-blue; 'Felicity', 1½–2 feet, deep pink, large; 'Foerster's Liebling', 1½ feet, deep pink, semi-double; 'Gartenmeister Walther', 2 feet, soft pink; 'Merstham Glory', 2 feet, deep lavender-blue, semi-double; 'Prosperity', 2 feet, deep blue; 'Quakeress', 2 feet, pale blue overlaid silvery pink; 'Quakeress White', 2 feet, white; 'Unity', 2 feet, bright pink; 'Vanity', 3 feet, clear pink, late flowering; 'Wupperthal', 2 feet, pale blue.

Cultivation Plant in the autumn or early

spring in a sunny position in ordinary soil on a rock garden, or towards the front of the border for the taller varieties. *E. mucronatus* is a good plant for paved areas or steps, where it can seed itself between the cracks. Cut down stems after flowering. Named varieties are propagated by division of the clumps in the autumn or spring, the species by seed sown in the open in light soil in a shady position from April to June.

Eryngium (er-in-je-um)

From the ancient Greek name *eryngeon,* the meaning of which is obscure *(Umbelliferae)*. A genus of over 200 species of hardy and nearly hardy perennial herbaceous plants, some with thistle-like leaves. Some species are seaside plants in the wild. All are more or less spiny and in some species a feature is the glistening, metallic bluish sheen that covers the stem, the inflorescence, and the floral bracts. If the stems are cut and allowed to dry slowly they retain their colour and sheen, thus providing useful winter decorations.

Species cultivated *E. agavifolium,* 5–6 feet, narrow spiny leaves up to 5 feet in length, flowers green, hardy in milder counties, Argentine. *E. alpinum,* 1–1½ feet, upper parts tinged blue, summer, Europe. *E. amethystinum,* up to 2½ feet, deep blue shiny flower-heads and upper stems, July to September, Europe. *E. bourgatii,* 1½–2 feet, leaves marked grey-white, flowers light blue on spreading branches, June to August, Pyrenees. *E. bromeliifolium,* 3–4 feet, long, slender leaves, flowers pale green to white, July hardy in the south and west, Mexico. *E. dichotomum,* 1–2 feet, blue, July and August, southern Europe. *E. giganteum,* up to 4 feet, rounded blue heads, July and August, Caucasus. *E. heldreichii,* 1–2 feet, bluish, summer, Syria. *E. leavenworthii,* 3 feet, purple, summer, North America. *E. maritimum,* sea holly, 1–1½ feet, pale blue, summer to autumn, Europe, including Britain. *E. × oliverianum,* 3–4 feet, teazle-like, metallic blue flowers, July to September, a hybrid. *E. pandanifolium,* 6–10 feet, narrow, spiny leaves up to 6 feet in length, purplebrown flowers, late summer, Uruguay, hardy in the south and west. *E. planum,* 2 feet, small, deep blue flowers, July and August, eastern Europe. *E. serra,* 6 feet, leaves up to 5 feet long, narrow, with spiny teeth, flowers white, to pale green, autumn, Brazil. *E. spinalba,* 1–2 feet, small bluish-white flowers, summer, Europe. *E. tripartitum,* 2–2½ feet, steel blue, with long bracts, summer, possibly a hybrid, origin unknown. *E. variifolium,* 1½–2 feet, leaves white veined, flowers whitish-green, summer, Europe. Cultivars include 'Blue Dwarf', 2 feet; 'Violetta', 2½ feet, violet-blue, both flowering in late summer.

Cultivation Plant in the autumn or in the spring, preferably in light sandy soil, although these plants are not particular,

so long as the drainage is good. They like a sunny site and dislike cold, wet soil in winter. The thong-like roots require the soil to be deeply cultivated. Generally speaking, eryngiums from South America are half-hardy or hardy in the south and west only. They are, however, striking plants where they can be grown. Propagation is by seed sown in boxes and placed in a cold frame in April or May; by division of the plants in October or April, or by root cuttings.

Erysimum (er-is-im-um)

From the Greek *erus,* to draw up; some species are said to produce blisters *(Cruciferae)*. Alpine wallflower. Hardy annual, biennial and perennial plants, closely related to *Cheiranthus*. Some are rather weedy, but others make good edging plants for a perennial border, or on gravelly banks and retaining walls.

Annual species cultivated *E. perofskianum,* 1 foot, reddish-orange, summer, Afghanistan.

Biennial *E. allionii* see *Cheiranthus allionii, E. arkansanum,* 1½–2 feet, goldenyellow, July to October, Arkansas and Texas. *E. asperum,* 1 foot, vivid orange, early summer, North America. *E. linifolium* (syn. *Cheiranthus linifolius*), 1–1½ feet, rosy-lilac, early summer, Spain.

Perennial *E. dubium* (syn. *E. ochroleucum*), 1 foot, pale yellow, April to July, Europe. *E. rupestre,* 1 foot, sulphuryellow, spring, Asia Minor.

Eryngium grandiflorum, like most of the eryngiums, prefers well-drained, sandy soil and a sunny site

Cultivation The alpine wallflowers like ordinary soil in dryish, sunny beds or on the rock garden. Propagation of annuals is by seed sown in April where the plants are to flower; biennials by seed sown out of doors in June in a sunny place, transplanting the seedlings to their flowering positions in August; perennials by seed sown in a similar manner, or by division in March or April, also by cuttings inserted in sandy soil in August in a cold propagating frame.

Erythronium (er-e-thro-ne-um)

From the Greek *erythros,* red, the flower colour of the European species *(Liliaceae)*. Small hardy bulbous plants grown here since the sixteenth century and coming mainly from the North American continent, although the species commonly grown, *E. dens-canis,* is a native of Europe. Some species have marbled leaves and others have plain green leaves, a general method of classification.

Species cultivated *E. americanum,* yellow adder's tongue, 6 inches, golden-yellow flowers speckled with red, May. *E. californicum,* 9–12 inches, creamy-white, petals spreading and reflexed at the tips, leaves heavily mottled. *E. citrinum,* 6 inches, creamy-white, lemon-yellow at the base, March and April. *E. dens-canis,* dog's tooth violet, 6 inches, the most popularly grown species, white to pale pink and reddish-mauve with a ring of orange-red marks at the base, March and April, leaves heavily marbled; vars. include *album,* white. *E. hendersonii,* 6 inches, pale lilac with dark purple markings at the base, early April, leaves heavily mottled, with pale green and pink lines. *E. revolutum,* trout lily, 6–9 inches, white to deep pink, April and May, mottled leaves. *E. tuolumnense,* 9–12 inches, golden-yellow flowers, April, light greenish-yellow leaves with pale mottling. Cultivars include: *E. dens-canis* 'Franz Hals', reddish-purple; 'Pink Perfection'; 'Purple King'; 'Rose Beauty'; 'Rose Queen'; 'Snowflake'. *E. revolutum* 'White Beauty'. *E. tuolumnense* 'Pagoda', 1–1½ feet, large golden-yellow flowers.

Cultivation Plant the bulbs in sheltered rock gardens, on banks or among shrubs which cast light shade, 3 inches deep and 2 inches apart, in August, in their permanent positions, because the plants do not like to be transplanted. Top dress annually with compost or rotted manure and loam and keep the soil moist; never let the bulbs dry out or they will shrivel. Bulbs can be grown in pots in a compost of equal parts of loam, peat and leafmould. Plant them in August, 1 inch deep only. Keep the pots free from frost through the winter, either in a cold frame or cold house and withhold water unless the soil dries out completely. In February put the pots into a greenhouse or living room and water regularly. The bulbs will then flower in March. Propagation is by offsets from the bulbs, separated at planting time, or by seed which is very slow to germinate and the resulting plants may take four or five years to flower.

Eschscholzia (esh-olt-se-a)

Commemorating Johann Friedrich von Eschsholz, physician and naturalist, member of a Russian expedition to north west America in the early nineteenth century *(Papaveraceae).* A small genus of hardy annuals from north west America, bearing saucer-shaped flowers which open to the sun and close up during damp and cloudy weather.

Species cultivated *E. caespitosa,* 6 inches, flowers yellow, 1 inch across, summer; 'Sundew' with lemon-yellow flowers is a cultivar. *E. californica,* the Californian poppy. This grows 1–1½ feet tall and has 2 inch wide bright yellow or orange flowers in summer; var. *alba flore pleno* has double white flowers. There are

1 Euphorbia pulcherrima, the Poinsettia, has flamboyant bracts. 'Mikkelsen Pink' is an example of a newer strain.
2 Erythronium 'White Beauty', a bulbous plant that can be grown in pots, the rock garden and the front of mixed borders. Also used for naturalising.

numerous named varieties and strains to be found seedsmen's lists, in which the flowers vary from the palest lemon and apricot to a clear orange-red. Both single and double varieties are available, in heights from 9 inches–1 foot or so. The foliage is a consistent pale silvery-green, light, feathery and an exquisite foil for the flowers. They will be found under such names as 'Monarch Art Shades'; 'Carmine King'; 'Golden Glory'; 'Mandarin' and 'Toreador'. New strains are constantly being developed.

Cultivation A light, well-drained soil is most suitable, although these annuals will grow in any ordinary garden soil. Where they flourish they will seed themselves freely. Sow seed out of doors, in open, sunny positions in September or March to April where the plants are to flower and thin the seedlings to 6 inches apart, as soon as they are large enough to handle, to prevent them from becoming spindly. Once the flowers begin to fade cut them off to prevent the formation of seed and thus prolong the flowering season unless, of course, self-sown seedlings are required.

Euphorbia (u-for-be-a)

Named after Euphorbus, physician to King Juba of Mauritania (*Euphorbiaceae*). A genus of about a thousand species, widely distributed, mainly in temperate regions, showing immense diversity of form and requirements. They include annual, biennial and perennial herbaceous plants, shrubs and trees and succulent plants. The decorative parts are really bracts, often colourful, round the small and inconspicuous flowers. Some are warm greenhouse plants others are hardy. The succulent species are mainly from Africa, most of them from South and West Africa. Many of those resemble cacti in appearance. For the purposes of this article the succulent species are dealt with separately. All euphorbias exude a poisonous milky latex when the stems are cut, which can burn the skin and eyes and which, in some species, is poisonous if taken internally.

Greenhouse species cultivated (non-succulent), *E. fulgens* (syn. *E. jacquinaeflora*), 2–3 feet, small leafy shrub, scarlet bracts carried on the upper side of young shoots, autumn and winter, Mexico. *E. pulcherrima* (syn. *Poinsettia pulcherrima*), poinsettia, 3–6 feet, brilliant scarlet showy bracts in winter, Mexico. The modern Ecke hybrids are increasing in popularity. They include 'Barbara Ecke', fluorescent carmine bracts; 'Pink Ecke', coral pink and 'White Ecke', white. Some have variegated foliage. Even more popular now is the Mikkelsen strain, introduced in 1964. These, with shorter stems and with bracts in scarlet, pink or white, are a good deal 'hardier' in that they will withstand lower temperatures and fluctuating temperatures, yet will retain

their bracts and remain colourful for 5–6 weeks.

Hardy *E. biglandulosa*, 2 feet, yellow, February and March, Greece. *E. cyparissias*, cypress spurge, ploughman's mignonette, 1–2 feet, small narrow leaves, small greenish-yellow flowers and yellow, heart-shaped bracts, May, Europe. *E. epithymoides* (syn. *E. polychroma*), cushion spurge, 1–1½ feet, rounded heads of golden-yellow bracts, early April to late May, Europe. *E. griffithii*, 1½–2 feet, reddish-orange flowers and bracts, April and early May; the cultivar 'Fireglow' has redder flower-heads, Himalaya. *E. heterophylla*, Mexican fire plant, annual poinsettia, 2 feet, scarlet bracts, annual, North and South America. *E. lathyrus*, caper spurge, 3 feet, large green bracts, biennial, Europe. *E. marginata*, snow-on-the-mountain, 2 feet, leaves banded white, bracts white, annual, North America. *E. myrsinites*, trailing, good when sprouting between stones of a dry wall, fleshy stems, blue-grey foliage, bright yellow flower-heads, late winter and spring, south Europe. *E. pilosa*, 18 inches, usually grown in its form *major*, with yellow foliage, turning bronze in autumn, Europe, north Asia. *E. portlandica*, 9 inches, blue-green leaves, yellow bracts, British native. *E. robbiae*, 1½ feet, rosettes of dark green leaves, bracts yellow, good ground cover plant for shade. *E. sikkimensis*, 2–3 feet, young shoots bright red, bracts yellow-green, summer, India. *E. veneta* (syn. *E. wulfenii*), to 4 feet, nearly 3 feet across, very handsome almost sub-shrubby plant, grey-green foliage, yellow-green flower-heads with black 'eyes', spring to summer, Europe. Other species and varieties of hardy spurges may be found in nurserymen's catalogues.

Succulent there are very many species in cultivation; some of the following are some of the more popular ones, *E. alcicornis*, to 2 feet, leafless, spiny shrub, stem five angled, Madagascar. *E. bupleurifolia*, dwarf, thick stem like a tight fir cone, large deciduous leaves growing from the top, pale green flowers, Cape Province. *E. canariensis*, shrub with small yellow flowers, many erect stems, 4–6 ribbed, short spines on edges, Canary Isles. *E. caput-medusae*, dwarf, thick main stem, making a large head from which radiate many thin branches a foot or more long, small yellow flowers. There is a cristate or monstrous form with thin, flattened branches, Cape Province. *E. echinus*, shrub with erect stem and many branches, 5–8 angled, stems similar in shape to the cactus, *Cereus eburneus*, south Morocco. *E. obesa*, one of the most popular euphorbias, plants round when young, coloured like plaid, becoming columnar, closely resembling the cactus, *Astrophytum asterias;* this plant does not make offsets so must be

grown from seed, Cape Province. *E. splendens*, crown of thorns, 2–3 feet, succulent, spiny, few-leaved shrub, pairs of round scarlet bracts, mainly in spring.

Cultivation Greenhouse, non-succulent species: a good compost is 4 parts of fibrous loam, 1 part of decayed cow manure and a half part of silver sand. Young plants should be potted into 6- or 8-inch pots in summer and kept in a cold house or frame until September. Then feed regularly with a liquid feed and bring into a temperature of 60–65°F (16–18°C) to bring the plants into flower in December. After flowering, reduce watering and temperature until the soil is quite dry. In April cut back to two buds and start to water. Repot in May when the young shoots are about 1 inch long. Pot on as required; in high summer the pots can be stood out of doors or kept in a cold frame and brought in again in September. Propagation is from cuttings of young shoots taken in summer and inserted in sand in a temperature of 70 F (21 C).

Hardy species Any good garden soil suits them. *E. veneta* (*E. wulfenii*) prefers a slightly sheltered position, but the others should be given sunny places. The dwarf kinds are suitable for the rock garden, although *E. cyparissias* tends to ramp, spreading by underground rhizomes. Propagation of perennial kinds is by division of the plants in spring or autumn but *E. veneta* (*E. wulfenii*) is best increased from seed or soft cuttings taken in early spring and inserted in a sandy compost out of doors or under a cloche. The annuals and the biennial, *E. lathyrus*, are easily raised from seed sown out of doors in April where the plants are to flower, thinning the seedlings later. *E. lathyrus* seeds itself freely.

Succulent species Most of these plants like a richer soil than some succulents but it must be porous. The compost should be made up from John Innes potting compost No 2 with a fifth part added of sharp sand, grit or broken brick. Repot in March every two years or when the plants become pot-bound; water well from April to September, keep fairly dry from October to March. Temperatures should be 65 F (18 C), in the growing period, 45–50 F (7–10 C) in winter. Plants should be given a light sunny place in the greenhouse, or on a window sill. Propagation is by seed sown in early spring in pans of John Innes seed compost. Cover the seed with its own depth of soil, keep moist at temperature of 70 F (21 C), shade from sun but give light when seedlings appear. Large seeds should be washed well before sowing. Plants may also be propagated by cuttings which should be dusted with powdered charcoal to prevent bleeding, then dried and rooted in sharp sand and peat in equal parts. Pot up the cuttings, when they have rooted, in the compost described above.

Exacum (eks-ak-um)

From the Latin *ex*, out of, *ago*, to drive; the plant was thought to expel poison *(Gentianaceae)*. Hot house annuals, biennials and perennials first grown here in the middle of the nineteenth century for their freely produced flowers.

Species cultivated *E. affine*, 6 inches, fragrant, bluish-lilac flowers, June to October, Socotra; var. *atrocaeruleum*, gentian-blue. *E. macranthum*, 1½ feet, purple, summer, Ceylon. *E. zeylanicum*, 2 feet, violet-purple, summer, Ceylon.

Cultivation Exacums like a compost of equal parts of loam, peat, sand and leafmould and need a minimum winter temperature of 50 F (10 C). Sharp drainage is essential as the plants are particularly liable to damp off. The atmosphere should be moist and shade is needed from hot sun. Propagation is from seed, sown in August and September, the seedlings over-wintered in small pots and potted on into 5 inch

pots in March for summer flowering.

Felicia (fel-is-e-a)

From the Latin *felix*, cheerful, a reference to the bright flowers *(Compositae)*. Half-hardy annual or greenhouse evergreen plants, some of them sub-shrubs, from South Africa and Abyssinia.

Species cultivated *F. amelloides* (syn. *Agathaea coelestis*), blue daisy, blue marguerite, 1–1½ feet, half-hardy perennial, blue daisies June to August, an attractive pot plant for the cold greenhouse or conservatory. *F. bergeriana*, kingfisher daisy, 6 inches, half-hardy annual, blue flowers, June onwards. *F. petiolata*, prostrate evergreen sub-shrub, pink to blue flowers, summer. *F. tenella* (syn. *F. fragilis*), 1 foot, half-hardy annual, small violet-blue flowers with yellow centres, July and August.

Cultivation Seeds of the half-hardy annual kinds should be sown in the greenhouse in March in light soil, and the seedlings gradually hardened off and

Freesias, South African cormous plants with heavily fragrant flowers, are available in a wide colour range

planted out in late May where they are to flower. The greenhouse kinds can be raised from seed sown at the same time, pricked off into small pots and then into 5 inch pots in which they will flower. Cuttings of young shoots can be made in spring or August and inserted round the edge of a pot in sandy compost in a propagating case or where a temperature of 55–65 F (13–18 C), can be maintained.

Freesia (free-ze-a)

In honour of Dr F. H. T. Freese of Kiel, nineteenth-century botanist *(Iridaceae)*. A genus of a few species of South African cormous plants with heavily fragrant flowers, especially noticeable in orange varieties. Hybridisation has produced varieties in a wide range of colours. These have superseded the species, especially as cut flowers, for they are available over a long season (October to May) and last well in water.

Species cultivated *F. armstrongii*, 10–15 inches, rose pink with yellow tube, the parent of many richly coloured hybrids. *F. refracta*, 1 foot, orange and white; vars. *alba*, white; *leitchlinii*, pale lemon with an orange blotch; *xanthospila*, flowers with a wider throat. Cultivars include, *White:* 'Snow Queen', 'White Madonna', 'White Swan'. *Cream:* 'Caro', 'Fantasy'. *Pink and Crimson:* 'Carnival', 'Margot Fonteyn', 'Red Chief', 'Rosamunde'. *Yellow-orange:* 'Buttercup', 'Orange Favourite', 'Orange Sun', 'Princess Marijke' (some purple marking). *Violet:* 'Apotheose', 'Royal Present', 'Sapphire', 'Vanguard'.

Cultivation A good firm compost of John Innes potting No. 2 is ideal and a 5 or 6 inch pot will take six to eight bulbs. Plant in August, about 1 inch deep, then put the pots in a cool spot out of doors to encourage rooting. Alternatively freesias can be raised from seed sown in April or May in a temperature of 65 F (18 C). At the end of May the seedlings can be stood in a cold frame, the glass being put on only during heavy rain. At this stage it is a good precaution to stand the pots on bricks or tiles to prevent the strong roots from growing out of the base of the pot.

Whichever way the young plants are raised, bring them into the greenhouse in September into a temperature of 45–50 F (7–10 C). Light staking is necessary and watering should be done with discretion, withholding it almost entirely once the flower buds form, until the stems lengthen. After flowering, a little liquid feed is helpful to build up the bulbs as the leaves die down. Dry off the pots out of doors during the summer. A strain of so-called 'hardy freesias' is available. Bulbs should be planted in August, 2 inches apart and 1½ inches deep in a rich light soil and sunny, warm position. Use cloches for protection during the winter.

Fritillaria (frit-il-air-e-a)

From the Latin *fritillus*, a dice box, an allusion to the marking on some flowers (*Liliaceae*). Fritillary. A large genus of hardy bulbous plants mostly of small stature with nodding, bell-shaped flowers. The bulbs of most species consist of two or three fleshy scales and are very fragile and dry out easily when out of the soil.

Species cultivated *F. acmopetala*, 1½ feet, jade-green and brown-maroon, greenish-yellow inside, early April. *F. bithynica* (syn. *F. citrina*), 9 inches, citron-yellow, with green markings, April. *F. graeca*, 9 inches, brown to purplish, April. *F. imperialis*, crown imperial, 3–4 feet, a plant of cottage gardens, the thick stem crowned with a whorl of leaves under which hangs a circle of large bell-shaped flowers varying in colour from brilliant orange-red to deep acid yellow, April to

May; vars. *lutea*, lemon-yellow; *maxima rubra*, red; *raddeana*, straw-yellow, dwarf. Cultivars include 'Aurora', red-orange; 'De Jager's Favourite', soft orange; 'Orange Brilliant', brownish-orange; *F. latifolia*, 6 inches, purplish-maroon, April; 'Erasmus', olive-green with chocolate-brown internal markings is a cultivar. *F. meleagris*, snake's head, chequered daffodil, guinea flower, 12–18 inches, a native plant, with pendulous bells in shades of purple, all chequered. Good cultivars are 'Aphrodite', white, vigorous; 'Artemis', grey-purple; 'Charon' a particularly dark purple form; 'Poseidon', white, veined purple; 'Saturnus', large reddish-purple flowers. *F. messanensis*, 9 inches, purplish, April. *F. nigra*, 18 inches, variable shades of purple, April. *F. pallidiflora*, 1–2 feet, pale greenish or cream flowers, rose or plum coloured dots inside. *F. persica*, 3 feet, violet-blue, March and April. *F. pontica*, 1 foot, brown-purple overlaid greenish-yellow, April. *F. pyrenaica*, 8–15 inches, purplish-red chequered flowers, April. *F. roylei*, 1½ feet, yellow-green, purple, April. *F. tuntasia*, 1 foot, deep

Fritillaria pyrenaica has chequered purple and green flowers in April

purple, April. Other species are occasionally offered by specialist bulb merchants or may be seen in botanic gardens.

Cultivation Out of doors the bulbs should be planted from September to November in a good loam with leafmould and decayed manure incorporated, in shady borders or naturalised in turf. Sharp drainage is needed for most species other than *F. imperialis* and *F. meleagris* which do well in moister, heavier soils. Topdress annually with compost or decayed manure.

Fritillarias do well in pots. Plant in September singly in 5 or 6 inch pots of John Innes potting compost with added leafmould. Water moderately and feed once when the flower buds show. Propagation is by seed sown as soon as it is ripe in a cold frame or greenhouse. Transplant seedlings at two years and do not expect flowers for five or six years. Offsets can also be planted separately in September.

Gaillardia (gal-ar-de-a)

Commemorating M. Gaillard de Marentonneau, a French patron of botany (Compositae). Blanket flower. A small genus of annuals and perennials, natives of America, with a long flowering period, useful for cut flowers. Somewhat untidy in habit, the long stalks falling about in wind and rain, gaillardias need some twiggy stakes to help to keep the flowers clean and in full view.

Annual species cultivated G. amblyodon, 2–3 feet, maroon-red flowers, autumn. G. pulchella, 2–3 feet, crimson and yellow flowers, late summer and autumn, best treated as a half-hardy annual; vars. lorenziana, double flowers in reds and yellows; picta, larger flower-heads. 'Indian Chief' with coppery-scarlet flowers is a named cultivar. In addition seedsmen usually offer mixed annual types under such names as 'Choice Double Mixed', 'Special Mixture', and 'Double Fireball'.

Perennial species cultivated All garden varieties originate from G. aristata (syn. G. grandiflora) and comprise a great range of colour from pale primrose-yellow to crimson and bold orange, all flowering from June to October. Named cultivars include 'Burgundy', 2 feet, rich wine red with a narrow yellow frill along the outer edges of the petals; 'Copper Beauty', 2 feet, smaller flowers of orange-yellow suffused with brown; 'Dazzler', 2 feet, yellow with brown-red central zone; 'Firebird', 2 feet, a vigorous variety with flame-orange flowers; 'Goblin', 1 foot, dwarf, yellow with red zone; 'Ipswich Beauty', 2½–3 feet, large deep yellow flowers touched with reddish-brown; 'Monarch Strain', 2½ feet, mixed colours; 'Nana Nieski', 1–1½ feet, red and yellow flowers on shorter stems; 'The Prince', 2½ feet, very large flowers up to 4 inches across, deep yellow tinged reddish-brown at the centre; 'Tokaj', 2 feet, wine-red and tangerine; 'Wirral Flame', 2½ feet, a strong growing variety, tangerine flowers tipped yellow; 'Yellow Queen', 2 feet, golden-yellow.

Cultivation A sunny border in a moderately light soil is ideal and the drainage should be good. The annual kinds are raised from seed sown in March in gentle heat and gradually hardened off and planted in the border in late May to flower for the remainder of the season.

Twiggy stakes are needed for good effects and bold planting repays in garden decoration. The perennial kinds prefer drier soils. Autumn and winter damp is their enemy and if they do not survive it is probably because of dampness. On the other hand, a sun-baked soil stunts the plants, so a mulch of leafmould or decayed manure in summer is helpful. Liquid feeds can be given to good advantage when the plants are

Gaillardia aristata is the parent of the colourful garden varieties

coming into flower. Named varieties are best propagated from root cuttings taken at any time between February and April and put in a sandy box in the frame or greenhouse. Those that are taken early and do well may flower the first year. Alternatively basal cuttings taken from August to October, put into a sandy compost in a cold frame or under a cloche will soon get away. The plants can be divided in either October or March and any roots left in the ground at this time will sprout again.

Galanthus (gal-an-thus)

From the Greek, gala, milk, anthos, flower (Amaryllidaceae). Snowdrop, Fair maids of February. Hardy bulbs of which one species only is commonly grown but which span much of the winter with their flowers in other species.

Species cultivated G. allenii, 6–9 inches, broad green leaves, flowers larger than those of many species, February and March; G. byzantinus, 9–12 inches, broad leaves, flowers large with green marks at the base of the inner segments, mid January to February; G. caucasicus, 6 inches, broad leaves, no green marks on flowers, but varying somewhat in form and flowering time, from early January to February; G. elwesii, 9–12 inches, broad leaves, flowers large with green marking at base of the inner segments, January; G. ikariae, 8 inches, unmarked white flowers with outer petals held well out and curved like a claw, March and April; G. nivalis, common snowdrop, naturalised in many woodland areas of the British Isles, 6 inches, flowers with a green spot at the tip of each inner segment, but rather variable. The most widespread and commonly cultivated species, early January to February. There is a double-flowered form, flore-plena. 'S. Arnott' ('Arnott's Seedling') and 'Straffan' are both large-flowered varieties. G. plicatus, Crimean snowdrop, 10–12 inches, large flowers with green marking at the mouth of the inner segments, March; 'Warham', is a fine, large-flowered form, which was given a first class certificate by the Royal Horticultural Society.

Cultivation Ordinary good garden soil is suitable for snowdrops, in woodland, under shrubs, on open edges, in turf, or in the rock garden. Put the bulbs in about 1 inch apart and 2 inches deep from September to December. They can be left in for several years until they deteriorate when they need to be lifted and replanted, either in the autumn or early winter or just after they have flowered, or even when in flower, provided their roots are not dried off.

The flowers can be slightly forced by planting the bulbs in pots and keeping them out of doors or in a cold frame until the flower buds are showing, when they should be put into a cold greenhouse or conservatory or brought into a warm living room. Plant the bulbs 1 inch deep

and 1 inch apart in September or October and water moderately only once the shoots are showing. After flowering these bulbs can be planted out of doors.

Galega (gal-ee-ga)

From the Greek gala, milk, ago, to lead; the plant was used as fodder for cattle and goats and was thought to stimulate the flow of milk (Leguminosae). Goat's rue. A small genus of hardy herbaceous plants with pinnate leaves, useful for the border. The only species likely to be found in cultivation is G. officinalis, 3–5 feet tall with spikes of bluish sweet-pea-shaped flowers in summer and autumn. It is variable in flower colour and has several varieties, including alba, white flowers, and hartlandii with larger flowers of a better lilac than the type. Cultivars include 'Duchess of Bedford', mauve and white; 'Her Majesty', clear lilac; 'Lady Wilson', blue and white flushed with pink.

Cultivation In the border, put the galegas well to the back, or towards the middle in an island border so that their tendency towards untidiness can be masked by other plants. Light twiggy stakes thrust in early in the season so that the leaf growth can hide the support and at the same time use it, are the best. Ordinary garden soil is all that is required and the plant does well on poor chalky soils. It remains fairly compact, so does not need dividing too often. Propagate by division of roots in October or March or from seed sown in April out of doors in a sunny position, thinned and later transplanted. Self-sown seedlings usually appear in large numbers.

Galtonia (gawl-to-ne-a)

Commemorating Sir Francis Galton, nineteenth-century anthropologist (Liliaceae). Spire lily, Cape hyacinth, summer hyacinth. A small genus of hardy bulbs from South Africa, related to Hyacinth. The only species likely to be found in cultivation is G. candicans (syn. Hyacinthus candicans), a plant 3 feet tall, which in late summer and early autumn bears spikes of white, drooping, hyacinth-like bells tinged green, which stand well above the tufts of strap-shaped, glaucous green leaves.

Cultivation The best time to plant the bulbs is in March or early April in a well-dug soil enriched with a little manure because they do not like too dry a soil. Choose a sunny spot and put the bulbs in 6 inches deep and 15 inches apart, because they make vigorous growth. Protection may be required in winter, in the form of ashes, bracken or a cloche. Alternatively the bulbs can be lifted in autumn, the dried soil removed and the bulbs stored in boxes or trays in a dry, frost-proof place.

The bulbs may also be planted in pots for conservatory decoration or for standing out of doors in the summer. A compost of 2 parts of loam, 1 part of decayed

manure and sand is suitable. Pot up the bulbs between October and December for spring flowering or from February to April to flower in August or September. The neck of the bulb should be just at soil level, and the bulbs are best when potted singly in 6 inch pots. Keep cold until growth appears and water freely once growth starts, drying off completely once the flowers have faded. Do not try to use the same bulbs for flowering in pots a second time; they should be planted out in the garden.

Gazania (gaz-ay-ne-a)

Commemorating Theodore of Gaza, fifteenth-century translator of the botanical works of Theophrastus (Compositae). Treasure flower. Half-hardy perennials from South Africa, with showy flowers, which open in the sun and close about 3 p.m. The species hybridise freely and gazanias have been much improved in recent years; seed is offered in red and orange shades and pink and cream shades, both groups coming true from seed. The ray petals are frequently beautifully marked with zones of contrasting colours. All flower from June to September.

Species cultivated G. longiscapa, 6 inches, golden-yellow. G. pavonia, 1 foot yellow and brown. G. rigens, 1 foot, orange. G. splendens, 1 foot, orange, black and white. This, which is probably the showiest species, will thrive out of doors in very favoured districts. Cultivars include 'Bridget' orange with black centre; 'Freddie', yellow with green centre; 'Roger', citron-yellow with a purple feathering at the centre; 'Sunshine', deep yellow with a brown ring dotted white. In addition, under the name G. hybrida, seedsmen offer seed in mixed colours, including shades of yellow, pink, red, brown orange and white, variously marked.

Cultivation Treat the gazanias as half-hardy annuals, sowing seed in gentle heat in February and hardening off and planting out in May. They are not fussy about soil, will do well on chalk, but

must be given the sunniest possible positions. G. splendens can be propagated from cuttings in August, rooted in a cold frame. The rooted cuttings should be taken into a frost-proof greenhouse for the winter unless the frame can be made frost proof. By potting these up in spring as an alternative to planting them out of doors, in a compost of 2 parts of loam to 1 part of peat and 1 part of sand, they will make fine greenhouse flowering plants in early summer.

Gentiana (jen-te-a-na)

Named after Gentius, King of Illyria who first used the plant medicinally (Gentianaceae). Gentian. A large genus of hardy perennials; most of those in cultivation are dwarf plants suitable for the rock garden, but a few are more at home in the border. Some of them are lime-haters.

Species cultivated G. acaulis (now considered to be a hybrid), gentianella, 4 inches, glossy green tufts of pointed leaves, stemless, deep blue trumpet flowers, spring; vars. alba, white; alpina, compact form; coelistina, pale blue; dinarica, short-stemmed, clear blue flowers. G. angulosa, 2–5 inches, deep lilac, May and June. G. asclepiadea, 2–3 feet, willow gentian, dark blue flowers, July and August; var. alba, white. G. brachyphylla, 2 inches, deep blue flowers, spring. G. cachemirica, 4–6 inches, pale blue, August. G. clusii, 1–4 inches, deep blue, spring. G. dahurica, 6 inches, dark blue, August. G. farreri, 4 inches, Cambridge blue flowers, August and September. G. fetisowii, 6 inches, purplish-blue, August. G. gracilipes, 6 inches, deep blue, summer; var. alba, white. G. freyniana, 4 inches, pale blue, July to September. G. grombezewskii, 9 inches, pale yellow, August. G. hascombensis, 1 foot, blue, summer. G. × hexa-farreri, 3-4 inches, deep blue, August, hybrid. G. hexaphylla, 3 inches, pale blue flowers heavily marked on the outside with darker bars, July and August. G. × 'Inverleith', prostrate, clear blue, August and September,

1 The Willow Gentian, Gentiana asclepiadea, has dark blue flowers in July and August
2 Gentiana acaulis, sometimes known as gentianella, has deep blue trumpet flowers in spring.
3 Gentiana sino-ornata flowers in the early autumn

hybrid. G. lagodechiana, 9 inches, blue, white spotted, August and September. G. lutea, 4–6 feet, pale yellow in tall, unbranched spikes, June to August, bog garden. G. × macaulayi, 4 inches, deep blue, September and October, hybrid. G. pneumonanthe, 6–9 inches, heather gentian, bog gentian or marsh gentian, a native, deep blue, heavily speckled outside with bands of greenish spots, August and September; var. depressa shorter, more prostrate; 'Styrian Blue' is upright (1½ feet) with larger, paler flowers. G. saxosa, 4 inches, ivory-white, summer. G. septemfida, 6–12 inches, bright blue, July. G. sino-ornata, 3 inches, deep blue, September. G. stragulata, 2–3 inches, deep purplish-blue, August. G. verna, 3 inches, deep blue, April and May.

Cultivation It is impossible to generalise about the cultivation of gentians. Some, such as G. cachemerica, hexa-farreri, hexaphylla, 'Inverleith', macaulayi, pneumonanthe, saxosa, sino-ornata and stragulata, will not tolerate lime. Most require a well-drained, gritty soil containing leafmould or peat, but both G. lutea and G. pneumonanthe are bog garden plants. These two, together with G. asclepiadea, will grow in partial shade. Others require sunny positions and although they like ample moisture in summer, they dislike winter wet, hence the need for good drainage. All should be planted firmly. Propagation is by seed sown in March in a cold frame or in pans in a frost-free greenhouse. Seed sometimes takes a year or so to germinate so the compost must be kept moist. G. sino-ornata and G. acaulis can be divided in spring but many other species resent this kind of disturbance.

4 A selection of true Geraniums, not to
be confused with the Zonal Pelargoniums or Bedding Geraniums:
1 Geranium atlanticum, 9 inches,
flowers in summer.
2 Geranium endressii may flower from
June until October or even later.
3 Geranium cinereum subcaulescens.
4 Geranium renardii, a dwarf kind.

Geranium (jer-ay-ne-um)

From the Greek *geranos*, a crane,
because the seed pod resembles a crane's
head and beak *(Geraniaceae)*. Crane's-bill.
A genus of hardy herbaceous summer-
flowering perennials with lobed or cut
leaves, widely distributed over the
temperate regions of the world. They are
easily cultivated, free flowering, and
some are useful rock garden plants,
others good border plants. For the
greenhouse 'geraniums' see Pelargonium.
Species cultivated *G. aconitifolium*, 15–18
inches, leaves finely divided, flowers
white with black veins, May and June.
G. anemonifolium, 1–2 feet, pale purple,
May and June, may need winter protection. *G. argenteum*, 4 inches, clear
pink, summer, scree plant. *G. atlanticum*,
9 inches, purple, red-veined, summer. *G.*

candidum, 1 foot, spreading, sprawling
habit, white, crimson-centred, cup-
shaped flowers, summer. *G. celticum*, 4
inches, white, all summer. *G. cinereum*,
6 inches, pale pink, June to August;
vars. *album*, white; *subcaulescens*,
cerise, dark-centred, May to October.
G. collinum, 9–12 inches, red to purplish-
violet, May and June. *G. dalmaticum*,
6–9 inches, pink, summer; var. *album*,
white. *G. delavayi*, 1 foot, crimson,
summer. *G. endressii*, 9–18 inches, light
rose, June to October or later; cultivars
include 'A. T. Johnson', silvery-pink;
'Rose Clair' salmon, veined purple;
'Wargrave Variety', deeper pink. *G.
grandiflorum*, 1–1½ feet, blue, red-veined,
spring to autumn; var. *alpinum*, 9–12
inches, deeper blue, larger flowered. *G.
ibericum*, 1 foot, violet-purple, all summer. *G. kotschyi*, 9 inches, soft purple,
darker veined, early summer. *G. macrorrhizum*, 18 inches, red to purple, all
summer; var. *album*, white. 'Ingwersen's
Variety', 9–12 inches, rose-pink, is a fine
cultivar. *G. napuligerum* (syn. *G. farreri*),
4 inches, soft pink, May and June, scree
plant. *G. phaeum*, mourning widow, 18
inches, dark purple, May and June. *G.*

platypetalum, 2 feet, deep violet, red-veined, June and July. *G. pratense,* meadow crane's-bill, 2 feet, blue, May to September, native; vars. *album,* white; *flore-pleno,* double blue; *roseum,* 1½ feet, rose-pink. *G. psilostemon* (syn. *G. armenum*), 2 feet, magenta-crimson, dark-centred, May and June. *G. pylzowianum,* 3–4 inches, clear pink, early summer. *G. renardii,* 9 inches, white, purple centred, summer. *G. sanguineum,* bloody crane's-bill, 6–24 inches, blood-red, summer, native; vars. *album,* white; *lancastriense,* 4 inches, pink; *prostratum,* 6 inches, rosy-pink. *G. sessiliflorum,* prostrate, white and purple, summer; var. *nigricans,* dark leaves. *G. stapfianum* var. *roseum,* 4 inches, crimson-purple flowers, summer, richly coloured autumn foliage. *G. striatum,* 15 inches, pale pink, reddish veins, May to October. *G. sylvaticum,* 18 inches, purple-blue, summer, native; vars. *album,* white; *roseum,* rose-pink. *G. tuberosum,* 9 inches, purplish, May; var. *charlesii,* pink. *G. wallichianum,* 1 foot, purple, August and September; 'Buxton's Blue', deep blue with a white eye, is the cultivar usually offered. *G. yunnanense,* 12–15 inches, white, purple-veined, summer.

Cultivation In general the crane's-bills are easy to grow, although, as noted above, some of the dwarf species need scree conditions in the rock garden. The others will grow in any kind of soil; most of them do best in a sunny position although *G. endressii,* one of the finest, as it produces its pink flowers over a very long period, will tolerate a good deal of shade, as will *G. aconitifolium, G. macrorrhizum* and *G. phaeum.* The taller species are apt to look a little untidy after they have flowered, and benefit from a trim over, just above the leaves to remove the spent flower stems. This will often result in a second flush of flowers being produced, especially if it is done before the seeds ripen. Most species form clumps (a few are tap-rooted) and these are very easily propagated by division in autumn or spring. With those that form vigorous, wide-spreading clumps, such as *G. endressii* and *G. grandiflorum,* it is not even necessary to dig up the clumps in order to divide them; it is sufficient to cut away pieces from round the clump and replant these. Seeds may also be sown, either under glass in the cold frame or greenhouse, or out of doors, in March or April.

Geum (jee-um)

From the Greek *geno,* to impart an agreeable flavour, referring to the aromatic roots of some species (*Rosaceae*). Avens. A genus of hardy herbaceous perennials, some of which are useful border plants, the dwarf species good rock garden plants. Several are natives of the British Isles but those valued for gardens are from Europe, South America and the Near East.

Species cultivated *G. borisii,* 1 foot, vivid orange flowers, May to August, hybrid. *G. bulgaricum,* 1–1½ feet, yellow flowers, summer. *G. chiloense* (syn. *G. coccineum* in some catalogues), 2 feet, scarlet flowers, summer. The species itself is rarely cultivated, but from it many cultivars, mostly with double flowers, have been produced. They include 'Dolly North', orange; 'Fire Opal', single orange overlaid with red; 'Lady Stratheden', golden-yellow; 'Prince of Orange', bright orange; 'Princess Juliana', golden-orange; 'Mrs Bradshaw', pillarbox red; 'Red Wings', semi-double, bright scarlet, late flowering. *G. heldreichii* 9–12 inches, orange-red, summer, hybrid. *G. montanum,* 6–12 inches, yellow flowers, May. *G. reptans,* 6 inches, yellow, late summer. *G. rivale,* water avens, 1 foot, reddish, May and June, a native; 'Leonard's Variety', with pink and orange flowers, is a cultivar. *G. triflorum,* 9–12 inches, soft pink, July.

Cultivation Geums are easily grown in any good, well-drained garden soil. They appreciate sunshine but the border kinds are tolerant of shade and damp conditions. Propagation is by division in spring or autumn or from seed sown out of doors in April or May, or in a cold frame or greenhouse in March or April.

Gladiolus (glad-e-o-lus or glad-i-ol-us)

From the Latin *gladiolus,* a little sword, referring to the shape of the leaves; plural: gladioli (*Iridaceae*). This genus

Gladiolus 'Caribbean' is a medium-flowered, mid-violet cultivar

comprises over 250 species of perennial herbs with the base of the stem swollen into a corm, producing usually 3 or 4 sword-shaped lateral leaves. They are natives of Europe, the Mediterranean region, Tropical and South Africa, and the Mascarene Islands, but about 15 species grow only north of the Sahara. From less than a dozen of the African species the summer-flowering garden cultivars have been bred and, therefore, these are not completely hardy in Britain, though many survive the winter in the ground. The main ancestors are (in order of their incorporation into the race): *G. cardinalis,* to 3 feet, salmon-scarlet with carmine and white lip-markings, a South African species preferring streamsides and other damp habitats. *G. oppositiflorus,* 3–4 feet, from Madagascar and Natal, with large white flowers striped amethyst, which gave added height and bud-count. *G. psittacinus,* to 3 feet, a very variable species found throughout Equatoria and usually with a yellow or green base-colour covered by maroon or scarlet flecking, which gave large-flowered, yellow-centred cultivars. *G. saundersii,* 3 feet, is bright carmine-rose, lower segments white with red spots, South African. *G. purpureo-auratus,* 3–4 feet, yellow and purple, which gave increased hardiness and striking throat-blotches, Natal. *G. cruentus,* 2–3 feet, which gave amaryllis-flowered types and bright red colouring. *G. papilio,* to 6 feet, violet to

may be had in bloom outdoors from late June until the frosts of October. Flowering dates are dependent upon choice of varieties, time of planting, site, and the season's weather. Gladioli are excellent for introducing height to an herbaceous border, as the foliage is tall even before the spikes emerge. They can also be planted in clumps in their own beds, with the smaller cultivars on the perimeters, or in rows in the vegetable garden for cut–flowers. Their range of colour and colour combinations is one of the widest in horticulture.

Two main types are officially recognized: the primulinus hybrids, which have short, slender, but strong and whippy stems, elongated buds, flowers in which the top segment of the perianth regularly forms a hood over the anthers and stigma, airily spaced flowers in 'stepladder' fashion with little or no overlapping and a tendency to face outwards; and the non-primulinus hybrids, with thicker, longer, straight stems, more bulbous buds set closer together, wide-open flowers facing forwards and overlapping to present a gapless ribbon of bloom. Terms such as 'Ruffled Miniature' and 'Butterfly' are convenient trade names only, often embracing wide variations in size and form. Most national gladiolus societies classify blooms by their diameter.

The gladiolus is not a bulb, but a corm, which is a compressed rhizome or underground stem consisting of a food-store crowned with new stem-shoots and having incipient roots encircling the basal plate underneath. It develops two forms of root: contractile roots to anchor the plant and pull the new corm down to its correct level, and fibrous feeding roots. The colour of the corm is no guide to the colour of the flower it will produce. High-crowned heavy corms with small root-scars (basal plates) will perform better than old flattish corms, especially if they are restricted to one spike each by rubbing out all but the apical bud on planting.

Gladioli will grow in most garden and allotment soils found in Britain, but attention to their specific requirements will be repaid by better spikes and fewer losses. The soil should be balanced and either neutral or slightly acid, the site must receive full sun for most of the day, the larger-flowering types need plenty of nourishment and continuously available water at the roots (but not water-logged conditions), and the corm needs to sit in a fast-draining pocket of light soil or sand. Soils not already rich in organic food should have plenty of old manure, garden compost, or other balanced fertiliser incorporated in the second spit down. A dusting of boneflour

bright purple with yellow shading. which gave purple-blue-lavender colouring and butterfly form, South Africa. G. primulinus, 1½ feet (now thought to be G. nebulicola from the Victoria Falls and Zambesi banks), which gave dainty hooded flowers and yellow and pastel tints.

Some species can be grown satisfactorily out of doors in England. especially in the south and west. G. byzantinus, 2 feet, rhodamine purple, is hardy and spreads vigorously by cormlets, but sets seed in England. North Africa. G. illyricus, 1–1½ feet, hardy, bright purple, is a very rare native of the New Forest, Europe. G. segetum, corn flag, 2 feet, is half-hardy, bright pink, and spreads rapidly by cormlets,

Mediterranean.

Other species are occasionally grown as cool house plants for flowering in March and April. They include G. alatus, 1 foot, orchid-flowered, strongly day-scented, scarlet and yellow. G. blandus, 1–1½ feet, white, often flushed pink, red lip-markings, unscented. G. carinatus, violet and cream, strongly day-scented. G. grandis, variable in height, brown or orange flowers, night-scented. G. tristis, 1½ feet, creamy-white, night-scented of carnation.

Half-hardy types raised from G. tristis, G. cardinalis and G. blandus, called 'Nanus' and 'Colvillii', will survive the winter outside in the south and flower in May and June.

Cultivation Summer-flowering gladioli

or bonemeal on top of the second spit will help root development. The top spit should be kept light and open, as a preventive against corm and neck rots. A four-yearly rotation is advised.

Planting depth will vary according to the nature of the soil; but on average soils large corms can be covered by 4–5 inches of soil, the medium-sized ones by 3 inches, and smalls and cormlets by 1½–2 inches. Plant when the soil has warmed up, in late March and throughout April. For later blooms, plant during May. Use a trowel, not a dibber; place a handful of sharp sand into the bottom of the hole, press the corm firmly into this, and sprinkle some more sand over the top before returning the soil into the hole. Plant the corms at least 6 inches apart (1 foot for exhibition purposes) and leave 9 inches between rows for subsequent hoeing. Inspect the site three or four weeks later and remove any stones or clods that are impeding emerging shoots.

On already rich soil a less laborious method of preparation is simply to kill all weeds by using a contact weedkiller

1 'Peter Pears' of 400-500 size has proved to be one of the best exhibition Gladioli of all time.
2 'Oscar', also 400-500 size, is one of the few successful exhibition Scarlets to be produced so far.

on their foliage a fortnight before planting-time. Then apply a soil-conditioner (any proprietary product that stimulates soil bacterial action). No digging is required. Rake the area flat, and plant the corms as detailed above; but add some soil-conditioner to the sand under each corm and finish with a sprinkling of it along each row. Thereafter, rely upon top dressings and liquid manuring to boost spikes for show purposes.

During dry periods an occasional thorough drenching is far better than frequent superficial wettings. Mulchings will help where water is not readily available; but keep rotting material away from the stems. Start early on a regular fortnightly protective routine, using insecticidal sprays in dry weather, dustings in wet weather, to prevent

infestation by thrips, aphids, or, later, caterpillars. For exhibition large-flowered varieties give sidedressings of fish manure or liquid manure every three or four weeks, with additional sulphate of potash a month before flowering-time. Ensure that there is adequate water once spikes begin to appear.

On exposed sites, stake the taller-growing plants early, to prevent rocking from causing loosened roots. Do not let a spike run to seed unless you are hybridising. On cutting, leave at least four leaves intact and continue to treat the plant as a growing entity until the foliage begins to turn brown. Then lift the plant, cut off the foliage close to the corm, trim off the roots, and dry the corm thoroughly as soon as possible. Never allow the corm to hang in humid conditions with its dying foliage attached. After two weeks or so, the old corm-husk will pull away cleanly. Clean the corm and cormlets, dust them with a mixture of insecticide and fungicide, and store them in a cool dry place that has adequate air-circulation. Do not allow your corms to suffer freezing or any dampness. Inspect your stock occasionally during the winter and discard any corm that has turned stone-hard or light and corky, or is obviously diseased. Black scabs in depressions (usually slug-damage) will lift out cleanly with a knife or thumbnail, revealing sound flesh underneath. Dust the exposed area with any fungicide and all should be well.

Keep your cultivars separate and labelled. Any you particularly like may be propagated next season by skinning the husks from the cormlets and planting the cormlets in prepared beds or deep boxes. There should be a moisture-retentive layer of plant-food, such as rich compost, only 4 inches below the surface and the cormlets should be pushed into the topsoil 2 inches deep and 2 inches apart. Keep the cormlet beds well watered and apply dilute liquid fertiliser fortnightly.

New scented gladioli are being produced along two lines: G. tristis hybrids that need coolhouse conditions and flower from the end of February to the middle of April, and the results of an Acidanthera × Gladiolus cross made successfully in New Zealand some twelve years ago, which flower in September in this country and are officially termed × Gladanthera.

Unfortunately, the best gladioli (other than primulinus hybrids) come from overseas and are still available only from specialist nurserymen and importers. It is wise to pay extra for good stock and to propagate from that, rather than to buy old cultivars that are losing their vigour or becoming disease-prone. The following cultivars are recommended both as good garden decoration and as delightful cut flowers. All can win on the show-bench.

Large- and Giant-flowered (sizes 400 and 500, 4½–5½ inches and over 5½ inches diameter): 'Antarctic', vigorous ruffled white; 'Landmark', giant cream; 'Green Ice', pale green-white; 'Sulphur Victory', ruffled sulphur-cream; 'Morning Sun', ruffled pale yellow; 'Gold Piece', ruffled deep yellow; 'Golden Waves', ruffled mid-yellow, late flowering; 'Ethereal', pastel pink and yellow; 'Metropole', pale pink and white; 'Salmon Queen', an aptly named giant; 'Christine', a heavily ruffled deep salmon with white throat; 'Peter Pears', orange-pink; 'Parnassus', a beautiful peachy colour; 'Thunderbird', a tall heavily ruffled strong orange; 'Bandwagon', tall scarlet, blotched white; 'Oscar', deep red; 'Flaming Jet', ruffled strong crimson, blotched white; 'Indrapoera', solid saturated red, almost black; 'Lavanesque', reliable lilac-lavender, blotched creamy-white; 'China Blue', giant pale blue-violet; 'K & M's Blue', velvety blue-purple; 'King David', blue-purple with white picotee; 'Picotee' (Dutch), cream with sharp pink picotee; 'Brown Lul-laby', red-brown smoky with redder blotch and white picotee; and 'Green Woodpecker', yellow-green with wine-coloured throat-marks.

Medium-flowered (300 size, 3½–4½ inches): 'Rainier', pure white, ruffled; 'Angel Eyes', ruffled pure white with crisp purple blotch faintly edged yellow; 'Ares', a tall cream blotched deep red; 'Summer Fairy', salmon-pink with brown-red blotch edged yellow; 'Jacqueline', apricot-pink, blotched cream; 'Femina', strong pink, blotched red on creamy-white, many buds, but very late; 'Blue Mist', pale blue-violet, blotched white; 'Caribbean', ruffled mid-violet, blotched deep violet on white throat; 'Gladiator', scarlet; 'Negus', black-red.

Small-flowered (200 size, 2½–3½ inches): 'Elite', ruffled white, blotched purple; 'Dido', ruffled white, blotched yellow; 'Goldilocks', ruffled deep yellow; 'Figurine', yellow with bronze picotee and dull red blotches; 'Red Ribbon', tall mid-scarlet with white picotee, many open; 'Frisky', heavily ruffled deep red with white picotee; 'Blue Sapphire', pale blue-violet with white blotch; 'Little Pansy', mid-violet with dark violet blotch edged white; 'Towhead', creamy-yellow, many open.

Miniature-flowered (100 size, under 2½ inches, mainly face-ups): 'Angelica', white, with many side-spikes; 'The Imp', yellow, blotched red on all petals; 'Pint Size', lavender and white; 'Red Dot', bright scarlet.

Primulinus (hooded): 'Ocean Spray', cream, blotched apricot; 'Chrysantha', strong yellow, blotched dark red; 'Pamela Mummery', apricot; 'Parfait', salmon with throat-marks; 'Aria', flame-pink, blotched pale yellow, good-opener; 'Richard Unwin', chestnut; 'Chocolate Chip', a brown smoky with faint white picotee; and 'Red Star', first of a new line that features star-shaped opening buds.

Godetia (god-ee-she-a)

Commemorating Charles H. Godet, nineteenth-century Swiss botanist *(Oenotheraceae)*. A genus of hardy annuals, popular and showy, greatly improved in recent years, related to the evening primrose *(Oenothera)* in which genus they were formerly included.

Species cultivated Few original species are grown, with the possible exception of *G. dasycarpa*, 9 inches, from the Andes, with mauve flowers and steely blue-green foliage, the parent of many lavender-flowered varieties. The original species have been superseded by the garden varieties now available, mainly the results of crosses between *G. grandiflora*, 6–12 inches, a showy plant of compact habit and the tall-growing *G. amoena*, 1–2 feet, with loose habit, both variable in colour.

Cultivars include 'Firelight', crimson; 'Kelvedon Glory', salmon; 'Orange Glory', a deeper salmon and 'Sybil Sherwood', salmon pink, orange and white, all 1–1½ feet tall. Double-flowered cultivars include 'Cherry Red'; 'Rich Pink'; 'Rosy Queen'; 'Schaminii', salmon-pink, all 2–2½ feet tall; 'Whitneyi azalaeiflora plena', pink with a crimson blotch, and 'Carmine Glow', about 1 foot tall.

Another kind, tall but with single flowers, is represented by such cultivars as 'Lavender Gem' and 'Lavender', with dark prominent stamens. These probably come from the 2 foot tall species *G. viminea*, from California.

Cultivation Sow in beds and borders in full sun in April; thin according to ultimate height. The tall double-flowered kinds are the hardiest and may be sown in autumn in a well-drained position and will produce spikes of flower up to 3 feet in height the following summer.

Grevillea (grev-ill-ee-a)

In honour of Charles F. Greville, 1749–1809, a founder of the Royal Horticultural Society *(Proteaceae)*. A large genus of evergreen shrubs, natives of Australia, Tasmania and New Caledonia, mostly tender, grown as pot plants for conservatory decoration and as indoor plants. Some are grown simply for their decorative foliage. A few are nearly hardy and may succeed in sheltered positions in south and west Britain.

Species cultivated *G. acanthifolia*, 4 feet, deeply jagged leaves, reddish flowers, June. *G. alpina*, 1–2 feet, a free flowering compact shrub, hardy in the south and west, red and white flowers, spring onwards; var. *dallachina* is a better form. *G. asplenifolia*, 12 feet, pink, flowers, July. *G. banksii*, 15 feet, red flowers, August; var. *forsteri* is a better form, with good red flowers. *G. glabrata*, to 6 feet, weeping habit, bright green leaves, white flowers, summer. *G. juniperina* (syn. *G. sulphurea*), 6 feet, pale yellow, May and June; hardy in the south and west. *G. punicea*, 6 feet, deep red flowers, spring. *G. robusta*, 2–20 feet (much more in nature), finely divided, fern-like leaves, does not flower in the young state, grown as a house plant and in sub-tropical bedding schemes. *G. rosmarinifolia*, 7 feet, red flowers, summer, hardy in the south and west. *G. × semperflorens*, 6 feet, flowers yellow, flushed pink, tipped green, hybrid, hardy in the south and west. *G. sulphurea*, 6 feet, flowers canary-yellow, summer, hardy in mild districts. *G. thelemanniana*, 5 feet, yellow, green and red flowers, early summer. *G. thyrsoides*, 4–5 feet, crimson, summer, hardy in the south-west.

Cultivation Pot every two or three years in a compost of fibrous loam and coarse sand and maintain a temperature of 50°F (10°C) in winter. Pinch and prune to encourage bushy growth. Those that may be grown out of doors should be planted with the shelter of a south-facing wall in spring or autumn and protected in severe weather. Propagation is from seed sown in a temperature of 65°F (18°C) in March or from cuttings with a heel in March, April or May inserted in sand in a temperature of 75°F (24°C). Seed is erratic and may take a couple of years to germinate. Plants can also be layered in autumn.

Gypsophila (jip-sof-ill-a)

From the Greek *gypsos*, chalk, *phileo*, to love; the plants prefer chalky soils *(Caryophyllaceae)*. Hardy annuals and perennials of great value in both the border and rock garden; the dwarf kinds also look well in pans in the alpine house. They are mainly natives of the eastern Mediterranean region.

Annual species cultivated *G. elegans*, 1–1½ feet, clusters of small white flowers; vars. *alba grandiflora*, larger flowered, *rosea*, bright rose. 'London Market Strain' and a crimson strain are sometimes offered. *G. muralis*, 6 inches, rose-pink flowers.

Perennials *G. aretioides*, 1 inch, a cushion plant for a sunny scree, with white, stemless flowers, spring. *G. cerastioides*, 3 inches, leaves in dense flat mats, white flowers much veined with purple, spring; var. *flore-pleno*, double flowers. There are various garden forms. *G. dubia*, mat-like dark green foliage, white, pink-flushed flowers, spring, good for walls or crevices. *G.*

pacifica (syn. *G. oldhamiana*), 3–4 feet, dark leaves, pink flowers in cloudy sprays, August and September. *G. paniculata*, baby's breath, chalk plant, 2½–3 feet, light sprays of white flowers occasionally pinkish, June to August; vars. *compacta*, 1½ feet, *flore-pleno*, double flowers, a better form. Cultivars include 'Bristol Fairy', 3 feet, 'Rosy Veil' (sometimes called 'Rosenchleirer'), 9 inches, 'Flamingo', 2½ feet, large double pink flowers. *G. repens*, 6 inches, white flowers June to August; vars. *fratensis*, compact form, pink flowers. *rosea* 9 inches, rose-pink. 'Letchworth Rose', 9 inches, is a named cultivar.

Cultivation Plant both rock garden and border kinds in autumn or spring, the rock garden sorts in pockets containing a large amount of mortar rubble or limestone chippings. Although the border kinds like limy soil, they are tolerant of other soils but need a sunny spot with good drainage. They provide useful cut flower material when well grown. Propagation of the annual species and *G. repens* and *G. pacifica* is from seed. *G. paniculata* itself comes true from seed but cuttings of the varieties should be taken in June. These should be of young growth with a heel, 2 inches long, inserted in silver sand with gentle bottom heat. Commercially named forms are propagated by root grafting. Trailing species can be increased by

cuttings or by division in spring.

Hardenbergia (har-den-ber-je-a)

Commemorating Franziska, Countess of Hardenberg, sister of Baron Hugel, a plant collector, whose plants she tended while he was on his travels *(Leguminosae)*. Australian sarsaparilla-tree, Australian lilac. A genus of three species, greenhouse evergreen twining plants from Australia.

Species cultivated *H. comptoniana* (syn. *Kennedya comptoniana*), 9–12 feet, long racemes of violet-blue flowers, early summer. *H. violacea* (syn. *H. monophylla*, *H. bimaculata*), Australian lilac, 8–10 feet, purple flowers, April; var. *rosea*, pink flowers. These species are very similar except in leaf form, the latter having only one leaflet, and *H. comptoniana* three to five.

Cultivation Plant in large pots or in the greenhouse border from February to May in a compost of equal proportions of loam and peat with some silver sand sprinkled on to the surface. Prune in February or March, cutting out straggly shoots and unwanted growth. The plants can be trained to stakes, wires or along the rafters. Propagation is from cuttings taken any time from March to July, 2–3 inches long, and

1 The double-flowered form of Gypsophila paniculata. 2 G. repens rosea

inserted in sandy peat in a temperature of 55–65°F (13–18°C). Seed may also be sown in spring in the same temperature.

Hebe (hee-be)

From the Greek, hebe, small (Scrophulariaceae). A genus of about 140 species of evergreen flowering shrubs, mostly natives of New Zealand, some hardy, some tender, formerly included in the genus Veronica. The tender sorts are the better plants, and although they may be killed or damaged by frost, they root so easily from cuttings and grow so quickly that losing a shrub need not be a disaster. Some, such as H. armstrongii, H. buchananii and H. cupressoides, have very tiny, overlapping leaves, resembling those of conifers, and are known as 'whipcord hebes'. These have small, insignificant white flowers, but make good foliage shrubs.

Species cultivated H. albicans, 2 feet, white flowers, summer. H. angustifolia, 3–6 feet, pale lilac, summer. H. anomala, 3–4 feet, small bright green leaves, white flowers, hardy in south-west, July to September. H. armstrongii, to 3 feet, tiny, cypress-like leaves, white flowers, July. H. brachysiphon, (syn. H. traversii) 5 feet, sometimes more, white flowers, June-July. H. buchananii, 2 feet, tiny leaves, white flowers, June and July. H. carnea, 3–4 feet, flowers pink fading to white, May to August. H. catarractae, 1–2 feet, white or blue flowers, July to September; var. diffusa less tall, mat-forming, white, purple-veined flowers. H. colensoi, 1–2 feet, small leaves, white flowers, July and August; var. glauca, glaucous-blue leaves. H. cupressoides, 4–5 feet, cypress-like leaves, mauve flowers, June-July. H. darwiniana, 2–3 feet, small leaves, white flowers, July-August. H. elliptica, 5–6 feet, or more, mauve, July and August, the commonest species, used for hedging near the sea; var. variegata, leaves edged with cream. H. gracillima, 3–4 feet, lilac, July and August; H. hulkeana, 4–6 feet, flowers pale lavender in panicles up to 1 foot long, May and June, needs wall protection. H. lindsayi, 1–2 feet, pink flowers, summer, hybrid. H. macrantha, 2 feet, large white flowers, summer. H. parviflora, 4–6 feet, lilac-flushed white flowers, July and August. H. pinguifolia, 1–1½ feet, small leaves, white flowers, June and July; vars. carnosula, 2–2½ feet, white June and July; pagei, 1 foot, white flowers, June and July. H. salicifolia, 5–10 feet, narrow leaves, lilac-tinged flowers, June to August. H. speciosa, 4–5 feet, purplish flowers, July to September, tender, parent of various hybrids. H. subalpina, 2–2½ feet, small leaves, white flowers, June and July. H. vernicosa, 1½–2 feet, tiny leaves, lavender flowers, June and July. Cultivars include 'Alicia Amherst', purple, summer, slightly tender; 'Autumn Glory', 1½–2 feet, deep violet, summer to

Hebe 'Autumn Glory' is probably the most popularly grown cultivar

winter, hardy; 'Bowles's Variety', 3–4 feet, white flowers, June-July; 'Carl Teschner', 9–12 inches, dense spreading habit, violet flowers, July and August; 'Diamant', 3–4 feet, bright crimson, summer, slightly tender; 'Ettrick Shepherd', 2 feet, violet, summer, moderately hardy; 'Hidcote', 3–4 feet, pale lilac, summer, hardy; 'Hielan Lassie', 2 feet, violet-blue, summer, hardy; 'La Seduisante', 4 feet, crimson, summer, slightly tender; 'Marjorie', 3 feet, violet, July to September, hardy; 'McEwanii', 1 foot, bright blue flowers, summer; 'Midsummer Beauty', 3–5 feet, flowers lavender in long spikes, July to September, hardy, one of the best; 'Mrs E. Tennant', 2½–3 feet, light violet, July to September, hardy; 'Purple Queen', 4 feet, rich purple, summer, slightly tender; 'Simon Delaux', 3–4 feet, rich crimson, summer, slightly tender.

Cultivation These shrubs are not fussy about soil, and will succeed in chalky soils. The slightly tender kinds thrive near the sea and one or two are used for making seaside hedges. Little pruning is required unless bushes become straggly, when they may be cut back in April. The dwarf species grown for foliage effect may be lightly trimmed over after flowering to remove spent flower heads. Propagation is from cuttings taken after the plants have flowered. These root very easily, even

in water. It is advisable to take a few cuttings of the tender kinds and over-winter them in a frame for use as replacements.

Hedera (hed-er-a)

The ancient Latin name (Araliaceae). Ivy. A small genus of evergreen climbing or trailing plants which attach themselves to supports by means of aerial roots. They are grown for their leathery, often decorative, variegated leaves. They were planted extensively in Victorian gardens, and there has been a renewed interest in them in recent years. Several species and hybrids are now used as house plants. When plants reach the top of their support they cease to produce aerial roots, growth becomes bushy, the leaves lack lobes and the plants produce flowers and fruits (usually black). Cuttings taken from mature growth will not revert to the climbing plant habit, but will remain bushy.

Species cultivated H. canariensis, Canary Island ivy, vigorous climber, 3–5 lobed leaves up to 8 inches across, leathery; vars. azorica, leaves with 5–7 lobes, tender; variegata, leaves green and silvery-grey, margined with white. H. chrysocarpa, Italian ivy, leaves 4 inches wide, fruits yellow. H. colchica, Persian ivy, strong growing, leaves up to 8 inches long, 4 inches wide, dark green; var. dentata, leaves toothed, dentata variegata, variegated yellow. H. helix, common ivy, a native plant which may grow 80–100 feet up trees, leaves variable in size and number of lobes; vars. *aureo-variegata*, leaves flushed yellow; 'Buttercup' (also known as 'Golden Cloud' and 'Russell's Gold'), small leaves, flushed yellow; *caenwoodiana*, small, narrowly lobed leaves; 'Chicago', large leaves, 3-lobes; 'Chicago' *variegata*, variegated cream; *conglomerata*, slow growing, growth dense, leaves small, wavy, suitable for rock garden; *congesta*, slow growing, growth dense, leaves more or less triangular, grey-green; *deltoidea*, leaves 3-lobed, the two basal ones overlapping; *digitata*, leaves broad, 5-lobed; *discolor*, small leaves, flushed red, mottled with cream; 'Eva', leaves small, margined cream, variegation very variable; 'Glacier', leaves grey, margined cream; *gracilis*, graceful, slender growth; 'Jubilee' (or 'Golden Leaf'), small leaves, central vein red, yellow mark at base; 'Little Diamond', central lobe long pointed, variegated cream and pale green; *lutzii*, dense growth, lime green and cream, darker green flecks; *palmata*, slow growing, palmately lobed leaves; 'Pittsburgh' mid-green, cream veins; *purpurea*, leaves bronze-purple in winter; 'Shamrock', very dark green leaves, basal lobes overlapping; *tortuosa*, curled and twisted leaves; *tricolor*, leaves grey-green, edged white, rosy in winter. Other varieties and cultivars may be offered in trade lists from time to time. *H. hibernica*, Irish ivy, strong growing, large leaves up to 6 inches wide, bright green in colour, usually 5-lobed, useful for ground cover under trees and in other shady places.

Cultivation Ivies will grow in any aspect out doors and in any kind of soil. Plant in autumn or early spring. When used as ground cover peg the shoots to the soil to encourage growth. Prune in April and feed as required for rapid growth. When grown in pots indoors John Innes potting compost No. 1 is suitable; provide good drainage. Plants may be allowed to trail, may be trained up sticks or bark-covered branches or trained to a fan or frame of any form. Water moderately in winter; freely in summer, when established plants should be fed occasionally. It should be noted that the varieties are more often grown as house plants and as such are liable to damage by frost, but if put out of doors in late May and gradually accustomed to lower temperatures, will then tolerate frost. Propagation is by cuttings rooted out of doors in autumn or in winter under glass.

Helenium (hel-ee-knee-um)

After Helen of Troy; according to legend the flowers sprang from her tears (*Compositae*). Sneezeweed. Hardy herbaceous perennials from North America, good for cutting and popularly grown for their late summer flowers. The disk of the flower head is very prominent, a

Helenium 'Wyndley' is yellow-orange; in front is 'Moerheim Beauty'.

characteristic of the entire genus.

Species cultivated *H. autumnale*, 3–5 feet, yellow flowers, July to October; var. *pumilum magnificum*, 3½ feet, golden-yellow. *H. bigelovii*, 4 feet, yellow and brown, July to September. *H. hoopesii*, 2 feet, yellow flowers, June onwards. There are many fine cultivars including 'Bruno', 3–3½ feet, bronze-red; 'Butterpat', 3–3½ feet, rich yellow. 'Chipperfield Orange', 4–5 feet, yellow streaked and splashed crimson; 'Copper Spray', 3½ feet, copper-red; 'Crimson Beauty', 2 feet, bronze-crimson; 'Goldlackzwerg', 2½–3 feet, gold and copper-red; 'July Sun', 3 feet, golden-bronze; 'Moerheim Beauty', 3–3½ feet, glowing bronze-red; 'Riverton Beauty', 4½ feet, yellow; 'Riverton Gem', 4½ feet, crimson streaked yellow; 'The Bishop', 3 feet, buttercup-yellow; 'Wyndley', 2–2½ feet, chestnut and orange.

Cultivation Almost any garden soil is suitable but a stiff loam is ideal. Plant in autumn or spring, the lower growing kinds towards the front of the border in clumps and taller growing varieties towards the back. Propagate by division or by seed.

Helianthemum (hel-ee-an-them-um)

From the Greek *helios*, the sun, and *anthemon*, a flower (*Cistaceae*). Sun Rose. A genus of evergreen and semi-evergreen shrubs, sub-shrubs, perennial plants and annuals, very free flowering. Numerous named varieties and hybrids are grown and four species are native plants.

Species cultivated *H. alpestre*, 1 foot, a tufted alpine, yellow flowers, summer, European alps. *H. apenninum*, 1 foot, spreading plant, grey leaves, white flowers, June short-lived sub-shrub, Europe (including south-west England), Asia Minor. *H. lunulatum*, 6–9 inches, sub-shrub, yellow, summer, Italy. *H. nummularium* (syn. *H. vulgare*, *H. chamaecistus*), common sun rose, 6–12 inches trailing, yellow, June, July, Europe (including England). There are many cultivars including 'Beech Park Scarlet', 'Ben Attow', primrose yellow, deeper centre; 'Ben Hope', carmine shading to orange; 'Ben Ledi', dark red; 'Butterball', clear yellow, double; 'Jubilee', double yellow; 'Lemon Queen', lemon yellow; 'Mrs C. W. Earle', scarlet, double; 'Rose of Leeswood', rich pink, large double; 'The Bride', white; 'Watergate Rose', deep carmine, foliage grey-green; 'Wisley Pink', clear pink. *H. tuberaria*, 9 inches, herbaceous perennial forming tufts of brownish leaves with yellow flowers, July, south Europe.

Cultivation As the name implies, a sunny spot is essential for the sun roses. Ordinary soil is suitable and they are excellent plants for dry walls, rock gardens and sunny banks. Most are not very long lived and need replacing in preference to cutting hard back to encourage new growth. Propagate from cuttings of young shoots in July or August, inserted in sandy compost. Once these are rooted they should be potted singly into small pots and over-wintered thus. Because they do not transplant well it is common practice to put them into their permanent positions from these pots, planting out in April.

Helianthus (hel-ee-an-thus)

From the Greek *helios*, the sun, *anthos*, a flower. *(Compositae)*. Sunflower. A genus of tall, coarse-growing plants, annuals and perennials, gross feeders, dominating the border in which they are planted. *H. annuus*, the common sunflower, is a plant of some economic importance as the seeds are fed to fowl and produce an edible oil, and the flowers yield a yellow dye.

Annual species cultivated *H. annuus*, 6–10 feet, common or giant sunflower, large yellow flowerheads, late summer, coarse growing; var. *floreplenus*, double flowers. Cultivars and strains include 'Dwarf Chrysanthemum-flowered', 3 feet, golden-yellow, fringed petals; 'Gaillardia flora', 5 feet, brown and yellow gaillardia-like flowers; 'Primrose', 5 feet, sulphur-yellow, darker disk; 'Red', 5 feet, a strain with chestnut-brown flowers; 'Russian Giant', 8 feet, large, yellow; 'Sungold', 6 feet, golden-yellow, double; 'Tall Chrysanthemum-flowered', 5 feet, golden-yellow, fringed petals; 'Yellow Pygmy', 2 feet, double yellow, dwarf. *H. debilis* (syn. *H. cucumerifolius*) 3–4 feet, branched plants with somewhat glossy leaves, yellow flowers, summer. Cultivars include 'Autumn Beauty', 2 feet, yellow, coppery zone; 'Dazzler', 3 feet, chestnut, orange-tipped rays; 'Excelsior', 3 feet, yellow, red zones; 'Starlight', 4 feet, yellow, twisted petals; 'Stella', 3 feet, golden-yellow, starry flowers.

Perennial *H. atrorubens* (syn. *H. sparsifolius*), 6–8 feet, golden-yellow, September. 'The Monarch', with flowers 6 inches across is a good cultivar. *H. decapetalus*, 4–6 feet, tough, sharply toothed leaves, sulphur-yellow flowers, August to October. Cultivars include 'Capenoch Star', lemon yellow, single, good for cutting; 'Capenoch Supreme',

1 Helianthemum, the Sun Rose, a very free flowering perennial plant.
2 The double flowered Helianthus 'Loddon Gold' has rich yellow flowers.

large, single, pure yellow 'Loddon Gold', double, rich yellow; 'Soleil d'Or', double, sulphur-yellow, quilled petals. *H. laetiflorus* (syn. *H. rigidus*), 5–7 feet, yellow, September and October. 'Miss Mellish', orange-yellow, is the best cultivar of this, but both are very rampant plants. *H. salicifolius* (syn. *H. orgyalis*), 6 feet, small yellow flowers, September and October, willow-like leaves. *H. tuberosus*, Jerusalem artichoke, 6–8 feet, yellow, October (see Artichokes).

Cultivation The best plants are grown in a stiff loam in full sun. Seeds of annual kinds can be sown *in situ* in April, and to get the largest flower-heads water, and give liquid feeds occasionally up to flowering time. The perennials can be divided in autumn or spring. *H. laetiflorus* needs constant checking to prevent it from dominating the surrounding area, and is best planted in rough corners where it will provide useful flowers for cutting.

Helichrysum (hel-ee-kry-sum)

From the Greek *helios*, the sun, *chrysos*, gold, referring to the yellow flowers of some species. (*Compositae*). Everlasting-flower, immortelle-flower. A large genus of plants ranging from alpines to shrubs, bearing daisy-like flowers. Some are commonly dried as everlasting flowers. Not all are hardy.

Annual species cultivated *H. bracteatum*, 2–4 feet, bracts yellow or pink, summer, Australia; *album*, white, *monstrosum*, flower-heads double. Cultivars and strains of *H. b. monstrosum* include 'Fireball', scarlet, 'Golden', 'Rose', and 'Salmon Rose'.

Perennial *H. arenarium*, yellow everlasting, 6–12 inches, bright yellow bracts, summer, Europe. *H. frigidum*, mat-forming, silvery leaves, rather moss-like, white flowers, May and June, suitable for scree or alpine house, Corsica. *H. marginatum* (syn. *H. milfordae*), 3 inches, forming hummocks of silvery rosettes, white, spring. *H. orientale*, 9 inches, yellow, August, south-east Europe. *H. plicatum*, 1–3½ feet, silvery foliage, small yellow flowers, needs warm position, south-east Europe. Shrubby and sub-shrubby *H. angustifolium*, 1 foot, yellow, summer, southern Europe. *H. bellidoides*, mat-forming, white flowers, summer, useful rock garden plant, New Zealand. *H. fontanesii*, 1 foot, narrow, silvery leaves, yellow flowers in loose sprays, summer, rock garden. *H. lanatum*, 1 foot, leaves white of a flannel-like texture, yellow flowers, summer, useful for bedding, South Africa. *H. petiolatum*, 12–15 inches, white, summer. *H. rosmarinifolium* (syn. *Ozothamnus rosmarinifolius*), 6–9 feet, branches and leaves sticky, flowers white, small, produced very freely, June, Tasmania; var. *purpurescens*, 4 feet, purple. *H. selago*, 9 inches, white summer, New Zealand.

H. splendidum, 2–5 feet, shoots and leaves grey-white, flowers bright yellow, summer, South Africa. *H. stoechas*, goldilocks, 1–2 feet, leaves silvery-white, flowers yellow in heads to 2 inches across, summer, southern Europe. *H. virgineum*, 9 inches, cream, summer.

Cultivation Treat the annuals as half-hardy, sowing in gentle heat in March, gradually hardening off and planting out in May. Late sowings can be made out of doors in early May. The rock garden kinds all like dry sunny spots with sharp drainage, and make good scree plants. The shrubby kinds are rather tender and need wall protection in all except mild localities. Plant in April and fasten the main branches to a trellis or wire support. Prune away unwanted branches early in April. They may be grown as attractive greenhouse shrubs in a gritty compost of sand, peat and loam. Propagation of the perennial species is by division in April or by cuttings in a cold frame in spring, and of the shrubby kinds from cuttings of half-ripened wood in August, inserted round the edges of a pot of sandy soil and put in a cold frame.

Heliophila (he-le-off-ill-a)

From the Greek *helios*, the sun, and *philein*, to love (*Cruciferae*). A genus of attractive plants, from South Africa, mostly annuals, particularly effective when grown in masses.

Species cultivated *H. linearifolia*, 1½ feet, blue flowers, summer, a sub-shrubby plant usually treated as an annual. *H. longifolia*, 1½ feet, blue flowers with a white eye, freely produced on long racemes in summer, annual.

Cultivation A light, well-drained soil in a sunny spot suits the heliophilas and they also make attractive pot plants for the cold greenhouse. The seedlings are raised under glass from a March sowing. Those to be grown on under glass are potted up singly into 5-inch pots in John Innes potting compost No 1, and those to be planted out of doors need hardening off and planting out 6 inches apart in May. Alternatively seed can be sown out of doors in May on a well-prepared seed bed.

Helipterum (hel-ip-ter-um)

From the Greek *helios*, the sun, *pteron*, a wing or feather; the seed pappus is plumed (*Compositae*). Australian everlasting, immortelle-flower. A genus of sun-loving annuals and perennials, some of them shrubby, the annuals bearing everlasting flowers excellent for winter decoration.

Species cultivated *H. humboldtianum*, 1 foot, yellow, summer. *H. manglesii* (syn. *Rhodanthe manglesii*), 12–18 inches, pink and white, June to September, out of doors; April to June under glass, Australia. *H. roseum* (syn. *Acroclinium roseum*), 15–18 inches, shades of pink and white with yellow or bronze-copper

1 Helleborus x nigricors, a pale green flowered hybrid, is slightly perfumed.
2 The Christmas Rose, Helleborus niger, has white saucer shaped flowers.

centres, from July onwards out of doors, earlier under glass; vars. *flore plenum album*, double white, *grandiflorum*, larger flowers, various colours, Australia. 'Red Bonnie' is a bright red cultivar.

Cultivation Seeds are sown under glass in March and the seedlings are pricked out and hardened off, ready for planting out of doors in May. Seed may also be sown under glass in September and the seedlings pricked out, and potted on through the winter to provide spring blooms under glass. Water freely and give a liquid feed weekly after the plants are 6 inches high. Light staking will be required, and a minimum temperature of 45–50°F (7–10°C).

Helleborus (hel-le-bor-us)

From the Greek *helein*, to kill, *bora*, food; some species are poisonous (*Ranunculaceae*). Hellebore. Hardy perennials, often retaining their leaves through the winter, with thick fibrous roots. All flower early in the year and the flowers are long lasting. Most of them have handsome, leathery, divided leaves, sometimes spiny. They are natives of southern Europe and western

Asia.

Species cultivated *H. abchasicus,* 1 foot, flowers purplish-green, January to March; vars. *coccineus,* wine red, *venosus,* rosy-purple with dark veins. *H. argutifolius* (syn. *H. corsicus*), 2–3 feet, apple-green flowers in February and March which persist until mid-summer. *H. foetidus,* stinking hellebore, 2–3 feet, pale green flowers, the petals tipped purple, February and March, native plant. *H. guttatus,* 1½ feet, white flowers, heavily spotted with crimson inside, January to April, the parent of most spotted hybrids in cultivation. *H. lividus,* 2 feet, green flowers soon turning brown; doubtfully hardy. *H. niger,* 1½–2 feet, Christmas rose, 1 foot, white, saucer-shaped flowers with a boss of golden-yellow anthers; vars. *altifolius* and *macranthus,* longer stems. 'Potters Wheel' is a fine cultivar. *H.* × *nigricors,* (*H. niger* × *H. corsicus*), 1½ feet, pale green, February, hybrid. *H. odorus,* fragrant hellebore, 1½ feet, greenish-yellow flowers with faint elderflower scent, March. *H. orientalis,* Lenten rose, 2 feet variable flowers, purple, pink or almost black and often spotted with other shades, February to May. 'Albion Otto' is a white, purple-spotted cultivar. *H. torquatus,* 1½ feet, flowers purple inside and blue-purple outside, February to March, rather shy-flowering, leaves die down in summer. *H. viridis,* green hellebore, 1–1½ feet, pale green flowers, February.

Cultivation A well-drained rich soil is best and although a shaded position is usually recommended, this is not essential, although partial shade is preferable to full sun. Once established, the plants like to be left undisturbed, although they quickly settle down if they are moved in winter with plenty of soil round their roots. In December, protect the flowers of the Christmas rose by a cloche or by mulching with peat to prevent the short-stemmed flowers from being splashed by soil. Plant in October November or March, 15 inches apart in groups, preparing the site well and incorporating some manure.

Plants can be forced in pots by lifting and potting up in October and maintaining a temperature of 40–50 F (4–10°C). Replant out of doors in April.

Propagate from seed or by division of roots after flowering.

Hemerocallis (hem-er-o-kal-lis)

From the Greek *hemero,* a day, and *kallos,* beauty, referring to the life of the flowers *(Liliaceae).* Day lily. Hardy perennials from temperate E. Asia and S. Europe, very adaptable, flowering for many weeks, but with the individual

1 The rich plum purple flowers of Helleborus orientalis, the Lenten Rose, vary slightly in colour.
2 Hemerocallis fulva 'Kwanso' is an example of a double flowered Day Lily.

funnel-shaped flowers lasting only for one day. There has been an almost bewildering number of cultivars both from America and our own country with the result that the species seem to have been somewhat neglected.

Species cultivated *H. aurantiaca,* Japanese day lily, 3 feet, orange-yellow flowers, July. *H. citrina,* 3½ feet, lemon-yellow, slightly fragrant flowers, July to September; var. *baronii,* larger flowers, citron-yellow. *H. flava,* 2–3 feet, orange-yellow flowers, June and July. *H. fulva,* 3 feet, vigorous, orange-brown, June to August; vars. *flore pleno,* double, *kwanso flore pleno,* double flowers and variegated striped foliage. *H.* × *luteola,* 3 feet, large, light yellow, June and July, hybrid. *H. middendorffii,* 1–1½ feet, rich yellow, fragrant, June. *H. minor,* 9 inches, clear yellow, reddish-brown on outside, June. *H. thunbergii,* 2–3 feet, light yellow, fragrant, July to September. There are many cultivars such as 'Ambassador', currant red rich yellow centre; 'Apollo' bright apricot-yellow; 'Bagette', dark brown; 'Ballet Dancer', soft pink; 'Black Prince', purple-red; 'Bonanza', soft golden-yellow, dwarf; 'Display', bright red; 'Golden Chimes', golden-yellow, a miniature with well-branched growth; 'Hyperion', canary yellow, 'Morocco Beauty', very dark purple with golden throat; 'Norma Borland', copper; 'Pink Prelude', flesh pink, yellow throat; 'Rajah', late flowering, orange, shaded mahogany and violet; 'Red Torch', cardinal red; 'Viscountess Byng', orange flushed rose, long flowering season. New ones appear each year; nurserymen's catalogues should be consulted for the latest varieties.

Cultivation Day lilies are most accommodating as to soil and position, provided they are not planted in full shade. They do not, however, give of their best in poor, chalky soils. Plant in autumn or spring, incorporating some compost or old manure. The plants will survive for many years unattended except for an occasional early summer mulch and a regular dressing of slug repellent.

Hepatica (he-pat-ik-a)

From the Greek *hepar,* liver, from a supposed resemblance of the leaves to that organ *(Ranunculaceae).* A genus of three or four species of low growing hardy perennials, sometimes included in the genus *Anemone* and growing wild in woodlands over the whole of the north temperate zone.

Species cultivated *H. americana* (syns. *H. triloba, Anemone hepatica),* 6 inches, almost stemless deep lavender-blue flowers, March; vars. *alba,* white, *rubra flore pleno,* double pink. *H. media,* 9 inches, offered in its var. *ballardii,* large clear blue flowers, spring. *H. transsilvanica* (syns. *Anemone transsilvanica, A. angulosa),* 3–5 inches, lavender-blue, slightly larger flowers than *H. ameri-*

cana, spring. A pink form is sometimes offered.

Cultivation The leaves appear after the flowers and form good green tufts for the remainder of the summer, and throughout the winter. Shady rock gardens or shrub borders in moist soil suit them best. They will tolerate lime in the soil. Propagation is from seed sown in pans of sandy compost in autumn and by division of the roots.

Herpolirion (her-po-lir-e-on)

From the Greek *herpestes,* creeping, *lirion,* lily, referring to the habit of the plant *(Liliaceae).* There is one species only, *H. novae-zelandiae,* which is native to S.E. Australia, Tasmania and New Zealand. It is a small perennial herb, 1–3 inches high, with a creeping rhizome. In its native habitat it grows in sub-alpine swamps. The leaves are long and narrow and spread out to form a fan, sheathing at the base. The flowers are relatively large (½ to ¾ inch wide), blue or white.

Cultivation This is not an easy plant to

grow; it requires alpine house treatment, that is, no heat in summer but sufficient heat in winter to keep the minimum temperature above 40°F (4°C). Stand the plant and its container in a saucer filled with water, so that the plant can be kept constantly moist in summer. It should be allowed to become drier in winter. A suitable compost consists of 1 part of loam, 2 parts of peat, 1 part of sand. Propagation is from seed sown in spring or by careful division of the branching rhizomes.

Hesperis (hes-per-is)

From the Greek *hesperos,* evening, when the flowers of some species become fragrant *(Cruciferae).* A genus of hardy plants including biennial and perennial species, similar in form to *Matthiola* and *Cheiranthus,* and native to Europe and

Hesperis matronalis, The Sweet Rocket or Dame's Violet, has white to pale lilac flowers in May and June. It is sweetly fragrant especially in the evening when the humidity is high.

90

W. and N. Asia.

Perennial species cultivated *H. matronalis*, sweet rocket, dame's violet, dame's rocket, 2–3 feet, flowers fragrant in evenings, variable between white and lilac, May to July; vars. *candissima*, 15 inches, pure white, *purpurea*, purple. Double forms have appeared from time to time but are rare in cultivation.

Biennial *H. tristis*, 1–2 feet, flowers ranging from white through brick red to purple, fragrant at night, summer. *H. violacea*, 6–12 inches, violet flowers, June.

Cultivation *H. matronalis* and its forms will thrive in an ordinary soil with a regular moisture supply, in full sun. Plant in autumn or spring. Plants do best if fed by mulching with well-rotted manure in May. Remove spent flower stalks in autumn. Double varieties, when obtainable, benefit from occasional extra feeding with liquid manure during summer, and replanting in alternate years. Single varieties can be raised from seed sown ¼ inch deep in a warm spot outside in April. Transplant seedlings in June or July. Double varieties can be perpetuated only by cuttings, 3 inches long, taken from July to September, and inserted in a shaded position outdoors. Later cuttings, taken in September or October, require glass protection. Transplant in March. Established plants may be divided in autumn or spring. Biennial species are raised from seed sown direct in sunny flowering positions in July. Thin seedlings to 9 inches apart. *H. violacea* can be established on stone walls where a roothold permits.

Heuchera (hu-ker-a)

Named in honour of Professor J. H. Heucher, 1677–1747, German professor of medicine, and a botanist *(Saxifragaceae)*. Alum-root. A genus of hardy perennials with dainty, small, bell-like flowers in loose panicles which are produced over a long period, blooming on and off from spring through to autumn. The leaves are evergreen and the flowers are attractive when cut for indoor use.

Species cultivated *H. americana*, 18 inches, red flowers, summer. *H. × brizoides*, 1 foot, pink flowers, hybrid. This name includes various hybrids, such as 'Coral Cloud', raised from crossing *H. americana* with *H. sanguinea*. *H. micrantha*, 2 feet, pale yellow flowers, summer. *H. pubescens*, 1 foot, flowers deep pink marked with yellow, summer, foliage mottled with brown. *H. sanguinea*, coral bells, 12–18 inches, red flowers, summer; vars. include *alba*, white, *atrosanguinea*, deep red, *grandiflora*, larger flowers, coral-scarlet; *rosea*, rose-red; *splendens*, dark crimson. *H. villosa*, 1–3 feet, small pink flowers, late summer. Cultivars include 'Bressingham Blaze', 2 feet, coral flame; 'Bressingham Hybrids' a fine modern strain with flowers from crimson to pink in all shades. 'Carmen', 2 feet, intense carmine-pink; 'Edge Hall', 2 feet, bright rose;

'Oakington Jewel', 2½ feet, deep coral rose, coppery tinge; 'Pearl Drops', 2 feet, white; 'Pluie de Feu', 1½ feet, bright red; 'Red Spangles', 20 inches, crimson scarlet, 'Rhapsody', 20 inches, glowing pink; 'Scintillation', 2 feet, bright pink, tipped carmine; 'Snowflake', 2 feet, white; 'Sparkler', 2 feet, carmine and scarlet; 'Splendour', 2½ feet, salmon-scarlet.

Cultivation Heucheras do best in light, but rich well-drained soil, or in ordinary soil with peat added, in full sun or partial shade. Plants do not thrive on clay. Plant in autumn or spring. Increase by dividing plants from March to May, or by sowing seeds in spring under glass protection, in a light compost. Seedlings are best grown on in pots for planting out when a year old.

Hibiscus (hi-bis-kus)

An ancient Greek name given to a mallow-like plant *(Malvaceae)*. Rose mallow. A genus comprising species which are mostly greenhouse perennial plants in this country, though one popular species is a hardy deciduous shrub. There are also hibiscus which, in their natural environment, produce tropical fruits. These can be grown as flowering annuals. They are mostly natives of the tropics.

Greenhouse species cultivated *H. ×*

A form of Hibiscus rosa-sinensis, with showy flowers in summer.

archeri (H. schizopetalus × H. rosa-sinensis), 6–8 feet, flowers red, summer, similar to those of the latter parent, hybrid. *H. cameronii*, 2 feet, rose-coloured flowers, July, Madagascar. *H. coccineus*, 6 feet, scarlet flowers, July and August, South N. America. *H. manihot*, to 10 feet, large flowers, 6 inches across, yellow with maroon centre, late summer, China, Japan. *H. rosa-sinensis*, blacking plant, 8 feet, showy crimson flowers, 4–5 inches across, summer, Asia. Many named varieties of this species have been raised, with single, semi- and fully double flowers in various shades. *H. schizopetalus*, 10 feet, brilliant orange-red pendulous flowers, summer, east tropical Africa.

Annuals *H. diversifolius*, 6–8 feet, whitish-yellow flowers, maroon centre, strictly, a perennial, from Africa, Australia, Pacific Isles. *H. esculentus*, gumbo, okra, 2–3 feet, flowers yellow, crimson centre, summer, fruit cooked in America and the Tropics. *H. trionum*, bladder ketmia, 2 feet, white or yellow flowers, dark centres, summer, Africa. N. America.

Hardy *H. syriacus* (syn. *Althaea fruticosa*), shrubby althaea, shrub to 10 feet,

flowering late summer and autumn, variable in colour. Many good cultivars have been raised in shades of red and blue, double and single. These include: single, 'Blue Bird', strong blue; 'Coeleste', deep blue; 'Hamabo', pale blush with crimson basal blotch, 'Woodbridge', rich red; 'W. R. Smith', white, crinkled petals; double, 'Ardens', rose tinted violet; 'Duc de Brabant', red; 'Jeanne d'Arc', white.

Cultivation Greenhouse species are usually trained to a support from pots or borders containing a well-drained compost. Prune as required, in February. Water freely during summer, less in winter. Summer temperature can go up to 75 F (24 C), with a winter minimum of 55 F (13 C). *H. manihot* can be grown from seed annually for flowering as a tender pot plant. All are propagated by seeds sown in a temperature of 75°F (24 C) in March, or by cuttings of near-ripe shoots rooted in a close frame, in a temperature of 75 F (24 C) in spring or summer. Of the annual species, seed of *H. trionum* is sown out of doors in April in the flowering positions; seed of the others is sown in February in a temperature of 60–65 F (16–18 C). The seedlings are potted on and planted out in June. They require a warm sunny position. *H. syriacus* varieties do best in a light, rich soil. A sunny position is essential, and shelter provided by other shrubs is preferable. Plant in autumn or spring. Pruning should be limited to cutting out weak or unwanted wood immediately after flowering. Propagation is by cuttings placed in a sandy peat mixture in a cold frame in summer.

Hippeastrum (hip-pe-as-trum)

Derived from the Greek *hippeus*, a knight, *astron*, a star, possibly in connection with a resemblance to knights and stars as seen in *H. equestre (Amaryllidaceae)*. A genus of S. American, greenhouse, bulbous plants often referred to as *Amaryllis*, to which they are closely related. The large, showy, trumpet flowers of the hybrids, ranging in colour from the richest velvety crimson to the more delicate shades of pink and white, also bicolored, rank them among the most prized of winter and spring flowering pot plants for the greenhouse. Most of the hippeastrums offered in trade lists are of hybrid origin.

Species cultivated *H. aulicum*, 2 feet, crimson and purple flowers, winter. *H. pardinum*, 2 feet, flowers green, yellow and scarlet, spring. *H. pratense*, 2 feet, scarlet flowers, spring and early summer. *H. procerum*, 3 feet, bluish-mauve flowers, spring. *H. psittacinum*, 2 feet, flowers orange and scarlet, summer. *H. puniceum* (syn. *H. equestre*), Barbados lily, 18 inches, red flowers, summer. *H.*

reginae, 2 feet, red and white flowers, spring. *H. reticulatum*, 1 foot, flowers rose or scarlet, spring. *H. rutilum*, 1 foot, crimson and green flowers, spring. *H. vittatum*, 2 feet, flowers crimson and white, spring. Cultivars include 'Fire Dance', vermilion; 'Picotee', pure white, petals edged red; 'Queen of the Whites', faintly grey inside; 'Rilona', pure salmon; 'Wyndham Hayward', dark red, deeper inside.

Cultivation Pot new bulbs in January, choosing a pot size to leave no more than ¾ inch width of soil between the bulb and the pot rim. Bulbs should be planted to half their depth only, in John Innes No 2 compost, or a mixture of 2 parts of turfy loam, and 1 part of sharp sand, plus a double handful of bonemeal to each bushel of the mixture. Start them into growth in a temperature of 60°F (16°C) and give no water for the first two weeks, then start with small amounts. As flower spikes appear, within about 3 weeks of being started, the temperature can rise to 65–70°F (18–21°C) by day, with a night minimum of 60°F (16°C). Keep the plants well watered and fed with liquid manure while growing, syringeing twice daily and maintaining a humid atmosphere. Remove dead flower heads if seed is not required. Gradually reduce the water supply from July to September (according to the time the bulbs were started into growth) until the pots are stored dry in a minimum temperature of 40 F (4°C) for winter. Examine and repot as necessary in January, removing all dead roots. Renew the surface compost of bulbs not repotted, and start them into growth.

Hostas are useful plants to grow where there is light shade.

Young plants raised from seed should not be dried off for the winter until after their first flowering, but will need less water while the older bulbs are resting. Sow seed as soon as it is ripe, in a temperature of 60–65 F (16–18°C). Grow on in quantities in large pots or boxes until plants are about 6 inches tall, then pot them individually into 4-inch pots for their first flowering. Named or selected forms are increased by offsets removed and potted separately when the plants are inspected in January.

Hosta (hos-ta)

Commemorating Nicolous Thomas and Joseph Host, Austrian botanists of the late eighteenth and early nineteenth centuries *(Liliaceae)*. Plaintain lily. Hardy herbaceous plants, natives of E. Asia, principally Japan, valued for their large decorative leaves in variable greens, some glaucous, some with variegated patterns in green, silver and gold. Their flower racemes carry tubular, lily-like blooms mainly in summer, in shades purple-lilac or white. Preferring partial shade, hostas are ideal for mass planting in woodland settings or other shady places. Used in clumps they discourage weeds from establishing in border edges where they make bold contrast with taller growing plants. As moisture-loving plants they are excellent for planting by streams or on the banks of ponds. When grown in pots or tubs and watered adequately hostas are fine for use in terrace or patio gardening, or

Hibiscus 'Blue Bird', a good cultivar of the shrubby althaea, Hibiscus syriacus, syn. Althaea fruticosa.

in greenhouses and conservatories. Their leaves and flowers last well in water and are used widely in floral arrangements.

Species cultivated *H. albo-marginata* (syn. *H.lancifolia albo-marginata*), 1 foot, leaves with a narrow white border, flowers violet. *H. crispula* (syn. *H. fortunei marginato-alba)*, 2 feet, large leaves with a broad pure white border, flowers pale lilac. *H. decorata,*broad oval leaves, narrowly edged with white, flower stems to 2 feet, flowers dark violet. *H. fortunei,* 2 feet, broad glaucous green leaves, flowers pale lilac; var. *albo-picta,* leaves yellowish-white, darkening later with a green edge. *H. lancifolia* (syn. *H. japonica*), 1½ feet, narrow, dark green leaves, flowers pale lilac. *H. plantaginea,* 1½ feet, large glossy, green leaves, flowers white, fragrant, early autumn. *H. rectifolia,* 1½ feet, leaves green, 1 foot long, flowers deep lilac, carried well above the foliage. *H. sieboldiana,* 2 feet, leaves grey-blue, flowers lilac-white, one of the most handsome species. *H. tardiflora,* 1 foot, narrow, shining green leaves, flowers lilac-mauve, late September to November. *H. undulata,* 15 inches, leaves green with a white central band, wavy edged or spirally twisted, flowers pale lilac; var. *erromena* (syns. *H. japonica fortis, H. lancifolia fortis*), 3 feet, leaves rich green, flowers dark lilac. *H. ventricosa,* 2½ feet long, heart-shaped green leaves, flowers dark lavender.

Cultivation Ground preparation should include the addition of plenty of well-decayed manure, and peat if the soil tends to dry out quickly. Mulch annually in spring with compost or manure. Plant in autumn or spring. Keep moist during dry spells. For pot culture, use John Innes No 3 compost or 2 parts of loam to 1 part of decayed manure and sand mixture. Pot in March or April and overwinter in a cold frame. Hostas are easily increased by dividing clumps, preferably when new growth starts in spring. Seed is available of some species; this should be sown in John Innes seed compost in spring under glass.

Hyacinthus (hi-a-sin-thus)

Named after Hyakinthos who was accidentally killed by Apollo and, according to Greek mythology, hyacinths sprang up where his blood was shed *(Liliaceae)*. A genus of some 30 species of bulbous plants, those in cultivation being mainly from the Mediterranean region, while a few are to be found in Tropical and South Africa. The many splendid hybrid hyacinths used for forcing and bedding purposes have been raised, mainly in Holland, from *H. orientalis.* In 1686 the Leyden Botanic Garden listed 35 varieties, both single and double. At present there are about 180 named varieties, but the number offered commercially is much less.

Species cultivated *H. amethystinus,* 8

inches, bright Cambridge blue, in drooping, tubular heads in March and April (there is a white form) Pyrenees, where they flower in the alpine meadows in May and June. *H. azureus,* 8 inches, deep azure-blue heads in dense clusters, similar to muscari, in March and April, Asia Minor. There is a white form of garden origin. *H. orientalis,* common hyacinth, 6 to 12 inches, with fragrant, nodding, funnel-shaped flowers of various colours in April, Eastern Mediterranean. Rarely seen in cultivation, having been replaced by florists' varieties. From the form 'Albulus' has been developed the dainty white Roman hyacinth. Florists' hyacinths have much larger and more substantial heads of flower than the original species, and have fortunately retained the exquisite fragrance. Leading varieties: white; 'Carnegie', 'L'Innocence', 'Queen of the Whites': yellow; 'City of Haarlem', 'Yellowhammer': pink; 'Flushing', 'Lady Derby', 'Pink Pearl', 'Princess Margaret': red; 'Cyclops', 'Madame du Barry': pale blue; 'Delft Blue', 'Myosotis', 'Queen of the Blues', 'Winston S. Churchill': dark blue; 'King of the Blues', 'Ostara', 'Purple King'.

Cultivation Bedding hyacinths are best

The florists' Hyacinths are derived from *H. orientalis,* now rarely seen.

planted in late October about 4 inches deep in well-drained soil and in a sunny position. Space the bulbs about 8 inches apart for maximum colour effect. Bone meal forked into the soil before planting at the rate of 4 oz to the square yard will ensure good heads of flower in April. Larger, specially prepared bulbs are used for growing in bowls filled with bulb fibre or Levington Compost for flowering indoors. Plant the bulbs in September and October to provide a succession of bloom from January onwards. The nose of the bulb should stand about an inch above the surface of the bulb fibre. Once planted the bowls should be stood in a cool, airy, dark place for about eight weeks to ensure good root growth. The bulb fibre must be kept moist at all times but must not be saturated. Then bring the bowls into a warm room, or greenhouse, and give them a reasonably light position. Do not stand them near a radiator where the dry atmosphere might shrivel the growth. As top growth develops move them to a sunny position. Avoid extremes of room temperature; about

65–70°F (18–21°C) is desirable at this stage to bring them gently into flower. After flowering the bulbs may be planted outdoors as they will not be satisfactory for flowering again in bowls. Roman hyacinths may be brought into flower for Christmas if planted in bowls in August. Hyacinth species for flowering in the open should be planted in groups about 2 inches deep, or a little deeper on light soil, and in a sunny position. Propagate by seed sown in boxes containing light sandy soil in September and placed in a cold frame. The seedling bulbs should start to flower when three years old. Or by offsets removed from old bulbs when lifted. These offsets should be planted out in the open in a nursery bed in October.

Hymenocallis (hi-men-o-kal-iss)

From the Greek *hymen,* a membrane, *kallos,* beauty, referring to the cup-like membrane which unites the stamens *(Amaryllidaceae).* A genus of bulbous plants, for the warm greenhouse or stovehouse, containing both evergreen and deciduous species, all but one (which is a native of Guinea) coming from America, mainly from South America. They are grown for their large, usually white, fragrant flowers, borne in clusters at the ends of long stalks. They are closely related to *Ismene* and *Pancratium.*

Species cultivated *H. calathina,* leaves narrow, 1 foot long, flowers white, very fragrant, several on a stem opening in succession, spring, Peru, greenhouse. *H. crassifolia,* leaves to 2 feet long, 2 inches wide, flowers white, borne in a cluster of four on a 2-foot tall stem, summer, Kentucky. *H. eucharidifolia,* leaves to 1 foot long, flowers white, funnel-shaped, with green tube, 4 or 5 in a cluster, on a 1 foot tall stem, spring, Tropical America, stovehouse. *H. macrostephana,* leaves strap-shaped, to 3 feet long, flowers white, tube green, up to 8 flowers on a stem, South America, stovehouse. *H. ovata,* leaves strap-shaped, to 10 inches long, flowers white, fragrant, tube greenish, on a stem to 1 foot tall, autumn, West Indies, stovehouse. *H. speciosa,* leaves narrow to 2 feet long, to 4 inches wide, flowers white, very fragrant, on stems to 1 foot tall, West Indies, stovehouse.

Cultivation All species will succeed in a compost consisting of 2 parts of sandy loam, 1 part of well-rotted manure and ½ a part of sharp sand. Pot in March every three or four years and keep the pots in a sunny part of the greenhouse. Plants will need ample water from April to September, less from September to December and should be kept quite dry from December to April. Once plants have started into growth, in May, they may be fed once or twice a week with weak liquid manure. *H. crassifolia* may be grown on the edges of indoor pools. Stove species require a minimum

winter temperature of 55–65°F (13–18°C), ranging up to 80°F (27°C) in summer; greenhouse species should have a winter minimum of 45–50°F (7–10°C), rising in summer to 65°F (18°C). Propagation of all kinds is by offsets detached at potting time and potted up as recommended above. In the very mildest parts of the British Isles *H. calathina* may be grown out of doors in a sheltered position, although the bulbs should still be lifted and stored in dry sand during the winter months. Plants may be attacked by mealybug, but the pest can be controlled with nicotine washes.

Hypericum (hi-per-ik-um)

Possibly from the Greek *hyper,* over, *ereike,* heath *(Guttiferae* or *Hypericaceae).* St John's Wort. A large genus of annuals, herbaceous perennials, sub-shrubs and shrubs, mainly hardy, widely spread throughout the northern hemisphere, many species and hybrids grown in our gardens for their attractive, usually yellow flowers, with numerous

The fruits and flowers of the small shrub Hypericum elatum 'Elstead', as they appear in late summer.

stamens. The sub-shrubs and shrubs are mainly evergreen or nearly so.

Species cultivated *H. androsaemum,* tutsan, 1–3 feet, sub-shrub, flowers bright yellow, ¾ inch across, June to September, followed by conspicuous fruits first red, then black, native plant. *H. × arnoldianum,* 3–4 feet, flowers numerous, ½ inch or so across, yellow, hybrid. *H. calycinum,* Rose of Sharon, Aaron's beard, 1 foot, sub-shrub, trailing habit, often forming dense carpets, much used for ground cover on banks or under trees, flowers bright yellow, over 3 inches across, June to September, leaves often bronze in winter. *H. chinense,* 2–3 feet, flowers 2½ inches wide, bright yellow, August and September, hardy in the south. *H. coris,* 6 inches, sub-shrub, leaves heath-like, flowers ¾ inch across, golden yellow, summer, plant sometimes succumbs to severe frosts. *H. dyeri,* 3–4 feet, shrub, flowers yellow, to 1½ inches wide, summer. *H. elatum* (SE), 4–5 feet, shrub, flowers yellow, 1 inch across, summer, not quite hardy in cold gardens. *H. empetrifolium,* 1–1½ feet, sometimes prostrate shrub, flowers golden-yellow,

95

The commonly grown Candytuft,
Iberis umbellata, in mixed colours.

$\frac{1}{2}-\frac{3}{4}$ inch across, July to September,
half hardy except in the south; var.
prostratum, 2 inches, mat-forming plant,
flowers orange-yellow, June to August,
rock garden. *H. fragile*, 4–6 inches,
flowers yellow, 1 inch across, July and
August, rock garden. *H. frondosum* (D),
3–4 feet, shrub, leaves bluish-green,
flowers orange-yellow, to 2 inches
across, July and August. *H. galioides*,
2–3 feet, sub-shrub, flowers yellow, July
to October. *H. hircinum*, stinking St
John's Wort (SE), 2–4 feet, sub-shrub,
flowers bright yellow, July to September;
var. *pumilum*, dwarf, compact variety.
H. kalmianum (SE), 2–3 feet, shrub,
flowers bright yellow, to 1 inch across,
August. *H. kouytchense* (SE), 3–4 feet,
shrub, narrow leaves, sometimes turning
bronze in autumn, flowers golden-
yellow, to 2 inches across, June to
October. *H. × moserianum*, 15–18 inches,
shrub, flowers rich yellow, to 2½ inches
across, July to October, excellent ground
cover plant, hybrid; var. *tricolor*, leaves

variegated white and pink on green.
H. napaulense, prostrate shrub, stems
to 2 feet long, flowers golden, summer.
H. olympicum, 1–1½ feet, sub-shrub,
flowers yellow, to 2 inches across, July
and August. *H. patulum*, 1–3 feet, shrub,
flowers bright yellow, to 2 inches
across, July to October, hardy in the
south; vars. *henryi*, leaves colour well in
autumn, larger flowers, hardier;
'Hidcote', to 6 feet, flowers to 3 inches
across, the finest variety; *uralum*, 2–3
feet, flowers to 1 inch across. *H. ×
penduliflorum*, 4–5 feet, shrub, drooping
habit, flowers yellow, 2–2½ inches across,
summer to early autumn, hybrid. *H.
polyphyllum*, almost prostrate, herbaceous, stems to 1 foot long, flowers
golden yellow, sometimes splashed with
scarlet, to 2 inches across, July to
September, rock garden; var. *sulphureum*, flowers sulphur-yellow. *H.
prolificum*, 3 feet or more, flowers
yellow, to 1 inch across, July to September. *H. repens*, 3 inches, herbaceous
perennial, trailing, heath-like foliage,
flowers yellow, summer, rock garden.
H. reptans, 3 inches, shrub, leaves

colour well in autumn, flowers rich
yellow, to 1¾ inches across, June to
September, rock garden. H. 'Rowallane
Hybrid', 5–8 feet, shrub, flowers rich
yellow, to 2½ inches across, summer,
one of the finest hypericums, but needs
a sheltered situation except in the
mildest counties. *H. trichocaulon*, 3
inches, trailing shrub, flowers red in
bud, pale yellow when open, July and
August, rock garden. Other species and
hybrids may be offered by nurserymen
from time to time.

Cultivation Hypericums do well in
ordinary garden soil, especially if it
is well drained. With the exception of
H. androsaemum and *H. calycinum*,
they should be planted in sunny positions. The less hardy kinds do better
if given the protection of a wall or fence.
Plants should be set out in autumn or
spring. *H. calycinum* and *H. moserianum*
will benefit from hand pruning, cutting
the plants hard back in March to
promote new growth; other species
require little pruning other than the
removal of frost-damaged shoots in
spring. *H. calycinum* is easily propagated
by division in spring; other species may
be increased by seed, or by cuttings
taken in late summer and rooted in sandy
soil in a cold frame.

Iberis (eye-ber-is)
From the ancient name for Spain, Iberia
(Cruciferae). Candytuft. A genus of about
40 species of hardy annual, biennial,
evergreen and perennial herbs, from
Spain and the Mediterranean region. All
the species are easily grown, provided
they have plenty of sun in a well-drained
ordinary soil. The annuals make a
useful addition to the annual border,
while the perennials are invaluable as a
margin plant, or for rock gardens and
pillars where there is no fear of damp
conditions.

Species cultivated Annual *I. amara*, 1
foot, white, summer. *I. umbellata*, 1
foot, purple, summer; vars. *albida*, white,
'Dunnett's Crimson,' bright crimson;
'Giant Pink', rose-pink, 15 inches;
purpurea, dark purple. Shrubby *I.
saxatilis*, 4–6 inches, white, tinged purple,
May. *I. sempervirens*, 9 inches, white,
May; vars. 'Little Gem', 9 inches;
'Snowflake', 1 foot.

Cultivation For summer-flowering species
sow the annual and biennials ⅛ inch
deep, in March or April in light workable
soil or in August for flowering in spring.
Thin seedlings to 2 inches apart. Prevent
the ground from drying out or the plants
will run to seed. Remove seed pods.
Propagate the sub-shrubs by seed sown
in boxes in April by cuttings 1–2 inches
long in July–October, or by division of
roots October–March.

Impatiens (im-pa-she-ens, or im-pat-e-ens)
From the Latin *impatiens* in reference to
the way in which the seed pods of some

species burst and scatter their seed when touched *(Balsaminaceae).* Balsam, or Busy Lizzie. A genus of about 500 species of annuals, biennials and sub-shrubs mostly from the mountains of Asia and Africa. The succulent hollow stems are brittle and much branched. Few species are now cultivated, those that are may be grown in flower borders or under glass, or in the home as house plants.

Species cultivated *I. balsamina,* 1½ feet, rose, scarlet and white, summer, annual. greenhouse. *I. holstii,* 2–3 feet, scarlet, almost continuous flowering, half-hardy, greenhouse perennial; var. Imp Series F_1, low growing, brilliant mixed colours, in shade and sun. *I. petersiana,* 1 foot, reddish-bronze leaves and stems, red, almost continuous flowering, half-hardy, greenhouse perennial. *I. sultanii,* 1–2 feet, rose and carmine, almost continuous flowering, greenhouse perennial. *I. amphorata,* 5 feet, purple, August, annual. *I. roylei* (syn. *I. glandulifera),* 5 feet, purple or rose-crimson, spotted flowers in profusion, summer, annual.

Cultivation Greenhouse plants are potted in a mixture of equal parts loam, leaf-mould and sharp sand in well-drained pots, during February or March. They do best in well-lit conditions, and require moderate watering March–September, but only occasionally otherwise. They require a temperature of 55–65°F (13–18°C) from October to March, 65–75°F (18–24°C) March to June, and about 65°F (18°C) for the rest of the time. Pinch back the tips to make them bushy during February. Hardy species do well in ordinary soil in a sunny position, about 6 inches apart. *I. holstii* can be grown as a bedding plant and prefers light shade out of doors; it will tolerate varied temperatures. Propagate by seed in spring, sown in heat for the greenhouse species, and out of doors where the plants are to grow, for the hardy species, or by cuttings taken March to August, and placed in sandy soil in a temperature of 75°F (24°C).

Ipheion (i-fee-on)

The name is ancient Greek of obscure origin *(Liliaceae).* Now subdivided from the genus *Brodiaea,* native of North and South America. These bulbous plants were first introduced in the early nineteenth century. There is only one species cultivated, *I. uniflorum* (syn. *Brodiaea uniflora),* commonly called the spring starflower, 6 inches tall, pale blue or white, flowering March–April. It is not a corm, but a true bulb which smells of garlic when bruised. It requires a rich sandy loam in a warm well-drained border, provided it is not heavily manured. Plant the bulbs in September or October 4 inches deep and the same distance apart.

Ipomoea (i-po-mee-ya)

From the Greek *ips,* bindweed, and

Ipomoeas include some of the prettiest of all climbing plants.

homoios, like, in reference to the twining habit of growth *(Convolvulaceae).* A genus of 300 species of evergreen and deciduous climbing and twining herbs, including the sweet potato, and a few trees and shrubs, mostly from the tropics, Asia, Africa and Australia. First introduced in the late sixteenth century. Some of the greenhouse species, which like plenty of root room, are amongst the prettiest of climbing plants. They do best if planted in borders.

Species cultivated *I. batatas,* sweet potato, 2–4 feet, tubers edible, greenhouse. *I. tricolor* (syn. *I. rubro-caerulea),* red, summer, greenhouse. *I. hederacea,* Morning Glory, blue, summer, half-hardy. *I. purpurea,* purple, summer, half-hardy. *I. pandurata,* white and purple, perennial, summer.

Cultivation The seeds of annual species, whether greenhouse or half-hardy, should be sown (notch seed slightly with file) 2–3 in a 3-inch pot in a warm house in early spring using a compost of fibrous loam, decayed manure and lumpy leafmould, otherwise the plants are prone to a chlorotic condition. Transfer the plants to a larger pot as required, without disturbing the roots. Train up a tripod of canes until ready for planting. The half-hardy species may be planted out at the beginning of June in a sheltered border on a south wall. Evergreen ipomoeas may be propagated by cuttings or layers.

Iris (eye-ris)

From the Greek *iris,* a rainbow *(Iridaceae).* A large genus of bulbous, creeping and tuberous rooted perennials, some of which are evergreen. They are natives of the north temperate zone from Portugal to Japan. Among the most varied and beautiful of flowers, irises have been compared to orchids by some gardeners who, without the required greenhouse facilities for orchids, have decided to specialise in this most interesting genus. They may be divided into six main sections: tall bearded, dwarf bearded, beardless, Japanese, cushion or regelia and bulbous-rooted.

Tall bearded These are known best as the flag or German irises, flowering in May and June, and suitable for growing in ordinary, well-drained borders, especially on chalk. *I. flavescens,* 2½ feet, pale lemon flowers, almost white, probably of garden origin. *I. florentina,* 2½ feet, white flowers tinged pale blue on the falls, May; grown near Florence for orris root. This iris is the fleur-de-lis of French heraldry. *I. germanica,* common iris, 2–3 feet, lilac-purple flowers, May. Other forms slightly differently coloured.

Dwarf bearded Growing requirements similar to those of the previous section. *I. chamaeiris* (syn. *I. lutescens),* 10 inches, blue, purple, yellow or white, tinged and veined brown, April–May, S. Europe. Most variable in colour and growth, and frequently confused with *I. pumila. I. pseudopumila,* 6–9 inches, purple, yellow or white, April, southern Italy. *I. pumila,* 4–5 inches, almost

Iris xiphium, the Spanish Iris.

stemless and much variation in colour, April, Europe, Asia Minor.

Beardless Species suitable for moist soils, margins of pools or streams: *I. douglasiana,* 6–12 inches, very variable in colour, violet, reddish-purple, buff, yellow white, May, leaves evergreen and leathery, California. *I. fulva* (syn. *I. cuprea),* 2–3 feet, bright reddish-brown, June–July, southern United States; var. *violacea* is a violet form. *I. foetidissima,* gladwyn iris, 2 feet, lilac-blue flowers followed by an ornamental seed capsule with breaks to expose brilliant orange seeds in winter, Britain. *I. ochroleuca,* 4–5 feet, creamy-white, with orange blotch, June–July, western Asia Minor. *I. pseudacorus,* yellow flag or water flag, 2–3 feet, bright orange-yellow, May–June, Europe including Britain; *variegata,* with variegated leaves. *I. sibirica,* 2–3 feet, blue, purple, grey, or occasionally white, June–July, invaluable for waterside or border planting, central Europe and Russia. *I. versicolor,* 2 feet, claret-purple, May–June, N. America.

Species requiring sunny borders: *I. chrysographes,* 1½ feet, deep violet with golden veins, for a moist place, June, Yunnan. *I. innominata,* 4–6 inches, golden-buff veined light brown, and there are lavender, apricot and orange-yellow forms, Oregon; 'Golden River' is an attractive named variety. *I. japonica* (syn. *I. fimbriata),* 1–1½ feet, lilac, spotted yellow and white, evergreen, sage-green leaves, April, Japan, China. The form 'Ledger's Variety' is said to be hardier than the type. *I. tectorum,* 1–1½ feet, bright lilac, flecked and mottled with deeper shades. There is a white form. Lift and divide after second year's flowering, May–June, Japan. *I. unguicularis* (syn. *I. stylosa),* 1 foot, lavender, blue, November–March, ideal in dry poor soil against south wall. One of the gems of winter. Japanese: These species thrive in 2–4 inches of water and do well in moist soil or on the margins of ponds. *I. kaempferi,* clematis iris, 2 feet, varying shades lilac, pink, blue and white, June and July. *I. laevigata,* 2 feet, deep blue, June and July.

Cushion or Regelia Very beautiful, easily grown hardy irises, doing best in a calcareous soil in a sunny sheltered site. *I. hoogiana,* 1½–2 feet, soft lavender-blue flowers, early May, Turkestan. *I. korolkowii,* 1–1½ feet, chocolate-brown markings on creamy-white ground, May, Turkestan.

Bulbous-rooted Other than the Spanish and English iris which may be planted on sunny borders, this section includes choice kinds which may be grown in pots in the alpine house or in the rock garden. *I. bucharica,* 1–1½ feet, golden-yellow falls and small white standards, April, Bokhara. *I. bakeriana,* 4–6 inches, deep violet, with a touch of yellow on the falls, January–February, Asia Minor. *I. danfordiae,* short, bright yellow, January and February. A gem but rarely survives to flower a second year. *I. filifolia,* 1–1½ feet, deep purple, June, southern Spain. *I. graeberiana,* 6–8 inches, mauve falls marked cobalt-blue and whitish veins. For a sunny position, April, Turkestan. *I. histrioides,* short, dark blue, purple, January, Asia Minor. *I. reticulata,* 6 inches, violet, purple and yellow, February, Caucasus. *I. winogradowii,* 3–4 inches, light yellow, January–February, Caucasus. *I. xiphioides,* English iris, 1–2 feet, various colours, June–July, Pyrenees. *I. xiphium,* Spanish iris, 1–2 feet, various colours, white, yellow or blue, with orange patch on blade, May–June, south Europe and North Africa.

Miscellaneous *I. cristata,* 4–6 inches, pale lilac with deep yellow crest. A delightful miniature for a sink garden in full sun, May–June, eastern United States. *I. vicaria* (syn. *I. magnifica),* 2 feet, white, tinged pale blue, April, central Asia. Other species are offered by specialist nurseries.

Cultivation The most widely grown of this large and varied family are the tall bearded irises. These colourful hybrids have been developed by plant breeders from the long-cultivated, dark blue *Iris germanica.* This type of iris is one of the few plants that may be lifted, divided and replanted soon after it has finished flowering, preferably in July. By planting in July the fleshy rhizomes will soon make new roots in the warm soil and will be firmly established before the winter.

Choose a sunny well-drained site, and if planting in wet, heavy soil is unavoidable, build the bed up a few inches above the surrounding level. On light soil, add leafmould or peat, but manure should be used sparingly, for it will only induce soft growth. These irises like lime, so if the soil is deficient in this, work in some builder's rubble. Bonemeal and bonfire ash are both useful for feeding irises. It is important not to bury the rhizome when planting. In nature, it grows along the surface of the soil, and if the rhizome is planted too deep a year's flowering may be lost. On light soil it is necessary to plant somewhat deeper, otherwise the plants are liable to topple over. It is usual at planting time to cut back the sword-like leaves, but this can be overdone, for the plants do depend, to some extent, on the leaves to assist them in making new roots; drastic cutting back should be avoided. When planting, leave ample

Iris japonica, 'Ledger's Variety', an evergreen which requires a sunny border but is hardier than most of its type.

room between each variety so that the rhizomes will not require lifting and dividing for three years.

For those who do not know one variety from another the best way to start a collection is to buy 12 varieties in 12 different shades of colour from a specialist iris nursery. With some 300 different named varieties listed in iris catalogues it will be an easy matter to obtain individual varieties to increase the selection. Among outstanding modern hybrids are: 'Berkeley Gold', a handsome tall deep gold; 'Blue Shimmer', ivory-white dotted with clear blue; 'Caprilla', yellow-bronze falls and blue-lavender standards; 'Chivalry', a ruffled medium blue; 'Cliffs of Dover', creamy-white; 'Dancer's Vale', with pale violet dottings on a white ground; 'Desert Song', a ruffled cream and primrose; 'Enchanter's Violet', violet; 'Golden Alps', white and yellow; 'Green Spot'; 'Harriet Thoreau', a large orchid-pink self; 'Inca Chief', a ruffled bronze-gold; 'Jane Phillips', intense pale blue; 'Kangchenjunga', pure white; 'New Snow', pure white with bright yellow beard; 'Pegasus', a tall white: 'Party Dress', a ruffled flamingo-pink; 'Patterdale', a clear pale blue; 'Regal Gold', glowing yellow; 'South Pacific', a pale shimmering blue: 'Total Eclipse', almost black with a similar coloured beard, and many Benton hybrids raised in Suffolk by Sir Cedric Morris. Another amateur iris breeder in this country, the late Mr H. J. Randall, made crosses of many of the best American hybrids with remarkable success.

Waterside irises are charming beside a formal pool or in a wild garden. The June-flowering *I. sibirica* and its hybrids have long been appreciated. They thrive in boggy conditions, although they will grow in a border provided the soil is deeply dug, reasonably moist and in partial shade. In the bog garden they flower happily in full sun. Good hybrids include; 'Heavenly Blue', 'Perry's Blue' with china-blue flowers on 3-foot stems, and 'Eric the Red' with heavily veined wine-red flowers. The elegant *I. kaempferi*, of Japanese origin, is in all its glory in July. The flowers are large and handsome, with blends of colour of great charm. There are both single and double varieties in shades of velvety purple, rosy-lilac, plum and white shaded blue, for instance, 'Morning Mist', purple, flecked grey, and a double white, 'Moonlight Waves'. They must have lime-free soil and, for that matter, lime-free water. They like a rich loam with ample moisture during the growing season but moderately dry roots during the rest of the year. Another handsome Japanese species, *I. laevigata*, is sometimes confused with the clematis-flowered *I. kaempferi*. The large, brilliant, violet-blue flowers of *I. laevigata* are borne on 2-foot stems at intervals from June to September, above a mass of deep

Ixias, the South African Corn Lily, can be had in various colours.

green, arching foliage. It does well in a bog garden or in water up to 4 inches deep. The North American, claret-coloured water-flag, *I. versicolor,* is also a good waterside plant.

These waterside irises are best propagated by division of the roots in the spring, although it can be done in the autumn if necessary. They may also be raised from seed sown in a cold frame in the autumn in well-drained soil, covering them with ½ an inch of sifted soil. They should germinate in the spring, but some may prove erratic, so do not discard the pans in too much of a hurry.

The bulbous irises are quite distinct from the tall bearded and waterside irises. They are admirable for the rock garden or in a sunny well-drained border containing plenty of sharp sand or grit. Plant the bulbs in September. The miniature varieties which flower in February and March may also be grown in pans in a cold greenhouse or frame—the violet-blue *I. reticulata,* and its pale

blue variety 'Cantab', *I. histrioides major,* bright blue with yellow markings, and bright yellow *I. danfordiae,* are particularly suitable for this purpose. The taller growing Dutch, Spanish and English irises are easily grown in any reasonably good soil in the garden and are most useful for cutting. Plant the bulbs in October about 4 inches deep, in a sunny position. The Dutch irises produced by crossing *I. xiphium* with other bulbous species, flower in June, followed a little later by the Spanish and then the English. The English irises prefer a cool moist position and should be left undisturbed for three or four years before being lifted and divided. Dutch and Spanish irises should be lifted every year after the foliage has died down and stored until planting time. There is a good selection of named varieties to be found in bulb catalogues.

By making a careful selection of the

many different types of iris, including the April-flowering Juno species and hybrids which have brittle swollen roots needing careful handling, it is possible to have irises of one sort or another in flower for many months of the year.

Ixia (iks-e-a)
From the Greek word for bird-lime, *ixia*, referring to the sticky sap *(Iridaceae)*. African corn lily. Ixias are a genus of South African cormous plants, first introduced in the eighteenth century. They are half hardy bulbous plants with fragrant, very brightly coloured flowers.

Species cultivated *I. campanulata* (syn. *I. speciosa*), 1 foot, purple and crimson, summer. *I. maculata*, 1 foot, orange-yellow, spotted black, spring. *I. patens*, 1½ feet, pink, spring. *I. viridiflora*, 1 foot, green, spring.

Cultivation Ixias do best in a sunny south border in well-drained soil. They should be planted outdoors in November, 4–6 inches deep, and the corms covered with litter until early spring. In May mulch with well-rotted organic matter, and after flowering leave in the ground until the leaves have died down, before lifting. They should be replanted annually. In colder districts plant 6–8 corms in a 5-inch pot in October, and plunge in an ash bed until the spikes begin to appear. Then move the pots into a cool house. No heat is required, but draughts must be avoided. Propagate by seed sown in autumn, and seedlings grown on in pans to flower in third or fourth year, or by offsets planted at the same time as the corms; they will take two years to flower.

Jasminum (jas-min-um)
A Latinised version of the Arabic name, *ysmyn (Oleaceae)*. Jasmine. A large genus of climbing, trailing, and erect shrubby flowering plants native of tropical and sub-tropical regions, introduced in the mid-sixteenth century. There are both evergreen and deciduous species, some of which have very fragrant flowers.

Species cultivated Stove: *J. gracillimum*, 4 feet, white, fragrant, winter, Borneo. *J. sambac*, 6 feet, evergreen, white, fragrant, autumn, tropical Asia. Coolhouse: *J. grandiflorum*, 30 feet, white, most beautifully fragrant, flowers early summer (hardy in sheltered parts in warm climate). *J. mesnyi* (syn. *J. primulinum*), 6–10 feet, yellow, winter. Hardy: *J. nudiflorum*, winter jasmine, 15 feet, deciduous, yellow, November–March. *J. officinale*, common jasmine, 30–40 feet, white, June–September, very fragrant. *J. stephanense*, 15–20 feet, pale pink, very sweetly scented, flowers June–August.

Cultivation Stove and coolhouse species should be potted or planted in February or March, in a compost of equal parts by volume of loam, peat and leafmould with a little sand. Prune them to shape in February and train the shoots to walls, pillars, or trellis. Watering should be moderate during the winter, but copious between March and October. Keep the stove species in a temperature of 55–65°F (13–18°C), and the coolhouse species 45–55°F (7–13°C) from September to March. Syringe daily March–April and give adequate ventilation when weather permits. Coolhouse species benefit from standing outdoors in a sunny place from June–September. The hardy species should be treated as slightly tender in cold districts and the north. Plant them in ordinary soil, rich but well-drained, preferably at the base of south or south-west walls October–November or February–March. After flowering, remove only those shoots which have flowered. Propagate greenhouse species by cuttings of firm shoots in March–September placed in sandy peat in a temperature of 65–75 F (18–24°C) or hardy species by cuttings 3–6 inches long placed in sandy soil in a cold frame September–December, or by layering in spring or summer.

Kennedya (ken-ned-e-a)
Commemorating Mr L. Kennedy, an original partner in the old nursery firm of Lee and Kennedy, Hammersmith, 1775–1818 *(Leguminosae)*. Semi-woody and herbaceous climbers for the greenhouse which were introduced into this country in the late eighteenth century from Australia. They need a temperature of around 65 F (18°C) in the summer and about 50 F (10 C) in winter.

Species cultivated *K. coccinea*, 15 feet, semi-woody with scarlet flowers in spring. *K. nigricans*, purple-black, April. *K. prostrata*, prostrate twining plant, scarlet flowers, April–June. *K. rubicunda*, 15 feet, dark red, April–June.

The white flowers of Jasminum officinale are very sweetly fragrant, especially in the evening during late summer.

Cultivation Use a compost of peat, loam and silver sand or John Innes potting compost and pot in February or late spring. Little pruning is required except to remove straggly, unwanted growths, and water freely in summer. When in flower give a balanced fertiliser. Propagate by seeds sown in a sandy compost in spring, or by cuttings placed in well drained sandy peat and kept close in a temperature of 65 F (18°C).

Kniphofia (nif-of-e-a)

Commemorating a German professor of medicine, Johann Hieronymus Kniphof, 1704–63 *(Liliaceae)*. Red-hot pokers. These herbaceous perennials from South and East Africa and Madagascar are tolerant of wind, but dislike badly-drained soil. They are often seen in seaside gardens where the milder climate suits them well, as they are not altogether hardy and need protection in the winter in the colder districts. There are many good garden hybrids and varieties of *K. uvaria* in colours ranging from pure yellow through to reds, some of them being shaded in the spikes. The leaves are strap shaped.

Species cultivated *K. caulescens*, 4 feet, buff changing to red, autumn. *K. foliosa*, 3 feet, yellow tinged with red, late summer. *K. galpinii*, 2–3 feet, slender plant, orange-red flowers, late autumn. *K. macowanii*, 2 feet, slender plant, orange-red, late summer. *K. nelsonii*, 2 feet, bright scarlet tinged orange, autumn. *K. northiae*, 2 feet, foliage grey-green, flowers yellow at base changing to red up the spikes, October. *K. pumila*, 4 feet, grey-green foliage, orange-red flowers, to orange-yellow and finally yellowish-green, August. *K. uvaria*, 4 feet, coral red, late summer. A hardy species from which many hybrids and cultivars have been developed; they include 'Buttercup', 3½ feet, yellow; × *erecta*, 4 feet, orange-scarlet; 'Maid of Orleans', 4 feet, ivory-white; 'Mount Etna', 5 feet, large terra-cotta spikes; 'Royal Standard', 3 feet, deep gold; 'Yellow Hammer', 3 feet, yellow to orange.

Cultivation Plant in autumn or spring, choosing an open sunny position, but divide the clumps in spring as this becomes necessary. Kniphofias prefer a rich soil. Propagate by seed, but seedlings will not reach flowering size for about three years and then may not breed true.

Kochia (kok-e-a)

Named after W. D. J. Koch, 1771–1849, a German botanist *(Chenopodiaceae)*. A half hardy annual that is prized as a foliage plant; the small bushes, growing to as much as 3 feet, are green in the early stages, changing to crimson later in the season. They make ideal specimen

Kniphofia 'Springtime', typical of the Red-hot Pokers.

plants dotted in sunny annual or other border, and they also look well as a low background for smaller plants. Only one species is cultivated, *K. scoparia*, belvedere, seldom grown, and its variety *trichophila*, the summer cypress.

Cultivation Seeds are sown in March in slight heat, and the seedlings pricked out and transplanted into their permanent quarters in June after being hardened off. They also make good plants for the unheated greenhouse.

Laelia (ley-lee-a)

From the Latin *Laelia*, the name for a vestal virgin, because of the delicacy of the flowers *(Orchidaceae)*. An important genus of epiphytic tropical orchids from South America closely related to *Cattleya*, with which they have been crossed to produce the many hundreds of varieties of × *Laeliocattleya*. One section has plants very similar in habit to *Cattleya*, especially in the clavate (club-shaped) pseudobulbs and in the leaves; another section has rather short pseudobulbs with long slender spikes of several brightly coloured flowers, and yet another section has plants of dwarf habit and large flowers, often in pairs.

Species cultivated *L. albida*, long spikes of white rose-flushed flowers, winter, Mexico. *L. anceps*, long spikes of flowers varying from rose to purple, winter, Mexico. *L. autumnalis*, long spikes of rose-purple flowers, winter, Mexico. *L. cinnabarina*, long spikes of brilliant orange-red flowers, spring, Brazil. *L. crispa*, clavate pseudobulbs, flowers white, flushed purple, lip purple, summer, Brazil. *L. gouldiana*, long spikes of deep rose-purple flowers, winter, Brazil. *L. grandis*, clavate pseudobulbs, flowers yellowish and rose-purple, summer, Brazil. *L. harpophylla*, slender pseudobulbs, flowers orange-red, winter, Brazil. *L. jongheana*, short plants, flowers lilac-purple, spring, Brazil. *L. lobata*, clavate pseudobulbs, flowers rose-purple, lip bright purple, summer, Brazil. *L. perrinii*, clavate pseudobulbs, flowers rose-purple and crimson, winter, Brazil. *L. pumila*, and its varieties *dayana* and *praestans*, dwarf plants, large rose-purple to bright purple flowers, Brazil. *L. purpurata*, clavate pseudobulbs, flowers white, flushed rose, lip deep red-purple, summer, Brazil. *L. rubescens*, long spikes of lilac-rose flowers, winter, Mexico. *L. speciosa*, whitish lilac and purple, summer, Brazil. *L. tenebrosa*, clavate pseudobulbs, flowers yellow-bronze and brownish-purple, summer, Brazil. *L. xanthina*, clavate pseudobulbs, flowers yellow lip, whitish flushed purple, summer, Brazil.

Cultivation A general compost of 3 parts of osmunda fibre and 1 part of sphagnum

moss in pots or pans is suitable. The clavate pseudobulbed group require a minimum winter temperature of 55 F (13 C) and a resting period with little water. The section with long spikes, such as *L. anceps*, should have a cool winter temperature and a very decided rest; the dwarf types prefer a warmer winter temperature and little or no resting period, and are best hung near the glass. All types appreciate warm, moist summer conditions with light shading. Propagation is by division of plants at potting time.

Lamium (la-me-um)
From the Greek *laimos*, a throat, in reference to the appearance of the flowers (*Labiatae*). Dead nettle. Belonging to the dead nettle family, this herbaceous perennial, from Europe and temperate Asia, is useful as ground cover where other plants, perhaps, would not grow.
Species cultivated *L. galeobdolon*, 1–1½ feet, yellow, June–July, a native plant; var. *variegatum*, white variegation on foliage. *L. maculatum*, 8–12 inches, white central stripe on leaves, purple, pink or white flowers, summer, a native plant; var. *aureum*, golden leaves. *L. orvala*, 2 feet, rosy-lilac, summer.
Cultivation Any garden soil will suit these plants, but *L. maculatum* does best in moist soils, lamiums can be planted in the autumn or spring and increased by division at any time of the year.

Lathyrus (lath-eye-rus)
Lathyrus is the ancient Greek name for the pea (*Leguminaceae*). A genus of hardy annual and herbaceous perennial climbers, from temperate zones and tropical mountains. The sweet pea, *L. odoratus*, is dealt with in detail under

1 Laelia anceps and 2 L. gouldiana are two attractive Mexican orchids.

Sweet peas.
Species cultivated Annual: *L. sativus azureus*, 2 feet, blue, June–July, southern Europe. *L. tingitanus*, 6 feet, purple and red, summer, North Africa.
Perennial: *L. grandiflorus*, 5 feet, rosy carmine, summer, southern Europe. *L. latifolius*, 10 feet, everlasting pea, bright carmine, August; var. *albus*, white flowers. *L. magellanicus*, 8 feet, bluish-purple, summer to early autumn, Straits of Magellan. *L. pubescens*, 5 feet, pale blue, mid to late summer, Chile. *L. rotundifolius*, 6 feet, pink, summer, Asia Minor. *L. splendens*, sub-shrub, 1 foot, carmine, summer, California. *L. undulatus*, 3 feet, rosy-purple, early summer, Turkey. *L. vernus*, 1 foot, purple and blue, spring, Europe.
Cultivation Any good rich soil is suitable. Plant the perennials in the autumn or spring, choosing a sunny position where the plants can climb over a trellis, wall or other support. These plants need a lot of water in the growing season and they should be fed during the summer with liquid manure of a balanced fertiliser. In the autumn cut down the stems and top-dress with manure in the spring. The perennial species are propagated by seeds or by division of the roots in the spring. The annual species are propagated by sowing seeds in spring, either under glass and then planting the seedlings out of doors after they have been hardened off, or out of doors where they are to flower.

Lavatera (la-vat-ear-a)
Commemorating a seventeenth-century Swiss naturalist J. K. Lavater (*Malvaceae*). A genus of some 20 species of

annuals, biennials, herbaceous perennials and sub-shrubs, mostly from southern Europe and the Mediterranean region. All bear mallow-like flowers.
Species cultivated *L. trimestris* (syn. *L. rosea*), 3–5 feet, pink, summer, annual; var. *alba splendens*, white. Named cultivars include 'Loveliness', 2 feet, deep rose, and 'Sunset', 2 feet, deeper in colour. *L. arborea*, tree mallow, 6–10 feet, flowers pale purple, summer to autumn, biennial; var. *variegata*, white variegated leaves. *L. cashmiriana*, 5–6 feet, pale rose, summer, perennial, India. *L. assurgentiflora*, 10 feet, purple, July, shrub, California. *L. olbia*, 6 feet, reddish purple, June–October; var. *rosea*, rose-pink.
Cultivation All these lavateras like hot, dry positions and make good plants for the back of a border. The tree mallow is not entirely hardy and may be cut down by frosts, but it usually shoots up again from the base in the spring. The perennial species are planted out in June from sowings made under glass in February or March in a temperature of 60 F (16 C) or from sowings made out of doors in late spring. The variegated tree mallow is propagated by cuttings taken in mid-summer and kept in a closed propagating case until rooted. The annual species are sown in September or April in the beds or borders where they are to flower.

Leeks
The leek is a valuable vegetable for winter and spring use and is often grown to replace onions when the last of the stored crop has been eaten. Sow the seeds outdoors in late March or early April on a prepared bed. A seed bed prepared for cabbage and lettuce sowings is suitable. Prevent annual weeds from

smothering the grass-like seedlings, and water, should May be a dry month. The seedlings are dug up and moved to their growing positions in June or July. June planting is preferable.

For leeks of good size, a well-manured or well-composted soil is necessary. Mark the rows with the garden line at 18 inches apart. The usual planting tool is a blunt-nosed dibber, such as may be made from an old spade handle. Make the planting holes 9 inches apart in the rows and sufficiently deep so that only the tops of the plants show above the soil when one plant is dropped into each hole. After planting, simply fill the holes with water. This washes sufficient soil down on to the roots; more loose soil fills the holes when the rows are hoed a week or two later. Following planting, inspect the bed for a day or two and replant any plants which may have been pulled out of the holes by birds. Mulching with sedge peat or, on rich soils, with weathered sawdust, in late July, saves all further cultivation.

Leeks are left in the soil throughout the winter in the same way as parsnips. Should the ground be needed for another crop in February or March, any leeks still in the soil may be lifted and heeled into a trench. All leeks should be used before May.

The leek is a favourite vegetable among exhibitors and for this purpose, seeds are sown in gentle heat in the greenhouse during January or February. The seedlings are pricked off into fairly deep trays and each seedling is allowed 1½ square inches of space. The seedlings are hardened off gradually in the cold frame for planting out in early May. Some keen showmen prefer to prick the seedlings into small clay pots and to pot on into the 5-inch or 6-inch sizes.

To obtain leeks blanched to a length of 2 feet or more, the plants are grown in trenches prepared similarly to those in which single rows of celery are grown (see Celery). The preparation of the trenches calls for deep digging and the addition of well-rotted manure or alternatives such as garden compost or spent mushroom compost. The trenches are spaced 3 feet apart with 12 inches between the plants. Soil from between the rows is drawn up towards the plants as they grow to form a steep ridge. Liquid manure feeds are given as well as frequent top-dressings.

'Musselburgh' and 'The Lion' are good standard varieties. The pot leek is a northern speciality.

Leontopodium (le-on-to-po-dee-um)

From the Greek *leon*, a lion and *pous*, a foot, because the shape of the flowers and leaves was supposed to resemble a lion's paw (*Compositae*). A genus of a few species of low-growing hardy herbaceous plants, closely related to *Gnaphalium*, widely distributed, as far east as China, west to the Andes, and as high up

Leontopodium alpinum is the well-known Edelweiss, one of the most popular plants for the rock garden.

as the Swiss Alps. One species, *L. alpinum*, known as edelweiss, is almost too well-known to need a description.

Species cultivated *L. alpinum*, edelweiss, 6 inches, greyish leaves with white down, yellow, star-shaped flowers surrounded by white bracts, June–July. *L. haplophylloides* (syn. *L. aloysiodorum*), 6 inches, leaves grey-white, flowers similar to above, summer, plant lemon-scented. *L. japonicum*, 9 inches, leaves dark shining green above, silvery below, flowers white, May. *L. palibinianum*, 9 inches, white, May, rare. *L. sibiricum*, 9 inches, white flowers, nearly twice as big as those of *L. alpinum*, May. *L. stracheyi*, 6 inches, similar to *L. alpinum*.

Cultivation Plant in the spring in a sunny, well-drained position in the rock garden and protect the plants from excessive rain in the winter by suspending a sheet of glass over them. They like a porous, gritty compost that contains a good deal of sand. Propagate by seeds sown in the spring in pans of leafmould,

loam and granite chips. Keep the pans in a cool shady position. When the seedlings are large enough to handle, plant them out into their flowering positions. Established plants may also be divided in the spring.

Leptosyne (lep-to-sy-knee)

From the Greek *leptos*, slender, describing the growth of these plants (*Compositae*). A small genus of hardy annuals and perennials that deserve to be better known, as they are showy in the garden and good as cut flowers. They are very similar in appearance to *Coreopsis*, to which they are closely related, and are natives of America.

Species cultivated Annual: *L. calliopsidea*, 1½ feet, yellow, late summer. *L. douglasii*, 1 foot, *L. stillmanii*, 1½ feet, bright yellow, autumn. Perennial: *L. maritima*, 1 foot, yellow, autumn.

Cultivation Any ordinary soil will suit these plants but they like an open, sunny position. Sow seeds of the annual species in the spring in the open ground where the plants are to flower, or sow them under glass and transplant the seedlings to their flowering positions in late May or early June. The perennial species can be planted in the autumn or spring and they are either raised from seed or from division of the plants in the autumn or spring. Cuttings of young growths can be taken and rooted in a frame.

Lettuce

This vegetable (*Lactuca* species and varieties) is the basic ingredient of most salads and a continuous supply is important. By full use of the greenhouse, cold frames and cloches, the good gardener is able to raise lettuces for at least six months of the year. The production of winter and early spring lettuces is not easy and these crops are a challenge to the gardener. Certain hardy varieties for April cutting may be over-wintered in the open in favourable areas, but much depends on the winter weather following the autumn sowing.

Lettuces fall into three groups—cabbage, cos and loose-leaf. The cabbage kinds are subdivided into crispheads and butterheads. Those sold by the greengrocer are almost always butterheads because crispheads do not travel well and wilt rather quickly after harvesting. The cos varieties have long, boat-shaped, very crisp leaves and they are preferred by many for their fine flavour. Loose-leaf lettuces are more popular in the United States than here, although one American variety, 'Salad Bowl', is liked by many gardeners.

Any check to steady growth is liable to result in rather poor lettuces. Water is very important, but the soil must be sufficiently porous to allow for good drainage. Although late summer lettuces will tolerate the shade cast by rows of taller vegetables, earlier sowings demand an open, unshaded site. The soil should have been dug well during the winter digging programme and organic manures in the form of farmyard manure, garden compost or spent hops applied generously. These manures are invaluable in helping to retain soil moisture and, at the same time, increasing the porosity of heavy soils.

The first sowings may be made under glass in January or February and a greenhouse temperature of 55–60 F (13–16 C) is suitable. Sow thinly and not deeply in shallow trays and prick off into deeper ones as soon as possible after germination, allowing each seedling 2 square inches of space. Harden off in the cold frame in late March and plant out on a mild day in April. Plant with a ball of the compost mixture adhering to the roots at 12 inches apart in the row. If cloches are available, the small plants may be set out beneath them in late March.

Outdoor sowings may be made in March in the south-west and during the first two weeks of April in other areas. Here again, cloches are useful. Sow as thinly as possible in 1-inch deep drills spaced 15 inches apart. Keep down weeds by hoeing and thin the seedlings to 1 foot apart when three or four leaves have formed. The thinnings from March, April and May sowings may be used to make further rows.

A sowing made in late July provides lettuces in November and December but here again, the weather plays an important part. The rows need cloche protection from October onwards. For early spring supplies, sow in the cold frame in September and, subsequently, replant the seedlings in the greenhouse or in frames. Alternatively, sow in the greenhouse in early October and transplant when the plants have four leaves. Deep planting at any time is unwise. It is particularly dangerous where lettuces are to be over-wintered. Over-crowding must also be avoided and correct ventilation is very important.

Birds often peck at lettuce seedlings and plants. A few strands of black cotton fixed above the rows prevents this trouble. Although present-day cos varieties are reputed to be self folding, better hearts form if the plants are tied rather loosely with raffia or soft string. Loose-leaf varieties are less prone to bolt than cabbage and cos plants. Instead of cutting the whole plant, leaves are picked as and when required from loose-leaf varieties.

Among the very many varieties on offer, the following may be relied upon for worth while crops.
For early sowings under glass 'May Queen' (syn. 'May King').
For outdoor sowings from March until July 'Sutton's Improved', 'Unrivalled', 'Trocadero', 'Webb's Wonderful', 'Giant White Cos', 'Salad Bowl'.
For sowing under glass for early spring cutting 'May Queen', 'Cheshunt Early Giant', 'Kordaat', 'Kloek'.
To stand the winter out of doors 'Stanstead Park', 'Arctic King', 'Brown Cos'.

Leucogenes (lew-codge-en-ees)

From the Greek *leuco*, white, *eugenes*, noble, an apt description of the white-felted bracts which surround the flowers (*Compositae*). These plants have the common name of New Zealand edelweiss because of the similarity of their flowers to those of their European namesakes of the genus *Leontopodium*, which however they surpass in beauty. They are alpines from the mountains of New Zealand, with prostrate stems and silvery foliage. These stems elongate and carry the inflorescences whose beauty is derived from the row of petal-like, white-felted bracts which surround the tiny, rather insignificant yellowish flowers.
Species cultivated *L. grandiceps*, to 8 inches, densely tufted growth, leaves tiny, silvery on both sides, flowerheads about 1 inch across. *L. leontopodium*, to 8 inches, leaves small, larger than in the above species, flowerheads similar to those of the edelweiss, up to 1 inch across.
Cultivation These are alpine plants which are easier to grow in the moister summer atmosphere of the north of this country than in the drier south. They are plants for a scree or for planting in a rock crevice where they have perfect surface drainage. The soil should be lime free, containing some peat, plenty of grit and should never be allowed to dry out. Where summer humidity is high, plant in full sun, but in dry areas plant in light shade or in a northerly aspect. If grown on the flat it is usual to suspend a sheet of glass over the plants during the winter to shed excess moisture rather than to give protection against cold.

L. leontopodium is possibly the choicer plant and is often grown as a pan specimen in the alpine house merely for the sake of its rosettes of silvery foliage which are attractive at all times, even when not in flower. For pot culture, use a mixture of equal parts of lime-free soil, peat and fine gravel; pot firmly and dress the soil surface with gravel chips. Plunge in moist peat in a cool position, housing the plants in a frame or glasshouse during the winter. Plants are easily propagated by seed which should be sown on a gritty compost and never allowed to dry out. Cuttings of non-flowering shoots taken in summer and inserted into a mixture of sand and peat in a frame or cool glasshouse, will root without much difficulty.

Leucojum (lew-ko-jum)

From the Greek *leukos*, white, and *ion*, a violet which may be because of the scent and colour of the flower (*Amaryllidaceae*). Snowflake. A small genus of hardy bulbous plants whose flowers look very like large snowdrops, from Central Europe and the Mediterranean region.
Species cultivated *L. aestivum*, summer snowflake, 2 feet, white, tipped green, May. *L. autumnale*, 8 inches, white tinted pink, autumn. *L. vernum*, spring snowflake, 1 foot, white and green, early spring.
Cultivation Plant the bulbs of *L. aestivum* and *L. vernum* in September, placing them 3 inches deep. Those of the autumn-flowering snowflake should be planted in mid summer. They resent disturbance and need dividing only about every five years when the bulb clusters can be divided and replanted. They are shade lovers and do best in light shade in leafy soil.

Lewisia (lew-is-e-a)

Commemorating Captain Meriwether Lewis, 1774–1809, of the Lewis and Clark expedition across America (*Portulacaceae*). A small genus of hardy herbaceous perennials from western North America, mostly grown in the rock garden. They are pretty little plants, with flowers with strap-shaped petals in shades of pink,

rose and salmon; there are also white-flowered species. Their growing period above ground is short, about six weeks.
Species cultivated *L. brachycalyx*, 3 inches, flowers white or pink, May; var. *angustifolia*, leaves narrower. *L. columbiana*, 9 inches, flowers white or pink, veined dark red, May; var. *rosea*, flowers purple-red. *L. cotyledon*, 9 inches, flowers white, pink veined, May; 'Apricot' is an apricot-yellow cultivar. *L. heckneri*, 9 inches, salmon-pink, May. *L. howellii*, 3 inches, apricot-pink, early summer. *L. leeana*, 3–4 inches, flowers pink, early summer. *L. rediviva*, 1–2 inches, soft pink, leaves wither before flowers appear, May–June. *L. tweedyi*, 6 inches, flesh-pink, May; var. *rosea*, flowers rosy-pink. A number of hybrids have been raised from various species and are available either as hybrid races such as 'Birch Hybrids' in colours ranging from pink to crimson, or in individual colours such as 'Old Rose', rich red; 'Pinkie', clear pink; 'Rose Splendour', clear rose; 'Trevosia', salmon red. All grow 6–12 inches tall.
Cultivation Lewisias grow best in soil containing equal parts of sandy loam, peat and sand in a moist and sunny position. Most of them prefer to be planted in vertical or horizontal crevices in walls. Plant in September–October or March–April, and keep well watered in dry weather. Propagation is by seeds sown in well-drained pans of sandy soil during the spring; they should be kept in the cool and the shade. They may also be propagated by careful root division in spring.

Ligularia (li-gu-lair-ee-a)
From the Latin *ligula*, a strap, referring to the strap-shaped ray florets (*Compositae*). A genus of about 80 species of herbaceous perennials, formerly included in *Senecio* but now placed in their own genus. These handsome members of the daisy family from the temperate zones of the Old World grow best in damp situations. In recent years they have been considerably hybridised and some striking varieties have been obtained.
Species cultivated *L. dentata* (syn. *L. clivorum*), 4–5 feet, orange-yellow, July–September, China; cultivars include 'Desdemona', large, heart-shaped leaves with a purple tinge, orange flowers; 'Gregynog Gold', 4 feet, large rounded leaves, orange-yellow flowers in pyramidal spikes; 'Othello', leaves veined purple, and large orange flowers. *L. x hessei*, 5 feet, flowers orange, August–September. *L. hodgsonii*, 1½ feet, rounded leaves, orange-yellow flowers. *L. japonica*, 3–5 feet, orange-yellow flowers, July, Japan. *L. przewalskii*, 3–4 feet, stems purple tinged, deeply cut leaves, tapering spikes of small yellow flowers, June and July; 'The Rocket', 5 feet, orange, August, is a cultivar. *L. tussilaginea*, 1–2 feet, softly hairy stems, light yellow flowers, August, Japan. *L.*

veitchiana, 4–6 feet, leaves large, roughly triangular, yellow flowers in long flat spikes, July and August. *L. wilsoniana*, 5–6 feet, similar to *L. veitchiana*, flower spikes more branched, June.
Cultivation These hardy perennials grow best in a good loamy soil, if possible fairly moist. They do well in slight shade, otherwise any position will suit them. *L. japonica* and *L. dentata* are most successful at the edge of a pool or stream. Mulching occasionally with rotted garden compost or similar material is beneficial. They are propagated by dividing the crowns in autumn or spring, by taking cuttings in spring, or by sowing seed in spring in the cold greenhouse or out of doors in early summer.

Lilium
Connected with the Persian word *laleh*, and the Greek word *leiron*, both meaning lily, referring to *L. candidum* whose cultivation goes back 35 centuries in parts of western Asia. A genus of 85 or more species of bulbous plants confined to the northern hemisphere, but distributed in a ring within the temperate zone around it. Of the recognised species there are approximately 49 Asiatic, 24 North American, 10 European and 2 Eurasian in origin.
Species cultivated *L. amabile*, 3 feet, intense lacquer-red blooms, spotted black, 3 inches wide of pendent bowl or Turk's cap form, with sharply reflexed margins, June and July. Does well in full sun and stands some drought. Stem roots are produced sparsely or are lacking; forms underground stem bulbs in profusion; vars. *luteum*, one of the loveliest of yellow-flowering species; *unicolor*, an unspotted orange-red. *L. auratum*, 4–7 feet, the golden-rayed mountain lily which created a sensation when first shown at the Royal Horticultural Society's Hall in 1862. It has large, 9-inch wide, bowl-shaped blooms in August, strongly scented, white with a yellow stripe and purple spots. It likes deep, rich, well-drained, lime-free soil and should be planted shallowly where it can have a moist, cool, growing season, Japan; vars. *platyphyllum* is superior though similar; *virginale* is a handsome, pure white, tall form with very broad glossy leaves. The cultivar 'Tom Thumb' grows only 16 inches tall and the blooms are only 4 inches across, but it is a difficult variety to grow. *L. brownii*, 3–4 feet, the trumpet lily of China, producing large fragrant, funnel-shaped flowers in July. These are creamy-white, shaded brown externally, with brown anthers. It is a stem-rooting type and should be planted deeply. Top dress with leafmould annually; var. *australe* is even more elegant and intensely coloured, forming many stem bulblets just under the soil. *L. callosum*, var. *flaviflorum*, 3 feet, bears 5–12 scentless, nodding pale lemon-yellow

flowers in August. It likes an ordinary sunny position and is stem rooting, Okinawa. *L. canadense*, 3 feet, orange-yellow, open bell-shaped, pendulous, 5–6 per stem, July, an easy lily with a preference for moist, peaty soil. North America. *L. candidum*, 4–5 feet, the famous madonna lily much associated with Christian symbolism. It was the only lily of the English garden until the sixteenth century. It is rather difficult to grow because it often gets disease, particularly botrytis. Plants are best raised from seed, or ensure that bulbs are obtained from a clean source. Bulbs should be planted immediately after flowering. The bowl-shaped flowers are pure white and large. It likes moderately heavy soil, but a well-drained site and some lime. *L. cernuum*, 2–3 feet, bears soft lilac-pink nodding blooms in July, fragrant, well reflexed, with purple spots. Very hardy, stem rooting, likes full sun but avoid lime. Suitable for the rock garden or among low-growing shrubs, Korea, Manchuria. *L. chalcedonicum*, scarlet Turk's cap lily, 2½–3½ feet, bright scarlet drooping flowers, up to 6 per stem, July, Greece. *L. concolor*, 1–2 feet, scarlet, starry flowers, 5–7 per stem, slightly fragrant, China; var. *coridion*, flowers larger, bright yellow, centre spotted brown, Mongolia. *L. croceum* (syn. *L. bulbiferum croceum*), orange lily, 3–4 feet, bright orange, 15–18 per stem, June and July, central Europe. *L. dauricum*, 2–2½ feet, red or scarlet, brown spotted, several on a stem, August, lime-free soil, northeast Asia; vars. *wallacei*, orange spotted maroon; *wilsonii*, apricot with yellow centres, black spots. *L. davidii*, 4–6 feet, up to 20 nodding, much reflexed, Turk's cap, bright orange-red flowers marked with black spots, in July and August, stem rooter, China. This species rarely suffers from virus; var. *willmottiae*, 3–4 feet, flowers brown-spotted, up to 30 per stem, sun or partial shade. *L. duchartrei*, 2–3 feet, white, reflexed blooms with purple spots, stem rooting, tolerates lime and increases quickly, a very attractive, graceful, small lily, China. *L. formosanum*, 5 feet, very graceful, with long tubular, funnel-shaped flowers, white with an irregularly coloured wine-purple exterior, late summer. They open widely at the mouth which has reflexing margins. They are fragrant, 6–8 inches long, poised horizontally. Heavily stem rooting, likes lime-free soil, flowers from seed very quickly. Not really hardy, best grown in the border or pots in a greenhouse. An excellent florist's lily, Formosa; 'Price's Variety' (var. *pricei*) has striped buds; 'Wallace's Variety' is pure white; 'Wilson's Variety' is the latest flowering of all lilies, white. *L. hansonii*, 4 feet, golden-yellow, spotted

The panther Lily, L. pardalinum, has long recurved orange-pink flowers.

brown, Turk's cap type, up to 12 per stem, June, Korea. *L. henryi*, 6 feet, a very late flowering, tall, graceful lily, very hardy and vigorous. Bears 15–20 orange yellow nodding blooms. Easy to grow, stem rooting, dislikes the acidity of peaty soils but otherwise lime is immaterial, likes partial shade, China. *L. humboldtii*, 4–5 feet, flowers reddish-orange, maroon-spotted, reflexed, up to 40 per stem, July, woodland conditions, California; var. *magnificum*, flowers deeper in colour, more heavily spotted, prefers sunny position but roots shaded. *L. japonicum*, 3 feet, rose pink to pale pink, trumpet-shaped, June, woodland in light soil, or cool greenhouse, Japan. *L. kelloggii*, 2 feet, Turk's cap shaped blooms, delightfully fragrant, white, turning to delicate pink and then dull purple, bright orange pollen. Blooms in July, must not be allowed to become short of water in the summer, North America. *L. lankongense*, 2–3 feet, rosy-purple, centres spotted crimson, Turk's cap type, up to 36 per stem, July, China. *L. leichtlinii*, 3–4 feet, citron-yellow, spotted purple, reflexed, July and August, stem-rooting, Japan; vars. *maximowiczii*, 2–3 feet, orange-red, spotted brownish-purple, lime-free soil, plant up to 8 inches deep depending on soil; *maximowiczii wadai unicolor*, 3–5 feet, salmon-red, unspotted, pendent. *L. longiflorum*, 2–3 feet, the Easter Lily, widely grown for floral work. Up to 5 large, fragrant, white funnel-shaped flowers. Stem rooting, does not mind lime, not properly hardy, best grown under glass, Formosa; 'Ace' is a 1-foot high cultivar, ideal for growing in pots; var. *formosum*, 2 feet, free-flowering, suitable for early forcing. Cultivars include 'Croft', 1½–2 feet; 'Holland's Glory', up to 12 flowers per stem. *L. mackliniae*, 1½ feet, a very slender-stemmed lily, with delicate pink bell-shaped flowers 2 inches across, in June, Manipur. *L.* × *maculatum*, hybrid group, with numerous cultivars, including *alutaceum*, 9 inches, flowers apricot-yellow, spotted black, June and July; *bicolor*, 1 foot, margins of flowers bright red, with central orange band, June and July; 'Mahogany', 1 foot, crimson, ageing to mahogany-red. *L. martagon*, 3–5 feet, the pink-flowered European or Turk's cap lily. Has up to 30 smallish pendent flowers per stem, strongly recurved, the colour varying to dull purple. Resents transplanting, but once established continues indefinitely. Though not stem rooting it likes planting moderately deeply. Seedlings take up to 7 years to flower, Europe, Asia; vars. *album superbum*, a large-flowered form; *dalmaticum*, dark wine-purple. *L. medeloides*, wheel lily, 1–1½ feet, 2–10 small reflexed flowers per stem, colour varying from scarlet to apricot, spotted red, July, partial shade, thin woodland with leafy soil, Japan, Kamchatka. *L. monadelphum*, 2–3 feet,

a striking early-flowering lily with 20 or more lemon-yellow blooms with a maroon base, in June. They are pendent or facing outwards, with recurved margins, spotted and have a good scent. Leaves arranged in spirals and curved. Likes light shade and moderately deep planting, resents disturbance and may not show top growth the first season after moving, Caucasus; var. *szovitzianum*, 3–4 feet, pale straw yellow, pendulous flowers. *L. nepalense*, 2–3 feet, a lovely species with broad, dark green, glossy foliage, and large emerald-green very sweetly scented pendent flowers, blotched claret-purple, Nepal. Not entirely hardy, best grown indoors in beds, as stems like to run underground, but also flowers early in pots. Plant fairly deeply; var. *robustum*, 1½–2 feet, flowers with dark purple centres. *L. nobilissimum*, 2–3 feet, flowers large, pure white with green throat, usually borne upright, 2–5 per stem, July, greenhouse or frost-proof positions only if grown out of doors, Japan. *L. papilliferum*, 1 foot, flowers crimson-maroon, 1–3 per stem, Turk's cap type, August, dislikes wet soils, Yunnan. *L. pardalinum*, panther lily, 4–5 feet, flowers orange, shaded and spotted crimson,

recurring habit, up to 20 per stem, July, sun or partial shade, moist but well-drained soil, western North America; var. *giganteum*, 5–6 feet, taller kind, flowers rich crimson, golden-yellow centres, spotted purple brown. *L. polyphyllum*, 3 feet, flowers creamy-white, fragrant, nodding, up to 12 per stem, shady, moist but well-drained conditions, rare, western Himalaya. *L. pumilum*, 1½ feet, dainty, dwarf lily, with wiry stems, bearing up to 18 nodding, bright scarlet Turk's cap blooms, June, stem rooting, suitable for the rock garden, does not mind lime, easily grown, north-east Asia. There are orange and yellow forms as well as named cultivars such as 'Golden Gleam', light orange, and 'Yellow Bunting', rich yellow. *L. pyrenaicum*, 2–3 feet, flowers greenish-yellow, spotted purple, recurved, heavily, somewhat unpleasantly scented, June, Pyrenees; var. *aureum*, flowers canary-yellow with green throat. *L. regale*, 5 feet, a handsome, large-flowered trumpet lily, one of the easiest to grow, tolerating most soils. Bears up to 30 funnel-shaped flowers, rosy-purple outside and white to creamy-yellow inside, June and July. Stem rooting, likes planting very deeply, with roots

1 The upright lemon flowers of Lilium Destiny (Div 1a) are speckled with brown spots and have prominent anthers. 2 Lilium Enchantment (Div 1a) produces magnificent orange flowers on long sturdy erect spikes.

shaded by low plants, but with the flowers able to reach the sun, China; var. *album*, pure white. *L. rubellum*, 2 feet, an attractive dwarf lily which produces 2–3 short, fragrant, pink trumpet-flowers per stem, June. Stem rooting, likes lime-free soil, partial shade, very hardy, Japan. *L. speciosum*, 3–4 feet, a first-class lily for pot culture or a well-drained open site, with shade from mid-day sun, but suitable out of doors only in the milder parts of Britain. Produces in late summer up to 10 large, flat, Turk's cap type blooms, margins recurving slightly with age. Very attractively spotted and suffused carmine on a cream ground, strongly scented. The several improved forms, have now superseded the type. It is a very good florist's lily because of its long stiff pedicels, Japan; vars. *album*, flowers pure white; *rubrum magnificum*, 5 feet, flowers ruby-red, to 8 inches across. There are also named cultivars

including 'Cinderella', pink, shading to white, spotted deep pink; 'Ellabee', pure white with green throat; 'Grand Commander', to 6 feet tall, crimson, edged white, up to 30 flowers per stem; 'Lucie Wilson', rose-pink, edged white, spotted red; 'Melpomene', deep carmine, edged white; 'Red Champion Strain', various shades and combinations of pink and white; 'Superstar Strain', shades of crimson; 'Uchida', dark red, edged white; 'White Champion', 2–3 feet, pure white. *L. superbum*, 5–6 feet, orange-red, yellow centres, spotted dark brown, 15–30 flowers per stem, July and August, woodland or full sun with shade for roots, North America. *L. sutchuenense*, 4–5 feet, vermilion-orange, dark spots, July, woodland conditions, Mongolia. *L. taliense*, 3–4 feet, white, purple-spotted, fragrant, recurved, up to 12 per stem, July, China. *L. tigrinum*, tiger lily, 2–4 feet, orange-red, dark purple spots, recurved, up to 20 per stem, August and September, easy in sun or partial shade in any soil provided it remains moist, China, Japan, Korea; vars. *flaviflorum*, yellow, spotted purple; *splendens*, orange, spotted black, one of the best varieties. *L. tsingtauense*, 1–2 feet, bright orange, dark spots, up to

6 per stem, star-shaped, June and July, prefers partial shade, China. *L. wallichianum*, 3–5 feet, creamy white, greenish at centre, solitary fragrant, up to 8 inches across, trumpet-shaped, August and September, stem rooting, needs shelter or cool greenhouse conditions, Nepal. *L. wardii*, 3 feet, purplish-pink, reddish spots, recurved, fragrant, up to 40 per stem, July and August, lime-free soil, Tibet. For cultivation details see Lily hybrids and their culture.

Lily hybrids and their culture

The lily has been something of a Cinderella in the British garden, and often thought to be 'difficult'. This false image has persisted too long. The lily is not only a producer of exotic-looking, often richly-scented flowers, suitable for both cool greenhouse and garden culture, but offers a wide range of size, form, colour of bloom and time of flowering.

Considering that many lilies come from extreme climates, such as those of the Himalaya, China and Tibet, they usually stand up to the British weather admirably.

Though the species are rewarding, it is the vast range of hybrids that have made lily-growing worthwhile for British gardeners today.

In recent years the much-improved forms and colours of the highly concentrated and specialised breeding programme of the world-famous lily-breeder, Jan de Graaf, of Oregon, USA, has begun to make an impact on the amateur. Hundreds and thousands of crosses between species and the resulting seedling hybrids have now evolved separate hybrid strains which are continually being improved upon.

The flowering period under glass can extend from March until December in pots or in the greenhouse border. Pot-grown lilies can be taken into the house when they come into flower, or may even be grown entirely in the house now that pre-cooled, 'instant' types are sold, complete with pot and growing compost. As far as the latter are concerned, all you need do is water the pot you buy and stand it on a windowsill. However, the varieties offered are restricted in range.

But good indoor lily-growing is not quite so lacking in interest. You can force a few kinds into flower with gentle warmth, so they bloom by Easter. For example *L. auratum* (the golden-rayed lily of Japan), *L. speciosum* and *L. longiflorum* (the Easter lily, so popular for weddings), may be potted in the autumn or early winter and may be grown in cool conditions to flower in spring or early summer.

Most lilies, however, do not respond to forcing, so you should pot them in January, February or March for fairly early flowering. The Mid-century hybrids are particularly good for this purpose.

You may also pot bulbs in the spring for general summer and autumn flowering. If space is restricted you can start them off in a cool frame.

The latest-flowering is *L. formosanum* which, with care, can be had in bloom at Christmas.

Often pot culture can be the answer to the problem of difficult outdoor soils, such as very light chalky or sandy ones or very heavy clay.

If the bulbs are stem-rooting kinds do not fill the pots completely, but leave sufficient space for you to top up with added compost consisting of 1 part of rich loam, 2 parts of well-rotted manure or leafmould when these roots start to form. You should never use fresh manure or compound artificial fertilisers for lilies. A good potting compost consists of 3 parts of fibrous loam, 1 part of gritty sand, 1 part of leafmould or peat. To each bushel add 1 part of old sifted cow manure or horse manure and 4 ounces of John Innes Base Fertiliser.

A number of lily enthusiasts find that proprietary all-peat composts are especially suited to pot lily culture. In any case some liquid feeding should be done during active growth and flowering.

After flowering and then leaf production, which builds up the bulbs, you can give them a partial rest by watering them less frequently. But remember that lily bulbs never really become dormant, either indoors or in the garden. Crudely the bulb's cycle is to grow downwards, forming roots, then grow upwards, forming stems and flowers; then it grows downwards again during its apparently dormant period above ground. This is why lilies always do best if the bulbs are transplanted soon after flowering, so that out of doors they have plenty of time to get their roots well established during late autumn and early winter.

For this reason many keen lily growers prefer to grow newly-bought bulbs in pots for the first year to acclimatise them. The bulbs are invariably imported and often arrive no earlier than Christmas, after a fairly long period out of the ground.

Though perfectly hardy in the garden *L. auratum* seems to do better indoors, and of course the tender species such as *Ll. formosanum, longiflorum* and *nepalense* must be grown under glass.

If you want lilies for a particular event you can retard the bulbs for several weeks in a refrigerator, and you can dwarf them by treating them with cyclocel. In general they all survive with a minimum winter heat of 40 F (4 C) though during flowering and active growth it pays to give them warmer conditions.

The most spectacular lilies for growing in pots include the very large *L. speciosum* 'Potomac Hybrid', much more

Lilium 'Imperial Crimson', an excellent strain, can be grown in pots.

brightly spotted cerise than the type and with very large strongly fragrant flowers. 'Empress of India', 'Empress of China' and the three 'Imperial' strains —'Silver', 'Gold' and 'Crimson' are outstanding, as is 'Golden Clarion'.

Lily bulbs have no outer protective envelope as have tulips and narcissi, and so need careful handling. They consist of tightly packed scales which often serve as a means of multiplying more expensive varieties you may occasionally buy. Long exposure to air dries the bulbs and insects can get between the scales and damage them. If they are allowed to stand in water too long they may rot, so that they should be planted in soil, whether in the open garden or in pots. If the bulbs must be kept out of the ground or out of their pots store them in trays, covered with moist peat or a mixture of moist peat and sand.

When preparing the soil out of doors, mix in plenty of compost, leafmould, or other organic matter, plus some well-rotted manure if you can get it, and plenty of gritty material to provide sharp drainage.

One method of growing lilies on heavy soils is to make raised beds surrounded with logs. Fill in with a load of grit, and then build up a bed of good organically rich soil on top of the grit.

Refuse to buy bulbs which have had their roots trimmed off because the roots are vital in establishing the bulb quickly. They also pull the bulb down to its correct depth—so planting depth need not be adhered to very accurately.

Stem-rooting types also produce roots above the bulb, but these perish when the flowering spikes wither down to ground level. But they largely take over during active growth and flowering. All lilies appreciate monthly liquid feeding during their most active above-ground growing period. Maxicrop and Phostrogen are particularly good for this purpose.

The basal-rooting types rely entirely on the roots below the bulb, so plant shallowly, at 2–3 inches, so that they are in the best soil. The stem-rooting types need to have both types of roots in good soil so plant these with about 6 inches of soil above the bulb, top-dressing with organic matter in the summer, especially on shallow soils.

Lily stems stand hot dry, sunny conditions, but not the bulbs, hence some slight ground shade from other plants is beneficial and so is plenty of organic matter in the soil to ensure an even supply of moisture. They can take all the organic matter you can give them on light soils. Leafmould from ditches and woods is especially good. But it is better to err on the side of exposure to full sun than to plant the bulbs in full shade. On very limey soils a really generous supply of organic matter is also essential, and if you have very poor, shallow soil in

your garden you may find it better to grow lilies in containers rather than in the open ground.

If you are unable to get bulbs early enough for late summer or autumn planting out of doors then plant them in the spring, storing them indoors in trays, covering them lightly with moist peat so that their scales and roots remain plump.

Attractive lilies for beginners in the garden include *L. henryi*, which tolerates almost any conditions, though it does not like peat, so use leafmould; 'Golden Clarion' is good; so are *L. regale, L. davidii*, the Aurelian hybrids, the Mid-century hybrids. The new Harlequin strain is a modern type that looks like being especially good for the garden. The martagons are also easy.

The modern types are divided into nine divisions.

Division 1 contains the Asiatic hybrids derived from *L. dauricum* and *L. concolor*, easily-grown lilies not over 4 feet tall, which resist wind. They are subdivided into three groups.

Sub-division 1a contains those with upright flowers borne singly or in clusters, mainly stem-rooters, early-flowering, which may be planted in full sun or partial shade. They include the lemon, orange and red Mid-century hybrids as well as a number of named cultivars.

Sub-division 1b has outward-facing flowers and most of the bulbs are stem-rooting and like sun or partial shade. They include 'Corsage', pink, 12 or more per stem; 'Fire King', orange-red, purple-spotted; 'Paprika', rich crimson.

Sub-division 1c has hanging flowers, including the 'Harlequin Hybrids' with 4-inch-wide flowers, 15–20 per stem, in a wide colour range, the 'Fiesta Hybrids' have as many as 30 blooms, lightly spotted, again in many colours, 'Sutter's Gold' strain and other named varieties.

Division 2 contains the *L. martagon* hybrids, which like light shade, and have pendent flowers, recurved at the margins, flowering in June and July. This division contains the Paisley strain *martagon-hansonii* hybrids with Paisley shawl-like colours, and various named cultivars. Most of them do not object to lime in the soil; all prefer semi-shady conditions. They are stem-rooting so should be planted 5–6 inches deep.

Division 3 contains the *L. candidum* hybrids, including *L.* x *testaceum*, the Nankeen lily, the oldest lily hybrid, derived from a cross between *L. candidum* and *L. chalcedonicum*, up to 6 feet tall, with up to 12 flat recurring flowers per stem, in June and July, apricot in colour, with a few red spots. This is a lime-loving lily, the bulbs of which should be planted 3–4 inches deep in sunny positions between September and December.

Division 4 consists of hybrids derived from American species such as *L. pardalinum* and *L. parryi*. It includes the 'Bellingham Hybrids' in shades of yellow, orange and red, well-spotted with maroon or black, up to 25 reflexed flowers on stems 5–6 feet tall, in July. All may be planted in sun or partial shade. They do best in light soils and should be planted 4 inches deep and top-dressed with leafmould during the growing season and in winter.

Division 5 contains the *L. longiflorum* hybrids, of which a few are occasionally offered, including 'Croft', 1½–2 feet; *formosanum* 'Erabu', 2 feet; 'Holland's Glory', 3–4 feet. All these have flowers indistinguishable from those of *L. longiflorum* but flower slightly earlier.

Division 6 consists of the hybrid trumpet lilies obtained from Asiatic species, but excluding the *Lilium auratum* and *L. speciosum* hybrids. The group is divided into 4 sub-divisions according to the shape of the flower.

Sub-division 6a contains the Chinese trumpet lilies, hybrids with funnel-shaped flowers. Most of them are easily grown, stem-rooting plants which should be planted 4 inches or so deep in rich soil and partially shaded places. They mainly flower in July. Fine strains include the 'African Queen' strain, 5 feet tall with flowers in shades of apricot pink; 'Aurelian Hybrids', 4–5 feet, pink, apricot, yellow or white: 'Black Magic' strain, 5–6 feet, mainly purplish-brown outside, white inside; 'Golden Clarion' strain, 3–5 feet, shades of yellow, many with brown or red stripes on the outsides; 'Olympic Hybrids', 4–5 feet, cream to pink and green; and such named kinds as 'Black Dragon', 5–6 feet, white inside, purple-brown outside; 'Green Dragon', 3–6 feet, chartreuse green, and 'Royal Gold', 3–5 feet, golden-yellow.

Sub-division 6b consists of lilies with bowl-shaped, outward-facing flowers. Typical of these are 'First Love', 5–6 feet, pink with a golden stripe and pale green throat, flowers up to 8 inches across; 'Heart's Desire' strain, 5–6 feet, shades of cream, yellowish-orange and white; 'Regina' 4–5 feet, sulphur-yellow.

Sub-division 6c consists of lilies with pendent flowers, including 'Golden Showers' strain, 4–5 feet, butter-yellow on the inside, brown outside; 'Golden Splendour' strain, 4–6 feet, deep golden-yellow with maroon stripe on the reverse.

Sub-division 6d has lilies with star-shaped flowers, opening flat, including 'Bright Star', 3–4 feet, silvery-white; 'Golden Spire', 5 feet, buttercup-yellow; 'Pink Sunburst' strain, 4–5 feet, fuchsia pink and white in various combinations; 'Whirlybird', 3–4 feet, white with bronze-yellow centres.

Division 7 is the oriental hybrids, again split into 4 sub-divisions.

Sub-division 7a consists of hybrids with trumpet-shaped flowers.

Sub-division 7b consists of those hybrids originating from *Lilium auratum* and *L. speciosum* crosses, mainly flowering in late summer. They are stem-rooting. They must be given well-drained, gritty soils with ample leafmould added, and should be planted in sunny places. Examples are 'Arabian Nights', 4 feet, blackish-mauve, fading to mauve; 'Bonfire', 4–5 feet, crimson in the centre, white at the edges, crimson dots, outside silvery flushed pink; 'Empress of India', crimson inside, pink outside, flowers up to 10 inches across.

Sub-division 7c contains oriental hybrids with recurved blooms, including 'Imperial Silver' strain, 5–6 feet, white, spotted with vermilion, up to 10 inches across; 'Imperial Gold' strain, 5–6 feet, white with gold central stripe and maroon spots; 'Julian Wallace', 5–6 feet, rosy-red, white margins, crimson dots.

Sub-division 7d consists of hybrids and cultivars with flat-faced flowers. Examples are 'Allegra', 5–6 feet, pure white with green centres; 'Black Beauty', 5–8 feet, dark red with green centre; 'Winston Churchill', 3–4 feet, dark reddish-mauve.

Division 8 is composed of those hybrids which do not fall into Divisions 1 to 7.

Division 9 contains the true species and their botanical forms. These have been described in the article Lilium.

Diseases As far as troubles are concerned there are two main bugbears for the lily grower. One is mosaic virus which dwarfs and cripples and which is spread by aphids. So destroy any mottled, stunted plants, and spray regularly with a good insecticide such as Pestex, which acts as both a contact and systemic. Malathion marks lily flowers. Spraying is most important indoors where aphids easily get a foothold.

The other trouble is botrytis which also can cripple, and regular spraying with captan, or better still the newer Elvaron is recommended. You can combine it with dimethoate (Rogor), which is contained in Pestex, and spray when you do your roses or other plants to save time.

Another trouble is fusarium rot which affects the basal bulb plate, so dip the bulbs in PCNB or Botrilex before planting indoors or out.

Propagation For multiplying stock of valuable hybrids scales can be detached from bulbs when transplanting and set in an upright position in boxes of peaty compost in the frame or greenhouse. They get a better start if they are put in a polythene bag of all-peat compost, in a warm propagating frame, until they show shoots. Then space them an inch apart in boxes of potting compost.

After the first season, when they produce young leaves, they can be potted up individually for growing on to planting size.

Some lilies also produce small grape-sized bulblets on the stems, below or above soil level. These can be detached in the late summer, when they are almost ready to drop off naturally, and can be stored over the winter in boxes or peaty compost, for growing on in boxes next spring.

Many amateurs find the cheapest method to start lily growing is to grow from seed, a method better suited to the species which come true, rather than the hybrid strains which do not.

Space seeds of smaller types ½ inch apart, larger ones 1½ inches. Sow in an all-peat compost: larger amounts can be sown in boxes. Sow in the spring—though experienced lily growers often sow some types in the autumn after breaking their dormancy in polythene in a refrigerator. You can save your own lily seed quite easily from your best plants. As with scales or stem bulbs, move the young seedlings to larger containers when their growth becomes large enough.

Limnanthes (lim-nan-thes)

From the Greek *limne*, a marsh, and *anthos*, a flower, referring to the liking some of these plants have for damp ground (*Limnanthaceae*). A small genus of hardy annuals from California, which deserve to be grown more. They will always have a cloud of bees hovering over them, to which they seem to be very attractive, and a common name for them is the bee-flower. In the right soil they are prolific in their production of flowers and if left to seed will bloom again in the same year, in September and October. One species only is cultivated, *L. douglasii*, which grows 6 inches tall and has delicate fern-like leaves and shining, lemon-yellow and white flowers, in May–June. The flower colours have also led to the plant being given the popular name, butter and eggs.

Cultivation Ordinary soil will do, but limnanthes grow best in moist soils. Plants should be given a sunny position and they give good displays if grown in clumps. Propagate by seed sown in autumn and spring where the plants are to flower, thinning the seedlings to 3–4 inches apart.

Limonium (li-mo-nee-um)

From the Greek *leimon*, a meadow, because certain species are found growing in salt marshes (*Plumbaginaceae*). Sea lavender. A genus of annuals, perennial herbaceous plants and sub-shrubs, hardy, half hardy and tender. Once known as *Statice*, these plants are natives of all parts of the world, particularly coasts and salt marshes. The numerous small flowers, usually borne in branched spikes, are easily dried and are much used for long-lasting flower arrangements. All flower in summer.

Species cultivated Perennial: *L. altaicum*, 15 inches, blue. *L. bellidifolium*, 9 inches, white or blue, Europe (including Britain). *L. dumosum*, 2 feet, silvery-grey. *L. incanum*, 1½ feet, crimson, Siberia; vars. *album*, dwarf, white;

late winter or early spring and rooted in a cold frame.

Linaria (lin-ar-ee-a)

From the Latin *linum*, flax, referring to the flax-like leaves *(Scrophulariaceae)*. Toadflax. Linarias are in the main hardy annual or perennial plants from the Northern Hemisphere; the European plant, once known as *L. cymbalaria*, the Kenilworth ivy or mother of thousands, widely naturalised in Britain, is correctly known as *Cymbalaria muralis*. The yellow flowers of the native species *(L. vulgaris)* can be seen on roadside verges, banks and in fields throughout the summer.

Species cultivated Perennial: *L. alpina*, 3–6 inches, yellow, purple and blue, summer–autumn, Alps. *L. dalmatica*, 3 feet, yellow, June–September, south-east Europe. *L. macedonica*, 3–4 feet, deep yellow flowers to 1 inch long, June to September, Macedonia; 'Canary Bird' is a deeper yellow cultivar. *L. purpurea*, purple toadflax, 3–4 feet, tall slender spikes of purple flowers, July to September, southern Europe; 'Canon Went' is a pink-flowered cultivar. *L. triornithophora*, 3 feet, blue-purple and yellow, summer, Portugal, Spain, half hardy, a good pot plant. *L. ventricosa*, 3 feet, creamy-yellow with brownish-red veins, June, Morocco. *L. vulgaris*, toadflax, 2 feet, yellow-orange, spring–autumn, Europe, including Britain.

Annual: *L. heterophylla*, 1–3 feet, yellow, July, Morocco. *L. maroccana*, 9–12 inches, violet-purple, June, Morocco; cultivars include 'Fairy Bouquet', mixed colours; 'Northern Lights', mixed colours, 'White Pearl' and Yellow Prince'. *L. reticulata*, 2–4 feet, purple and yellow, summer, Portugal. *L. tristis*, 1 foot, yellow and brown, summer, Portugal and Spain.

Cultivation The soil should be well-drained and rather moist. Sunny borders or rock gardens are suitable positions. Plants can be moved and replanted in autumn or spring. Propagation is by seeds sown where the plants are required to flower, in September for flowering in spring, and in April for summer flowering. The perennials may also be divided in autumn or spring.

Linum (li-num)

From the old Greek name, *linon*, used by Theophrastus *(Linaceae)*. Flax. This important genus contains, besides the economically valuable annual which supplies flax and linseed oil, a number of very decorative garden plants. The flower colour which seems characteristic of the genus is a fine pale blue but there are a number of shrubs with yellow blossoms, and a lovely scarlet annual. The genus is widely distributed in the temperate regions of the world.

nanum, 6 inches, dwarf; *roseum*, 6 inches, rosy-pink. *L. latifolium*, 2–3 feet, blue, south Russia. *L. minutum*, 6 inches, violet, Mediterranean area. *L. peticulum*, 4 inches, white. *L. puberulum*, 6 inches, violet to white, hardy in the milder counties only, Canaries. *L. sinense*, 1 foot, yellow, China. *L. tataricum*, 1 foot, red and white, south-east Europe and Siberia. *L. vulgare*, 1 foot, purple-blue flowers, Europe (including Britain).

Annual: *L. bonduellii*, 1 foot, yellow, North Africa, strictly a perennial but treated as a half hardy annual. *L. sinuatum*, 1–2 feet, blue and cream, Mediterranean region; there are several cultivars including 'New Art Shades', a strain containing a mixture of colours; 'Chamois Rose', shades of apricot-pink; 'Lavender Queen', 'Market Grower's Blue'; 'Pacific Giants Mixed', large-flowered strain in mixed colours; 'Purple Monarch', rich purple. *L. spic-atum*, 6 inches, rose and white, Caucasus, Persia. *L. suworowii*, 1½ feet, lilac pink, Turkestan.

Greenhouse: *L. imbricatum*, 1½–2 feet, blue, Canary Isles. *L. macrophyllum*, 1–2 feet, blue, Canary Isles. *L. × profusum*, 2–3 feet, blue, late summer to autumn, hybrid.

Cultivation All the limoniums prefer well-drained, sandy loam and a sunny position. The outdoor species are suitable for borders, the dwarf kinds for rock gardens. Plant the hardy perennials in spring and the annuals in late May. Greenhouse species are potted in the spring and fed occasionally with a weak liquid fertiliser. They require a summer temperature of 55–65 (13–18 C) and 40–50 F (4–10 C) in the winter. Propagation is by seeds sown in sandy soil in early spring, when the temperature should be 55–60 F (13–16 C). Root cuttings of the perennials can be taken in

Species cultivated Perennial: *L. alpinum*, 6 inches, blue, July–August, Alps. *L. campanulatum*, 1 foot, yellow, June–August, south Europe. *L. capitatum*, 9 inches, yellow, June–August, south Europe, Asia Minor. *L. flavum*, 1–1½ feet, yellow, June–August, Germany, Russia. *L. hirsutum*, 15 inches, blue with white eye, summer, south Europe, Asia Minor. *L. monogynum*, 2 feet, white, June–July, New Zealand. *L. narbonense*, 2 feet, blue, May–July, south Europe. *L. perenne*, 1½ feet, blue, June–July, Europe. *L. salsoloides*, 9 inches, pink, June–July, south Europe.

Annual: *L. grandiflorum*, 6–12 inches, rose, summer, North Africa; vars. *coccineum*, rose-crimson; *rubrum*, brighter than type; 'Venice Red' is a large-flowered cultivar with carmine-scarlet flowers. *L. usitatissimum*, common flax, 1½ feet, blue, June–July, Europe. Historically this is the world's most famous fibre plant; it was known to the Egyptians. Shrubby: *L. arboreum*, 1 foot, yellow, May–June, Crete.

Cultivation The flaxes are not fussy about soil provided it is well-drained and will do very well on an alkaline medium. The annuals need the standard treatment for this group. Sometimes *L. grandiflorum* is sown in pots in July to decorate

Lithospermum oleifolium, not often grown, is an attractive rock garden plant, with deep blue flowers.

the greenhouse in the autumn, but whether grown outside or in, it is one of the best annuals for display. Most of the perennials and shrubby species will be happy and certainly look well on the rock garden in full sun. *L. arboreum* is not entirely hardy. Propagate by seed sown in April outdoors, or by firm cuttings taken in summer and kept close until rooted.

Lithospermum (lith-o-sper-mum)

From the Greek *lithos*, a stone, and *sperma*, a seed, in reference to the extreme hardness of the seed *(Boraginaceae)*. Gromwell. A genus of about 40 species of biennials, herbaceous perennials and sub-shrubs, grown for their flowers, which are predominantly bright blue. Those in cultivation are mostly trailing evergreen sub-shrubs or perennials from the Mediterranean region, and are generally grown among other plants on a sunny rock garden, though *L. diffusum* and its garden forms are somewhat invasive, and *L. purpureo-caeruleum*, a rare native plant is even more so. Some species are now included in *Moltkia*.

Species cultivated *L. canescens*, puccoon, red root, 1 foot, yellow, July, North America. *L. diffusum* (syn. *L. prostratum*), 6 inches, blue, summer, southern Europe; cultivars are 'Grace Ward', 3 inches, bright blue, late spring; 'Heavenly Blue', smaller flowers. *L. doerfloeri*, 1 foot, erect, deep purple, May and June. *L. gastoni*, 1 foot, blue, summer, western Pyrenees. *L. oleifolium*, 6 inches, prostrate shrub, violet to blue, summer, rare, Pyrenees. *L. purpureo-caeruleum*, 1 foot, creeping habit, purple, summer, native. *L. rosmarinifolium*, 1½ feet, bright azure blue, February, Italy, does best in the alpine house.

Cultivation A well-drained coarse soil is suitable for these plants, and they do best in alkaline soils, except for *L. diffusum*, which requires a lime-free acid one. Keep the soil just moist in winter. Cut back *L. diffusum* after flowering. Propagate by means of green cuttings in June, or seed may be sown. *L. diffusum* is grown most easily from cuttings of the preceding year's shoots, rooted in fine peat and sand, and kept cool and shaded for a few weeks.

Lobelia (lobe-ee-lee-a)

Commemorating Matthias de L'Obel, 1538–1616, a Fleming, botanist and physician to James I *(Campanulaceae)*. A genus of some 200 species of annuals, herbaceous perennials or sub-shrubs, widely distributed over temperate and tropical regions of the world. All should be regarded as half hardy, although the herbaceous perennials will survive out of doors in the more favoured parts of the country. Elsewhere, the bright red-flowered species from America may well be grown in the garden from June onwards but usually need protection in winter, or should be lifted and over-wintered in a frame or in a frost-proof greenhouse, since prolonged frost will kill them. These red flowered lobelias have the additional charm of dark purple-bronze leaves.

Species cultivated *L. cardinalis*, cardinal flower, perennial, 3 feet, scarlet, late summer, North America; var. *alba*, white; 'Queen Victoria' is a cultivar with bronze foliage, deep scarlet flowers. *L. erinus*, annual, 6 inches, blue, summer, South Africa; cultivars include 'Blue Gown', dwarf, sky blue; 'Blue Stone', clear blue without eye; 'Crystal Palace', bronze foliage, intense blue flowers; 'Emperor William', compact, bright blue, very good for bedding; 'Prima Donna', wine; 'Rosamund', deep carmine-red with white eye. This is the lobelia much used for summer bedding. *L. fulgens*, perennial, 3 feet, scarlet, May–September, Mexico. *L.* × *gerardii*, perennial, 3–4 feet, pink to violet-purple, July, hybrid. *L. syphilitica*, perennial, 2 feet, blue, autumn, Eastern United States, nearly hardy. *L. tenuior*, annual, 1 foot, blue, September, Western

Australia, the lobelia of trailing habit, used for hanging baskets. *L. tupa*, perennial, 6–8 feet, reddish-scarlet, autumn.

Cultivation The scarlet-flowered *L. cardinalis* and *L. fulgens* when planted in the border need frequent watering since in their native habitat they are stream-side plants. They are otherwise not difficult and, except in the mildest localities, should be lifted and stored in October. Propagation of these is by seeds, sown in sandy compost in autumn in a cold frame, or in a temperature of 55°F (13°C) in March, or by cuttings rooted in a warm propagating frame. Plants may also be divided in March. The bedding lobelias with blue flowers may be grown from seed sown in February, in the greenhouse, in the orthodox half hardy annual method, but in September these plants may be lifted and stored in the greenhouse to provide cuttings for rooting in a heated propagating frame in March.

Lupinus (lu-py-nus)
From the Latin *lupus*, a wolf (destroyer), because it was thought that the plants depleted the fertility of the soil by sheer numbers (*Leguminosae*). Lupin. A genus of over 300 species of annuals, perennials and sub-shrubs, mainly from North America, though there are a few Mediterranean species which, since Roman times, have been used for green manuring. This is surprising since the Roman farmers did not know that within the root nodules were colonies of bacteria capable of utilising nitrogen to produce valuable nitrates. The fine Russell hybrid lupins are among the most showy of herbaceous perennials and have a wide colour range embracing the three primary colours: red, yellow and blue. They do not, however, thrive on alkaline (chalky or limy) soils.

Species cultivated Annual: *L. densiflorus*, 1½–2 feet, yellow, fragrant, July–August, California. *L. hartwegii*, 2–3 feet, blue, white and red, July–October, Mexico. *L. hirsutissimus*, 1 foot, with stinging hairs, purple flowers, July, California. *L. hirsutus*, 2–3 feet, blue and white, July–August, Mediterranean region. *L. luteus*, 2 feet, yellow, June–August, south Europe. *L. mutabilis*, 5 feet, white, blue and yellow, summer, Colombia. *L. pubescens*, 3 feet, violet, blue and white, summer, Mexico. *L. subcarnosus*, 1 foot, blue and white, July, Texas.

Perennial: *L. nootkatensis*, 1 foot, blue, purple and yellow, May–July, north-west America. *L. polyphyllus*, 4 feet, blue, white or pink, June–August, California. Shrubby: *L. arboreus*, 6 feet, short-lived, yellow, white or violet, fragrant, summer, California. *L. excubicus*, 1–5 feet, blue, violet, summer, California var. *hallii* (syn. *L. paynei*), larger flowers. Russell hybrids: These well-known hybrids have developed from a cross

made at the end of the last century between *L. arboreus* and *L. polyphyllus*. Some years later a seedling with rose-pink flowers appeared, *L. p. roseus*, and with the help of this, Mr George Russell was able to develop and select the superb colours and strong spikes that are available today in the now famous Russell strain.

Some good cultivars are: 'Betty Astell', 3 feet, deep pink; 'Blue Jacket', 3 feet, deep blue and white; 'Fireglow', 3 feet, orange and gold; 'George Russell', 3 feet, pink and cream; 'Gladys Cooper', 4 feet, smoky blue; 'Joan of York', 4 feet, cerise and pink; 'Josephine', 4 feet, slate blue and yellow; 'Lady Diana Abdy', 3½ feet, blue and white; 'Lady Fayne', 3 feet, coral and rose; 'Lilac Time', 3½ feet, rosy-lilac; 'Mrs Mickleth-waite', 3 feet, salmon-pink and gold; 'Mrs Noel Terry', 3 feet, pink and cream; 'Thundercloud', 3 feet, blue and rose-mauve.

Cultivation The most popular section is that of the perennial species, which are easily grown in any sunny border that

Lupin hybrids, with their wide range of colour, particularly strong in red, yellow and blue, make excellent herbaceous perennials. Lupin 'Serenade' shows the typical shape.

has not too much lime or chalk. Mulch with compost in spring, and cut down the old flower stems in October.

The Russell lupins are now available from seed, though the named forms are still raised from cuttings of young growths in March. These are not among the longest lived plants and it is wise to renew them from time to time. Since they are hardy they may be raised from seed sown in drills ¼ inch deep in April and put in their final places in the autumn. Many will flower during the following summer.

The annuals are also treated as hardy and seeds are sown in drills in April. In May the seedlings must be thinned out to 9 inches apart. It is important with both annual and perennial lupins to remove the forming seed pods before they can grow large enough to retard the flowering capacity of the plants.

The tree lupin, *L. arboreus*, may be raised from seed with extreme ease. These shrubs make rapid growth and will flower in their second season. They are, however, not long-lived, but generally manage to renew themselves by self-sown seedlings. The shrubby lupin, *L. excubicus*, makes a fine large plant, but needs some frost protection. Like most lupins this has very fragrant flowers.

Lychnis (lik-nis)

From the Greek *lychnos*, a lamp, alluding to the brilliantly-coloured flowers (*Caryophyllaceae*). This small genus from the north temperate zone of the Old World contains some good herbaceous perennials and one good hardy annual. Two of our most impressive wild plants, the red and the white campion belong here, and, in fact, are worthy of garden cultivation, the white one in particular for its extreme fragrance in the evening. There is a natural hybrid between these two plants which has delicate pink flowers. The ragged robin, *L. flos-cuculi*, is also a native plant quite worth growing in the wild garden. It is interesting that *L. chalcedonica* gives us the brightest scarlet in the herbaceous garden, while *L. flos-jovis* (syn. *Agrostemma flos-jovis*), *A. coronaria* (syn. *L. coronaria*) gives us the most saturated magenta to accompany its greyish foliage.

Species cultivated *L. alba* (syn. *Melandrium album*), white campion, 3 feet, Europe. *L. alpina* (syn. *Viscaria alpina*), 6 inches, pink, summer, May to August, Europe. *L. arkwrightii*, 1½ feet, scarlet, summer, hybrid. *L. chalcedonica*, 3 feet, scarlet, summer, Russia. *L. coeli-rosa* (syn. *Silene coeli-rosa*), rose of heaven, 1 foot, purple and various other colours, annual, Levant. *L. coronaria*, 2½ feet, magenta, July and August, south Europe. *L. dioica* (*Melandrium rubrum*), the red campion, 3 feet, strong pink, summer, Britain. *L. flos-cuculi*, 1½ feet, ragged robin, rose-pink, May and June, Britain. *L. fulgens*, 9 inches, vermilion, May to September, Siberia. *L. grandiflora* (syn. *L.* x *haageana*, 9 inches, salmon, summer, Japan. *L.* x *haageana*, 18 inches, very large scarlet flowers, hybrid. *L. lagascae* (syn. *Petrocoptis lagascae*), 3 inches, rose and white, summer, Pyrenees. *L. viscaria* (syn. *Viscaria vulgaris*), catchfly, 1 foot, reddish-purple, summer, Europe.

Cultivation Most lychnis are very easily grown in any kind of soil and can withstand dry conditions better than many other herbaceous plants. However, *L. alpina* and *L. lagascae* need rather richer soil. Some of these herbaceous plants are rather short-lived perennials —*L. alba* is almost biennial. All may be readily raised from seed sown in March in the open garden, as they are supremely hardy. The one annual species needs the standard hardy annual treatment.

Lyperanthus (ly-pe-ran-thus)

From the Greek *lyperos*, mournful, *anthos*, flower, referring to the dark colour of the dry flowers of some species (*Orchidaceae*). A genus of about 12 species of seldom-grown terrestrial orchids with fleshy or tuberous roots, natives of Australia, New Caledonia and New Zealand. The upper sepal is helmet-shaped; the flowers have large basal bract.

Lysimachia (lis-e-mak-e-a)

Probably from either *Lysimachus*, King of Thracia, or from the Greek *luo*, to loose, and *mache*, strife, hence the common name of *L. vulgaris*, (*Primulaceae*). This genus, most species of which in cultivation are hardy herbaceous perennials, has some species which have long been cultivated. There are about 120 species in all from temperate and sub-tropical regions of the world, three of them being British natives. The yellow loosestrife and creeping jenny are cultivated in gardens the latter plant making an excellent specimen for a hanging basket, with its neat leaves and abundance of yellow flowers.

Species cultivated *L. atropurpurea*, 2 feet, purple, summer, Greece. *L. clethroides*, 3 feet, white, summer, foliage brightly coloured in autumn, Japan. *L. ephemerum*, 3 feet, white, summer, Europe. *L. fortunei*, 3 feet, white, summer, China and Japan. *L. leschenaultii*, 1 foot, rose-red, summer, India, does best in light, sandy soil. *L. nemorum*, creeping, yellow, summer, Britain. *L. nummularia*, creeping jenny, yellow, summer, Britain; var. *aurea*, golden leaves. *L. punctata* (syn. *L. verticillata*), 3 feet, yellow, summer, Europe. *L. thyrsiflora*, 3 feet, yellow, summer, north Europe. *L. vulgaris*, yellow loosestrife, 3 feet, yellow, summer, Britain.

Cultivation Rich moist soil is appreciated by these plants, and many species do best by the sides of pools or streams. They will tolerate some shade. The soil needed in hanging baskets or pots for *L. nummularia* consists of 1 part of leafmould and coconut-fibre and 1 part of sand. The baskets should be suspended in partial shade. This plant also makes useful ground-cover under trees etc., particularly in its golden-leaved form. Propagation is by division of plants in spring or autumn.

Lythrum (lith-rum)

From the Greek *lythron*, black blood, in reference to the colour of the flowers of some species (*Lythraceae*). Loosestrife. This is a small genus, mainly consisting of hardy herbaceous and shrubby perennials from temperate regions. One of them, *L. salicaria*, makes beautiful banks of many British streams, and grows abundantly in wet meadows, its long flower spikes coming in late summer when flowering wild plants are beginning to be scarce.

Species cultivated *L. alatum*, 3 feet, crimson-purple, July to October, North America. *L. salicaria*, purple loosestrife, 3 feet, crimson-purple, July, Britain; cultivars include 'Brightness', rose; 'Prichard', rose-pink; 'The Beacon', deep crimson. *L. virgatum*, 2-3 feet, purple, summer, Taurus; 'Rose Queen', rosy-red, is a less tall cultivar.

Cultivation These are ideal plants for the borders of ponds and streams. However, provided the soil is moist, these loose-strifes will grow in any border. It is as well to lift and divide the plants periodically, and this is, in fact, the best method of propagation. It is best carried out in October or April.

Macropidia (mak-ro-pi-dee-a)

A corruption or typographical error from the Latin name for the kangaroo, *macropodia*, meaning long foot. It refers to the shape of the flowers which also give rise to the common name of black kangaroo paw (*Haemadoraceae* or, according to some authorities *Amaryllidaceae*). There is one species only, *M. fuliginosa* (syn. *Anigozanthus fuliginosus*), which is restricted in its distribution to south-west Australia. It is an attractive flowering plant, 3-4 feet high, with iris-like leaves up to 2-3 feet long. The flowers are borne on a long slender stalk and are like those of the related *Anigozanthus* except that they are yellow and black and are normally produced in midsummer.

Cultivation The plant grows very slowly, taking several years to flower from seed. Since it grows in desert areas with limited rainfall, it is very important to keep the plant on the dry side in winter as it can easily be over-watered and killed. It is rare in cultivation, perhaps because of this susceptibility. The compost should be freely draining, as used for cacti. Normally grown in a cool greenhouse with sufficient heat in winter to avoid a stagnant atmosphere, in summer the pots may be plunged out of doors. Propagation is by seed which has to be imported.

Malcolmia (often spelt Malcomia) (mal-ko-me-a)

Commemorating William Malcolm, nurseryman, botanist, and associate of the naturalist Ray (*Cruciferae*). Though there are 35 species in this genus of hardy annual and perennial plants, and many quite decorative plants among them, there is one only which is commonly grown, the Virginian stock, *M. maritima*. The vernacular name is a misnomer as this plant is a native of Southern Europe and has been grown in British gardens since its introduction in 1713. *M. maritima*, which is perhaps the simplest of all hardy annuals to grow, is a 1-foot tall plant with a colour range including white, pink, red, yellow and

Malope (mal-o-pe)

The old Greek name for a kind of mallow, meaning soft or soothing, from the leaf texture, or the plant's medicinal properties (Malvaceae). This is a small genus of hardy annuals from the Mediterranean region, with showy rose or purple flowers.

Species cultivated M. malacoides, 1 foot, rose-pink and purple, June, Mediterranean region. M. trifida, 2–3 feet, purple, summer, Spain; vars. alba, white; grandiflora, large rosy-purple flowers; rosea, rose.

Cultivation Good soil and full sunshine are appreciated and water should be given in dry periods. Soluble stimulants should be given occasionally when the plants are in full growth. Propagation is by seed sown in boxes or pots under glass in March in a temperature of 50°F (10°C), potting the seedlings on as necessary and planting them out 6 inches apart in their flowering positions in May or June. Or seed may be sown ½ inch deep out of doors in April or May where the plants are to flower.

Malva (mal-va)

From the Greek malakos, soft or soothing, probably in reference to an emollient yielded by the seeds (Malvaceae). A genus of hardy herbaceous perennial and annual plants. M. moschata, the musk mallow, is one of the most decorative of our wild flowers, quite suitable for the herbaceous border. It is even more lovely in its white variety. All parts of the musk mallow are said to give off a musky odour when taken indoors, especially in warm dry weather. It is unfortunate that in some areas all malvaceous plants are afflicted by Puccinia malvacearum, the hollyhock rust.

Species cultivated M. alcea, 4 feet rosy-purple, summer, hardy perennial, often grown as annual, Europe; var. fastigiata, flowers red, July to October. M. crispa, 5 feet, purple and white, summer,

lilac. There is a 6-inch tall variety in various colours, known as nana compacta. It is sometimes used to edge beds of annual plants and may be sown quite thickly where it is intended to grow, thinning the seedlings to ½–1 inch apart when they are 1 inch tall. The seeds may be sown in spring for summer blooming, in early summer to flower in late summer and autumn, or in September to bloom in the following spring. Plants may also be grown in 5-inch pots to decorate a sunny windowsill or cold greenhouse.

1 A plant from South-west Australia, Macropidia fuliginosa or Black Kangaroo Paw, reaches about 4 feet and has yellow and black flowers.
2 Lythrum salicaria, the Purple Loosestrife, a British plant, has several cultivars such as 'Rose Queen'.

Marrow cultivation

The marrow is a popular, half-hardy vegetable, and plants are generally raised from seeds sown under glass in April or early May. Sow two or three seeds in pots filled with John Innes compost, in colder parts of the country a little heat may be necessary to assist germination. Thin the plants to leave one seedling in each pot and wait until all risk of a late spring frost has passed before setting the plants in their growing positions in the open. Alternatively, give the plants cloche protection until late June or early July.

A very rich bed is essential for a marrow and the site chosen should have received a generous dressing of well-rotted farmyard manure or garden compost is ideal. Planting distances depend on the type of plant. A bush variety needs almost one square yard of surface area; a trailer needs a great deal more if allowed to roam at will over the ground. Trailing or vining marrows may also be trained on tall supports. These may be bamboo canes or even the garden fence.

Water is essential and the plants must on no account be permitted to become dry at the roots. Liquid manure feeds should be given weekly when the first marrows begin to swell. To ensure that both water and liquid manure reach the roots, many gardeners sink a clay pot alongside each plant. The water and the liquid feeds are poured into the pots and run directly to the root area. Weeding is necessary until the large leaves shade the surrounding soil and inhibit weed growth.

The plants bear male and female flowers. Bees, flies and other insects transfer ripe male pollen to the female blooms. Where female flowers fall off without setting fruits, natural fertilisation is not occurring. In such cases, hand pollination is advisable. Do this before noon. Pick a male flower for each female to be hand pollinated. Strip the petals from the male and twist its core into the centre of the female. The females may be recognised quite easily because they carry an embryo marrow behind them. Bush plants need little attention. Trailers may be guided between other crops or, if they are to be trained to supports, the main shoot must be tied in regularly. Cut the marrows when they are young and tender. They are old if the thumb nail does not pierce the skin easily. Marrows for jam or for storing are allowed to ripen on the plants until September. The storage place should be cool and dry. The marrows are sometimes hung up in nets for storage purposes. Smaller marrows are now preferred. Up-to-date varieties include 'Zucchini F₁ Hybrid' (bush), 'Productive' (bush), 'Prolific' (trailer), 'Clused Roller' (trailer). 'Rotherside Orange' is a prolific variety of excellent flavour. 'Cocozelle' (the Italian vegetable marrow), a bush variety, produces dark green, yellow-striped fruits up to 2 feet long.

Courgettes, or French Courgettes, have become increasingly popular in recent years. In the natural course of events the fruits do not grow very large but, in any case, to obtain the best results, they should be cut when not much bigger than thumb size and cooked unpeeled. Constant cutting will ensure the steady production of fruits throughout the summer. Cultivation is otherwise the same as for the larger marrows. For exhibition purposes, 'Sutton's Table Dainty' is a popular variety.

Matthiola (mat-te-o-la)

Commemorating Pierandrea Mattioli 1500-77, Italian physician and botanist (Cruciferae). This genus of 50 species is important for the gardener's benefit because it contains those annual and biennial species known as stocks. They are showy plants and most have the additional quality of sweet scent. In the wild state stocks are found in the Mediterranean, Egypt, South Europe and in South Africa, and two species, M. incana and M. sinuata, are among the rarer British natives. M. incana is, in fact, the parent plant from which the annual ten-week stocks have arisen; it is also the parent of the biennials: the East Lothian, Brompton, queen and wallflower-leaved stocks.

The sweetly fragrant night-scented stock, M. bicornis, looks a dowdy thing during the daytime but as evening comes the air is filled with its scent. For the sake of its fragrance it may well be grown beneath a window, but not in too prominent a place as it has no beauty of appearance. It is sometimes listed as Hesperis tristis.

Species cultivated M. bicornis, the night-scented stock, 1 foot, purplish, fragrant, annual, Greece. M. fenestralis, 1 foot, scarlet or purple, biennial, Crete. M. incana, 1½ feet, purple, summer, biennial. It is from this last species that most of the showy garden stocks have arisen, and any seedsman's catalogue will offer a great choice of colours in various strains. Named cultivars and strains include:

Beauty or Mammoth stocks, all 1½ feet tall 'Abundance', crimson-rose; 'American Beauty', carmine rose; 'Beauty of Naples', old rose; 'Beauty of Nice'; flesh-pink; 'Côte d'Azur', light blue; 'Crimson King', scarlet, double; 'Monte Carlo', yellow; 'Queen Alexandra', rosy-lilac; 'Summer Night', purple; 'Violette de Parme', violet.

Brompton stocks, mainly 15-18 inches tall 'Crimson King'; 'Giant Empress Elizabeth', rosy carmine; 'Ipswich Carmine King', 2 feet; 'Ipswich Pink King', 'Lavender Lady', 'White Lady';

Hybrida 'Harbinger', early-flowering, East Lothian stocks, 15 inches to 2 feet tall, available in lavender, rose, crimson, scarlet and white and in strains such as 'Giant Imperial', 1½ feet, double flowers in various colours; 'Giant Perfection', 2 feet, mainly double, various colours; 'Improved Mammoth Excelsior' non-branching strain, mainly double flowers, various colours.

Ten-week stocks, 15 inches tall, various colours.

Of both Brompton and ten-week stocks there are available strains known as 'Hanson's Double'. With these it is possible at the seedling stage to select the double varieties as these have light green leaves, whereas those with darker green leaves will produce single flowers if grown on. This colour distinction can be emphasised by sowing seeds in a temperature of 54-60°F (12-16°C), lowering it to below 50°F (10°C) when the seedlings have formed their first pair of leaves.

In addition to the above there is a newer strain called 'Trysomic Seven Week Stocks', earlier to flower than all others, which produces single plants above 1 foot tall with mainly double flowers in carmine, pink, light blue and white.

Cultivation Ten-week stocks are grown from seed sown under glass in March. Plant out the seedlings in May or June, leaving 9 inches between plants. The soil should be deep and well manured. The night-scented stocks are sown out of doors in April where the plants are intended to remain. The biennials of the Brompton group etc, should be sown in frames in June and July. Transplant when 1 inch high to the places where the plants are to flower in the following year. Or, over-winter them in pots in a frame to plant out in the following March. The intermediate and the East Lothian stocks may be given much the same treatment as the Bromptons but will flower much earlier in the year. Though some seedsmen apply the term 'hardy annual' to many of the stocks, it is in fact not advisable to give hardy annual treatment to any but the night-flowering M. bicornis.

Mazus (ma-zus)

From the Greek mazos, a teat, in reference to the tubercles at the mouth of the flowers (Scrophulariaceae). This genus of dwarf perennial plants, related to Mimulus, has a few species natives of

annual, Europe, naturalised in Britain. M. moschata, 3 feet, rose or white, summer, perennial, biennial, Europe, including Britain: var. alba, white. M. sylvestris, 3 feet, purple, summer, biennial, Europe, including Britain.

Cultivation In general, these plants will grow in any kind of soil and in most aspects, though the annuals need sunny conditions to give their best. All can be easily raised from seeds sown in sandy soil in spring under glass in a temperature of 55°F (13°C). The perennials will flower in their second season.

China, Australia, New Zealand and Malaya. The species cultivated in Britain are dwarf hardy plants suitable for the sunny rock garden.

Species cultivated *M. pumilio*, creeping, purplish-blue with yellow centre, summer, New Zealand and Australia. *M. reptans*, prostrate, rosy-lavender, white and brown, May to October, Himalaya. *M. rugosus* (syn. *M. japonicus*), low-growing, lilac-blue, summer, east Asia.

Cultivation Moist sandy soil suits these dwarf plants, which should be grown on a sunny rock garden. Propagation is easily effected by dividing the straggling stems, or seed may be sown in April in a cold frame. The seedlings should be grown on until the following spring before planting out.

Meconopsis (mek-on-op-sis) From the Greek *mekon*, a poppy, and *opsis*, like (*Papaveraceae*). This genus of poppy-like and very showy annual, biennial and perennial plants generally attracts much attention in those fortunate gardens which provide the necessary conditions for their cultivation. Most of the showy Chinese and Himalayan species need light woodland conditions and a moist soil or climate. Very many of these plants are monocarpic, that is, they will die when they attain flowering age whether it be in one, two, three or more years' time. It is probably the bright blue species which are most admired, though some of the delicate yellow ones are extremely fine. One species, *M. cambrica*, the Welsh poppy, is a British native which, with its golden-yellow or orange flowers will brighten sunny or shady places in the garden and will successfully seed itself, often in such inhospitable places as between the cracks in paving stones or even between the bricks in old walls where the pointing has decayed.

Species cultivated (monocarpic unless otherwise noted) *M. aculeata*, 15 inches–2 feet, pale blue-violet, summer, western Himalaya. *M. betonicifolia* (syn. *M. baileyi*), blue poppy, blue Himalayan poppy, 4 feet, azure blue, June to July, Himalaya. *M. cambrica*, 1½ feet, yellow, summer, Europe, including Britain, perennial; vars. *aurantiaca*, flowers orange; *plena*, flowers double, orange or yellow. *M. delavayi*, 6 inches, violet, summer, western China. *M. dhwojii*, 2½ feet, primrose-yellow, summer, Nepal. *M. grandis*, 3 feet, blue, June, Sikkim, perennial; 'Branklyn' is a form with large, rich blue flowers. *M. horridula*, 3½ feet, blue, red or white, Asia. *M. integri-*

1 The various types of Stock have been derived from Matthiola incana. They can be obtained in various shades of pink and purple, and in white.
2 The erect-growing Matthiola vallesiaca is a native of Mediterranean regions and likes dry situations. It produces unspectacular mauve flowers in summer.

folia, 6 inches, violet, Central Asia. M. napaulensis, 5 feet, pale mauve and pink, June, Himalaya. M. paniculata, 5 feet, yellow, July to August, Western China. M. punicea, 1½ feet, crimson, autumn, Tibet. M. quintuplinervia, 1½ feet, lavender-blue, Tibet. M. sarsonii, 2-3 feet, sulphur-yellow, summer, hybrid. M. simplicifolia, 2 feet, purple to sky blue, summer, Himalaya. M. sinuata, 2 feet, pale blue, May to June, east Himalaya. M. superba, 4 feet, pure white, May and June, Tibet, Bhutan. M. villosa, 2 feet, buttercup-yellow, July, Himalaya, perennial.

Cultivation A woodland soil containing leafmould is most suitable, and some light overhead shade during part of the day is appreciated. It is well to sow the seeds as soon as they are available in autumn, but if you get your seeds from a commercial source they will not be available until the spring. A few species, such as M. quintuplinervia may be propagated by division; others, for example, M. grandis, may be increased by removing and rooting side-shoots. Many of the species, especially those with rosettes of silvery leaves, are suited to the lower stratum of a rock garden. Water generously in summer but keep dry in winter. In general the meconopsis found in the moister conditions do better in Scotland and western Britain than in the drier east and south.

Melon

Most of the melons grown in the garden are classified as Cucumis melo cantalupensis. Generally considered a fruit, the melon is in fact a vegetable. If the plants are to be grown in heat, seeds of 'Hero of Lockinge', 'King George' or 'Superlative' may be sown as early as January. 'Tiger' and 'Dutch Net' are hardier and are preferred by many gardeners with a slightly heated or cold greenhouse, and the seeds are sown in May. Sow one seed in each small clay pot filled with John Innes or other suitable seed compost. A temperature of around 65°F (18°C) is needed for germination. The bed for melons is similar to that advised for cucumbers, and consists of turfy loam, well-rotted manure, bonemeal and wood ashes. The plants are set out on the bed when they have made three true leaves. Setting the plants on slight mounds is advisable to prevent stem rot. A trellis of vertical and horizontal wires should be erected, to which the plants are tied until they are stopped at a height of 4 or 5 feet. In the meantime, the sideshoots are stopped when a foot long and tied to the horizontal wires. Watering and ventilation must be attended to carefully. Do not permit fruits to set on the main stem as it is more desirable to have four fruits on separate side-growths. Hand pollination is often necessary and the ripe male pollen should be transferred with a camel hair brush from the male to the female blooms. Pollinate at noon on a bright, sunny day. As soon as the four small fruitlets begin to swell, all others on the plant should be removed. Any surplus growth may also be cut away at this stage. Top-dressings of well-rotted manure may be applied when white rootlets appear on the surface of the bed. No other feeding is necessary. To support the large fruits, slip each melon into a special melon net. Stop all watering as soon as the melons on a plant have reached maximum size. An indication of this and of ripening is when the stalks start to crack near the fruit, or, where the variety 'Dutch Net' is concerned, when the skin develops a network of fine cracks. A 6-foot by 4-foot frame provides sufficient room for two plants of one of the hardier varieties. Set out the plants in late May and pinch out the growing point after the fourth leaf. Peg the sideshoots to the bed, using pieces of wire bent to the shape of a hairpin. Stop the runners when they reach the sides of the frame. Allow either two or three fruits on each plant, and prune away all surplus growth.

Mertensia (mer-ten-se-a)

Named in honour of Francis Karl Mertens, 1764-1831, Professor of Botany, Bremen (Boraginaceae). A genus of low-growing hardy, perennial plants, mostly with blue flowers.

Species cultivated M. ciliata, 1½-2 feet, large greyish-green leaves, clusters of bright blue bells, pink in bud, May and June, North America. M. echioides, 9 inches, racemes of dark blue flowers, summer, Himalaya. M. virginica, Virginian cowslip, 2 feet, leaves soft, bluish-grey, purplish-blue heads of forget-me-not-like flowers on arching sprays, May, Virginia.

Cultivation Suitable for a deep loamy soil and partial shade, although they will succeed in sun provided the roots are moist. The dwarf species may be grown in partial shade on the rock garden; M. virginica is a good plant to grow in light woodland. Propagation is by division of the roots in autumn or by seed sown as soon as it is ripe.

The Virginian Cowslip, Mertensia virginica, flowers in May.

Mesembryanthemum (mes-em-bre-an-the-mum) From the Greek *mesos*, middle, *embryon*, fruit, and *anthemon*, flower; not from *mesembria*, mid-day and *anthemon*, as is usually suggested. The earliest species known flowered at mid-day, but when night-flowering species were discovered the name was changed to give a change of sense without a change of sound (*Aizoaceae*). These are greenhouse suc-culent plants, many suitable for bedding out for the summer. Fleshy leaves and habit of growth. **Species cultivated** *M. albatum*, branch-ing, green and pinkish-red flowers, Cape Province. *M. crystallinum*, ice plant, spreading branches, white flowers, south-west Africa, annual. *M. falleri*, white flowers, Cape Province. *M. intrans-parens*, erect stem, white and pink flowers, Cape Province. *M. macro-phyllum*, prostrate, violet-pink flowers, Namaqualand. *M. nodiflorum*, cylind-rical leaves, white flowers, Africa, the Middle East and California. *M. setosum*, pink and greenish flowers, Cape Pro-vince. *M. striatum*, prostrate, white flowers, Cape Province. The plant now called *Dorotheanthus criniflorum* popularly known as *M. criniflorum* is

Cultivation They should be grown in a very porous compost, for instance John Innes potting compost No 1 with ⅓ part added of coarse sand, grit, broken brick and granulated charcoal. The green-house kinds require a sunny position, with plenty of ventilation in hot weather. Give them a minimum winter tem-perature of 45°F (7°C), and normal greenhouse temperature during summer. Water only when the soil has dried out and keep dry during the winter. Propa-gate from seed sown in John Innes seed compost in March in a temperature of 65-70°F (18-21°C). Do not cover the seed, but keep it moist and shaded until the seedlings are pricked out. These can then be put out in a sunny position in well-drained soil as bedding plants, or on a rock garden.

Microseris (my-kro-ser-iss) From the Greek *mikros*, small, and the Latin *seris*, chicory, endive, referring to the appearance of the flowers which resemble those of chicory (*Cichorium intybus*) (*Compositae*). A genus of 14 species, mainly natives of western North America, but 1 species found in Chile and another in Australia, Tasmania and New Zealand. One species only is likely to be found in cultivation and that only in botanic gardens and the like. This is *M. forsteri* (syns. *Scorzonera scapigera*, *Phyllopappus lanceolatus*) from south-eastern and south-western Australia and New Zea-land. It is a variable plant, sometimes growing up to 2 feet tall, the leaves narrow, up to 6 inches long, sometimes deeply lobed. The flowers are yellow, chaffy in appearance, about ½ inch across. The roots are tuberous and edible, being sweet and milky with a flavour resem-bling that of coconut. They were used as food by the Australian aborigines.

Mimulus (mim-u-lus) From the Greek *mimo*, ape; the flowers were thought to look like a mask or monkey's face (*Scrophulariaceae*). Monkey flower, monkey musk, musk. A genus of hardy annual, half-hardy perennial and hardy perennial plants, grown for their showy flowers. They are found in many temperate parts of the world, particularly in North America.

Species cultivated *M. brevipes*, 1½-2 feet, yellow flowers, summer. *M. fremontii*, 6-8 inches, crimson flowers, summer. Hardy perennial *M. x burnetii*, 1 foot, yellow, spotted bronze; var. *duplex*, flowers double. *M. cardinalis*, cardinal monkey flower, 1-2 feet, red or yellow flowers, summer. *M. cupreus*, 8-12 inches, flowers yellow to copper-red, summer; cultivars include 'Monarch Strain', 1 foot, various colours; 'Red Emperor', 6 inches, scarlet flowers; 'Whitecroft Scarlet', 4 inches, bright orange-scarlet flowers. *M. langsdorfii*), 1-1½ feet, yellow, red spotted flowers, summer. *M. lewisii*, 1-1½ feet, red or white flowers, late summer. *M. luteus*, 1½ feet, yellow monkey musk, summer. *M. moschatus*, monkey musk, 9 inches, yellow flowers, summer. *M. primuloides*, 2-3 inches, creeping habit, yellow, June and July. *M. ringens*, 2 feet, violet to white flowers, summer. *M. variegatus*, 1 foot, blotched flowers, summer, best grown as a half hardy annual. Cultivars include 'Bonfire', 9 inches, orange-scarlet flowers; 'Queen's Prize', 9 inches, white, cream and yellow, blotched red flowers. The plant usually referred to as shrubby mimulus is in fact the Diplacus.

Cultivation Annual species do best in moist, shady positions, though they will grow in sunny places provided the soil is sufficiently moist. Propagation is by seed sown under glass in a temperature of 55-65°F (13-18°C) in spring. The seedlings are pricked out, and gradually hardened off, finally in a cold frame, before being planted out at the end of May or the beginning of June. The hardy perennials grow well in sun or shade provided the soil is moist. They should be planted from spring to early summer. Propagation is by seed sown from spring to early summer, in a temperature of 55-60°F (13-16°C), by cuttings of young growths inserted in sandy soil at almost any time, in a temperature of 55-65°F (13-18°C) or by division of established plants in spring.

Monarda (mon-ar-da) Named after a sixteenth-century Spanish physician and botanist, Nicholas Monar-des (*Labiatae*). A small genus of annual and perennial herbs from North America, with fragrant leaves and flowers, related to *Salvia*. The leaves are nettle-like and the flowers have a spiky appearance and are clustered together in whorls in the colour ranges from white through pinks, mauves and purples to red.

Species cultivated *M. didyma*, bee balm, Oswego tea, 2-3 feet, scarlet flowers, sometimes in twin whorls, late summer; cultivars include 'Adam', 2½ feet, cerise; 'Beauty of Cobham', purple leaves, pink flowers; 'Cambridge Scarlet', crimson-scarlet; 'Croftway Pink', soft pink; 'Dark Ponticum', dark lilac; 'Melissa', soft pink; 'Pale Ponticum', lavender; 'Pillar Box', bright red; 'Sunset', 4 feet, purple-red. *M. fistulosa*, wild bergamot, 2-5 feet, purple lilac flowers, not as showy as *M. didyma*; var. *violacea* (*violacea superba*), deep violet-purple with mint-like foliage. *M. menthaefolia*, similar to *M. fistulosa*.

Cultivation Any ordinary garden soil will suit these plants but there must be plenty of moisture and good drainage. They will grow in sun or partial shade. They can be planted in the autumn or spring and need top-dressing. Propaga-tion is by division in February or March out of doors in a semi-shaded position in spring or in boxes placed in the greenhouse or cold frame in March. Seeds germinate easily but the plants will need rogueing and any drab coloured varieties discarded.

Montbretia (mont-bre-she-a) Named after A. F. Conquebert de Montbret, a botanist of the French expedition to Egypt in the eighteenth century (*Iridaceae*). The familiar com-mon montbretias are now listed under *Crocosmia crocosmiiflora* and allied to this genus is *Tritonia*, leaving only *M. laxifolia* of those species grown in the British Isles under *Montbretia*. This cormous perennial is a native of South Africa and generally requires the pro-tection of a cool greenhouse in the British Isles. The leaves are very narrow and grass-like and the funnel-shaped flowers are carried on 18-inch stems and are creamy-pink, appearing in September.

Cultivation Although the protection of a cool greenhouse is best, this plant may be grown out of doors in warm, sheltered places in a well-drained sandy loam. In all but the most favoured places the corms should be lifted and placed in boxes of soil and stored in an unheated frame or greenhouse during the winter months. In very sheltered gardens they can be left in the ground and protected during the winter but they may not survive if the winter is particularly wet and cold. Propagation is by separating the corms at planting time in late spring.

Muscari (mus-kar-ee)

From the Greek *moschos*, musk, which describes the musky scent of some species (*Liliaceae*). Grape hyacinth, musk hyacinth. A genus of about 50 species of bulbous plants from the Mediterranean region. Some botanists have divided the muscari into three groups, *Moscharia*, *Leopoldia* and *Botryanthus*, and recognise these as separate genera, but for the purpose of this article they are all considered as belonging to the genus *Muscari*. The bulbs are hardy and spring-flowering in shades of blue, some white. They are most commonly seen naturalised in gardens, often in association with spring-flowering trees and shrubs, and other bulbs.

Species cultivated *M. ambrosiacum*, 6 inches, soft lilac flowers, scented, March–April. *M. argaei album*, 7 inches, flowers white; *armenia-cum*, 8 inches, flowers cobalt blue, March–May; vars. 'Blue Spike'; 'Cantab'. *M. botryoides*, grape hyacinth, 6 inches, deep sky blue flowers, April; var. *album*, pearls of Spain, white flowers. *M. comosum*, tassel hyacinth, 7–9 inches, greenish-white, purple topped flowers, May; var. *monstrosum* (syn. *M. c. plumosum*), feather hyacinth, violet-blue flowers, May. *M. latifolium*, 7–10 inches, indigo blue, April. *M. neglectum*, 8–9 inches, fragrant flowers, dark blue, April. *M. paradoxum*, starch hyacinth, 8–9 inches, blue-black, May. *M. racemosum*, 9 inches, navy-blue flowers strongly scented, April. *M. tubergenianum*, Oxford and Cambridge grape hyacinth, 6–7 inches, flowers dark blue in lower half, top half light blue. March–April.

Cultivation Plant the bulbs in September and October, in sunny, well-drained sites, 3 inches deep and as much apart. The smaller kinds can go 2 inches deep and 1 inch apart. Leave them to natura-lise or lift them and replant every third year. Bulbs may also be pot-grown for early flowering in a cool greenhouse. Propagation is by seeds sown in boxes of sandy soil in a cold frame or out of doors in September, or offsets may be removed from old bulbs at planting time and treated in the same way as mature bulbs. Seedling bulbs flower after three or four years from sowing.

1 The Oxford and Cambridge Muscari, *M. tubergenianum*, has flowers of pale and dark blue in March and April.
2 The flowers of the Musk Hyacinth, *M. moschatum*, are blue at first and then become yellow and fragrant.
3 The almost navy-blue flowers of *Muscari racemosum* are strongly scented and bloom in April.

Mushroom cultivation

From the time of the Greeks and Romans, various fungi have been eaten as a delicacy and the expert can find many varieties growing wild which are equal, if not superior, in flavour to the mushroom (*Psalliota campestris*). But there are also a number of poisonous fungi, some deadly. The field mushrooms which appear in profusion in meadows in the moist autumn days are perfectly safe, but the inexperienced townsman would be well advised to make sure first that he is actually picking field mush-rooms, because some poisonous fungi are very similar. Cultivated mushrooms are absolutely reliable and a valuable food as well as a delicacy.

Since the war, the production of mushrooms on specialised farms has increased rapidly all over the Western world, in answer to a growing demand. There is a very wide gap between the results achieved by the amateur and the commercial growers, but provided atten-tion is paid to a few essential factors, useful crops can be grown in sheds or cellars, in the greenhouse during the winter and in outdoor beds. The amateur has one big advantage; he can enjoy the flavour of ripe mushrooms taken straight from the soil, the very best way to eat them. Most commercial growers pick the mushrooms as buttons or cups with the veils unbroken. If they are picked fully open, the delicate pink under-surface often becomes brown and dry before they reach the shops, and the flavour suffers.

Mushrooms are grown in a prepared compost which enables the spores to produce cotton-like threads called mycelium which, after a few weeks, emerge on the surface to form pin-heads. These develop in a week to 12 days (according to the temperature), into fully grown mushrooms and successive flushes appear for 10 to 12 weeks or even longer.

The first and most important task is to prepare the compost making certain that it is the right texture for the development of the mycelium and at the same time provides nutrient and moisture. If the compost is right, there will be no difficulty in getting a crop; if it is incorrectly prepared, the result can be a complete failure.

Fresh horse manure with plenty of straw is the easiest material to use and is generally recommended. But any sort of manure and breaks down organic activity which creates bacterial material will produce good mushroom compost. Horse, pig and cow manure have all been used. One Belgian research station produced excellent results using elephant manure from the local circus. Compost can also be made by breaking down straw with chemicals. If horse manure cannot be obtained, one of the special activators obtainable from horticultural suppliers should be used to break down straw or chaff.

Manure is stacked in a heap about 4 feet wide and 5 feet high and watered during stacking so that it is moist but not wet. If an activator is used, this is sprinkled on successive layers of straw and chaff and watered in, until a similar sized heap has been made. The temperature of the heap goes up very quickly because the type of bacteria which develop in the presence of oxygen requires the type of bacterial activity; a good compost requires the type of bacteria which develop in the presence of oxygen. This means that air must reach all parts of the heap during composting. The process can be helped by a wire frame in the form of an upright triangle along the length of the heap. After seven days, the heap is turned, water being applied sparingly where the material is dry. Four or five more turns are made and at the end, all unpleasant smell should have disappeared. The material should be rich brown and exudes liquid when squeezed.

The compost is then put into boxes or shelves to any depth between 5 and 15 inches. The deeper the compost, the longer the crop will continue; on the other hand, the shallower beds give a larger area and a quicker crop. The beds are then spawned with one of the pure culture spawns available commercially. Manure spawn is inserted into the compost and firmed in. Grain spawn is ruffed in.

After 10-14 days, the tiny white threads will be seen running into the compost and at this point the beds are cased. Commerical growers use a mixture of peat and chalk for casing and this can easily be made up by mixing the peat, after it has been thoroughly wetted, with a quarter of its volume of chalk. If soil is used it should be taken from the second spit and heat sterilised. The casing is spread 1 inch deep.

From spring to autumn, mushrooms can be grown without artificial heat. If the temperature falls below about 50°F (10°C) the mycelium will not grow, but this will only delay the crop. Beds can be frozen solid and still produce mushrooms, when the weather gets warmer. Too hot weather will quickly ruin a crop. That is why the greenhouse is suitable only in winter and an insulated building is preferable in summer.

Provided the temperature is satisfactory, the first pinheads will appear about four weeks after casing. For a winter crop, the temperature should be kept at about 65°F (18°C). The beds should be kept fairly dry until the pin-heads develop, enough water being given to keep the casing just moist. After that, rather more water is needed and the surroundings should be sprayed to keep up humidity. There should be a free movement of air round the beds. If a puff of cigarette smoke blown over the bed slowly moves away, ventilation is adequate. The ripe mushrooms are pulled out, not cut, and the holes filled with a little peat.

The compost can also be made up into outdoor beds. These should be on a well-drained site and are best built deeper than the indoor beds with a 3-feet wide base and sloping sides. They are spawned and cased as for indoor beds, but are then given a thatch of straw. Extra care must be taken to deal with slugs and woodlice. Mushrooms are subject to a number of insect and other pests, particularly two types of fly, *Phorids* and *Sciarids*, which breed in the manure, and mites, which eat holes in the caps and stems. These can be controlled by modern insecticides, but it is advisable to buy preparations made up specially for the mushroom crop.

Spent mushroom compost is excellent for the garden. Tests at experimental horticulture stations have shown that it is just as valuable as farmyard manure.

Myosotis (my-o-so-tis)

From the Greek *mus*, a mouse, and *otes*, an ear, in reference to the leaves (*Boraginaceae*). Forget-me-not, scorpion grass. The common forget-me-not is a popular plant for use in spring bedding schemes in combination with other plants such as tulips and wallflowers. There are some 40 species of annuals, biennials or perennials in the genus. Those natives of temperate regions, particularly Europe and Australia. Those used for bedding purposes are hardy perennials but are usually treated as biennials.

Species cultivated *M. alpestris*, 3-8 inches, azure-blue with yellow eyes, June-July, European mountains; vars. *alba*, white flowers, *aurea*, golden yellow leaves. *M. australis*, 1-1½ feet, yellow leaves, sometimes white, summer, New Zealand. *M. azorica*, 6-10 inches, violet-purple, summer, Azores; var. *alba*, white flowers. *M. caespitosa*, 6 inches, sky-blue, yellow centre, summer, European mountains; var. *rehsteineri*, 2 inches, tufted, April-May. *M. dissitiflora*, 8-10 inches, sky-blue, May to July, European Alps; var. *alba*, white. *M. scorpioides* (syn. *M. palustris*), forget-me-not, 6-12 inches, blue flowers with yellow eye, May and June; vars. *alba*, white flowers, *semper-florens*, dwarf, *M. sylvatica*, 1-2 feet, blue with yellow eye, spring, Europe, including Britain, North Asia. Cultivars. 'Anne Marie Fischer', deep blue flowers, compact plant; 'Blue Ball', deep blue, compact plant; 'Blue Bird', deep blue, winter flowering; 'Carmine King'; 'Compindi', deep indigo-blue, compact; 'Marga Sacher', deep sky-blue; 'Royal Blue'; 'Rosea', pale rose; 'Ruth Fischer', very large blue flowers, 'Star of Love', blue, dwarf, 'Victoria', blue.

Cultivation *M. alpestris* requires a lightly shaded place in the rock garden, and should be planted in March or April. Other kinds are best grown as biennials by sowing seed in shallow drills outdoors from April to June. Transplant the seedlings to spring-flowering beds, in October, planting them 4-6 inches apart in ordinary soil. Perennial plants may be increased by division in March or October. *M. azorica* may not prove reliably hardy as a perennial in some years.

Narcissus (nar-siss-us)

Either from the Greek *narke*, or *narkao*, to be stupefied, as some species have narcotic properties (*Amaryllidaceae*). Daffodil. A genus of 60 species, but many thousands of cultivars, plants with tunicated bulbs, natives of Europe, North Africa and western Asia, grown for the beauty of their flowers, borne in spring.

Narcissus is the botanical name for the genus and daffodil is its common name. Many refer to yellow trumpet daffodils as jonquils but more correctly a jonquil is a sweetly-scented, rich yellow species of narcissus with slender round flower stems and rush-like leaves, or a hybrid derived from the species.

The narcissus stems from a handful of species or wild daffodils which flourished long before the time of Christ. In Greek mythology Ovid related a tender story of a lad called Narcissus, the son of Cephissus and Leirope, who was led to believe that a long and happy life would be his provided he never gazed upon his own features. In a moment of vanity one day Narcissus peered at his own reflection in a quiet pool and, falling in love with his own image, soon pined away.

From the earth where he died there sprang a beautiful nodding flower which thereafter was called Narcissus.

In Greek mythology these plants were consecrated to the Furies, who are alleged by ancient writers to first stupefy those whom they wished to punish.

English poets, from Herrick to Shakespeare and Wordsworth, have praised and popularised the narcissus under its common name of daffodil. It was also given such names as Lent lily, ostensibly because the flower bloomed in the Lenten season. Another name was chalice flower, probably because the corona of the flower closely resembles in shape the cup or chalice used for holding sacramental wine.

The daffodils in Shakespeare's day were only a meagre reflection of the massive daffodil family today. In Shakespeare's time some two dozen different daffodils only were grown in British gardens. By 1629 there were 90 known varieties and when the first list was published by the Royal Horticultural Society in 1908 the list had mounted to over 8,000. Today, although 4,000 varieties are obsolete, there are over 10,000 named varieties in the *Classified List and International Register of Daffodil Names* published by the Royal Horticultural Society in consultation with the Royal General Bulb Growers' Society of Haarlem, Holland. Many of the varieties are rare or in limited supply but the gardener has access today to over 500 varieties which are commercially cultivated.

The narcissus grows wild only in the Northern Hemisphere, mainly in Europe in the Mediterranean region. The northern limit is the north of Britain and southern-most limit the Canary Islands. Tazetta forms grow through Asia as far as Japan.

With the exception of one or two kinds, such as tazettas, narcissi are hardy, tolerant and adaptable plants. They will grow in almost any situation except heavy shade or in badly-drained soil. In open ground they flower from February to the end of May. Normally most varieties remain in flower for three to four weeks and if they are picked in bud for cut flowers they will last in water for ten days or more.

Narcissi will flourish in beds and borders, naturalised in meadows, open woodlands, lawns, orchards or under scattered trees, among shrubs, in tubs and window boxes. The smaller kinds do well in rock gardens and many varieties are suitable for forcing.

The bulbs of the different varieties and species of narcissi vary enormously in size and shape. Those of the smallest of species (*N. minimus*) are no larger than a pea, while some of the trumpet and large-cupped daffodils have bulbs which measure 5 or 6 inches in circumference. In shape the bulbs range from the round onion form of some of the N.

Narcissus 'February Gold' is an early-flowering, long-lasting plant with bold trumpets of a fine golden-yellow.

tazetta hybrids to the long narrow bulbs of some of the *N. poeticus* hybrids.

Wild daffodils increase mostly by seed but garden daffodils increase by offsets produced on the two opposite sides of the bulb. These start as small buds between the scales on the upper surface of the base plate, and within a year or two arrive at the side of the bulb. As they develop, their own system of scales presses some of the parent bulb scales outwards, which eventually become the desiccated outer skins. These split in time, permitting the enlarged offsets to become detached from the parent bulb.

Hybridisation and development of the narcissus, particularly in Britain and Holland, have produced flowers of far greater beauty and more varied form than nature alone provides. The ancestry of the many varieties, going back to their origin in species, is often complex and confusing. But even a superficial study of the classification key reveals the diversity of the family.

There are far more kinds than the popular yellow trumpets and the starry poet's narcissus. It soon becomes evident why increasing numbers of gardeners have made a hobby of growing and collecting daffodils. There are flourishing daffodil societies in Britain, the United States, Holland, Australia and New Zealand.

As in any key, under the revised system for the classification of daffodils which came into force on 1st January 1950, there are a few terms to learn. These terms are used in defining each of the eleven classes or divisions of daffodils.

The corona (trumpet, cup, or crown) is the centre portion of the flower varying in shape from long and tubular to a flattened disc.

The perianth is the wheel or circle of petals surrounding the central corona.

The length of perianth segment is the extreme length measured on the inside from its junction with the corona along the midrib to the extreme tip.

The length of the corona is the extreme length measured from its junction with the perianth to the end of its furthest extension when the edge is flattened out.

Coloured means yellow or some colour other than white.

White means white or whitish.

Out of doors daffodils will flourish in any well-drained soil although *N. bulbocodium* prefers sandy soil and *N. cyclamineus* peaty soil. The best sites are in sun or light shade with shelter from sweeping winds. Plant the bulbs as early in the autumn as they can be obtained. Robust kinds that have large bulbs should be planted 5–6 inches deep, less vigorous kinds with smaller bulbs 3–4 inches deep, and tiny species 3 inches deep. Space vigorous growers 6–9 inches apart, moderately vigorous growers 4–5 inches apart, and small species 2–4 inches apart. In naturalised plantings these distances are varied considerably and it is best to scatter the bulbs at random, in groups or drifts, planting them exactly where they fall.

For planting bulbs out of doors, especially in turf, special planting tools are available. Some of these are long-handled tools, shod with a circular metal cutter which is forced into the soil. When the tool is lifted a core of

---

Narcissus classification
Examples of varieties available in Britain are given in each division

Division I   **Trumpet narcissi:** distinguishing characters—one flower to a stem; trumpet or corona as long or longer than the perianth segments
- **a** Perianth coloured; corona coloured, not paler than the perianth (yellow trumpets)—'Dutch Master', 'Golden Harvest', 'Golden Top', 'Irish Luck', 'King Alfred', 'Magnificence', 'Rembrandt', 'Unsurpassable'
- **b** Perianth white; corona coloured (bicolor trumpets)—'Celebrity', 'Music Hall', 'President Lebrun', 'Queen of Bicolors'
- **c** Perianth white; corona white, not paler than the perianth (white trumpets)—'Beersheba', 'Mrs E. H. Krelage', 'Mount Hood'
- **d** Any colour combination not falling into the above—'Spellbinder' (greenish sulphur-lemon, inside of trumpet almost white)

Division II   **Large-cupped narcissi:** distinguishing characters—One flower to a stem; cup or corona more than one-third but less than equal to the length of the perianth segments
- **a** Perianth coloured; corona coloured, not paler than the perianth—'Carbineer', 'Carlton', 'Fortune', 'Yellow Sun'
- **b** Perianth white; corona coloured—'Flower Record', 'Mrs R. O. Backhouse', 'Sempre Avanti'
- **c** Perianth white; corona white, not paler than the perianth—'Castella', 'Silver Lining', 'White Queen'

- **d** Any colour combination not falling into the above—'Binkie' (perianth sulphur-yellow, corona sulphur, ageing to white)

Division III   **Small-cupped narcissi:** distinguishing characters—one flower to a stem; cup or corona no more than one-third the length of the perianth segments
- **a** Perianth coloured; corona coloured, not paler than the perianth—'Chungking', 'Edward Buxton'
- **b** Perianth white; corona coloured—'Pomona', 'Verger'
- **c** Perianth white; corona white, not paler than the perianth—'Chinese White', 'Polar Ice'
- **d** Any colour combination not falling into the above—'Green Elf'

Division IV   **Double narcissi:** distinguishing character—double flowers —'Inglescombe', 'Mary Copeland', 'Texas'

Division V   **Triandrus narcissi:** distinguishing characters—characteristics of *Narcissus triandrus* clearly evident.
- **a** Cup or corona not less than two-thirds the length of the perianth segments—'Liberty Bells', 'Thalia'
- **b** Cup or corona less than two-thirds the length of the perianth segments—'Dawn', 'Hawera', 'Moonshine'

Division VI   **Cyclamineus narcissi:** distinguishing characters—characteristics of *Narcissus cyclamineus* clearly evident

- **a** Cup or corona not less than two-thirds the length of the perianth segments—'February Gold', 'March Sunshine', 'Peeping Tom'
- **b** Cup or corona less than two-thirds the length of the perianth segments—'Beryl'

Division VII   **Jonquilla narcissi:** distinguishing characters—characteristics of any of the *Narcissus jonquilla* group clearly evident
- **a** Cup or corona not less than two-thirds the length of the perianth segments—'Golden Sceptre'
- **b** Cup or corona less than two-thirds the length of the perianth segments—'Cherie', 'Lintie', 'Trevithian'

Division VIII   **Tazetta (Poetaz) narcissi:** distinguishing characters—characteristics of any of the *Narcissus tazetta* group clearly evident—'Cheerfulness', 'Cragford', 'Geranium', 'St Agnes', 'Scarlet Gem'

Division IX   **Poeticus narcissi:** distinguishing characters—characteristics of any of the *Narcissus poeticus* group without admixture of any other—'Actaea', *N. poeticus recurvus* (pheasant's eye)

Division X   **Species and wild forms and wild hybrids:** all species and wild, or reputedly wild, forms and hybrids—*N. bulbocodium conspicuus* (yellow hoop petticoat daffodil), *N. minimus* (tiniest of daffodils)

Division XI   **Miscellaneous narcissi:** all narcissi not falling into any of the foregoing divisions—'Brilliant Star', 'Canasta'

A selection of Daffodils

For the garden

Division I
  a 'Golden Harvest'—giant trumpet of solid golden colour, beautifully flanged and deeply serrated at mouth
  b 'Patria'—smooth overlapping creamy-white perianth of enormous size and bold, beautifully finished pale primrose trumpet elegantly rolled back at mouth
  c 'Mount Hood'—broad pure white perianth of thick smooth texture, the ivory trumpet with rolled back brim soon passes to pure white throughout
  d 'Spellbinder'—large, even erect perianth of greeny lime-yellow; smooth trumpet, neatly turned back at mouth, opens the same lime shade but becomes nearly white except for brim which remains yellow

Division II
  a 'Fortune'—soft yellow broad and well overlapping perianth and well-proportioned fluted cup of bright orange
  b 'Sempre Avanti'—broad shovel pointed creamy-white perianth and well-proportioned fluted cup of bright orange
  d 'Binkie'—reversed bicolor of distinct and beautiful form; on opening the whole flower is pale clear sulphur-lemon, but the cup gradually passes to almost white

Division III
  b 'Verger'—large white, rounded perianth segments, flatly overlapping and at right angles to the stem and corona. The small, flat crown is lemon-yellow with a narrow border of bright orange

Division IV 'Mary Copeland'—double flower of exquisite beauty, outer petals creamy-white and centre interspersed with orange-red

Division V
  a 'Liberty Bells'—head of two to four flowers of deep lemon-yellow on a slender stem, corona slightly paler at the margin

Division VI
  a 'Peeping Tom'—long, rich, narrow golden-yellow trumpet attractively rolled at the mouth, the reflexing perianth segments of slightly paler colour

Division VII
  a 'Trevithian'—beautiful and graceful jonquil hybrid with an average of two sweetly-scented flowers per stem. The perianth and shallow corona are clear grapefruit-yellow throughout

Division VIII 'Geranium'—a tazetta hybrid of remarkable beauty, bearing on strong stems heads of three to five flowers with broad paper-white petals and a golden-orange corona, colour deepening towards the edges

Division IX 'Actaea'—large, striking flower with broad snow-white perianth, petals well overlapping, canary-yellow eye edged red

Division X N. bulbocodium conspicuus (yellow hoop petticoat daffodil)—very quaint with hooped cup of rich golden-yellow, the much reduced perianth paler and protruding from the cup, the anthers curl upwards; rush-like foliage.

For naturalising

Division I
  a 'Irish Luck'—broadly overlapping but pointed petals of rich golden-yellow at right angles to the smooth trumpet which is frilled at the mouth
  c 'Mrs E. H. Krelage'—broad, massive snow-white perianth, the elegant trumpet neatly rolled back opens soft primrose and passes to ivory white
    'Mount Hood'—see under garden selection
  d 'Spellbinder'—see under garden selection

Division II
  a 'Carlton'—broad, flat, well overlapping soft yellow perianth, large clear yellow corona, beautifully frilled and expanded
  b 'Bizerta'—pure white perianth segments and balanced cup of soft honey-amber, delicately fringed at the edge
    'Brunswick'—overlapping pure white perianth and evenly frilled trumpet-shaped corona of lime-yellow
    'Kilworth'—broad white perianth and bowl-shaped corona of vivid orange-red with a touch of dark green in the eye
  d 'Binkie'—see under garden selection

Division III
  b 'Pomona'—perianth pure white with neatly shaped petals, short cup of apricot with a tangerine frill

Division IV 'White Lion'—broadly overlapping perianth segments behind a fully double creamy-white centre, interspersed with smaller petals of soft coppery ochre

Division VI
  a 'February Gold'—clear yellow perianth slightly reflexing and deep golden-yellow trumpet, prettily frilled at the margin
    'March Sunshine'—narrow perianth petals of canary-yellow, reflexing, and straight trumpet of deepest gold, frilled

Division IX N. poeticus recurvus (pheasant's eye)—pretty flower with reflexed snow-white perianth and yellow eye, rimmed orange-red, fragrant

Division X N. bulbocodium conspicuus—see under garden selection
    N. minimus—resembles the wild narcissus in miniature, delightful little golden flower, tiniest of the daffodils
    N. triandrus albus (angel's tears)—produces a cluster of pretty creamy-white flowers with globular cup

For indoor cultivation

Christmas-flowering (specially prepared bulbs)

Division I
  a 'Golden Harvest'—golden-yellow
  b 'Patria'—pale primrose and creamy-white

Division II
  a 'Yellow Sun'—clear yellow perianth and frilled golden-yellow cup
  b 'Patriarch'—pure white perianth and frilled tangerine corona
    'Smiling Queen'—pure white perianth and frilled golden-orange cup

Division III
  b 'Verger'—white rounded perianth and lemon-yellow cup bordered orange

Division IV 'Texas'—immense double flower of cream, gold and tangerine

Division VI
  a 'Peeping Tom'—rich golden-yellow trumpet

Flowering from January onward

Division I
  a 'Dutch Master'—rich gold
    'Golden Harvest'—golden-yellow
    'Golden Top'—canary-yellow
    'King Alfred'—deep golden-yellow
  c 'Beersheba'—white
    'Mount Hood'—white
    'W. P. Milner'—mimosa yellow trumpet turning cream

Division II
  a 'Carlton'—soft clear yellow
    'Galway'—intense gold
    'Scarlet Elegance'—golden-yellow with orange-red cup
  b 'Flower Record'—white perianth, golden-yellow cup with orange-red band
    'Mrs R. O. Backhouse'—white with pink cup

Division III
  b 'Barrett Browning'—white perianth, neatly ruffled flat flame cup
    'La Riante'—white perianth, brilliant orange-red crown (not to be forced before February and then in cool conditions)

Division VI
  a 'February Gold'—deep golden-yellow
    'March Sunshine'—deep gold
    'Peeping Tom'—rich golden-yellow

Division VIII 'Cheerfulness'—white with yellow centre
    'Geranium'—white with orange cup
    'Scarlet Gem'—brilliant orange cup, two to three flowers per stem

Division IX 'Actaea'—white with canary-yellow eye edged red

For growing on pebbles in water

Division VIII 'Cragford'—three to four dainty flowers per stem with milk white petals and brilliant orange-scarlet cup
    'Grand Soleil d'Or'—multi-flowered, golden-yellow
    'Paperwhite grandiflora'—white

1 Narcissus watieri (Div X) is one of the dainty little species, growing to about 4 inches tall, which is suitable for planting in the rock garden, or, better still, for growing in pans in the cool greenhouse, where the beauty of the flowers can be appreciated best.

2 N. bulbocodium (Div X) is popularly known as the Hoop Petticoat Narcissus, because of the shape of its flaring trumpets. It is another species which is ideal for the rock garden, for naturalising or for the alpine house.

3 N. nanus, at 8 inches, is a little taller; it is one of the earliest to flower, producing its trumpets in early March. It is often listed under its synonym, N. lobularis.

4 'Beersheba' (Div Ic) is one of the most popular of white Daffodils.

5 N. odorus (Div X), the Campernelle, bears up to 4 flowers per stem in April. It grows to about 1 foot tall.

6 N. rupicola (Div X) is, at 3 inches, one of the tiniest of all daffodils, with deep-yellow flowers in April.

turf and soil is removed intact. A bulb is then placed in the hole and the core of turf replaced over it and firmed with the foot. To enable the cutter to be driven easily into hard turf the tool is fitted with a foot bar. There are versions of this tool with short handles, without the foot bar. Otherwise, when planting in soil or in the rock garden it is always advisable to do so with a trowel, never with a dibber. If a dibber is used an air pocket may be left below the bulb, into which the roots will not grow, thus preventing proper development. If the soil is dry, water thoroughly after planting.

Where winters are severe, protect bulbs which are not planted in grass with a covering of leaves or other suitable material. Feed established plantings in early autumn and early spring, using a complete fertiliser in spring and a slower-acting organic fertiliser in the autumn. Water copiously during dry spells when the foliage is above ground. Never remove the foliage until it has died down naturally. When plantings become crowded so that the bloom deteriorates in quantity and quality, lift, separate and replant the bulbs as soon as the foliage has died down.

Daffodils will root, grow, and flower indoors in a perfectly natural manner if planted early in 5–8 inch pots, deep pans or other containers. Plant the bulbs in light, loamy well-drained soil or bulb fibre, placing the bulbs close together but not touching each other and with their tips just showing above the surface. Daffodil bulbs must be made firm in the soil or fibre as the masses of roots tend to lift bulbs from their place. On the other hand the fibre below them must not be packed too tightly or root action may force the bulbs out of the containers. Bulbs intended for forcing indoors must be planted no less than 12–16 weeks before they are brought indoors for flowering. When they are first planted, place the containers in a cellar, temperature 40–45°F (4–7°C), or plunge them out of doors under 6–8 inches of soil, peat, sand or ashes, except 'Paper White', 'Grand Soleil d'Or', and those of the tazetta division which may be placed out of doors in a temperature of 40–45°F (4–7°C) without plunging them. When flower buds are clearly visible remove the containers to the greenhouse, sunroom or window, shading them until the shoots turn green, then place them in full sun, temperature 50–55°F (10–13°C), at first, then 55–60°F (13–16°C). Water them freely, as dryness causes the buds to blast. After flowering is over continue to water the plants, harden them off gradually, and plant the bulbs out of doors after the danger of frost is past; or keep them watered as long as the foliage remains green, then dry and store the bulbs in a cool, dry place, and

plant them out of doors in early autumn.

'Paper White', 'Soleil d'Or' and tazetta hybrids are suitable for growing on pebbles in water. Bulbs planted in pebbles and water are set so that their lower half only is below the surface of the pebbles. Water is then poured in until its surface is about level with the bases of the bulbs.

Species cultivated N. biflorus, 1 foot, white and yellow, May, Europe. N. bulbocodium, hoop-petticoat daffodil, 6 inches, flowers solitary, yellow, April, southern Europe; vars. citrinus, lemon-yellow; conspicuus, yellow hoop-petticoat daffodil, golden-yellow; obesus, clear yellow; romieuxii, primrose-yellow, early-flowering. N. cyclamineus, 4–8 inches, flowers solitary, lemon and yellow, segments much reflexed, February and March, Spain, Portugal. N. gracilis, 1 foot, 1–3 flowers per stem, yellow, April, southern France, possibly a hybrid. N. incomparabilis, chalice-cup narcissus, 1 foot, flowers solitary, yellow, April, 1 foot. N. jonquilla, jonquil, 9 inches, 2–6 flowers per stem, bright yellow, southern Europe, Algeria; there is a double form known as Queen Anne's jonquil. N. juncifolius, 6–8 inches, foliage rush-like, flowers 1–4 per stem, yellow, April, southern Europe. N. minimus (syn. N. asturiensis), pygmy daffodil, 4 inches, flowers solitary, sulphur-yellow, February to April, Europe, the smallest of all trumpet narcissi. N. moschatus (syn. N. cernuus), musk daffodil, 1 foot, foliage bluish-green, flowers solitary, white, Pyrenees. N. nanus (syn. N. minor conspicuus), 6–8 inches, flowers solitary, sulphur-yellow and bright yellow, southern Europe. N. obvallaris, Tenby daffodil, 8–12 inches, flowers solitary, golden-yellow, March, Europe, including Britain. N. odorus, campernelle, 1 foot, 2–4 flowers per stem, bright yellow, April, Mediterranean region eastwards. N. x poetaz, narcissus, 1 foot or so, up to 8 flowers per stem, yellow, March, hybrid. N. poeticus, poet's narcissus, pheasant eye narcissus, 1 foot, flowers solitary, white, May, southern Europe, from France to Greece; var. ornatus, flowering earlier. N. pseudo-narcissus, daffodil, Lent lily, trumpet narcissus, 12–15 inches, flowers solitary, yellow, March, Europe, including Britain, a variable plant; var. bicolor, yellow and white. N. rupicola, 3 inches, leaves rush-like, flowers solitary, to 1 inch across, deep yellow, April, Portugal, Spain. N. scaberulus, similar to N. rupicola, but flowers smaller, deeper yellow, 2 per stem, Mediterranean area. N. serotinus, 1 foot, flowers solitary, occasionally 2–3 per stem, white and yellow, September and October, southern Europe. N. tazetta, polyanthus narcissus, 1 foot, up to 8 flowers per stem, white and yellow, March, Canary Isles eastwards to Japan; var. orientalis, Chinese sacred lily, more erect in habit. N. triandrus, angel's tears, 6–9 inches,

to 6 flowers per stem, white, April and May, Portugal, Spain; vars. albus, to 1 foot, flowers creamy-white; concolor, pale yellow. N. watieri, 3–4 inches, flowers solitary, white, April, Morocco.

Nemesia (nem-e-ze-a)

An ancient Greek name used for a similar plant (Scrophulariaceae). Although there are some 50 species in the genus, of annuals, perennials and sub-shrubs, mainly natives of South Africa, the majority of plants grown by gardeners are hybrid races and cultivars originating mostly from the South African species N. strumosa. In Britain these are mainly grown as half-hardy annuals, chiefly to provide bright mixtures of colour in summer-flowering bedding schemes. Cultivars include N. strumosa, 'Aurora', 9 inches, carmine and white flowers; 'Blue Gem', 9 inches, pale blue flowers; 'Fire King', 9 inches, flowers crimson scarlet; 'Orange Prince', 9 inches, rich orange flowers, superbissima grandiflora, 9 inches, a strain with large flowers in a wide range of colours. N. strumosa suttonii is a selected race with large flowers and a range of all colours found in nemesias. Other hybrid selections include 'Dwarf Compact Hybrids', 9 inches; 'Dwarf Gem Mixture', 9 inches; 'Dwarf Triumph Strain', 9 inches; 'Carnival Mixture', 9–12 inches; 'Red Carnival', 9–12 inches, a tetraploid cultivar.

Cultivation Sow seed, in well-drained pans, pots or boxes in the greenhouse in April, in a temperature of 55°F (13°C) and transplant the seedlings 1 inch apart in seed boxes until the plants are ready for setting out in the open garden in June, at 4 inches apart. Keep the plants cool at all stages, at a temperature not above 55°F (13°C), and ensure that seedlings are never allowed to dry at the roots, nor become overcrowded in their boxes. Seed may also be sown directly into flowering beds, in May and June, thinning the seedlings to 4 inches apart when they are large enough to handle. A sowing under glass in July or August will provide winter-flowering pot plants for the greenhouse. For flowering under glass in early spring sow seed between mid-September and mid-October. Prick off the seedlings first into seed boxes and later pot them on individually into 3-inch pots, finally moving them to 5-inch pots. Forcing in extra heat should not be attempted.

Nemophila (nem-of-il-a)

From the Latin nemos, a glade, and the Greek phileo, to love, because the plant was found growing in glades or groves (Hydrophyllaceae). Baby blue eyes. A genus of nearly 20 species of annual plants from North America of which a few are grown in gardens in Britain as hardy annuals.

Species cultivated N. maculata, 6–12 inches, flowers white, prominently

veined flowers blotched violet, summer.
N. menziesii (syn. *N. insignis*), 6 inches,
spreading in habit, flowers light blue
with white centres, summer; var. *alba*,
flowers white with black centres.
Cultivation These little annuals are
easily grown in any ordinary garden
soil. Seeds are sown in March or April,
where the plants are to flower in
summer, choosing sunny places. Spring-
flowering plants are raised from seed
sown in August or September, but they
may need cloche protection during
severe spells. The seedlings should be
thinned when young to 3 inches apart.
Nemophilas make attractive pot plants
for unheated greenhouses or sunny
window-sills, if seed is sown in pans or
pots and the seedlings into potted-on
3½-inch pots and later into final 5–6-inch
pots. Keep them in a cool, shady place
until the plants are about to flower.

Nepeta (nep-ee-ta)

An early Latin name, probably taken
from an Italian place name Nepi
(Labiatae). A genus of about 150 species
of hardy herbaceous perennials and
annuals, a few of which are grown partly
for their aromatic foliage. Some were
once used for their remedial properties.
One, grown commonly under the name
of *N. mussinii*, often used for edging, is
of hybrid origin and is more correctly
called *N. × faassenii*. Creeping kinds can
be usefully grown as ground cover in
shady places.
Species cultivated *N. × faassenii* (syn. *N.
mussinii* of gardens), 1–1½ feet, silvery
foliage, flower spikes formed by whorls
of soft lavender-blue flowers with darker
spots, May to September, hybrid. *N.
cataria*, catmint, catnip, catnep, 2–3 feet,
flowers whitish purple in whorls on
upright stems, summer. *N. macrantha*
(syn. *Dracocephalum sibiricum*), 3 feet,
blue flowers clustered on stems, summer.
N. nervosa, 1–2 feet, light blue flowers in
dense spikes, July–September. Cultivars
include 'Six Hills Giant', 2½ feet, light
violet flowers, summer; 'Souvenir
d'André Chaudron', 1 foot, rich lavender-
blue flowers, July–September.
Cultivation The nepetas will do well in
ordinary, well-drained soil in sunny
borders, grouped or as edging plants. As
growth is vigorous and sprawling, it is
inadvisable to plant nepetas too near
smaller plants which may easily be
smothered. Plant in autumn or spring.
Cutting back of dead autumn growth
should be delayed until the spring when
the new growth begins. Then the plants
should be trimmed over to remove the
dead stems. Propagation is by seed sown
in spring, division in spring or cuttings
taken from new growth made from base

**Nemesia strumosa suttonii is a selected
race with large flowers in the wide
range of colours to be found in this
genus. The plants are used here to add
colour to the mixed border.**

129

of plants cut back in summer after flowering. Young shoots root readily in sandy compost in a cold frame and can be planted out in the following spring

Nerine (ne-ri-nee)
From Nereis, daughter of Nereus, a sea nymph of Greek mythology *(Amaryllidaceae)*. A genus of about 30 species of South African bulbous plants, mostly grown in cool greenhouses though some can be grown successfully out of doors where conditions are favourable, especially *N. bowdenii* and its cultivars. The genus is divided into two groups, one comprising species with the characteristics of *N. flexuosa*, whose leaves and flowers appear together; the other with species similar to *N. sarniensis*, which flower before the new foliage appears. Nerine flowerheads consist of many flowers which radiate in an umbel from the top of a fleshy stem. Colours range from shades of pink mostly through salmon to deep crimson, and some white.
Species cultivated *N. bowdenii*, 18 inches, pink flowers, September; cultivars include 'Blush Beauty', satin-pink; 'Pink Triumph', large-flowered. *N. flexuosa* (syn. *N. pulchella*), 15–20 inches, pale pink flowers, September; var. *alba*, flowers white. *N. humilis*, 10–15 inches, rose-pink, September. *N. sarniensis*, Guernsey lily, 10–15 inches, flower colour variable, from crimson through vermilion to pink, autumn. *N. undulata* (syn. *N. crispa*), 10–18 inches, rose-red flowers, autumn. Cultivars: species have been crossed to give many first-cross hybrids and dozens of named cultivars have been bred or selected from these. They include the 'Borde Hill' hybrids, in a wide colour range. Others are listed and described in specialists' catalogues.
Cultivation Hardy kinds will grow in well-drained soils in warm, sheltered positions, such as those often conveniently found at the base of a south-facing wall. Plant the bulbs in a site enriched with rotted manure, compost or bonemeal, in July or August. In cold areas bulbs may be planted to a depth of 9 inches at their base as protection from frost. A mulch of straw, bracken or other dry litter will also insulate the bulbs from frost. Feed the bulbs during growth, using a weak liquid fertiliser. Top dress them each August with rotted cow manure or leafmould. Lift and divide the bulbs when they become overcrowded, usually about every four years.

Greenhouse kinds should be potted in August, in rich compost, one bulb per 4-inch pot or up to four in a 6-inch pot. Keep the compost just moist until growth is seen, then water freely with an occasional feed throughout the winter period while the bulbs are in leaf, keeping them in good light and

Nerine 'Stephanie X', one of the many cultivars of this varied genus.

cool conditions at about a temperature of 40–45°F (4–7°C). Allow the bulbs to dry off after the first sign of the leaves yellowing in the following spring or summer. Keep the soil dry until growth starts again in August, when watering should be started again. Repot the bulbs every three or four years.

Nertera (ner-ter-a)
From the Greek *nerteros*, referring to the prostrate habit of the plant *(Rubiaceae)*. Bead plant. There are about 6 species in the genus, herbaceous perennials of creeping habit, natives of mountains in many parts of the southern hemisphere. There is one species only in common cultivation, *N. granadensis* (syn. *N. depressa*). It is a low-growing, spreading plant, its main decorative feature being its dense crop of bright orange, pea-sized berries. Coming from New Zealand, Australia and South America, it is almost hardy in Britain and is sometimes grown permanently on rock gardens, with winter protection.
Cultivation *N. granadensis* is normally grown as a greenhouse pot plant, in sandy compost, such as 2 parts of sandy loam, 1 part each of sand and leafmould. Plants should be shaded from strong

Nicotiana tabacum, Tobacco, is grown commercially for its dried leaves.

sunlight. Pot in spring in warmth and afterwards, when the plants are established, move the pots to a cool place to assist flower and berry formation. Keep the plants well watered. Out of doors they may be grown on shady parts of the rock garden in ordinary light rich soil, but will need some protection in winter. They are easily raised from seed sown in warmth in spring or may be increased by potting small pieces separated from established plants.

Nicotiana (nik-o-shee-a-na)
In honour of Jean Nicot (1530–1600), a French Consul in Portugal, who introduced the tobacco plant into France and Portugal *(Solanaceae)*. A genus of some 66 species, mainly annual and perennial herbaceous plants, treated as half-hardy plants, 45 species from the warmer regions of north and south America, 21 from Australia. The most important economic species is *N. tabacum* and its many varieties, grown commercially for the sake of its leaves which when dried provide the tobacco of commerce, although *N. rustica*, still used for this

131

purpose, was the first species used to provide tobacco for smoking in Europe. They all have sticky stems and very hairy leaves, exceptionally large in *N. tabacum*. The long-tubed flowers of the ornamental species are carried in racemes or panicles. The colours vary considerably, due mostly to hybridisation between the white of *N. alata* and carmine of *N. x sanderae*. The flowers of most of the ornamental species are very fragrant, some of them particularly so at night.

Species cultivated *N. alata*, 2 feet, flowers white with greenish-yellow reverse, very fragrant, summer; var. *grandiflora* (syn. *N. affinis*) has large flowers which are yellowish on the reverse; cultivars include 'Daylight', 2½ feet, flowers pure white, remaining open all day; 'Dwarf White Bedder', 15 inches, flowers remaining open all day; 'Lime Green', 2½ feet, greenish-yellow, popular with flower arrangers; 'Sensation', 2½ feet, a strain with flowers in various colours. *N. glauca*, half-hardy shrubby plant, normally about 8 feet tall, sometimes considerably more, leaves glaucous, flowers yellow, August to October, naturalised in southern Europe. *N. x sanderae*, 2–3 feet, flowers in shades of pinks and carmines, summer hybrid; cultivars are 'Crimson Bedder', 15 inches, deep crimson; 'Crimson King', 2½ feet, crimson-red; 'Knapton Scarlet', 3 feet. Mixed colours are also available. *N. suaveolens*, 1½–2 feet, white flowers, greenish-purple outside, summer. *N. sylvestris*, 5 feet, leaves to 1 foot long, flowers white, long-tubed, fragrant. *N. tabacum*, the common tobacco, to 6 feet, very large hairy leaves, insignificant pink flowers, summer; cultivars include 'Burley', a popular kind for making home-grown tobacco; 'Havana', leaves used for cigar making; 'New Zealand Gay Yellow'; 'Virginica No. 25'. All the above species and hybrids are annuals, except where stated, and all are from north or south America.

Cultivation The ornamental species, grown as half-hardy annuals, will thrive in full sun or partial shade in any good garden soil. The seeds are sown in the greenhouse in a temperature of 55–60°F (13–16°C), in March or April in John Innes seed compost. The seedlings are hardened off and planted out 1 foot or so apart in June. Seeds may also be sown out of doors in May, where the plants are to flower. In the southern part of the country, at least, self-sown seedlings often appear in late spring. Although *N. alata* is treated as an annual, it is, in fact, a perennial and in sheltered gardens plants may survive through a mild winter, especially if the roots are protected in some way, to flower again the following summer. The roots are thick and tuberous, not unlike those of the dahlia. The common tobacco is also treated as a half-hardy annual, the leaves being gathered in September

for curing. For greenhouse decoration *N. suaveolens* is suitable and also the 'Daylight' and 'Sensation' hybrids. The taller species and varieties need a good deal of space but otherwise make good greenhouse plants. Seeds can be sown in September in a temperature of about 50°F (10°C), the plants being potted on eventually into 6-inch pots For early summer flowers sow seeds again in February. A fairly rich compost should be used or the plants will be of poor quality. Water plants freely when they are in full growth.

Nigella (ni-jel-la)
From the Latin *nigellus*, a diminutive of *niger*, black, referring to the black seeds (*Ranunculaceae*). Fennel-flower. A genus of 20 species, natives of the region stretching from Europe to eastern Asia. Those in cultivation are popular, easily-grown hardy annuals with feathery foliage and, in the main, blue flowers though other colours have been introduced in recent years. *N. damascena* has given us the majority of cultivated forms. The dried seed heads may be used for ornamental purposes.

Species cultivated *N. damascena*, love-in-a-mist, devil-in-a-bush, 1–2 feet, flowers blue, summer, vars. *alba*, white flowers; *flore-pleno*, double flowers. Cultivars include 'Miss Jekyll', bright blue flowers; 'Oxford Blue', flowers open light blue and become darker; 'Persian Jewels', mixture including shades of rose, pink, carmine, mauve, lavender, purple and white; 'Persian Rose', flowers open pale pink and become darker; seeds of mixed colours are also available. *N. hispanica*, 1–2 feet, deep blue flowers with red stamens, summer.

Cultivation Sow seed in ordinary garden soil, in March or April, where the plants are intended to flower, later thinning the seedlings to 6 inches apart. Seed may also be sown in early September in sheltered borders with a minimum of winter protection, to provide the best plants. If they are raised in a nursery bed, seedlings may be transplanted in spring.

Notothlaspi (no-to-thlas-pe)
From the Greek *noto*, southern, and *thlaspis*, cress, referring to their resemblance to the northern hemisphere *Thlaspi*, or pennycress (*Cruciferae*). This is a genus of 2 species, both of which are confined to the mountains of the South Island of New Zealand. Although they are hardy rock garden plants, their cultivation is difficult and they are probably much more suited for growing in pots in an alpine house. Both species are rare in cultivation.

Species cultivated *N. australe*, perennial, smaller than the following species, branched from the base; the creamy-white flowers are fragrant, and borne in small heads. *N. rosulatum*, penwiper plant, grows only on loose shingly

screes and as well as being a unique plant it is the most outstanding of the two. It is monocarpic and from a flat rosette of grey, fleshy leaves eventually sends up a flower spike 3 to 9 inches high, densely crowded with sweetly scented, white flowers.

Cultivation As it is monocarpic, *N. rosulatum* can be propagated only by seed and as it is extremely difficult to transplant, the seed should be sown where it is to grow. Alternatively, the seedlings could be transplanted into their permanent quarters before they grow out of the first true-leaf stage. A suitable potting mixture for this species is 3 parts of ½-inch stone chips, 2 parts of sharp sand, 2 parts of peat or leafmould and 1 part of loam. Water may be given frequently throughout the summer but during winter very little should be given. *N. australe* is easier to grow and can be propagated by seed or division. Pot in a well-drained, gritty compost to which some crushed limestone has been added. Seeds of both species should be sown in a very sandy soil. Gentle heat will hasten germination.

Nymphaea (nim-fee-a)
Named after the Greek goddess of springs, *Nymphe*; a name given to water nymphs (*Nymphaeaceae*). Water-lily. A genus of 50 species of tuberous-rooted perennials, natives of tropical and temperate regions. They grow with their roots in mud at the bottom of ponds, their foliage and flowers on the water surface. Water-lilies are well known for the beauty of their large, rounded floating leaves and many-petalled cupped flowers in a variety of shades. The majority that are grown are perfectly hardy. Those from tropical regions require at least frost protection in winter indoors, if they are not grown permanently in tanks or tubs under glass, which is perhaps preferable.

Hardy species cultivated *N. alba*, common water-lily, white flowers, summer, Europe, including Britain; var. *rubra*, rosy-pink flowers. *N. candida*, flowers white, summer, northern and arctic Europe. *N. fennica*, small white flowers, summer, Finland. *N. nitida*, small white flowers, June, Siberia. *N. odorata*, white flowers tinged red, fragrant, to 6 inches across, opening in the morning, closing after noon, North America. *N. pygmaea alba*, white flowers with golden stamens. *N. pygmaea helvola*, flowers primrose yellow, smallest of water-lilies. *N. tuberosa*, white flowers lightly scented, north-eastern America; var. *rosea*, pale-rose flowers, spreading freely. Cultivars: *N. marliacea* is a name given to a group of hybrids raised by a Frenchman, M.

1 The deep pink, cup-shaped flowers of Nymphaea 'James Brydon' float on the water surrounded by dark green leaves.
2 N. lactea is a garden form of N. odorata. Its white flowers have golden centres.

Latour-Marliac. These are described in specialists' lists as *Marliacea albida*, white; *M. rosea*, rose pink and *M. flammea*, wine-red, etc. Another similar group contains the *laydekeri* hybrids. Dozens of other named varieties are listed in their main colour groups—white, pink, salmon and rose, crimson and red, orange and yellow.

Tender species cultivated *N. caerulea*, blue lotus, flowers light blue, north and central Africa. *N. capensis* (syn. *N. emirensis*), Cape blue water-lily, sky blue flowers, southern and eastern Africa, Madagascar; vars. *azurea*, leaves spotted purple, *zanzibariensis*, dark blue flowers, fragrant, *rosea*, deep rose to pink flowers. *N. elegans*, flowers creamy-white, tinged light purple, New Mexico. *N. flava* (syn. *N. mexicana*), canary yellow flowers, south-eastern America. *N. gigantea*, golden-yellow flowers, Australia. *N. lotus*, Egyptian or Indian lotus, sacred lotus, sacred bean, large flowers mostly white, tinged pink or red at base of outer petals, opening at night, tropics; var. *dentata*, pure white flowers. *N. odorata gigantea*, pure white, fragrant flowers. *N. polychroma* (syn. *N. colorata*), bright blue flowers tinged mauve, Tanganyika. *N. rubra*, deep red flowers, nocturnal, Bengal. *N. stellata*, pale blue flowers; vars. *cyanea*, blue, *purpurea*, flowers red-purple, south and east Asia. Cultivars: 'Blue Beauty', cerulean blue, 'Emily Grant Hutchings', amaranth red, 'General Pershing', deep pink, scented, 'Golden West', peach to apricot pink, 'Juno', white, 'Peach Blow', pale rose. Others are available from specialist nurseries.

Cultivation of hardy kinds *N. flava*, although listed as a tender species, is hardy enough to be grown out of doors in mild districts. Species and varieties, vary in the depth of water required. Some nurserymen usefully catalogue the collections in groups accordingly. The following is a selection only:

For water 15–36 inches deep

'Charles de Meurville', pink to wine-red; 'Gladstoniana', pure white; 'Colonel Welch', canary-yellow; 'Masanjello', rose-pink.

For water 10–24 inches deep

'Escarboucle', crimson; 'Marliacea alba', white; 'Sunrise', yellow; 'Rose Arey', cerise pink.

For water 7–15 inches deep

'Conqueror', rosy-crimson; 'Gonnère', white; 'Aurora', buff-yellow; 'Laydekeri Rosea', rose-pink.

For water 3–10 inches deep

'Froebelii', bright red; 'Candida', white with yellow centres; 'Pygmaea Helvola', yellow; 'Laydekeri Lilacina', pink.

It should be noted that although for the most part water-lilies which are suitable for planting in deep water will

The heavily marked flowers of Odontoglossum 'Royal Serenade' are of very fine form.

also succeed in shallower pools, those that are suitable for shallow water will not succeed in deeper water. Planting is done from May to July, in special water-lily pots or baskets containing rich loam with well-rotted manure or bonemeal added. Moulded polythene containers, which do not rot, are now available in various sizes. The containers whether of polythene or more traditional materials, are lowered gently into place in the pond. Or, where the pond is empty and is to be planted up, place the baskets in position and gradually run the water in, over a period of several weeks. Choose a sunny area of water for planting. The rhizomes remain dormant during the winter, after the foliage has died back, and plants should be in-

creased, or overcrowded plants thinned out, by division of the rhizomes in March or April, when new growth begins.

Cultivation of tender kinds This is similar to that of the hardy types but they are grown in suitable containers that can be housed in the greenhouse or conservatory. These may be moved outside for plants to flower in the open during fine summers. Take in the containers again before the first frosts and allow the water level to drop when the foliage dies down. Either leave the rhizomes to dry in the containers through the winter or remove them and store them in moist sand. Repot them in fresh compost in February or March. Plant in March or April.

Nymphoides (nim-fo-eye-deez)
From *Nymphaea,* another genus, and the Greek *opsis,* like, referring to the habit of the plant (*Gentianaceae* or *Menyanthaceae*). This genus is sometimes found listed under its former name of *Limnanthemum.* There are about 20 species from tropical and temperate regions, some tender, some hardy, aquatic perennials with broad leaves, heart-shaped at the base, which float on the water surface.
Species cultivated *N. aquatica* (syns. *Villarsia aquatica, Limnanthemum trachyspermum, L. lacunosum*), fairy water-lily, white flowers, June–August, eastern North America. *N. cordata* (syn. *Villarsia cordata*), floating heart, white flowers, July–August, tender, eastern North America. *N. indica,* water snowflake, white flowers, yellow centres, summer, tender, northern Australia, tropics. *N. peltata* (syns. *Limnanthemum peltatum, L. nymphoides, Villarsia nymphoides*), water fringe, golden-yellow flowers, July–September, Europe (including Britain), Asia.
Cultivation Hardy species grow easily if planted in a rich loam with shallow water over them in ponds or by lakesides. Plant these in March. Plants need thinning occasionally to prevent them from spreading too much. Propagation is by dividing plants in spring. Tender species are grown under glass in suitable tubs or tanks two-thirds full of loam, then filled with water to the brim. These are planted in spring. For propagation purposes sow seeds in pots of light compost immersed in water at a temperature of 65°F (18°C) in spring. Maintain a minimum winter temperature of 45°F (7°C).

Odontoglossum (o-don-to-gloss-um)
From the Greek *odons,* a tooth, and *glossa,* tongue, in reference to the shape of the lip of the flower (*Orchidaceae*). A large genus of epiphytic orchids from South and Central America. Most of the species and many thousands of hybrids have large very pretty flowers and are deservedly popular. Long spikes are produced from the base of the leading pseudobulb and carry many flowers although some have a few flowers only on each spike. Fine form and a great variety of lovely colours are very much in evidence among the many modern hybrids.
Species cultivated (A selection only.) *O. apterum,* white, red-brown-spotted, spring, Mexico. *O. bictoniense,* yellowish-green with blotches of chestnut-brown, the lip rose, spikes 2–3 feet long, autumn, Guatemala. *O. cervantesii,* rose-white, barred with chocolate-red, spring, Mexico. *O. cirrhosum,* white with crimson-purple spots, spring, Ecuador. *O. citrosmum,* rose flushed white, spikes

long and pendent, spring, Mexico. *O. cordatum,* chestnut-brown marked with yellow, spring, Mexico. *O. coronarium,* chestnut-brown margined with yellow; it is best grown on a raft, Colombia. *O. crispum,* varying from white to rose-tinged or red-blotched, various forms can be found in flower at any time of the year, Colombia. *O. grande,* very large yellow and chestnut brown flowers, autumn, Guatemala. *O. hallii,* brownish-red and yellow, spikes up to 4 feet, spring, Ecuador. *O. luteopurpureum,* large, yellow and chestnut-brown flowers, spring, Colombia. *O. oerstedii,* dwarf type, white, winter and spring, Venezuela. *O. pulchellum,* small flowers, very fragrant, spring, Costa Rica. *O. rossii,* very pretty, small growing, white, rose-flushed, spring, Mexico. *O. schlieperianum,* yellow barred with brown, autumn, Costa Rica. *O. triumphans,* very fine, bright yellow and chocolate-brown, spring, Colombia. *O. uro-skinneri,* greenish, chestnut-brown and rose, the spike up to 3 feet long, spring, Guatemala. *O. wilckeanum,* large flowers, yellow blotched with red-brown, spring, Colombia. Cultivars: a small selection only is given here; specialist catalogues should be consulted for new varieties. Colour expectancy of the new crosses is usually given. 'Aireworth', 'Aristocrat', 'Bandor', 'Brimstone Butterfly', *O. crispum* 'Premier Type' and the many improved forms of this species, 'Diplomat', 'Elpania', 'Golden Guinea', 'Renton', 'Stropheon' and 'York'.
Cultivation The species are generally easy to grow, as are many of the hybrids though with these greater care may be necessary for them to give of their best. A good general compost is 3 parts of osmunda fibre and 1 part of sphagnum moss (by bulk). For *O. crispum* and most hybrids a little more moss can be used and, as the roots are more slender, the finest grade of fibre should be used.

The white flowers of Oenothera caespitosa, a plant native to western North America.

Repot in spring or during September. The ideal temperature is 60°F (16°C) and this should be as equable as is possible. In winter this can drop to 55°F (13°C) or even to 50°F (10°C) if the conditions are dry. In summer temperature will rise by sun heat but this should be kept down to as near 70°F (21°C) as is possible by careful use of the ventilators and blinds. Use the ventilators freely at night when the weather is suitable and also during the daytime, provided the ventilation is not so excessive as to allow moisture to escape. Fresh, moist, airy conditions should prevail at all times, but avoid draughts. Plants should be watered all through the year but can have less water during colder weather. The harder bulbed types (*O. grande* and *O. citrosmum*) prefer a little more light and a decided rest, and the latter warmer winter conditions. *O. rossii* and *O. cervantesii* require a rest but not such a severe one. Propagation is by division of the large plants at potting time. Each division should have four bulbs and a new growth or bud. Sound bulbs, singly or in twos, can be placed in well-crocked pots topped with fresh sphagnum moss and kept shaded. Pot them up into small pots when growth and roots appear.

Oenothera (ee-noth-er-a)
From the Greek *oinos,* wine, and *thera,* pursuing or imbibing, the roots of one plant being thought to induce a thirst for wine (*Onagraceae*). A genus of 80 species of annuals, biennials and numerous good herbaceous and shrubby perennials for the herbaceous border and rock garden, natives of America and the West Indies, but now widely

naturalised in many parts of the world. The flowers, fragrant in many species, are fragile in appearance, carried in racemes, or singly in the leaf axils and generally yellow but there are white, pink and red forms. The common name, evening primrose, relates to *O. biennis* in particular, the flowers opening in the evening.

Species cultivated *O. acaulis*, trailer, flowers white, ageing to rose, spring to autumn, hardy perennial. *O. biennis*, biennial, 3 feet, yellow, very fragrant, June–October. *O. erythrosepala* (syn. *O. lamarckiana*), 4 feet, flowers yellow, ageing to reddish, to 3½ inches across, summer to autumn, probably of garden origin. *O. fruticosa*, about 2 feet, lemon-yellow flowers, July and August, one of the best of the herbaceous perennials. *O. glaber*, 1½ feet, foliage bronze-green, flowers golden-yellow, summer. *O. missouriensis*, about 9 inches, trailing and spreading in habit, bright, light yellow flowers, July, perennial. *O. odorata*, to 1½ feet, flowers yellow, turning red, to 2½ inches across, opening in the evening, April to June, perennial; var. *sulphurea*, taller, later flowering, leaves, buds and stems, tinted red. *O. perennis* (syn. *O. pumila*), 1 foot, flowers yellow, opening in daylight, July, perennial. *O. speciosa*, 2 feet, white flowers, scented at night, appearing throughout the summer and early autumn, perennial, United States, Mexico. *O. tetragona* (syn. *O. youngii*), 2 feet, flowers yellow, to 1½ inches across, opening by day, summer; var. *riparia*, 1½ feet, flowers larger. Cultivars: 'Fireworks', 1½ feet, bright red buds opening to yellow flowers, makes a very good plant for the front of the border; 'Yellow River', 1–1½ feet, canary yellow, very free-flowering.

Cultivation These plants are sun lovers; they do well in any ordinary soils, including those that contain much chalk. The trailing kinds are suitable for the rock garden, taller kinds for sunny borders. They can be propagated by division in spring or they may be grown from seed. Seed of the biennial species is best sown in May or June where the plants are required to flower, the flowers being produced the following year in July and August. Cuttings can also be taken of the perennial species in May and rooted in a sandy compost.

Omphalodes (om-fa-lo-des)

From the Greek, *omphalos*, a navel, and *eidos*, like, referring to the shape of the calyx *(Boraginaceae)*. A genus of 28 species of herbaceous perennials and some annual species with forget-me-not-like flowers from the Mediterranean region, east Asia and Mexico. The leaves are large and liable to slug damage in the spring.

Species cultivated *O. cappadocica*, 1 foot, with blue-grey leaves and sprays of dark blue flowers, May and June, a strong grower in either sun or shade,

Omphalodes cappadocica, a strong-growing plant for both sun and shade.

north-eastern Turkey; 'Anthea Bloom', 9 inches, with gentian-blue flowers, is a cultivar. *O. luciliae*, 6 inches, flowers rose at first, then sky blue, May, suitable for the rock garden with a sunny position and perfect drainage, or in the alpine house, Greece, Asia Minor. *O. verna*, 9 inches, vigorous, white-eyed, bright blue flowers, spring, south Europe; var. *alba*, flowers white.

Cultivation A partially shaded position is best and there must be ample moisture. They are excellent for naturalising in a light woodland. Plant in the autumn or spring and make sure the drainage is good. Any ordinary garden soil suits these plants, provided it is fairly moist. Water well in dry weather and mulch with well-rotted cow manure in spring. Propagate by dividing the roots in spring, or sow seeds in semi-shade in April.

Onion

In the past, a special bed was reserved for the onion crop. The onions from this heavily-manured site were often massive, but the growing of the same crop on the same soil season after season generally resulted in a build-up of onion pests and diseases. The monster onions were not noted for their good-keeping qualities.

Nowadays, onion cultivation is fitted into rotation and manuring programmes and can be managed in kitchen gardens. Onions may be raised from seeds or from sets. Sowings may be made in the open or in the cold frame in August, in January or February in the heated greenhouse, or in the open garden in March and April.

Cultivation For the August sowing, choose a sunny position and fork the soil lightly, removing all weeds and their roots. Do not add any manure or fertiliser. Firm the bed and rake it well before making 1-inch deep seed drills at 9 inches apart. Sow the seed reasonably thinly, fill the drills with soil and firm it gently. Hoe between the seedlings in late September or October to keep down weeds. In March, use the fork to lift all of the seedlings and set them on a prepared bed, allowing 8 inches between the plants and 15 inches between the rows. Spread out the roots in the planting holes made with the trowel and if the plants do not remain upright, draw some fine soil round them. Rake away this covering when the plants have become established. If you make this sowing in the cold frame, do not set the light in position until October. Use the onion hoe to remove weeds, and give plenty of ventilation throughout the winter except in very severe, frosty weather. The seedlings may also need watering around

Christmas and in February. Choose mild days for watering and leave the light fully open for several hours afterwards. Set out frame-protected plants in March. The winter sowing in a slightly heated greenhouse is made in boxes or pots of seed compost. Sow seeds 1 inch apart or, if they are sown closer together, prick off the seedlings when they are large enough to handle. Harden them off in the cold frame in March and plant them out late that month.

When the seeds are to be sown directly in the soil where the plants are to grow, the bed should be well prepared. Digging and manuring will have been carried out during the late autumn or winter and the soil needs raking before sowing so that the bed is level, even and free of large clods and stones. Sow thinly in 1-inch deep drills, spaced 1 foot apart. After sowing, fill in the drills and firm. Do not tread heavily on a clay soil. Keep the seedlings free of weeds by hoeing between the rows during April and May, and pull out any weeds in the rows. Start thinning the plants in mid-June and continue thinning until mid-July by which time those which are to remain should have at least 6 inches of row space. When thinning, take great care not to break roots or foliage and never leave either on top of the soil. The odour of the broken plants attracts female onion flies and their small maggots ruin many onion crops. If the soil is on the dry side, water both before and after thinning. Use the immature onions in salads.

Continue weeding the onion bed until July. During that month, or in August, the foliage becomes yellow and topples to the soil. Here and there it may be necessary to bend the foliage of a plant downwards. No further weeding is necessary and the crop is left to ripen. When the foliage is brown and brittle, choose a dry, sunny day, pull up or dig the onions from the soil, and spread them in the sun to complete the drying process. In wet weather, spread the onions on the greenhouse bench or under cloches. When the onions are quite dry, rub off soil, dead roots and dry, loose scales. Store the ripe onions in trays in a cool dry place, or better still, rope the crop. Hang the ropes in an outhouse or in the garage.

Onion sets These are small onions grown by specialist nurserymen. The crop is dug and dried in the previous summer and offered for sale in the early winter and spring. One pound of sets is sufficient for the average garden. Small sets are considered of better quality than large ones. Do not leave onion sets in bags after purchasing them, but spread them in a tray in a cool place before planting them in March. Prepare the bed as for seed sowing and plant the sets 6–8 inches apart in 1-inch deep drills. Except for hoeing to keep down weeds, little in the way of cultivation is

necessary. The feeding of the plants with fertilisers may result in 'bolting'. In late July, loosen the soil around the swelling bulbs to expose them to the sun. This must be done carefully because the plants may be blown down by strong winds if the roots are broken. The foliage will topple to the soil in August and from then on harvesting and storing are as for onions from seeds.

Spring onions Where maincrop onions are raised from sets, 'spring' or salad onions are grown by sowing seeds of 'White Lisbon' in August or in March. In colder parts, the August sowing needs cloche protection from October until the spring. Although the bed should not be a rich one, it must be well-drained. Sow quite thickly and hoe to remove weeds in September and again in March. Start pulling the small onions for salad use in May and continue to pull until July. The March sowing provides salad onions from July until the autumn.

Exhibiting onions The onion is one of the few vegetables allowed 20 points at shows where the organisers follow the rules laid down in The Horticultural Show Handbook of the Royal Horticultural Society. For this reason, keen showmen very often choose this vegetable as one of their exhibits. The plants are raised in gentle heat in the winter and the seedlings are potted into 3-inch peat or clay pots. After they have been

hardened off the plants are set out on a well dug and richly manured bed in early April. At least 1 foot is allowed between the plants and 18 inches between rows. Weeding and watering are carried out, when necessary, together with small but regular feeds of liquid manure or fertiliser. Great care must be taken to prevent over-feeding which leads to 'bolting' or to bulbs with thick necks. All watering and feeding must cease when the onions reach their full size. Size and uniformity can earn 10 points.

Onions for Pickling 'Marshall's Super Pickle' is a new onion with the round shape and size as favoured by the commercial pickler. Seeds of this variety or of any maincrop suitable for spring sowing are sown rather thickly in ½-inch to 1-inch deep drills spaced at 9 inches apart in soil of low fertility during March or April. Weeding must be attended to regularly but the onion plants are not thinned. Harvesting is carried out when the foliage is dead, brown and brittle.

For white cocktail onions seed of 'Silver Skin' or 'Pearl Pickler' is sown quite thickly in April or early May. The soil should be reasonably fertile. If grown in a poor soil the onions are liable to be too small for use. Apart from weeding no cultivation is necessary and the plants are not thinned. The crop is harvested when the foliage dies. Unless harvested promptly, there is new foliage.

Maincrop onion varieties

'Ailsa Craig' Large, globular, handsome. Suitable for both spring and late summer sowing. One of the best for exhibition.

'Autumn Queen' Flattish shape. Good keeper. For spring and late summer sowing.

'Bedfordshire Champion' Large, globe-shaped, straw-brown skin usually tinged with pink. For spring sowing only.

'Big Ben' (A) Large, semi-flat shape, golden skin. Practically non-bolting. Exhibition quality. Good keeper. Sow in August.

'Blood Red' Medium-size, deep red skin, flat, pungent. Very hardy and especially recommended for cold areas. Good keeper.

'Crossling's Selected' A globe onion much liked by exhibitors.

'Early Yellow Globe' Flattish-round, medium-sized, golden skinned, quick maturing and reasonably good keeper. For spring sowing only.

'Excelsior, Cranston's Selected' Pale-skinned, large, round exhibition variety.

'Giant Rocca' (Brown) (A) Brown-skinned, flattish globe. For August sowing only. Does not store well. There is also 'Yellow Rocca'.

'Giant Zittau' (A) Medium to large, semi-flat, golden-brown skin. Good keeper. Strongly recommended for August sowing.

'James' Long Keeping' Oval, brown skin, medium size, stores well.

'Marshall's July Giant' (A) Large, semi-globe shaped, early maturing. For August sowing.

'Marshall's Leverington Champion' Globe-shaped, pale golden skin, very large, fairly good keeper. Recommended for exhibition use.

'Red Italian' (A) Medium-sized, red-skinned, flat bulbs. Sow in August.

'Reliance' (A) Large, flattish, golden skin. Sow in August.

'Rijnsburger Globe' Large, pale-skinned, globe-shaped, long-keeping.

'Rousham Park Hero' White Spanish type, semi-flat, greenish-yellow skin, mild flavour. Can crop well on light soils.

'Sutton's A1' Large flat bulbs, a good keeper. For spring or August sowing.

'Sutton's Solidity' (A) Large, flattish bulbs. Plants do not bolt. A good keeper. Especially recommended for August sowing.

'Superba' A new F₁ hybrid. Medium-sized globular bulbs with smooth golden-brown skin. Early maturing and noted for uniformity. Stores well.

'The Sutton' Globe-shaped, early-ripening, excellent keeper.

'Up-to-Date' Globe-shaped, straw-coloured skin, remarkably good keeping qualities.

'White Spanish' Flattish onion, golden skin, mild flavour, good keeper.

'Wijbo' An early maturing selection of 'Rijnsburger'. Noted for uniform appearance of the crop.

(A) = Recommended for August sowing. Onions from this sowing are referred to as Autumn-sown among exhibitors.

Orchis (or-kis)

From the ancient Greek name *orchis*, testicle, in reference to the form of the oblong tuberous root of some species *(Orchidaceae)*. A genus of about 35 species of terrestrial orchids, having deciduous leaves and underground tubers which are either rounded or long-fingered. They are native to Britain, Europe, Africa, and North America.

Species cultivated *O. latifolia,* marsh orchis, 10–20 inches, flower flesh colour or rose, lip darker, spring, Britain, Europe. *O. maculata* (syns. *Dactylorchis maculata, Orchis ericetorum*), heath spotted orchid, 1 foot, pinkish and purplish, summer, Britain, Europe. *O. maderensis,* 1–2 feet, purple, summer, Madeira. *O. mascula,* early purple orchis, 8–24 inches, crimson-purple, spring, prefers damp loam, Britain, Europe. *O. militaris,* military orchis, 1 to 2 feet, reddish-pink, striped purple, summer, southern England (very rare), Europe. *O. morio,* 6–8 inches, purplish, petals green and veined, spring, Britain, Europe. *O. pallens,* 9 inches, pale to deep yellow, spring, Europe. *O. pardalina* (syn. *Dactylorchis praetermissa*), southern marsh orchid, purplish-red to white, summer, Europe. *O. purpurea,* lady orchis, 1–2½ feet, purple and pink, or purple and white, May–June, Britain. *O. purpurella* (syn. *Dactylorchis purpurella*), northern marsh orchis, 4–6 inches, dark purple, summer, northern England, Scotland. *O. sambucina,* 9 inches, yellow or purple, summer, Europe. *O. simia,* monkey orchis, whitish and pink, summer, England (very rare), Europe. *O. spectabilis,* 4–7 inches high, pinkish-purple, summer, North America. *O. tridentata,* 9 inches, purplish-rose, lip flesh-coloured, spotted red, spring, Europe. *O. ustulata,* burnt-tip orchid, brownish-purple and pinkish-white, Britain, Europe.

Cultivation For most species a well-drained loam with limestone chips and sand is the best soil mixture. A few species prefer moister conditions. Sunny positions in the rock garden suit most kinds. The taller growing types are more suitable in a border. Propagation can be effected by division of well-established clumps. Disturbance is in general resented. It should be noted that the British species described above are often very rare natives and may be protected by law.

Ornithogalum (or-nith-og-a-lum)

From the Greek *ornis, ornithos,* a bird, and *gala,* milk; 'bird's milk' was supposed to be a colloquial expression among the ancient Greeks for some wonderful thing, or the name may be in reference to the egg-like colour of the flowers of some species *(Liliaceae).* There are about 150 species in this genus, bulbous plants, natives of southern Europe, South Africa and Asia Minor and other temperate regions of the eastern hemisphere. The flowers are star-like, usually white or whitish and some of the species in cultivation need greenhouse protection.

Species cultivated *Greenhouse O. arabicum,* 2 feet, flowers white with black ovary in centre, fragrant, May and June, Mediterranean region. This species can be grown out-of-doors if it is protected in the winter. *O. thyrsoides* (syn. *O. lacteum*), chincherinchee, 1½ feet, flowers white with prominent yellow stamens, very long-lasting when cut. Often imported from South Africa as cut flowers at Christmas time.

Hardy O. balansae, 6 inches, flowers white, starry, with green stripe, March–April, Asia Minor. *O. nutans,* 1–1½ feet, flowers drooping, silver and green rather than white, April and May, southern Europe. *O. pyrenaicum,* 2 feet, flowers pale yellow, tinged green, spring, southern Europe. *O. umbellatum,* star of Bethlehem, 1 foot, white flowers, May, Europe, North Africa.

Other species may be offered from time to time by specialist bulb growers.

Cultivation Bulbs of the greenhouse species are potted up in the autumn, placing several in a 5-inch pot; John Innes potting compost No 1 is suitable. Place the pots in a cold frame so that they will form a good root system—this will take two to three months—then bring the pots into the greenhouse and place them in a good light and water them well.

1 Ornithogalum umbellatum, the Star of Bethlehem, produces an umbel of white flowers in May. It is a bulbous plant from North Africa and the Mediterranean regions.
2 Ornithogalum nutans, has slightly drooping flowers in spring.

After flowering gradually dry off the bulbs as the foliage begins to wither.

The hardy species are not difficult to cultivate and they grow in most soils in sun or partial shade. When planted in the autumn, 4 inches deep and about 8 inches apart, leave them undisturbed for some years. Propagation is by seeds sown in the open or in a cold frame in spring, or by offsets detached and grown on at planting time.

Orthrosanthus (or-thro-san-thus)

From the Greek *orthros*, morning, and *anthos*, flower, in allusion to the short-lived flowers and their habit of opening very early in the morning *(Iridaceae)*. Short, woody rhizomatous plants closely related to *Sisyrinchium*, these plants have very stiff and often grass-like foliage. There are about 8 species, which come from South America and Australia, and they are suitable for the cold greenhouse.

Species cultivated *O. chimboracensis*, 1½ feet, leaves grass-like, about 15 inches long, lavender-blue flowers, South America. *O. multiflorus*, 1 foot, tufted grassy foliage up to 2 feet long, sky-blue flowers in a panicle of 4 to 6 inches long, May–July, Australia.

Cultivation These plants are suitable for cultivation in the cold greenhouse in an open compost or they may be planted out in the greenhouse border. Propagation is by division of the tufted rootstock in early spring or by seed sown in spring in the warm greenhouse.

Ourisia (owr-is-e-a)

Commemorating Governor Ouris of the Falkland Islands *(Scrophulariaceae)*. These are pretty little plants for the rock garden, mostly hardy and low-growing. They are natives of the Andes, antarctic

parts of South America and New Zealand. Although not much seen in this country they could make a very attractive addition to the alpine and rock garden.

Species cultivated *O. alpina*, 6 inches, red or pink semi-pendent flowers with red dots in the throat, June, Argentinean Andes. *O. coccinea*, 6–12 inches, scarlet trumpet-shaped flowers in small clusters, May–July, Chilean Andes. *O. crosbyi*, 6 inches, dark green leathery leaves, white flowers in sprays, shade-loving, New Zealand. *O. elegans*, 18 inches, red tubular flowers in summer, Chile. *O. macrocarpa*, to 20 inches, white flowers 1 inch wide, New Zealand. *O. macrophylla*, 6–9 inches, white flowers with yellow hairs in throat, July, prefers shade, New Zealand. *O. sessiliflora*, 6 inches, purple flowers with a white margin, New Zealand.

Cultivation Ourisias do best in a lightly shaded place in the rock garden, with their roots close to soft porous stone. They like to be fairly dry in winter and should be protected from excessive wet then. During the growing season they should be watered freely. *O. macrocarpa* and *O. sessiliflora* have not yet been grown in the British Isles, but it is to be hoped that they are eventually introduced. Propagate by seed sown when ripe or by division of the plants in April.

Paeonia (pe-o-ne-a)

Commemorating *Paeon*, an ancient Greek physician, said to have first used *P. officinalis* medicinally. Although

the genus has long been considered a member of the buttercup family, *Ranunculaceae*, some modern botanists now place it in a family of its own, *Paeoniaceae*. A genus of 33 species of hardy herbaceous and shrubby perennials and a few shrubs, among the noblest and most decorative plants for a sunny or shaded border. The main division of the genus is between the herbaceous and the tree paeony, but botanically the matter is much more complex. Stern's monograph, *A Study of the Genus Paeonia*, published by the Royal Horticultural Society in 1946, deals with the whole classification. The wild herbaceous species are single-flowered and vary in height from about 1 foot up to 3 or 4 feet. The double varieties have been developed by breeding and selection. The tree paeonies, although woody shrubs, are deciduous and are often grown in association with other hardy perennial plants. They enjoy a sunny position but are liable to be broken by summer gales so should be planted in a reasonably sheltered place. Long established specimens—they live many years—may attain a height of 7 feet or more with a considerable spread. Accordingly it is necessary to allow ample space when planting tree paeonies for no paeony likes being moved once it has been planted. Tree paeonies are often grafted on to the rootstock of *P. officinalis*, the common garden paeony, and when planting care should be taken to bury the point of the union between the stock and the scion 3 inches below the surface. It is at this point that a young specimen may get broken in rough weather. If possible choose a site that does not get the early morning sun because tree paeonies come into growth earlier than herbaceous varieties and the young shoots may be damaged by late spring frosts.

Species cultivated *P. anomala,* 1–1½ feet, foliage finely cut, flowers bright crimson, May, Russia, central Asia. *P. bakeri,* 2 feet, flowers purplish-red, May, possibly of garden origin. *P. broteri,* 1–1½ feet, purplish-red, May, Spain and Portugal. *P. cambessedesii,* 1½ feet, deep rose-pink, April–May, Balearic Isles, liable to damage by spring frost. *P. clusii* (syn. *P. cretica*), 1 foot, white, May, Crete. *P. coriacea,* 1½–2 feet, rose, April, Spain, Morocco. *P. delavayi,* up to 5 feet, shrubby, dark red, May, China; var. *angustiloba,* leaves finely divided. *P. emodi,* 1–3 feet, white, May, Himalaya. *P. humilis,* 15 inches, distinct small leaflets, dark pink to red, May, southern France, Spain. *P. lactiflora* (syns. *P. albiflora, P. edulis*), up to 2 feet, white, fragrant, June, Siberia, northern China, Mongolia. *P. lutea,* shrubby, up to 4½ feet, yellow, June, China, Tibet. *P. × lemoinei (P. lutea × P. suffruticosa),* shrubby, 4–5 feet, flowers large, yellow, May–June, hybrid race. *P. mascula* (syn. *P. corallina*), 2–3 feet, deep rose, May, Europe,

Paeonia 'Lady Alexandra' is a good rose-pink and flowers in June.

naturalised in Britain. *P. mlokosewitschii,* 1½ feet, foliage, grey-green, flowers yellow, coral stamens, April, Caucasus. *P. officinalis,* up to 2 feet, red, May, southern Europe; vars. *albo-plena,* the old double white paeony; *rosea plena,* the old double rose paeony; *rubra plena,* the old double crimson paeony. *P. peregrina* (syns. *P. decora, P. lobata*), up to 3 feet, deep maroon-red, May, southern Europe, Asia Minor. *P. potaninii* (syn. *P. delavayi angustiloba*), shrubby, up to 5 feet, deep maroon, May, western China. *P. suffruticosa* (syn. *P. moutan*), tree paeony, up to 6 feet, rose-pink, May, China, Tibet. *P. tenui-*

folia, 1–2 feet, leaves finely dissected, fern-like, flowers deep crimson, May, Transylvania, Caucasus. *P. veitchii*, 1–2 feet, purplish-red, June, China. *P. wittmanniana*, up to 3 feet, yellowish, April, Caucasus.

Hybrid Double Paeonies (a selection) 'Adolphe Rousseau', 3 feet, maroon, golden anthers, large, June. 'Alice Harding', 2½ feet, pale pink, cream within, fragrant, excellent foliage on strong stems, May and early June. 'Baroness Schroder', 3 feet, free flowering, white, with yellow centre, large globular blooms excellent for cutting, fragrant, late May and June. 'Claire Dubois', 3 feet, satiny pink and silver, June. 'Duchesse de Nemours', 3 feet, free flowering, white to pale sulphur-yellow, medium-size, incurved bloom, fragrant, May and June. 'Edulis Superba', 3 feet, old rose-pink, edged silver, fragrant. Early May onwards, much used as a commercial variety for cut bloom. 'Eugene Verdier', 3 feet, soft pink, silver-edged, free-flowering, a famous old variety, June. 'Felix Crousse', 2½ feet, bright deep carmine, large, a popular variety. 'Festiva Maxima', 3 feet, pure white, flecked crimson, fragrant, a splendid old variety, the name meaning the largest and gayest, May. 'Germaine Bigot', 2½ feet, semi-double, glistening white, shaded pale salmon, fragrant, June. 'Karl Rosenfeld', 2½ feet, bright crimson, June. 'Kelway's Glorious', 2½ feet, creamy-white, large, fragrant, among the best of the doubles, May–June. 'Sarah Bernhardt', 2½ feet, bright pink, tipped silver, large, June.

Hybrid Single Paeonies 'Eva', 2½ feet, deep salmon-pink, June. 'Lady Wolseley', 2½ feet, deep rose, large, June. 'Lord Kitchener', 3 feet, deep maroon-red, May. 'Pink Delight', 2 feet, pale pink, becoming white, May.

Cultivation Paeonies are easily grown in sun or partial shade and in deep fertile soil, preferably containing lime, where they can remain undisturbed for many years. Top dress with old manure or garden compost in February every two or three years. Named varieties of herbaceous and tree paeonies are increased by division in September or October, which gives the newly-planted pieces time to make fresh roots before the ground is frozen. Great care must be taken when lifting the clumps for division as the thick root-stock is very brittle. Paeonies can be raised from seed, but it is a slow process and the seedlings may vary considerably in colour and form. Seed should be sown about 2 inches deep in sandy loam in a cold frame in September. Newly gathered seed is best. With old seed the covering may be hard and the seed should be soaked in water for a few days before sowing. Some seeds may germinate the first spring, but the majority may take up to two years. Placing seed in a

refrigerator for 48 hours or so before sowing sometimes accelerates germination. Seedlings may take five years or more to develop into plants large enough to produce mature blooms. One cannot assess accurately the quality of the blooms from those produced in the first and second year of flowering as they are not usually typical. Grafting in August is done by commercial growers, usually on to stock of *Paeonia albiflora*. Tree paeonies can also be layered, but it is a slow process, and air layering has been attempted on a small scale without great success.

Pansy

The pansy and the viola are very similar and belong to the same family (*Violaceae*). Pansies are used mainly for summer bedding although they can be treated as perennials and increased by means of cuttings. This is, in fact, what is done to perpetuate outstanding varieties for show purposes. In most gardens, however, pansies are treated as biennial plants and discarded after flowering. There are a number of different colourful strains which have been produced by crossing *Viola tricolor* with selected varieties—'Monarch Strain', 'Engelmann's', 'Roggli' of Swiss origin, and 'Morel's'—or by hybridising different strains. The work continues and there is no telling what splendid flowers will appear in the years to come. What is known as the Fancy Pansy is grown for exhibition purposes, particularly in the North of England and has superseded the Show Pansy. For show work the flower should be large, circular in outline, with smooth, thick, velvety petals without serrations. The middle of the flower should be slightly convex with the petals gently reflexed. The colours should be harmonious, with a margin of uniform width, and the yellow eye large, bright and clearly defined. The flower should be not less than 2½ inches in diameter.

Cultivation Pansies thrive in well-drained, deeply dug soil that has been enriched with bonemeal or well-rotted horse manure. Choose an open position, preferably with some shade from the midday sun. Where the soil is heavy fork in gritty material—old weathered ashes, sharp sand, brick dust—or compost and a dressing of lime may help to break up to soil. With such a soil the bed should be raised about 6 inches above the surrounding level. On light soil dig in cow manure and garden compost some weeks before planting time.

Planting may be either in the autumn or in the spring, but this depends upon local conditions. Plants put out in the autumn will usually start to flower earlier than those bedded out in spring; however, on heavy soil it is wise to defer planting until the spring. Where plants are put out in the autumn top-dress the bed or border with equal parts of loam,

sedge peat or leafmould and sharp sand, a week or two after planting. This will prove a useful protection to the roots during the winter. The plants are reasonably hardy but will not withstand excessive winter wet. When planting is done in the spring this should be during the second half of March so long as there are not bitter east winds. Set out the plants about 10–12 inches apart and during dry weather water them freely in the evenings.

Propagation is by seed sown in light soil in boxes or pans in July or August and placed in a cold, shady frame. Transplant the seedlings into their flowering positions in September or early October, or prick out and over-winter in a cold frame. Outstanding plants may be increased by cuttings taken in August or September and inserted in sandy soil in a cold, shady frame, or by division in September or October. For exhibition purposes allow one bloom only to grow on each shoot, removing other buds at an early stage. Plants grown for exhibition should be fed with weak liquid fertiliser once a week throughout the growing season (see also Viola).

Strains and cultivars include 'Cardinal Giant', brilliant red. 'Chantreyland', apricot. 'Coronation Gold', yellow flushed orange. 'Early Flowering Giant', sky-blue. 'Engelmann's Giant', mixed colours. 'Felix' strain, large flowers, various colours, yellow centres. 'Feltham Triumph', various colours. 'Indigo Blue', blue with dark blotches. 'King of the Blacks'. 'Masquerade', various light colour combinations. 'Pacific Toyland F_2 Hybrids', mixed colours. 'Paper White'. 'Roggli', mixed colours, very large flowers. 'St Knud', lower petals orange, upper apricot. 'Westland Giants', mixed colours, very large flowers.

Winter-flowering kinds (flowering from February onwards). These include 'Celestial Queen', sky-blue. 'Helios', golden-yellow. 'Ice King', white with dark spots. 'Jupiter', sky-blue with a purple blotch. 'March Beauty', velvety purple. 'Moonlight', primrose-yellow. 'Orion', golden-yellow. 'Winter Sun', golden-yellow with dark spots.

Papaver (pap-a-ver)

An ancient Latin plant-name of doubtful origin, but possibly derived from the sound made in chewing the seed (*Papaveraceae*). Poppy. A widespread genus of 100 species of colourful hardy annual and perennial plants. Poppies like full sun, although some will flower reasonably well in partial shade. The newly unfolded petals have the appearance of crumpled satin and many varieties have a glistening sheen on the blooms. They produce seed freely and many hybrids have been raised which are most decorative and easily grown. When used as cut flowers they will last longer if the stems are burned when they are cut and

before putting them in water. This seals the milky sap in the stems.

Species cultivated Annual *P. commutatum* (syn. *P. umbrosum*), 18 inches, bright crimson flowers with a conspicuous black blotch on each of the four petals, summer, Caucasus, Asia Minor. *P. glaucum,* tulip poppy, 18 inches, deep scarlet, summer, Syria. *P. rhoeas,* corn poppy, 1–2 feet, scarlet flowers with a black basal blotch, summer, Europe, including Britain. *P. somniferum,* opium poppy, 2–3 feet, pale lilac, purple, variegated or white flowers in summer, widely distributed in Europe and Asia.

Species cultivated Perennial *P. alpinum,* 6 inches, bluish-green foliage in neat tufts, yellow, orange, salmon and white flowers, summer, Europe. *P. atlanticum,* 18 inches, orange flowers, summer, Morocco. *P. nudicaule,* Iceland poppy, yellow, white and orange flowers, summer, sub-arctic regions. *P. orientale,* Oriental poppy, 3 feet, orange-scarlet, June, Asia Minor. *P. pilosum.* 2 feet, leaves form a green hairy rosette, orange-buff flowers, summer, Asia Minor. *P. rupifragum,* Spanish poppy, 2 feet, soft terra-cotta pink flowers, summer, Spain. Cultivars: There are many delightful varieties of the poppies in many and diverse colours; the following

Papaver orientale has given many good perennial varieties, mostly scarlet.

is a selection from those currently available. The annual varieties include the Shirley poppies, derived from *P. rhoeas,* single, and one of the best of all annuals; the double 'Ryburgh' hybrids and the begonia-flowered, also double in many colours and both also derived from *P. rhoeas*; from *P. somniferum* come the 'Daneborg' hybrids, scarlet with fringed petals and four white inner petals, the carnation-flowered, also fringed, the paeony-flowered doubles, and 'Pink Beauty', $2\frac{1}{2}$ feet, with grey leaves and double salmon-pink flowers. The perennial varieties include those from *P. nudicaule,* such as 'Coonara', salmon pink and rose; 'Golden Monarch', 'Kelmscott Strain', rich mixed colours; 'Red Cardinal', crimson-scarlet' 'Tangerine', brilliant large orange flowers. Also varieties of *P. orientale* such as 'Beauty of Livermere', scarlet frilled flowers; 'Grossfurst', crimson; 'Lord Lambourne', orange-scarlet; 'Princess Victoria Louise', cerise-pink; 'Olympia', light orange-scarlet, double early; 'Queen Alexandra', rose; 'Perry's White', white with dark blotches; 'Rembrandt', orange-scarlet; 'Salmon Glow', salmon-pink, double; 'Watermelon', single large, cherry-red.

Cultivation Sow annual varieties in April in patches where they are to flower. They prefer a sunny position and reasonably good soil. Thin the seedlings to 2 or 3

inches apart when quite small. Plant the perennial varieties in October or early spring in deeply dug, loamy soil in full sun, and top-dress with old manure or compost in March or April. Propagation of the perennials is by means of root cuttings in winter, by division of the roots in March or April, or by seed sown in pans or boxes in a cold-frame in spring, or on a finely broken-down seed bed out of doors in early summer, scarcely covering the fine seeds. *P. alpinum* and *P. nudicaule* are frequently grown as annuals or biennials (for the Welsh poppy see Meconopsis cambrica).

Paphiopedilum (paf-ee-o-ped-i-lum) From *Paphos*, the city sacred to Venus, and the Latin *pedilus*, sandal or slipper, referring to the shape of the flower *(Orchidaceae)*. A genus of about 50 species of epiphytic and terrestrial orchids, from the Far East, commonly known as slipper orchids. At one time they were included in the genus *Cypripedium*, but they are distinct from these in not having plicate (folded) foliage. All are without pseudobulbs. The foliage is either plain green or mottled with grey or yellowish-green. Plain-leaved types flower mainly in the winter, and the mottled kinds in spring and summer, but some, such as P. 'Maudiae', flower at various times, and by good cultivation and having several plants, a bloom can be had in nearly every month. Flowers are very long lasting, up to 12 weeks. Most have single-flowered spikes but one section contains plants which have up to 4-flowered spikes. All are very handsome, and many thousands of hybrids have been raised.

Species cultivated P. appletonianum, 12–18 inches, greenish-white and mauveish, spring, Thailand. P. argus, 1 foot, greenish, purple striped, brownish-purple, summer, Philippines. P. barbatum, 1 foot, greenish, white, striped and flushed purplish-brown, spring to summer, Malacca. P. bellatulum, large flowers, cream, spotted with purple-maroon, spring, Burma. P. callosum, large, white, purple-striped, brownish-purple, winter to summer, India; var. sanderae, white and green. P. chamberlainianum, spiralled petals, greenish, rose or greenish-rose, purplish, New Guinea. P. charlesworthii, rose suffused mauve, summer, Burma. P. ciliolare, 1–1½ feet, whitish, green-veined, purplish-brown, summer, Philippines. P. concolor, small, very pretty, short-stemmed, yellowish spotted red, summer, Thailand, Burma. P. curtisii, large, greenish-purple, summer, Sumatra; var. sanderae, whitish, striped green. P. dayanum, greenish-white, pinkish, brownish-purple, summer, Borneo. P. delenatii, 9–12 inches, very fine, smallish, pink, rounded shape, summer, Tonkin (China). P. druryi, yellowish, black median lines, spring, India. P. exul, yellowish and white, spring, Thailand. P. fairieanum, very pretty, small, whitish, purple striped and flushed, flowers at various times of the year, Assam. P. glaucophyllum, flowers in succession, greenish, dull purple, winter, Java. P. godefroyae, whitish or yellowish marked brown-purple, summer, eastern Asia. P. haynaldianum, 3 to 6 flowers on a stem, rose, yellowish-green, brownish-purple, summer, Philippines. P. hirsutissimum, 1 foot, large, to 6 inches across, green, purple, shaded brownish-purple, autumn, northern India. P. hookerae, greenish-yellow to purplish, summer, Borneo. P. insigne, very variable, greenish-brown, white, purplish spotted, winter, northern India. P. javanicum, green or brownish-green, summer, Java. P. lawrenceanum, large, white striped purple, greenish-purple, summer, Borneo. P. niveum, 6 inches, very pretty, pinkish to white, summer, Malaya. P. parishii, 3 to 7 flowers on a spike, petals twisted, purplish brown, summer, Burma. P. philippinense, petals twisted and tapered, black warted, brown-purple, brown-green, summer, Philippines. P. purpuratum, white, reddish striped, purplish-red, summer, Hong Kong. P. rothschildianum, 2 to 7 flowers on a spike, large, yellowish-white, black striped,

reddish-brown, spring, very fine, Borneo. P. spicerianum, white brownish-purple, winter, Assam. P. tonsum, greenish-white, striped green, summer, Sumatra. P. venustum, whitish, green-veined, purple flushed, winter, northern India. P. villosum, white, yellow-brown, winter, Burma. P. wardii, white veined green, purplish, spotted reddish, winter, Burma. Cultivars: the following is a small selection of the very great number available. For the newest varieties, the catalogues of the specialist orchid nurserymen should be consulted: 'Alain Gerbault'; 'Alma Gavaert'; 'Atlantis', a reddish cultivar; 'Blagrose'; 'Bordube'; 'Bruno'; 'Cappa Magna'; 'Desert Song'; 'Dreadnought'; 'Dusty Millar', very fine; 'F. C. Puddle', white; 'Maudiae'; 'Moreton Bay'; 'Redstart'; 'Wendbourn'.

Cultivation A general compost of 2 parts osmunda fibre and 1 part of sphagnum moss suits these orchids, and they should be potted in well-drained pots. P. insigne and some of the early hybrids should have a winter minimum temperature of 50–55°F (10–13°C). All other species and hybrids do best in a winter minimum of 60–65°F (16–18°F), and with a few, such as P. rothschildianum, 65–70°F (18–21°C) is required. Well shaded, moist and warm conditions in summer produce the best results. Never allow the plants to remain dry for more than a few days, and water them freely in summer. Less water is required in winter according to the conditions prevailing. Provide ventilation, but avoid draughts. The section containing P. niveum, P. bellatulum, P. concolor and P. godefroyae can have a layer of limestone or mortar rubble over the crocks before the compost is added. Pot during early spring if conditions are suitable. This allows time for the growths to reach a good size before the autumn. Propagation is by division, ensuring that each new part has several growths.

Parahebe (pa-ra-he-be)
From the Greek para, near, and Hebe, the ancient Greek goddess of youth and cup-bearer to the gods. The genus is very closely related to Hebe (Scrophulariaceae). They are a group of plants which have been removed from the genus Veronica mainly on account of their chromosome number. Closely related to the shrubby veronicas, or hebes as they are now called, they differ largely in the form of their fruits. There are 15 species, natives of New Zealand. All are very easily grown soft-wooded shrubs, suitable for planting in the rock garden or in paved areas, and flower from early July to late September.

Species cultivated P. catarractae, branches usually almost prostrate, rooting at the nodes, with purple-tinged ascending shoots up to 2 feet tall, flowers white, veined with pink or purple in 3 to 9-inch long slender racemes. P. lyallii, low, much-branched, almost prostrate

shrub, often rooting at the nodes, the young leaves sometimes tinged reddish when young, flowers white to pink, small, in erect slender racemes.

Cultivation Almost any soil will suit most of the parahebes, and they will thrive on a sunny bank. As they are not always winter hardy it is often advisable to overwinter replacement plants under glass. One of the easiest ways of doing this is to take cuttings in late summer, lining them out in sandy soil in a cold frame. The frame should be kept closed, humid, and shaded from direct sun for about a fortnight, afterwards slowly hardening off the plants. In times of severe frost the frames should be covered with sacking or similar material, to give the plants a little extra protection. The rooted cuttings are either potted up or planted out in the following spring.

Parsnip
This hardy root vegetable, known botanically as Peucedanum sativum or Pastinaca sativum, needs a long period of uninterrupted growth and it must also be remembered that the seed is rather slow in germinating. These facts make it imperative that the seed be sown in the open as early in March as possible. Another point in connection with this seed is that germination is somewhat irregular.

Cultivation It is essential if you expect to produce good-sized specimens to trench the soil deeply so that the desirable, long, straight, unforked roots are produced. The large seeds are sown in 1-inch deep drills in small groups at intervals of 4 inches, the drills spaced 1½ feet apart. Choose a calm day for sowing as the seeds are light and liable to blow away in windy weather. Do not try to transplant as this will generally result in some injury to the essential tap root. Should all your seeds germinate you may remove alternate plants in the drills leaving the remaining ones at 8-inch intervals.

The best soil is one which has been well manured for a previous crop, and no animal manure should be applied later. However, a stimulant may well be given in the form of a mixture of 3 ounces of superphosphate, 1 ounce of sulphate of ammonia and 1½ ounces of sulphate of potash per square yard. The roots will be ready for use at the end of October but, since they are frost resistant, they may be left in their rows until they are needed; or, if the soil has to be dug in preparation for further cropping, the roots may be lifted and packed away in a shed or cellar with a covering of dry soil or sand. In any event it is always wise to lift and store a few roots in case the ground freezes hard, making it impossible to dig up the roots.

Cultivation for exhibition When growing parsnips for exhibition a somewhat more

1 Parsonsia heterophylla, a climber from New Zealand, is hardy in milder localities in Britain.
2 The yellowish-brown, white-centred flowers of Parsonsia brownii.

elaborate method of cultivation is advisable. The winter trenching may well be 2 feet deep and the soil subsequently left in ridges to be properly pulverised by the frosts, the subsoil as well as the topsoil being exposed to the weather. The next stage in the production of exhibition quality roots comes with the March seed sowing, when instead of the method of sowing described above, a series of 2-foot holes are forced in the soil by using an iron rod or crowbar. These should be 1 foot apart and in rows 1½ feet apart. The holes should have a good light potting soil dribbled into them, and in each three seeds are to be sown, covered by 1 inch of soil. When the seeds germinate the weakest are removed until each hole is left with a single seedling. The tap root will easily penetrate into the fine soil prepared for it.

Harvesting of exhibition parsnips is also a matter requiring a special technique since it is most important to secure the specimens without damage, right down to the very tip of the root. Starting at one end of the row a trench is opened up beside the row of parsnips and cautiously the roots are approached until the full length of root is obtained intact. This operation is continued patiently to the end of the row, when you will have a large number of long straight roots from which to select your exhibition specimens.

The seedsmen offer a few named kinds of which the variety 'Hollow Crown' seems to be very popular for exhibition purposes, though for the normal kitchen use other kinds such as 'Lisbonnais' may well be preferred for their superior flavour, and the fact that what they lose in length they gain in girth.

Parsonsia (par-son-se-a)
Named after Dr John Parsons (1705–1770), a Scots physician and writer on natural history *(Apocynaceae).* A genus of about 100 species, nearly all woody climbers with opposite leaves and small whitish flowers in early summer, suitable for a cool greenhouse. Most of the species in cultivation are from Australia and New Zealand, the others are found elsewhere in Polynesia and in tropical Asia.

Species cultivated *P. capsularis,* a slender evergreen climber with narrow leaves up to 3 inches long and small white bell-shaped flowers, New Zealand. *P. heterophylla,* a slender evergreen climber with fragrant creamy-white flowers, May–June, hardy in mild locations in Britain, New Zealand. *P. velutina,* a pubescent (velvety) tall woody climber with very small white flowers, July, Australia.

Cultivation John Innes potting compost will suit this genus. The growths may be trained round canes in a pot or planted out and trained up the inside of the greenhouse. Propagation is by seed.

Passiflora (pas-se-flor-a)
From the Latin *passus,* suffering, and *flos,* a flower, hence Passion-flower, the Spanish Roman Catholic priests arriving in newly colonised South America found in the plants features which they regarded as symbols of the Crucifixion *(Passifloraceae).* This genus of 500 species of tender tendril climbers, mostly from tropical America, has many species with arrestingly beautiful blossoms, and some with edible fruit. The only species which may be grown upon an outside wall in the south and west of Britain is *P. caerulea.* There is some disagreement among experts about the colour of the five petals and five sepals. W. J. Bean, the British shrub expert, says they are blue and the American horticulturist, L. H. Bailey, says they are pink, though to the man or woman with normal sight they are apparently greenish-white. About the remarkable circle of thread-like radiating filaments called the corona there is no disagreement; it is purple, inclining to blue. This plant was used by the Spanish priests to give the native 'Indians' a lesson on the Crucifixion as prophetically figured by the leaves, tendrils, petals and sepals, the stamens and stigmas.

Species cultivated *P. alata,* tall climber, flowers fragrant, to 5 inches wide, sepals and petals crimson, outer filaments banded with red, white and blue, spring to summer, Brazil, stovehouse. *P. × allardii,* vigorous climber, flowers large, sepals and petals white, shaded with pink, corona deep blue, hybrid, cool greenhouse. *P. antioquiensis* (syn. *Tacsonia van-volxemii*), vigorous climber, flowers 5 inches or more across, bright red, summer, Colombia, greenhouse, but hardy in the extreme south-west, particularly on the Isles of Scilly. *P. × belottii,* strong climber, flowers to 5 inches across, sepals pink flushed green, petals rose, filaments blue, hybrid, warm greenhouse. *P. caerulea,* vigorous climber, described above, June to September, sometimes into November in mild autumns, fruits egg-shaped, orange,

The strangely beautiful flowers of Passiflora caerulea are typical of the genus. The plant is hardy in warmth

inedible, hardy in the south and west against warm walls, Brazil; the parent of many hybrids; var. 'Constance Elliott', flowers ivory-white. *P. edulis,* purple granadilla, woody climber, flowers to 3 inches across, sepals green outside, white inside, petals white, filaments white with purple bands, summer, fruit egg-shaped, yellow ripening to deep purple, pulp edible, Brazil, warm greenhouse. *P. incarnata,* maypop, may apple, vigorous climber, flowers to 3 inches across, sepals lavender, petals white or lavender, filaments purplish-blue, summer, fruits yellow, egg-shaped, edible, south-eastern United States, cool greenhouse. *P. mixta,* climber, flowers 3 inches or more across, sepals and petals orange-red, corona lavender or purple, summer, tropical South America, greenhouse or out of doors in the mildest places; var. *quitensis,* differing in minor botanical details. *P. quadrangularis,* giant granadilla, vigorous climber, flowers up to $4\frac{1}{2}$ inches across, sepals greenish outside, pink or white inside, petals pale pink, corona banded with blue and reddish-purple, summer, fruits egg-shaped, purple, 8 inches to 1 foot long, pulp edible, tropical South

America. *P. racemosa,* vigorous climber, flowers 4–5 inches or more across, sepals and petals crimson, corona purple, white and red, stove greenhouse, Brazil. *P. umbellicata,* vigorous climber, flowers small, purplish-brown, hardy in the milder counties against protected walls, South America.

Cultivation The soil mixture for the stove species should consist of equal parts of loam and peat and $\frac{1}{4}$ part of coarse potting sand. Pot cultivation is quite suitable if a large pot is used, for underpotting encourages the plant to flower rather than produce too much extension of growth. The plants should be pruned in February, removing weak growth completely and shortening the strong shoots by one third. These climbers may be trained up to the greenhouse roof and will stand full sun. The temperature from March to October should be 65–75°F (18–24°C), and from October to March 55–65°F (13–18°C). Water them generously April to September, but sparingly at other times. The greenhouse plants should have a temperature from March to October of 55–65°F (13–18°C) and October to March of 45–50°F (7–10°C).

Passiflora caerulea may be planted in ordinary garden soil, preferably at the foot of a warm wall, though even here a severe winter may destroy all the top growth; however, some new shoots

generally appear later from the unharmed roots. All species may be propagated from seed, or very easily from 6-inch cuttings, rooted under glass in a propagating frame with bottom heat, from April to September. They may also be propagated by layering young shoots in summer.

Peas

The garden or green pea *(Pisum sativum)* is a highly nutritious legume widely grown as a farm crop and a popular vegetable among gardeners. Varieties are sub-divided into First Early, Second Early, Maincrop and Late. Pea seeds may be round and smooth (round-seeded) or wrinkled (marrowfats). Round-seeded peas are hardier than marrowfats, but marrowfats are considered of better flavour and to have a higher sugar content. Light soils suit the production of First Early peas; for later maturing crops a loamy soil which does not dry out quickly is ideal providing that soil drainage is good. A heavy clay soil is unsuitable for peas unless drainage has been remedied. Although peas grow readily in alkaline soils, the growth of plants in an acidic soil is invariably poor. A desirable soil pH value for garden peas lies between pH 6·0 and pH 7·5. No highly nitrogenous manure or fertiliser should be applied when the ground is being prepared for this crop. Like other legumes, the pea plant develops nitrogen-fixing nodules on its roots. When pea bine is removed after harvesting the roots should be allowed to decompose in the soil and enrich it by releasing nitrogen into it.

In a normal three-year rotation of Kitchen crops, peas follow brassicas, for which the soil will have been generously dressed with manure or garden compost in the previous season. The plot reserved for pea growing is dug with the spade or garden fork during the late autumn or winter and this may be followed by a light forking to a depth of 4 inches to 6 inches just before a sowing of peas is contemplated. During the diggings, all weeds and their roots should be removed as should any wireworms, leatherjackets or slugs.

There are dwarf and taller pea varieties. Although plants of the short, dwarf varieties may be grown without supports it is the custom to provide all garden peas with supports of some sort. Twiggy brushwood of the height the plants will attain is much liked by gardeners. Bamboo canes linked together with strong thread or garden twine often replace the traditional brushwood. Garden netting for pea growing is offered at garden shops and by horticultural retailers. The tall supports needed by tall growers should be augmented by several strong, tall stakes to prevent strong winds in summer from blowing down the plants when bearing their heavy crops.

Seed is sown in a 2-inch deep furrow, which is 6 to 8 inches wide, made with the draw hoe. The seeds are sprinkled thinly into the furrow so that each seed is between 2½ to 3 inches from the next. Should the soil be dry, the furrow should be flooded with water and sowing undertaken when this has drained away. After sowing, the seeds are covered with soil raked over them. During the raking any large stones should be removed. The distances between rows of peas vary. It is generally accepted that the distances between the rows should be the same as the height of the variety being grown, but with very dwarf peas 30 inches between rows is the rule. Supports, if to hand, should be set in position immediately after the seed has been sown. The tendrils of the pea plant cannot grasp thick supports and where these are in use young pea plants are encouraged to climb by the insertion of short pieces of twiggy wood on either side of the row. The twigs also afford some protection to the young plants by breaking the force of cold winds.

Pea seeds and pea seedlings are attractive to birds and black cotton or small mesh chicken wire are useful protectors. The wire mesh should be removed when the seedlings are a few inches tall. The old-fashioned scarecrow is a useful bird deterrent as are large polythene bags fixed to tall stakes. Where mice are known to take freshly-sown seeds, traps should be set or a proprietary poison used with care and according to the manufacturer's instructions. Slugs are a great nuisance in some gardens and a slug bait may have to be laid down. Weevils also attack pea seedlings. Weevil damage may be distinguished from that caused by slugs. Leaves bitten by weevils have a scalloped-like shape. Hoeing around the rows regularly and the dusting of the plants when dry with derris powder or soot are ways of combating weevils.

The pea plant is very susceptible to mildew infection in dry weather. The mildew shows clearly as a white powder on the pods and foliage. Watering the rows regularly and copiously during dry weather is the preventive measure. Mulching between the rows with straw or granulated sedge peat assists the retention of moisture in the soil and is also a weed preventive measure. The pea moth, *Laspeyresia nigricana,* is a common pest of garden peas in the south of England. The caterpillars bore into and devour the peas. Damage is more likely to occur in a very dry season. Spraying the plants with nicotine when the flowers are setting is a control. 'Kelvedon Wonder' and 'Foremost' are said to be less susceptible to pea moth damage than some other varieties.

Garden peas should be harvested before the pods are drum-tight and but a few hours before the cook needs them. If left to become old on the plants or if

The flowers of Pelargonium 'Degeta'.

they are not used quite quickly after harvesting, peas lack flavour and sugar. Pea bine should on no account be burnt. It is a useful waste material for the compost heap.

Pelargonium (pel-ar-go-knee-um)

From the Greek *pelargos,* a stork, referring to the resemblance between the beak of the fruit and that of a stork *(Geraniaceae).* This is the correct name for the plant which is grown in public parks and our gardens and greenhouses. The zonal pelargoniums have in the past 70 years mostly been called 'Geraniums' which is a complete misnomer. The true geraniums were described in an earlier article in this Encyclopedia.

Within the past 10 years the horticultural public has been made aware of the misnomer, mainly by the efforts of the specialist societies throughout the world, and are now using the correct term for the zonal and regal pelargoniums in increasing numbers.

To help to sort out the confusion that has existed it is worth stating that the cultivars of the genus *Pelargonium,* both regal and zonal types, have definitely been bred from the true *Pelargonium* species and not from the genus *Gera-*

nium; this is the key to the correct definition.

In the genus *Pelargonium* there are over 300 recorded species; this does not include the sub-species and other varieties not recorded yet, of which there must be a considerable number.

The species are identified in one way by the fact that the plants breed true from seed, although some have individual races within the species which also breed true from seed and a lot of cross-pollination is done by insects on plants growing in their natural habitat, causing much confusion among taxonomists. Many of these natural hybrids are very closely identified with the original plant but may have slightly different leaves, form or flowers.

The species were mainly brought to England from many parts of Africa, although several places in other parts of the world have also contributed, such as Australia, New Zealand and Tasmania, during the last three centuries. They are not hardy here and have to be protected during the winter months, although a wide range of species is grown out of doors in the Abbey Gardens at Tresco,

Isles of Scilly.

What is so remarkable is that such a large number of colourful cultivated varieties could ever have been bred from plants that have only very small flowers. It shows the tenacity and enthusiasm of the breeders who performed this task, mainly during the last century, although this work has been carried on into the present era.

The species are fascinating to explore and there is no doubt that they are more important than the cultivars in many ways, especially in their use for hybridising purposes and also for experimentation and research.

There are all kinds of fantastic shapes and forms among the various kinds and a great number have perfume in their leaves. Although this scent is often clearly defined it cannot be assessed absolutely in all varieties because so many factors have to be taken into consideration, which contribute to the amount of volatile oil in the tissues. Variations of this can be caused by environment, feeding, soil structure, age of plants, time or season of year, etc., all of which can vary from county to county and country to country. One of the main reasons why smells or perfumes seem to vary is because the sense of smell varies widely between one person and another.

The volatile oil is distilled from many of the species to be used in cosmetics and perfumes.

The scented-leaved kinds are listed here because they are mainly species and thus they are easy to classify.

The leaves of the pelargonium are edible and are used a great deal in cooking and can add at least ten different flavours to any cake or sweetmeat. It is, therefore, worthwhile growing certain species for this purpose alone.

The following is a list of the species most commonly known and grown and obtainable in Britain. If they do have a perfume this is described in terms which are generally accepted for the particular species. Except where stated all species are natives of South Africa, and, in general, they all flower in summer and normally grow to between 9 inches and $2\frac{1}{2}$–3 feet in height.

Species cultivated *P. abrotanifolium,* flowers white or rose veined with purple, leaves fragrant of southernwood (*Artemisia abrotanum*). *P. acetosum,* leaves silvery-green, tasting of sorrel, single carmine flowers, can be used in cooking. *P. angulosum,* plant hairy, leaves 5-lobed, flowers purple, veined maroon. *P. australe,* flowers rose or whitish, spotted and striped carmine, Australia, New Zealand, Tasmania. *P. capitatum,* rose scent, pale mauve blooms. *P. crispum,*

A selection of Pelargoniums. *Top l. to r.* 'Verona', 'A Happy Thought', 'Distinction'; *centre l. to r.* 'Mrs Parker', 'Henry Cox', 'Wilhelm lan Guth', 'Marechal MacMahon'; *below l. to r.* 'Mrs Mappin', 'Harry Hieover', 'Flower of Spring', 'Black Douglas'.

strong lemon scent, flowers pink or rose; vars. *major,* larger; *minor,* smaller; *variegatum,* lemon scent, grey-green leaves with cream edges, very elegant for floral display work. *P. cucullatum,* rose-scented cupped leaves, flowers red with darker veins, late summer, a parent of the regal pelargoniums and very good for outdoor pot plant growing. *P. denticulatum,* sticky leaves with strong undefined scent, flowers lilac or rosy-purple, best species with fern-like foliage. *P. echinatum,* sweetheart geranium, tuberous-rooted, stems spiny, leaves heart-shaped, lobed, flowers purple, pink or white, nearly hardy. *P. filicifolium* (syn. *P. denticulatum filicifolium*), fern-like leaves, very pungent scent, small rose flowers. *P. formosum,* salmon flowers, white-tipped, upright habit. *P. × fragrans,* nutmeg-scented geranium, small dark green leaves smelling of spice, flowers white, veined red; var. *variegata,* a miniature plant with a very pleasant scent, tiny light green leaves edged with cream, easily grown and propagated, should be in every collection. *P. frutetorum,* prostrate habit, salmon flowers. *P. gibbosum,* gouty pelargonium, so named because the joints are similar to those on elderly people so afflicted, flowers greenish-yellow, early summer. *P. graveolens,* rose-scented geranium, strong rose scent, flowers pink, upper petal with dark purple spot; much used in the distillation of perfume. *P. inquinans,* scarlet flowers, plain leaves, one parent of the zonal pelargoniums. *P. multibracteatum,* leaves heart-shaped, deeply lobed, with dark green zones, flowers white. *P. odoratissimum,* apple-scented geranium, leaves heart-shaped or kidney-shaped, fragrant of apples, flowers small, white. *P. peltatum,* ivy-leaved geranium, leaves fleshy, flowers pale rosy-mauve, a parent of the ivy-leaved cultivars. *P. quercifolium,* oak-leaved geranium, leaves roughly oak-leaf shape, grey-green, strongly scented, flowers mauve. *P. radula,* fern-like leaves, fragrant of verbena, flowers rose, upper petals blotched purplish-carmine, very attractive if grown out of doors during the summer when it grows into a small shrub. *P. saxifragioides,* very dainty plant with tiny leaves similar to some ivy-leaved kinds, flowers mauve, marked purple. *P. tetragonum,* often called the cactus-type pelargonium because of its four-sided stems; its growth should be controlled by stopping because of its vigorous habit, flowers small, white, single. *P. tomentosum,* strong peppermint scent, leaves grey-green, soft and spongy, sometimes difficult to keep during the winter period, flowers tiny, white. *P. tricolor,* foliage sage green, small tricolor flowers, lower petals white, upper petals magenta, with dark spots, a good plant for pots in the greenhouse, a prize collector's piece. *P. triste,* the sad geranium, tuberous rooted, long, much-divided leaves, flowers brownish-yellow with a pale border; sweetly scented in the evening. *P. zonale,* flowers single, mauve, pink or red, leaves lightly zoned. 'Lady Plymouth', foliage as *P. graveolens* except that the leaves are variegated green and lemon. 'Mabel Grey', strong lemon scent, upright grower that needs frequent stopping. 'Prince of Orange', orange scented, small pale mauve flowers.

The 'Uniques' are another group that have sprung up in recent years and are stated to be *P. fulgidum* hybrids. *P. fulgidum,* a sub-shrubby species with bright red flowers, is prominent in their ancestry. They are best grown in pots and hanging baskets. There are many different perfumes in the leaves of the

1 Pelargonium 'Carisbrooke' has soft rose-pink petals with darker markings.
2 The white flowers of Pelargonium 'Muriel Harris' are feathered with red.
3 Pelargonium 'Black Prince'.

varieties listed below:
'Crimson Unique', red and black flowers; 'Scarlet Unique', lemon scent, red flowers, parent of 'Carefree' and 'Hula'; 'Paton's Unique', verbena scent, rose flowers; 'Purple Unique', peppermint scent, purple flowers; 'Rose Unique', rose scent, rose flowers; 'White Unique', white flowers with purple veins. Cultivars: one of the most important sections of the cultivars are the regal or domesticum Pelargoniums which have very beautiful flowers and green leaves, but recently some sports have been discovered with golden and green bicolor leaves which should make these beautiful plants much sought after if hybridisers are successful in breeding these coloured leaves into this section.

The main parents of the regals are *P. cucullatum* and *P. betulinum* which are indigenous to the coastal regions of South Africa. Hybridisation started on the species mainly here in England, in France and also in central Europe well over a century ago. These plants should be grown under glass or in the house throughout the year in the British Isles, although they may be grown out of doors in summer in exceptionally protected places. Two lovely cultivars have

been produced that will grow out of doors well in all kinds of weather during the summer months. These are 'Hula' and 'Carefree', from America. These two are the result of crossing the cultivars back to the species. 'Hula' and 'Carefree' do not have flower umbels as large as the true regals but have the advantage of being able to stand up to bad conditions out of doors.

Some recommended cultivars are as follows (dominating colours only are mentioned): 'Annie Hawkins', pink; 'Applause', pink and white; 'Aztec', strawberry pink and white; 'Blythwood', purple and mauve; 'Caprice', pink; 'Carisbrooke', rose pink; 'Doris Frith', white; 'Grand Slam', red; 'Marie Rober', lavender; 'Muriel Hawkins', pink; 'Rapture', apricot; 'Rhodamine', purple and mauve; and the outstanding sport from 'Grand Slam', 'Lavender Grand Slam'.

The flowering season of the regals has been greatly lengthened within the last five years by the introduction of the new

There are over 300 species of Pelargoniums and literally thousands of cultivars, including 1 'Aztec', 2 'Lavender Grand Slam', 3 'Rapture' and 4 'Blythwood', which are all recommended.

American cultivars.

A great advantage in growing plants in this section is that they are rarely troubled by disease. The worst pest is the greenhouse white fly which appears at all times and can spread rapidly. It can, however, easily be controlled by using a good insecticide.

The section which dominates the genus consists of the hortorums, usually referred to as zonals. These are divided into many groups which are classified as follows (selected cultivars are listed under each heading):

Single-flowered group (normally with not more than five petals):
'Barbara Hope', pink; 'Block', scarlet; 'Countess of Jersey', salmon; 'Doris Moore', cherry; 'Elizabeth Angus', rose; 'Eric Lee', magenta; 'Francis James', bicolor flowers; 'Golden Lion', orange; 'Highland Queen', pink; 'Maxim Kovaleski', orange; 'Mrs E. G. Hill', pink; 'Pandora', scarlet; 'Pride of the West', cerise; 'Victorious', scarlet; 'Victory', red.

Semi-doubles:
American Irenes of various shades and colours are extremely useful for bedding purposes; many named cultivars are very similar to each other. Other cultivated

varieties include 'Dagata', pink; 'Genetrix', pink; 'Gustav Emich', scarlet; 'King of Denmark', pink; 'Pink Bouquet', pink; 'The Speaker', red.

Double-flowered group:
'Alpine Orange', orange; 'A. M. Maine', magenta; 'Blue Spring', red-purple; 'Double Henry Jacoby', crimson; 'Jewel', rose; 'Jean Oberle', pink; 'Lerchenmuller', cerise; 'Monsieur Emil David', purple; 'Maid of Perth', salmon; 'Mrs Lawrence', pink; 'Paul Reboux', red; 'Rubin' red; 'Schwarzwalderin', rose; 'Trautleib', pink.

Cactus group (single or double flowers with quilled petals):
'Attraction', salmon; 'Fire Dragon', red; 'Mrs Salter Bevis', pink; 'Noel', white; 'Spitfire', red with silver leaves; 'Tangerine', vermilion.

Rosebud group (flower buds tight and compact, centre petals remaining unopened, like small rosebuds):
'Apple Blossom Rosebud', pink; 'Red Rambler', red; 'Rosebud Supreme', red.

Miniature group:
'Alde', pink; 'Caligula', red; 'Cupid', pink; 'Goblin', red; 'Jenifer', carmine; 'Grace Wells', mauve; 'Mephistopheles', red; 'Mandy', cerise; 'Pauline', rose; 'Piccaninny', red; 'Taurus', red; 'Timothy Clifford', salmon; 'Wendy', salmon; 'Waveney', red.

Dwarf group:
'Blakesdorf', red; 'Emma Hossler', pink; 'Fantasia', white; 'Miranda', carmine; 'Madam Everaarts', pink; 'Pixie', salmon.

Fancy-leaved group (the colours given are those of the flowers):
Silver leaves: 'Flower of Spring', red; 'Mrs Mappin', red; 'Mrs Parker', pink; 'Wilhelm Langguth' (syn. 'Caroline Schmidt'), red.
Golden leaves: 'Golden Crest'; 'Golden Orfe'; 'Verona'.
Butterfly leaves: 'A Happy Thought'; 'Crystal Palace Gem'; 'Madame Butterfly'.
Bronze bicolor leaves: 'Bronze Corrine'; 'Bronze Queen'; 'Gaiety Girl'; 'Dollar Princess'; 'Maréchal MacMahon'; 'Mrs Quilter'.
Multi-coloured leaves: 'Dolly Varden'; 'Lass o' Gowrie'; 'Miss Burdett-Coutts', 'Henry Cox'; 'Mrs Pollock'; 'Sophie Dumaresque'.

Ivy-leaved group:
One of the best in this group is *P. peltatum,* the original species from which this section has been derived. Cultivars are: 'Abel Carriere', magenta; 'Beatrice Cottington', purple; 'Galilee', pink; 'La France', mauve; 'L'Elegante', leaves cream and green with purple markings; 'Madame Margot', white and green leaf; and two with green leaves and white veins, 'Crocodile' and 'White Mesh'.

In general the large-flowered cultivars described above will grow under normal garden and greenhouse conditions as will the coloured-leaved cultivars, which benefit from being left out of doors

Pelargonium 'Doris Frith' has ruffled white flowers with red markings.

during the summer months to get full sunshine and rain.

The miniature and dwarf sections are best grown in the greenhouse in pots, or they are very useful plants to grow out of doors in containers such as window boxes or urns. They are especially good for hanging baskets when used in conjunction with ivy-leaved kinds.

Hanging baskets are very useful for enhancing a display out of doors, especially under porches. One of the best cultivars for this purpose is 'The Prostrate Boar', a newer introduction which grows very quickly and produces an abundance of flowers throughout the summer. Make sure that you get the prostrate type and not the ordinary 'Boar' which does not grow so vigorously, nor flower so freely. 'The Boar', or *P. salmonia,* is inclined to grow vertically.

P. frutetorum has had in the past, and should have in the future, a great influence on the pelargonium genus because of its great vigour and its ability to influence the pigments in the leaves of the many cultivars crossed with it. Among the well-known hybrids are:
'Dark Beauty'; 'Filigree'; 'Medallion'; 'Magic Lantern'; 'Mosaic', and 'The Prostrate Boar'; large flowers have now been introduced into this group.

Hybridisation The hybridisation of pelargoniums is very easy as most cultivated varieties will cross with each other, especially if they are in the same section. Among these are the large zonals, dwarfs, miniatures, and coloured-leaved cultivars.

Hybridisation merely consists in taking the pollen from one flower and transferring it on to the stigma of another compatible cultivar. This method will give some good results, but if you are going to go in for a proper breeding programme you should isolate those plants intended for breeding purposes and keep clear records of each individual cross. This is very necessary should any of your seedlings turn out to be good ones and you wish to register them as new introductions. The miniatures and the dwarfs are very adaptable for cross-breeding, so it is advisable to work on these for primary experiments.

Cultivation In general pelargoniums grown in pots will do well in the John Innes potting composts, though it is advisable to add a little extra lime to neutralise the acidity of the peat. Alternatively, particularly for potting on rooted cuttings, a suitable soil mixture consists of 2 parts of good loam, 1 part of sand, 1 part of peat, all parts by bulk, not weight, plus 1 pint of charcoal and 1 cupful of ground limestone per bushel of the mixture. The ingredients should be thoroughly mixed together and then watered with a liquid fertiliser with a high potash content. Some growers have been successful with the 'no-soil' composts (peat/sand mixtures plus balanced fertilisers), while others use ordinary good garden soil which has been cleared of worms and sterilised to kill harmful soil organisms.

Pelargoniums should never be overpotted. When repotting becomes necessary it is often possible, by removing old

The Pelargonium can be put to many decorative uses where it is afforded protection from frost. Here it clothes the wall of a conservatory.

compost and slightly reducing the size of the root-ball, to repot into pots of the same size; otherwise the plants should be moved into pots one size larger only. They should always be potted firmly.

Although plants should be watered freely during the growing period, in spring and summer, they should never be over-watered and, in any case, the pots in which they are grown should be properly crocked and the soil mixture should be free-draining so that surplus moisture can get away quickly, otherwise various root-rots and stem-rots may be encouraged. In winter plants will need little water, though the soil in the pots should not be allowed to dry out.

Some shading will be required in the greenhouse from late April or early May onwards. A light application of 'Summer Cloud' or other proprietary shading compound to the glass will be sufficient.

In order to prevent damping-off of the flowers the atmosphere in the greenhouse should be kept as dry as possible during the summer. This means that proper use should be made of the ventilators and that every attempt should be made to keep the air circulating to avoid an over-humid, stagnant atmosphere. During the winter, when it is equally important to keep the air dry, though warm, good circulation can be provided by using an electrical blower heater.

To keep the plants growing freely and to maintain good leaf colour it is necessary to feed them during the growing season. Regular weak applications of proprietary liquid fertiliser should be given from about a month after the plants are in their final pots, until September. It should be noted, however, that plants in the fancy-leaved group should either not be fed at all, or the feed they are given should not contain nitrogen. These kinds should, in any case, be given less water than others.

A number of zonal varieties can be induced to flower in winter, when blooms are always welcome. The method is to take cuttings in the spring, by normal propagation methods described below. The young plants are grown on steadily during the summer and all flower buds are removed until late September. Plants treated in this way should flower throughout the winter months. It is best to maintain a minimum temperature of 60°F (16°C) and the plants should be given as much light as possible. During the summer the plants may be placed in a sunny cold frame or the pots may be plunged in a sunny, sheltered place out of doors. They should be brought into the greenhouse in September.

Plants which are to be used for summer bedding purposes are raised from cuttings taken in August or September, rooting several in each 5-inch pot, or in boxes, spacing the cuttings 2 inches apart. In February the rooted cuttings are potted into individual 3-inch pots and kept in a temperature of 45–50°F (7–10°C) until April. They are then hardened off in a cold frame before planting them out of doors in late May or early June, when all danger of frost is over. Do not plant shallowly; it is best to take out a hole large enough and deep enough to take the plant up to its first pair of leaves. Leggy plants may be planted more deeply. Remove dead leaves and flowers as soon as they are seen and pinch out long, unwanted shoots from time to time to keep the plants bushy. Keep the plants well watered in dry weather. A gentle overhead spray in the evenings in hot weather is beneficial. In September before the first frosts, the plants should be lifted and brought into the greenhouse for the winter. The shoots should be cut back, long roots trimmed and the plants potted into small pots. The minimum winter temperature in the greenhouse should be around 42°F (5°C).

Propagation of regal pelargoniums is by cuttings, which, like those of the other types, root easily. They should be about 3 inches long, taken from the top of the lateral shoots. They are trimmed back to a node and the bottom leaves are removed. They will root quickly in a sterile rooting compost, in pots or in a propagating frame in the greenhouse. Bottom heat is not required. Cuttings of this type are usually taken in July or August.

Propagation of the hortorums or zonal pelargoniums may be effected in several ways. Cuttings of the type described above may be taken and either rooted singly in 2½-inch pots or three cuttings may be inserted round the edge of a 3-inch pot. If large numbers are to be

rooted they may be inserted in a suitable rooting compost in a frame, or 2 inches apart in shallow boxes. Cuttings are usually taken in June, July or August in this country, to enable them to form roots early. If they are taken later they may not root properly before the end of the season and thus may be lost. However, they may be rooted later in a propagating case in the greenhouse, and commercially they are rooted in quantity by mist propagation methods, using bottom heat.

The leaf-axil (or leaf-bud) method of taking cuttings has become popular in recent years. This consists in taking a leaf and ½ inch of stem from the parent plant, ¼ inch above and below the node or joint. The stem section is cut vertically through the centre of the stem. The cuttings thus formed are inserted in rooting compost in the normal way, just covering the buds. If some bud growth is seen in the leaf axils you are more certain of rooting the cuttings. Such cuttings are normally taken in the summer months.

Whichever method you adopt, make sure that you use clean stock only. Almost any piece of a zonal pelargonium containing stem and leaves can be used for propagation purposes, provided the conditions are right. It is quite normal to root stem cuttings of these plants out of doors during the summer months, in the open ground.

Plants may also be raised from seed obtained from a reliable source. It is unwise to buy unnamed seedlings as they may produce large plants with few flowers. Seeds should be sown ¹⁄₁₆ inch deep in light sandy soil, in pans or boxes,

in the greenhouse, from February to April, in a temperature of 55–65°F (13–18°C).

Tuberous-rooted pelargonium species may be divided in spring for propagation purposes.

The principal pests of pelargoniums grown under glass are aphids and greenhouse white fly. These may be controlled by insecticidal sprays or by fumigation methods. The disease variously known as black leg, black rot, black stem rot or pelargonium stem rot, is very liable to attack cuttings and sometimes mature plants. It first appears on the lower part of the stem, which turns black. It spreads rapidly up the stem and soon kills the plant. It seems to be encouraged by too much moisture in the compost and in over-humid conditions. Some control may be obtained by spraying or dusting plants with captan in the autumn. It is also important not to damage the skin of the stem when taking cuttings, otherwise disease spores may enter through the skin at this point. Always use a sharp sterile knife or razor blade when taking or trimming cuttings.

Grey mould *(Botrytis cinerea)* will attack plants under glass, especially in close, humid conditions. It appears as a grey furry mould on stems, leaves or flowers. Proprietary fungicides based on copper or thiram will control this

disease, but it is more important to maintain the correct conditions in the greenhouse, with ample ventilation and a dry atmosphere. When plants are overwintered remove all dead, furry leaves, but make sure that the leaf is quite dead. When taking away discoloured leaves do this by removing the leaf only at first, leaving the stalk intact until the abscission layer has formed between stalk and stem, when the stalk may be removed easily. To attempt to remove it before the abscission layer has formed will result in the stem being damaged with the consequent risk of disease spores entering.

Penstemon (pen-ste-mon)

From the Greek *pente,* five, and *stemon,* stamen, in reference to the five stamens *(Scrophulariaceae).* This genus of over 250 species of hardy and half-hardy herbaceous annuals, perennials and sub-shrubs is almost exclusively North American. The name is sometimes erroneously spelt *Pentstemon.* Though many are grown in British gardens, some of the species do not thrive and it seems likely that the continental climate, with its colder winters and hotter summers, is needed to make these plants really happy. The very popular late summer bedding penstemons were derived from an initial crossing of *P. cobaea* and *P. hartwegii,* and they have a fairly wide colour range through pinks and reds to deep maroons and purples. *P. heterophyllus* is a fine sub-shrub with blue flowers which usually attracts interest when well grown. Another striking plant is the herbaceous *P. barbatus* (syn. *Chelone barbata),* a tall grower, to 3 feet, with bright vermilion-scarlet flowers.

Species cultivated *P. angustifolius*, 1 foot, soft blue, July, western United States. *P. antirrhinoides*, 3 feet, lemon-yellow, July, California. *P. azureus*, 1 foot, blue, August, North America. *P. barbatus*, 3 feet, scarlet, summer, Colorado. *P. barrettiae*, 1 foot, bright violet, May–June, western United States. *P. bridgesii*, 2 feet, scarlet, July to September, North America. *P. campanulatus*, 2 feet, rosy-purple, violet or white, June, Mexico and Guatemala. *P. centranthifolius*, 3 feet, scarlet, summer, California and western Arizona. *P. cobaea*, 2 feet, purple or white, August, United States. *P. confertus*, 1 foot, purple and blue, summer, Rocky Mountains. *P. cordifolius*, 4 feet, scarlet, summer, partial climber, southern California. *P. davidsonii*, 1–2 inches, ruby-red, summer, spreads by underground stems, rock garden, California. *P. diffusus*, 2 feet, blue or purple, September, western North America. *P. fruticosus*, 9–12 inches, purple, summer, north-western United States; var. *crassifolius*, with minor leaf differences. *P. glaber*, 2 feet, purple, July, United States. *P. glaucus*, 15 inches, purple, July, Rocky Mountains. *P. hartwegii*, 2 feet, scarlet, summer, Mexico. *P. heterophyllus*, 1–3 feet, sky blue, July, California. *P. hirsutus* (syn. *P. pubescens latifolius*), purple or violet, 1–3 feet, July, United States. *P. isophyllus*, sub-shrubby, 4–5 feet, crimson-scarlet, white within, late summer, Mexico. *P. laevigatus*, 3 feet, white or pink, summer, United States. *P. menziesii*, 6 inches, purple, June, north-western America. *P. ovatus*, 2 feet, blue to purple, August to October, United States. *P. richardsonii*, 2 feet, violet, summer, United States. *P. rupicola*, 4 inches, ruby, north-western America. *P. scouleri*, 1½ feet, purple, May to June, United States. *P. spectabilis*, 4 feet, rosy-purple, summer, Mexico and southern California. Cultivars: The following are some good modern varieties; 'Blue Gem', azure-blue, summer; 'Chester Scarlet', summer; 'Evelyn', pink, May–October; 'Garnet', wine-red; 'George Home', summer; 'Newberry Gem', pillar-box red; 'Six Hills Hybrid', rosy-lilac, May–June.

Cultivation A rich, slightly acid soil is most suitable, or a compost mixture of 1 part of leafmould or peat and 2 parts of good loam. A sunny aspect is required. A weekly watering with a soluble fertiliser or liquid manure is needed by the summer bedding penstemons to keep them growing and flowering well. Seed is available for many species. This is

sown under glass in February or March in a temperature of 55–65°F (10–18°C) and the young plants are set out in May after they have been hardened off. But to get exactly similar plants of hybrids it is necessary to take cuttings and raise them under glass in August. They should not be disturbed till the following April. Plants may also be divided in April.

Perilla (per-il-la)
Possibly from the native Indian name *(Labiatae)*. This is a small genus, containing 4 to 6 species only, of which there is one plant which is of value in the garden. This is *P. frutescens nankinensis*, a half-hardy annual from China, which has been grown by gardeners for the sake of its striking purple-bronze foliage, the margins of which are crisped and fringed. It was much in favour during the late Victorian vogue for

carpet bedding and is still seen today, particularly in public parks. There is a form *laciniata* (syn. *N. frutescens foliis atropurpurea laciniata*), in which the leaves are cut nearly to the middle, and *rosec*, the leaves of which are red, pink, light green and whitish.

Cultivation Seed should be sown under glass in sandy compost during mid-March, in a temperature of 65–70°F (18–21°C). Transplant the seedlings when they are large enough to handle to individual pots and keep the temperature at 55–65°F (13–18°C) until May. Then transfer the pots to a cold frame and gradually harden off the plants until they are planted out 6 inches apart in June, in ordinary good garden soil and sunny positions. The leaf colour of seedlings varies to some extent. To form bushy plants the growing points should be pinched out from time to time. The

Petunias are among the gayest summer bedding plants and should be treated as half-hardy annuals in the open garden. Petunia 'Cascade' *(this page)* is an F₁ hybrid with a wide range of colours. *Opposite* A group of mixed Petunias.

full effect is gained when plants are massed together.

Petunia (pe-tu-ni-a)

From *petun*, the Brazilian name for tobacco to which petunias are nearly related *(Solanaceae)*. A genus of 40 species of annual or perennial herbaceous plants from South America, two of which have been crossed to produce the many named varieties given in catalogues.

Species cultivated The two species concerned are *P. nyctaginiflora* and *P. integrifolia,* from the Argentine, and the resultant plants, though in fact perennial, are best treated as half-hardy annuals for the open garden. They are handsome plants, very varied in colouring, marking and form, and make extremely effective and colourful displays when used as bedding plants,

in sunny situations, during late summer and autumn. Cultivars include 'Bedding Alderman', dark violet; 'Blue Bee', violet-blue; 'Blue Lace', light-blue fringed flowers with violet throat; 'Blue Danube' (F₁), lavender-blue, double; 'Blue Magic' (F₂), velvety blue; 'Canadian Wonder' (F₁), double flowers, fine colour range; 'Cascade' (F₁), large-flowered, wide range of colours; 'Cheerful', bright rose; 'Cherry Tart' (F₁), rose-pink and white; 'Confetti' (F₂), wide colour range; 'Commanche Improved' (F₁), scarlet-crimson; 'Fire Chief', fiery scarlet; 'Great Victorious' (F₁), double flowers, up to 4 inches across, wide colour range; 'Gypsy Red', brilliant salmon-scarlet; 'Lavender Queen'; 'Moonglow', yellow; 'Mound Mixed', various colours, useful for bedding; 'Pink Beauty'; 'Plum Dandy' (F₁), reddish-purple; 'Red Satin' (F₁),

bright red, dwarf; 'Rose Queen'; 'Salmon Supreme'; 'Snowball Improved'; 'Sunburst' (F₁), light yellow, ruffled petals; 'Tivoli', scarlet and white bicolor; 'Valentine' (F₁), red, double, large flowered; 'White Magic' (F₁). There are also strains with fimbriated (fringed) petals in various colours. It is wise to consult current seedsmen's catalogues as very many other kinds are available and new ones appear annually.

Cultivation For growing out of doors, petunias should be treated as though half-hardy annuals and you should sow the very fine seed carefully in boxes in February or March in the greenhouse. Use a compost of equal parts of loam, leafmould and sand or the John Innes seed compost. Make the surface firm, with a layer of finely-sifted compost on top and do not cover the seed with any further compost once it has been sown. Keep the seed boxes in a temperature of 65–75°F (18–24°C) and do not allow the soil to dry out. Transplant the seedlings when they are large enough to handle; begin to harden them off and continue this operation until the plants are set out at the beginning of June. If seed-raised plants are required for increase, overwinter the mature plants in the greenhouse, and take cuttings in the spring, placing them in a sandy compost in a frame in a temperature of 55–65°F (13–18°C). Greenhouse cultivation is similar, but cut the plants back in February or March. Water them freely during the growing season, but moderately at other times. Feed them with a liquid fertiliser twice a week while growing, and keep them in a temperature of 55–65°F (13–18°C) during the summer. In winter do not allow the temperature to fall below 40°F (4°C), and it should preferably be higher. It may be necessary to train the growths, which can be lax and rather sappy, to stakes. For cultivation in hanging baskets or window-boxes or ornamental plant containers it is best to choose such strains as 'Cascade', or 'Pendula Balcony Blended'.

Phacelia (fa-se-lee-a)

From the Greek *phakelos*, a bundle, in reference to the arrangement of the flowers *(Hydrophyllaceae)*. A genus of 200 species, natives of North America and the Andes, of hardy annual and perennial plants, of which a number of blue, purple, mauve or white flowering annuals are of great value in the garden. One species in particular, *P. campanularia* has flowers of great depth and intensity of blue colouring, comparable with those of certain gentians.

Species cultivated *P. campanularia,* 9 inches, flowers bell-shaped, intense blue, June to September, southern California. *P. ciliata,* 1 foot, flowers fragrant, lavender, June to September, California. *P. congesta,* 1½ feet, lavender-blue, July to September, Texas, northern Mexico. *P. divaricata* (syn. *Eutoca*

divaricata), 1 foot, flowers large, bright blue, July to September, California. *P. grandiflora,* 2 feet, large flowers lavender veined violet, July to September, southern California. *P. minor* (syn. *Whitlavia minor*), Californian bluebell, 1½ feet, flowers bell-shaped, deep violet, July to September, California. *P. parryi,* 1½ feet, flowers cup-shaped, deep violet, July to September, California. *P. tanacetifolia,* to 3 feet, soft lavender heliotrope-like flowers, July to September, California. *P. viscida* (syn. *Eutoca viscida*), 2 feet, flowers deep rich blue with white centre, July to September, California; 'Musgrave Strain' is an improved strain.

Cultivation All the species listed should have hardy annual treatment. Sow seeds thinly in April, where the plants are to flower and thin the seedlings to 6–8 inches apart in June. Any garden soil suits them, and they should be grown in the sunniest position possible. Seedlings transplant badly. As these are hardy annuals, seeds may be sown in September and will generally survive to make excellent plants for early flowering the following summer. Seed is available of most of the species described above.

Phlox (flocks)

From the Greek *phlego,* to burn, or *phlox,* a flame, referring to the bright colours of the flowers (Polemoniaceae). A genus of nearly 70 species of hardy, half-hardy, annual and perennial herbaceous plants all, with one exception, natives of North America and Mexico. Almost all the most important species are from the eastern United States, though the popular annual, *P. drummondii,* is from Texas and New Mexico. The fine herbaceous plants derived originally from *P. paniculata,* the garden forms of which may sometimes be listed as *P.* × *decussata,* have a most important part to play in the garden as they give colour at a time—July and August—when it very much needs their bright colours. They are extremely easy to grow and all have fragrant flowers. Our rock gardens would be much poorer if they lacked the various forms of either *P. douglasii* or *P. subulata* or their hybrids.

Herbaceous perennial species cultivated *P. carolina,* 2 feet, phlox-purple to pink and white, May and June, eastern United States. *P. glaberrima,* 2 feet, red, May and June, eastern North America in swamps. *P. maculata,* wild sweet william, 3 feet, violet and purple, summer, eastern North America. These three species are the parents of the early flowering taller phlox. *P. paniculata* (syn. *P.* × *decussata*), 1½–4 feet, violet-purple, summer, eastern North America.

Alpine species cultivated *P. amoena,* 6–9 inches, rose, May to June, south-eastern United States; var. *variegata,* leaves variegated with white. *P. bifida,* sand phlox, prostrate, tufted habit, spiny leaves, flowers pale violet to white, spring, eastern North America. *P. divaricata* (syn. *P. canadensis*), 6–15 inches, blue-lavender, May, eastern North America. *P. douglasii,* 4 inches, lilac, May to August, western North America. *P.* × *frondosa,* pink, spring, hybrid. *P. kelyseyi,* 6 inches, flowers lilac, spring, eastern North America. *P. ovata,* 1 foot, rose, summer, eastern North America. *P. pilosa,* 10–20 inches, purplish-rose, summer, eastern North America. *P.* × *procumbens,* 6 inches, lilac-blue, June, a hybrid. *P.* × *stellaria,* 6 inches, pale blue, April to May, hybrid. *P. stolonifera* (syn. *P. reptans*), 6–12 inches, stoloniferous habit, flowers violet to lavender, 1 inch across, April to May, eastern North America. *P. subulata,* moss phlox, 6 inches, purple or white, eastern United States.

Annual species cultivated There is one annual, *P. drummondii,* to 1 foot, flowers in a wide colour range, July onwards, from Texas and New Mexico. This is among our most floriferous of annuals.

Opposite **Phlox paniculata 'Frau A Buchner', a border cultivar.** *Below* **Phacelia campanularia, from southern California, has flowers of an intense blue in summer, from June to September. It should be treated as a hardy annual and sown in a sunny position where it is to flower.**

Border cultivars P. *paniculata* is the border perennial phlox which has given rise to many good plants, flowering from July to October, sweet smelling, and very colourful. 'Antoine Mercie', deep mauve with white centre; 'Border Gem', deep violet; 'Brigadier', orange-red; 'Europe', white with a red centre; 'Frau Antonin Buchner', white; 'Jules Sandeau', pure pink; 'Le Mahdi', rich purple; 'Leo Schlageter', dark red; 'Lofna', rose-pink; 'Mrs A. Jeans', silvery-pink; 'Rijnstroon', rose-pink; 'Starfine', red; 'Thor', salmon-red. Many more will be found in nurserymen's lists.

Alpine cultivars P. *douglasii*, 'Boothman's Variety', clear mauve; 'Eva', pink with deeper centres; 'May Snow', white; 'Rose Queen', silvery pink; 'Snow Queen', white; 'Supreme', lavender-blue. P. *kelseyi*, 'Rosette', stemless pink flowers. P. *stolonifera* 'Blue Ridge', soft blue. P. *subulata* 'Appleblossom', pink; 'Benita', lavender-blue; 'Brilliant', bright rose; 'Camla', clear pink; 'Fairy', mauve; 'G. F. Wilson', mid-blue; 'Model', rose; 'Pink Chintz', pink; 'Sensation', rose-red; 'Temiscaming', magenta-red; 'The Bride', white.

Annual cultivars P. *drummondii cuspidata* (stellaris), star phlox, 6 inches, flowers starry, mixed colours; 'Brilliant', deep rose with darker eye; 'Isabellina', light yellow; *kermesina splendens*, crimson with white eye; *rosea*, bright rose; *rosea-albo ochlata*, rose with white eye; *nanum compactum*, dwarf strain available in various named colours including blue, pink, red, violet, white. Others are listed by seedsmen.

Cultivation The tall herbaceous phloxes need a moist loam, preferably on the heavy side. They do perfectly well on chalky soils, provided these are enriched. Though in the past shady positions have been given to phloxes, and this does not actually kill them, they do better in sunny positions. Plant from October to March, and feed generously thereafter with manure, or compost and inorganic fertilisers, as they are greedy feeders. Lift, divide and replant every three years. They are readily raised from root cuttings and this has the advantage of providing plants free from the stem eelworm, by which the herbaceous phlox are all too often attacked.

Alpine phlox species also like a rich

1 Phlox 'Brigadier' is a magenta-red cultivar of P. paniculata.
2 Phlox decussata, is a catalogue name wrongly applied to the forms of P. paniculata.

soil, and a sunny ledge on the rock garden or on top of a wall. Many of them may be easily increased by layering, or they may be divided into separate plants each possessing roots, and this is best done in March. A few of the more dwarf or less vigorous kinds may be given alpine house treatment. Winter wet is their bane. The annual species, P. *drummondii,* needs the standard half-hardy annual treatment. Sow in pans or boxes in March, under glass, and harden off the seedlings and plant them out in June, 6 inches apart. Nip out the points of the shoots to induce bushy growth, and water generously. They make excellent edging plants and, if allowed to develop naturally, make good plants for tubs, ornamental containers, hanging baskets or window boxes.

Phormium (for-mee-um)
From the Greek *phormos,* basket, the fibres of the leaves being used for basket making (*Liliaceae* or *Agavaceae).* There are two species in this New Zealand genus, and both are occasionally seen in gardens. They do best in the south of Britain and in the south-west they often make most strikingly decorative plants. They have huge evergreen sword-shaped leaves and clusters of lily-like flowers.

Phormiums are sometimes potted and grown in conservatories, to be brought into the house on occasions when their noble leaves can be used to decorate the corner of a room or entrance hall. In the past the plant supplied a fibre called New Zealand flax or hemp, but it is not now of much commercial value. An old leaf, if torn into strips, will provide a remarkably strong material for tying plants to stakes and so on.

Species cultivated *P. colensoi* (syn. *P. cookianum*), the wharariki, leaves 2–3 feet long, flower spikes to 7 feet, flowers yellow, summer. *P. tenax*, New Zealand flax, leaves 8–9 feet long, with reddish or orange margins, flower spikes to 15 feet, dull red flowers, summer; vars. *purpureum*, reddish-purple leaves; *variegatum*, leaves striped with cream and white; *veitchii*, broad yellow stripes on leaves.

Cultivation A light loamy soil is suitable and these plants look particularly well on the margins of ponds or streams, or they may be used as specimen plants in isolated places. They may be grown in large pots in a cold greenhouse or conservatory in a soil mixture of 1 part each of peat and sand and 2 parts of loam. Water generously from April to October, but moderately only after this. Repot in February when necessary. Plants may be raised from seed sown in March in a greenhouse, or they may be propagated by root division in April.

Phyllachne (fill-ak-nee)

The derivation of the name is uncertain, but it possibly comes from the Greek *phyllon*, a leaf, and *achne*, a fruit, referring to the leaf-like fruits *(Stylidaceae)*. A small genus, consisting of 4 species of small, cushion-forming plants from the mountains of Tasmania, New Zealand and Tierra del Fuego. One species only is likely to be found in cultivation. This is *P. colensoi*, the rock cushion, a native of the New Zealand alps, which forms a hard tight cushion of tiny leathery leaves. In June and July it bears small starry, almost stemless flowers, with protruding anthers.

Cultivation This is a difficult plant to grow and it needs great skill in cultivation. Success is more likely in the north of England and in Scotland where the summers are both cooler and moister. While it may be possible to grow it in a shady peat garden or on a scree, with plenty of peat in the soil mixture, it is more usual to treat it as a pot plant. The pot should be very well-drained and the compost should consist of 2 parts of natural peat, 1 of sharp sand and 1 of lime-free soil. Wedge two or three pieces of sandstone around the rosette and dress the surface of the soil with gravel. Plunge the pot to its rim in peat which should never be allowed to dry out, in a north-facing frame. Water freely during the summer but sparingly in the winter. Cover the frame in winter with a light to

The Bladder Cherry, or Chinese Lantern Plant, Physalis alkekengi, has bright orange, air-filled, papery calyces.

give protection against damp. For propagation purposes portions of the cushion can be detached in July after flowering and inserted into a mixture of 2 parts of peat to 1 of sand, around the edge of a pot. Place the pot in a larger one and fill the space between the two pots with peat, which should be kept moist by standing the larger pot in a saucer of water.

Physalis (fy-sa-lis)

From the Greek *physa*, a bladder, in allusion to the inflated calyx *(Solanaceae)*. A genus of 100 or more species of which the two most well known are *P. alkekengi*, the bladder cherry or Chinese lantern plant, with its brilliant, flame-coloured, air-filled calyces, and *P. peruviana*, the Cape gooseberry, which is a greenhouse species. They are annual and perennial herbaceous plants, mostly from Mexico and North America.

Species cultivated *P. alkekengi* (syns. *P. alkekengi franchetii*, *P. bunyardii*, *P. franchetii*), bladder cherry, bladder herb, Chinese lantern plant, winter cherry, hardy perennial, 1–2 feet, flowers whitish, similar to those of the potato, summer, fruit a single scarlet berry enclosed in the much inflated showy calyx, up to 2 inches long, turning orange in autumn, south-eastern Europe to Japan, naturalised in many other parts of the world; vars. *gigantea*, calyces larger; *pygmaea*, 9 inches, dwarf form. *P. ixocarpa*, tomatillo, half-hardy annual, 2 feet, flowers yellow, ¾ inch or more across, with blackish-brown blotches in the throat, fruit purple, sticky, almost filling the yellow, purple-veined calyx. The fruits are edible and may be stewed or used for jam making, Mexico, southern United States. *P. peruviana* (syns. *P. edulis*, *P. peruviana edulis*), Cape gooseberry, 3 feet, flowers yellow, blotched purple, summer, fruit yellow, edible, South America,

159

greenhouse. *P. pruinosa,* dwarf Cape gooseberry, strawberry-tomato, half-hardy annual, 2 feet, flowers bell-shaped yellowish, fruits yellow, edible, southern United States.

Cultivation The hardy species require a rich, well-drained soil in a sunny or partially shaded position and should be planted in the spring. The fruits, popularly called 'lanterns' (the inflated calyces) can be used for winter decorations and can be picked and dried in the autumn. If left out of doors, they become skeletonised. The tender species require a compost of loam, leafmould and a little sand, and should be planted singly in 5–6 inch pots placed in a sunny position. Water freely during the summer and feed regularly with a liquid fertiliser. Pot up or plant in early spring. Propagate hardy species by division every three years, and greenhouse species from seed sown in sandy soil in heat in the spring, or from cuttings placed in sandy soil in heat between January and April. *P. alkekengi* grows very vigorously and spreads by means of underground runners. It may be used as a deciduous ground cover plant in sun or semi-shade. Where it is suited it can become something of a nuisance, difficult to eradicate unless every piece of root is removed.

Pink
This is an old and attractive name used by John Gerard who wrote in 1597; 'a wild, creeping pink which groweth in our pastures neere about London'. Pink is an old English word meaning 'an eye' and probably referred to the maiden pink, *Dianthus deltoides,* and had nothing to do with the colour of that little flower which is crimson-red to purple. The name pink has lead to some confusion, for the old favourite pink 'Mrs Sinkins', which was introduced by a nurseryman of Slough, Buckinghamshire, in 1868, is white, although this variety has produced a pink-coloured sport. There are also show pinks, laced pinks, garden pinks, imperial pinks, Herbert's pinks, and others, in a variety of colours. The main colour classifications are: *Selfs*—flowers of one colour; *Bicolors*—flowers with a ground of one colour and a central zone or 'eye' of a darker colour; *Fancies*—flowers in which colours are blended or have irregular markings of two or more colours. The predominant parent of the hybrid pink race is *Dianthus plumarius,* a native of south-eastern Europe, which was introduced to the British Isles in 1629. This fringed, white species is reliably hardy, which cannot be said for all modern hybrids, although it is excessive wet, rather than frost, that they cannot withstand. They are bred from a line that inhabits sunny cliffs and well-drained hillsides in southern Europe, and so to plant them out in heavy, wet soil and expect them to thrive in fog, rain and wet snow, is expecting too much.

In 1910, Montagu Allwood started work on crossing the perpetual-flowering carnations with *Dianthus plumarius,* which eventually gave rise to the race known as *Dianthus x allwoodii,* and this hybrid strain has in turn led to the beautiful colours now to be seen in the modern and diverse pink family. In the 1950s a group called 'London' pinks was raised by Mr F. R. McQuown, mainly from the Allwoodii pinks, Herbert's pinks and garden pinks, though perpetual-flowering carnations played a later part in the breeding programme. Most of this group are 'laced' pinks, that is, bicolored varieties in which the colour of the central eye or zone is continued in a loop round the edge of the petal. This is the 'lacing' and many growers consider laced varieties to be the most beautiful of all pinks. They are, in fact, among the oldest of types, bred some 250 years ago or more by the weavers in Lancashire and later in Paisley, though the original varieties so developed have long been lost to cultivation.

The following are recommended varieties:

Garden pinks 'Dad's Favourite', white, laced red, with chocolate-purple markings, semi-double (does not like heavy soil); 'Inchmery', semi-double, shell-pink; 'Mrs Sinkins', fragrant, double, white; 'Sam Barlow', white, with almost black centre; 'White Ladies', pure white.
Allwoodii pinks 'Alice', white with dark crimson eye; 'Daphne', pale pink with crimson eye, single; 'Doris', salmon-pink with red eye; 'Fortuna', rose-cerise, self; 'Ian', rich crimson; 'Thomas', deep red with bold maroon eye.
Imperial pinks (raised from Allwoodii pinks and Herbert's pinks) 'Crimson Glory', rich crimson, double, fringed petals; 'Freckles', dark salmon-pink, flecked with red, a fine fancy pink; 'Salmon Queen', bright salmon-pink, edges serrated; 'Snow Queen', white.
London pinks 'London Girl', white ground, eye and lacing Indian red; 'London Glow', deep dark crimson ground, edged pink; 'London Lady', pale pink, eye and lacing dark crimson; 'London Poppet', white ground with pink flush, eye and lacing ruby-red.
Show pinks 'Show Beauty', deep rose-pink with a maroon eye; 'Show Enchantress', rich salmon-pink, double; 'Show Glory', bright orange-scarlet with a salmon-scarlet sheen; 'Show Pearl', pure white, of almost perfect form and structure.

Cultivation A well-drained, ordinary garden soil and an open sunny position are the main requirements of the pinks. Avoid over-light and over-heavy soils. The connoisseur likes what is called a good deep friable loam in which to grow his plants to perfection. Pinks like lime and where this is deficient fork in 8 ounces of carbonate of lime to the square yard on light soil, or 4 ounces of hydrate of lime to the square yard on heavy

soil, help to break up the clay. Where there is any doubt about drainage the bed should be raised about 6 inches or more above the surrounding level, for pinks will not survive in waterlogged ground. October or March are the best months for planting out young stock. Propagation is by cuttings or pipings taken in summer and inserted in sandy soil in a cold frame, or by seed sown in April or early May in boxes and placed in a cold greenhouse or cold frame. Pink seedlings are better raised without artificial heat. It should be noted that named cultivars will not come true from seed, but must be propagated vegetatively, by cuttings or pipings as described above. Seeds, even taken from the same pod may show great variation of form and colour.

Plectranthus (plek-tran-thus)
From the Greek *plectron,* spur, and *anthos,* flower, in reference to the base of the corolla tube *(Labiatae).* This genus of 250 species of herbaceous plants, sub-shrubs and shrubs, gives us a small selection of plants suited to the stove-house or greenhouse. They are nearly related to the hemp nettle or *Coleus,* and need the same treatment. They are natives of a wide area from tropical Africa to Japan, Malaysia, Australia and the Pacific Islands.
Species cultivated *P. australis,* herbaceous plant, to 3 feet, flowers purple, summer, Australia, greenhouse. *P. chiradzulensis* (syn. *Coleus ruwenzoriensis*), herbaceous plant, to 3 feet or more, flowers bright blue, in a panicle up to 8 or 9 inches long, winter, tropical Africa, greenhouse. *P. mahonii* (syn. *Coleus mahonii*), 2 feet, flowers violet in large panicles, winter, tropical Africa. *P. saccatus,* to 2 feet, flowers blue, October, Natal; this is quite the most showy species of the genus.
Cultivation A soil mixture consisting of 2 parts of loam, 1 part of well-rotted manure (or compost), leafmould and sand is suitable. If possible these plants should spend the summer in a greenhouse, but the winter in the stovehouse. Pot firmly in February or March. The temperature from September to March should be 60–70°F (16–21°C); from March to June it should be 75–85°F (24–30°C), and June to September, 65–75°F (18–24°C). Water freely from March to September, but sparingly afterwards. Propagation is by seed sown in a temperature of 75°F (24°C) from February to April. Cuttings may be taken and rooted in a warm propagating frame at any time.

Pleione (pli-o-ne)
From the ancient Greek name, *Pleione,* mother of the Pleiades in Greek mythology *(Orchidaceae).* A genus of 10 species of epiphytic and terrestrial orchids, sometimes known as the Himalayan or Indian crocus. The pseudobulbs are

small, smooth and rounded, or flask-shaped and warted. Flowers are produced either before, or with, the new growth from the base of the bulb, which persists into the following year and then shrivels away. The leaves are deciduous. The flowers, mainly one or two to a spike, are large and showy. The genus is rightly very popular with both the alpine enthusiasts and the specialist orchid growers.

Species cultivated *P. formosana* is a former species now divided into a number of distinct cultivars: 'Oriental Splendor' formerly known as *P. pricei;* 'Bush of Dawn', and 'Polar Sun'. *P. hookeriana,* whitish or rose flushed and blotched brownish-purple and yellow, early summer, Sikkim. *P. humilis,* pale lilac, purple-lined, winter, northern India. *P. lagenaria,* lilac, purple-lined, blotched with crimson-purple and yellow, winter, Assam. *P. maculata,* whitish, crimson-purple blotches, autumn, northern India. *P. praecox,* rose-purple, winter, northern India.

Cultivation An ideal compost consists of equal parts of osmunda or peat fibre, loam fibre, and sphagnum moss with a little leafmould and sand, although the plants will grow very well in standard John Innes composts or even in leafmould alone. Repot every year either before or just after flowering in well-drained pans, placing the bulbs at 1-inch intervals with their bases on the compost surface. Little or no water is required in winter, but the plants should be watered frequently in summer after the growths have advanced. Weak liquid feeding when in full growth helps to make up large bulbs. Some types may just be on the borderline of hardiness, and a sheltered position in the alpine garden may be suitable in warmer districts. Cold frames or the alpine house are particularly good places in which to grow them. If they are to be grown with other orchids, the cymbidium section is suitable, as the time for their winter rest coincides with that of the pleiones. They seem to grow equally well in any temperature, so they can be housed in any orchid section where there is room. Propagation is by division, as strong bulbs frequently produce two new ones. Several species, especially *P. humilis,* produce clusters of tiny bulblets at the apex of the bulbs, and these can be detached and grown on.

Podolepis (pod-o-lep-iss)

From the Greek *podos,* foot, and *lepis,* a scale, referring to the scaly flowerhead stalks *(Compositae).* A genus of about 20 species of annual and perennial herbaceous plants, hardy or nearly so, natives of Australia. The inflorescences are terminal heads of florets bearing daisy-like, ray and disc flowers, yellow, purple or pink. They are grown as everlastings.

Species cultivated *P. acuminata,* annual, 12–18 inches, flowers yellow, summer. *P. aristata,* annual, to 12 inches, inflorescence 1 inch wide, yellow, ray flowers small, pink, summer. *P. canescens,* annual, to 12 inches, inflorescence $\frac{3}{4}$ inch wide, yellow, summer. *P. gracilis,* perennial but treated as an annual, 1–3 feet, much-branched inflorescence, lilac, purple or white, late summer.

Cultivation A sandy soil and a sunny situation are ideal for podolepis where they will produce good quality flowers suitable for drying as everlastings. Seeds may be sown out of doors in beds or annual borders, in May or June, in rows 1 foot apart, $\frac{1}{2}$ inch deep, thinning the seedlings to 1 foot apart. Or seed may be sown in boxes in the greenhouse in a temperature of 60–65°F (16–18°C) in April. Prick out the seedlings into seed trays and plant them out late May to June, 1 foot apart, after they have been hardened off. Little or no staking is necessary. *P. aristata* may be grown as an individual pot plant for use in the conservatory or greenhouse. Seeds are sown in January to produce flowers in late April to May. Pot up the seedlings in a fairly sandy compost.

1

2

Pleiones are very popular orchids, mostly native to northern India.
1 The light purple flowers of Pleione pogonioides, from China, are about 3 inches across.
2 Pleione formosana is a former name of a number of distinct cultivars of which this is one.

Polyanthus (pol-e-an-thus)

From the Greek *polys,* many, and *anthos,* flowers, in reference to the flowers being in clusters *(Primulaceae).* This name is now applied to the garden forms of primulas which have originated from a supposed hybrid between the primrose *(Primula acaulis)* and the cowslip *(Primula veris).* They are hardy perennials, mostly opulent-looking plants with massive flowerheads. Essentially these plants are for positions where eye-catchers are required, for in the latest strains the flowers are very large, 3 inches or more across. They are often seen in bedding schemes in public parks, for which purpose they are admirably suited. The very large-flowered kinds are, however, unsuitable for woodland settings, though the older, small-flowered kinds look well when massed under trees.

Seedsmen's catalogues give a large selection of variously coloured but unnamed forms, from which to choose. The 'Pacific' strain raised in the United States is among the largest and brightest flowered, in yellow, red, pink, blue and white. The 'Festival' and the 'Giant Bouquet' strains are almost as showy. More old-fashioned in appeal are the modest gold-laced forms of polyanthus, in various colours, the petals narrowly edged with gold or yellow. Blue polyanthus appear occasionally; a fine strain is Blackmore and Langdon's, with colours ranging from purplish-blue to

pale blue. Seedsmen's catalogues list and describe many named cultivars and strains, and others appear from time to time, the result of work carried out by plant breeders. Heights range from 6 inches or less to 1 foot or more.

Cultivation Polyanthus are easily grown in rich soil in places where they have a little overhead shade, although magnificent displays are often seen growing in fully open situations. Seed may be sown in early spring in the open garden, under frame lights, or in the unheated greenhouse. The seeds usually germinate quickly and the tiny plants should be well thinned out. By August they are ready to be planted out into their final positions spaced at least 9 inches apart. The modern polyanthus is such a vigorous plant that it should be divided each year after flowering, and in this way a fine stock will rapidly be built up. Division ensures that all your plants have the original's colour and habit.

Plants are often grown in pots, especially the gold-laced forms. A suitable soil mixture consists of a good loam, and an equal quantity of a mixture of well-rotted manure, leafmould, and sharp sand. Potted in August, the plants are overwintered in a cold frame, and ventilated at all times except during frosty weather. When the plants are in flower they may be placed on the staging of a shaded greenhouse, for direct sunlight will damage the blossoms (see also Primula).

The Polyanthus is a hardy perennial with opulent flowers, velvety in texture. There are many strains and forms, many of them unnamed. They are often used in spring bedding schemes, for which they are admirably suited and provide the necessary eye-catching colour in mass. They can also be used for naturalising among shrubs.

1 Gold-laced forms have narrow-edges of gold or yellow.
2 A rose-purple hybrid Polyanthus.
3 Polyanthus 'Reinelt'.
4 A pale yellow form of Polyanthus.
5 An orange Pacific Strain Polyanthus.
6 A blue form of Polyanthus.
7 A collection of mixed Polyanthus.

6

7

Polygonum (pol-ig-on-um)

From the Greek *polys,* many, and *gonu,* a small joint in allusion to the many joints in the stems *(Polygonaceae).* Knotweed. There are 300 species in this cosmopolitan genus, and they are mostly annuals or hardy herbaceous plants, with a few sub-shrubs. There are a dozen or so British native species, among them the bistorts and knot grasses. A form of the bistort, *P. bistorta,* is the only native sometimes grown in the garden. *P. bilderdyckia baldschuanicum* (syn. *P. baldschuanicum*), the Russian vine, is perhaps the most useful climbing plant to obscure quickly a garden eyesore. Because of the rapidity of its growth it also has another most appropriate common name: mile-a-minute plant. Its racemes of white blossoms are very decorative and long-lasting as they pass into the fruiting stage without much change of colour.

Species cultivated *P. affine,* 9–12 inches, rose, June to October, foliage turns bronze-red in autumn, Himalaya, an excellent rock plant; cultivars include 'Darjeeling Red', less tall, flowers crimson; 'Lowndes 1357', shorter, flower spikes thicker, deepening from rose to garnet-red. *P. alpinum,* to 3 feet, white, August, southern Europe. *P. amplexicaule,* 2–3 feet, red, autumn, Himalaya, somewhat invasive. *P. aubertii,* climber to 30 feet, pink or white, similar in habit and rapidity of growth to *P. bilderdyckia baldschuanicum,* but with narrower flower panicles, autumn, western China. *P. bilderdyckia baldschuanicum* (syn. *P. baldschuanicum*), to 30 feet, white, summer and autumn, Turkistan. *P. bistorta superbum,* to 2 feet, deep carmine, summer, Europe, Asia. *P. campanulatum,* 3 feet, bluish-white, summer, Himalaya. *P. capitatum,* 6 inches, spreading in habit, leaves with dark green V-shaped bands, flowers pink in rounded heads, July to September, northern India, tender, best overwintered in a frame. *P. compactum,* 2 feet, white, autumn, Japan. *P. equisetiforme,* 1½–2 feet, white, summer, Mediterranean area, not fully hardy. *P. tenuicaule,* 3–4 inches, white, spring, Japan, shady rock garden or alpine house. *P. vacciniifolium,* 6 inches, rose, autumn, Himalaya. *P. viviparum,* 6–15 inches, white, May to June, arctic regions, a good rock garden or wall plant. (For *P. cuspidatum, P. reynoutria, P. sachalinense* and *P. sieboldii,* see Reynoutria.)

Cultivation Any soil suits these plants, but to get maximum growth from the climbers a rich moist soil is advisable. Plant in autumn or spring. All plants need watering in summer in dry weather. *P. amplexicaule* can be invasive and it is best not to plant it where it can overwhelm nearby, less tough plants. *P. capitatum* is easily killed by frost and in order to keep it from one year to another it is best to dig up rooted pieces of it in September, pot them up and overwinter them in a frost proof frame or in the alpine house. The rock plants in the genus are valuable for their late flowering. Propagation is by root division in autumn or spring, or by seed sown in the cold frame in spring or out of doors in summer. Propagate *P. bilderdyckia baldschuanicum* and *P. aubertii* by cuttings rooted in sandy soil in a cold frame in August.

Portulaca (por-tu-lak-a)

An old Latin name, possibly from the Latin *porto,* to carry, and *lac,* milk, in allusion to the milky juice *(Portulacaceae).* These are succulent annual and perennial herbaceous plants, with fibrous or thickened roots and small fleshy leaves. Of the 200 or more species in this genus, widespread in tropical and sub-tropical regions, many are considered to be weeds and the group is not very important for garden cultivation. The leaves of *P. oleracea* can be used in

**1 Polygonum paniculatum produces cloudy cream flower spikes in summer.
2 Polygonum affine 'Darjeeling Red' has crimson flowers.**

salads.

Species cultivated *P. grandiflora*, annual, stems procumbent and spreading, flowers white, yellow, pink, red or orange, June–July, Brazil. *P. lutea*, coarse-stemmed perennial, yellow flowers, summer, Pacific Islands. *P. oleracea*, purslane, annual, a fleshy-leaved plant, flowers yellow, summer, southern Europe.

Cultivation The half-hardy annual species are grown from seeds sown in John Innes or other seed composts at a temperature of 60°F (16°C) and the seedlings pricked off when they are large enough to handle into small pots. Finally they are planted out on rock gardens or in sunny borders in well-drained soil. When grown in the greenhouse in pots, they are placed in very sandy soil and kept in a sunny position, being watered freely in late spring and summer. The temperature in summer should be between 65–70°F (18–21°C), and in winter about 50°F (10°C). Propagation is by seed, as for most succulents, covered very lightly or not at all, or from cuttings, rooted in sandy soil at any time.

Potato

All of the many potato varieties fall into three different groups—First Early, Second Early and Maincrop. The tubers of First Early varieties bulk up quickly and are dug during June, July and August when the haulm is still green. Second Earlies are lifted in August and September. Maincrop varieties are harvested in the autumn when the foliage is quite dead and brittle. Although all potatoes keep reasonably well in store, the gardener relies on the long-keeping maincrop varieties for winter supplies.

The principal requirements of the potato plant are adequate available food, sufficient water, good drainage and the type of soil in which tubers may swell easily. An open, unshaded site is very necessary. Light soils are considered very suitable, provided they have been dressed with large quantities of moisture-retaining organic matter. A heavy soil may also be improved structurally by the addition of organic material. A reasonably light, easily worked loam is probably the ideal. Where farmyard manure is available, it may be dug in during winter digging at the rate of up to 1 cwt to 6 square yards. Garden compost may be applied even more generously during winter digging or as a mulch after planting. If a compound potato fertiliser is raked into the soil before planting, use it at the rates advised by the manufacturer.

Potato plants are raised from seed tubers taken from plants grown in parts of Britain which are free of virus-carrying aphids. The potato fields are visited by Ministry of Agriculture officials who issue certificates regarding the freedom from disease of the plants.

Tubers from these plants are known as 'Certified Seed'. It is unwise to plant any but certified seed tubers. They should be purchased in January or February and sprouted in trays housed in a light but frost-proof room (a process known as 'chitting'). It is believed that sprouted potatoes result in earlier crops. The gardener may also see which tubers have not sprouted and these are not planted. At planting time—in late March or April—each potato has two or three short, sturdy sprouts. The actual planting date depends on the condition of the soil and on the weather.

There are many planting methods. Perhaps the simplest is to make 8-inch deep trenches with the draw hoe or with the spade. First Earlies are planted at 12 inches apart with 2 feet between rows. Other varieties need more space; 15 inches between the tubers and 30 inches between the rows are satisfactory distances.

The black plastic method of growing potatoes is favoured by many gardeners because it obviates almost all cultivation. The planting holes are made with the trowel. A tuber—with its sprouts uppermost—is set in each hole. The holes are then filled in and the black plastic sheeting is unrolled over the row. It is important to ensure that the sheeting is securely anchored into the soil. One way of doing this is to make slits with the spade on either side of the row and also at each end of the row. The edges of the 3-foot wide sheet are tucked into the slits when the material is unrolled. When growth starts in May, the shoots of the potato plants are drawn through small holes (made with scissors) in the polythene sheeting.

Rows not treated in this way need weeding now and then. Many gardeners earth up the plants, too. This process consists in drawing soil up and around the plants, using the draw hoe. Earthing up is done in two or three stages. Finally, the plants appear to be growing on low hills. Earthing up is no longer considered necessary but the practice is advantageous on heavy soils where the plants benefit from the improved drainage provided.

There is only one way of ascertaining when First Earlies are ready for use. This is by examining a root. Scraping away some earth may reveal reasonably large tubers. If this fails, dig up a root in late June. If some of the potatoes are as large as a hen's egg, continue digging as and when required. If the potatoes are far too small for use, wait a fortnight before starting to dig.

Plants of Second Earlies and Maincrop varieties are sprayed with Burgundy or Bordeaux mixture in early July. A further spraying may be necessary later that month. The fungicide prevents an attack of potato blight for which there is no cure. It is most important to cover all parts of the plants with the spray—including the underside of the leaves.

Choose a fine, dry day for harvesting maincrop potatoes and take great care not to spear the tubers with the fork. Leave the crop on the soil for an hour or two after lifting so that the potatoes are quite dry before being stored. Remove any damaged, diseased or very small potatoes and store the rest in boxes or trays in a dark, frost-proof place. Darkness is essential to prevent greening. Greened potatoes are not edible. Sort through your stored potatoes at least once each month during the winter and spring. Rub off all shoots which form on the tubers and remove any which show signs of rotting.

Potato varieties

First Early

Arran Pilot A very popular potato and a good cropper. Very suited to light soils. Seldom badly affected by common scab. The flavour of the potatoes grown in fertile soil is excellent. Kidney shape, white flesh. Immune.

Di Vernon Not widely grown among gardeners but crops can be very heavy. Kidney shape, purple eyes, white flesh. Immune.

Duke of York Once also known as Midlothian Early. Does well in most soils. Kidney shape, yellow flesh.

Epicure An old favourite among gardeners who appreciate its good flavour when first lifted for 'new' potatoes. The flavour deteriorates as the potatoes increase in size during August. The rather deep eyes do not please the cook. This potato is much liked in colder parts of the country because of its hardiness. The plants recover better from frost damage than those of most other varieties. Round shape, white flesh.

Home Guard Quite popular but does not appear to have the cropping potential now that it had when it was introduced around thirty years ago. Round, white flesh, shallow eyes. Immune.

Sharpe's Express Very suited to medium and heavier soils of reasonably high fertility. Not the earliest of first earlies but cooks well and stores satisfactorily. Kidney shape, white flesh.

Sutton's Foremost Awarded Certificate of Commendation by Department of Agriculture for Scotland. Not as early as some and plants are best left to grow on until late July. Heavy cropper. Cooks well. Pale skin, oval, white flesh. Immune.

Ulster Chieftain Possibly the earliest of the First Earlies and an excellent cropper. At its best in July. Oval shape, white flesh. Immune.

Second Early

Ben Lomond Not well-known among gardeners. Does best in medium and heavier soils. Kidney shape, white flesh. Immune.

Catriona A heavy cropper and a potato which can crop quite well in less fertile

The Potentillas are a large genus of plants, mostly herbaceous in habit. Potentilla fragiformis has trifoliate leaves typical of the genus and bright yellow flowers in May and June. It reaches 9 inches in height.

soils. Does not store well. Liked by exhibitors. Long oval, white kidney with purple patches. Immune.

Craig's Royal Attractive tubers, long oval white kidney with shallow pink eyes. White flesh. Immune.

Dr McIntosh Good cropper. Tubers of medium size. Kidney, white flesh, shallow eyes. Immune.

Great Scot A well-known second early. Suits most types of soil, crops well and stores well. Excellent for baking. Round, white flesh. Immune.

Maris Peer Needs a soil which does not dry out in hot weather. Shows some resistance to common scab and blight. Oval, white flesh.

Pentland Dell From the Scottish Pentland-field Station now releasing several new, good varieties among which Pentland Dell was one of the first. Good cropper, oval to kidney shape, pale skin, shows resistance to potato blight, white flesh.

Immune.
Red Craig's Royal Does best on heavy soils Very suitable for exhibition use. Long oval-shaped tubers light pink, smooth skin with eyes mostly shallow. Immune.

Maincrop

Arran Banner May also be considered as a Second Early. Stores well until March. A very good cropper and particularly suited to light soils. Tubers are large but they are not considered highly flavoursome. They sometimes occur quite deep down in the soil. Popular among gardeners. Flattish round, white flesh. Immune.

Arran Consul Not a well-known potato among gardeners but noted for its good storing quality. Oval, white flesh. Immune.

Arran Peak Does best on heavier soils and stores well. Reputed to stand up well to diseases. Round to oval, white flesh. Immune.

Aura Bred by Vilmorin-Andrieux of Paris and introduced to Britain via Ireland. The plants need a very fertile soil. Not a heavy cropper but the kidney, yellow-fleshed tubers are by far the best for chipping. The flesh is pale gold. Until

1968 supplies came from Kent. Now certified seed tubers are grown in Scotland.

Dunbar Standard Won much praise when introduced thirty years ago but better known among Scots gardeners than others in the United Kingdom. Long oval-shaped tubers. The plants show little if any resistance to blight. White flesh. Immune.

Golden Wonder Considered by many as the best-flavoured potato of all and at its best after Christmas. It requires a light, well-manured soil and enthusiasts say that only farmyard manure applied to the soil can lead to fine flavour. Not renowned for its crop but, although an old variety, much liked by present-day exhibitors. Kidney shape, yellow flesh. Immune.

Kerr's Pink Introduced over fifty years ago and still popular in Scotland but not in England. Not a handsome potato. Has a floury texture when cooked. Heavy cropper and stores well. Fairly resistant to blight. Flattish round, pink tubers. White flesh. Immune.

King Edward An old but still very popular potato once also known as Pink-Eyed Majestic and Scottish King. Not renowned for heavy cropping and its popularity is greater among farmers than among gardeners. Does not thrive on every kind of soil, doing best in a medium loam. Large, kidney-shaped tubers with shallow eyes and a few pink markings at the crown end. Stores well. Very susceptible to blight. Good flavour. Pale yellow flesh.

Majestic Once also known as Tremendous and Allangrove. Introduced in 1911 and was once very popular among gardeners. Its cropping potential, once very high, appears to be decreasing. May be grown as a Second Early or Maincrop. Plants mature early. Large kidney, shallow eyes, good flavour, suitable for boiling or chipping. Shows resistance to blight. Immune.

Pentland Crown A new potato bred by the Scottish Society for Research in Plant Breeding. It is claimed that the plants show immunity to some virus diseases and to blight. Vigorous grower and heavy cropper. Seldom affected by common scab. Stores well. Good flavour. Oval, white flesh. Immune.

Pink Fir Apple Needs very good soil to produce a good crop of long tubers many of which are of very uneven shape. Tubers are formed just below the surface and often at some distance from the crown of the plant. The skin is pink; flesh pale yellow. Much liked as a salad potato.

Red King Edward Once also known as Red King. Similar to King Edward but tubers are red-skinned. It is claimed that the red variety can crop better than King Edward.

Note, in listing the varieties the word 'immune' refers only to immunity to wart disease.

Potentilla (po-ten-til-la)

From the Latin *potens,* powerful, some species having active medicinal properties *(Rosaceae).* Cinquefoil. The 500 species of this genus are mostly hardy herbaceous plants, with a few shrubs and sub-shrubs, natives mainly of northern temperate and arctic regions. Among the species are nine British natives. Reginald Farrer praised the tubers on the roots of the silverweed, *P. anserina,* which he preferred to new potatoes (see Farrer). In Britain, if you can find them at all, they are no worthy addition to our vegetables. Farrer was writing of the Chinese form of the plant which seems in this matter to be unlike our native. Of the shrubs, *P. fruticosa* and its varieties is a very valuable small shrub which is found sometimes wild in Yorkshire on soils overlying limestone.

Herbaceous species cultivated *P. alba,* 6 inches, white, spring, Europe. *P. alchemilloides,* to 1 foot, white, summer, Pyrenees. *P. ambigua,* 6 inches, yellow, summer, Himalaya. *P. aurea,* 3–6 inches, flowers golden-yellow, May to July, European Alps, Pyrenees; var. *plena,* flowers double. *P. atrosanguinea,* 1½ feet, crimson, summer, Himalaya. *P. clusiana,* 6 inches, milk white, June to July, Europe. *P. crantzii* (syn. *P. alpestris*), 9 inches, yellow, May to June, Europe. *P. fragiformis,* 9 inches, yellow, May to June, north-western America. *P. grandiflora,* 1 foot, yellow, summer, Alps. *P. × hopwoodiana,* 1 foot, rose to white, summer, hybrid. *P. nepalensis,* 1½ feet, rosy-red, summer, Himalaya; var. 'Miss Willmott' *(willmottiae),* 9 inches, carmine. *P. nitida,* 4 inches, rose, summer, Europe; vars. *alba,* white; *grandiflora,* pink. *P. recta,* 1½ feet, yellow, June and July, southern Europe to Siberia; var. *warrenii,* flowers golden yellow, larger. *P. rupestris,* 1½ feet, white, May to July, Europe. *P. tabernaemontani* (syn. *P. verna*), 1–2 inches, mat-forming, yellow, spring and summer, Europe, including Britain; var. *nana,* dwarf form. *P. ternata* (syn. *P. chrysocraspeda*), 3 inches, flowers bright yellow, May to July, Europe. *P. tonguei,* 3 inches, terra-cotta, summer, hybrid.

Shrub species cultivated *P. arbuscula,* low shrub, flowers large, rich yellow, summer to autumn, China, Himalaya; vars. *bulleyana,* leaves covered with silky hairs below; 'Logan's Form', taller. *P. davurica,* 1½ feet, yellow, May to September, China. *P. × friedrichsenii,* to 6 feet, pale yellow, June to September, a hybrid. *P. fruticosa,* 4 feet, yellow, May to September, northern hemisphere; vars. include *grandiflora,* larger flowers; *tenuifolia,* very narrow grey leaves; *veitchii,* 3 feet, white flowers; *vilmoriniana,* silvery-white leaves and creamy-white flowers. *P. glabra,* to 2 feet or more, stems red, flowers white, summer, northern China, Siberia. *P. rigida,* compact, dwarf shrub, flowers bright yellow, summer. *P. salesoviana,* dwarf,

dark green leaves, white beneath, flowers white tinted rose, June to July, Siberia. *P. tridentata,* sub-shrub, 1 foot, flowers white, summer, arctic North America. Cultivars: the following are some excellent garden forms, which are well-worth growing, as well as the species. *Herbaceous* 'Etna', 1½ feet, silvery leaves and deep red flowers; 'Fireflame', 2 inches, silvery leaves, bright scarlet flowers; 'Gibson's Scarlet', 1½ feet, brick red; 'Gloire de Nancy', 1½ feet, double yellow; 'Monsieur Rouillard', 1½ feet, large flowers, crimson-mahogany and orange; 'Roxana', 9 inches, salmon-orange; 'White Beauty', 12-15 inches, white flowers 1 inch wide; 'William Rollison', 1½ feet, orange-red, yellow centre, semi-double. *Shrubby* (all 3–4 feet tall unless otherwise stated). 'Daydawn', peachy-pink and cream; 'Elizabeth', 2½ feet, yellow, perpetual flowering; 'Gold Drop', 1–2 feet, small, golden yellow flowers; 'Katherine Dykes', primrose yellow; 'Primrose Beauty', grey-green leaves and primrose-yellow flowers with deeper coloured centres; 'Sunset', deep orange to brick red; 'Tangerine', 1–1½ feet, pale coppery-yellow; 'Walton Park', large, very freely

The mat-forming Potentilla nitida rubra is covered with silky hairs which give the plant a soft appearance. Out of doors it needs a sunny position.

produced bright yellow flowers.

Other cultivars, both herbaceous and shrubby, are offered by nurserymen.

Cultivation These plants are easy to cultivate and have no special requirements except for the herbaceous species where the soil should be deep and rich but well-drained, and dwarf species, which are rock plants and need positions in full sun. Plant in autumn or spring. Feed the tall herbaceous kinds in the summer-flowering period. The shrubby species also do best in deep loam, but do not mind chalky soils, provided the drainage is good. Propagation of both herbaceous and shrubby species may be by seeds sown under glass in March in a temperature of 55–65 F (13–18 C), transplanting the seedlings out of doors in May or June. Division of roots is also possible with herbaceous species and varieties. Shrubs may be easily raised from cuttings of ripe wood taken in August or September and placed in sandy soil in a frame.

Primula (prim-u-la)

The name is derived from the Latin *primus,* first, referring to the early flowering of some of the species, such as the primrose *(Primulaceae).* A diverse and widely distributed genus of over 500 species including those from the high alps, moisture-loving perennials and tender greenhouse varieties. All are natives of the northern hemisphere. The one thing most primulas demand is a cool, moist soil containing plenty of peat or leaf soil. Most of the Asiatic primulas —and this is a considerable number of species—are lime haters, but they can be grown in neutral or acid soil, together with the European species. The genus has been divided by botanists into 30 or so different sections, some of which are large and have been further sub-divided, but of these sections, about a dozen or so only are of importance to the gardener. The section to which the species belongs is indicated in brackets after the name of the species.

Hardy species cultivated   *P. allionii*

Forms of Primula vulgaris can be had in a wide and decorative range of colour.

(Auricula), 2 inches, grey-green leaves, rose-pink to deep red flowers, March and April, Maritime Alps; var. *alba,* a pure white form; easy plants to grow in pans in an alpine house or cold frame. *P. alpicola* (Sikkimensis), 1–1½ feet, with variable, cowslip-like, fragrant flowers in shades of yellow, violet or white, May and June, Tibet. *P. anisodora* (Candelabra), 2 feet, purple flowers with a green eye in June, Yunnan. The whole plant is aromatic. *P. altaica* (Vernales), of gardens, is now *P. vulgaris rubra,* a pale pink primrose of European origin. *P. aurantiaca* (Candelabra), 1 foot, flowers reddish-orange, bell-shaped, in whorls, July, Yunnan; moist soil. *P. auricula* (Auricula), 3–6 inches, yellow, fragrant flowers in spring and more or less farinose leaves about 3 inches long, European Alps. (See also Auricula). *P. beesiana* (Candelabra), 1½–2 feet, bright rosy-purple flowers with a yellow eye,

borne on erect stems in tiers, June and July, Yunnan. It will soon naturalise itself in moist soil and partial shade. *P. bulleyana* (Candelabra), 1½–2 feet, orange, shaded apricot, June and July, for similar conditions, Yunnan. *P. capitata* (Capitatae), 6–9 inches, with heads of fragrant, violet flowers from June to August, Tibet, Sikkim. Suitable for a moist place on the rock garden. *P. carniolica* (Auricula), 4–6 inches, soft rose-purple, bell-shaped, fragrant flowers in May, Maritime and Julian Alps. *P. chungensis* (Candelabra), 2 feet, flowers light-orange, bell-shaped, tube red, borne in whorls, June, Burma, China, Assam; moist soil. *P. clarkei* (Farinosae), 2–3 inches, foliage coppery-red, flowers rose-pink, April, Kashmir, rock garden or alpine house. *P. cockburniana* (Candelabra), 1 foot, with dark orange-red, bell-shaped flowers, June, China. Best treated as a biennial in fairly moist soil and partial shade. *P. denticulata* (Denticulata), the drum-stick primula, 1 foot, with large, globular heads of lilac flowers from March to May, Himalaya; var. *alba,* is a good white form and 'Prichard's Ruby' is a rich ruby-red; easily grown in moist soil in the border or rock garden in light shade. *P. florindae* (Sikkimensis), 2–4 feet, with large heads of sulphur-yellow, drooping flowers June and July, Tibet. Requires a really moist soil and is admirable beside a pool. *P. frondosa* (Farinosae), 3–6 inches, with rosy lilac flowers with a yellow eye, April, Balkans. *P. gracilipes* (Petiolares), almost stemless blue or mauve flowers with a yellow eye produced in spring from a rosette of leaves up to 6 inches long, Nepal, Sikkim, Tibet. A charming little plant for the alpine house. *P. helodoxa* (Candelabra), 2–8 feet, with golden-yellow, bell-shaped flowers in June and July, Yunnan. The common name, glory of the marsh, indicates that it likes a boggy place. *P. involucrata* (Farinosae), 6–9 inches, flowers white with a yellow eye in May and June, Himalaya. *P. ioessa* (Sikkimensis), 9 inches, flowers bell-shaped, pinkish mauve to violet, summer, Tibet, moist soil *P. japonica* (Candelabra), 1½ feet, with purplish-red flowers in whorls in May and June, Japan; var. 'Miller's Crimson' is a striking plant, and 'Postford White' is a clear white with a pink eye. These will seed themselves readily in moist conditions. *P. juliae* (Vernales), 2 inches, forms mats of foliage, flowers lilac-purple, winter and early spring, Transcaucasia, parent of a number of hybrids, requires moist soil. *P. marginata* (Auricula), 6 inches, with umbels of fragrant, deeply farinose lavender flowers in May, Maritime and Cottian Alps; var. 'Linda Pope', rich lavender-blue with a white eye. *P. minima* (Auricula), almost stemless rose-pink flowers in April, and short, shiny green leaves, southern European Alps. *P. nutans* (Soldanelloideae), 9–12 inches, with compact heads of lavender-blue, fragrant flowers in June, Yunnan. Charming, but short-lived and requires to be kept on the dry side during the winter, so should be grown in an alpine house. *P.* × *pubescens* (Auricula), 3–6 inches, flowers rosy-purple, April–May, hybrid group; 'Faldonside', 3 inches, flowers rich crimson; 'Mrs J. H. Wilson', 3–4 inches, flowers rich purple with paler centre. *P. polyneura* (Cortusoides), 9–12 inches, pale pink to wine-red flowers in whorls in May and leaves up to 4 inches in length, sometimes hairy, Yunnan, Tibet. *P. pulverulenta* (Candelabra), 2–3 feet, with whorls of claret-red flowers with a darker eye in June and July, China. The 'Bartley Strain' has delightful soft pink flowers. *P. rosea* (Farinosae), 3–6 inches, brilliant carmine flowers in April before the leaves develop, Himalaya; var. 'Delight' is a brilliant carmine-red. For a moist, reasonably sunny place in the rock or bog garden. Once established self-sown seedlings will appear. *P. rubra* (syn. *P. hirsuta*) (Auricula), 3 inches, with rose or lilac trusses of flowers in March and narrow leaves, central European Alps and Pyrenees. *P. rusbyi* (Parryi), 6 inches, red-purple, nodding heads in loose clusters in late summer. The tufts of leathery leaves are lance-shaped and toothed, Rocky Mountains. *P. sieboldii* (Cortusoides), 6 inches, variable rose to purple, with tufts of soft, heart-shaped leaves, Japan, suitable for the alpine house. *P. sikkimensis* (Sikkimensis), 2 feet, with pendent, funnel-shaped, fragrant flowers in May and June, Sikkim, Tibet, Yunnan. Admirable beside a pool. *P. veris* (Vernales), cowslip, 2–6 inches, deep yellow, fragrant flowers in April and May, Europe, including Britain (rare in parts of Scotland and Ireland), western Asia. *P. vialii* (syn. *P. littoniana*) (Muscarioides), 1½ feet, a slender spike of lavender flowers with bright red buds at the tip in June and July, Yunnan. *P. viscosa* (Auricula), 4 inches, deep violet flowers in one-sided umbels in May, Swiss Alps and Pyrenees. Often confused with *P. rubra. P. vulgaris* (syn. *P. acaulis*) (Vernales), primrose, 1–4 inches, creamy-yellow, March and April, western and southern Europe, including Britain. Coloured primroses include: 'Garryarde Guinivere', 6 inches, leaves reddish-bronze, large pink flowers in big heads; 'Garryarde Victory', 4 inches, leaves tinted crimson, flowers wine-red; 'Lingwood Beauty', cherry-red, leaves bright green; 'Wanda', deep claret-crimson and unnamed blue and pink shades. *P. whitei* (Petiolares), rosettes of ovate leaves, almost stemless pale blue flowers in April covered with farina, Bhutan.

1 The large pale flowers of Primula bhutanica bloom in March and April.
2 The deep magenta flowers of Primula werringtonensis in early summer.

Greenhouse species cultivated *P. × kewensis* (*P. floribunda × P. verticillata*) (Floribundae), 9–12 inches, yellow, fragrant flowers in winter and early spring in a cool greenhouse; a hybrid which originated at the Royal Botanic Gardens, Kew. *P. malacoides* (Malacoides), 12–18 inches, whorls of lavender flowers in winter and early spring, China; vars. 'Pink Pride', 8 inches, carmine-pink; 'Rose Bouquet', 15 inches, carmine-rose; 'Snow Queen', 15 inches, white. *P. obconica* (Obconica), 6 inches, pale lilac with a yellow eye in winter, continues to flower for months, China. The hairs on the stems and underside of the leaves are liable to cause a skin rash on some people; var. *alba* is a white form; 'Red Chief', scarlet-crimson; 'Salmon King', salmon-pink. *P. sinensis*

1 The flowers of Primula denticulata alba, the white form of the Drumstick Primula, are borne in April.
2 The yellow flowers of Primula 'Broadwell Gold' have white eyes, and the leaves are covered with white 'meal'.
3 The golden-yellow flowers of Primula helodoxa are borne in a series of whorls.

(Sinensis), Chinese primrose, 9 inches, purplish-rose with a yellow eye in spring, China; vars. *alba*, white; 'Dazzler', vivid orange-scarlet; 'Pink Beauty', rose suffused salmon.

Cultivation of hardy species These are best planted in September and October, or March and April. Those suitable for the alpine house, in pans containing an open, gritty sandy loam with peat or leaf soil in it, are: *P. allionii, P. carniolica,*

P. frondosa, P. marginata and *P. nutans.* For waterside planting or in moist soil in partial shade suitable species are: *P. alpicola, P. beesiana, P. bulleyana, P. denticulata, P. florindae, P. japonica, P. pulverulenta, P. rosea* and *P. sikkimensis.* Mulch plants growing in the open with old manure or compost in February. Propagation is by seed sown as soon as it is ripe in a cold frame or by division of the plants soon after they have finished flowering.

Cultivation of greenhouse species Sow seed of *P. malacoides* in June and July on the surface of a compost consisting of leaf soil, loam and sharp sand. Cover the pan with a piece of glass, shade from the sun and germinate in a temperature of 55–60°F (13–16°C). Prick out the seedlings when they are large enough to

170

handle, and when they have grown larger pot them into individual 3-inch pots, harden them off and place the pots in a cold frame. Finally, pot them into 5-inch pots in John Innes potting compost No 1 and bring them into the greenhouse in September. Keep them in a temperature of about 50–55 F (10–13 C) and feed them with a liquid fertiliser when they are flowering. When potting, allow the base of the leaves just to touch the compost, and pot fairly firmly. *P. x kewensis, P. obconica* and *P. sinensis*, may be sown from April to August and treated in a similar way (see also Auricula and Polyanthus).

Prunella (proo-nel-a)
From *Brunella,* from the German *Die Braune,* quinsy, which the plants were supposed to cure *(Labiatae).* This genus has 7 species, one of which, *P. vulgaris,* is a weed widely distributed over the northern hemisphere. It is the native self-heal, which in past time was renowned as a herbal dressing for wounds. The plants are all hardy herbaceous perennials of moderate height, with dense whorls of flowers, borne in terminal spikes. As they are apt to spread widely if not checked, they are best grown in wild gardens in damp, shady or semi-shady places, where their spreading habits can be tolerated.
Species cultivated *P. grandiflora,* 6 inches, flowers purple, July and August, Europe; vars. *alba,* white, *rubra,* red. *P. vulgaris,* to 12 inches, flowers purple, summer. *P. webbiana,* 9 inches, flowers purple, June to September; var. *rosea,* pink.
Cultivation Prunella species are not exacting in their needs. They will grow in shade, and are not choosy about soil. Every alternate year the plants should

The bizarre appearance and shape of the Pterostylis has earned them the name of Greenhoods. Most of them are terrestrial orchids. They are plants for a greenhouse; but they may be grown out of doors in summer in the milder counties of Britain.
1 Pterostylis pedunculata.
2 Pterostylis grandiflora.

be divided and replanted, as they spread rapidly. It would be unwise to grow these plants in close association with choice rock plants as not only are their roots invasive, but they seed themselves freely.

Pterostylis (ter-o-ste-lis)
From the Greek *pteron,* a wing, and *stylos,* a style, in reference to the winged style or column of the flower *(Orchidaceae).* A genus of some 95 species of terrestrial orchids which, because of their hood-shaped and generally greenish flowers, bizarre rather than beautiful, are commonly known as greenhoods. Most of the species are confined to Australia but about 15 are natives of New Zealand, two or three of New Caledonia, and one or more of New Guinea. They are deciduous, coming up from late summer to spring from the tuber-like pseudobulbs. The flowers are either solitary and terminal or several may be produced on each stem. The species are quite amenable to cultivation although they are too tender to be grown out of doors except in the milder counties and are really only suitable for growing in a shady alpine house or a cool greenhouse. Few of the species are likely to be cultivated, but some of those worth seeking are described below.
Species cultivated *P. banksii,* flowers green, streaked with white and reddish

brown, 2 to 3 inches long, New Zealand. *P. baptisii,* flowers translucent greenish-white with brown stripes, 3 inches long, Australia. *P. coccinea,* flowers light crimson to greenish with darker stripes, 1 to 2 inches long, Australia. *P. nutans,* flowers green and white, 1 to 2 inches long, Australia. *P. oliveri,* flowers green and white, 1 to 2 inches long, New Zealand.
Cultivation In nature the pseudobulbs are found several inches deep in the soil and so they should be planted in pots rather than shallow pans. The compost should be well-drained and consist of 2 parts of fibrous loam, 4 parts of peat or leafmould and 3 parts of sharp sand. A layer of sand around the pseudobulbs will help to prevent them from rotting. During winter those species which are dormant should have a minimum temperature of about 40 F (4 C). Species which make their growth during the winter should have a minimum temperature of 50 F (10 C). Watch out for slugs, which are very fond of the young succulent growths, and take the necessary precautions against them. If the plants are grown out of doors they should be planted in shade, in leafmould to which some sharp sand has been added. The soil should never be allowed to dry out. Propagation is by seed or the off-set pseudobulbs which are freely produced with some species. Importing of tubers from overseas is the only satisfactory method of introducing these plants to the garden.

Pulmonaria (pul-mon-air-ee-a)
From the Latin *pulmo,* lung; derivation uncertain; either because the spotted leaves bore a resemblance to diseased lungs, or because one species was regarded as providing a remedy for

diseased lungs *(Boraginaceae)*. Lungwort. This is a genus of 10 species of hardy herbaceous perennials, natives of Europe. *P. angustifolia* is a rare native, an excellent garden plant. The charm of these early flowering lungworts is in their flowers, which change from red to blue—they also have the name soldiers-and-sailors on this account—and in their hairy leaves which, in some species, are spotted with a much paler green or with white. The spotted leaves suggested to some herbalists the human lungs, and it was thus in accordance with the 'doctrine of signatures' that the plant was used to dose unfortunate sufferers from lung complaints.

Species cultivated *P. angustifolia*, blue cowslip, to 1 foot, leaves lacking spots, flowers pink, changing to blue, spring, Europe, including Britain; vars. *alba*, white; 'Mawson's Variety' is a selected garden form. *P. officinalis*, Jerusalem cowslip, spotted dog, to 1 foot, leaves spotted white, flowers pink then violet, spring, Europe. *P. rubra*, 1 foot, leaves usually lacking spots, flowers brick red, Transylvania. *P. saccharata*, to 1 foot, leaves blotched white, flowers pink, April to July, Europe.

Cultivation Any soil is suitable and the plants will grow in sun or shade. Quite the best companions for lungworts are other early spring flowering plants including bulbs, primroses and so on, interspersed with native ferns. Plant in autumn or spring and lift and divide the plants every four to five years. Propagation is by seed sown in a shady border out of doors in March or April, or by division of the roots in spring or autumn.

Pulsatilla (pulse-a-til-a)

The name was first used by Pierandrea Mattioli, a sixteenth-century Italian botanist and physician, and possibly means 'shaking in the wind' *(Ranunculaceae)*. This genus of 30 species, distinguished from *Anemone* only by minor botanical differences, includes some of the most beautiful of low-growing flowering plants, and one in particular, *P. vernalis*, which is so lovely that it must have converted many to the growing of alpine plants. The plants are very suitable for alpine house cultivation. One of their attractions is the feathery foliage, and another is the equally hairy and feathery seedheads. They are natives of the temperate regions of Europe and Asia.

Species cultivated *P. alpina*, 1 foot, blue buds opening white, May to June, European Alps; var. *sulphurea* with pale yellow flowers. *P. halleri*, 10 inches, flowers of deep violet, finely cut leaves,

1 A red form of Pulsatilla vulgaris, in which the colour is more pronounced on the inside of the petals.
2 In this form Pulsatilla vulgaris, the Pasque Flower, produces outstanding purplish flowers with orange centres.

There are many hybrids, both single and double, of Pyrethrum roseum. Pyrethrum 'Eileen May Robinson' is a clear pink, while P. 'Kelway's Glorious' is a deeper pink. They mix well.

April to May, Swiss Alps and the Austrian Tyrol. *P. slavica* (syn. *P. vulgaris slavica*), 6 inches, flowers plum-purple with golden centres, April. *P. vernalis,* 6–9 inches, evergreen, finely cut foliage, hairy bronze-violet buds opening to a glistening crystalline white with a boss of golden stamens, April, high Alpine meadows. *P. vulgaris,* Pasque flower, 1 foot, rich purple flowers covered with shaggy fur, April, Europe, including Britain; vars. *alba,* white; 'Budapest'; large powder-blue flowers; red-flowered seedlings are offered by some nurserymen.

Cultivation A light open soil is suitable; *P. vulgaris* is found naturally on chalk and limestone formations. A well-drained rock garden suits most species, but they *must* be protected from wet during the winter. It is for this reason that they are so eminently suitable for the alpine house. Seed, sown as soon as it is ripe in July or August, in sandy soil in a cold frame, is quite the best method of propagation.

Pyrethrum (py-re-thrum)

From the Greek *pyr,* fire, probably with reference to fever, since the plant was used medicinally to assuage fevers (*Compositae*). These hardy plants are admirable for a sunny border and last well as cut flowers. Long known as pyrethrum they are botanically classified under *Chrysanthemum.*

Species cultivated *P. roseum* (syn. *Chrysanthemum coccineum*), 1–2 feet, with large, daisy-like flowers in May and June. The colour is variable from red to white, occasionally tipped with yellow. The leaves are vivid green, graceful and feathery, Caucasus, Persia. There are many hybrids, both single and double. *Single* 2–2½ feet, 'Allurement', rich pink; 'Avalanche', pure white; 'Brenda', bright carmine; 'Bressingham Red', large crimson; 'Eileen May Robinson', clear pink; 'Kelway's Glorious', glowing scarlet; 'Salmon Beauty', bright salmon-rose. *Double* 2–2½ feet, 'Carl Vogt', pure white; 'Lord Rosebery', velvety red; 'Madeleine', lilac-pink; 'Yvonne Cayeux', pale sulphur-yellow. For the plant sometimes listed as *Pyrethrum parthenium,* the feverfew, see *Chrysanthemum parthenium.*

Cultivation A well-drained loamy soil and a sunny position suits pyrethrums best, though they will grow well on chalky soils. They require ample moisture when coming into bud and during the growing season. Plant in March and leave them undisturbed for three or four years. If left longer the plants will deteriorate and the flowers become smaller and fewer. Lift and divide in March or after flowering in July, discarding the old, woody pieces. Each year cut the plants hard back after flowering. This often results in a second crop of blooms in late summer or autumn. Slugs and rabbits can be a menace but if coarse, weathered ashes are scattered around and over the crowns in the autumn this will deter them, as will slug pellets. The plants are somewhat floppy in habit so some light staking should be provided. Propagation is by division in March or after flowering in July, or by seed sown in a cool greenhouse or frame in spring (see also Chrysanthemum, *C. coccineum*).

Radishes

Seeds of this quick-growing vegetable may be sown for salads at intervals from early March to October. It is generally treated as a catch crop, being sown on a piece of ground which is intended for cabbages or some other crop to be planted subsequently. A rich, moist soil and cool conditions yield the most succulent radishes. Slow growth may cause them to have a rather hot, unpalatable taste.

Sowings in March or early April may be made in the cold frame or under cloches. Sow the seeds in 1-inch deep drills, the drills being six inches apart. Sow thinly to avoid having to thin out. Remember each radish needs at least 1 square inch of surface area. Sow similarly in open ground. Prevent annual weeds from smothering the seedlings and soak the rows with water if the soil is on the dry side. There are many varieties and 'French Breakfast' is probably the most popular. 'Sutton's Red Forcing' is suitable for cloche and frame sowings. The long, white radish, 'Icicle', is liked for its flavour.

Winter radishes are large and may have a black skin, as in the variety 'Black Spanish', or a red skin such as 'China Rose', or a white skin like 'All Season'. Do not sow winter radishes until June and space the rows 1 foot apart. Thin the seedlings to 9 inches apart, and keep the rows free of weeds. Water well in dry summer weather. Lift the roots in October and store them in slightly moist sand.

Ranunculus (ra-nun-ku-lus)

From the Latin *rana,* a frog, some species inhabiting marshy places where frogs abound (*Ranunculaceae*). This genus of 400 species, cosmopolitan in distribution, includes many fine garden plants and a number of British native plants, several of the buttercups being among the gardener's (and farmer's) most invasive weeds. The family itself always seems to the gardener, though not to the botanist, to contain some strangely assorted genera. The great spearwort, *R. lingua,* is a pretty aquatic weed with large flowers carried high above the water. It is not, unfortunately,

173

Ranunculus asiaticus, a plant native to Asia, has single red flowers.

as common as *R. repens*, the creeping buttercup. In the English Tudor and Elizabethan garden double forms of our native buttercups were among the few flowers which would generally be found. The showiest of these plants, *R. asiaticus*, has a wide colour range, but it is more at home in Mediterranean gardens.

Species cultivated *R. aconitifolius*, fair maids of Kent, 2 feet, white, May, Europe; var. *flore-pleno*, double. *R. acris*, common buttercup, 8 inches to 3 feet, yellow, spring Europe (including Britain); cultivated in its var. *flore-pleno*, yellow bachelor's buttons, flowers double, non-weedy in habit. *R. alpestris*, to 4 inches, flowers white, March to August, European Alps. *R. amplexicaulis*, 1 foot, flowers white with golden stamens, spring, Pyrenees; var. *grandiflorus*, flowers larger. *R. asiaticus*, to 1 foot or so, various colours, double in cultivation, May, June, Asia. *R. bulbosus flore-pleno*, 1 foot, flowers yellow, double, spring, Europe. *R. bullatus*, 6–12 inches, orange, yellow, May, Mediterranean region. *R. carpaticus*, 1 foot, golden-yellow, May, Hungary. *R. crenatus*, 3–4 inches, white, April to July, Transylvania. *R. ficaria*, lesser celandine, pilewort, 3–6 inches, flowers bright yellow, March to May, Europe, including Britain; cultivated in its varieties: *albus*, flowers white; *aurantiacus*, flowers coppery-yellow; *flore-plena*, flowers double, rich yellow; *major*, 9 inches, flowers much larger than the type, pale yellow; 'Primrose', a cultivar with soft pale yellow flowers. *R. geranifolius* (syn. *R. montanus*), 4 inches, yellow, May to June, Alps. *R. glacialis*, 6 inches, white and rose, June to

August, European mountains, arctic. *R. gouanii*, 6–12 inches, leaves deeply cut, the flowers golden-yellow, summer, Pyrenees. *R. gramineus*, 6–12 inches, narrow shining leaves, flowers golden-yellow, April to June, Europe. *R. lingua*, greater spearwort, 2–3 feet, yellow, 2 inches across, July to September, Europe (including Britain), the plant for the bog garden or for marshy places, best in its form *grandiflorus*, with larger flowers. *R. lyallii*, 3–4 feet, leaves up to 1 foot wide, flowers white, single or semi-double, up to 4 inches in diameter, spring to summer, a very striking rock plant, New Zealand. *R. monspeliacus*, 1 foot, flowers yellow, April to May, Mediterranean region. *R. parnassifolius*, 3–6 inches, flowers white with a pink tint, June, Europe. *R. pyrenaeus*, 1 foot, flowers white, summer, southern Europe. *R. repens*, creeping buttercup, flowers yellow, spring, Europe (including Britain); worth growing in its var. *plena*, with double flowers and much less invasive. *R. seguieri*, 4 inches, flowers white to rose, May to July, Europe. *R. thora*, 6 inches, flowers yellow, May to July, southern Europe.

Cultivation The hardy herbaceous species need no special soil, and will grow well in partly shaded borders. Plant either in autumn or spring, and lift and divide the plants at least every three years. The Asiatic tuberous species need a rich soil, preferably containing one third part of decayed manure. The tubers (usually offered by bulb growers as *Ranunculus asiaticus grandiflorus*, or *R. grandiflora*) are planted 'claws' down, from October or November until April; those described as 'Persian' ranunculus are best planted in late February. All kinds should be planted 2 inches deep and 3–4 inches apart. They are often grown in rows 6 inches apart, for cutting purposes. Apply liquid manure once a week from the time the leaves are seen and water freely if the weather is at all dry. When the flowering season is over the tubers must be sun dried and stored until planting time comes round again.

Raoulia (ra-oo-lee-a)
Commemorating Edouard Raoul (1815–52), a French naval surgeon, who collected and wrote about plants from New Zealand (*Compositae*). This genus of 25 species, all natives of Australia or New Zealand, includes a few which are used in the rock garden to give a close-growing silvery-white carpeting effect. *R. eximia*, in its native New Zealand, is called the vegetable sheep, for the shepherd, when he sees it on the distant hillside, has some difficulty in telling the plant from an injured and immobilised sheep.

Species cultivated *R. australis*, carpeting, silvery foliage, New Zealand. *R. eximia*, silvery rosettes, New Zealand. *R. glabra*, emerald foliage, fluffy white flowers, New Zealand. *R. lutescens*,

leaves very tiny, greyish-green rosettes, flowers stemless, yellow, summer, New Zealand. *R. subsericea*, green foliage, minute white flowers, New Zealand. *R. tenuicaulis*, grey-green máts of foliage, flowers yellow, spring, New Zealand. All the above species grow ½ inch or less in height.

Cultivation A well-drained ledge on a rock garden or a position on a moraine in a sheltered sunny position, is the most suitable place. Plants may be divided in March, or propagated from seed.

Reseda (re-se-da)
Derived from *resedo*, to heal, a name given by Pliny (the Elder) for a species of mignonette which was credited with certain medicinal qualities in healing external bruises (*Resedaceae*). A genus of some 60 species of annual and biennial hardy plants, two of which are decorative in gardens. Sprays of flower cut from the garden in late autumn will keep indoors in a cool room in water throughout the winter and retain their refreshing fragrance. They are natives of southern Europe and North Africa to central Asia.

Species cultivated *R. alba*, 1½–2 feet, a biennial producing spikes of white flowers with brownish anthers from May to September, southern Europe; it is sometimes grown as a decorative pot plant in a cool greenhouse. *R. odorata*, mignonette, hardy annual, 9 inches, with heads of fragrant, yellowish-white flowers from June to October, North Africa, Egypt; vars. 'Goliath', 10 inches, large, very fragrant, reddish spikes; 'Red Monarch', 10 inches, large, deep red heads.

Cultivation Seed of mignonette should be sown in April or May where it is to flower, in a sunny position; it is not particular about soil. The seed should be covered with a thin layer of fine soil only and will germinate better when the soil is made firm after sowing. Plants do not transplant readily, but a few seeds sown in a pot will make most attractive cool greenhouse plants.

Rheum (ree-um)
From the Greek *rha* or *rheon*, rhubarb (*Polygonaceae*). A genus of some 50 species of hardy perennial herbaceous plants, frequently with woody rhizomes, natives of temperate and subtropical Asia. Many of those in cultivation are handsome plants of noble aspect suitable for the waterside, wild garden or for architectural planting. They may also be used in selected positions in shrub or herbaceous borders where a bold effect is required. The leaves are large, often palmately lobed, the flowers are mainly borne in tall spikes in summer, dock-like

Ranunculus is a very cosmopolitan genus of over 400 species, which vary widely in appearance. Many are dangerous weeds but they also include some striking garden plants, many native to Britain.

but frequently with attractively coloured bracts. *Rheum rhaponticum* is probably the main parent of our culinary rhubarb, and *R. officinale* the chief source of medicinal rhubarb.

Species cultivated *R. alexandrae,* 3–4 feet, compact rosettes of ovate-oblong leaves, remarkable for its conspicuous pale yellow bracts which clothe the inflorescences; often shy-flowering, June, China and Tibet. *R. emodii,* 6–10 feet, leaves large with undulating margins, tall spikes of white flowers, Himalaya. *R. nobile,* 4–6 feet, leaves large, green, glossy, with red leaf stalks, flowers greenish with shining straw-coloured bracts, Himalaya. *R. officinale,* 8–10 feet, distinctly lobed, untoothed foliage of roundish, kidney-shaped outline, flowers pink-white or greenish, Tibet. *R. palmatum,* 5–6 feet, leaves large, roundish or near heart-shaped and palmately lobed with near cylindrical leaf-stalks, flowers in large panicles varying from creamy-white to deep red, China; 'Bowles' Crimson' has leaves flushed crimson, flowers deep-red; var. *tanguticum* has more deeply lobed leaves. *R. rhaponticum,* common rhubarb, 4–5 feet, leaves large, roundish with long stalks, flowers whitish in leafy panicles, Siberia.

Cultivation Most rheums are easily grown in any deep fertile soil. Ample space should be allowed for the spread of their large leaves. An exception is the choice *R. alexandrae,* which needs well-drained, even scree-like conditions, tending to rot in badly-drained soil in British winters. Propagation is by division in winter or early spring or by seed sown in autumn or early spring in cold frame or open ground (see also Rhubarb).

Rhubarb

Because the roots continue to crop for up to ten years after planting, special attention should be given to choosing a suitable site for rhubarb and preparing it well. The bed should not be shaded and should be dug deeply. Any roots of perennial weeds must be removed when digging. Where dung is available, this should be dug in at the rate of 1 cwt to 10 square yards. Otherwise garden compost may be incorporated into the soil or spread over the bed after planting; a barrowload to the square yard is not excessive. Plant the roots 3 feet apart, using the spade. November, February or March are suitable planting times. Plant firmly and leave the pink buds at soil level. Supplies of rhubarb are appreciated early in the season. This is why 'Timperley Early' is favoured. 'Hawke's Champagne' is better known but this variety crops later and the flower stems which the plants make in June or July should be cut away as soon as they are noticed. 'Glaskin's Perpetual' may be raised from seed. Sow seed in the cold frame in March or April and thin the seedlings to 6 inches

apart. A year later, set the plants in the specially prepared bed.

Do not pull any sticks in the first season after planting and, in subsequent years, do not over-pull as this weakens the plants. Hand weeding should be carried out during the first summer but, in future seasons, no weeding is necessary because the large leaves inhibit weed growth. To ensure that the plants continue to crop well, mulch the bed each autumn with well-rotted farmyard manure or garden compost.

Forcing There are two ways of forcing rhubarb. If this is to be done in the shed or greenhouse, the roots should be lifted as and when required and exposed to frost for a few days. Plant the frosted roots closely together in boxes of soil or beneath the greenhouse staging. Water them well and exclude light by draping black polythene sheeting or sacking over and around the roots. At a temperature of between 60–70°F (16–21°C), sticks will be ready for use within a month or so. In unheated sheds and

Rodgersia pinnata is handsome both in leaf and flower. It is a native of China and Japan and useful for under-planting in the woodland garden.

greenhouses, growth will be considerably slower and the roots may need watering occasionally. Use a fine rose on the can when doing so. Discard all roots after they have been forced in this way.

Rhubarb forcing pots are seldom seen these days. Instead, grape barrels or large boxes are used to force rhubarb roots on the bed. Pack straw or autumn leaves around the containers and exclude all light. If strawy, fermenting stable manure mixed with leaves is used, the heat generated will induce quicker growth. Roots forced in this fashion may be retained for future use, but should be allowed to rest from early April onwards.

Rodgersia (rod-ger-see-a)

Commemorating Admiral John Rodgers,

United States Navy (1812–82), commander of an expedition during which *Rodgersia podophylla* was discovered (*Saxifragaceae*). A genus of six species of hardy herbaceous perennials with scaly rhizomes. Handsome both in leaf and flower, the rodgersias are natives of China and Japan. They are ideal for waterside or wild gardens in shade or sun and are particularly appropriate where their striking and unusual foliage can be seen to good advantage.

Species cultivated *R. aesculifolia,* 3–4 feet, leaves deeply-cut, chestnut-like, up to 18 inches across, flowers blush-white, July. *R. pinnata,* 3–4 feet, leaves 5-lobed, handsome, often tinged bronze or crimson, flowers pink in branched panicles; vars. *alba,* flowers white; *superba,* a rare and much improved form with deep pink flowers and bronzed leaves. *R. podophylla,* Rodger's bronze leaf, 3–4 feet,

leaves palmately lobed, flowers in drooping panicles, buff-yellow, June or July. *R. sambucifolia,* 2–3 feet, leaves, pinnate, elder-like, flowers white in rather dense panicles. *R. tabularis,* unusual and decorative umbrella-like large apple-green leaves on stalks 2–3 feet high, flowers creamy-white in spikes 3–4 feet high, summer.

Cultivation Rodgersias require moist, deep, preferably peaty soil and a situation away from wind. Propagation is by seed or by division of the rhizomes in the spring; the latter method is particularly desirable when increasing cultivars of *R. pinnata* which have good flower or leaf colour.

Roses and their cultivation

Almost no garden subject has been written about at greater length, or with more enthusiasm, than roses and their

cultivation. Nevertheless, there is plenty that can be said on the matter, and the fact that roses grow easily in most parts of Britain only makes the keen gardener more than ever determined to think of everything in order to cultivate the flower to its greatest perfection.

Certainly roses will repay your attention. Whether they are grown on a fairly large scale, as, for example in the Italian rose garden at Trentham, Staffordshire, or in smaller groups in the home garden, roses provide tremendous pleasure at a reasonably small cost and minimal effort.

In an article which concentrates on the technical side of the subject it would be wrong to forget entirely the historical and romantic associations of the flower. Chaucer's *Romaunt of the Rose*, with its associations of courtly love, and the Scene in the Temple Garden, London, in Act II of Shakespeare's King Henry VI, Part 1, when the rival factions in the 'Wars of the Roses' plucked the red or the white rose, are just two examples of how the rose from the earliest times has come to symbolise the deepest feelings of countless men and women.

Modern roses fall mainly into the following groups: hybrid tea, floribunda, shrub, climbing and rambling, polyantha pompon and miniature.

Hybrid tea These include the large flowered, shapely bedding and exhibition roses, many with a strong fragrance. The group merges the few remaining hybrid perpetuals in general cultivation and what used to be known as 'Pernetianas', representing all the original pure yellow, orange, flame and bicolor varieties. The first hybrid tea varieties were obtained crossing the hybrid perpetuals with the tea-scented roses.

Hybrid Tea Roses are the most popular of all types of rose and new varieties are being added every year.
1 Hybrid Tea 'Super Star'.
2 Hybrid Tea 'Peace'.

Fifty first-class hybrid tea roses

Name	Habit of growth	Colour	Fragrance	Name	Habit of growth	Colour	Fragrance
Anne Watkins*	T/U	Apricot, shading to cream	S	Mischief*	T/B	Rich coral-salmon	S
Beauté	M	Light orange and apricot	S	Miss Ireland*	M	Orange-salmon, reverse peach	S
Belle Blonde	M/B	Deep tawny gold	M	Mme L. Laperrière	D	Dark crimson	M
Blue Moon	M	Lavender-mauve	R	Mojave*	T/U	Burnt orange and flame	S
Buccaneer*	T/U	Rich golden-yellow	S	Montezuma	T/B	Rich reddish-salmon	S
Caramba*	M/U	Crimson, with silver reverse	S	My Choice	M	Pale carmine-pink, reverse buff-yellow	R
Chrysler Imperial	M/U	Dark velvety crimson	R	Peace*	T/B	Light yellow, edged pink	S
Diorama*	M/B	Apricot yellow, flushed pink	M	Perfecta	T/U	Cream, shaded rosy red	S
Doreen*	M/B	Chrome-yellow, shaded orange	M	Piccadilly*	M/B	Scarlet, reverse yellow	S
Dorothy Peach*	M	Golden-yellow, shaded peach	S	Pink Favourite*	T/B	Deep rose-pink	S
Eden Rose*	T	Rose-madder, paler reverse	R	Prima Ballerina*	T/U	Deep carmine-rose	R
Ena Harkness*	M/B	Velvety scarlet-crimson	R	Rose Gaujard*	T/B	White, shaded carmine-red	S
Ernest H. Morse*	M/U	Rich turkey-red	R	Sarah Arnot	T	Deep rosy-pink	S
Fragrant Cloud*	M/B	Scarlet changing crimson-lake	R	Signora*	T	Flame, pink and orange shades	M
Gail Borden*	T/B	Peach and salmon, shaded gold	S	Silver Lining	M/U	Silvery rose, paler reverse	M
Gold Crown	T/U	Deep gold, shaded red	M	Spek's Yellow*	T/U	Rich golden-yellow	S
Grand'mère Jenny*	T/U	Light yellow and peach-pink	S	Stella	M/B	Carmine-pink, shading to white	S
Grandpa Dickson*	T/U	Lemon yellow, paling to cream	S	Sterling Silver	M/U	Lavender-mauve, shaded silver	R
Helen Traubel*	T	Pink and apricot blend	M	Summer Sunshine	T	Intense golden-yellow	S
Josephine Bruce	M/S	Dark velvety crimson	R	Super Star*	T	Light pure vermilion	M
Lady Belper	M	Light orange	M	Sutter's Gold*	T	Orange-yellow, shaded pink and red	R
La Jolla	M	Pink, cream and gold blend	S	Tzigane	M	Scarlet, reverse chrome-yellow	M
Lucy Cramphorn*	T/B	Geranium-red	S	Virgo	T/U	White, tinted pale pink	S
Margaret*	M/B	China-pink, paler reverse	M	Wendy Cussons*	M/B	Rich cerise	R
McGredy's Yellow*	M/U	Light yellow without shading	S	Westminster	T	Cherry-red, reverse gold	M

Key *Habit of growth* T=tall U=upright M=medium B=branching D=dwarf S=spreading
Fragrance S=slight M=moderate R=rich *Exceptionally good in autumn

There are hundreds of Hybrid Tea Roses from which to make a selection including dwarf and climbers. A few of the best are recommended on this page. It is now possible to find Hybrid Teas in almost any colour other than a true blue, or a green. All the following are Hybrid Tea varieties:
1 'Blue Moon'.
2 'Helen Traubel'.
3 'Ernest Morse'.
4 'McGredy's Yellow'.
5 'Miss Ireland'.
6 'Silver Lining'.
7 'Ena Harkness'.
8 'Margaret'.
9 'Piccadilly'.
10 'Grand'mère Jenny'.
11 'Lady Seton'.

Fifty first-class floribunda roses

Name	Habit of growth	Colour
Allgold	D	Rich golden-yellow
Anna Wheatcroft	M	Light vermilion
Arabian Nights	T	Deep salmon-red
Arthur Bell	T/U	Deep golden yellow, paling to cream
Chanelle	M	Peach and buff
Circus	M	Yellow, pink and red
Copper Delight	D	Bronze-yellow
Daily Sketch	T	Pink and cream
Dearest	T	Coral-rose
Dorothy Wheatcroft	T	Bright orange-scarlet
Elizabeth of Glamis	M	Light salmon
Elysium	T	Pale rose, shaded salmon
Evelyn Fison	M	Bright scarlet
Europeana	M	Deep blood-red to crimson
Faust	T	Yellow shaded pink
Fervid	T	Bright poppy red
Frensham	T	Scarlet-crimson
Golden Slippers	D	Orange and yellow shades
Golden Treasure	M/B	Deep yellow, non-fading
Goldgleam	M/B	Canary yellow, unfading
Gold Marie	T/S	Deep tawny gold, tinged red
Highlight	T	Orange-scarlet
Iceberg	T	White flushed pink
Joyfulness	M	Apricot shaded pink
Korona	T/U	Orange-scarlet, fading deep salmon
Lilac Charm	D/B	Silvery lilac, single flower
Lilli Marlene	M	Scarlet-crimson
Lucky Charm	M	Yellow, pink and red
Manx Queen	M	Orange-yellow shaded pink
Masquerade	M	Yellow, changing to pink and red
Meteor	D	Orange-scarlet
Orangeade	M	Orange-vermilion
Orange Sensation	M	Vermilion-scarlet
Paddy McGredy	D/B	Deep carmine-pink
Paprika	M	Bright turkey-red
Pernille Poulsen	D/B	Salmon-pink, fading lighter
Pink Parfait	M	Pastel shades of pink and cream
Queen Elizabeth	T/U	Rose-pink
Red Dandy	M	Scarlet-crimson, large flowers
Red Favourite	D	Dark crimson
Rumba	M	Orange-yellow, edged scarlet
Ruth Leuwerik	D	Bright scarlet shaded crimson
Scented Air	T/B	Rich salmon-pink
Shepherd's Delight	T/U	Scarlet, flame and orange
Sweet Repose	T	Soft pink shaded apricot
Tambourine	T/U	Cherry-red, reverse orange-yellow
Toni Lander	M/U	Coppery salmon-red
Vera Dalton	M	Medium rose-pink
Violet Carson	M	Peach-pink, reverse silvery pink
Woburn Abbey	T	Tangerine-orange and yellow
Zambra	D	Rich orange and yellow

Key T=tall   M=medium   D=dwarf   S=spreading
U=upright   B=exceptionally branching

Floribunda These include all the original hybrid polyanthas evolved by the rose breeder Svend Poulson of Denmark. He crossed poly-pompons with hybrid teas, and all the many-flowered roses (other than the poly-pompons), the climbing and rambling groups and the Pemberton, so-called 'hybrid musks'. The term 'hybrid polyantha' was discontinued soon after the Second World War, because varieties were being added to the group each year with little or no true polyantha 'blood', resulting from crossing hybrid teas with various groups of shrub roses.

Shrub This group covers a very wide range of modern hybrids of species and also includes all the old types of garden roses, often referred to as 'old-fashioned' roses.

Climbing and rambling Practically all rambling and climbing roses derive from the Synstylae section of the genus. They include hybrid tea climbing sports.

Polyantha pompon These have largely

A wide selection of Floribunda Roses is available for garden decoration:
1 'Iceberg'.
2 'Queen Elizabeth'.
3 'Daily Sketch'.
4 'Ambrosia'.
5 'Irish Mist'.
6 'Arthur Bell'.
7 'Sweet Repose'.
8 'Zambra'.
9 'Evelyn Fison'.
10 'Telstar'.

been superseded by modern floribundas and the miniatures. They are compact-growing, cluster-flowered bedding roses, with small rosette type flowers similar in appearance to those of the old wichuraiana ramblers.

Miniature These are tiny replicas of the hybrid teas and floribundas, with flowers, foliage and growth scaled down in proportion. They are mainly hybrids from *R. chinensis minima* and may never exceed 6–12 inches in height.

Selecting and ordering It is important to order your roses early in the season, that is between June and August, when most of the rose shows are held. During this period the roses may be seen in flower at the nurseries and by ordering promptly you can be sure of the most popular varieties being available.

It is advisable to order from a rose specialist, and from one who buds his own plants, rather than from a man who is not a producer. This is because the grower selling under his own name has a reputation to maintain, and no well-known rose specialist can afford to sell plants which do not give satisfaction. When you visit the nursery, or display garden adjoining it, watch for the habit of growth, disease and weather resistance and freedom of flowering of any of the species provisionally selected.

There is a great deal of variation in the quality of maiden rose plants supplied from various sources, and cheap offers are often the dearest in the long run, as the quality is normally very inferior. Bearing in mind that a healthy rose, when once properly planted, may last from 12 to 20 years or more, with reasonable treatment, it is false economy to attempt to save a few shillings on the initial cost when this may mean the difference between success and failure. It is essential to obtain plants from a reliable source. This is because of the need for them to be hardy and well-ripened, true to name, budded on a suitable rootstock which will transplant readily and not sucker freely and free from disease spores.

Bare root roses are sometimes still on offer in overheated departmental stores, but nowadays these are normally offered packed in individual polythene bags. The trouble with these roses is that they are frequently subjected to this overheated atmosphere for considerable periods, with consequent dehydration showing in bone-dry roots and shrivelled stems. A rose purchased in this condition is unlikely to flourish unless measures are taken to plump up the wood again by burying the entire plant for about ten days in moist soil, before planting it in its permanent quarters. Another disadvantage of these pre-packaged roses is that each package acts as a miniature greenhouse, and the stems are forced into tender premature growth while they are awaiting sale. This tender growth receives a severe check when the plants are taken out of their packages and exposed to the hazards of the open garden.

Container-grown roses are offered at many nurseries and garden centres. These enable the planting season to be extended throughout the year, as no root disturbance should occur in planting from containers into the permanent beds. They may even be planted when in full bloom.

Although it is unwise to succumb to

1 When Roses are purchased in containers for planting from autumn to early spring, the growths should be cut back to within a few inches of ground level.
2 Slitting the container after the hole has been dug to receive the plant.
3 The roots should be spread out and fine soil worked among them before the soil is firmed with the feet.

cheap offers in end-of-season sales, nearly all rose specialist firms offer collections, their selection of varieties, at an all-in price lower than the aggregate cost of ordering the same varieties individually. For the beginner who is not fussy about varieties he starts with, provided that they are popular, this is as good a way as any of placing a first order, as the quality of the plants should be equal to the nurseryman's normal standard.

Soil Ordinary well-drained soil which has grown good crops of vegetables will suit most roses. Ideally a medium heavy loam, slightly acid (pH 5.5 to 6.5) is best. The site should be open and away from large trees and buildings, but not in a draughty position between two houses. On poor soils plenty of old chopped turf, compost, hay and straw and vegetable waste should be added to the subsoil when preparing the beds by double digging, together with any animal manure available. The top spit will be improved by adding granulated peat, compost and bonemeal (at the rate of 4 ounces per square yard) and hoof and horn meal (at 2 ounces per square yard). These should be thoroughly mixed with the soil and not left on the surface or in layers. On heavy land the beds should be raised a few inches above the general level, but sunk slightly on sandy soil. Perfect drainage is vitally important.

Planning and design The planning of a rose garden is essentially a matter of personal choice depending on individual requirements. The first question to settle is whether the layout is large enough to take roses grown in beds and borders on their own, or whether the roses must fit in with other plants in mixed borders. In a formal rose garden there are separate beds for individual varieties, whether of hybrid tea or floribunda type. These beds are cut in lawns with the possible inclusion of several standard or half standard roses of the same variety to give added height.

Although well-kept turf is the best setting for roses it involves a great deal of labour to maintain in first-class condition and it is always advisable to have at least one dry path crossing the rose garden, so that barrowing can be done in wet weather without cutting up the turf. Crazy paving or formal stone paving slabs are best for this dry path, with cement run between the crazy paving stones to provide a firm surface and to reduce the labour of weeding. Normally rose beds about 5 feet wide are to be preferred to rose borders against a wall or fence, on the grounds of accessibility for weeding, pruning and cultivation generally. A bed of this width will accommodate three rows of plants, 18 inches between the rows with 1 foot at each side between the outside rows and the edge. This will be sufficient to

A bold and satisfactory effect is always obtained from Roses when varieties are planted in groups.

avoid an overhang with nearly all varieties, which would otherwise interfere with mowing and trimming the edges, if the setting is grass.

The shape of the rose beds is a matter for personal taste, but a simple design is normally best, and it involves less labour for maintenance. It should always be borne in mind that numerous small beds cut in a lawn, apart from looking fussy, require the edges trimming regularly and also slow down the operation of mowing the lawn.

Few amateurs can afford the space to have beds confined to one variety, but mixed beds should be selected carefully, and the varieties chosen for either tasteful colour blending or for similar habit of growth. Alternatively, the centre of the bed should be planted with a variety of taller growth and the perimeter with one of more compact habit. It is far better to plant six or more of the same variety in a group than to dot them about in ones and twos, and this holds good whether beds or borders are being planted.

In a rose border or a mixed border featuring roses and other plants, bold groups are essential for maximum display. In a deep rose border, the grading of groups of varieties according to height will be desirable, with the tallest at the back, although monotony may be avoided by breaking up the gradings with an occasional group of taller varieties running towards the front, or a single pillar or tripod with recurrent-flowering climbing roses about the middle.

Colour grouping with roses is again a matter of personal taste. Some people delight in the extreme contrast between a pure scarlet and a deep golden yellow, whereas others might find this garish, and prefer colour harmonies in blends of soft pink, apricot and orange shades. Some may prefer to group the same, or similar, colours together. The object of colour blending, of course, is to bring out the best in each colour by careful association of adjacent colours. Thus, white and orange-scarlet next to each other will emphasise, by contrast, the purity of the white and the brilliance of the orange-scarlet. On the other hand, orange-scarlet next to deep carmine pink would be an unhappy combination, as the blue in the carmine pink would look crude and harsh by contrast with the orange-scarlet.

As a general guide shades of yellow will associate well with shades of red. Orange, flame and apricot contrast well with dark crimson. Deep pink, especially carmine pink and cerise, is safest with cream, primrose yellow or white, and the same is true of lilac, lavender and mauve. These shades in roses are often dull in the garden and may need enlivening with bright yellow close by. Scarlet, orange-scarlet, crimson, deep pink and cerise are better separated from each

other by using buffer groups of the soft pastel shades of cream, flesh, amber and off-white.

The question of whether to use other plants for carpeting rose beds often arises, bearing in mind that the roses do not normally provide much colour until June. Violas as ground cover or border plants add colour in the spring. Low growing plants, such as aubrieta, arabis and the 'mossy' saxifrages may also be used for edgings, but they will need shearing back after flowering. There is no reason either why shallow-rooted annuals should not be used, such as eschscholtzias, love-in-a-mist and night-scented stocks.

Slow growing conifers may also be used for effect. These have the advantage of being evergreens, and will improve the appearance of the rose garden, although the rank growers should be avoided. The Irish juniper, *Juniperus communis hibernica*, is excellent and takes up little space with its narrow, erect growth. The same is true of *Chamaecyparis lawsoniana columnaris glauca* in blue-grey, and the Irish yews, *Taxus baccata fastigiata*, and the golden *aurea*. Two very splendid slow-growing forms are *Chamaecyparis lawsoniana ellwoodii* and *fletcherii*. Both of these will remain below or about 5 feet in height for many years. Clematis may also be planted either by themselves or with recurrent

flowering pillar roses, and will often be outstanding, introducing colours not found among roses. *Clematis jackmanii* in rich violet-purple will make a splendid pillar when planted with roses 'New Dawn' or 'Aloha'.

Planting This may be done safely from late October to the end of March whenever the soil is friable and free from frost. Autumn planting usually gives the best results, provided the soil is not too wet for planting firmly; otherwise it will be better to wait for suitable conditions. On receipt of the bushes they should be heeled in temporarily in a trench, throwing plenty of soil over the roots and treading firmly. When the soil in the bed is friable, a large bucket of moist granulated peat, into which a couple of handfuls of meat and bonemeal have been mixed, should be prepared. The position of each bush

1 When preparing to plant Roses mark out the area to show the positions.
2 Take out one hole at a time deep enough to ensure that the union of stock and scion is at soil level.
3 Spread out the roots.
4 Fill the hole with fine soil and work it well round the roots.
5 Firm the area around the bush and cut back the growth to a few inches.
6 A stout stake is inserted in the ground before planting a standard Rose.

in the bed is marked with a stick. Distance apart will depend on the vigour and habit of the variety, but on an average soil about 18 inches each way will be about right for most. Exceptionally vigorous kinds, such as 'Peace', which need light pruning, may be better at least 2 feet apart. The roots should be soaked for a couple of hours before planting. A shallow hole is taken out wide enough to take roots when fully spread. The plant should be inspected carefully for suckers emerging from the root system, and any found should be pulled off. Damaged and broken roots must be trimmed and unripe or damaged shoots removed, also all leaves and flower buds. The prepared plant is then tested in the hole for correct depth; the union of the stock and scion should be just covered with soil. A few handfuls of the peat mixture are thrown over and between the roots and the hole half filled with fine soil and trodden firmly before filling up to the correct level. Standard roses are staked before covering the roots to avoid possible injury. It is beneficial to mulch new beds with 2 inches of granulated peat, to conserve moisture.

Pruning All dead or decadent wood should be cut out as soon as it is noticed at any time. Full-scale pruning should be done when the bushes are dormant, or nearly so. This may be done at any

1

3

5

2

4

6

184

time from January to mid-March, depending on the weather and the area. In the first spring after planting all groups, except climbing sports of hybrid tea roses, should have weak or twiggy shoots removed entirely, together with any sappy growth. The remainder should be cut back just above a dormant shoot bud pointing away from the centre of the plant and not more than 6 inches from the base. Spring planted roses may be pruned in the hand just before planting. Climbing sports of hybrid teas should just be tipped and the main shoots bent over by securing the ends to canes or wires, to force the lower buds into growth. On light hungry soils it may be advisable not to prune any groups the first year, but to encourage as much new growth as possible by mulching and watering.

1 The head of a standard Rose before pruning with twiggy and dead wood.
2 After pruning, when the growth has been tidied up.
3 The pruning of climbing Roses varies with the group to which they belong, but dormant buds can be encouraged to grow by cutting back the laterals.
4 Pruning a newly-planted climbing Rose by shortening the long growths.
5 Pruning a newly-planted bush Rose by cutting the growth down to within a few inches of ground level.

1

2

4

3

5

1 An overgrown rambler Rose much in need of pruning.
2 Dead shoots are cut away, together with old flowered growths and very thin, unwanted shoots. The work is best carried out in late summer immediately after flowering is over.
3 Cutting down the old canes.

Subsequent years Pruning of hybrid teas may be hard, moderate or light, according to circumstances. Light pruning is generally preferable on poor sandy soils which do not encourage a lot of new wood. This means cutting back new shoots formed in the previous season to about two-thirds of their length and removing all weak or twiggy growth. On average soils moderate pruning may be done, involving cutting back all new wood about half way and removing entirely the weak and twiggy shoots. Hard pruning is seldom necessary for modern varieties, but some will respond to it on a good soil with ample feeding. It requires the cutting out of all but two or three of the main growths and reducing these to just above a dormant bud about 6 inches from the base.

Floribundas require different treatment. The object is to ensure as continuous a display of colour during the season as possible. This requires the application of a differential pruning system, based on the age of the wood. Growth produced from the base in the previous season should merely be shortened to the first convenient bud below the old flower truss. The laterals on two-year-old wood should be cut back half way and any three-year-old

wood cut hard back to about three eyes from the base. As with all groups, all dead, decadent, unripe and twiggy wood should be removed entirely.

Shrub roses and the old garden roses in general do not require much pruning. Apart from the cutting out of dead and exhausted wood and cutting back a main growth near the base occasionally to encourage new basal growth, pruning is mainly confined to remedying overcrowding and ensuring a shapely outline.

The treatment of climbers varies with the group to which they belong. Generally, the more recurrent flowering

the variety, the less rampant is its growth and the less the pruning required. The once-flowering wichuraiana ramblers, which renew themselves with new canes from the base each season after flowering, should have all old flowering wood cut out and the new canes tied in to take its place. Climbing sports of hybrid teas and other climbing hybrid teas require little pruning, but should be trained fanwise or horizontally to force as many dormant eyes into growth as possible. Flowers are borne either on laterals or sub-laterals. Recurrent flowering pillar roses, such as 'Aloha', 'Coral

1 The new canes are tied in carefully.
2 Rambling Roses can be trained horizontally over beds to provide a good cover. The long growths are tied down to pegs in the ground.
3 Removing dead flowerheads.
4 A complete rose fertiliser should be applied during April.

Dawn' and 'Parade', require only the removal of dead or exhausted wood and any which is weak or twiggy, plus sufficient thinning out of the remaining wood to avoid overcrowding.

General cultivation Suckers must be removed before they grow large. They may come from any point below the inserted bud and with standards they may appear either on the standard stem below the head or anywhere on the root system. The roots of roses should not be disturbed any more than is essential to the removal of weeds and suckers.

Where light or moderate pruning is practised, summer thinning or de-shooting may be necessary, and this will be routine procedure for the keen exhibitor. All side shoots appearing before the terminal buds have opened should be pinched out as soon as they are large enough to handle. While watering is not a practical proposition on a large scale, newly planted roses may need the roots soaking thoroughly at weekly intervals during hot weather. Roses planted in dry positions, against walls or close-boarded fences, will also require regular watering in the summer.

Removal of spent flowers is essential if a later crop is to be produced and seed pods should never be allowed to develop. Dead-heading should be a routine operation throughout the season. In the first summer after planting merely the flower and foot of the stalk, without any leaves, should be removed, but in subsequent years the growth from the pruning point may be reduced to half way, to ensure a fine second display. Disbudding will also be necessary for the keen exhibitor and those who insist on high quality blooms. Not more than three buds are left on hybrid tea stems for garden display or a single bud for exhibition. In the autumn any long growths should be shortened to minimise possible gale damage.

Feeding Before embarking on a feeding programme you should find out whether your soil is naturally acid or alkaline. There are a number of soil-testing kits available. Lime, if required, is best applied in the form of ground chalk (calcium carbonate) during the early winter months, at 3 or 4 ounces per square yard, sprinkled evenly over the surface of the beds and left for the winter rains to wash it down. By the time the spring mulch is due, the lime should have done its work. As roses prefer a

slightly acid soil, it may be necessary to apply lime every year, though never on chalky soil

During February and March it is beneficial to apply a dressing of meat and bonemeal at 4 ounces per square yard, pricking it just below the surface. If this proves difficult to obtain in small quantities sterilised bonemeal may be used instead. About the middle of April a complete rose fertiliser can be applied to established beds, according to the makers' instructions. There are many of these available, or a useful compound fertiliser may be made up quite cheaply from 16 parts of superphosphate of lime, 10 parts of sulphate of potash, 5 parts of sulphate of ammonia, 2 parts of sulphate of magnesia (commercial Epsom Salts) and 2 parts of sulphate of iron. These parts are in terms of weight, and the ingredients must be mixed thoroughly, any lumps being crushed. The fertiliser should be sprinkled evenly at about a *level* tablespoonful per plant, afterwards hoeing and watering in if necessary. The temptation to use a double dose in the hope of obtaining spectacular results should be resisted.

Alternatively, for those who do not wish to go to much trouble, many firms market a rose fertiliser to the well-known 'Tonks' formula, which was based originally on the chemical analysis of the ashes of a complete rose tree

1 Peat used as a summer mulch round rose bushes to conserve moisture.
2 Peat being worked into the soil prior to planting Roses.
3 Around the middle of May a mulch of animal manure is applied.

after burning it in a crucible. The formula comprises 12 parts of superphosphate of lime, 10 parts of nitrate of potash, 8 parts of sulphate of lime, 2 parts of sulphate of magnesia and 1 part of sulphate of iron. It should be applied at the rate of 3 or 4 ounces per square yard and pricked in with a border fork.

About the middle of May, when the soil will have started to warm up, a mulch of animal manure or, if this is unobtainable, compost, granulated peat,

leafmould or spent hops should be applied evenly to the beds, preferably 2 inches deep. If peat, leafmould or spent hops are used they should be well moistened and fortified with a further application of the compound rose fertiliser, at the same rate as in mid-April. It is a good plan to wash this in with a hose jet applied at pressure to the mulch. The keen grower, with ambitions to produce excellent specimen blooms, may wish to try liquid stimulants from the stage of bud formation. Apart from liquid animal manures, which should *always* be applied in very dilute form (no stronger than a pale straw colour) and at intervals of ten days or so, soot water and soluble blood are useful nitrogenous fertilisers. Nitrate of potash (at $\frac{1}{2}$ ounce per gallon) and superphosphate of lime (at 1 ounce per gallon) may also be used safely at these strengths. The important points to watch in liquid feeding are: to use the feed in very dilute form only; to ensure that there is already plenty of moisture in the soil before applying and to discontinue application at the end of July.

About the end of August, especially in a wet season, it is a good plan to apply a dressing of sulphate of potash to the rose beds at the rate of 3 ounces per square yard. This will help to ripen and harden the wood in readiness for the winter. It should be pricked in along with what

remains of the mid-May mulch.

Pests Rose pests should be tackled in the early stages before damage becomes widespread. Common pests include caterpillars of all types, the rose slugworm sawfly and leaf rolling sawfly.

Caterpillars These cause the familiar 'holed' appearance of leaves and indented leaf edges. Both leaves and stems should be sprayed with an approved insecticide from early May onwards, as soon as the first symptoms of caterpillar attacks appear.

Rose slugworm sawfly The leaves take on a skeletonised appearance, which is the result of feeding by the yellowish larvae on the green leaf tissue. They are controlled by spraying in the same way as caterpillars.

Leaf rolling sawfly The leaves become rolled downwards and inwards. The maggot feeds on the tissue inside the rolled leaf. Pressing these leaves and then pulling them off and burning them seems to be the only fully effective treatment, but encouraging results can be obtained by spraying with trichlorphon at least three times between mid-May and mid-June.

Tortrix moth The leaves folded inward show the presence of the larva, which may be brownish or green. Pressing the folded leaves between the finger and thumb, and then pulling them off and burning them is the only really effective treatment.

Shoot borer sawfly The tip of a young shoot will sometimes wilt, though lower down the growth seems healthy. The brownish maggot of this sawfly bores down inside the shoot, feeding on the pith. Pressure applied just below the drooping tip will often cause the maggot to wriggle out backwards. Growing points should be sprayed or dusted with an approved insecticide from early May at fortnightly intervals.

Chafer Beetle Typical damage consists of flower buds eaten on one side only in early summer. The larvae feed on the rose roots in light soils, especially in the Home Counties. Top growth should be sprayed regularly as soon as the first symptoms are noticed. Where the damage is extensive, an appropriate insecticide should be forked into the soil near the bushes to a depth of 6 inches to destroy the larvae.

Rose leafhopper Pale mottled areas on leaves in May and June are caused by the small yellowish nymphs sucking the sap. The undersides of leaves and the soil beneath should be sprayed early in May with malathion or gamma-BHC.

Greenfly The familiar colonies are to be seen on tender growing points of young

**1 Rose Slugworm Sawfly larvae, and the damage caused by them.
2 The distinctive mottling of the leaves of Roses attacked by Rose Leafhopper.
3 Aphids, or Greenfly, are the commonest pests of Roses.**

1 The pale green Capsid Bug causes
punctures on and distortion of Rose
leaves, as well as browning of the buds.
2 A Cuckoo Spit Insect emerging from
the frothy 'spit' deposited on the leaf.
3 Powdery mildew, a disease of Roses.

shoots, on the undersides of leaves and
below the flower buds and on the footstalks. They suck the sap and multiply at
an alarming rate. Any of the proprietary
contact sprays, other than DDT, may be
used, applying with a mist-like spray to
ensure full coverage over both surfaces
of leaves. A follow-up spray should be
applied about three days later.

Thrips Early flowers may develop with
blackened or stained petal edges, pre-
senting a withered or scorched appearance. Leaves may also be mottled and
marbled. Foliage, buds and opening
flowers are best sprayed in May with
either derris or malathion.

Capsid bug Withered young flower buds
and punctured and distorted foliage,
sometimes with brown areas round the
punctures, show the presence of nymphs
of the green capsid bug. They are active
and drop to the soil or hide beneath a
leaf at the first sign of danger. Early in
the season the growing points, foliage
and soil beneath the plants should be
sprayed with gamma-BHC (Lindane) or
dusted with pyrethrum extract.

Cuckoo spit insect (frog hopper) The yellowish-green nymphs conceal themselves
inside the frothy 'spit', usually found at
the leaf axils, and suck the sap. A coarse
spray applied at pressure, using derris,
pyrethrum or malathion, controls them.

Diseases The three main rose diseases
are black spot, rust and mildew. The
first two will rarely affect roses grown
in industrial or built-up areas.

Powdery mildew This disease may affect

190

1 Black Spot is a disease of Roses caused by the fungus Diplocarpon rosae. **2** The disease known as Rose Rust may affect both leaves and stems.

all areas. Roses planted in a dry spot or in a draughty bed between two houses, or near a brick wall or a dense hedge seem particularly prone to the disease. It is a surface fungus only, which does not invade the tissue of the leaf. Spraying the upper and under surfaces of the leaves at the first sign with a recognised mildew specific will control the disease, or a dilute solution of washing soda (1 ounce of crystals to 1 gallon of soft water, together with a little liquid soap to act as a spreader) may be used instead.

Black spot In rural areas black spot seems to be present in greater or lesser degree every season. Once the black spots have appeared, that leaf cannot be cured. The spots have fringed edges, are quite black and gradually increase in size until several may merge to form a completely black area of irregular shape. The remainder of the leaf turns yellow and is shed prematurely. This disease is controlled by regular preventive spraying, which provides a protective coating over the leaf surface. Maneb 80 and captan preparations, such as orthocide or zineb, are mostly favoured nowadays and should be made up exactly to the makers' instructions. Picking off and burning leaves bearing the ominous black spots in the early stages will help to control the disease, but preventive spraying at fortnightly intervals, avoiding overcrowding, and proper pruning are the best answer. Trees which have suffered from a severe attack should be pruned fairly hard the following winter and sprayed with copper sulphate solution (1 ounce of copper sulphate to 1 gallon of water). Any leaves which have fallen on the beds should be raked up and burnt during the winter.

Rose rust This is the most serious rose disease, but fortunately the spores seem unable to flourish in industrial and built-up areas. The disease may be identified by the orange coloured pustules (uredospores) appearing on the undersides of the leaves from June onwards; these show as yellow patches on the upper surface. Later in the season the over-wintering teleutospores are produced. These are black, thick-walled spores which remain on the undersides of the leaves or winter on the wood and carry the disease forward to the following season. The thread-like mycelium of the fungus beneath the bark of shoots will also carry the disease over, and in advanced cases vertical cracks will appear in the wood which will have a scarred appearance.

As with black spot preventive spraying is the only effective control. Just after pruning, the dormant wood should be sprayed with a copper preparation, such as Bordeaux mixture. When the leaves are unfolding and following this at about fortnightly intervals, and also after heavy rain, protective spraying with maneb or zineb, at the rate of $\frac{3}{4}$ ounce per gallon of soft water, will be necessary in gardens where rust has been troublesome before. The leaves should be well covered with the solution, paying particular attention to the underneath. Leaves showing the orange-coloured pustules should be removed and burnt, as should any fallen leaves.

Propagating *Seed* Roses may be raised from seed, but as modern hybrid teas and floribundas have such a complex ancestry, they do not come true, and the vast majority of seedlings will be inferior to their parents. Raising from seed is usually only done by raisers of new varieties, who deliberately cross two selected parents under controlled conditions. Nevertheless there is nothing very difficult about raising roses from seed. People often express surprise that it is quite easy to have a rose in flower in three months after sowing the seed. The great difficulty is not to flower rose seedlings, but to raise a really good one of commercial value.

Many of the cluster-flowered groups will provide a source of interest to amateurs interested in growing from seed. Three groups which are recommended for the beginner are the Pemberton hybrid musks, the hybrid rugosas and the miniature roses, the seed of which is sometimes offered under the heading of 'Fairy Roses'. The heps (or hips) may be gathered as late in the autumn as is safe before severe frosts, usually up to mid-October, and stored under cover in a box or a flower pot filled with a mixture of moist peat and sand or just sand until March. Then rub them between the palms of the hands,

when you will find that the seeds will separate from the pulp. The seed may be sown in March in pots, seed pans or boxes of good compost—say John Innes No 1. They should be spaced 1 inch apart each way and covered with ½ inch of soil, finishing off with a sprinkling of sharp sand. A high temperature is not desirable —between 50° and 60°F (10–16°C) is about right. Germination is irregular and uncertain and the individual seedlings may be transferred to thumb pots when one true leaf has developed. Some will flower on tiny plants before the end of June and may be transplanted outside if of attractive colouring.

An alternative method, just as easy, is

Rose hips are prepared for seed sowing by stratification in pots.
1 Placing Rose hips on moist sand.
2 A further layer of sand is added.
3 The sand is firmed by hand.
4 A cross-section showing the hips.

to sow the seed in shallow drills out of doors, applying a dressing of moist granulated peat to the surface to avoid too rapid drying out of the soil. Some of the seedlings will not flower until the second or third season, and these usually develop a climbing habit.

Cuttings These may be taken of the stronger groups, notably the wichuraiana ramblers, some of the old shrub

roses and the most vigorous floribundas. Ripe growths of the current season are selected in September, shortened to 9 inches by rejecting unripe ends and all but two leaves at the top are removed. The cuttings thus prepared are placed upright in a narrow trench, about 6 inches deep, to which coarse sand has been added. The trench is filled in and the cuttings made firm, leaving the top 3 inches above the surface. They are left undisturbed for at least the whole of the following season, apart from watering and weeding, as necessary. Layering may also be successfully employed with the stronger growing climbing, rambling and shrub types.

192

Budding or grafting roses Some of the most vigorous hybrid teas and floribundas may be grown on their own roots from cuttings, but most roses make better plants, and in a shorter time, when budded or grafted on a suitable rootstock. There is a range of such stocks used, mostly species or selected strains of such. In this country the seedling briar *(R. canina)* is the most popular, as it thrives on most soils, transplants well, has a long life and is hardy. There are also many selected strains of *R. canina* used to ensure greater uniformity or comparative freedom from thorns or other characteristics, as well as *R. multiflora* and *R. rugosa,* the latter being largely used for standard rose stems.

Budding is carried out in early summer when the sap is running freely in both rootstock and cultivar. For bush and climbing forms a 'T' cut is made in the bark of the stock at or about soil level, with the vertical cut not more than an inch long. The two flaps of bark are then carefully raised with the handle of the budding knife, to enable a shoot bud of the selected cultivar, suitably prepared on its own shield of bark, to be pushed down behind the flaps to the bottom of the cut, so that the bud faces outwards. The top of the shield of bark on the bud is then trimmed flush with the top of the 'T' cut and the bud tied in securely with raffia or fastened with a plastic tie.

The preparation of the shield of bark, carrying an 'eye' or shoot bud, is the part which usually causes most difficulty. This must be in the correct stage of development—not too ripe and not immature. Usually a stem carrying a terminal flower which is just about ready to shed its petals will provide suitable material. The stem should be cut about 8 or 9 inches below the flower, and the flower and footstalk cut away, leaving the stem with perhaps three leaves. The leaves are cut off about half an inch from the main stem, leaving this length of leaf stalk to facilitate handling of the bud, which may be identified as a tiny nob at the angle between the stalk and the main stem. There will then be three buds, each with half an inch of stalk attached, and the centre bud of these three is most likely to be in the right stage of development.

The object is to remove the bud with a shield of bark about 1 inch long with the bud as its centre, without cutting so deeply into the wood that the bud is injured in the process of removing the piece of wood behind it. It is best to use a special budding knife, which has a single blade and a smooth bone handle which tapers to a point at the end, this point being used for lifting the bark of the rootstock before inserting the bud on its shield. Starting half an inch above the bud make a cut gradually going deeper so that it is deepest just behind the bud. Then reduce the depth so that the knife blade emerges about half an

1 A T-cut is made in the stock with a sharp budding knife.
2 The bud is prepared and the pith removed from behind the bud of the scion.
3 The prepared bud is slipped into place behind the two flaps of the T-shaped cut, and pushed firmly down.
4 The union is bound with tape.

inch beyond the bud. There will then be a boat-shaped piece of bark carrying an eye or shoot bud, with a small piece of stalk attached and with a thin slice of wood behind the bark and the bud. This wood must be removed without injuring the bud, and this is best done in two

stages. Holding the shield with the thumb nail of one hand pressed hard against the wood behind the bud, with the first finger and thumb of the other hand separate the wood and bark above the bud, using the blade of the knife to give a start. A sudden sideways snatch will remove this wood without damaging the bud, which is protected by the thumbnail of the other hand. Reverse the shield and proceed similarly with the other half, and then trim the base of the shield flat with a cross cut, ready for insertion behind the bark of the rootstock.

All of this may sound rather involved, but with a little practice it becomes automatic. Speed is essential to a successful union, as the cambium layer is very thin and must not be allowed to dry—otherwise failure is certain.

If the shield and the bud remain green, nothing more is done until the following February, when the whole of the top growth is cut away immediately above the inserted bud, which should start to grow in late March or April. In the one season this will make the maiden plant as sold by the rose nurseryman.

Standard roses are formed by inserting two or three buds in the main stem of rugosa stocks at the desired height, or in the case of canina stems, into two or three laterals of the current season's growth. All non-budded growth is removed in the following February and the budded laterals shortened to about 6 inches. The maiden growth will need tying to small canes as it develops, or pinching back to reduce the need for staking and to encourage a bushy head.

Grafting, as distinct from budding, which is a form of shield grafting, is normally done under glass and is often resorted to by nurserymen in order to work up a stock of a new variety.

Simple hybridisation New commercial varieties are produced by the cross-pollination of two chosen parents under carefully controlled conditions. The resultant seeds are sown and grown on. The weather in this country is such that it is wiser to make the cross in a greenhouse, so that the hips or seed pods will become sufficiently ripe before the cold weather.

Much thought is devoted to the choice of parents. The seed parent must be a variety which sets seeds freely, and one that flowers at the same time as the chosen pollen parent—otherwise it may not be possible to make the cross at all. Such qualities as freedom of flowering, disease resistance, vigour, weather resistance and attractive foliage are taken into consideration when selecting parents, although it does not follow that because both parents have these excellent qualities, the progeny will necessarily inherit them. Very often the undesirable qualities tend to be dominant and reveal themselves in subsequent generations.

Having decided on the parents, it is usual to lift plants in the autumn and to pot them into 8-inch or 10-inch pots, according to their size, trimming the roots to fit into the pot. Sufficient heat

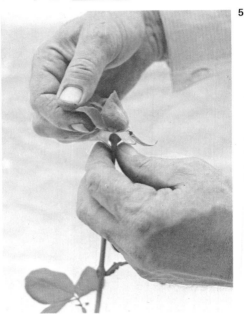

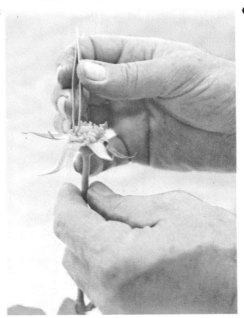

1 New varieties of Roses are produced by cross-pollination of selected parents. *Left* **The pollen parent and** *right* **the seed parent.**
2 Remove petals from the seed parent.
3 Remove anthers from the same flower, thus emasculating it.
4 and 5 The pollen is transferred from the pollen parent on to the stigma of the seed parent either by brush or by direct contact.
6 Label the parents, seed and pollen.

should be turned on to exclude frost, and flowers should be available towards the end of May when plenty of sunshine may reasonably be expected for cross-pollination, which should take place preferably on a sunny day. Not later than the half-open stage, the flower of the seed parent should have the petals pulled off one at a time, making sure that no small portion remains to set up decay. The flower should then be emasculated by removing all the anthers to prevent self-pollination. A small pair of nail scissors or tweezers may be used.

The stigma of the chosen seed parent remains, and if there are any insects about, this should be covered with a polythene or paper cap to prevent chance pollination. The stigma should be ready to receive the pollen by the following day, when it will be seen to be shiny and sticky. The best method of transferring the pollen of the male parent is directly from the anthers of the male flower, holding the petals well back to ensure that the stigma receives a generous dusting of the pollen. After this, replace the cap at once and tie a small label to the footstalk of the seed parent, giving particulars of the cross, with the seed parent named first, e.g., 'Ena Harkness' x 'Margaret'. If all goes well the pollen will germinate and pollen tubes will grow down to the ovary inside the seed pod, there fertilising the ovum in the ovule to form an embryo. The seed pod will swell and begin to change colour in the autumn, when it should be cut off with a couple of inches of footstalk for after-ripening. This involves storing the pods in a mixture of moist peat and sand for at least three months, usually outside in a mouse-proof container.

By about February the fleshy part of the seed pod will have rotted, and the seeds can be separated easily by rubbing the pods between the palms of the hands. The seeds may be tested in water for viability, those that sink, the 'sinkers', normally being regarded as fertile, and those that float, the 'floaters', being considered unlikely to germinate. The sinkers should be sown straight away in John Innes potting compost No 1, in pots, pans or boxes, ½ inch deep and 1 inch apart each way. The surface should be firmed with a piece of flat board and a good sprinkling of coarse sharp sand applied to discourage moss. A watering through a fine rose completes the operation. A temperature of 55° to 60°F (13–16°C) is suitable and better than a higher temperature. Germination will be irregular and the first seedlings are usually through in about six weeks. Some seeds may remain dormant until the second season or even later.

It is usual to pot up the seedlings into individual thumb pots when the first true leaf has developed, and to grow them on under glass until they flower. Many will be discarded at this stage, but a few may show some promise, either in colour or fragrance. The most promising seedlings are usually budded on small rootstocks outside, and it is only after being grown in this way for several seasons that the merits and faults of a seedling can be accurately assessed.

Exhibiting The rose is not always as easy as other flowers for exhibiting, as it may conform to show standards for but a very short time in hot weather. Pruning should be undertaken towards the end of March for a show in the latter part of June. In the specimen bloom classes, large flowers of good form, young and fresh, with firm petals of thick substance, are necessary. The colour should be rich and typical and the centre conical or spiral, high pointed, with two rows of outside petals reflexing to form a background. The petals should be free from insect holes and other blemishes; flowers with split, quartered or confused centres are useless for showing. In classes for 'decorative' roses size is less important, but brilliance of colour, freshness, perfection of form (HT) or truss (floribunda) are required, as well as tasteful and pleasing arrangement and healthy foliage.

Pruning, feeding, spraying and dis-budding will have been attended to at the proper time. Preparation immediately prior to the show will start in earnest three days before, when tying and shading of the promising buds may be started (this is not desirable for the 'decorative' classes). Tying involves encircling opening buds with a length of thick soft wool placed inside the outside

1

2

3

1 The popular Rose 'Masquerade' is a hybrid. Its parentage is 'Goldilocks' x 'Holiday'.
2 Like all plants grown for showing, exhibition Roses must be given extra care, and the growths thinned.
3 Spraying is of utmost importance when growing Roses for exhibition.

row of petals, two-thirds of the way down from the point of the bud and drawing it firm with a double loop. The object is to restrict the expansion of the petals laterally in the hope that they will develop with greater length. Buds are at the right stage when the sepals have curled back and the outside row of petals is just separating from the hard centre. The petals should be dry at the time and a shade must be placed over the bud immediately for protection.

Flowers should be cut, allowing plenty of spares, either the evening before or very early on the show day. Each stem should be examined for insect pests, the prickles removed from the lower part, the bottom inch or so split and the leaves washed under running water. The bloom must be tested by removing the tie carefully and replacing it if the centre holds. Slightly damaged petals may be trimmed with nail scissors. Trusses of floribunda and other cluster roses may need tidying by removing faded flowers, including their footstalks. As many fresh young flowers as possible should be open in each truss.

All blooms intended for showing should have the stems immersed in water up to their necks for several hours beforehand in a cool place. The show schedule should be studied and if your own containers are permitted, these should be washed out in advance and rushes or coarse grass obtained for packing vases to facilitate arrangement. Florist's wire may be obtained for wiring of stems with weak necks, which is permissible.

For a local show roses may be transported in buckets. Entries are usually confined to vase and bowl classes nowadays. Equipment needed will include a sharp knife, secateurs, florist's

1 Roses exhibited at a show. Presentation is important and the show schedule rules must be followed closely.
2 Rose 'Nevada' makes a good hedge because of its thorns.
3 Rose 'Fritz Nobis', a good hedge Rose.

wire, a soft camel's-hair brush, nail scissors, bowls and vases, a pen and packing material. Ample time should be allowed for staging. All vases are better packed loosely with rushes or grass; trim the packing flush with the rim and select the appropriate blooms.

In arranging three stems in a vase an inverted triangle is best, using the largest bloom for the base. For a vase with six stems of flowers, three levels—with two blooms in the highest, three in the middle and one in the lowest—are most effective. Any leaves below the waterline should be removed. The entry card is placed face downwards against the vase and the variety names shown on a separate card. Leave any ties in position until shortly before judging time. Where there is no background bowl classes usually require an all-round effect. Otherwise a frontal effect is best. Always select the brightest colours for the bowl, avoiding delicate shades except to separate the strong colours. The top of the bowl or grill should be hidden by the foliage and the stems so arranged that the flowers face in several directions and are on different levels, with pleasing colour contrasts.

Shortly before judging time carefully remove all ties from specimen blooms, taking care not to tear any petals. The centre should remain intact—if any fly open, revealing the anthers, they must be replaced. No blown bloom, nor any left tied, will score points. Assuming the centre holds, using the camel's-hair

brush, the other petals should be pressed gently outwards and downwards, at the same time placing the middle finger of the free hand behind each, so as to ensure a symmetrical outline.

Roses as hedges These may be divided into two groups, internal and boundary hedges. Internal hedges need not be as tall as boundary hedges and may include vigorous hybrid tea type roses, lightly pruned, such as 'Peace', 'Eden Rose', 'Tahiti', 'Rose Gaujard', 'Buccaneer', 'President H. Hoover', 'Super Star', 'Golden Masterpeice', 'Gold Crown', and the new blood-red 'Uncle Walter'. It does not matter about them being gappy at the base as they are not functional. The more upright growers should be planted fairly close together, and a staggered double row with the trees about 18 inches apart in each direction will help them to grow together quickly.

Strong-growing floribunda roses are also suitable and perhaps the best of all for a continuous display of colour. Such varieties as 'Queen Elizabeth', 'Frensham', 'Faust', 'Honeymoon', 'Lubeck', 'Daily Sketch', 'Shepherd's Delight', 'Sweet Repose' and 'Ama' will make a lovely mass display and seldom be without colour from June to October. There are too, the modern shrub roses, hardly less floriferous than the floribundas, which they closely resemble in flower type, but which have even stronger growth. Such excellent examples as 'Elmshorn', 'Dorothy Wheatcroft', 'Fred Loads', 'Lavender Lassie', 'First Choice', 'Nymphenburg' and 'Chinatown' offer a wide choice of colour.

Those who find an appeal in the soft, refined colouring of the old Pemberton hybrid musks may derive great pleasure from a hedge of such favourites as 'Penelope', 'Prosperity', 'Moonlight', 'Felicia', 'Cornelia', 'Vanity' and 'Thisbe', as well as enjoying their distinctive fragrance. All varieties mentioned for internal hedges are recurrent flowering.

1 Rose 'Pink Supreme' used to form a decorative hedge in a Rose garden.
2 One of the old Pemberton Hybrid Musk Roses, 'Penelope' forms a good hedge.

For boundary hedges rather different qualities are required. If animals have to be discouraged, very strong growers with thorny wood, such as the hybrid rugosa 'Conrad F. Meyer', are very useful, as are most of the hybrid rugosas, including 'Blanc Double de Coubert', 'Sarah van Fleet', *R. rugosa rubra* and *R. rugosa alba*. While not as recurrent flowering as modern types, they have the attraction of brilliant scarlet tomato-like hips in the autumn and leaves which then change colour to an attractive gold and russet and crimson shades. To obtain plenty of colour in a boundary hedge it may be necessary to introduce some of the modern recurrent flowering climbers and shrub roses. 'Queen Elizabeth' will easily reach a height of 7 feet. Unfortunately most of the really thorny varieties bear their flowers early in the season and are not reliably recurrent.

Some of the species and hybrids of species would also be very useful as boundary hedges because of their thorns. These include 'Nevada', pale creamy-white, tinted pink; 'Fritz Nobis', flesh pink shaded salmon; 'Frühlingsgold clear yellow; 'Frühlingsmorgen', deep pink, with yellow centre; *R. moyesii*, blood red, followed by bottle-shaped scarlet hips; and *R. sericea pteracantha* (syn. *R. omeiensis pteracantha*) with huge, broad translucent ruby-red thorns on young red wood, and small white flowers.

The wichuraiana rambler roses may be interplanted with those of more rigid, upright growth in boundary hedges. They mostly have lax canes which need some support. This may take the form of a post and wire fence, individual uprights or adjacent shrub roses of erect habit. They mostly have a short but glorious burst of colour in June and July. 'Alberic Barbier', 'Emily Gray', 'François Juranville' and 'Sanders' White' are four with a particular appeal because, even when they are not in flower, the glistening foliage is beautiful in itself and retained for much of the winter.

Finally, when considering roses as hedges, the claims of the modern recurrent-flowering pillar roses should not be overlooked. These could be alternated with the hybrid wichuraianas to give colour over a longer season. Such varieties as 'Joseph's Coat', yellow, orange and red; 'Maigold', coppery yellow; 'Golden Showers', medium yellow; 'Danse du Feu', orange-scarlet; 'Bantry Bay', rose pink; 'Pink Perpétué', rose pink with carmine pink reverse; 'New Dawn', flesh pink and 'Schoolgirl', apricot-orange; are all highly recommended for this purpose. They need little pruning and have a high proportion of flowers to wood.

Standard roses Hybrid tea and floribunda varieties may be obtained budded on 3½-foot stems (full standard), or stems 2 feet 3 inches tall (half standard). These forms are useful to provide an extra dimension where beds of bush roses might be too flat. They also enable the flowers to be admired at eye level.

Several modifications in cultivation are advisable to obtain the best results. Planting should be shallow, the top roots being covered with not more than 3 inches of soil. Staking is essential and a stout oak stake should be driven home before the roots are covered. It should be long enough to reach well up into the head of the standard to give effective support, and ties must be durable—old rubber-insulated electrical cable is excellent. Pruning must be rather lighter than for the same variety in bush form. A large symmetrical head is the objective and thinning, by cutting out the weaker growth, will be desirable. Suckers appearing on the stem below the head must be pulled off while small, and a watch kept for any springing from the root system. Insecurely staked standard roses will often throw many suckers.

Weeping standards budded on 5-foot to 6-foot stems are still in demand for planting as isolated specimens on lawns. The old wichuraiana ramblers 'Dorothy Perkins', 'Excelsa' and 'François Juranville' are among the most popular.

Both Hybrid Tea and Floribunda Roses may be obtained budded on to standards. In addition to being decorative they are useful for varying the interest of a Rose garden.
1 'Alberic Barbier' grown as a standard.
2 A weeping standard.
3 Rose 'Prestige' as a standard.

They may be allowed to form natural bouquets or the growths may be secured to wire umbrella trainers. The new canes produced after flowering are retained for next season's flowering, and wood which has flowered is cut out in the autumn. There are also many hybrid wichuraianas and modern recurrent-flowering climbers which will make large heads when budded on a 6-foot briar stem. These have stiffer growth than the true

care should be taken to provide a deep pocket filled with rich soil, and water copiously in dry weather. Similarly, any window-boxes or stone troughs in which they may be planted should be deep and well drained, and they should never be allowed to dry out.

Propagation may be either by cuttings or by budding on to small rootstocks. The advantage of cuttings is that the dwarf habit of growth is retained, whereas growth may become more vigorous on rootstocks, and there is always the risk of suckers developing.

A few of the best varieties are given below under two headings, according to whether growth is very dwarf or somewhat taller.

Very dwarf

Colibri Orange-yellow, flushed pink.
Perla de Alcanada Carmine.
Perla de Montserrat Light Pink.
Pour Toi Creamy-white.
Presumida Orange-yellow in the centre, paling to cream.
Robin Cherry Red.
Simple Simon Deep Pink.
Sweet Fairy Lilac pink.
Yellow Doll Yellow, paling to cream.

Somewhat taller

Baby Gold Star Deep yellow.
Baby Masquerade Yellow, pink and red.
Cinderella Blush pink to white.
Coralin Bright salmon-red.
Easter Morning Pale yellow buds, opening cream.
Eleanor Coral pink.
Little Flirt Flame red, with pale yellow reverse.
New Penny Salmon pink to coral.
Red Imp Deep crimson.
Rosina Rich golden yellow.
Scarlet Gem Bright orange-scarlet.

Miniature roses are not house plants. While they will tolerate the dry atmosphere of living rooms for a time, they should be brought into the house only when in flower and kept well watered. As soon as the flowers are past their best the pots should be sunk outside up to their rims in soil, top-dressed with moist granulated peat and watered with a little weak fertiliser. They should provide a further crop or even two later in the season if they are looked after.

The old shrub roses It is uncertain how these roses began to be propagated, but it is believed that four species, *R. gallica, R. phoenicea, R. moschata* and *R. canina,* all natives of the Mediterranean region interbred and their progeny eventually became the popular roses of the nineteenth century.

R. gallica, said to have been a religious emblem of the Medes and Persians in the twelfth century BC, is a small, compact, upright bush with tiny thorns and a few prickles, neatly toothed and pointed leaves and light crimson flowers

weeping standard, so the effect is not as graceful, and the growth needs to be tied down to a wire trainer or some other device, such as a hoop. Although not as attractive as individual specimens as the true weeping standards, these can make a striking display of colour, often for a longer period than the three or four weeks of the true weepers. Varieties such as 'Dr W. Van Fleet' and its recurrent sport, 'New Dawn', flesh pink; 'Albertine', coppery-pink; 'Danse du Feu', orange-scarlet; 'Paul's Scarlet Climber'; 'Dortmund', crimson, with a white eye, single; and 'Parkdirektor Riggers', blood red, semi-double; are in this category.

Miniature roses These delightful roses may be regarded as a self-contained group, partly because they lend themselves to planting where there would not

Miniature Roses need all the attention afforded to ordinary Roses, but are useful for cultivating in places where Roses would not normally be grown.
1 'Baby Masquerade'.
2 'Red Imp'.
3 'Pixie'.

be facilities for planting other groups of roses. Thus, they will fit into deep stone troughs or sink gardens, window-boxes, tubs or miniature gardens of their own, with tiny beds and grass paths to scale. They are also sometimes used for planting on rock gardens and in pots. However, a word of warning is necessary. These are true roses and, as such, they need a deep, cool root run, with ample moisture, to give of their best. Therefore, when planting them on rock gardens, followed by small rounded hips. *R. phoenicea* is a lax shrub with long shoots, few prickles, small leaves, bearing tiny white or creamy flowers in bunches and small hips. It is not reliably hardy in Britain. *R. moschata,* the musk rose, has similar botanical characters to *R. phoenicea. R. canina,* the dog briar, is an arching shrub with large prickles, neat greyish leaves, pink flowers and oval hips.

Three of the species flower around midsummer. The exception is *R. moschata,* which flowers from August onwards. The resulting hybrids which bear flowers singly or in branching sprays fall into several distinct classes described below.

Gallica Mostly forms and close hybrids of *R. gallica,* usually compact, upright bushes with neat, pointed leaves, flowers semi-double or very double, with petals arranged into sections, 'quartered', often overlapping or tucked into the receptacle in the centre, 'button-eyed'; colours blush white, pink, light crimson, mauve, purplish crimson and maroon. Tiny thorns, few prickles, rounded hips.

Examples include *R. gallica officinalis,* said to have been brought from Damascus by the crusaders and hence known as the 'Red Damask' (but it should not be confused with the Damask type), 'Red Rose of Lancaster', 'Apothecary's Rose', 'Rose of Provins'. The last named is derived from the French in connection with the production of rose petal conserves, to which this rose is specially suited as its dried petals long retain their fragrance. Provins is a small town in northern central France, an agricultural centre noted for its roses. The industry of producing rose petal conserves was carried on in France and also in England. The flowers are large and open, loosely semi-double, showing stamens, light crimson. *R. gallica versicolor,* 'Rosa Mundi', a sport of the above, first recorded in the sixteenth century. The petals are striped and splashed with palest pink. Often confused with 'York and Lancaster' (see under *R. damascena*).

Other varieties, which are probably very old, include 'Conditorum', semi-double flowers, rich magenta-crimson, flushed and veined with purple, showing stamens. It is said to have been used in Hungary for the making of attar of roses and for preserving. 'Tuscany' or 'Old Velvet Rose', many petals opening flat, showing stamens, darkest maroon-crimson. 'Sissinghurst Castle', semi-double, showing stamens, petals plum-coloured, with magenta-crimson edges and flecked with the same tint.

Damask R. gallica × *R. phoenicea* (the type is named after the city of Damascus). Spindly erect or lax shrubs, thorny and prickly, leaves mostly soft and downy, small and rounded, long narrow hips, flowers mostly semi-double, pink.

Examples include *R. damascena tri-*

Rosa gallica versicolor, 'Rosa mundi', has been grown since the sixteenth century when it was first recorded.

gintipetala, soft pink, semi-double, showing stamens, leaves pale green. Forms the main plantings at Kazanlik, Bulgaria, and is planted there and elsewhere for the extraction of rose water and attar of roses. *R. damascena versicolor,* 'York and Lancaster', known before 1629, flowers pink or white or parti-coloured (not striped and splashed as in *R. gallica versicolor);* perhaps a sport of, or closely related to, *R. d. trigintipetala.* 'Celsiana', known before 1750, pale downy leaves, large loosely semi-double flowers, blush pink, showing stamens. 'Petite Lisette', recorded 1817, downy greyish foliage, flowers double, blush pink, each with 'button eye'.

Alba R. damascena × *R. canina.* Inheriting the strong growth, sparse but large prickles, greyish leaves and oval hips of

R. canina, to which *R. damascena* brought double flowers, white or pink.

Examples include *R. alba semi-plena,* 'White Rose of York', seven-foot stems, few big prickles, hard greyish leaves, semi-double, pure white flowers, showing stamens, oval hips. Used as surrounding hedges for the Damask rose fields at Kazanlik; and yields an inferior essence for extraction. *R. alba maxima,* 'Jacobite Rose', 'Great Double White', double sport of the above, creamy flesh in centre on opening, showing a few stamens, few hips. 'Maiden's Blush', also known as 'Cuisse de Nymphe', 'La Royale', 'La Seduisante'; similar to *R. alba maxima,* but on opening the flowers have a warm flush of pink in the centre, fading paler.

Centifolia 'Rose of a Hundred Leaves', 'Cabbage Rose', 'Provence Rose'. Probably evolved during the seventeenth century from the above roses; to be seen in many Flemish pictures of the period (and hence called the 'Rose des Peintres'),

1 Rosa damascena versicolor, the 'York and Lancaster' Rose was known prior to 1629. The flowers are pink or white or parti-coloured, but not striped as in Rosa gallica versicolor ('Rosa mundi').
2 The old variety 'Tuscany' opens flat and is a form of Rosa gallica.
3 Rosa gallica officinalis.

Moss', R. damascena bifera alba muscosa, 'Quatre Saisons Blanc Mousseux'. Like its parents it produces more than one crop of bloom.

Moss Apart from the above Damask Moss rose, *R. centifolia* gave rise in 1727 or earlier to a sport with 'mossy' buds, called *R. centifolia muscosa*, 'Common Moss'; similar to the parent but with less globular blooms, and with 'moss' all over the calyces and pedicel; the 'moss' is soft, sticky and fragrant.

Examples include 'Shailer's White' ('White Bath', 'Clifton Moss', *R. centifolia muscosa alba*); Shailer's sport was recorded in 1790, the others were probably identical to it. Similar to the pink form in every way except colour. 'Réné d'Anjou', recorded 1835, closely related to the 'Common Moss'; flowers opening rather flat, of lilac-pink, fully double, bronze young foliage. 'Single Moss', sports with fertile flowers occurred in England in 1807 and in France in 1814; they opened the way for seed raising and many hybrids occurred between the Damask Moss (which gave harsh 'moss' and a recurrent flowering habit), and the Centifolia Moss (which gave soft 'moss' and more handsome foliage and flowers).

Examples include 'Comtesse de Murinais' (recorded 1843), 'moss' green and harsh, flowers large, white, with pronounced 'button eye', not recurrent. 'Madame Delaroche-Lambert' (1873), rich purplish crimson, green 'moss' on long foliaceous sepals; recurrent. 'Salet' (1854), very similar to the 'Common

---

also on cretonnes and wallpapers up to the present day. Lax stems, thorny and prickly, making an open bush; large, rounded, coarsely toothed leaves, big, nodding, fully double flowers.

Examples include *R. centifolia* (of which the above description is typical). The variation *parvifolia (R. burgundica,* 'Pompon de Burgoyne', 'Pompon de St François'), believed to be a sport from the above, first recorded in 1664. Neat upright bushlet, tiny pointed leaves, tightly double rosette-flowers, deep pink. Probably arose as a witch's broom, a tightly bunched set of shoots stemming from the base (see Witch's Broom). There are two forms in cultivation, one stronger than the other. 'Unique Blanche' ('White Provence', 'Unique', 'Vierge de Cléry'), a sport from *R. centifolia,* recorded 1775; less vigorous than *R. centifolia,* otherwise similar but with less shapely white flowers opening from reddish buds. Variation *bullata* (lettuce-

leafed rose, 'Rose à feuilles de laitue'), a sport which originated in 1801. Distinguished by its large bullate leaves, brownish when young. Variation *cristata,* 'Crested Moss', 'Chapeau de Napoléon', a sport which originated in 1826, distinguished by the proliferous or crested calyx wings, so that the bud appears shrouded in greenery.

Autumn Damask R. gallica × R. moschata. R. d. semperflorens (R. damascena bifera, 'Quatre Saisons'), a small bush, with small thorns and prickles, downy leaves, bearing loose, double pink blooms at midsummer and again later, a character inherited from *R. moschata.* The 'Old Monthly' rose dates back to Roman and probably pre-Roman times. In 1835, it was reported that it had given rise to a sport bearing white flowers with pedicel and bud enclosed in bristly, 'mossy' excrescences; the 'moss' also appears on the surface of the leaves; this was named the 'Perpetual White Damask

Moss', but is markedly recurrent.

Further hybridisation The French empress, Napoleon Bonaparte's wife, Joséphine, collected in her garden at Malmaison, near Paris, all the roses she could acquire, and so started a fashionable interest in roses which has continued ever since. Her roses were recorded in the three series of paintings by Pierre Joseph Redouté (1759–1840). Copying the example of the Empress Joséphine seedlings were raised in ever-increasing quantities. Formerly distinct groups became hybridised and many of the most superb of the popular roses of the nineteenth century were difficult to ascribe to one group or another, except the Alba type which were less interbred.

Examples of highly bred Old Roses not distinctively attributable to any one group include 'Koenigin von Danemarck' (1816), showing considerable Alba influence in its greyish leaves, wide flat flowers, quartered and with 'button eyes', intense vermilion-pink in the centre on opening, fading paler. 'Madame Hardy' (1832), white, very full and cupped, faintly blush in the centre on opening, reflexing later and with green central pointel, Centifolia leaves. 'Cardinal de Richelieu' (1840), intense velvety maroon, cupped and reflexing, petals rolled at edges; smooth leaves.

Portland Roses At the end of the eighteenth century 'Slater's Crimson China' rose was introduced from Asia and in due course became hybridised with the Autumn Damask, the result being the 'Scarlet Four Seasons', 'Portland Rose' or *R. paestana*. Several more were subsequently raised, eventually giving rise to a group called Portland Roses, which bore at least two crops during the summer and autumn, some being in almost constant production.

Examples include 'Blanc de Vibert' (1847), yellowish green soft foliage, fully double, cupped blooms of white with a hint of lemon in the centre when opening. 'Comte de Chambord' (1860), pointed light green leaves, well filled flowers opening flat and reflexing, clear pink.

All of these roses distinctly derived from the Portland Rose inherit a very short pedicel; the leaves are gathered in a sort of collar quite closely under the flower. This is noticeable in 'Jacques Cartier' and also in some hybrid moss varieties, such as 'Gloire des Mousseux' and 'Mousseline'. The same character is also found in several hybrid perpetuals which are most closely linked to these roses, such as 'Baroness Rothschild' and 'Reine des Violettes'.

The style of flower most admired was one which was full of petals, expanding in a circle, flat or reflexing, apart from those mainly derived from *R. centifolia*, which were inclined to be globular or cup-shaped. Most appreciated was the fully open flower, not the bud. The colours range from white, blush white, maroon to purplish mauve and pink to bright crimson. 'Henri Martin' and 'Surpasse Tout' most nearly approached crimson, a colour which did not occur in roses except in those inheriting this true colour from 'Slater's Crimson China'. Flaked and striped varieties were much sought after and the subtly changing shades of the purplish varieties varied with the effect of light on them.

1 The deep-pink flowers of Rosa gallica 'Surpass Tout' are fully double.
2 Rosa gallica 'Cardinal Richelieu' has maroon flowers and reaches 4 feet.
3 Another old-fashioned Rose, Moss Rose, 'Henri Martin'.

Old shrub roses—a selection of 22, chosen for their floral perfection and garden value, including the historic main forms and hybrids

Name	Colour	Height
Belle de Crécy	Mauve	3 feet
Camaieux	Striped, mauve and white	3 feet
Capitaine John Ingram (Moss)	Maroon crimson	5 feet
Cardinal de Richelieu	Maroon	4 feet
Céleste	Clear pink	6 feet
Charles de Mills	Crimson purple	5 feet
Comte de Chambord	Pink	3 feet
Duc de Guiche	Crimson	5 feet
du Maître d'Ecole	Lilac	3 feet
Empress Josephine	Deep pink	3 feet
Fantin Latour	Blush pink	5 feet
Félicité Parmentier	Blush	4 feet
Général Kléber (Moss)	Bright pink	5 feet
Henri Martin (Moss)	Crimson	5 feet
Koenigin von Dänemarck	Pink	5 feet
Madame Hardy	White	6 feet
Maiden's Blush	Blush	6 feet
Président de Sèze	Mauve	5 feet
Réné d'Anjou (Moss)	Pink	4 feet
Surpasse Tout	Crimson	4 feet
Tour de Malakoff	Cerise and purple	7 feet
Tuscany Superb	Maroon	3 feet

were still being raised well into the 1850s which were untouched by either recurrent parent. At the same time the recurrent roses were eventually to come to the fore. There are the hybrids between the Autumn Damasks and 'Parson's Pink China', which we know today as the 'Old Blush' or '.Common China Rose'. In 1817, a seedling occurred between these two in the French island of Bourbon, and a subsequent seedling from this, raised in France about 1823, was called the Bourbon Rose. From this seedling many popular varieties were raised, which, while retaining much of the old style of flower, had smooth leaves; the most favoured were those which were recurrent.

Examples include 'Bourbon Queen' (1835), not recurrent, yet it is one of the roses most frequently found in old gardens; warm lilac pink, tall lax growth. 'Souvenir de la Malmaison' (1843), blush, very large, flat and full of petals, quartered, constantly in flower. The climbing sport, which has two good crops only, occurred in 1893 in Australia. 'Boule de Neige' (1867), white, double, camellia-like, an upright bush, constantly in flower. 'Reine Victoria' (1872), mallow pink, cupped, continuously in flower, spindly upright bush. The blush pink sport 'Madame Pierre Oger' has always been more popular.

Later developed varieties These include the semi-climbers 'Madame Isaac Pereire' (1880), large full flowers, quartered, of deep magenta pink, with two good crops, and the noted purple and white semi-climber 'Variegata di Bologna' (1909), which has fine, well-filled·flowers but is not recurrent.

The selections from seed gradually produced tall bushes, bearing good rounded flowers in profusion at mid-summer, with bunches of bloom later at the tips of the long new summer's growth. This led to them being called Hybrid Perpetual.

Non-recurrent varieties In addition to this ever-popular move towards perpetual roses many non-recurrent varieties continued to be raised, and several were tall lax bushes which today are used for covering stumps, hedgerows, etc. Good examples include *R. gallica violacea,* before 1802, semi-double, violet crimson, 6–7 feet. *R. dupontii,* before 1817, of *R. moschata* derivation, greyish leaves, single blush-white flowers, tall lax bush. *R. polliniana (R. macrantha* of gardens), before 1820, large single blush-pink, sprawling; 'Daisy Hill', 'Raubritter', 'Complicata' and 'Scintillation' are close relatives. 'Constance Spry', though introduced in 1960, being a hybrid between 'Belle Isis' *(R. gallica)* and 'Dainty Maid', assorts best with these roses. It makes a vigorous lax bush.

Other old hybrids Species other than those discussed above are mentioned in the selection of old shrub roses on the opposite page.

1 Rose 'Constance Spry' is one of the recent introductions (1960) of the old-fashioned type of flower.
2 'Louise Odier', a Bourbon Rose.

Further Chinese hybrids The roses bred during the ancient Chinese civilisation reached Europe very early in the nineteenth century. They are believed to be hybrids between two species, *R. chinensis* and *R. gigantea,* and not only produced the rich crimson colouring found in 'Slater's Crimson China' but also pale yellow, as well as a habit of flowering from early summer until the onset of severe frost, coppery colouring. In popular esteem the pale yellow and coppery colours of the flowers outweighed the long flowering habit and made up for the small loose blooms, smooth small leaves, smooth weak stems with few prickles and general lack of vigour in all but the most suitably warm climates. While growers sought the recurrent habit by sowing seeds of these new types interpollinated with the established favourites, many varieties

In 1583 *R. francofurtana* was described, said to be a hybrid between *R. gallica* and *R. cinnamosnea*. Two roses probably decended from this are *R. francofurtana* 'Agatha' and the much later rose known today as 'Empress Joséphine'. Once-flowering roses of *R. gallica* type, these are unique in having no thorns, ribbed leaves and large turbinate receptacles. 'Empress Joséphine' is worthy of inclusion in any collection of old roses.

Rambling and climbing roses All wild roses are shrubs but some are of lax habit and grow in somewhat shaded positions, reaching the sunlight by means of their hooked thorns which enable their stems to lodge in neighbouring bushes. All species of the *Synstylae* section of the genus, together with *R. chinensis, R. gigantea, R. laevigata, R. banksiae* and *R. bracteata* have these characters, and from these all climbing and rambling roses are derived. The last three species have produced little groups of related varieties but are not in the mainstream of breeding. The hybrids of *R. gigantea* and *R. chinensis*, evolved in China before their introduction into Europe between 1792 and 1824, were bushes not climbers, flowered from summer till autumn, and were comparatively large flowered. Practically all of the *Synstylae* species would be termed in horticulture 'ramblers', making long lax growths, bearing, with one exception, once only during the summer bunches of small single flowers. The exception is *R. moschata* whose flowers are borne from August onwards. British garden ramblers were derived from the *Synstylae* species *R. arvensis, R. sempervirens, R. multiflora, R. luciae* and *R. l.* var. *wichuraiana* (a few other species have played a small part) hybridised with other garden roses derived from the breeding together of *R. gallica* (see the section Old shrub roses), *R. moschata* and *R. phoenicea* on the one hand and the China hybrids mentioned above.

Rambling roses today include varieties raised from *R. arvensis* and *R. sempervirens* in the early nineteenth century, 'Félicité et Perpétué' and 'Adelaide d'Orleans'; from *R. multiflora*, 'Blush Rambler', 'Goldfinch'; from *R. luciae* var. *wichuraiana*, 'Dorothy Perkins', 'Excelsa', and *R. luciae*, 'Alberic Barbier', 'François Juranville', all in the early decades of this century. Very few have been raised since; one example is 'Crimson Shower'. Practically all rambling roses, apart from the hybrids of *R. luciae* itself (which had mainly tea roses for their other parent) are of white, pink, crimson or purplish colouring; those descended from *R. luciae* itself are mainly of yellowish or salmon colouring. Yellow also crops up in 'Aglaia' (*R. multiflora* × 'Rêve d'Or') which is the ancestor of the hybrid musk roses. Dwarf sports or hybrids of these roses gave rise to the polypoms or dwarf polyantha roses.

R. moschata crossed with the ancestral Chinese rose hybrids gave rise to the noisette class; the main selections, 'Blush Noisette', 'Aimée Vibert', bear small flowers in clusters repeatedly from summer till autumn. By hybridising more closely with the yellowish, ancestral Chinese roses the climbing teas were evolved, 'Gloire de Dijon', 'Maréchal Niel', in the middle decades of the eighteenth century. These may be regarded as among the first developments of what have come to be known in horticulture as 'climbing' roses, as opposed to 'rambling' roses; their distinguishing features are large flowers borne singly or in small clusters and a recurrent flowering habit. During the heyday of the hybrid tea roses numerous climbing sports occurred and are known as climbing HTs ('Climbing Madame Butterfly', 'Climbing Mrs Sam McGredy'); these reproduce the large flowers and leaf characters of the bush form and flower at least twice during the year. Their interest historically is mainly during the first half of this century. With the advent of the floribunda roses, towards the middle of this century, varieties have been bred with medium to large flowers borne singly and in clusters, flowering usually more repeatedly through the season than the climbing HTs ('Leverkusen', 'Soldier Boy'). With the fusion of the HTs and

1 Rambler Rose 'May Queen'.
2 Climbing Rose 'Frances Lester'.
3 'Chaplin's Pink Companion' a climber.
4 'Paul's Scarlet Climber'.
5 'Albertine' and 'Zéphirine Drouhin'.
6 'Emily Gray' (cream) and 'Danse du Feu'.
7 Climbing Rose 'Mme Grégoire Staechelin'.

Rambling and climbing roses

Good ramblers mainly descended from *R. multiflora* and *R. luciae*, variety *wichuraiana*

Name	Colour
Crimson Shower	Crimson
Débutante	Pink
Excelsa	Scarlet crimson
Félicité et Perpetué	Milk white
Francis E. Lester	Blush, single
Goldfinch	Pale yellow
Sanders' White	White
Violette	Purple

Large-flowered ramblers mainly derived from *R. luciae*

Albéric Barbier	Creamy yellow
Albertine	Coppery pink
Breeze Hill	Straw yellow
Emily Gray	Yellow
François Juranville	Salmon pink
Mary Wallace	Pink
May Queen	Lilac pink
Paul Transon	Coppery pink

Climbers of hybrid tea style

Climbing Etoile de Hollande	Dark crimson
Climbing Mme Butterfly	Light pink
Climbing Mme Caroline Testout	Pink
Climbing McGredy's Ivory	White
Climbing Mrs Sam McGredy	Coppery Red
Easlea's Golden Rambler	Yellow
Guinée	Maroon
Mme Grégoire Staechelin	Deep pink
Paul's Lemon Pillar	Lemon white

Floribunda climbers

Climbing Allgold	Yellow
Coral Dawn	Coral pink
Danse du Feu	Orange red
Dream Girl	Coppery salmon
Kassel	Coppery red
Leverkusen	Pale yellow
Nymphenburg	Salmon pink
Parade	Crimson pink
Pink Cloud	Clear pink

the 'floribundas' we may expect to see this group considerably increased in the future, augmented by sports from floribundas, and hybrids of 'Max Graf', which is descended from *R. rugosa* (*R. kordesii* and descendants).

While some of the species of the *Synstylae* section may climb to 30 or 40 feet on trees (*R. filipes, R. brunonii*), the garden ramblers are usually not taller than 18 feet; the noisettes rather shorter; the climbing HTs up to 20 feet, and the floribunda-type moderns achieve 8–15 feet. These shorter roses, together with the tallest Bourbon roses and hybrid perpetual roses are frequently termed 'pillar' roses. A further variation is when rambling roses are budded on to stems of briar and develop umbrella-like heads; these are termed 'weeping standards'.

As the first crop of flowers of all of these classes is produced on shoots arising from the leaf-axils of the previous year's growth, the training of them on to pillars or poles, upright arches or vertically on walls will not tend to produce the maximum quantity of flower. By training the shoots nearly horizontally, flowering shoots will appear in every leaf axil. The modern pillar roses or floribunda climbers will benefit in the same way. Where they are growing vigorously, the pruning of most rambling roses is by removing the wood of the previous season that has flowered immediately after flowering; if left for two seasons the flowering side-shoots may be shortened to one eye in winter. The hybrids of *R. luciae* do not require so much pruning as the hybrids of *R. multiflora* and *R. luciae*, var. *wichuraiana;* they are more bushy and flower freely from old twiggy branches. The same applies to 'Mermaid'. The recurrent flowering climbing roses should be pruned in winter, removing old twiggy growth and tying in long new shoots; and occasionally removing old wood as far as the base to encourage fresh growth.

R. banksiae and its forms and hybrids flower best on small side shoots; pruning consists in the occasional removal of old weak stems to encourage new, during the youth of the plant; thereafter little attention is required if the plants have sufficient space to develop on warm sunny walls.

The most natural way of enjoying rambling and climbing roses, particularly the more graceful varieties, is to train them over hedgerows, stumps, arbours, and into trees. In ramblers the extreme grace of the falling sprays can then be appreciated, which is so much greater than when the sprays are trained upwards. An ideal method is to grow two roses in one tree, large and small flowered together to appreciate the contrast of style and form, and in such cultivation pruning is scarcely needed, nor possible. To any collection of rambling and climbing roses such old and unsurpassed favourites as 'Gloire de Dijon', 'New Dawn', 'Gruss an Teplitz', 'Mme Alfred Carrière', 'Climbing Monsieur Paul Lédé', 'Alister Stella Gray', 'Mermaid' and 'Climbing Lady Hillingdon' should be added, for their distinctive fragrance and strongly recurrent flowering habit. For warmer counties on sunny walls *R. banksiae* and its varieties are recommended, with small flowers early in the season, and 'Mermaid', a hybrid of *R. bracteata* with large single yellow flowers in long succession.

Rudbeckia (rud-beck-ee-a)

Commemorating Olaf Rudbeck (1660–1740) Swedish professor of botany and counsellor of Linnaeus (*Compositae*). Cone flower. A genus of about 25 herbaceous plants, mostly perennial and hardy, natives of North America (related to *Echinacea*). The flowers are showy daisy-like, often with drooping petals and

1 'Mermaid' is one of the few evergreen or semi-evergreen climbing Roses. It is vigorous and may even reach a height of 30 feet.
2 'Golden Showers' may be grown as a climber or as a vigorous shrub Rose.

conspicuous conical centres. Most of them are excellent herbaceous border plants and are valuable for late summer effect in the garden.

Species cultivated *R. bicolor,* 1–2 feet, half-hardy annual, yellow, ray petals yellow, sometimes with purplish bases, disk purplish, conical, July; var. *superba,* flowers 2 inches across, petals brown on the under-sides; cultivars include 'Golden Flame', golden-yellow; 'Kelvedon Star', 3 feet, golden-yellow with mahogany-red zone; 'My Joy' ('Mon Plaisir'), dwarf habit, flowers golden-yellow. *R. fulgida deamii* (syn. *R. deamii*), 2–3 feet, a somewhat hairy plant of erect habit; flowers deep yellow 2–3 inches across with purple-black centres freely produced, July to September; var. *speciosa* (syns. *R. speciosa, R. newmanii*), 2½ feet, black-eyed Susan, similar but of laxer habit, an old favourite; 'Goldsturm', 2 feet, an excellent larger flowered form of stiffer habit and less hairy, August–September, a good garden plant. 'Goldquelle', 2½–3 feet, a newer hybrid of erect growth with lemon-yellow flowers three or more inches across, August–September. 'Herbstsonne' *(R. laciniata × R. nitida),* 6–8 feet, a tall, erect-growing plant with large, deeply-cut leaves and golden-yellow flowers with green cones, September. *R. hirta hybrida,* 2 feet, usually grown from seed as an annual or biennial, a bristly-hairy plant, striking flowers in shades of gold, orange and mahogany, summer. *R. laciniata* 'Golden Glow', 6 feet, deeply-lobed green leaves and fully double yellow flowers, 3 inches across, August to September. *R. maxima,* 4–6 feet, a rather rare and very ornamental species with large handsome glaucous leaves and rich yellow flowers with dark centres, August–September, Texas. *R. purpurea* see *Echinacea purpurea. R. tetra* 'Gloriosa', Gloriosa daisy, 2–3 feet, half-hardy annual, flowers to 7 inches across, colours various including yellow, mahogany-red, bronze, and bicolors; double-flowered forms are also offered.

Cultivation Most rudbeckias are easy to grow. A sunny or semi-shaded site with good but well-drained loamy soil is preferable, though the plants grow well on chalk. Some of the taller species and their varieties prefer moister soils and are particularly useful when grown in groups among shrubs or in the wild garden where they provide an early autumn display. Hybrids or cultivars have now largely replaced many of the species in general cultivation. The perennial sorts do best if they are divided and replanted every third or fourth year. *R. hirta* is best treated as an annual and succeeds in a sunny position in well-drained soil. Seeds of the half-hardy annual kinds should be sown under glass in gentle heat in early spring. After they have been hardened off the seedlings should be planted out 9 inches apart in late May or early June, where

they are to flower. *R. maxima* is rather slow to become established and requires a moist soil. Propagation of the perennials is easily effected by seed or by division in the spring.

Saintpaulia (pronounced in England as written, but san-pole-ee-er elsewhere) Named in honour of Baron von Saint-Paul-Illaire (1860–1910), who discovered *S. ionantha* in 1892 *(Gesneriaceae).* A genus of about 12 species, one only of which is in general cultivation. This is *S. ionantha,* the popular African violet which is much cultivated in rooms as well as in greenhouses. It is a dwarf plant with dark green, hairy, heart-shaped leaves about 2 inches long borne on reddish stalks about 4 inches long. The flowers of the wild plant are dark violet with yellow anthers, but numerous cultivars have been selected to give plants with white, pink, reddish-purple and lavender flowers. There are also some double-flowered cultivars. The flowers are borne in few-flowered cymes. Some cultivars have leaves that are a paler green than normal and these may be lobed.

The plants flower practically without stopping in the greenhouse and about three times a year in dwelling rooms. In the wild it is a native of Tanzania.

Rudbeckia flowers are distinguished by their prominent, conical, dark centres. R. 'Bambi' has a red zone at the base of each petal.

Cultivation The plants like a light soil mixture and that generally used is composed of 3 parts of peat, 1 part of loam and 1 part of sharp sand. The plants could be expected to do well in soilless composts. Saintpaulias have a small root system only and rarely require to go beyond a 5-inch pot. For this plant plastic pots have been found to be more satisfactory than clay pots. The other requisites for the plants are shade, warmth and a moist atmosphere. This latter is not easy to provide in dwellings and it is best either to stand the pot on pebbles, which are standing in water in such a way that the base of the pot is clear of the water, but so that the vapour can ascend round the plant as the water evaporates, or to plunge the pot in another container, filling the interstices with some water-retentive medium such as peat, moss, sand or vermiculite. This is kept moist at all times. The plants themselves do not take great quantities of water, but this should always be given at the same temperature. The best temperature appears to be 60°F (16°C) but provided it is not too cold or too

1 and 2 Two large-flowered 'Diana' hybrids of Saintpaulia ionantha.

warm, the exact temperature does not seem to matter as much as seeing that this temperature is always maintained. Waterings where the temperature fluctuates will cause the appearance of unsightly white blotches on the leaves. The temperature should ideally be 55°F (13°C) at night, and 70°F (21°C) during the daytime, and if this can be kept going throughout the year the plants will do particularly well. However, this is not always possible and lower readings will slow down growth, but will not cause any damage, provided that the temperature does not fall for long below 50°F (10°C). When temperatures are low the soil should be kept rather dry and the atmosphere should also not be too moist. In dwellings this will occur automatically as the water will evaporate more slowly, but in greenhouses this means that the house should not be damped down too frequently. Established plants should be given weak feeds at fortnightly intervals between April and October. Between November and mid-February no shading is necessary, but after this date the sun may get rather fierce and light shading should be supplied which will require intensifying at the end of April. This is a good time for doing any potting on that may be necessary.

Propagation is by seed or by leaf-cuttings. The seed is very fine and should be placed on the surface of the pot, which is then encased in a polythene bag. A temperature of 70°F (21°C) is necessary to ensure germination. The seed should be sown as early in the year as is possible, having regard to the temperature needed. The seedlings are subsequently pricked out and potted up. The various cultivars must be propagated by leaf cuttings. A leaf is taken with its stalk and the end is inserted shallowly in the propagating medium. Under warm conditions a number of plantlets will form at the base. As soon as they are large enough to handle, these plantlets should be separated and pricked out and then potted up individually when large enough. The young plants should not be allowed to flower until they are of a good size, otherwise they become weakened and never become really healthy.

Salpiglossis (sal-pi-glos-sis)

From the Greek *salpin*, a tube, and *glossa*, a tongue, referring to the tongue-like style in the corolla tube *(Solanaceae).* A genus of 18 species of half-hardy annuals, biennials and herbaceous perennials, of which the only species cultivated is *S. sinuata,* sometimes called the scalloped tube tongue or painted tongue, a plant of Chilean origin, which is remarkable for the

richness of colour of the large trumpet-shaped flowers and the elegant veining and flushing. It makes an admirable pot plant for a cool greenhouse, and is useful as a cut flower. *S. sinuata* grows 2–3 feet tall and has flowers in shades of rose-pink, crimson, purple, yellow and cream, many of which are beautifully veined. Various improved strains are offered from time to time under such names as *grandiflora*, and 'Splash' is a modern F₁ strain, compact in habit, free-flowering, in a good colour range.

Cultivation Sow the seed in late February or March under glass in a temperature of about 55°F (13°C) in John Innes seed compost, and when they are large enough to handle prick out the seedlings singly into small pots of John Innes potting compost No 1 and grow them on steadily until they are planted out in early June in a sunny border, to flower in late July and August. Seed may also be sown in the open in late April or May where they are to flower. Such plants will come into flower somewhat later than those sown under glass and will thus prolong the display. If they are required to flower in the greenhouse in the spring, sow the seed in July and August and transplant when three leaves have formed, into a 2½-inch pot containing John Innes potting compost No 1. Keep them close to the light in a temperature of 55–65°F (13–18°C), and move to 5-6-inch pots when well-rooted.

When 6 inches high, take out the tips of the shoots to encourage bushy growth. These fast-growing plants require ample water in dry weather and when grown in a cool greenhouse. An occasional application of liquid fertiliser is also of help.

Salvia carduacea, the Thistle Salvia, has bluish-purple flowers.

Salvia (sal-vee-a)

From the Latin *salveo,* meaning save or heal, used by Pliny with reference to the medicinal qualities of some species *(Labiatae).* A large genus of over 700 species of hardy, half-hardy and tender annual, biennial, perennial plants and shrubs, some with aromatic leaves, widely distributed in the temperate and warmer zones. It includes the common sage, *S. officinalis,* a valuable culinary plant, as well as many colourful summer and autumn flowering border plants.

Species cultivated *S. ambigens,* about 5 feet, perennial or sub-shrub, flowers deep sky-blue, September–October, South America, slightly tender. *S. argentea,* 2 feet, most decorative, leaves large, silvery-grey, felted, flowers white, small, in spikes, June and July, Mediterranean region; for a dry soil and a sunny position. *S. aurea,* shrub, leaves rounded, covered with fine hairs, flowers yellowish-brown, South Africa, hardy in mild areas. *S. azurea,* 4 feet, sub-shrub, flowers deep blue, autumn, North America, hardy; var. *grandiflora,* flower spikes denser. *S. fulgens,* Mexican red sage, 2–3 feet, shrub, flowers scarlet, in whorls, July, Mexico, tender. *S. gesneraeflora,* 2 feet, sub-shrub, flowers bright scarlet, summer, Colombia, tender. *S. grahamii,* shrub, to 4 feet, flowers deep crimson, July onwards, Mexico, somewhat tender. *S. greggii,* shrub, 3 feet, flowers scarlet, summer, Texas, Mexico, tender. *S. haematodes,* biennial, 3 feet, leaves large, wrinkled, heart-shaped, light blue flowers on branching stems from June to August, Greece. *S. interrupta,* 2–3 feet, sub-shrub, leaves 3-lobed, aromatic, flowers violet purple with white throat, May to July, Morocco, nearly hardy. *S. involucrata,* sub-shrub, 2–4 feet, flowers rose, summer and autumn, Mexico, not quite hardy; var. *bethelii,* flowers rosy crimson in longer spikes. *S. juriscii,* perennial, 1 foot, flowers violet, June, Serbia, hardy. *S. lavandulifolia,* perennial, 9–12 inches, leaves grey, flowers lavender, early summer, hardy. *S. mexicana minor,* sub-shrub, to 12 feet in nature, flowers violet-blue, February, Mexico, tender. *S. neurepia,* sub-shrub, 6–7 feet, flowers scarlet, late summer and autumn, Mexico, hardy in the milder counties. *S. officinalis,* common sage, sub-shrub, 2–3 feet, leaves wrinkled, aromatic, flowers variable purple, blue or white, June and July, southern Europe, hardy; vars. *purpurascens,* reddish-purple stems and leaves, strongly flavoured; *aurea,* leaves golden, flowers rarely produced. *S. pratense,* perennial, 2 feet, flowers bright blue, June to August, Europe, including Britain, hardy; var. *rosea,* flowers rosy-purple. *S. rutilans,* pineapple-scented sage, sub-shrub, 2–3 feet, flowers magenta-crimson, summer, tender. *S. sclarea,* clary, biennial or short-lived perennial, leaves and stems sticky, flowers pale mauve, bracts white and rose, conspicuous, June to September, Europe; various strains are offered; var. *turkestanica,* flowers white, bracts and stems pink. *S. splendens,* scarlet sage, sub-shrub, 3 feet, flowers scarlet, in spikes in summer, Brazil, usually grown as half-hardy annual; vars. for summer bedding: 'Blaze of Fire', 9–12 inches, scarlet; 'Fireball', 15 inches, rich scarlet; 'Harbinger', 15 inches, long scarlet spikes; 'Salmon Pygmy,' 6 inches. *S.* × *superba* (syn. *S. nemorosa*), 3 feet, bracts reddish, persistent, flowers violet-purple in spikes, July to September, hybrid, hardy; var. *lubeca*, identical but 1½ feet tall only. *S. uliginosa*, bog sage, 4–5 feet, leaves shiny green, deeply toothed, flowers azure-blue in spikes, August to October, eastern North America, hardy.

Cultivation Salvias are easily grown in ordinary, well-drained garden soil and in a sunny position. *S. argentea* particularly likes dry soil, as well as sun, and *S. officinalis* should be cut back in spring to encourage new bushy growth. *S.* × *superba* makes a particularly good border plant when planted in a bold group. *S. uliginosa* prefers moister conditions than the others, and its creeping rootstock should be given a covering of bracken or dry peat in cold districts. Those described as tender will succeed in the milder counties, given the shelter of a warm wall, or they may be grown in the greenhouse in pots in a compost of loam and well-rotted manure or leafmould plus some sand to provide drainage. The pots may be placed out of doors in June and brought in again in September. Water freely form spring to autumn, moderately in winter. Maintain a temperature in winter of 45–55°F (7–10°C). Propagate the shrubs, sub-shrubs and hardy perennial kinds by division in the spring or by soft-wood cuttings, rooted in sandy soil in a propagating case in spring in a temperature of 65°F (18°C). *S. splendens* is increased by seed sown under glass in February or March in a temperature of 60°F (16°C) and planted out in late May or June

Saponaria (sap-on-air-ee-a)

From the Latin *sapo*, soap, the crushed leaves of *S. officinalis* producing a lather when mixed with water, and at one time used as a soap substitute *(Caryophyllaceae)*. Soapwort. A genus of some 30 species of hardy perennials and annuals, mainly from the Mediterranean area. They are easily grown, and some of them can become invasive.

Species cultivated *S. caespitosa*, perennial, 3 inches, flowers large, pink on a green turfy cushion of leaves, May and June, Pyrenees. *S. calabrica*, hardy annual, 9 inches, flowers deep rose, freely produced, summer, Italy, Greece. *S. ocymoides*, perennial, 6 inches, a vigorous trailer, flowers rose-pink, on slender, ruddy-brown 2-inch stems, June to August, southern Alps, Sardinia, Caucasus; it may seed itself too freely. *S. officinalis*, bouncing Bet, 1–3 feet, flowers rose-pink, in panicles, August and September, central and southern Europe to Japan, naturalised in Britain. Its spreading roots must be watched; vars. *alba plena*, double white, *rosea plena*, semi-double pink, are better garden plants.

Sarcochilus australis has fragrant white flowers scattered along the whole length of the stems.

Cultivation Plant the perennial kinds from October to April in a sunny position and in deep, good soil. They are propagated by seed sown under glass in early spring, or out of doors in April, by cuttings rooted in a cold frame in autumn, or by division of the clumps from October to March. Sow seed of the annual species in a sunny border in ordinary garden soil in April for summer

flowering, or sow in the open in September for spring flowering.

Sarcochilus (sar-ko-chil-us)

From the Greek *sarkos*, flesh, and *cheilos*, lip, in allusion to the lip being very fleshy *(Orchidaceae)*. A genus of epiphytic orchids, from the Pacific Isles and Australia, mostly dwarf growing but with very pretty flowers in the Australian species, which are the ones mostly grown. The genus once contained about 200 species but most of them have been transferred to other genera, leaving about a dozen species. The plants have leafy stems and are without pseudobulbs. They vary very much in habit and appearance. All those described below are natives of Australia.

Species cultivated *S. ceciliae,* flowers fragrant, pink, late summer. *S. falcatus,* flowers whitish, lip has red and orange markings, spring. *S. fitzgeraldii,* flowers white, spotted red, lip spotted rose-purple, a very attractive species, spring. *S. hartmannii,* flowers creamy-white spotted with red, another very attractive species, spring.

Cultivation A warm, moist atmosphere is required, and the plants grow best if the minimum temperature is kept around 60 F (16 C) throughout the year. Pot them in small pans and hang these up near the glass. A suitable compost is osmunda fibre and sphagnum moss in equal parts. Do not give them as much water in winter as in summer, but do not allow the compost to dry out for long periods. During summer spray overhead frequently. If propagation is required, divide established plants having several stems in spring, but propagation is difficult.

Savoy

This hardy plant, a type of cabbage, has been grown in Britain since the seventeenth century. The leaves are quite distinct from those of other cabbages, being very puckered or crimped. Although there are early varieties, most gardeners prefer those which are of use during the winter and early spring. Successional crops are obtained by choosing drumheads for cutting between November and April. Its botanical name is the tongue-twisting *Brassica oleracea bullata sabauda.*

Cultivation Cultivate as for winter cabbage—the seeds being sown in the seed bed in April for plants to be set out on fertile soil in June. Allow 2 foot of space between the rows, setting the plants from 15–18 inches apart. If the soil is on the dry side, water the planting holes and plant very firmly when the water has drained away. During July and August, hoe or mulch to prevent weeds. Particular care must be taken to prevent cabbage caterpillars from establishing themselves in savoys. Varieties to grow to provide a succession for cutting include 'Ormskirk Medium', for cutting from November to February; 'Ormskirk Late Green', very hardy and the solid, medium-sized heads are cut between January and late March; 'Ormskirk Extra Late', a large, flattish, dark green savoy for use in March and April.

Saxifraga (sax-ee-fra-ga)

From the Latin *saxum,* rock or stone, and *frango,* to break, alluding either to its ancient medicinal use for 'breaking' stones in the bladder, or to the supposed ability of the roots to penetrate and assist the breakdown of rocks *(Saxi-*

fragaceae). Saxifrage, rockfoil. A genus of some 370 species of mainly dwarf tufted perennial and annual plants inhabiting the mountain regions of the northern and southern temperate regions. The many species, varieties and cultivars are usually grown on the rock garden or in the alpine house.

For the convenience of classification, the genus is divided into 15 or 16 sections, largely on the basis of the characteristics of its foliage and habit. From the gardener's point of view, however, it is best divided as below into fewer larger groupings according to cultivational requirements.

Species cultivated *S. aizoides,* yellow mountain saxifrage, a loosely tufted mat-forming species with yellow, orange or red flowers and linear fleshy leaves. *S. aizoon* (see *S. paniculata*). *S. apiculata (S. marginata × S. sancta),* a cushion or Kabschia hybrid, forming wide mats of green, silver-tipped rosettes and primrose-yellow flowers on 3-inch stems. *S. × arco-valleyi (S. burseriana × S. lilacina),* a Kabschia hybrid with compact silvery cushions and soft pink flowers on 1-inch stems. *S. aretioides* produces hard, grey-green cushions and yellow flowers; a Kabschia that has given rise to many good hybrids easier to grow. *S. × assimilis* (probably *S. burseriana × S. tombeanensis*) has firm grey cushions and white flowers on 1–2-inch long stems. *S.*

There are several forms of Saxifraga cotyledon, some of which have arching sprays of flowers that are useful for the rock garden.

biternata is an ally of the meadow saxifrage from the Mediterranean area. It has tufts of hoary, kidney-shaped, divided leaves and large glistening white flowers on 6–8-inch long stems. *S. × borisii (S. ferdinandi-coburgii × S. marginata),* is a Kabschia hybrid with blue-grey cushions and large citron-yellow flowers on 3-inch stems. *S. boryi,* allied to *S. marginata,* but more compact in habit. *S. × burnatii (S. paniculata × S. cochlearis),* is a silver or encrusted hybrid showing a blend of the parental characteristics; white flowers in loose panicles are borne on reddish stems. *S. burseriana* is the finest of the Kabschias and a parent of many excellent hybrids and cultivars. The type plant forms large cushions of crowded, silver-grey rosettes composed of many narrow, somewhat spiny, leaves. Each rosette bears a 2-inch long reddish stem surmounted by one or more large glistening-white flowers in early spring. *S. b.* 'His Majesty' is a splendid form with the flowers flushed pink; *S. b.* 'Gloria' has larger flowers on redder stems; *S. b. sulphurea* may be a hybrid, but looks like the type plant with soft-yellow flowers. *S. cespitosa* (syn. *S. caespitosa*), tufted saxifrage, is one of the

'mossy' species and a rare native in Wales and Scotland. It makes dense cushions of somewhat glandular-hairy deeply divided leaves and bears small white flowers on short slender stems. *S. caucasica* is a green-leaved Kabschia with yellow flowers on 1-inch high stems. *S. cernua* may be likened to a mountain form of the meadow saxifrage *(S. granulata)* with a drooping inflorescence bearing both white flowers and red bulbils in the leaf axils. It is a very rare Scottish native. *S. cochlearis* is an encrusted species, with small spoon-shaped silver leaves forming the hummock-like plants, from which arise slender panicles of milk-white flowers on reddish glandular stems. *S. c. minor* and *major* are smaller and larger forms. *S. cortusifolia* belongs to the Diptera section, to which the better known *S. fortunei* belongs, and has rounded, deeply cut leathery leaves on stiff 3-inch long stems, and panicles of white flowers with irregularly sized narrow petals. *S. cotyledon* is one of the largest encrusted species, with broad rosettes of wide strap-shaped leaves rimmed with silver and huge airy panicles of white flowers that may be 1½ feet or more long. *S. c. caterhamensis* and 'Southside Seedling' are superior forms with red-spotted flowers. *S. crustata,* also an encrusted sort, is smaller, the rosettes forming cushions or mats with off-white flowers on branched 6-inch stems. *S. cuneata* is a loose 'mossy' species with toothed deeply lobed leathery leaves and open panicles of white flowers. *S. cuneifolia* belongs to the Robertsonia section whose chief representative in gardens is London pride *(S. umbrosa)*. It is a small species with flat rosettes of leathery daisy-like leaves and flowering stems reminiscent of London pride in miniature. *S. cuscutiformis* is a smaller edition of mother of thousands *(S. stolonifera)* with the leaves prettily veined white. Abundantly produced red stolons, or runners, resemble the leafless stems of common dodder *(Cuscuta)*. *S cymbalaria* is an annual, with smooth shining kidney-shaped leaves and numerous starry yellow flowers. *S. decipiens* (see *S. rosacea)*. *S.* × *engleri (S. crustata* × *S. hostii)* resembles the first parent, and has pink flowers on 3-inch stems. *S. exarata* is a distinctive 'mossy' saxifrage, with dark green, strongly-nerved, deeply-cleft leaves, and flowers that may be either white, yellow or purplish. *S. ferdinandi-coburgii* belongs to the encrusted group, forming neat mounds of silver-grey, spiny-leaved rosettes topped by 4-inch high stems bearing red buds and bright yellow flowers. *S.* × *florariensis (S. hostii* × *S. lingulata)* is an encrusted hybrid eventually forming mats of handsome 3-inch

Saxifraga fortunei is one of the best known of the genus, with striking leaves and white flowers.

wide silvered rosettes that turn red in autumn, and has foot long sprays of white flowers. *S. fortunei* is undoubtedly the finest member of the Diptera section, with large, glossy, thick-textured, kidney-shaped leaves which are often red beneath, and tall airy, elegant panicles of glistening white flowers, each with one or more extra long tail-like petals. The plant is completely deciduous after the first severe frost of late autumn. *S.* × *frederici-augusti* (probably *S. media* x *S. porophylla)*, is a hybrid in the Engleria section, noteworthy for the flowering stems being clad in leafy often coloured bracts. This hybrid has silver-rimmed rosettes and flowers composed of a bell-shaped calyx covered with claret hairs below the small pink petals. *S. geum* (see *S. hirsuta). S.* × *godseffiana (S. burseriana* × *S. sancta)* produces mats of narrow spiny-leaved rosettes and lemon-yellow flowers on reddish stems. *S. granulata,* the meadow saxifrage of Britain and also known as fair maids of France, is a deciduous species, the kidney-shaped, rounded-toothed leaves dying away soon after the plant has flowered; milk-white flowers are borne on branched stems up to 1 foot tall; var. *plena* has double flowers. *S. grisebachii* belongs to the Engleria section, eventually forming humped mats of 3-inch wide grey rosettes set with leafy flowering spikes 9 inches tall. The bell-shaped calyces and bracts are set with deep red glandular hairs. *S.* × *haagii (S. ferdinandii-coburgii* × *S. sancta)* is a Kabschia with dark green rosettes in cushions and bears rich yellow flowers. *S. hederacea* rather resembles a small creeping *Linaria* or *Cymbalaria*, with small ivy-shaped leaves and starry white flowers. *S. hirculus* is placed in a section of the same name, and forms tufted mats of narrow leaves and branched stems set with quite large yellow flowers speckled with orange. It is a rare British native and known as yellow marsh saxifrage. *S. hirsuta,* probably better known as *S. geum,* is a Robertsonia saxifrage akin to London pride, but with longer leaf stalks and rounded, leaves heart-shaped at the base, set with long hairs on both surfaces. The flower stems, covered with short hairs, support open panicles of small white blossoms, each petal bearing a yellow spot at its base. *S. hostii* is one of the finest encrusted species, forming wide mats of silvery rimmed rosettes set with creamy-white flowers in short corymbs. *S. huetiana* is a small bushy annual with starry yellow flowers freely produced. *S. hypnoides* or Dovedale moss, is a cushion or mat-forming 'mossy' species native to Britain and most of the hilly regions of the northern temperate zone. It is very variable in habit, flower size and colour, the type being white; var. *condensata* is very compact with yellow flowers; var. *kingii* is close-growing, the leaves turning red in winter; var. *purpurea* has reddish

flowers. *S.* × *irvingii* (probably *S. burseriana* × *S. lilacina*) was raised at Kew and is one of the free-blooming Kabschia hybrids with lilac-pink flowers. *S.* × *jenkinsae,* is similar to the preceding and probably of the same parentage. *S. juniperifolia* has dark green, spine-tipped leaved rosettes in humped cushions, usually only sparingly set with small yellow flowers. *S. lilacina* produces wide dense mats of small green rosettes set with amethyst flowers on 1–2-inch tall stems. This distinctive Kabschia has entered into the parentage of many fine hybrids. *S. lingulata* should now be known as *S. callosa.* It is a very garden-worthy encrusted species with mats of large iron-grey rosettes and 1–1½-feet long, gracefully-arching panicles of pure white flowers; var. *catalaunica* has shorter broader leaves and shorter, stiffer flowering stems. *S. longifolia* is perhaps the finest of the large encrusted species with huge, densely leafy rosettes and elegant flowering stems up to 2 feet, long branched right to the base. *S. marginata* is another Kabschia that has contributed to some good hybrids; it forms mats or loose cushions of small green rossette rimmed with silver and bearing short-branched stems set with large white flowers. *S. media* is another Engleria somewhat smaller than *S. grisebachii* and which has entered into the parentage of many hybrids. *S. moschata* covers most of the common 'mossy' hybrids seen in gardens; it is similar to *S. decipiens* in appearance, but usually a little more dwarf and in various shades of red and pink, but sometimes yellow. *S. m.* 'Cloth of Gold', has golden-green foliage and white flowers; 'Mrs Piper' is a good bright red; 'Elf' is pink; 'James Bremner' is white; and var. *sanguinea superba* is scarlet. *S. oppositifolia* is the familiar purple saxifrage of the mountains of the northern temperate zone, extending down to sea-level in the more northern latitudes. This is a variable species as regards flower colour and leaf size, though always mat-forming with leafy interlacing stems and solitary terminal almost stemless purple flowers; var. *splendens* has large red-purple flowers; 'R. M. Prichard' is lilac-purple; *alba* is a poor form with white flowers, and *rudolphiana* is bright rose-purple. *S. paniculata* is still usually grown under the name of *S. aizoon,* a very variable encrusted species of great charm; var. *baldensis (minutifolia)* is very dwarf and compact-growing with small silvery-rimmed rosettes in low mounds and 4-inch stems of pure white flowers; var. *lutea* is similar to the type with mounds of stoloniferous rosettes and soft yellow flowers; var. *rosea* has clear pink flowers and reddish leaves; var. *orientalis* has green rosettes and milk white flowers on 4-inch stems. *S. porophylla* is akin to *S. media* and others of the Engleria group, but with purple calyces and small pink petals. *S. retusa* is akin to *S.*

213

oppositifolia but with smaller foliage and the rose-purple flowers in short terminal clusters. *S. rosacea* is still better known as *S. decipiens* and is the main 'mossy' species in cultivation, often as one parent with *S. granulata, S. moschata* and others. Most of the cultivars form loose cushions or are mat-forming with divided leaves and a profusion of short-stemmed flowers in all shades of pink, red and white. Some of the cultivars listed under *moschata* may well belong here. *S. rotundifolia* belongs to the Miscopetalum section which is close to Robertsonia and London pride. It has rounded or kidney-shaped leaves in tufts and airy panicles of small starry flowers, white speckled pink; var. *heucherifolia* is smaller, more hairy and with flowers more heavily spotted. *S. sancta* forms wide carpets of small rosettes of dark green spine-tipped leaves and bears rich yellow flowers on 2-inch tall stems. It is one of the most frequently grown green-leaved Kabschias. *S. scardica* is a blue-grey Kabschia, forming hard mounds topped by 4-inch stems of large white flowers sometimes flushed pink. *S. spathularis*, St Patrick's cabbage, is an Irish native belonging to the Robertsonia section. It resembles a smaller edition of London pride with airy panicles of starry white flowers spotted with yellow and crimson. Crossed with *S. umbrosa* it gives the familiar London pride which thrives so well in shady town gardens. *S. stolonifera* (syn. *S. sarmentosa*), mother of thousands, has long, red, branched runners like those of a strawberry, large round marbled rather fleshy leaves and graceful panicles of white flowers spotted with yellow and red. Typical of the Diptera section, each flower has one or two extra elongated petals. *S. trifurcata* belongs among the 'mossy' species with deeply cut recurved leaves somewhat aromatic when bruised and 6-inch stems of large white flowers. *S. umbrosa* is akin to *S. spathularis* but with shorter, long-hairy leaf stalks and the leaf blades with a cartilaginous border. *S. valdensis* is similar to, but smaller and slower growing than, *S. cochlearis,* with stiff glandular stems surmounted by heads of round white flowers. Cultivars: 'Amitie' (*S. lilacina* × *S. scardica obtusa*) is a Kabschia with firm cushions of grey-green rosettes and lilac flowers on 1-inch stems. 'Apple Blossom' ('mossy' hybrid) has small pale pink flowers in profusion. 'Boston Spa' (Kabschia hybrid) bears deep yellow flowers with red buds over green cushions. 'Buttercup' (Kabschia) has rich yellow flowers on grey-green cushions. 'Cecil Davies' (*S. lingulata* × *S. longifolia)* has very compact mounds of silvered rosettes and elegant sprays of white flowers. 'Cranbourne' is probably the finest of the Kabschia hybrids with neat grey-green mounds of ½-inch wide rosettes and almost stemless large clear pink flowers. 'Dr Ramsay' (*S. cochlearis*

× *S. longifolia*) is an encrusted cultivar with symmetrical silvered rosettes and sprays of white flowers on 1-foot stems. 'Edie Campbell' and 'Elf' are both 'mosses', the former with large pink flowers in profusion, the latter smaller and neater. 'Ester' (*S. paniculata lutea* × *S. cochlearis*) bears soft yellow flowers in short sprays over vigorous masses of silvered rosettes. 'Faldonside' (*S. aretioides* × *S. marginata*) is a first-rate Kabschia with citron-yellow flowers, the overlapping petals of which are charmingly crimped at the margins. 'Gem' (*S. burseriana* 'Gloria' × *S. irvingii*) is another good Kabschia with neat blue-grey spiny mounds and pale pink flowers with a ruby eye. 'Four Winds' is a rich red 'mossy' sport. 'Iris Pritchard' (*S.* × *godroniana* × *S. lilacina*) bears flowers of apricot-rose over neat grey hummocks. 'James Bremner' is one of the few good white-flowered 'mosses' and 'Kingscote White' is a larger flowered pure white 'mossy' variety. 'Kathleen Pinsent' (encrusted) may be a *S. ligulata* × *S. callosa* hybrid, with 1-foot long stems and sprays of yellow-eyed pink flowers. 'Myra' (Kabschia) is probably a *S. lilacina* hybrid, with compact, slow-growing mounds of silvery rosettes and deep pink blossoms. 'Mrs Piper' ('mossy'), forms wide mats of soft green foliage studded freely with bright red flowers on 3-inch stems. 'Pearly King' is a similar 'mossy' with pearly-white flowers. 'Pixie' is a compact growing 'mossy' with rose-red flowers. 'Riverslea' (*S. lilacina* × *S. porophylla*) is a Kabschia × Engleria hybrid, with silvery rosettes in compact mounds and purple-rose flowers on 3-inch stems. 'Salomonii' (*S. burseriana* × *S. marginata)* produces free-growing silvery mats and 3-inch stems bearing large vase-shaped white flowers that are pink in bud. 'Sir Douglas Haig' ('mossy') bears dark velvety-crimson flowers. 'Southside Seedling' is a comparatively new *S. cotyledon* hybrid with large silver-rimmed rosettes and long sprays of white, intensely red-spotted blossoms. 'Tumbling Waters' (*S. lingulata* × *S. longiflora*) is the finest large encrusted hybrid with huge silvered rosettes and magnificent 2-foot long plumes of white blossoms. 'Winston Churchill' ('mossy') bears soft pink flowers on 6-inch stems.

Cultivation With the exception of species in the section Hirculus, a few of the 'mossy' group, and *S. aizoides,* which need moist to wet conditions to thrive well, practically all saxifrages require a well-drained site either on the rock garden, dry wall, raised bed, moraine, or in pots and pans in the alpine house. The Robertsonia species, typified by London pride, the Miscopetalum section, and such species as *S. hederacea*, require a shady site, the first mentioned doing particularly well even in complete shade or in woodland. Kabschia species require particularly good drainage and are best grown in a scree or raised bed.

Flowering very early, they are ideally suited to alpine house culture where their delicate-looking flowers may be appreciated unsullied by heavy rain and mud splash. Most of the encrusted group are ideal for the open rock garden, in rock crevices or dry walls; *S. cotyledon* and *longifolia* should always be grown in the latter habitat if at all possible. All the popular mossy hybrids and some of the species are good all-rounders on the rock garden and are also suitable for paved areas and as ground cover for small bulbs. Generally speaking they will stand partial shade well and seem to thrive better if the site is not too sun drenched. Propagation is effected by seeds sown in pots or pans in early spring, stood in a cold frame, by division after flowering, or by offset rosettes inserted as cuttings in a sand frame from spring to late summer.

Scabiosa (skay-bee-o-sa)
From the Latin *scabies*, itch, for which some of these plants were used as remedies, or from the Latin *scabiosus,* rough or scurfy, referring to the grey felting on the leaves of some species (*Dipsacaceae*). Scabious. This genus of 100 species of hardy biennial and perennial herbaceous plants, mainly from the Mediterranean region, gives a number which are good decorative plants for the garden. The three species which are British native plants, *Scabiosa arvensis, S. columbaria* and *S. succisa,* are among our prettiest-flowering wild plants and are quite suited to garden cultivation. *S. succisa*, the devil's bit, is especially good as it has flowers of a bright blue colour. In the plants in the *Dipsacaceae* family the so-called flower is made up of a large number of small florets gathered into a head, or *capitulum,* somewhat as in *Compositae*.

Perennial species cultivated *S. arvensis* (syn. *Knautia arvensis*), field scabious, 1 foot, flowers bluish-lilac, July–August, Europe (including Britain). *S. caucasica,* 1–1½ feet, flowers mauve, blue or white, June to October, Caucasus; vars. 'Clive Greaves', flowers mauve, large; 'Miss Willmott', large, white; 'Moonstone', large, lavender-blue. *S. columbaria,* 1–2 feet, lilac or blue-purple, July to September, Europe (including Britain). *S. graminifolia,* 9 inches, leaves narrow, silvery-white, flowers pale mauve to rose, summer, southern Europe. *S. ochroleuca,* 2 feet, yellow, July to November, south-eastern Europe; var. *webbiana,* 6 inches, flowers creamy-white. *S. succisa* (syn. *Succisa pratensis*), devil's bit, 1–2 feet, blue-purple or white, July to October, Europe (including Britain).

Annual species cultivated *S. atropurpurea,* sweet scabious, mournful widow, pincushion flower, 2–3 feet, flowers deep crimson to purple, July to September, south-western Europe; cultivars include 'Azure Fairy', blue; 'Blue Moon', pale blue; 'Black Prince', very dark purple;

'Cherry Red'; 'Cockade Mixed', large almost conical flowers in various colours; 'Coral Moon', light to dark salmon; 'Fire King', scarlet; 'Loveliness', salmon-rose; 'Parma Violet'; 'Peach Blossom', pale rose; 'Rosette', deep rose and salmon; 'Snowball', white.

Cultivation These plants all do well in chalky or limy soil, which, however, should be enriched. *S. caucasica* is suitable for the herbaceous border, but may also be grown to supply cut flowers, for which purpose its long clean stems make it very suitable. These plants should be lifted and divided every three or four years, moving them in spring as disturbance in autumn can kill them. *S. graminifolia* and *S. ochroleuca webbiana* are suitable for the rock garden. *S. atropurpurea* can be raised from seed sown in February or March in a temperature of 60°F (16°C). Plant out the seedlings in May to flower as annuals, or later disturbance (July) will cause them to behave as biennials. In the latter case, over-winter them in a cold frame and plant out in April. They are good for cutting. Other species may be propagated by division of the clumps in March.

Scaevola (skee-vo-la)

A Roman family name meaning 'left-handed', taken from *scaevus*, left, referring to the form of the corolla (*Goodeniaceae*). A genus of 80 to 100 species, of which more than half are Australian; they are herbaceous plants, undershrubs, or shrubs with white, blue or reddish flowers produced in the leaf axils or forks of branches. The undermentioned species are probably in cultivation and are all suitable for the cool greenhouse.

Species cultivated *S. chamissoniana*, flowers white and purple, Sandwich Islands. *S. crassifolia*, under shrub, 3 feet, flowers in dense, terminal spikes, southern and western coasts of Australia. *S. frutescens*, flowers white. *S. suaveolens* (syn. *Goodenia calendulacea*), perennial, prostrate or decumbent, may be silky-hairy or glabrous, flowers blue, stemless, August, Australia.

Cultivation Most species are suitable for cultivation in pots but grow and look better if planted out in the greenhouse border. Any general potting soil, such as John Innes potting compost, will suffice, and propagation may be by cuttings of half-ripened wood, placed in sandy compost, or by seed.

Schizanthus (skiz-an-thus; shy-zan-thus)

From the Greek *schizo*, to cut, and *anthos*, flower, in reference to the deeply cut corolla (*Solanaceae*). A genus of 15 species of showy and attractive annual plants from Chile, sometimes

1 Scaevola chamissoniana has purple flowers with white centres. It is a native of the Sandwich Islands.
2 A fine form of Scabiosa caucasica.

known as the butterfly flowers, or the poor man's orchids. They are suitable for cold greenhouse cultivation, or can be sown in heat and bedded out in late spring or early summer.

Species cultivated *S. grahamii,* 2 feet, lilac, rose and yellow, June to October. *S. pinnatus,* 2 feet, violet and yellow, but may be other colours, June to October. *S. retusus,* 2½ feet, rose and orange, July to September. *S. × wisetonensis,* hybrid of first two species, combines their characteristics. Garden strains which have evolved from hybridising include: 'Danbury Park Strain', pansy-flowered, pink, crimson, purple and white; 'Dr Badger's Hybrids Improved', large flowers, colours ranging from white and yellow through lilac and rose; 'Dwarf Bouquet', bright rose, crimson, salmon, amber, and pink; Wisetonensis 'Monarch Signal', feathery leaves, cherry red orchid-like flowers.

Cultivation Schizanthus are usually grown as cold greenhouse plants and provide a most attractive display in late winter and early spring. Sow the seeds in August in John Innes seed compost, in a frame or cool greenhouse, and transplant the seedlings when large enough to handle, to 3-inch pots containing John Innes potting compost No 1, giving them as much light as possible, and a tem-

The showy hybrid Schizanthus, Butterfly Flower or Poor Man's Orchid, makes a colourful display in the greenhouse in spring from an autumn sowing.

perature of 45–55 F (7–13 C) until January. Then put them in 6-inch pots and grow them in a light position, but do not allow them to become pot-bound. Stop the plants frequently to keep them bushy, and support them by tying them to stakes. In winter they should be moderately watered, but freely at other times, and they benefit from the application of liquid fertilisers occasionally while flowering.

When grown as half-hardy annuals for planting out of doors, seed is sown under glass in February–March in a temperature of 65–75 F (18–24 C). The seedlings are pricked off when they are about 1 inch high, and then planted out in May after being hardened off. They can also be sown where they are required to grow, in May, but require a warm sheltered site if this is to be done; they will then flower in August.

Scilla (sil-la)

An ancient Greek or Latin name, used for *Urginea maritima,* or from the Latin, *squilla* (Greek, *skilla*), the squill *(Liliaceae).* Squill. A genus of 80 species of

bulbous plants from Europe and the non-tropical regions of Asia and Africa, and a few from tropical Africa, which have racemes of decorative flowers, making them well worthy of cultivation. The English and Spanish bluebells were for some time known as scillas, but have now been renamed *Endymion,* and are called, respectively, *E. non-scriptus* and *E. hispanicus.* Scillas are also closely related to *Chionodoxa.*

Species cultivated *S. amoena,* Byzantine squill, star hyacinth, 6 inches, flowers indigo blue, April to May, central Europe. *S. autumnalis,* 6 inches, flowers rose-lilac, July to September, Europe (including Britain), North Africa. *S. bifolia,* 6 inches, flowers blue, reddish, or white, March, mountains of southern Europe (not the Alps). *S. messeniaca,* 6 inches, flowers pale blue-mauve, March to April, Greece. *S. peruviana,* 9 inches, flowers deep lilac-blue, May to June, Mediterranean region. *S. pratensis,* 1 foot, bluish-lilac, fragrant, May to June, Yugoslavia. *S. sibirica,* Siberian squill, 8 inches, flowers deep blue, March. *S. tubergeniana,* 4 inches, flowers very pale blue, with deeper central stripe, late February–early March, north-western Persia. *S. verna,* 8 inches, flowers pale blue-mauve, April and May. Europe (including Britain).

Cultivation If grown out of doors, the scillas need no special soil other than a well-drained one, and are equally at home in a sunny border, a ledge in the rock garden, or naturalised in grass. Plant in early autumn in groups, to give the maximum effect, putting the bulbs at a depth which is twice that of their own height. For indoor cultivation, a compost consisting of equal parts of loam, sand and leafmould is suitable, potting the bulbs up in September and keeping them plunged under ashes until growth appears. Then transfer to the frame or greenhouse. Propagation is by offsets, or by seed, sown in September, out of doors or in sandy soil in boxes in a cold-frame. Plants take five years to flower from seed.

Scutellaria (sku-tel-lar-ee-a)
From the Latin *scutella,* a small shield, in allusion to the shape of the persistent calyx *(Labiatae).* Sometimes known as the skullcaps. A genus of 300 species of annual or perennial herbaceous plants from temperate regions and tropical mountains throughout the world, except South Africa. There are two native species, rather rare, one of which is of use in the garden because of its paired blue flowers.

Hardy species cultivated *S. albida,* 1 foot, flowers white, summer, south-eastern Europe, central Asia. *S. alpina,* 1 foot, flowers purple, sometimes yellow, August, Europe, central Asia. *S. baicalensis,* 1 foot, flowers blue, August, eastern Asia. *S. galericulata,* 6–18 inches, blue, July to September, Europe (including Britain). *S. indica,* 1½ feet, flowers blue, June to August, China; var. *japonica,* flowers violet-purple. *S. scordifolia,* 6 inches, bright blue, July and August, Siberia.

Stovehouse species cultivated *S. costari-*

Scilla tubergeniana has very pale mauve flowers with a slightly deeper central stripe.

cana, 1½–3 feet, scarlet and yellow, June, Costa Rica. *S. mociniana,* 3 feet, yellow and scarlet, summer, Mexico. *S. violacea,* 2 feet, violet and white, July, India and Ceylon.

Cultivation The hardy species are handsome, easily grown plants, happy in any soil and situation, in a border or a rock garden. *S. alpina* makes a good specimen for the alpine house; *S. albida* and *S. galericulata* are particularly suitable for the wild garden. Plant in spring. The stovehouse species require a compost of equal parts of loam, leafmould (or peat) and coarse sand, and should be potted in February or March. From September to June they do best in a sunny part of the stovehouse; for the rest of the year they can be put out in a sunny frame. The

217

Scutellaria costaricana is a stovehouse
perennial with scarlet-orange flowers
of arresting form.

pots should be well drained, and the
plants watered freely during the summer,
moderately at other times. They should
be pruned after flowering to within 3
inches of the basal growth, and also you
should take out the tips of the main
shoots when 3 inches long, and of the
side shoots so as to make the plants
bushy. An occasional feeding with
liquid fertiliser while growing is beneficial, and so also is overhead spraying
in the summer. The minimum temperature, between September and March,
should be not less than 55°F (13°C).
Propagation of the hardy species is by
seeds sown out of doors in April or by
division of roots at the same time.
Cuttings of firm shoots of the greenhouse
species, taken in spring, and placed in
sandy soil, will root in a temperature of
75–85°F (24–30°C).

Seakale

This vegetable (known botanically as
Crambe maritima) is much appreciated
by those who know its taste. The plants
are generally raised from cuttings taken
from growing plants in the autumn.
Sideshoots, varying in thickness from
that of a lead pencil to your thumb, are
suitable. They may be from 4–10 inches
long and, after severing them from the
plants, the base of each cutting should be
cut at a slanting angle and the top
cut squarely across. This is done so that
tops and bottoms may be recognised at
planting time to avoid planting them
upside down.

Tie the prepared cuttings in bunches
and store them in sand or ashes in a
sheltered part of the garden. Lift the
bunches in early March and plant them
in deeply dug, well-manured soil, or
ground into which plenty of garden
compost has been dug. Use the cabbage
dibber and make the dibber holes sufficiently deep so that the top of each
cutting is ½ inch below the surface of
the soil. Suitable spacings are 1 foot
between plants and 18 inches between
rows. Hoe or mulch during spring and
summer to keep down weed growth.

The plants are grown for their tender
young shoots. Unless blanched, they are
bitter and unpalatable. For the earliest
crop of blanched shoots, lift a few
plants in November and cut off the
thongy side growths for the preparation
of cuttings for new plants for spring
planting. Plant the strong main roots
and crowns closely together in large
clay pots, using old potting soil as the
compost. Water moderately and stand
the pots in a dark, heated place. If
blanching is carried out in the garden
shed, cover the window, if beneath the
greenhouse staging, drape a sheet of
black polythene over and around the
pots to exclude light. Further roots may

be dug and forced in the same way on
and off between November and February.
A temperature of between 60–75°F (16–
24°C) should be maintained. Late supplies may be forced out of doors. Cover
the crowns of the plants with inverted
clay pots or by heaping fine sand, sandy
soil or ashes over them to a depth of 9
inches. The drainage holes of pots
should be covered with pieces of tile or
bricks to prevent light from entering.
Cut the white shoots when they are from
6–9 inches long. Forced roots are of no
further use and should therefore be
composted.

It is important to obtain your original
cuttings from a reliable source offering
those of a good strain.

Sedum (se-dum)

From the Latin *sedo,* to sit, in reference
to the manner in which some species
attach themselves to rocks and walls
(Crassulaceae). A genus of some 600
species of annual, biennial or perennial,
succulent, xerophytic plants, natives of
the temperate or colder regions of the
northern hemisphere, with a few natives
of warmer regions such as central Africa
or Peru. The plants have very fleshy
leaves, and several species spread over
the ground as creepers. *S. acre,* the stone
crop, is one of a number of native British
plants. Many species and hybrids are
suitable for growing on rock gardens or
dry walls; others are excellent plants for
the herbaceous border.

Hardy species cultivated The following
is only a selection of the many that can
be grown. *S. acre,* stone crop, wallpepper,
mat-forming, flowers yellow, May and
June, Europe (including Britain), Asia;
vars. *aureum,* leaves and stem ends
bright gold in spring; *elegans,* silver. *S.
aizoon,* 12 inches, yellow to orange,
July, China. *S. album,* 4 inches, flowers
white or red, summer, Europe (including
Britain), Africa, Asia. *S. cauticola,* 4–6
inches, rose-crimson, autumn, Japan. *S.
elongatum* (syn. *S. bupleuroides*), hairy
leaves, flowers dark purple, May and
June, Himalaya, China. *S. kamtschati-*

cum, 6 inches, orange-yellow, June to
September, northern Asia; var. *variegatum*, leaves with cream margins, flowers
bright yellow. *S. maximum*, 1–3 feet,
flowers greenish-white, summer, Europe;
var. *atropurpureum*, stem and leaves
deep red, flowers deep pink, late summer.
S. middendorffianum, 4–6 inches, purplish leaves, flowers yellow, July to
August, Siberia. *S. oreganum*, cushion-forming to 3 inches, flowers golden, July
to August, western North America. *S.
roseum*, rose root, 6–12 inches, greenish
or yellow, May, northern hemisphere. *S.
rupestre*, mat-forming, flowers yellow,
July, Europe (including Britain). *S.
spathulifolium*, 3–4 inches, yellow, May
to June, North America; var. 'Cappa
Blanca', leaves with white meal, flowers
bright yellow. *S. spectabile*, 1–1½ feet,
wide, flat-topped clusters of pink flowers,
late summer, China; the cultivar 'Brilliant' has deeper coloured flowers. *S.
spurium*, 6 inches, white to crimson, July
to August, Persia, Caucasus; vars.
roseum, mat-forming, flowers deep pink;
'Schorbusser Blut', coppery coloured
foliage, flowers deep red, late summer,
autumn. *S. stribrnyi*, to 6 inches, bright
yellow, July, Bulgaria, Greece. *S. telephium*, orpine, 1–1½ feet, red-purple,
August to September, Europe (including
Britain); vars. 'Autumn Joy', salmon-pink and bronze, September to October;
'Munstead Red', deep red; *variegatum*,
cream variegated leaves. *S.* 'Weihenstephener Gold', mat-forming, flowers
golden, summer.

Tender species cultivated *S. alamosanum*,
3–5 inches, reddish-white, March, north-western Mexico. *S. bellum*, 3–6 inches,
mealy leaves, flowers white, April–May,
Mexico. *S. dasyphyllum*, 1–2 inches,
pink, June, Mediterranean coast. *S.
hintonii*, leaves and stems covered in
white hairs, flowers greenish-white,
Mexico. *S. longipes*, 8 inches, purple,
January, Mexico. *S. modestum*, hairy,
flowers whitish-red, Morocco. *S. morganianum*, long trailing stems, flowers
purple, at ends of stems, good for hanging
baskets in the greenhouse, summer,
Mexico. *S. pachyphyllum*, almost cylindrical leaves with red tips, flowers light
yellow, April, Mexico. *S. pulvinatum*,
flowers white, Mexico. *S. stahlii*, 4–8
inches, reddish leaves, flowers yellow,
late summer, Mexico.

Cultivation The hardy species will grow
in any porous soil, on sunny borders, or
rock gardens; some will grow in wall
pockets, or on the tops of walls themselves. Plant between November and
April. The tender species require a
compost such as John Innes potting

compost No 1 with ⅛ part added of sharp sand, grit and broken brick. A sunny position in the greenhouse, in pots or pans, suits them, and they should be potted in spring. Keep the soil dry in winter, and in summer water as the soil dries out. The minimum temperature in winter is 40°F (4°C), and 55–65°F (13–18°C) in summer. Propagation is by cuttings or divisions of plants or, with many species, by taking leaf cuttings and placing them in sharp sand. Also by seed sown in John Innes seed compost, the seedlings being pricked out when they are large enough to handle.

Sempervivum (sem-per-vi-vum)

From the Latin *semper*, always, and *vivo*, I live, an allusion to the tenacity of life common to these plants *(Crassulaceae)*. House leek. Hardy succulent perennials from the mountains of Europe; some species are found in Britain. There are 25 species but many varieties and hybrids, can be difficult to identify accurately. The plants consist of close rosettes of leaves, some pointed, and many with fine cobweb-like hairs which form from tip to tip of the leaves. The flowers appear in a terminal inflorescence and the rosettes from which they come die when flowering has finished, but are replaced by others.

Species cultivated *S. arachnoideum*, cobweb house leek, groups of small rosettes of leaves joined together at the tips with fine white hairs, flowers pinkish-carmine, July, Pyrenees, Alps. *S. arenarium,* leaves light green, flushed red, tall flower stem, flowers pale yellow, August, Tyrol. *S. ciliosum,* large hairy rosettes, leaves grey-green, flowers greenish-yellow, July, Bulgaria. *S. grandiflorum,* very large rosettes, flowers greenish-yellow to yellow with violet markings near the base, June, Switzerland. *S. ingwersenii*, dense rosettes, flowers pink, edged with white, summer, Caucasus. *S. nevadense,* forms a compact mass of rosettes with small leaves, turning red in summer, flowers red, summer, Spain. *S. tectorum,* St Patrick's cabbage, and numerous other vernacular names, flattish rosettes 2–3 inches across, sometimes to 8 inches, leaves green, purple-tipped, flowers pinkish-red, July, a very variable species, European Alps. *S. wulfenii,* leaves grey-green, flowers yellow in a hairy panicle, July, central Europe.

Cultivation These are easily grown plants in any light sandy, porous or gritty soil in the sun. Rock gardens, walls, edgings to borders and sink gardens are all suitable places to grow them; even the house roof will suit *S. tectorum* which was once planted on cottage roofs to help to keep the slates in place. Plant from March to June and topdress each spring with well-rotted garden compost or similar material. Propagation is by division or offsets in March, or by seed, but the plants

hybridise so freely that it is difficult to be sure of obtaining the required plant by this means.

Senecio (sen-e-see-o)

From the Latin *senex*, an old man, in allusion to the grey and hoary seed pappus *(Compositae)*. The largest genus in the plant world; containing between 2,000 and 3,000 species, it covers a wide range of plant types including greenhouse and hardy annuals, evergreen herbaceous plants, climbers, shrubs, an aquatic species and a dozen or more species of tree-like dimensions. The genus is of world-wide distribution. The greenhouse cinerarias are hybrids of one species, *Senecio cruentus* (for their cultivation see Cineraria).

Annual species cultivated *S. arenarius*, 1 foot, flowers lilac, summer, South Africa. *S. elegans,* 1–2 feet, single and double flowers of various colours, summer, South Africa.

Greenhouse species cultivated *S. cineraria* (syn. *Cineraria maritima*), dusty miller, 2 feet, yellow flowers, summer, silver leaves, Mediterranean. *S. cruentus* (syn. *Cineraria cruentus*), parent of the greenhouse cineraria hybrids, 1–2 feet, purple, summer, Canary Isles; many cultivars are available in a wide range of colours from light pink to deep blue. *S. glastifolius,* shrub, 4 feet, flowers

purple and yellow, June South Africa. *S. grandiflorus*, to 5 feet, purple and yellow, August, South Africa. *S. heretieri*, 3–4 feet, white and purple, May to July, Teneriffe. *S. leucostachys*, 2–3 feet, yellow, summer, silver foliage, Patagonia. *S. macroglossus*, Cape ivy, climbing, thick, ivy-shaped leaves, flowers yellow, winter, South Africa. *S. mikanioides*, German ivy, climbing, ivy-shaped leaves, flowers fragrant, yellow, winter, South Africa. *S. petasites* (E), velvet groundsel, shrub, 5 feet, yellow, winter, Mexico, hardy in Cornwall.

Hardy herbaceous species cultivated *S. adonidifolius*, 8–18 inches, orange, July and August, Spain. *S. doronicum*, 1–2 feet, yellow, summer, Europe. *S. incanus*, 3–4 feet, silver leaves in a rosette, flowers yellow, August, Europe. *S. macrophyllus*, 4–5 feet, yellow, summer, Caucasus. *S. palustris aurantiacus*, 12 inches, woolly leaves, orange-brown to yellow flowers, summer, Europe. *S. pulcher*, 1–2 feet, plant hairy, flowers red-purple, late summer and autumn, Uruguay. *S. smithii*, 4 feet, white, June, Falkland Islands, Chile. *S. tanguticus,* 6–7 feet, golden-yellow, in large pyramidical panicles, July to September, China. *S. uniflorus*, 3 inches, silvery-hairy, yellow, July, southern Europe.

Shrub species cultivated *S. bidwillii*, dwarf shrub, rigid habit, leaves thick,

shining above, felted below, flowers white, New Zealand. *S. compactus*, 2–3 feet, shoots and undersides of leaves covered with white hairs, flowers yellow, New Zealand. *S. elaeagnifolius,* to 10 feet in nature, leaves thick, leathery, brown-felted below, flowers yellow, New Zealand; var. *buchananii,* less tall. *S. greyi* (E), to 8 feet, leaves grey on undersurface, yellow flowers, summer, New Zealand. *S. hectori,* to 12–14 feet, leaves oval to 10 inches long, white below, flowers white, to 2½ inches across, New Zealand, tender. *S. laxifolius* (E), 4 feet, grey-green leaves and shoots, yellow flowers, summer, New Zealand. *S. monroi* (E), 2–6 feet, yellow, July, New Zealand. *S. rotundifolius,* 6 feet or more, shoots and undersides of leaves densely covered with white down, flowers small, yellowish, summer, New Zealand. *S. scandens,* rampant climber to 15 feet or more, flowers small, daisy-like, yellow, autumn, China, Japan; usually dies back in winter.

Cultivation of annuals Sow seeds ⅛ inch deep in patches or drills where they are to grow in ordinary soil which has been previously enriched. A sunny aspect in beds or borders is suitable. Thin the

**1 The purple Senecio or Wild Cineraria.
2 Senecio laxifolius has lemon-yellow, daisy-like flowers.**

seedlings to 3–6 inches apart.

Cultivation of greenhouse species Use a compost of 2 parts of sandy loam, 2 parts of peat and 1 part of coarse sand and sow the seeds in well-firmed, well-drained compost, in 6-inch pots in April. Use the seed sparingly and cover with sifted compost very thinly. Place the pots in a cool greenhouse, frame or window, and when the seedlings are 1 inch high, thin to 2 inches apart. The climbing species should be given a permanent position where they can be trained up to the greenhouse roof or round a window frame, and the seedlings potted up separately rather than thinned. Water freely during the growing season and feed also, but give little water in winter. The minimum winter temperature should be 40 F (4 C).

Cultivation of hardy perennials A rich loamy soil in a lightly shaded, moist border provide suitable growing conditions. *S. uniflorus* does best in the rock garden on a sunny bank. Plant in spring and mulch heavily, water freely in dry weather. Propagate in spring by root division or by seed sown outside.

Cultivation of hardy shrubs Sheltered sunny borders and ordinary soil are required for the hardy shrubs, which can be planted in autumn or spring. They are admirable shrubs for coastal gardens as they stand up well to salt-laden gales. Propagation is by placing cuttings of semi-ripe shoots in sandy soil in a frame in July. See also Cineraria; Ligularia.

Shallots

Some people prefer the milder flavour of the shallot, *Allium ascalonicum,* which they grow in place of onions. Generally, however, shallots are grown for pickling. When stocks of non-bolting onion sets were not available, many gardeners found shallot growing far easier than onion growing. The soil in which they are to be grown must be well-drained and, unless very large bulbs are required, without manure or fertilisers. A very poor soil is greatly improved by being mulched with garden compost just prior to planting time.

Traditionally, shallots were planted on the shortest day in December and lifted on the longest day in June. The soil is seldom suitable for planting during the winter, and planting between late February and early April produces good results. Simply press the bulbs into the ground at intervals of 8 inches in the row, and allow 12 inches between rows. Birds, earthworms and severe frost may loosen the bulbs so, about a week after planting, inspect the bed and replant or replace where necessary. If birds continue to pull out the bulbs, the bed should be netted.

Unless the plants are to be fed with liquid manure for the production of very large shallots, little is needed in the way of cultivation. Weeds may be removed by hand or hoeing. Alternatively, use sedge peat as a mulch around the plants in late April.

In early June, draw a little of the mulch or surrounding soil away from the bulb clusters to allow more sunlight to reach them. The foliage will yellow in July, when the clusters should be lifted with the garden fork and spread out to dry. In fine, sunny weather dry them in the open; in wet weather under cover. The greenhouse staging, the cold frame or under cloches are suitable places.

When quite dry, split the clusters into separate bulbs and store them in a cool, airy place for use when required. The bulbs are best stored in Dutch trays or in vegetable nets. Do not store in sacks or polythene bags. Some of the medium-sized bulbs may be set aside for planting in the following season. There are both yellow and red shallots. These include 'Giant Long Keeping', yellow; and 'Giant Long Keeping', red; and 'Giant Red'. 'Hâtive de Niort' and 'The Aristocrat' are favoured by exhibitors.

Sidalcea (sid-al-see-a)

A compound of two related genera, *Sida* and *Alcea*. The former comes from an ancient Greek name used by Theophrastus for the water-lily, the latter from *Althaea*, the generic name for hollyhock *(Malvaceae)*. These hardy perennial herbaceous plants belong to the same family as the hollyhock and the mallow. Their flowers have delicate, papery petals in varying shades of pink and purple. There are 25 species, all from western North America.

Species cultivated *S. candida,* 2–3 feet, flowers white, summer, Colorado. *S. malvaeflora,* 1½–3 feet, rather twiggy in habit, flowers lilac, summer, California; var. *listeri,* pink. *S. spicata,* 1–3 feet, rosy-purple flowers, July–September, western North America. Some good cultivars include 'Brilliant', crimson; 'Elsie Heugh', pink, fringed flowers; 'Interlaken', pink; 'Puck', large, clear pink flowers; 'Rev Page Roberts', soft pink; 'Rose Queen', tall; 'William Smith', salmon-red.

Cultivation Ordinary, slightly sandy soil is suitable; the position should preferably be a sunny border. Plant in the autumn or spring, and lift and divide every three or four years. Propagation is by seeds sown in light soil in April, transplanting the seedlings in April, or by division for the named varieties, doing this in October or March.

Silene (si-le-ne)

Probably from the Greek *sialon,* saliva, in reference to the gummy exudations on the stems which ward off insects *(Caryophyllaceae).* Catchfly. A genus of 500 species of annual, biennial and herbaceous perennials of the northern hemisphere and South Africa, having a wide range of colour through white, pink and red to purple. Some make good rock plants, but some can only be considered as weeds and should be banned from the garden.

Annual species cultivated *S. armeria,*

Sidalcea malvaerflora has lilac flowers in mid-summer. Several reliable cultivars are available.

1–2 feet, flowers pink, summer, Europe. *S. pendula,* 12 inches, rose to white, summer, Europe.

Biennial species cultivated *S. compacta,* 1½ feet, flowers pink, summer, Russia, Asia Minor. *S. rupestris,* 4–6 inches, flowers white to pink, June to August, western Europe, Siberia.

Perennial species cultivated *S. acaulis,* cushion pink, moss campion, 2 inches, flowers pink, June, northern hemisphere. *S. alpestris* (syn. *Heliosperma alpestre*), 4 inches, white, summer, eastern Europe; var. *plena,* flowers double. *S. laciniata* (syn. *Melandrium laciniatum*), 8–10 inches, flowers scarlet, summer, United States. *S. maritima,* sea campion, 6 inches, flowers white, large, July to September, Europe (including Britain); var. *plena,* flowers double. *S. saxifraga,* 6 inches, flowers white and brown, summer, Greece. *S. schafta,* 6–9 inches, flowers pink, summer and autumn, Caucasus. *S. virginica* (syn. *Melandrium virginicum*), fire pink, 1–1½ feet, flowers

crimson, North America. *S. zawadskyi* (syn. *Melandrium zawadskyi*), 4–6 inches, flowers white, large, summer, Romania. Some good cultivars include *S. pendula compacta,* pink; *rubervina,* ruby red; 'Peach Blossom', single pink; 'Triumph', crimson-rose; 'Special Dwarf Mixture', double white through pink and lilac to crimson.

Cultivation The soil for annual and biennial species should be light and sandy, in a sunny bed or border. For perennials a sandy loam mixed with well-rotted organic material is suitable. *S. acaulis* requires equal parts of loam, peat and stones, and prefers a sunny crack or shelf on a rock garden, as does *S. virginica.* Planting is carried out in the spring, and lifting and replanting should be undertaken only when absolutely essential. Propagation for annuals is by seed, sown in September. transplanting the seedlings, when they are 1 inch high, and then planting them in their permanent positions in March for spring flowering, or by seed sown in April, transplanting to flowering positions when 1 inch high for summer blooming, or by sowing seed where

1 A good rock plant, Silene schafta, has pink flowers in summer.
2 Silene elizabethae.
3 Some Silenes are regarded as garden weeds, although in themselves they are attractive plants. The inflated calyces of Silene inflata, the Bladder Campion, make this plant distinctive.

required to grow and thinning out in May. Perennials are propagated from seed sown in spring, in pans placed in cold frames, from cuttings and by division in spring.

Smilacina (smi-las-ee-na)

The diminutive of *Smilax,* literally a little smilax, which it resembles. Smilax is an ancient Greek name of obscure meaning *(Liliaceae).* A genus of 25 species of hardy rhizomatous perennials from America and Asia, with white flowers growing in a loose feathery spike, atypical of the lily family, and with parallel-veined leaves.

Species cultivated *S. oleracea,* 4 feet, flowers white and pale pink, May, fruit a dark-spotted, rose-purple berry, Sikkim. *S. racemosa,* false spikenard, 3 feet, flowers white, May, followed by red berries, North America. *S. stellata,* 2 feet, flowers white, May, north-western America.

Cultivation The soil should be a good loam, moist but not wet. Slightly shaded positions are preferred, in damp woodlands, on banks, in shrub borders or herbaceous borders. Planting is carried out in October or March. Propagation is by division of the roots in the same months as planting.

Solanum (so-la-num)

From the Latin *solamen,* quieting, in allusion to the narcotic effects of some species *(Solanaceae).* A genus of some 1,700 species of annuals, perennials, shrubs, trees and climbers, with a worldwide distribution in temperate and tropical regions, some having tuberous roots and edible fruits (e.g. potato and aubergine), some grown for their ornamental flowers.

Species cultivated *S. aculeatissimum,* prickly annual with lobed leaves and small white potato-like flowers in summer, followed by large fruits the size of a tangerine, tropics. *S. aethiopicum,* annual, leaves lanceolate, flowers large, white, red, in drooping racemes, fruits edible, Asia, tropical Africa. *S. aviculare,* kangaroo apple, shrubby in habit, leaves long, lanceolate, sometimes deeply cut, flowers violet, 1½ inches across, borne in short axillary clusters, fruits large, greenish or yellow, Australia, New Zealand. *S. capsicastrum,* Christmas or winter cherry, sub-shrub grown as a pot plant, leaves ovate, dark green, flowers white, small, berries orange-scarlet, Brazil; var. *variegatum* leaves splashed with creamy-yellow. *S. cornutum,* prickly annual, to 4 feet tall, leaves pinnately-lobed, flowers bright yellow, each with one curiously enlarged horn-shaped anther, Mexico. *S. crispum,* tall, almost climbing shrub, leaves ovate, flowers showy, purplish-blue in panicles, fruits yellowish-white, pea-sized, Chile. *S. demissum,* comes from the high pine forests of Mexico and is a low, tufted, tuberous-rooted plant with leaves that may be pinnate or almost simple, and small cymes of blue potato-like flowers; it has been crossed with the domestic potato to produce cultivars resistant to virus diseases. *S. dulcamara,* common native woody nightshade or bittersweet, a shrubby trailer, stems to 6 feet long, flowers purple or white, summer, fruits usually red, poisonous; var. *variegatum,* sometimes grown in gardens, its leaves handsomely splashed with creamy white. *S. etuberosum,* shrubby habit, leaves pinnate, flowers showy, blue-purple, in large clusters. *S. integrifolium,* Chinese scarlet egg-plant, with bright scarlet (or yellow) globular fruits and lobed leaves prickly on the veins, habitat unknown, possibly Africa. *S. intrusum,* garden huckleberry, resembles a large-growing black nightshade, with somewhat larger flowers and edible fruits which are variously described as pleasantly palatable and insipid. *S. jasminoides,* potato vine, deciduous climber, clusters of bluish-white flowers borne in profusion, summer, South America; vars. *album,* white flowers; *variegatum,* leaves blotched creamy-white. *S. laciniatum* resembles *S. aviculare,* but is a tetraploid and has flowers 2 inches across. *S. marginatum,* 3–4 feet, biennial, leaves and stems white-hairy, prickly, flowers bluish-violet, about 2 inches across, fruits yellow, Abyssinia. *S. melongena* (see Aubergine). *S. muricatum,* melon pear, bushy sub-shrub, leaves lanceolate, flowers small, blue, fruits yellow,

splashed with purple, egg-shaped, edible, Chile, Peru. *S. nigrum guineense* see *S. intrusum. S. pseudocapsicum,* Jerusalem cherry, shrub to 4 feet, with a similar appearance to *S. capsicastrum* when grown as an annual for pot plant work, Madeira. *S. pyracanthum,* to 6 feet, may behave as a biennial or a short-lived sub-shrub, leaves and stems are prickly, flowers purple-blue, tropical Africa. *S. quitoense* bears fruits like small oranges, the juice of which is used for soft drinks in its native South America. Known as the Quito orange or naranjilla, it forms a tall sub-shrub up to 10 feet with ovate sinuately lobed leaves often 2 feet long, woolly beneath and set with prickles on the veins and petioles. *S. rostratum,* prickly annual, flowers yellow, fruits globose surrounded by an inflated prickly calyx, Mexico. *S. seaforthianum,* produces trailing stems set with mainly pinnate leaves and spreading cymes of small reddish or lilac flowers, South America; var. *album* has white flowers. *S. sisymbrifolium* can be either an annual or short-lived perennial, with prickly stems and leaves and light bluish or white flowers 1 inch across, South American. *S. wendlandii,* vigorous climber, leaves simple or variously lobed, bright green, flowers large blue-lilac, up to 2½ inches across, in showy terminal cymes, Costa Rica.

Cultivation All the annual species are

Solanum jasminoides, Potato Vine.

suited to pot culture in a cool greenhouse or planted out of doors in a sheltered sunny border in late May. They are raised from seeds sown in a minimum temperature of 60–65°F (16–18°C) during March. *S. capsicastrum* and *S. pseudocapsicum* may be either planted out in a cold frame or stood in their pots in the frame with the lights off during summer, then brought into a cool house for fruiting in late September. *S. intrusum* is grown out of doors to maturity. The shrubby and climbing sorts such as *S. etuberosum, S. jasminoides* and *S. aviculare* need a cool greenhouse in most parts of the country or a sheltered sunny wall in the south and west. *S. crispum* is hardy on a sheltered wall in most parts of the country (at least in its 'Glasnevin Form'), as is the variegated form of *S. dulcamara, S. seaforthianum* and *S. wendlandii* require a warm greenhouse with a minimum winter temperature of 55°F (13°C) and are best planted out in a border and trained up under the glass. All these woody, shrubby or climbing sorts can easily be propagated by soft or semi-hard cuttings of short side shoots in a warm propagating case in summer.

Solidago (sol-id-a-go)
The healing properties of these herba-

Solanum crispum autumnale.

7-foot stems; 'Goldenmosa', 3 feet only, with golden-yellow flowerheads which appear in late summer; 'Lemore', 2 feet, soft primrose; 'Leraft', early-flowering with large heads on 2–3-foot stems; 'Lesden', 3 feet, compact habit, flowers bright yellow; 'Peter Pan', 2½ feet, large flowerheads, bright yellow.

Cultivation The golden rods will grow in most soils but appreciate good feeding. The taller species and varieties are better if staked. *S. canadensis* is an invasive plant, but this does not apply to the dwarfer growing modern cultivars. Division of the clumps is the best means of propagation and may be carried out in the autumn or spring. It is essential to divide and replant every three years. Seeds are best sown out of doors in April but it is necessary to throw out any inferior forms observed when flowering.

Sollya (sol-ee-a)
Named in honour of Richard Horsman Solly (1778–1858), a British naturalist *(Pittosporaceae)*. A genus of two species of western Australian evergreen twining plants, suitable for a cool greenhouse or they can be grown in the open where the winter temperature does not drop below 40°F (4°C). The slender stems trail naturally and they make most decorative plants for growing in a hanging basket or cascading over a bank to form a dense mat.

Species cultivated *S. fusiformis* (syn. *S. heterophylla*), bluebell creeper, 3–6 feet, leaves lance-shaped, flowers sky-blue, bell-shaped, in loose clusters. *S. parviflora* (syn. *S. drummondii*), 4–6 feet, similar to *S. fusiformis* but the flowers are a darker blue and the more slender shoots bear smaller leaves.

Cultivation The genus thrives in a moist, well-drained light loam in sun or partial shade, and requires ample moisture during the spring and summer. It tolerates heat but does not like a dry atmosphere when grown under glass. In early spring thin out and remove any dead shoots. Propagation is by cuttings taken in spring or summer and inserted in sandy soil in a propagating frame with a temperature of 65°F (18°C).

Specularia (spek-ul-air-ee-a)
From the Latin *speculum*, a mirror; Venus's looking-glass was the common name of one of the species *(Campanulaceae)*. Once known as *Legousia*, under which name they are still known by many botanists, these are hardy annuals from the northern hemisphere. They are much like campanulas. Of the 15 species there is one only commonly grown, *S. speculum* (syn. *Campanula speculum*), a native of Europe. This grows about 1 foot tall and bears purple, somewhat bell-shaped flowers in summer; var. *alba* has white flowers.

ceous perennials are responsible for the name, from the Latin *solido,* to make whole, heal *(Compositae)*. Golden rod. A genus of over 100 species of hardy herbaceous perennials from North America, the remaining are from Europe. They are of easy cultivation in sun or partial shade and any soil. The small, yellow daisy-like flowers are carried in sprays and mingle well with the Michaelmas daisies flowering at the same time, in late summer or autumn. *S. canadensis* is the most widely-grown species, of which there are many lovely hybrids and varieties.

Species cultivated *S.* × *ballardii,* 4 feet, flowers golden-yellow in branching heads, August to September, hybrid.

S. brachystachys, 6–9 inches, golden-yellow, September to October. *S. canadensis,* to 4 feet, sometimes more in favourable conditions, bright yellow panicles in late summer, eastern North America. *S. graminifolia,* 3 feet, narrow leaves, large flowerheads, eastern North America. *S. odora,* grown chiefly for its aromatic foliage, which when rubbed has an aniseed-like perfume, eastern North America. *S. virgaurea,* 2–4 feet, fluffy flowerheads, Europe (including Britain); var. *minuta,* a good plant for the rock garden, less than 1 foot in height, which also applies to the varieties *alpestris* and *cambrica*. Named cultivars include 'Golden Wings', very showy panicles produced in quantity on

Cultivation Ordinary soil and a sunny position suit these plants. Seeds should be sown in April, thinly, about $\frac{1}{16}$ inch deep. Thin when the seedlings are 1–2 inches high, to 3–6 inches apart. When the plants are over 3 inches tall they should be supported with twigs.

Spinach

It has been estimated that a 30-foot row of spinach supplies just about the right amount for a family of four during the summer months. But one sowing is not sufficient. Fresh young foliage is demanded and where spinach is much appreciated, successional sowings should be made fortnightly between late March and mid July. For later autumn supplies and for pickings in the following spring, a sowing should be made in a sheltered position in mid-August.

Spinach needs a rich, well-dug soil and one which retains moisture during the summer months. For the leaves to be really succulent, the plants need soaking with water during dry spells. Some gardeners find that their plants need less water if rows sown in May, June and July are partially shaded by other, taller vegetables.

Well-rotted farmyard manure or garden compost should be used in the preparation of the bed. A suitable dressing for sandy soils is 1 cwt of manure to 6 square yards. Garden compost may be used more generously. Provided the soil contains sufficient plant nutriments, no feeding of the plants is necessary. Rows of August-sown spinach are sometimes fed with nitrate of soda, applied at the rate of 1 ounce to each 10 feet of row, in early April.

Sow the seeds as thinly as possible in 1 inch deep seed drills spaced 9 inches to 1 foot apart. Thin the seedlings to 3 inches as early as possible and start harvesting the leaves as soon as they are of usable size. Do not wait until they are on the tough side. Regular hard picking is essential for summer spinach and almost all of the leaves of a plant may be removed at any one time. Plants from the August sowing should not be treated in this manner. Take only the largest leaves from them.

'Round Seeded' and 'Long Standing' are popular kinds for spring and early summer sowings. 'Long Standing Prickly' is hardier and is sown in August. The word 'prickly' refers to the seeds and not to the smooth leaves.

Perpetual spinach or spinach beet is less well known. Those who know it prefer it for its larger leaves. Sow in April, allowing 15 inches between the rows. Thin the seedlings to 8 inches apart. Successional sowings are not necessary because leaves may be pulled from the plants on and off between early summer and September (see also Beet, Spinach).

The Betony, Stachys macrantha, comes from the Caucasus and has violet flowers from May to July.

The cultivation of spinach consists of regular hoeing to keep down weeds. This work may be reduced by mulching the plants with sedge peat or chopped straw.

Spinach (New Zealand) New Zealand spinach is not a form of true spinach. True spinach is *S. oleracea* (prickly-seeded) and *Spinacia oleracea* var. *inermis* (round-seeded). Spinach beet is *Beta vulgaris* var. *cicla,* and New Zealand Spinach is *Tetragonia expansa.* This is an annual producing leaves and young shoots which are used as a replacement for summer spinach. The plants might be mistaken for a very large-leaved form of mint. Sow seed under cloches in late March, or in late April to early May in the open. Sow very thinly because each plant needs 2 feet of row space. Up to 3 feet must be left between the rows. Hoe to keep down weeds until all bare soil is well covered by the plants. Although the plants can withstand far drier and hotter conditions than ordinary spinach, the new growths are more succulent if water is given in dry spells.

Stachys (stak-is)

From the Greek *stachus,* a spike, alluding to the pointed inflorescences of this plant *(Labiatae).* A genus of 300 species of herbaceous perennials, annuals, sub-shrubs, with a few shrubby species, widely dispersed throughout the world. One tuberous-rooted species, *S. affinis,* is the Chinese or Japanese artichoke or crosnes. Some species are also known as woundwort or betony; they are closely related to the dead-nettles *(Lamium)* and are nearly all weeds.

Species cultivated *S. affinis* (syn. *S. sieboldii, S. tuberifera),* Chinese or Japanese artichoke, crosnes, 1–1½ feet, roots edible, flowers pink, rarely seen, summer, China, Japan. *S. coccinea*, 2 feet, flowers scarlet, summer, Central America. *S. corsica*, 1 inch, a good rock garden plant, forms carpets of small leaves, flowers pale pink, almost stemless, all summer, Mediterranean region. *S. lanata*, lamb's-ear, 1 foot, grey, densely woolly foliage, flowers small, purple, July, Caucasus to Persia. *S. lavandulifolia*, 6 inches, lavender-leaved, flowers purplish-rose, July to August, Armenia. *S. macrantha* (syns. *S. grandiflora, Betonica macrantha*), betony, 1 foot, violet, May to July, Caucasus. *S. officinalis*, bishop's wort, wood betony, to 3 feet, flowers purple, June to August, Europe.

Cultivation The hardy perennials thrive in ordinary soil in a warm sheltered border. The most attractive is *S. corsica*, which is a little tender and needs good drainage and sun. It is better under glass in winter. *S. lanata* is good for edgings to border or beds, and there is a form obtainable which does not flower. It should be planted in autumn or spring. Propagation is by division in autumn or spring. For the cultivation of *S. affinis*, see Artichokes.

Stephanotis (steff-an-o-tis)

From the Greek *stephanos*, a crown or wreath, and *otos*, an ear, a reference to the arrangement and shape of the stamens *(Asclepiadaceae)*. A genus of five species of evergreen twining climbers whose stems exude a milky latex if damaged. All are natives of Madagascar. The only species now cultivated is *S. floribunda*, the clustered wax flower, Madagascar chaplet flower or Madagascar jasmine, which produces its highly fragrant white flowers sporadically throughout the year. These flowers are much used in floristry, especially in wedding bouquets. It is a plant for a tropical house where the minimum winter temperature is 60 F (16°C). Plant it in a greenhouse border in an ordinary, well-drained soil against a wall where support is provided either in the form of wires or a trellis. When first planted it may be slow to grow away but once established it will grow rampantly. Train the shoots as they develop. Once growth really begins it develops so rapidly, twining as it grows that if training is neglected such a tangle develops that it becomes difficult to control. Reduce unwanted and thin shoots whenever they develop, and before growth begins again in the spring, cut back all side shoots to within an inch of the main stems and maintain only enough of these to form a reasonable framework. All surplus shoots should be removed. Top dress annually with well-rotted compost or a dressing of a complete fertiliser. Plants may be grown in pots but they need more attention than do plants in a greenhouse border. After the cuttings have rooted, put three

plants to a pot and pot on as each pot fills with roots, finishing, usually, in an 8-inch pot. As the young plants establish themselves in each pot, the developing shoots should be shortened. When the final pot is reached, make a framework either with canes or wire and train the shoots over this. Pinch back all shoots that develop to about two leaves and the sublaterals which form, back to one leaf. Each year cut out some of the older stems and tie in their place some younger ones. Feeding is necessary at regular intervals every year but use nitrogenous fertilisers cautiously and always balance these with potash so as to prevent vigorous growth at the expense of flowering. Mealy bug and scale can become serious pests if control is neglected. Spray with malathion when the pests are first noticed and continue until control is achieved. Propagation is by cuttings which can be taken at almost any time of the year. It is probable that cuttings of young shoots taken in spring as growth is beginning to give best results. Detach them with a heel and dip them into a rooting hormone powder to stop bleeding. Insert them in sand, with a bottom heat at a temperature of 75°F (24°C), either in a closed propagating case or under mist.

Strelitzia (strel-its-ee-a)

Named in honour of Queen Charlotte, the wife of George III, who was also Duchess of Mecklenburg-Strelitz *(Musaceae)*. Bird of paradise flower. A genus

Stephanotis floribunda, the only species in cultivation, has very fragrant waxy, white flowers.

of five species of large perennial herbaceous plants from southern Africa, grown for their large, strikingly beautiful flowers.

Species cultivated *S. augusta*, a very large plant with leaf stems up to 6 feet long bearing an elliptic rounded leaf that may be 3 feet long. The inflorescence is composed of two spathes, shaped like a bird's head, from the middle of which emerge the white flowers, so that the plant suggests the head of a crested bird, spring. *S. reginae*, leaf stalk about 18 inches long, leaf-blade about the same length; the leaves radiate out in a fan; the flowers are orange and purple and very brilliant, emerging from the purplish spathes on a stem some 3 feet long. The plant is variable and among the varieties are the more compact, var. *humilis;* the attractive glaucous-leaved, var. *glauca;* and the more brilliant, var. *rutilans*, in which the leaves have a purple midrib, late spring.

Cultivation John Innes potting compost No 3 suits these plants admirably. The winter temperature should not fall below 50°F (10°C) and during the summer high temperatures are relished. However, the plants resent a stuffy atmosphere and the ventilators should be opened whenever the temperature exceeds 65°F (18°C). During the summer the plants require abundant supplies of water and liquid feeding should be given  at fortnightly intervals to established plants from the end of May until the beginning of September. The plants are kept on the dry side during the winter. Any potting on is best done about mid-March. During the summer the glass should be slightly shaded, but all possible light should be admitted from the end of September until late March or early April. Propagation is generally by detaching suckers and potting them up, but if the plants are hand-pollinated, seed will be set and will germinate in rather high temperatures. They take many years to arrive at flowering size. The plants are of relatively easy cultivation but take up a lot of room.

Streptocarpus (Strep-toe-karp-us)
From the Greek *streptos*, twisted, and *karpos*, fruit; the seed capsules are twisted into a spiral *(Gesneriaceae)*. A genus of 100 species of tropical herbs, mainly natives of tropical and sub-tropical Africa, grown for their showy tubular flowers. The genus is divided into two subgenera. Plants with a main stem and stalked leaves in opposite pairs belong to the subgenus *Streptocarpella* and are rarely cultivated. In the subgenus *Streptocarpus* the leaves spring directly from the rootstock. The various species are now rather rare in cultivation, but a hybrid strain is among the most popular of greenhouse plants.
Species cultivated *S.* × *hybridus*, many parents have entered into this strain but the two most important are the single-leaved, brick-red *S. dunnii* and the variable *S. rexii* (see below). The plants have the leaves in rosettes; the leaves are wrinkled and about 6 inches long. The flower scapes are about 9 inches long and bear usually about 5 flowers. These are tubular with an extended limb, up to 2 inches long and about as much across. They are in varying shades of  pink, purple, blue, violet and white, sometimes with pencilling in the throat, and they flower throughout the summer. *S. rexii*, leaves up to 10 inches long, in a rosette, flower stems about 6 inches long and bearing one or two flowers only, which may be white, bluish or violet-mauve and are about 1½ inches long with purple stripes on the lower lip, Cape Province. *S. wendlandii*, the plant carries only a single ovate leaf, which may be up to 2½ feet long and 2 feet across, the underside is reddish-purple, while the upper surface has a purplish tinge, flowers violet, about 2 inches long and 1½ inches across, borne on a many-flowered scape (up to 30 flowers have been recorded) about 1 foot high, Natal.
Cultivation Streptocarpus are generally treated as greenhouse annuals and so loamless composts will suit them well, although they will also thrive in the John Innes mixtures. The seed is very fine and should be placed on the surface of the soil and the pot covered with a

**1 Strelitzia reginae has orange flowers which emerge dramatically from the purple-red spathe.
2 One of the varied Stylidium species from Australia and New Zealand.
3 Streptocarpus hybrids are in various shades of pink, blue, mauve and white.**

pane of glass or enveloped in a polythene bag. A temperature of at least 65°F (18°C) should be provided. Seed can be sown at any time in the late winter or spring when such temperatures are easily provided. As soon as the seedlings are large enough to handle they are pricked out into boxes, then potted into 3-inch pots and finally into 5-inch pots, although it is possible to pot on still further. S. x hybridus and S. rexii will flower in four months, but S. wendlandii may not flower until the second year. The plants like a warm, moist atmosphere and to be shaded from very bright sunshine, but they should also be given plenty of air. They will take ample

water while making their growth, but if they are to be over-wintered they should then be kept on the dry side. A temperature of 50°F (10°C) is satisfactory for over-wintering. S. wendlandii is sometimes monocarpic and dies after flowering, but this is not invariable. Apart from seed, plants can be propagated by means of leaf cuttings. The leaves are scored with a knife on the underside and laid on the propagating medium, much as is done with Rex begonias. If plants are over-wintered and can be given some heat in the spring they can be got into flower much earlier in the year. Plants that are to be kept for more than one year are probably better grown in John Innes potting compost.

Stylidium (sty-lid-ee-um)
From the Greek stylos, a column, referring to the joined stamens and styles of the flowers (Stylidaceae). A genus of some 136 species, native mainly to Australia and New Zealand,

and an odd one in south-eastern Asia. They are evergreen herbaceous or woody perennials, most of them forming a rosette of leaves or a spreading tuft of foliage. The flower spike emerges from the middle. In some species the tufts are immediately above the previous year's leaves; in others, they may be more widely spaced out. The flower spike may be a corymb or a simple raceme. The flowers usually have five petals, forming two lips.

Species cultivated S. adnatum, to 1 foot, flowers pink, July. S. brunonianum, to 1½ feet, flowers pink, June. S. ciliatum, to 1 foot, flowers usually yellow with pink and white variations, June. S. crassifolium, 2 feet, flowers pink, summer. S. dichotomum, to 1½ feet, flowers yellow, June. S. graminifolium, to 1½ feet, flowers pink, summer. S. hirsutum, to 1½ feet, flowers red and pink in hairy spikes, June. S. laricifolium, subshrub to 1 foot, flowers pink, summer. S. scandens, climbing, 1½–2 feet, flowers pink, summer. All the above are natives of Australia.

Cultivation A compost of loam, sand and peat or leafmould will give good results. Grow the plants in a cool temperate greenhouse in pots or in beds. The minimum winter temperature should be 45–50°F (7–10°C). The herbaceous species are best propagated by seeds sown in spring, the shrubby species by cuttings rooted in a sandy compost, with a bottom temperature of 65–70°F (18–21°C).

Styphelia (sty-fe-lee-a)
From the Greek styphelos, rough, hard, alluding to the stiff prickly-pointed leaves (Epacridaceae). A genus of 11 species from Australia, Tasmania and New Guinea, all of which can be grown in the cool greenhouse in the same way as the genus Epacris, but they are rarely met with in cultivation. They are shrubs with small, almost stemless, stiff leaves; the flowers are mostly single and have small narrow cylindrical corollas.

Species cultivated The following four species have been recorded as being in cultivation and all are from New South Wales; they attain a height of between 3 and 5 feet. S. longifolia, flowers green. S. triflora, flowers pale pink or yellow. S. tubiflora, flowers red. S. viridis, flowers green. S. suaveolens is from New Guinea and is a many-branched shrub about 2 feet tall and bears numerous pale pink flowers followed by small dark red fleshy fruits about the size of a blackcurrant. Both fruit and flowers can be had at the same time. The leaves are very small and stiff, mid-green above and glaucous below. It is altogether a most attractive small woody shrub but at present rare in cultivation.

Cultivation These plants should be grown firmly in an acid, open peaty compost and given full sun in a cool greenhouse. They resent root disturbance and should never be allowed to dry out at the roots, but watering must be undertaken very carefully. Propagation is by seed or by stem cuttings, but these are very difficult to root.

Sweet Corn

Zea mays rugosa is known in Britain as sweet corn. This cereal is a native of America and is boiled as a vegetable. The John Innes hybrid varieties remain popular, but 'Kelvedon Glory' is a newer introduction of merit.

In the south, seeds may be sown out of doors in May. Choose a sunny position and in areas exposed to gale force winds in August, provide a windbreak. The soil should have been well dug and dressed with dung or garden compost. These organic fertilisers not only supply plant foods but assist in providing good drainage on heavy soils and in retaining moisture on lighter ones. Sow the seeds 1 inch deep in rows 15 inches apart. Several short rows are preferable to one or two long ones. When the plants are grown in compact blocks wind pollination is more effective.

In other parts of the country, sow two or three seeds in 3½-inch pots in the cold frame or under a cloche in early May. Reduce the seedlings to leave one strong plant in each pot. Set the plants in the open when all danger of frost has passed or protect the rows with cloches until early July.

In dry summers, water as necessary and feed the plants with liquid manure if the soil was not supplied with sufficient organic matter before sowing or planting. Hand weeding is safer than using the hoe which is liable to sever surface anchorage roots. Mulching the bed with straw in July saves weeding and watering.

Harvest the cobs when the silks which hang from them are brown-black in colour and quite brittle. A check on the state of maturity may be made by carefully opening the top of the green sheath and by pressing a grain with the finger nail. If a watery juice exudes, the cob is too young. If the grain contains paste, it is too old. At the correct stage a creamy liquid spurts out. Cobs are twisted from the plants. The sooner the cobs are cooked after harvest-

1 Three popular varieties of the common Sweet Pea: from left to right Zetra, Percy Izzard and Pink Pearl. The Sweet Pea first gained popularity in Great Britain towards the end of the nineteenth century thanks to the enthusiasm of one Henry Eckford, a Scotsman who was a gardener in Gloucestershire at the time. The popularity of the Sweet Pea grew so rapidly that in 1912 a national newspaper offered a prize of £1,000 for the best vase of 12 stems. The competition brought in some 35,000 entries.
2 In the cordon method of growing Sweet Peas all unwanted tendrils and side growths are pinched out.

ing, the higher the sugar content.

Popcorn This is a form of maize, *Zea mays everta*, producing hard grains which, when cooked in fat, explode to form into the familiar popcorn breakfast cereal. There are many varieties. Those with a dwarf habit of growth and producing off-white, rice-like grains are more suited to gardens in southern parts of England than taller growers with cobs similar to those of sweet corn. The season of growth is fairly long, and because the plants resent transplanting seed is sown in 3½-inch pots under glass in April. Popcorn should be grown on sites similar to those suitable for sweet corn. The soil must be very fertile and should contain a high proportion of organic matter as for sweet corn. Compact block planting assists wind fertilisation. A typical 'block' would consist of four short rows in which the plants are spaced at 15 inches apart. Plant out in the open garden when all danger of frost has passed. This is generally during the first two weeks of June. If the soil is dry, water the planting holes and then plant firmly after the water has drained away. Frequent cultivation is unnecessary and may sever the surface anchorage roots. A light hoeing in late June will deal with the first flush of weed seedlings. This may be followed in early-to-mid July by a straw or peat mulch. The mulch may save watering but it may be necessary to water if

there is a dry spell between late July and late August. During the last fortnight of September the plants appear dead, the cob sheaths dry and almost white in colour, and the silks black-brown. Choose a dry, sunny day for harvesting. Tear back or remove the paper-like sheaths and hang the cobs in a warm room for a month. The grains may then be rubbed from the cobs and stored for use.

Sweet Pea

The annual sweet pea, *Lathyrus odoratus,* was introduced to England from Sicily in 1699. It was not until 1870, however, that the breeding of sweet peas started to interest Henry Eckford, a Scot, who was a gardener in Gloucestershire at that time. Later he moved to Wem in Shropshire where he made his name for raising sweet peas. The fragrant flowers of the species are in various colours: shades of purple and red, or white and red. In 1901 a new frilled rose-pink variety, 'Countess Spencer', was shown in London and caused a great sensation as it was the first with frilled petals. It was raised by Silas Cole, gardener to Earl Spencer, at Althorp Park, Northamptonshire. Many new varieties were raised and the popularity of the sweet pea became so great that in 1912 a national newspaper offered a prize of £1,000 for the best vase of 12 stems shown at the Crystal Palace. The competition brought in some 35,000 entries.

Of recent years breeding has been continued apace in the British Isles and the United States, and there are now many distinct types in a wide range of colours and heights. The 'Spencer' varieties have the most elegant flowers and are widely grown for exhibition and for decoration. They are available in many beautiful separate colours. The new, early-flowering 'Galaxy Hybrids' produce as many as seven large, fragrant flowers on a stem, many of them opening at the same time. These are also now obtainable in separate colours.

'Knee-Hi' varieties are less tall and grow to about 3 feet in English gardens, although they are reputed to be of shorter growth under Californian conditions where they were raised. They are free-flowering, with five to seven flowers on quite a long, straight stem which makes them useful for cutting, and they have the advantage of requiring light support only. This is a useful sweet pea for the small, modern garden, or even for growing in a deep container on a reasonably sheltered balcony. The 'Bijou' type do not exceed 1½ feet in height, yet they carry a good crop of flowers and have long-lasting, short-stemmed flowers. With all these types fading flowers should be snipped off, for if they are left to produce seed the flowering season will be much reduced.

Those who grow for exhibition pur-

Sweet Pea 'Bijou', a low-growing type which carries a good crop of flowers.

poses or like to have an early display of sweet peas, sow the seed in October, five seeds in a 3-inch pot and over-winter in a cold frame or cold greenhouse. Once the seed has germinated the seedlings should be ventilated freely except in the coldest weather. Mice can be a menace as they devour the seed and, during the winter, they are liable to eat off the young green shoots, particularly in hard weather when they may be covered in a frame. By making a further sowing in February or March, flowers will then be available over a long period, well into September. Seed may also be sown in the open, where it is to flower, in late March or April, and if the rows are covered with cloches these will assist germination.

Some varieties have particularly hard-coated seed and to assist germination such seeds should be chipped. With the aid of a sharp knife a small piece of the outer coat is removed—on the opposite side to the eye—care being taken not to injure the inner white tissue. For a large number of seeds an easier method is to soak them in water for about 24 hours before sowing. This will cause the seeds to swell and any that remain hard can be chipped so that all should germinate about the same time.

Another important point, particularly with spring-sown seedlings is the question of stopping. The growing tip is pinched out immediately the first or second pair of leaves has opened which will ensure that a strong, bushy plant develops.

Sweet peas are deep-rooting, hungry plants making rapid growth when the days are warm, therefore they require a deeply dug trench and a rich soil. Those who grow prize-winning stems go to a great deal of trouble in preparing trenches two or three spits deep and work in generous quantities of manure, but perfectly good flowers for cutting purposes can be produced when only the top spit is dug and hop manure, or processed animal manure, obtainable in polythene bags, is worked into the soil. During the growing season occasional doses of liquid manure should be given and the plants require ample watering in dry spells.

Plants that have been over-wintered under glass should be planted out in the prepared ground in March or early April, and in some districts it may be necessary to protect the young plants with short pea-sticks or netting against damage by pigeons and other birds. With tall-growing sweet peas the pea-sticks should be placed in the ground first and then plant one pea beside each stick, or 8–10-foot cane, if it is intended to grow them on the cordon system for exhibition. However they are grown the supports should be in a double row 8 inches apart in the row and about 1 foot between the rows. Sweet peas may also be grown on netting, trellis or polythene covered mesh, securely fixed to stout metal or wooden stakes. Where sweet peas are grown in a mixed border the pea-sticks can be in the form of a wigwam with the top tied together so that it will withstand summer gales.

When planting out pot-grown seedlings care must be taken not to break the long, slender roots and these should be spread out as much as possible in a deep hole made by a trowel. Or cut the soil with a spade and then firm the soil around the roots leaving the bottom side-shoot joint at soil level.

It may not always be possible to raise one's own seedlings but seedlings may be purchased from reliable sweet pea growers. As stocks of strong seedlings are limited it is usually necessary to order not later than January for delivery in March. Seedlings may also be purchased at market stalls, but beware of thin, weedy seedlings that may have a yellow, starved appearance through lack of water and poor soil, for it is a waste of time to plant out such miserable specimens.

Sweet pea seedlings are reasonably hardy and will withstand normal spring frosts but perishing east winds can be damaging to newly planted seedlings in exposed gardens and any form of temporary windbreak should be made use of.

Straw or bracken can be laid along the rows, or hessian or polythene stretched along the canes or pea-sticks. This may appear a little unsightly but it is likely to be required for a short period only, in the early days after planting, and it is one of those little attentions that will make all the difference between success and poor results.

Among the leading prize-winning varieties at National Sweet Pea Society's and other shows, are 'Leamington', deep lilac; 'White Ensign'; 'Royal Flush', salmon-pink on a cream ground; 'Herald', orange-cerise on a white

There are many cultivars and strains of Tagetes, varying in height and size of flower. All bloom over a long period.
1 A fine variety, Tagetes 'Cordoba'.
2 Tagetes patula 'Dainty Marietta'.
3 Tagetes erecta is a particularly full-flowered form.

ground; 'Gipsy Queen', crimson; 'Larkspur', pale blue; 'Margot', cream and ivory; 'Noel Sutton', rich blue, and 'Festival', salmon-pink on a cream ground. See also Lathyrus.

Tagetes (ta-ge-tez)

From the Latin *Tages*, an Etruscan divine *(Compositae)*. A genus of 50 species of half-hardy annuals or herbaceous perennials commonly called marigold, but not to be confused with the English or pot marigold *(Calendula officinalis)*. There are now many cultivars with single or double flowers of various forms. They have acquired the names African and French marigold, although the original species from which they have been bred were introduced from Mexico and the southern United States.

Species cultivated *T. erecta*, African marigold, annual, 2 feet, leaves much divided, flowers yellow to orange, 2–4 inches across, July, Mexico. There are numerous cultivars and strains, ranging in height from 1 to 4 feet, free-flowering, branching plants. A selection includes: 'All Double Orange', 2½ feet; 'All

Double Lemon', 2½ feet; 'Carnation-flowered Alaska', 2 feet, flowers pale primrose, to 4 inches across; 'Cracker-jack', 3 feet, golden-yellow to orange; 'First Lady' (F₁), 1 foot, pale yellow, double; 'Golden Age', 2 feet; 'Guinea Gold', 2½ feet; 'Hawaii', 2 feet, bright orange; 'Cream Puff', 1½ feet, creamy-white, ageing almost to white, double; 'Chrysanthemum-flowered Super Glitters', 2½ feet, lemon; 'Golden Fluffy', 'Orange Fluffy', 'Yellow Fluffy', all 2½ feet; 'Collarette Crown of Gold', 2 feet, centre petals incurved, outer petals broad; 'Diamond Jubilee' (F₁), 2 feet, yellow; 'Golden Jubilee' (F₁), 'Orange Jubilee' (F₁), both 2 feet; 'Climax Toreador', 3 feet, flowers mid orange, ruffled; 'Sunset Giants', 4 feet, flowers yellow, broad-petalled. *T. lucida,* sweet-scented 'Mexican Marigold, annual 1 foot, yellow, August, Mexico, South America. *T. minuta,* annual, 4–6 feet, pale yellow, October, South America; secretions from the roots are said to keep down weeds and research on this is proceeding at present. *T. patula,* French marigold, annual, 1½ feet, leaves much divided, flowers brownish-yellow, July onwards, Mexico. Numerous strains and cultivars are available, in a wide colour range and in heights ranging from 6 inches to 2 feet. These include: 'Sovereign', 2 feet, early-flowering, golden-yellow and brown to brownish-red, double: 'Dainty Marietta', 6 inches, golden-yellow blotched maroon;

'Flame', 9 inches, deep scarlet, double; 'Golden Ball, 1 foot, large flowers, double; 'Gold-laced', 9 inches, dark red, petals edged orange; 'Harmony', 9 inches, centres orange, collar dark red; 'Golden Bedder', 9 inches, double; 'Legion of Honour', 9 inches, yellow, flecked brown at base, single; 'Lilliput Fireglow', 6 inches, dark scarlet, golden centres; 'Miniature Lemon Drop', 9 inches, golden-yellow, blotched maroon; 'Pygmy Mixed', 6 inches, various colours; 'Samba', 1 foot, various colours; 'Spanish Brocade', 9 inches, golden-yellow, tipped dark red. *T. tenuifolia* (syn. *T. signata*), striped Mexican marigold, annual, 1½ feet, yellow, summer, Mexico; var. *pumila,* 6 inches. Cultivars and strains include: 'Gnome', 6 inches, deep orange; 'Golden Gem Selected', 6 inches; 'Lulu', 6 inches, canary-yellow. 'Irish Lace', 9 inches, is a foliage plant, recommended for edging, which makes mounds of slender, lacy-green foliage.

Cultivation Sow seed thinly in boxes of light soil in a heated greenhouse in March or cold greenhouse in April. Prick out seedlings into seed trays when they are large enough to handle and place in a cold frame and after hardening off, plant out, 12–15 inches apart (dwarf kinds, 6 inches apart) in a sunny bed in late May or June. Water freely during dry weather, and give a liquid feed occasionally. Seed of *T. minuta* is sown under glass in April and the young plants set out 8–9 inches apart in May,

after weeds have been cleared.

Thalictrum (thal-ik-trum)

From the Greek *thaliktron,* a name used to describe a plant with divided leaves, possibly of the same family *(Ranunculaceae)*. Meadow rue. A genus of 150 species of hardy perennials, herbaceous plants, mainly from north temperate regions but also represented in tropical South America, tropical Africa and South Africa. Those cultivated have elegant, fern-like foliage and dainty flowers. They are most effective when planted in bold groups.

Species cultivated *T. aquilegiifolium,* 3–4 feet, flowers pale purple in fluffy panicles, May to July, Europe, northern Asia. *T. chelidonii,* 2–3 feet, flowers large, mauve, July to August, Himalaya. *T. diffusiflorum,* 2–3 feet, finely cut, grey-green foliage, sprays of clear lilac flowers, July and August, Tibet; a difficult plant to establish. *T. dipterocarpum,* 3–5 feet, leaves dainty, blue-green, smooth, flowers deep lavender, with prominent yellow anthers, borne on slender stems, July and August, western China; vars. *album,* a graceful white form; 'Hewitt's Double', bright violet-mauve, fully double flowers, freely produced. *T. flavum,* 2–3 feet, grey-green, glossy, finely cut foliage, soft yellow, feathery heads of flowers, July and August, Europe (including Britain). *T. glaucum* (syn. *T. speciosissimum),* 5 feet, foliage glaucous, flowers yellow, summer, southern Europe, North Africa. *T. kuisianum,* 4 inches, foliage fern-like, flowers rosy-purple, spring, Japan, rock garden or alpine house. *T. minus* (syn. *T. adiantifolium),* 1½–2 feet, grown purely for its decorative, maidenhair fern-like foliage, borne on wiry stems which make it admirable for use with floral decorations, inconspicuous yellowish-green flowers in loose panicles, Europe (including Britain). *T. rocquebrunianum,* 4 feet, stems and leaf stalks purplish, flowers lavender-blue in large heads, summer.

Cultivation Thalictrums will grow in almost any soil, preferably of reasonable depth, but including those that contain much chalk, provided they do not bake dry. Plant them in full sun or dappled shade. Propagation is by seed or by division in the spring.

Thunbergia (thun-ber-gee-a)

Named after Dr Carl Pehr Thunberg (1743–1822), professor of botany at Uppsala *(Acanthaceae)*. A genus of 200 species of twining and dwarf annuals and perennials, mainly from Africa. Most require warm greenhouse conditions.

Species cultivated *T. affinis,* hairy-stemmed shrub, flowers violet, 2 inches

across, tube yellow, September. *T. alata,*
black-eyed Susan, twining annual,
flowers yellow and purple, 1½ inches long
but varying greatly in colour, summer;
vars. *alba,* white with dark centre;
aurantiaca, deep yellow, dark centre;
bakeri, white; *doddsii,* leaves white-
bordered, flowers orange with a purple
centre; *fryeri,* pale yellow, white centre;
lutea, yellow; *sulphurea,* sulphur-yellow.
T. grandiflora, large climber, leaves up
to 6 inches long, flowers blue, 3 inches
long and across, July to September,
India; var. *alba.* white. *T. gregori* (syn.
T. gibsonii), perennial climber, orange
waxy flowers 1½ inches across with lobes
half as long as the tube, summer.

Cultivation A well-drained, rich fibrous
compost is most suitable. Keep the
greenhouse at a minimum winter temperature of 60 F (16 C). Some kinds of
T. alata will tolerate lower temperatures
but it is necessary to maintain the
humidity. Propagate from seed, for
T. alata and *T. gregori* in March–April,
or from soft cuttings, using mild bottom
heat.

Thyme

Common or black thyme, *T. vulgaris,*
and lemon thyme, *T. citriodorus,* are the
two *Thymus* species preferred for use as
culinary flavourings. Both are grown in
the same way, preferably in a light, well-
drained soil containing lime on a sunny,
warm border.

The 1-foot-high bushes are generally
propagated by plant division in March
or April when portions, each with a few
roots, are set out deeply at 1 foot apart.
Propagation may also be effected from
cuttings of 2–5 inches, taken in May and

1 Thunbergia mysorensis.
2 Thunbergia alata, the Black-Eyed
Susan, is a twining annual with yellow
and purple flowers.

planted firmly. Propagation from seed
is seldom practised.

Apart from weeding when necessary,
no cultivation is carried out. Harvesting
takes place on and off between May and
August and always before flowering.
An application of nitrate of soda at
2 ounces to the square yard, followed by
a thorough watering, encourages fresh
growth after the first cut. Care must be
taken to prevent the fertiliser from
touching and damaging the foliage. The
harvested shoots are spread out to dry
in a warm, sunny place. They dry rapidly
and are ready for breaking up and sifting
preparatory to storing, within a week.
See also Thymus.

Thymus (ty-mus)

Possibly from the Greek *thymos,* thyme,
derived from *thuo,* to perfume *(Labiatae).*
A genus of between 300 and 400 species
of dwarf, aromatic shrubs or sub-shrubs,
distributed widely through Europe and
Asia. Very few exceed 1 foot in height.

Culinary species cultivated *T.* × *citriodorus,* shrub, 4–12 inches, flowers lilac,
summer, hybrid; numerous forms including 'Silver Queen', leaves silvery,
flowers pink. *T. vulgaris,* common thyme,
6–8 inches, shrub, flowers lilac, summer;
var. *aureus,* leaves golden, both grown
for flavouring, the variety grown on the
rock garden.

Ornamental species cultivated *T. caes-
pititius,* 2–3 inches, dense mat of woody
shoots and dark green leaves, flowers

lilac-mauve, July–August, Spain, the
Azores, Madeira. *T. carnosus,* 5–9 inches,
stiffly erect bushy habit, flowers white
or pale mauve, June–July, Portugal.
T. comosus, 3–6 inches, mat-like habit,
flowers pink, June, scent likened to
turpentine, eastern Europe. *T. doerfleri,*
mat-like sub-shrub, to 2½ inches, leaves
white-hairy, flowers rose-purple, summer, Albania, Yugoslavia. *T. herba-
barona,* 2–5 inches, mat-forming sub-
shrub, foliage dark green, caraway-
scented, flowers pink, June, Corsica,
Sardinia. *T. hirsutus,* tiny, carpeting
sub-shrub, 1–2½ inches, foliage grey,
hairy, flowers lilac to pink, summer,
Crimea, Balkans. *T. mastichina,* 6–12
inches, erect bush, leaves grey, strongly
aromatic, flowers in small fluffy heads,
cream, summer, Spain, North Africa.
T. × 'Porlock', 6–9 inches, leaves grey-
green, flowers deep pink, summer,
hybrid. *T. serpyllum,* low, bright green
aromatic mat, 1–3 inches, flowers purplish, summer, Europe, including
Britain, ideal for paved areas; a plant
with numerous varieties and cultivars
including *albus,* flowers white; 'Annie
Hall', flesh-pink; *coccineus,* crimson;
'Pink Chintz'; *roseus,* soft pink.

Cultivation The culinary species may be
grown with other herbs or as an edging
if the site is well drained and sunny.
Hardy flowering and carpeting species
require, warm, light soil conditions. Sow
seed or plant young stock in spring. Top
dress with sandy compost in late
summer or autumn. Trim the tops after
flowering to keep the plants compact.
For the cultivation of culinary species
see Thyme.

Tiarella (tee-ar-ell-la)
From the Greek *tiara,* a turban, literally
a little turban, in reference to the shape
of the seed pod *(Saxifragaceae).* A genus
of five species of perennial herbaceous
plants from the Himalaya, North
America and eastern Asia. *T. cordifolia*
has been crossed with a hybrid *Heuchera*
to give the inter-generic hybrid x
Heucherella.
Species cultivated *T. cordifolia,* foam
flower, 6–12 inches, leaves heart-shaped,
shallowly lobed, turning reddish in
autumn, flowers starry white in a cluster,
April to July, North America; after
flowering the plants spread by sending
out stolons. *T. polyphylla,* 9–24 inches,
leaves broadly ovate, to 3 inches wide,
flowers tiny, white or pink, in a cluster,
April to June, India, China, Japan.
T. trifoliata, 6–20 inches, leaves 3 inches
wide with three leaflets, flowers pale
pink, in a cluster, May to August,
Oregon to Vancouver. *T. wherryi,* to
14 inches, leaves heart-shaped, to 4
inches wide, becoming reddish in
autumn, flowers white or pale pink,
rather larger than in the other species,
with conspicuous orange anthers, May
to June, southern United States.
Cultivation The plants grow in woodland
in nature, and like a position in dappled
shade with preferably, ample leafmould
in the soil. However, they are very
adaptable in cultivation and any
reasonably cool root-run will accommodate them. They may be grown on
the rock garden, but they must be given
ample room, particularly *T. cordifolia.*
Plant in spring and propagate by seed
or by division.

Thymus serpyllum, Creeping Thyme.

Tigridia (tig-rid-ee-a)
From the Greek *tigris,* tiger, and *eidos,*
like, with reference to the spotted
flowers *(Iridaceae).* A genus of 12 species
of bulbous plants, natives of Mexico,
Peru and Chile, of which one species
only is in general cultivation. It is
remarkable for the shape of the petals
and the brilliant colour and markings of
the flowers which last one day only but
are produced, six or more from one bulb,
over a period. *T. pavonia,* the tiger
flower, grows 1–2 feet tall, with orange-
scarlet flowers up to 4 inches across,
often with crimson spots, from July to
September. There are various forms in
shades of orange, deep yellow, reddish
crimson, white, some spotted, some
without spots; it is a native of mountain
regions of Mexico and Peru.
Cultivation Plant in April or early May,
about 3–4 inches deep, in well-drained
soil and in a really sunny, sheltered
position. In mild districts bulbs may be
left in the ground, but elsewhere they
should be lifted in the autumn and stored
in the same manner as gladiolus corms.
Where the bulbs are properly established
in mild districts, self-sown seedlings
may appear. Propagation is by seed
sown in pans containing a light compost,
in spring, with a temperature of about
60°F (16°C), or by offsets removed from
the mother bulbs in April.

Tomato cultivation
Cultivation under glass Seed is sown in
January or February at a day tempera-
ture of between 65–70 F (18–21 C) falling

to around 60 F (16 C) at night. At these
temperatures gemination occurs in six
to eight days. To prevent a great deal of
heat having to be used to keep the entire
greenhouse at these relatively high
temperatures in winter, a seed propa-
gator is sometimes employed. A suitable
seed compost is essential and many
gardeners prepare their own. A typical
home-made mixture consists of four
buckets of garden topsoil, one bucket of
finely ground sedge peat, half a bucket
of coarse sand, a 5-inch pot of lime
rubble and one dessertspoon of superphosphate of lime. Such a mixture is left
to stand for ten days. It is then mixed
once more and passed through a ¼-inch
sieve. Any large lumps are removed for
use as drainage material at the base of
the containers in which the seeds are
to be sown.

Containers which have been in use
should be washed well with water containing a mild disinfectant and left to
drain for some hours beforehand. New
clay pots and pans should be soaked in
water for several hours. After the containers have been filled to within a ½
inch of the top with the compost this is
levelled and firmed and the seeds are
then sown on the surface. Seeds may be
broadcast as evenly as possible so that a
standard seed tray is sown with around
300 seeds (see below) or the seeds may be
spaced individually at about 1 inch
apart. A piece of perforated metal sheet
is of help where many trays are being
sown. The sheet has holes, spaced at 1
inch apart. Through each hole one seed
is inserted. The seeds are then covered
by sieving a ¼ inch layer of the compost
over them, and then watered thoroughly
with water of a similar temperature to
that of the compost. A sheet of glass is
then placed over each container to
prevent too much evaporation, and
brown paper laid on the glass to provide
dark conditions. The glass sheet is
turned each day to rid the underside of
excess moisture. As soon as signs of
germination are observed, the glass and
brown paper are removed. To prevent
any drying out of the containers during
this critical period the greenhouse
staging and paths should be damped
down twice daily.

Seedlings raised by broadcast sowings
must be pricked off into other seed trays
or small pots when the first true leaf
shows. It is usual to prick off so that a
standard tray holds 50 seedlings and
these are potted on later into 3-inch or
3½-inch pots filled with John Innes or
Levington potting or similar soilless
composts. Seedlings from an evenly-
made sowing may grow on in the original
containers, until several true leaves and
a good root system have been made,
before being potted up.

During pricking out each seedling is
carefully removed from the container
with a table fork, plant label, etc. The
stems of the seedlings must never be
handled. Where any handling is neces-

235

sary take hold of the seedling gently by one of the two seed leaves. In potting, the pot is filled with the compost (using one hand) and the young plant is held by the other. The compost is sprinkled round the roots until they are covered. The compost is then firmed slightly with the fingers and a little more compost then added. The plant should be in the centre of the pot with the seed leaves resting on the compost.

After the pots are stood close together on the greenhouse staging, they are watered well. To prevent any check to continued good growth due to potting, a night temperature of around 65°F (18°C) and a day temperature of at least 70°F (21°C) are maintained until the seedlings are making new growth. During favourable weather some ventilation is given for a half hour or so at midday. Keep the containers moist but not over-wet. Gradually more and more ventilation is given during the day as and when possible, and night temperatures may drop to 55°F (13°C). Paths and staging should be damped down daily and, as the plants grow, the pots should be spaced further apart.

Greenhouse border cultivation The soil in the greenhouse borders is dug during the late autumn and manure or garden compost incorporated. The greenhouse may also be fumigated. After soil preparation, the borders are flooded.

Planting out takes place about ten weeks after sowing. Before setting out, any plants untrue to type should be discarded. Purchased plants should also be inspected so that poor 'rogue' plants, known as 'jacks', are not planted. Each plant needs 18 inches of growing space. Planting holes made with the trowel should take the soil ball comfortably and leave the top of the soil ball level with the surrounding soil. Fine soil is worked around the soil ball to fill in any spaces. After planting, water is applied—take care not to splash the foliage. Greenhouse-grown tomato plants are provided with supports which should be set in position immediately after planting. The supports may be bamboo canes, wires or strings. Tying in is a weekly job when the plants are making good, rapid growth. Take care to make the first tie quite loose and remove all side shoots from the leaf axils regularly. Remove all weeds and water regularly. Ensure adequate ventilation, and in very warm weather the door as well as ventilators should be left open during a part of the day.

Ring culture In this method of cultivation the top 6 inches of soil in the greenhouse borders are replaced with an aggregate which may be washed clinker, weathered ash or clean shingle. Each plant is grown in a bottomless container or 'ring'. The rings, often of bituminised paper, are filled with a suitable compost. After the plants have become established in the rings the main watering of ring

culture tomatoes is to the aggregate and liquid feeds to the compost.

Pot culture Good crops of tomatoes may be obtained from plants grown in 10-inch pots. John Innes potting No 3 is a suitable compost. In high summer it may be necessary to water pot-grown tomato plants several times each day. Standing the pots on a solid bench covered with a ½-inch layer of pea gravel prevents the pots from drying out.

Electrically-heated troughs Suitable troughs are 2 feet wide and 10 inches deep. Soil-warming wires are secured to wooden battens in the bottom of the trough. If you experiment with this method of cultivation, you should have soil-warming equipment installed by a competent electrician and the installation checked by the local electricity board. Here again, John Innes No 3 potting compost is suitable.

The straw bale method This new way of cultivation is primarily of use to the large commercial grower with a greenhouse soil heavily contaminated with fungi. The soil in the greenhouse is covered with black polythene sheeting. Bales of straw are laid flat—not on edge. Each bale is soaked with 9 gallons of water applied in two or three applications. This is followed by chemical treatment. According to one formula, each bale is treated with 1 lb of Nitro-chalk, 10 ounces of triple-super-phosphate of lime, 18 ounces of potassium nitrate and 4 ounces of magnesium sulphate. The chemicals are damped in with water and, within a matter of days,

Cordon-trained tomatoes which have been layered once.

the bales start to ferment and decompose. When the fermentation has passed its peak and the temperature within the bales has fallen to below 100°F (38°C) planting is carried out at normal 18-inch spacing. A double handful of John Innes potting compost No 2, or similar compost, is placed at each planting position and the plants are set in this.

During the initial fermentation ammonia gas is produced which is harmful to greenhouse plants. At the end of the season all decomposed straw may be dug into the garden soil or used as a mulch.

Apply tomato fertiliser when the bottom truss of fruit has set and the tomatoes have begun to swell. Only fertilisers advised by the manufacturers as of use in tomato growing should be used. The application of an unsuitable fertiliser or excessive doses of a tomato fertiliser are likely to lead to unbalanced growth, etc.

For a good set of fruit both temperature and humidity must be suitable. A temperature of 50°F (10°C) should be maintained at night. Temperatures may soar in spring and summer to well over 80°F (27°C). Excessive heat is controlled by adequate ventilation. Judicious waterings and damping down ensure a moist but not wet atmosphere. Syringing the plants in summer helps towards a good set of fruit. In late spring syringeing could result in excessive humidity. Tapping the flower trusses with the

Tomato varieties

AILSA CRAIG Fruit of uniform, medium size, good colour and very good flavour.

AMATEUR IMPROVED (bush) A new, improved selection of 'The Amateur'.

AMBERLEY CROSS (F₁) Greenback-free, resistant to cladosporium disease (leaf mould). Heavy cropper and early.

ANTIMOULD A Introduced by the John Innes Institute. Resistant to mildew. First-class quality medium fruits.

ATOM (bush)* Very dwarf, self-stopping bush needing no more than 18 inches of soil surface. The small tomatoes are of good flavour.

BEST OF ALL* Large, deep scarlet fruits with solid flesh. Heavy cropper.

BIG BOY Very large tomatoes, scarlet-red, handsome and has very good flavour.

CARTERS FRUIT Peels easily and slices readily. Flesh is solid and flavour is good. Very few seeds. Recommended for eating as an apple.

DWARF CLOCHE (bush)* Medium-sized, good quality fruits on plants about 6 inches high and 15 inches across.

EASICROP (bush)* Similar to 'The Amateur' but a more compact plant. Heavy cropper, good flavour, introduced 1968.

ES1* Good cropper in the open or in the greenhouse.

ESSEX WONDER* Singularly robust and hardy. Good cropper and good flavour. For the greenhouse or outdoors.

EUROCROSS A (F₁) Similar to 'Moneymaker' but earlier ripening. Greenback-free, resistant to cladosporium disease.

EUROCROSS B (F₁) Larger fruits than 'Eurocross A'. Recommended for early greenhouse crop. Does well in soils below optimum fertility.

EUROCROSS BB (F₁) Recommended for early crops in heated houses. Large fruited and high-yielding.

EXHIBITION (Stonor) Shapely fruits of uniform size. Good cropper.

FIRST IN THE FIELD* Dwarf habit and distinct foliage. Best grown as a single stem standard or with two or three stems trained to a trellis. Foliage is dark green and curled. Superseded by newer, earlier varieties.

FLORISSANT (F₁) Similar to 'Ailsa Craig' but stronger growing.

GARDENERS' DELIGHT* Long trusses of small tomatoes of sweet, fine flavour. Much liked for eating raw.

GOLDEN AMATEUR (bush)* Similar to 'The Amateur' but fruits are gold/yellow.

GOLDEN BOY Large, orange-yellow tomatoes. Not a heavy cropper but noted for the meatiness and fine flavour of the fruits.

GOLDEN SUNRISE Medium size, gold-yellow, round tomatoes of good flavour.

HARBINGER Early ripening, heavy cropper. Tomatoes of medium size.

HUNDREDFOLD* Short-jointed, early ripening, heavy cropper. Fruits are deep red, medium-sized and of good flavour.

ITALIAN PLUM Plum-shaped, deep red fruits without much juice. Flavour is distinctive. Excellent for canning.

KELVEDON CROSS (F₁) Trusses are closely spaced. Early ripening and fruits are exceptionally uniform. Noted for its fine flavour. Recommended for both heated and unheated greenhouse.

KONDINE RED Deep scarlet fruits. Heavy cropper. Under dull conditions the tomatoes may suffer from blotchy ripening.

MARKET KING* A popular variety producing medium-sized very uniform fruits. For the greenhouse or out of doors.

MM (F₁) Similar to but earlier-ripening than 'Moneymaker'. Resistant to cladosporium disease.

MONEYCROSS Matures 10–14 days earlier than 'Moneymaker'. Fruits have the good shape and colour of 'Moneymaker'. Resistant to cladosporium disease.

MONEYMAKER Medium-sized, well-shaped scarlet fruits of non-greenback type. The most popular commercial variety. Exceptionally heavy cropper.

MONEYRES (F₁) Evenly-shaped tomatoes of good flavour. A good cropper.

ORNAMENTALS* Small red or yellow tomatoes resembling cherries, currants, plums and pears. The 'currant' type is a bush.

OUTDOOR GIRL* Very early ripening. Plants bear from 5 lb. to 7 lb of fruit. The bottom truss is exceptionally large. Not suited for the greenhouse.

POTENTATE Fruits are medium to large, of good colour and borne on large trusses. A popular commercial tomato.

PUCK (bush)* Dwarf variety liked for cloche and frame growing.

SIOUX (F₁)* Good cropper. Very evenly-shaped tomatoes of good flavour. Suitable for outdoor and greenhouse cultivation.

SLEAFORD Abundance (F₁) (bush)* The first English bred F₁ hybrid dwarf bush. Heavy cropper.

SUNRISE* Medium-sized fruits. Suitable for both indoor and outdoor cultivation.

SUPERCROSS (F₁) Shows tolerance to mosaic virus and is immune to cladosporium disease. Non-greenback fruits of 'Moneymaker' size and colour. Excellent flavour.

SUTTON'S ALICANTE Greenback-free, resistant to cladosporium disease and stands up well to low temperatures. Tomatoes are handsome and crops good.

SUTTON'S LEADER* Hardy, early ripening. For greenhouse or outdoors. Large crops of even, good coloured fruits.

THE AMATEUR (bush)* Considered by many as the earliest and best self-stopping bush tomato. Fruits are deep red, even and handsome. A good cropper.

TINY TIM (bush)* A very compact bush. Suitable for window-box growing. The scarlet tomatoes are seldom more than 1 inch across and are almost seedless.

TIGER TOM A new red tomato with yellow stripes when ripe.

TRIP-1-CROP Pale red tomatoes of excellent flavour and weighing up to 1 lb each. Uneven shape.

WARECROSS (F₁) Early ripener. Good quality fruit.

WHITE Yellowish-white, very ridged tomatoes. Flesh is rather dry but very sweet.

YELLOW PERFECTION* Early-ripening, good cropping yellow fruited. Tomatoes are small to medium in size.

Key: F₁ = F₂ hybrid. Noted for uniform appearance. Seeds should not be saved from F₁ hybrids for propagation. *Suitable for outdoor growing

Below **Popular Tomato 'Moneymaker'**

Tradescantia fluminensis variegata.

fingers helps to release the ripe pollen. In some seasons weather conditions hinder a good natural set of the bottom trusses and a tomato fruit setting spray can be helpful.

Let the plants grow on until the desired height is reached. In the greenhouse this final height is around 6 feet for plants grown in the border, in rings or in straw bales. Plants grown in containers are normally stopped by pinching out the central growing point when from three to five trusses have set. Tomatoes should be allowed to ripen off on the plants.

Unheated greenhouse cultivation Tomato plants for growing in an unheated greenhouse may be bought in late April or early May. In colder parts wait until mid-May unless the house can be given temporary heat with an oil heater at night to prevent frost damage.

Plants in an unheated greenhouse usually ripen four or five trusses in August and September. In a very cool summer a part of the crop may not ripen until October.

Outdoor Tomato growing Provided that an early-ripening variety is chosen, worthwhile crops of tomatoes may be grown in the garden in most parts. 'Outdoor Girl' is outstanding for its early-ripening quality. In colder parts

frames and cloches give protection to the plants during June and early July. Plants may be raised from seed in a cold frame, in an unheated greenhouse, or under a cloche during April in warmer areas.

Many gardeners prefer to buy plants for outdoor growing but this limits the choice of variety and most plants on sale are of varieties which are more suited to greenhouse conditions. The tomato plant is not only killed by frost but is adversely affected by sudden temperature changes and in most parts it is seldom possible to set plants outdoors without protection until early June. About 15 inches should be allowed between plants in rows 30 inches apart. Before planting, the planting holes should be filled with water and planting done when this has drained away. Supports for the plants may be bamboo canes, stakes or a wire trellis. Weeds must be controlled. Growing the plants in a black plastic substitute for mulch saves time and work, a straw mulch may be laid down in mid-July. The plants need tying in regularly to the supports and the central growing point of each plant is removed in late July, when three or four trusses of fruit will have set. Remove all side shoots.

Where a very early-ripening variety was not chosen a great part of the crop may not have ripened by mid-September. Plants may then be defoliated and cloches placed over them. Untie them from the supports and lower them on to clean straw. The cloches are then set over the bed and pickings continue until late October. Where no cloches are to hand all tomatoes on the plants should be harvested during the latter half of September. Most of the fruit will ripen off well in a drawer in a warm room. Any small green tomatoes may be used for chutney.

Dwarf bush tomatoes Self-stopping bush varieties are particularly suitable for frame and cloche growing; they may also be grown successfully in the open.

Tradescantia (trad-es-kan-tee-a)
Commemorating John Tradescant (died 1637), gardener to Charles I *(Commelinaceae)*. A genus of 60 species of hardy perennial and greenhouse plants from North America and tropical South America. The hardy varieties are commonly called spiderwort, flower of a day, Moses-in-the-bulrushes, or devil-in-the-pulpit. According to some botanists the garden plants grown under the name *T. virginiana* belong to a hybrid group known as *T.* × *andersoniana*.

Species cultivated *T. albiflora,* wandering Jew, trailing, fast-growing greenhouse or house plant with shiny stems, swollen at the nodes, leaves narrow, pointed, South America; several variegated forms are known with cream and yellow-striped leaves, green and white, or with faint red markings. *T. blossfeldiana,* creeping or trailing greenhouse or house plant, dark green leathery leaves, purple and whitely-hairy beneath, Argentine. *T. fluminensis,* wandering Jew, trailing greenhouse or house plant, often confused with *T. albiflora,* leaves slender-pointed, green, purplish-red beneath; several variegated forms, South America. *T. virginiana* (or *T.* × *andersoniana*) spiderwort, etc., hardy perennial, 1½–2 feet, flowers violet-blue from June to September, eastern United States; vars. *alba,* a white form; *coerulea,* bright blue; 'Iris Prichard', white, shaded violet at the centre; 'J. C. Weguelin', large, azure-blue; 'Osprey', large, white, with feathery blue stamens; *rosea,* pink, *rubra,* dark ruby-red.

Cultivation The tender species and varieties require a minimum winter temperature of 55 F (13 C), and should be potted in March or April, in ordinary potting soil. Avoid a rich compost which may cause the leaves to turn green and lose their variegations. Hardy varieties can be grown in ordinary garden soil in sun or partial shade. Lift and divide in autumn or spring every three or four years. Propagation of tender species is by cuttings taken from April to August

Opposite page **Tradescantia virginiana.**

and inserted in pots of sandy soil in a warm propagating frame; they will root in four to six weeks. Hardy varieties may be increased by division in the spring.

Trillium (tril-lee-um)

From the Latin *triplum*, triple, alluding to the three-part leaves and flowers *(Trilliaceae)*. Wood lily. A genus of 30 species of shade-loving hardy perennials from North America and extra-tropical Asia, of immaculate beauty when in flower in spring. They are reputed to be difficult, but respond to correct cultivation. *T. grandiflorum* is the most handsome and widely grown species.

Species cultivated *T. erectum*, birth root, 1 foot, flowers deep purple, unique in that the three petals are almost erect and have a curious scent, May, eastern North America; var. *album*, white. *T. grandiflorum*, wake robin, 1–1½ feet, large, stem-clasping leaves, flowers large, pure white, becoming pink, petals held horizontally, April and May, eastern North America. *T. luteum*, 6–12 inches, leaves strongly-mottled, flowers yellow, early spring, eastern North America. *T. nervosum*, 1–1½ feet, flowers white with rosy margins, spring, south-eastern United States. *T. nivale*, 6–9 inches, leaves spotted purple, flowers white, early spring, south eastern United States. *T. undulatum*, 1 foot, slender-pointed, coppery-brown, waved leaves, flowers white, striped purple at the base of the petals, April and May, eastern North America.

Cultivation Plant in August or September in leafy woodland soil which is well-drained but does not dry out in summer. Wood lilies should be planted in dappled shade and left undisturbed, until overcrowding of the tuberous roots makes division necessary. This should be done in late summer. Top dress established plants in March with compost, leaf soil or moist peat. Plants can also be raised from seed sown in pans of sandy peat, placed in a shady cold frame. Seedlings usually flower in their fifth year. By gentle forcing flowers may appear early in the year, or the rootstock can be retarded by refrigeration to produce flowers out of season.

Trollius (trol-lee-us)

From the German common name *troll-blume*, or the Latin *trulleus*, a basin, referring to the flower shape *(Ranunculaceae)*. Globe-flower. A genus of 25 species of hardy perennials with large buttercup-like blooms, and usually with palmately lobed leaves. They are natives of northern temperate and arctic regions, and are at their best beside a pool or stream.

Species cultivated *T. europaeus*, 1–2 feet, flowers lemon-yellow, May and June, Europe (including northern Britain and South Wales); vars. 'First Lancers', deep orange; 'Earliest of All', lemon-yellow, April–June; 'Goldquelle', orange-

Trillium grandiflorum, with large, white flowers is the most common species.

yellow, May; 'Helios', citron yellow; 'Orange Princess', bright orange-yellow. *T. ledebourii* (syn. *T. chinensis*), 2–3 feet, flowers deep orange with bright orange stamens, June, northern China; a cultivar is 'Golden Queen', 2 feet, bright orange with conspicuous stamens. *T. pumilus*, 6–12 inches, buttercup-yellow, rock garden, June and July, Himalaya. *T. yunnanensis*, 1½–2 feet, flowers golden-yellow, western China.

Cultivation Plant in early autumn in semi-shade or in full sun, provided the soil is deep, moist and loamy. Every three or four years lift and divide them in autumn. Seed may also be sown, preferably on ripening, in pans or boxes of a loamy compost in September or April, and placed in a shaded cold frame or stood in the open in the shade.

Tropaeolum (trop-e-o-lum)

From the Latin *tropaeum* (or Greek *tropaion*), a trophy, possibly in allusion to the likeness of the flowers and leaves to helmets and shields displayed after Roman victories *(Tropaeolaceae)*. A diverse genus of 90 species of annuals, perennial herbaceous climbers, some tender, others hardy, natives of Mexico and temperate South America.

Species cultivated *T. majus*, nasturtium, hardy or half-hardy annual climber, flowers orange, summer in the wild, Peru; cultivars include 'Golden Gleam', double; 'Indian Chief', flowers scarlet, double, dark leaves; 'Mahogany', mahogany-red, double; 'Orange Gleam', deep orange and mahogany, double; 'Primrose Gleam', double; 'Salmon Gleam', golden salmon, double; 'Scarlet Gleam', orange and scarlet, double; var. *nanum* is a non-climbing form commonly called the Tom Thumb nasturtium. Cultivars of this are: 'Cherry Rose', cerise, rose, double; 'Empress of India', deep crimson, dark leaves; 'Feltham Beauty', bright scarlet, compact; 'Fire Globe', brilliant red, double; 'Golden Globe', compact, double, gold and crimson. 'Jewel Mixed', double, various colours, flowers held well above the leaves; 'King of Tom Thumbs', scarlet, dark leaves; 'Mahogany Gem', deep mahogany-red, double; 'Queen of Tom Thumbs', various, silver-variegated leaves; 'Rosy Morn', rose-scarlet; 'Vesuvius', salmon-rose, dark leaves. *T. peltophorum* (syn. *T. lobbianum),* hardy or half-hardy annual or perennial climber, flowers yellow or orange, summer, Chile, Argentine. *T. peregrinum,* Canary creeper, 3–10 feet, half-hardy annual or perennial climber in mild districts, flowers golden-yellow fringed, July onwards, entirely different from the common nasturtium, and requiring a richer soil, Peru. *T. speciosum,* flame nasturtium, hardy perennial, 6–9 feet when established and climbing through a shrub or hedge, flowers brilliant scarlet, June to September, Chile. *T. tuberosum,* tuberous-rooted perennial, 4–5 feet, flowers orange-scarlet, September, Peru.

Cultivation The annual nasturtiums should be sown in spring where they are to flower, in well-drained soil and a sunny position. The young seedlings are tender and are liable to frost damage, therefore nothing is gained by sowing before the end of April or later in cold districts, although following mild winters self-sown seedlings often appear. Sow *T. peregrinum* in light soil under glass in March with a temperature of 50°F (10°C), and harden off the seedlings before planting out against a fence or wall in mid-May. It does well on a north-facing wall. The perennial species like a well-drained loamy soil, *T. speciosum* thriving in a cool, north-facing aspect beside a wall on which there are plants up which it can clamber. It does best in the north, where it is often seen scrambling into yew hedges. *T. tuberosum* does best in poorish, lime-free soil and a sunny position; the tubers should be planted in March or April and in colder districts lifted in autumn and stored in the same way as dahlia tubers. *T. speciosum* is raised from seed, although seed is difficult to germinate. The seedlings are best grown on in separate pots as they can prove tricky to transplant.

Tulipa (tew-lip-a)

Either from the Persian *thoulypen,* turban, or from the Turkish *tul-ban* or *tulipam,* turban, referring to the flower shape *(Liliaceae).* A genus of about 100 species of bulbous plants, natives of temperate Eurasia. Using some of these species as parents, breeders over the last 400 years have developed thousands of cultivars. Today over 3,000 cultivars are recognised, although about 800 only are in commercial cultivation, in 23 main groups or classes (see below).

Some tulips flower early (in mid-April, some in mid-season (late April), and others bloom late, in May. The colour range is from white to almost black, from softest pink to deepest purple; there are broken colours, self-

colours, striped, streaked, shaded and tinged. Some have oval flowers, some are shaped like turbans, and others are square at the base. Some tulips resemble paeonies, others have lily-like flowers. There are tulips with fringed or curled petals and others with pointed petals. A number produce several flowers on a stem. Some have tiny flowers, while others produce blooms up to 15 inches in diameter. Heights range from a few inches to nearly 3 feet.

Tulips are officially classified into four divisions, comprising the 23 groups. The first three divisions, early, mid-season and late or May-flowering, comprise 15 groups, all referred to as garden tulips. There are three categories in the early-flowering division: (1) Duc van Tol, (2) Single Early, and (3) Double Early. The Duc van Tol tulips are very early-flowering single tulips, with stems rarely exceeding 6 inches in height and with large, long, pointed flowers. They are no longer generally sold and their place has been taken by the sturdier, taller Single and Double earlies.

Single Early tulips (2) are 10–14 inches tall and single-cupped in form. The flowers range in colour from rich red, to orange, yellow, pink and white. They are the earliest garden tulips to bloom, flowering in mid-April, excellent for bedding, edging and window-boxes and many do well indoors. Varieties suitable for indoor and outdoor cultivation include: 'Bellona', golden-yellow; 'Brillant Star', scarlet; 'Couleur Cardinal', velvet red; 'General de Wet', golden-orange stippled orange-scarlet; 'Ibis', rose-scarlet flushed pink; 'Keizerskroon', brilliant red with yellow margin; 'Sunburst', coral-red edged old gold; 'Van der Neer', dark purple.

Double Early tulips (3), 10–14 inches tall, have cups filled with rows of petals in pink, red, yellow, white and orange. There are both self-coloured and variegated kinds. They flower in late April and prefer sunny, partially sheltered positions. Most varieties are suitable for indoor cultivation. Varieties suited to indoor and outdoor cultivation include: 'Electra', soft carmine pink with paler margin; 'Goya', orange-red, base yellow; 'Marechal Niel', canary-yellow, tinted orange; 'Mr van der Hoef' soft yellow; 'Murillo Max', pale rose flushed white; 'Peach Blossom', rosy-pink; 'Schoonoord', white; 'Willemsoord', carmine-red edged white.

The mid-season division consists of (4) Mendel, and (5) Triumph tulips. Mendel tulips (4) are chiefly the result of crosses between Duc van Tol and Darwin tulips. They have large, single flowers on 16–20-inch stems, flowering out of doors from late April. They are valuable for forcing and will bloom in greenhouses from January. Their blooms are self-coloured or edged with deeper or contrasting hue. Varieties include: 'Athleet', pure white; 'Beauty of Volen-

dam', feathered and flamed purplish-red on white; 'Her Grace', white,edged deep pink; 'Krelage's Triumph', deep geranium-red; 'Orange Wonder', orange-red; 'White Sail', opening cream turning to pure white.

Triumph tulips (5) are the result of crossing Single Early tulips with late-flowering tulips, particularly Darwins. They are generally of stouter build than the Mendels, but seldom exceed 16–20 inches in height. They have large, single-cup flowers in shades of self-colours, bicolors, edged, flushed, striped and margined, not to be found in other types of tulips. They are valuable for the garden because of their strong stems, vigorous habit and weather resistance. They flower immediately after the Mendels, are ideal for indoor cultivation, and excellent for cutting. Varieties include: 'Aureola', scarlet-red margined yellow; 'Blizzard', pure white; 'Crater', dark red; 'Edith Eddy', carmine-rose edged white; 'First Lady', reddish-violet flushed purple; 'Kansas', creamy-white, becoming pure white; 'Merry Widow', glowing red with white band; 'Reforma', butter yellow; 'Sulphur Glory', sulphur yellow.

The biggest and most varied group is the late or May-flowering division comprising (6) Darwin, (7) Darwin hybrid, (8) Breeder, (9) Lily-flowered, (10) Cottage, (11) Rembrandt, (12) Bizarre, (13) Bijbloemen, (14) Parrot, and (15) Double Late or paeony-flowered tulips. All bloom in May although the Cottage and Lily-flowered groups tend to flower earlier than the others, except the Darwin hybrids.

From the Darwin tulips stem the twentieth century groups of Mendel, Triumph, Rembrandt, Darwin hybrid and Lily-flowered tulips. Darwins (6) are sturdy, resistant to wind and rain, and are suited to beds, borders, orchards, etc. They have stems 26-32 inches in height and are excellent for cutting. Many can be grown in pots or bowls. The large-cupped flowers, in virtually all colours, are mostly self-coloured, and have a satiny texture. Over a hundred varieties are available in Britain, including: 'Aristocrat', magenta-pink; 'Bleu Aimable', lavender-mauve; 'Campfire', rich crimson; 'City of Haarlem', deep scarlet; 'Clara Butt', soft pink, flushed rose, base white; 'Golden Age', buttercup-yellow, flushed golden-orange; 'Insurpassable', lilac; 'La Tulipe Noire', blackest of all tulips; 'Pink Supreme', rich deep pink; 'Queen of Bartigons', delicate pink; 'Red Pitt', deep red; 'Sweet Harmony', butter-yellow merging to creamy-white; 'The Bishop', deep lavender-purple.

Darwin hybrids (7), the result of crossing the Darwin and Fosteriana (species) tulips, have the largest flowers yet produced, some reaching as much as 15 inches in diameter. They are brilliant in colour and have stems 22–28 inches

**1 'Johann Strauss', a variety of the attractive Tulipa kaufmanniana.
2 The bicoloured flowers of Tulipa tarda, good plants for the rock garden.**

tall. The single flowers are noted for their shades of red. They are ideal for massing. Varieties include: 'Apeldoorn', reddish-orange; 'General Eisenhower', guardsmen's red; 'Gudoshnik', creamy-peach, flecked rose; 'Holland's Glory', orange-red; 'Jewel of Spring', primrose-yellow, edged red; 'London', crimson-scarlet; 'Oxford', orange-red; 'Parade', scarlet-red; 'President Kennedy', golden-yellow.

Originally the name 'Breeder' signified a tulip that Dutch growers thought most likely in succeeding years to 'break' and produce the striped or streaked flowers that were so popular. Breeders (8) have long, large, oval flowers in shades of purple and gold, bronzy orange, yellow, soft copper and combinations of rich tints. Stems range from 24–36 inches in height. They are superb in sunny borders. Varieties include 'Barcarolle', violet-blue; 'Dillenburg', salmon-orange shaded rose; 'Georges Grappe', soft mauve; 'Louis XIV', bluish-violet, flushed bronze; 'Orange Delight', cinnamon bronze; 'Papago', deep red, glowing orange inside; 'Yuma', geranium-red with an orange band.

By crossing the species *T. retroflexa* with Darwins the Lily-flowered tulips (9) were created a century ago. They have beautifully reflexed and pointed petals and wiry stems 20–24 inches tall.

They come in reds, rose, bright pinks, yellows, lilac, violet and white. Superb for cutting, the look best when grouped Varieties include: 'Aladdin', crimson red, rimmed clear gold; 'Captain Fryatt', soft burgundy, flushed purple; 'China Pink', rose-pink, flushed bronze; 'Gisela', chinese-rose, tinged salmon; 'Golden Duchess', yellow; 'Maybole', bright pink; 'Queen of Sheba', scarlet-brown, margined yellow; 'Red Shine', deep red; 'White Triumphator', pure white.

Cottage tulips (10) are so named because they were originally found in the old cottage gardens of England, Ireland and France. With stems 20–32 inches tall, many have slender buds with long pointed petals, but there is considerably more variation in the form of the Cottage group than in any other. They come in pastel blends, pastel shades and in light red hues, etc. They are excellent in borders and with care may be naturalised. Varieties include: 'Advance', orange-scarlet; 'Artist', terracotta and green; 'Chappaqua', cherry-pink; 'G. W. Leak', orange-red; 'Inglescombe Yellow', canary-yellow; 'Marjorie Bowen', salmon-pink, flushed buff; 'White City'.

The history of tulips starts with 'broken' tulips which have since been classified as Rembrandt, Bizarre and Bijbloemen tulips according to parentage and colour. They are useful for floral decoration and in beds and borders. Rembrandts (11) are broken Darwin tulips with large, single, squarish cups, striped and streaked against the self-colours of Darwins. They grow 22–26 inches in height and look best planted in small groups. The few varieties include: 'American Flag', dark red stripes on white ground; 'Cordell Hull', flamed and splashed cherry red on white; 'Montgomery', pure white, edged rosy-red.

Both the Bizarre and Bijbloemen tulips are broken Breeder and Cottage tulips. They are commercially produced in small quantity and limited variety. All varieties in the Bizarre (12) group have yellow ground with brown and purple markings, while Bijbloemen (13) have violet, rose or purple markings on a white ground. Both have large, single cups and stems 20–24 inches in height. They are primarily grown for cutting. Bizarre varieties include: 'Black Boy', chocolate-black on brown; 'Golden Brocade', brownish-red, flamed yellow and bronze; 'Insulinde', violet on yellow ground; 'May Blossom', veined bluish-purple on a creamy-white ground, is a Bijbloemen variety.

Parrot tulips (14) have been known since the seventeenth century but the stems were too weak originally to support the huge, heavy flowers with deeply cut, curled and twisted petals. In recent years new varieties with strong 20–26 inch stems have been introduced. Ideal for focal points in the garden they should be planted 8 inches apart because of the large flowers. They are good for cutting and come in white, pink, red, orange, violet and yellow and the outside is often tinged with green. Varieties include: 'Black Parrot', almost black; 'Blue Parrot', lavender-mauve, crested green; 'Discovery', delicate pink; 'Fire Bird', scarlet-red; 'Orange Parrot', mahogany-brown with pencilled gold lines; 'Red Parrot', warm red, inside brilliant scarlet; 'Sunshine', golden-yellow; 'White Parrot'.

The Double Late or paeony-flowered tulips (15) have large, double flowers like paeonies on stems 20–24 inches in height, in shades of red, violet, yellow, white and two-toned, and are ideal for sunny borders and as cut flowers. Varieties include: 'Eros', old-rose; 'Gold Medal', golden-yellow; 'Livingstone', cherry-red; 'May Wonder', pink; 'Mount Tacoma', white; 'Nizza', cream-yellow with bright crimson markings; 'Orange Triumph', soft orange, flushed brown; 'Pride of Holland', carmine-red; 'Uncle Tom', glossy maroon.

The remaining eight groups of tulips consist of species or botanical tulips and their hybrids and form a division of their own, which contains the earliest of all tulips to flower and the shorter-stemmed tulips so useful for the rock garden, the alpine house or for naturalising. The groups are (16) *T. batalinii*, (17) *T. eichleri*, (18) *T. fosteriana*, (19) *T. greigii*, (20) *T. kaufmanniana*, (21) *T. marjoletti*, (22) *T. tubergeniana*, and (23) other species and their varieties and hybrids.

The pale yellow flowers of the 4-inch tall *T. batalinii* show up well against the creeping ribbon-like leaves; they look excellent in the rock garden and flower in May. There is a 6-inch tall hybrid, 'Bronze Charm', with yellow flowers, flushed warm cinnamon.

T. eichleri, 1 foot tall, has shining scarlet flowers with slightly reflexing petals. The centre is black with a narrow band of yellow. It flowers in April and should be planted with early-flowering daffodils for striking effect in borders. The hybrid 'Clare Benedict' is 20 inches tall, blooms cone-shaped in vivid scarlet. The centre is black with a narrow golden-yellow margin.

The *T. fosteriana* hybrids should be planted in clumps in beds, in the rock garden, at the base of trees, in tubs or urns, to bloom in early April. Among the new hybrids are 'Cantata', 12 inches, vermilion-red; 'Easter Parade', 16 inches, pure yellow, flushed red; 'Madame Lefeber' ('Red Emperor'), 15 inches, bright oriental scarlet; 'Princeps', 10 inches, scarlet; 'Purissima', 15 inches, milky white; 'Tender Beauty', 18 inches, white, edged rosy-red.

The purple mottling of the leaves of *T. greigii* has changed in some of the hybrids into broad, well-defined striping and the hybrids tend to have leaves that

Tulipa greigii 'Corsage'.

spread out almost flat on the ground, covering the soil in a way no other tulips do. *T. greigii* hybrids not only have the distinctly marked foliage of the species but their brilliant colouring as well. They flower in April and although only a few varieties are currently available, they are destined to become one of the most important groups of tulips for garden decoration. Those available include: 'Angel Bright', 9 inches, scarlet-orange, edged gold; 'Bokhara', 16 inches, crimson-scarlet, leaves heavily marked; 'Plaisir', 6 inches, vermilion-red, edged sulphur, leaves mottled; 'Red Riding Hood', 5 inches, pillar-box scarlet; 'Rockery Master', 12 inches, rich strawberry-scarlet; 'Yellow Dawn', 15 inches, yellow with a wide blaze of soft carmine-rose.

Kaufmanniana or Water-lily tulips, growing 4–9 inches tall, and with large cone-shaped flowers with petals curling back gracefully, flower in March–April and are the first tulips to bloom. They are excellent for rock gardens, tubs and window-boxes, and can be naturalised. They have flowers in yellow, scarlet, crimson, red and pastel shades and many hybrids have leaves that are beautifully marked or striped with brown or purple.

Varieties include: 'Alfred Cortot', 8 inches, bright red; 'César Franck', 8 inches, orange-red, edged yellow; 'Fair Lady', 7 inches, crimson-red and ivory; 'Heart's Delight', 9 inches, carmine-red, edged rosy white; 'Johann Strauss', 6 inches, ivory white and brick red; 'Shakespeare', 6 inches, salmon, apricot and orange, inside pale yellow, flushed red; 'The First', 6 inches, carmine-red outside shading to gold at the base, inside ivory merging to gold in the centre.

At present no varieties of *T. marjolettii* are in commercial cultivation and it is difficult to obtain any varieties or hybrids of *T. tubergeniana*. Among the other species tulips available, however, are *T. biflora*, 6 inches, 3–8 blooms per stem, petals delicately pointed, greenish, grey-purple on the outside, shading to yellow at the base, April. *T. hageri*, 5 inches, copper-red, two or three flowers per stem, April–May. *T. linifolia*, 6 inches, scarlet, black centre, April. *T. praestans*, 12 inches, 3–4 blooms per stem, flowers orange-red, April; var. 'Fusilier', 6 inches, 2–3 scarlet flowers per stem, April. *T. tarda* (syn. *T. dasy-*

The Lily-flowered Tulip 'Dyanito', descended from Tulipa retroflexa, has reflexed, pointed petals.

stemon), 3 inches, up to four white, green and yellow star-like flowers, April. *T. turkestanica*, 6–8 inches, 5–8 flowers per stem, grey-green on the outside shading to yellow at the base, inside off-white with a yellow centre, March–April. All are ideal for the rock garden in sunny positions.

Cultivation Bulbs can be planted out of doors between mid-September and mid-December. Species or botanical tulips should be planted 4 inches deep and about 5 inches apart with the exception of *T. fosteriana,* which should be planted 5–6 inches deep and some 6 inches apart, like all divisions of garden tulips. Good drainage is essential; they will thrive in virtually any well-drained soil, but in light sandy soils the bulbs should be planted an inch or two deeper than normal. Tulips can be interplanted with roses or with annuals or with other bulbs flowering at the same time, taking into account the differing heights of other plants when interplanting. Species tulips do best in sunny positions, but garden tulips can be planted in sun or in partial shade. Early-flowering garden tulips planted in sheltered sunny spots will come into flower sooner, or if late-flowering tulips are planted in partial shade, they will last longer.

Apart from *kaufmanniana* tulips which are naturalised, all tulips should be lifted every year when the foliage has turned completely yellow and begun to die off. The old flower stems should be cut off an inch or so above the newly formed bulbs at the end of June or early July. They should, under no circumstances, be left on the bulb in storage trays. If the bulbs must be cleared from the ground before the foliage begins to die, to make way for other bedding plants, they may be lifted and heeled into a shallow trench in a spare corner until the leaves yellow. The lifted bulbs should be kept out of sunlight, cleaned and stored in a cool, airy, frost-free place until planting time comes round again. Indoor cultivation is as for narcissus (see Narcissus), but forced tulip bulbs are not really worth keeping for later outdoor planting.

Propagation is by offsets or seed. Offsets are produced freely and can be easily detached when lifting and cleaning the bulbs. They are planted 3 inches deep, with room to develop, in light, rich soil in a sunny position during November. Flowers are produced when the offsets are three to four years old, and will be exactly like the parent plant, unlike those produced from seed. It is by the latter method that new varieties are produced.

Seed can be sown as soon as it is ripe, or in February, in light, sandy soil in a cold frame. Seedlings will start to appear in March–April, and should be left where they are, with protection during the winter until the following autumn, about 18 months after sowing, when they can be planted out of doors in rich light soil. There they can be grown on until they flower at four to six years old.

Turnip

This root vegetable, *Brassica campestris rapa* (syn. *B. rapa*), has been grown in Britain since the sixteenth century. The roots are global or flattish round. A well-drained sandy loam is suitable for both types—summer and winter. But if the soil is light and sandy, it dries out rapidly and turnip flea beetles flourish. A heavy soil is unsuitable for summer turnips but is usually suitable for the winter type. Both very light and heavy soils are improved by regular winter dressings of manure, etc. A site that was manured for a previous crop should be chosen. If liming was not carried out during the previous winter, ground chalk should be dusted on to the surface at the rate of 4 ounces to the square yard before seed sowing.

The first sowing, out of doors or under cloches, may be made from mid-March to mid-April with a second successional sowing in May. Sow seed thinly ½ inch deep in rows 1 foot apart. Dust seedlings with derris to control flea beetles and hoe to keep down weeds. Thin the seedlings to 4 inches or so apart and water in dry spells. Quick growth with no checks at all is essential for succulent summer turnips. Start pulling for use when the turnips are sufficiently large. If left to age they become coarse and fibrous. Sow seed of winter turnips similarly, in late July or early August. Water seed drills if the soil is dry and sow after the water has drained away. Dust the seedlings with derris and thin to 9 inches apart. Winter turnips are often left in the ground and pulled when wanted. In colder parts the roots are best lifted in the autumn when the outer leaves are yellowing. Cut back the foliage to about ½ inch from the crown and shorten long tap roots by a few inches before storing the roots in moist sand or ashes.

For a supply of turnip tops for 'greens in spring sow seed of a suitable variety in August quite thickly in ½-inch-deep drills spaced at 18 inches apart. In colder areas the plants benefit from cloche protection during the winter. When picking leaves for use take but one or two from each plant (see Brassica).

Turnip varieties *Summer* 'Early Snowball', 'Early White Milan', 'Red Top Milan', 'Golden Ball'; *winter* 'Manchester Market'; *for turnip tops* 'Hardy Green Round', 'Green Globe'.

Ursinia (ur-sin-ee-a)

Commemorating Johann Ursinus of Regensburg (1608–66), author of *Arboretum Biblicum (Compositae).* A genus of 80 species of annuals, herbaceous perennials or sub-shrubs, natives of South Africa, with one species found in Abyssinia. Those grown in Britain are treated as half-hardy annuals. The daisy-like flowers, in shades of orange and yellow, remain open through the day which is not true of all South

the base of the petals.

Cultivation Sow seed in a cool greenhouse in April, and prick off into small pots and plant out in late May or early June, in a sunny position in a soil that is not too rich. Seed may also be sown in the open in late April where plants are to flower. Germination is often erratic.

Verbascum (ver-bas-kum)
Possibly from the Latin *barba*, a beard, many species having a hairy or downy look *(Scrophulariaceae)*. Mullein. A genus of 300 species of hardy herbaceous plants, mostly biennials, or short-lived perennials, from temperate parts of Europe and Asia.

Species cultivated *V. blattaria*, moth mullein, to 4 feet, flowers yellow or cream, Europe (including Britain). *V. bombyciferum* (syns. *V.* 'Broussa', *V.* 'Brusa'), biennial, 4-6 feet, stem and leaves covered in silvery hairs, flowers golden-yellow, embedded in silvery hairs, June–July, western Asia Minor. *V. chaixii* (syn. *V. vernale*), 3 feet, stems purple, leaves covered with whitish hairs, flowers yellow, June–August, Europe. *V. dumulosum*, 1 foot, perennial, leaves grey felted, flowers lemon-yellow, May–June, needs a hot, dry place or alpine house, Asia Minor. *V. nigrum* (syn. *V. vernale*), normally perennial, 2–3 feet, yellow, blotched reddish-brown, June to October, Europe (including Britain). *V. olympicum*, perennial, 5–6 feet, leaves grey felted, flowers golden, June to September, Bithynia; several cultivars in shades of amber, terra-cotta, purple and yellow. *V. phoeniceum*, purple mullein, 3–5 feet; hybrids available in pink, lilac, purple. *V. pulverulentum*, hoary mullein, leaves white hairy, flowers yellow, July, Europe (including Britain). *V. thapsus*, Aaron's rod, hag taper, to 3 feet, very woolly, flowers yellow, summer, Europe, Asia.

Cultivation Verbascums grow easily in sunny positions and ordinary or chalky soil. Propagation of species is by seed sown in light soil outdoors in April. Hybrids, some of which are sterile, are increased by root cuttings in autumn or winter.

African annuals.

Species cultivated *U. anethoides* (syn. *Sphenogyne anethoides*), 1–2 feet, flowers bright orange-yellow with a central zone of deep purple, July to September; the cultivar 'Aurora' is bright orange with conspicuous crimson-red base. *U. versicolor* (syn. *U. pulchra*), 9 inches, flowers orange with dark centre, summer; the cultivar 'Golden Bedder' is light orange with deeper orange centre.

Cultivation These brightly coloured daisy-like plants require a light well-drained soil and full sun. They associate well with arctotis, as in the wild in Cape Province. Sow the seed under glass in late March and plant out in mid-May, or when the danger of frost is past.

Vallota (val-lo-ta)
In honour of Pierre Vallot, a seventeenth century French botanist *(Amaryllidaceae)*. A genus of one species, a bulbous plant from Cape Province, South Africa, where it is known as the George lily, but in Britain as Scarborough lily, after some bulbs were washed ashore there from a shipwreck. It is not reliably hardy in Britain, but is an admirable pot plant for a sunny window-sill. *V. speciosa* (syn. *V. purpurea)* reaches 1–2 feet, and has broad leaves, to 18 inches long and erect stems bearing up to 10 large, funnel-shaped, glowing scarlet-red flowers in August and September; there is a white variety, *alba,* and other varieties have been recorded.

Vallota speciosa, a bulbous plant from South Africa, has funnel-shaped, scarlet-red flowers.

Cultivation The bulbs are best potted in July in a compost of equal parts of fibrous loam, leafmould and sharp sand. The tip of the large bulb should be just below the surface, and potted firmly. Do not repot for several years, but give regular feeds with liquid fertilisers while the bulbs are growing, before flowering. Ample water is required during the growing season, but the soil should be kept nearly dry while the plants are dormant, after the leaves die down. Propagation is by offsets removed when repotting.

Venidium (ven-id-ee-um)
Possibly from the Latin *vena*, a vein, referring to the ribbed fruits *(Compositae)*. A genus of up to 30 species of South African half-hardy annuals and perennials.

Species cultivated *V. decurrens*, 1½ feet, flowers orange-yellow with a paler zone around a dark disc, July to October, perennial, best treated as a half-hardy annual. *V. fastuosum,* Namaqualand daisy, 2–3 feet, flowers orange, to 5 inches across, with a dark purple zone around a shining black central disc, June to September, annual; the strain 'Dwarf Hybrids', 15 inches, is available in shades of cream, ivory, yellow and orange with black centres and maroon markings at

Verbena (ver-be-na)
Possibly from the Latin *verbenae*, the sacred branches of laurel, myrtle or olive, or a corruption of the Celtic name *fervain* for *V. officinalis (Verbenaceae)*. A genus of 250 species of half-hardy perennials and annuals, widely distributed, notable for the bright colouring of the flowers. Those described are from South America.

Species cultivated *V. bonariensis*, perennial, 3–6 feet, flowers purple-lilac, July to October. *V. corymbosa*, perennial, 3 feet, flowers heliotrope-blue in dense, terminal heads, late summer. *V.* x *hybrida*, florist's verbena, to 1 foot, hybrid, summer bedding plant, many cultivars with flowers in shades of blue,

Verbena rigida has claret purple flowers in summer and autumn and is a good plant for mild localities.

red, pink, many with white eyes, also pure white. *V. peruviana* (syn. *V. chamaedrifolia*), half-hardy perennial, semi-prostrate, flowers brilliant scarlet, July to October, bedding plant. *V. rigida* (syn. *V. venosa*), perennial, 1½–2 feet, flowers claret-purple to violet, July to October; cultivars include: 'Amethyst', 1 foot, blue; 'Blaze', 9 inches, scarlet; 'Compliment' 1 foot, pink with yellow eye; 'Miss Susie Double', 9 inches, salmon pink, double; 'Olympia Strain', 9 inches, various colours; 'Ellen Wilmott', 1 foot, salmon-pink with white eye; 'Rose Queen', 1 foot; 'Royal Blue', 1 foot, blue with white eye; 'Scarlet Queen', 1 foot, scarlet with white eye; 'Snow Queen', 1 foot, white eye. *V. tenera*, trailing, South America; var. *maonettii*, reddish-violet and white, summer. *V. tenuisecta*, moss verbena, trailing, flowers in shades of blue, summer.

Cultivation Plant in spring in ordinary well-drained soil in a sunny position. In cold districts *V. bonariensis*, *V. corymbosa* and *V. rigida*, should be lifted and over-wintered in boxes of ordinary soil in a frost-free place. In March they should be started into growth in a temperature of 55 F (13 C) and the roots divided when new growth begins. Pot these and plant out in late May. Cuttings of *V. peruviana* should be rooted in late summer in boxes of sandy soil and over-wintered in a frost-free place. *V. bonariensis* is raised from seed sown outdoors in spring. Seed of half-hardy annual hybrids should be sown under glass in February; after the seedlings have been hardened off, plant them out in mid-May.

Veronica (ver-on-ik-a)
Origin doubtful, possibly named after St Veronica *(Scrophulariaceae)*. Speed-

well. A genus of some 300 species of hardy perennials, annuals and sub-shrubs, mainly from northern temperate regions. Those described are hardy perennials, their flowers often borne in spikes. Dwarf kinds are suitable for the rock garden.

Species cultivated *V. agrestis*, procumbent speedwell, prostrate, flowers pink, annual weed, Europe (including Britain). *V. chamaedrys*, germander speedwell, 1–1½ feet, bright blue, May onwards, Europe (including Britain). *V. cinerea*, 6 inches, leaves grey, flowers pale blue, early summer. *V. exaltata*, 5 feet, mauve in tall spikes, late summer. *V. fruticans* (syn. *V. saxatilis*), rock speedwell, 3 inches, sub-shrub, deep blue with red eye, late summer. *V. gentianoides*, 2 feet, pale blue in slender spikes, May–June; vars. *nana*, 1 foot; *variegata*, leaves variegated, flowers deeper blue. *V. x guthrieana*, 3 inches, flowers large, blue, hybrid. *V. hederifolia*, ivy-leaved speedwell, similar to *V. agrestis*, Europe (including Britain). *V. incana*, 1–2 feet, leaves grey, flowers dark blue, summer; var. *rosea*, pink. *V. longifolia*, 2–4 feet, lilac-blue, late summer; var. *subsessilis*, royal blue. *V. pectinata*, 3 inches, mat-forming, leaves grey, flowers deep blue with white eye, May; var. *rosea*, pink. *V. prostrata*, 6 inches, creeping, blue, summer; vars. 'Mrs Holt', pink; *rosea*, rosy-pink; 'Shirley Blue', deep blue; 'Trehane', leaves golden, flowers light blue. *V. spicata*, 2 feet, bright blue, late summer; vars. *alba*, white; many varieties in blue, purple, and pink. *V. scutellata*, marsh speedwell, creeping, flowers pale blue, pink or white, Europe, North America. *V. teucrium*, 1–2 feet, lavender-blue, late summer; vars. 'Blue Fountain', 2 feet, intense blue; 'Royal Blue', 1½ feet. *V. virginica*, 4–5 feet, light blue, late summer; var. *alba*, white. *V. whitleyi*, 3–4 inches, tufted, blue with white eye, June to August.

Cultivation Veronicas will grow in ordinary soil and a sunny position. Propagation is by division in August or in spring, or by seed sown in the open in spring in light soil and in part shade. For the shrubby veronicas see Hebe.

Vinca (vin-ka)
The Latin name used by Pliny, probably from *vincio*, to bind, referring to the long, tough runners *(Apocynaceae)*. Periwinkle. A genus of seven species of trailing plants, mostly hardy, widely spread over Europe and western Asia.

Species cultivated *V. difformis* (E), flowers pale blue, 1½ inches across, autumn, Mediterranean area, hardy in the milder counties. *V. herbacea* (E), flowers blue-purple, to 1 inch across, May and June, eastern Europe; double forms are occasionally found. *V. major* (E), flowers blue, large, April onwards, Mediterranean region, North Africa, naturalised in Britain; vars. *pubescens*, leaves and petals narrower; *variegata*, leaves margined creamy-white. *V. minor*, similar to the foregoing but more prostrate, flowers blue, to 1 inch wide, April and May, Europe, naturalised in Britain; vars. *alba*, white; *atropurpurea*, deep purple; *aureo-variegata*, leaves blotched yellow; *azurea flore pleno*, sky-blue, double; 'Bowles's Variety', large, single, azure-blue; 'Le Grave', flowers larger, deeper blue; *multiplex*, plum purple, double; *variegata*, leaves variegated creamy-white. *V. rosea* (E), shrubby, 1–2 feet, flowers rosy-red, spring to autumn, tropics, greenhouse.

Cultivation The hardy periwinkles are useful trailing ground cover plants that flower best in the sun, but are quite happy in dry shade beneath a hedge or under trees, in ordinary soil. Once planted leave them undisturbed and allow them to spread, cutting back when necessary in early spring. Propagation is by division or by digging up rooted layers in autumn or early spring. *V. rosea* may be grown in pots of loam and peat; the tips of the shoots should be pinched out to encourage bushiness.

Viola (vi-o-la)
An old Latin name for violet *(Violaceae)*. A genus of some 500 species of hardy perennials, mainly from northern temperate regions, including violas, pansies and violets of which there are many hybrids and strains.

Species cultivated *V. adunca*, hooked spur violet, to 4 inches, violet or lavender with white eye, spring, North America. *V. arvensis*, field pansy, 6 inches, cream, Europe (including Britain), Asia, annual weed. *V. cornuta*, horned violet, 4–12 inches, flowers violet, June to August, Pyrenees; cultivars, including the 'Violettas', derived mainly from this species, are available in shades of yellow, plum-purple, rosy-lilac, blue and white with a yellow eye. *V. cucullata*, 6 inches, white, veined lilac, April to June, North

America. *V.* × *florairensis,* 4 inches, mauve and yellow, spring and summer, hybrid. *V. gracilis,* 4–6 inches, deep violet, April to August, Balkans, Asia Minor; vars. *alba,* white; 'Black Knight', purplish-black; *lutea,* golden-yellow; *major,* violet. *V. hispida,* Rouen pansy, to 8 inches, violet, summer, Europe. *V. labradorica,* 4–6 inches, porcelain-blue, summer, North America. *V. odorata,* see Violet. *V. palmata,* 6 inches, violet-purple, summer, North America. *V. rupestris,* Teesdale violet, to 2 inches, bluish-violet, Asia, Europe (including Britian), North America. *V. saxatilis,* 4–8 inches, violet, summer, Europe, Asia Minor. *V.* × *wittrockiana,* see Pansy.
Cultivation Violas do best in a moist, well-drained soil and in light shade. Propagation of cultivars is by cuttings rooted in late summer in sandy soil in a cold, shaded frame. Species and strains are raised from seed sown in late summer in light soil in a cold, shaded frame. See also Pansy, Violet.

Violet

Viola odorata, the sweet violet, is a hardy perennial, parent of the florist's violets, many of them sweetly scented. The soil should be rich, moist but well-drained. Plant the crowns in the open in a sheltered, shady position in April or in September for winter flowering in a cold, sunny frame. Propagation is by runners removed in April, other runners that are produced during the summer months should be removed and discarded.

Named varieties include: 'Coeur d'Alsace', pink; 'Czar', blue; 'De Parme', pale lavender, double; 'Governor Herrick', deep blue; 'Marie Louise', mauve, double, good for frame cultivation; 'La France', violet-blue; 'Princess of Wales', large violet-blue; 'Sulphurea', creamy-yellow; 'White Czar', single white.

Vriesea (vree-zee-a)

Commemorating W. de Vriese, a Dutch botanist of the nineteenth century *(Bromeliaceae).* A genus of some 190 species, mainly epiphytic, from South and Central America, with attractive, handsome unarmed leaves, borne in rosettes, and/or flowers. *V. splendens* is a popular house plant. The generic name is usually, but incorrectly spelt Vriesia. **Species cultivated** *V. carinata,* leaves 8 inches long, about 1 inch wide, bracts conspicuous, red and yellow, flowers yellow, in a spike about 3 inches long, autumn, Brazil. *V. fenestralis,* leaves handsome, 18 inches long, light green with darker reticulations, bracts green, brown-spotted, flowers tubular, greenish-yellow in a spike to 1½ feet, Brazil. *V. hieroglyphica,* to 5 feet, leaves dark green with bands, black on the upper surface and purple below, bracts dull yellow, flowers yellow in a branched inflorescence, 3 feet high, Brazil. *V. saundersii* (syn. *Encholirion saundersii*), leaves 10 inches long, grey to green with red blotches at the base, bracts pale yellow, flowers tubular, yellow, in a branched inflorescence, Brazil. *V. splendens,* leaves 12–15 inches long, dark green, with wine-coloured bands until the flowers appear, bracts bright red, flowers yellow in a 15-inch long inflorescence, bracts remain coloured for

1 Vinca major, the Periwinkle, an evergreen plant useful for banks.
2 The white form of Viola cornuta, the Horned Violet, from the Pyrenees.
3 Viola gracilis.

at least 6 weeks, Guyana. *V. tessellata*, 6 feet, variable plant, leaves 15 inches long, chequered white, yellow and green, Brazil; vars. *roseo-picta*, large pink dots; *sanderae*, white and yellow bands on a chequered green ground.

Cultivation A compost of equal parts of peat, sharp sand and osmunda fibre is best for mature plants. The 'vase' in the centre of the rosette should be kept filled with rainwater and this should be warmed to a temperature of 55°F (13°C) in winter. Winter temperatures should be 50°F (10°C) for *V. carinata*, *V. saundersii* and *V. splendens*, 55°F (13°C) for the other species, which require to be shaded from early spring until the end of September. The species that will tolerate cooler conditions will also appreciate more light, and no shading need be applied until the end of May. Mature plants should receive fresh air whenever the inside temperature reaches 70°F (21°C). During late spring and summer, very minute quantities of liquid feed can be added to the water in the 'vase' at three-weekly intervals. No harm will be done if the species which will winter at 50°F (10°C) are given the higher temperature that the tessellated-leaved species require. After flowering the adult rosette dies away, when the side-rosettes may be detached and potted up separately in a mixture of equal parts of leafmould, sphagnum moss and peat and rooted with bottom heat of between 70–80°F (21–27°C). They should be heavily shaded. Once rooted, they are gradually hardened off and brought into more light. Propagation by seed is slow and a temperature of 80°F (27°C) is necessary.

Water Cress
This is *Nasturtium officinale*, a hardy annual belonging to the *Cruciferae*. Of the two types the green is best for summer supplies, the brown for winter and spring.

If you are growing it to eat you should not plant water cress in a garden pool. To grow it in a natural stream you must be certain the water is free from pollution. It is best grown in a permanently moist and partially shaded position from seed sown in April or August, or from rooted cuttings. You dig the soil deeply and incorporate moisture-holding peat, etc. The surface of the bed should be an inch or so below that of the surrounding soil. After being firmed somewhat and raked well, the bed should be flooded with water. When the water has drained away the seed may be sown broadcast but not be covered with soil. All weed seedlings must be removed. Water cress offered for sale often has roots which may be cut off and planted into a bed prepared as above. Sprigs without roots will put forth roots in water which should be changed daily. Plant the rooted cuttings quite thickly to cover the bed. Water cress may also

be grown in pots or clay pans stood in shallow containers of fresh water, well shaded, or in a sink sunk in the ground. For winter and early spring supplies, protect an August-made bed with frame lights when colder weather comes. The containers may also be stood in a slightly heated greenhouse.

Xanthosia (zan-tho-see-a)
From the Greek *xanthos*, yellow, in reference to the yellow hairs which cover some species *(Umbelliferae)*. A genus of 15 to 20 species, natives of Australia.

Species cultivated *X. pilosa*, 1–2 feet, shrub, erect or sometimes sprawling, flowers white. *X. rotundifolia*, southern cross, 1–2 feet, flowerheads terminal, arranged in cross-like shape, bracts showy white, petal-like, anthers red.

Cultivation *X. rotundifolia* is the most attractive species and is the only one likely to be seen in cultivation. Plants may be raised easily from seed sown in light compost in spring.

Zantedeschia (zan-te-desh-ee-a)
Commemorating Francesco Zantedeschi (1773–1846), Italian physician and botanist *(Araceae)*. Arum or calla lily. A genus of eight or nine species of greenhouse rhizomatous perennials, natives of tropical Africa, grown for

their handsome usually arrow-shaped leaves and arum-like flowers. *Z. aethiopica*, in particular, is much grown for the cut flower trade and is the 'arum lily' sold by florists.

Species cultivated *Z. aethiopica* (syn. *Richardia africana*), lily of the Nile, trumpet lily, 3–4 feet, flowers white, spathes to 10 inches long, winter and spring; varieties have been recorded with double or treble spathes. *Z. albomaculata*, 2 feet, leaves spotted white, flowers yellow or milk-white, summer. *Z. elliottiana*, 3 feet, flowers yellow, spathes 6 inches long, August. *Z. melanoleuca*, 18 inches, flowers yellow and purple, summer. *Z. rehmannii*, 2 feet, flowers rosy-purple, summer.

Cultivation For *Z. aethiopica* use a compost of equal parts of loam, cow manure and coarse silver sand. From October to May the plants should be in a greenhouse or indoors, but they can be either planted out of doors or the pots can be sunk up to their rims in moist, rich soil in summer. Repotting is needed annually in August or September. Moderate watering is required from September to March, but water freely from March to May. During the flowering period stimulants should be applied weekly. Out of doors water freely in dry

Vriesa fenestralis from Brazil.

1 The white Arum-like flowers of Zantedeschia aethiopica, Lily of the Nile, Trumpet Lily or Galla Lily.
2 Zinnia can be had in many colours. This is Z. haageana 'Persian Carpet'.

weather. Temperatures should be 40–55°F (4–13°C) from September to March and 50–60 F (10–16°C) from March to May. Suitable stimulants are one teaspoonful of Clay's fertiliser; ½ ounce of guano; or ¼ ounce of nitrate of soda or sulphate of ammonia to 1 gallon of water. In mild areas Z. aethiopica may be grown in ponds, etc., provided the rhizomes are about 2½ feet below the surface to protect them from frost.

For the other species the compost is the same, but they should be grown in the greenhouse from October to June and in a cold frame for the rest of the year, repotting each year in February. Watering should be moderate from February to April and from August to October, and liberal from April to August, but keep the soil nearly dry from October to February. Stimulants should be applied during the flowering period. Temperatures should be 55–65 F (13–18 C) from October to March, and 65–75 F (18–24 C) from March to October.

Propagation is by division when planting out of doors or repotting; by seeds sown ⅛ inch deep in loam, leafmould and sand in a temperature of 65–75 F (18–24 C) in spring, or from suckers removed at potting time.

Zephyranthes (zeff-er-an-thez)

From the Greek *zephyr,* the west wind, and *anthos,* a flower *(Amaryllidaceae).* Flower of the west wind, zephyr lily. A genus of 35–40 species of hardy and half-hardy bulbous, flowering plants with funnel-shaped flowers, natives of the warmer parts of America and of the West Indies.

Half-hardy species cultivated *Z. atamasco,* Atamasco lily, 1 foot, flowers white, tinged with purple, May. *Z. grandiflora* (syn. *Z. carinata*), 6–12 inches, flowers pink, summer.

Hardy species cultivated *Z. candida,* 6–12 inches, flowers snowy-white, September.

Cultivation *Z. candida* likes light, sandy loam and a sunny well-drained position in borders or rock gardens. It should be planted between August and November, the bulbs placed about 4 inches apart and 3–4 inches deep. A layer of cinders will protect them from extreme cold in winter. The other species are far more tender. They will survive in warm, sheltered places and sandy soils only. A compost of 2 parts of loam, 1 part of peat, leafmould and silver sand suits their cultivation in the cool greenhouse or frame. Pot them between August and November, inserting one bulb about 2 inches deep in a 6-inch pot. Water sparingly until growth begins, but then water freely. When the flowers die the

soil should be kept dry until potting time. Propagation is by offsets, treated in the same way as the large bulbs.

Zinnia (zi-nee-a)

Commemorating Johann Gottfried Zinn (1727–59), a German professor of botany *(Compositae).* A genus of 20 species of half-hardy annuals and perennials with beautiful flowers of various colours, natives of the southern United States to Brazil and Chile.

Species cultivated *Z. elegans,* 2–3 feet, flowers of various colours, summer; cultivars and strains are numerous; they include 'Aztec', bright orange; 'Big Snowman', white; 'Envy', green; 'Ice Cream', pure white; 'Chrysanthe-mum-flowered Hybrids', various colours; 'Giant Dahlia-flowered Strain', various colours; 'Mammoth', various colours; 'Polynesian', pink; 'Scabious-flowered Strain', various colours; 'Peppermint Stick', various striped colours. *Z. haageana,* 1 foot, flowers orange-scarlet, summer; 'Persian Carpet' is a double-flowered strain in various colours. *Z. linearis,* 9–12 inches, flowers golden-yellow, summer. *Z. pauciflora,* 1 foot, flowers yellow or purple, summer. *Z. tenuiflora* (syn. *Z. multiflora*), 2 feet, flowers scarlet, summer. Other strains and cultivars include 'Button-flowered Mixed', 1½ feet; 'Pink Buttons', 1 foot, salmon-pink; 'Red Buttons', 1 foot, bright scarlet; 'Thumbelina', 6 inches, flowers semi-double or double in various colours.

Cultivation Zinnias do best in deep, loamy soil with decayed manure added, in sunny beds and borders. Sow seed in early April $\frac{1}{16}$ inch deep in light soil in a greenhouse, in a temperature of 55 F (13 C) and transplant the seedlings when the third leaf forms, 2 inches apart in shallow boxes. When established they should be removed to a cooler house and then planted out in early May, 4 inches apart in a cold frame, gradually hardened off and finally planted out in early June, 8–12 inches apart. Seed may be sown directly out of doors in May and this has the advantage that the seedlings can grow undisturbed. Rapid changes of temperature should be avoided and the plants should be freely watered in dry weather. The taller species may be staked in windy conditions, as the blooms produced are often double and very big. When flowering starts the application of stimulants is helpful to the blooms.

Zygocactus (si-go-kak-tus)

From the Greek *zygon*, a yoke, and *Cactus*, possibly referring to the shape of the stem joints *(Cactaceae)*. Christmas cactus. A genus of a single species, an epiphytic greenhouse cactus, placed by some botanists as a hybrid in the genus *Schlumbergera*. The species is *Z. truncatus*, from eastern Brazil. It has flat, short stems with small areoles, minute spines and claw-like joints. Cerise-red flowers are freely-produced from the ends of the joints from December to February; vars. *altensteinii*, teeth on stems more pronounced, flowers brick-red; *crenatus*, flowers small, bluish-violet; *delicatus*, growth more erect, flowers pale pink.

Cultivation *Z. truncatus* is easy to grow, either on its own roots or grafted on to a tall stock to make an umbrella-shaped specimen. Use John Innes potting compost No 2 with added leafmould. Repot every two years or when the plant becomes too large for its pot, repotting when flowering has ceased. In winter maintain a minimum temperature of 50°F (10°C), increasing this to 60°F (16°C) as buds form. Water when the soil has almost dried out, throughout the winter. In June plants may be placed out of doors in semi-shade. Plants do not like a sunny position in an unshaded greenhouse; they do better in a medium-lighted room in the house. Give them a weak liquid feed after flowering. When plants are in bud do not move them and at this time, in particular, protect them from draughts. The causes of bud drop are too wet or too dry a soil or a changeable atmosphere. Propagation is by cuttings which are best taken in early summer and rooted in sharp sand, spraying them occasionally. Or plants may be grafted on to *Pereskia* stock.

1 Zygocactus truncatus, the Christmas Cactus, is easy to grow and produces cerise-red flowers in winter.
2 Zygopetalum × blackii, a hybrid between Z. crinitum and Z. perranaudii, was raised in 1957.

Zygopetalum (zy-go-pet-a-lum)

From the Greek *zygon*, a yoke, and *petalon*, a petal, referring to the way in which the perianth segments are joined at the base *(Orchidaceae)*. A genus of 20 species of epiphytic orchids, from Central and South America and Trinidad. Botanical classification of the genus is somewhat confused. The spikes are mainly tall and have large, long-lasting flowers.

Species cultivated This selection includes *Z. burkii*, flowers green, brown, white and purple, winter, Guyana. *Z. coeleste*, lacking pseudobulbs, flowers violet-blue and yellow, summer, Colombia. *Z. mackayii*, flowers fragrant, white, yellowish-green, blotched purplish-brown, lined purple-violet, autumn and winter, Brazil. *Z. maxillare*, creeping, flowers green, violet-blue, barred chocolate-brown.

Cultivation Pot these orchids in a compost of osmunda fibre and sphagnum moss, with fibrous loam added for the more vigorous types. Water frequently in summer, less so in winter. Temperatures should be about 55–60°F (13–16°C) in winter, and higher than that in summer. They prefer a moist atmosphere, but with plenty of ventilation. Propagation is by division of large plants in the spring.

Zephyranthes grandiflora, a half-hardy species, best in a cool greenhouse, has pink flowers in June.

INDEX